D1368464

WINDOWS® NT™
WORKSTATION 4.0
ADVANCED
TECHNICAL
REFERENCE

WINDOWS® NT™ WORKSTATION 4.0 ADVANCED TECHNICAL REFERENCE

Written by Jim Boyce with

Christa Anderson • Axel Larson • Richard Neff II • Sue Plumley
Chris Turkstra • Brian Underdahl • Serdar Yegulalp • Craig Zacker

Windows NT Workstation 4.0
Advanced Technical Reference

Library of Congress Catalog No.: 96-070612

ISBN: 0-7897-0863-9

98 97 96   6 5 4 3 2 1

Interpretation of the printing code: the rightmost double-digit number is the year of the book's printing; the rightmost single-digit number, the number of the book's printing. For example, a printing code of 96-1 shows that the first printing of the book occurred in 1996.

Screen reproductions in this book were created using Collage Plus from Inner Media, Inc., Hollis, NH.

Credits

PRESIDENT
Roland Elgey

PUBLISHING DIRECTOR
Brad R. Koch

EDITORIAL SERVICES DIRECTOR
Elizabeth Keaffaber

MANAGING EDITOR
Michael Cunningham

DIRECTOR OF MARKETING
Lynn E. Zingraf

ACQUISITIONS MANAGER
Elizabeth South

PRODUCT DIRECTOR
Kevin Kloss

ASSISTANT PRODUCT MARKETING MANAGER
Kim Margolius

PRODUCTION EDITOR
Lori A. Lyons

EDITORS
Kate Givens
Sarah Rudy
Linda Seifert
Brian Sweany
Nick Zafran

TECHNICAL EDITORS
Robert Bogue
Don Doherty

TECHNICAL SPECIALIST
Nadeem Muhammed

ACQUISITIONS COORDINATOR
Tracy Williams

OPERATIONS COORDINATOR
Patty Brooks

EDITORIAL ASSISTANT
Mark Kane

BOOK DESIGNER
Ruth Harvey

COVER DESIGNER
Barb Kordesh

PRODUCTION TEAM
Marcia Brizendine
Joan Evan
Daryl Kessler
Sossity Smith

INDEXER
Craig Small

Composed in *Century Old Style* and *Franklin Gothic* by Que Corporation.

About the Authors

Jim Boyce, the lead author for *Windows NT Installation and Configuration Handbook*, is a Contributing Editor and columnist for *WINDOWS Magazine* and a regular contributor to other computer publications. He has been involved with computers since the late 1970s, and has worked with computers as a user, programmer, and systems manager in a variety of capacities. He has a wide range of experience in the DOS, Windows, and UNIX environments. Jim has authored and coauthored over two dozen books on computers and software.

Christa Anderson started working with computers in the 1980s, long before anyone let it slip to her that you could make a living with them. Since 1992, she has written on such subjects as PC troubleshooting, data communications, and PC security, with her current interests centered on local and wide-area networking issues. Previously a member of a cutting-edge consulting team in the Washington, D.C. area, since her move to a city with better parking, she is now an independent technical writer and researcher.

Axel L. Larson (MCSE) has over 30 years of computer experience. He has delved into the internals of mainframe operating systems, beginning with the RCA Series 70 TDOS and continuing through Unisys OS1100, IBM DOS/VSE, and IBM VM. Axel's first home computer (before the term Personal Computer came into use) was a Commodore Personal Electronic Transactor (PET) with 8K of memory and Basic from a tiny company called Microsoft.

Axel switched to Local Area Networks in the late 1980s and is currently a consultant specializing in Windows 95 and Windows NT LANs. He can be reached by e-mail at AxelLarson@MSN.com.

Richard Neff is a Microsoft Certified Professional, certified as a Systems Engineer with elective exams in Microsoft Mail and Systems Management Server (SMS) and as a Product Specialist in Microsoft Excel 5.0 and Microsoft Word for Windows 2.0/6.0. He has a BS in Computer Science from VMI and has worked with personal computers for over 15 years. He currently writes a column called Unleashing Windows for the electronic magazine ChipNet found on America Online (keyword: Chipnet) or on the World Wide Web. He has formed his own computer consulting company, Network Technologies Group, which specializes in Novell NetWare, Microsoft Windows NT, and Microsoft BackOffice solutions. Network Technologies Group is located in Blacksburg, VA, and also has a Web site at http://www.bnt.com/~netech. He can be reached by e-mail at RickNeff on America Online (RickNeff@AOL.COM over the Internet) or at 70761,3615 on CompuServe (70761,3615@COMPUSERVE.COM).

Sue Plumley has owned and operated her own business for eight years. Humble Opinions provides training, consulting, and network installation, management, and maintenance to banking, education, medical, and industrial facilities. In addition, Sue has authored and co-authored over 50 books for Que Corporation and its sister imprints, including *10-Minute Guide to Lotus Notes 4, Special Edition Using Windows NT 4.0 Workstation,* and *Easy Windows 95.* You can reach Sue via the Internet at splumley@citynet.net or on CompuServe at 76470,2526.

Chris Turkstra is the kid who was always disassembling his toys. He has been involved with PC technology since his first IBM PC in 1983. Chris is a technical architect who spends much of his time designing and implementing networked systems for clients. You can reach him at 75507.720@compuserve.com or turkstra@cris.com.

Brian Underdahl is an author, independent consultant, and custom application developer based in Reno, Nevada. He's the author or co-author of over 25 computer books, as well as numerous magazine articles. He has also acted as a product developer and as a technical editor on many other Que books. His e-mail address is 71505,1114 on CompuServe.

Serdar Yegulalp is a technical editor with *WINDOWS Magazine,* and a regular beta tester for Windows 95, Windows NT, and NT products. Other research responsibilities include SCSI and document imaging hardware and software. You can reach Serdar at syegul@cmp.com.

Craig Zacker got his first experience with computers in high school on a minicomputer "with less memory than I now have in my wristwatch." He has worked in the industry as a technical support engineer, a network administrator, an online services engineer, and a technical writer and editor. He spends most of his time working on, playing with, and writing about computers, networks, and operating systems.

Acknowledgments

Many people helped in the creation of this book in one way or another. Jim Boyce offers his thanks to:

Brad Koch for his support and developmental direction of this project.

Elizabeth South for her invaluable help in putting together the project and authoring team.

Kevin Kloss, who did a great job molding and directing the project.

The editors involved in fine-tuning the book.

Brian Underdahl, for putting together a terrific CD and related online materials.

Robert Bogue and Don Doherty, for their outstanding job of technical editing. The book is much better because of their thoroughness and testing.

The staff of the Production department of Macmillan Computer Publishing, for their usual fine job of turning text and illustrations into a real book.

We'd Like to Hear from You!

As part of our continuing effort to produce books of the highest possible quality, Que would like to hear your comments. To stay competitive, we *really* want you, as a computer book reader and user, to let us know what you like or dislike most about this book or other Que products.

You can mail comments, ideas, or suggestions for improving future editions to the address below, or send us a fax at (317) 581-4663. For the online inclined, Macmillan Computer Publishing has a forum on CompuServe (type **GO QUEBOOKS** at any prompt) through which our staff and authors are available for questions and comments. The address of our Internet site is **http://www.mcp.com** (World Wide Web).

In addition to exploring our forum, please feel free to contact me personally to discuss your opinions of this book: I'm **74201,1064** on CompuServe, and I'm **kkloss@que.mcp.com** on the Internet.

Thanks in advance—your comments will help us to continue publishing the best books available on computer topics in today's market.

Kevin Kloss
Product Director
Que Corporation
201 W. 103rd Street
Indianapolis, Indiana 46290
USA

N O T E Although we cannot provide general technical support, we're happy to help you resolve problems you encounter related to our books, disks, or other products. If you need such assistance, please contact our Tech Support department at 800-545-5914 ext. 3833.

To order other Que or Macmillan Computer Publishing books or products, please call our Customer Service department at 800-835-3202 ext. 666. ■

Contents at a Glance

Table of Contents

11 Exploring NTFS   247

12 Optimizing CPU Performance   273

18   Integrating Windows NT in Microsoft Environments   407

V | Using TCP/IP and Internet Features

VI | Working with the Registry

Appendixes

Introduction

by Jim Boyce

From the threads of its beginnings as OS/2 to its current release as Windows NT 4.0, Windows NT has grown into a powerful operating system that suits the needs of the network administrator as well as the average user. With the introduction of the popular Windows 95 interface to Windows NT 4.0, Windows NT Workstation is the ideal operating system for desktop business users. It offers all the robustness, speed, and reliability of the core Windows NT operating system with an easy-to-use interface.

The comparison between Windows 95 and Windows NT, however, ends at the interface. Windows NT is a complex, powerful operating system. You need a good source of detailed technical information to take full advantage of Windows NT, and that's where this book can help. ■

What This Book Is About

Windows NT Workstation 4.0 Advanced Technical Reference covers a broad range of topics to help you configure and use Windows NT's many advanced features on both Intel- and RISC-based systems. In the majority of chapters, the material focuses on technical concepts and implementation rather than on the typical tutorial material provided in other Windows NT books. For example, *Windows NT Workstation 4.0 Advanced Technical Reference* does not offer an explanation of how to use the accessory applications included with Windows NT or other features that are self-evident to the typical, experienced user. Instead, the book focuses on these key areas:

- Understanding Windows NT's architecture, components, and new features
- Employing advanced Setup and customization techniques for installation
- Optimizing operating system, hardware, and software performance
- Optimizing network performance
- Understanding and implementing TCP/IP and TCP/IP utilities, as well as advanced Internet topics
- Managing the Registry
- Administering workstation and user properties and accounts

Although the focus of this book is on concepts and implementation of advanced features, some chapters do cover a limited amount of information on using certain features in Windows NT. For example, Chapter 3, "What's New in Windows NT 4.0," provides a brief overview of the new Windows NT 4.0 interface and other features.

The authors who have contributed to *Windows NT Workstation 4.0 Advanced Technical Reference* are experts in their areas, but have the unique ability of explaining their subjects in ways that a layman can easily understand. Most important, the authors write from practical experience.

Who This Book Is for

Windows NT Workstation 4.0 Advanced Technical Reference is intended for the intermediate to advanced user who needs a solid explanation of Windows NT topics and their applications. This includes advanced features such as Internet Information Server, DHCP, WINS, and PPTP (Point-to-Point Tunneling Protocol).

Because of the increasing popularity of Windows NT as a workstation operating system for business users, *Windows NT Workstation Advanced Technical Reference* is geared toward not only the experienced network or system administrator, but also to the average experienced user looking for detailed information on performance optimization and other advanced topics.

We assume that you have experience with Windows 3.x, Windows 95, or Windows NT 3.x and are able to use the Windows interface. For example, you should know how to use the mouse, work with program menus and dialog boxes, and perform other common Windows tasks.

How This Book Is Structured

Windows NT Workstation 4.0 Advanced Technical Reference is divided into eight parts that take you from an overview of Windows NT Workstation's architecture and features to system administration tools and techniques. The chapters are written to stand alone, so you don't have to keep referring from one chapter to another to set up or configure a particular feature in Windows NT. The following sections explain the parts of the book and what topics are covered in each one.

Part I: Overview of Windows NT Workstation

Part I serves as an introduction to Windows NT Workstation, including its structure and capabilities. You'll learn not only how Windows NT works, but also what new features are available in version 4.0. The chapters in Part I include the following:

- Chapter 1, "Operating Systems Overview," provides an introduction to the topics covered in Part I.

- Chapter 2, "Understanding Windows NT Workstation Architecture," explains the internal architecture of Windows NT and its core components, such as the executive, protected subsystems, and file system.

- Chapter 3, "What's New in Windows NT 4.0," provides an overview of the new features in Windows NT Workstation 4.0 to give you an understanding of its new capabilities.

Part II: Installing and Configuring Windows NT Workstation

Part II provides detailed coverage of important installation and configuration topics that will help you install and distribute Windows NT locally and across a LAN. The chapters in Part II include the following:

■ Chapter 4, "Installation and Configuration Overview," serves to introduce the topics covered in Part II.

■ Chapter 5, "Preparing for Installation," explores the many critical issues to consider when planning to install Windows NT Workstation. Covered topics include compatibility, security, hardware setup and preparation, system backup, and file system planning.

■ Chapter 6, "Advanced and Custom Setup Issues," provides a broad look at the Setup program and issues relating to installing Windows NT Workstation. Covered topics include understanding how Setup works, customizing Setup, various installation delivery methods, automation, and more.

Part III: Optimizing System and Application Performance

Part III covers a wide range of topics that will enable you to fine-tune your system operation and improve the performance not only of the operating system, but of your applications and hardware as well. The chapters included in Part III are the following:

■ Chapter 7, "Performance Optimization Overview," serves as an introduction to the topics covered in Part III.

■ Chapter 8, "Monitoring Performance," examines techniques and tools available to help you monitor the performance of your hardware, Windows NT, and your applications. In particular, Chapter 8 focuses on Performance Monitor, the performance testing tool included with Windows NT Workstation.

■ Chapter 9, "Optimizing Physical and Virtual Memory," will help you understand how Windows NT makes use of your system's physical memory and the disk subsystem for paging (virtual memory). You'll find tips in Chapter 9 to help you evaluate and improve memory and paging performance.

■ Chapter 10, "Optimizing the File System," explores the FAT and NTFS file systems to help you understand their similarities and differences, as well as advantages and disadvantages. Chapter 10 also examines disk subsystem performance and testing with a focus on optimizing the file system's performance.

■ Chapter 11, "Exploring NTFS," provides a more comprehensive look at NTFS than that provided in Chapter 10, exploring the structure of NTFS in more detail. Chapter 11 also examines NTFS's data compression mechanism and shows you how to migrate to an NTFS file system.

- Chapter 12, "Optimizing CPU Performance," helps you understand how to evaluate and improve the performance of your system's CPU. Included in Chapter 12 is a discussion of multiprocessor systems and their relative performance versus uniprocessor systems.

- Chapter 13, "Enhancing Video and I/O Performance," explores the issue of video performance and general I/O performance. You'll find discussions on performance testing and optimization through hardware and operating system changes.

- Chapter 14, "Ensuring Data Security," looks at the important issues surrounding data security. In addition to a discussion of backup strategies and implementation, you'll find an explanation of various types of fault-tolerance for the file system and overall system.

Part IV: Optimizing Network Performance

Part IV provides a detailed look at non-TCP/IP networking issues. Through the chapters in Part IV, you'll learn about networking in general and also how to integrate Windows NT with various network environments. The chapters in Part IV include the following:

- Chapter 15, "Networking Overview," serves as an introduction to the chapters in Part IV.

- Chapter 16, "A Brief Primer on Networks," introduces you to some general network concepts, as well as concepts that are specific to Windows NT. You'll learn about network structure and performance and learn the importance of domains and various security models available to you with Windows NT.

- Chapter 17, "Integrating Windows NT in Novell Environments," explores the many issues relating to the use of Windows NT in both client and server roles in networks involving Novell NetWare. You'll learn about the differences between Microsoft's and Novell's network client software and their respective advantages and disadvantages. Chapter 18 also covers NetWare-specific features in Windows NT, including File and Print Services for NetWare, NDS, using print queues, and other topics.

- Chapter 18, "Integrating Windows NT in Microsoft Environments," explores the issues surrounding implementation of Windows NT in environments containing DOS, Windows 3.x, and Windows 95 networking clients.

- Chapter 19, "Integrating Windows NT in UNIX Environments," will help you understand the unique problems and solutions for integrating Windows NT in both client and server roles in a UNIX environment. You'll learn about connection options, printing to UNIX printers, and using X-Windows clients under Windows NT to run UNIX-based applications on your Windows NT workstation.

- Chapter 20, "Using Dial-Up Networking," provides detailed coverage of Remote Access Services, which now are collectively termed Dial-Up Networking. You'll learn how to configure, use, and manage Dial-Up Networking features in Windows NT. You'll also find tips on implementing PPP, SLIP, and CSLIP connection protocols for dial-up connections.

Part V: Using TCP/IP and Internet Features

Part V examines a wide range of issues relating to use of the TCP/IP protocol and related utilities, as well as general Internet-related topics. The chapters in Part V are the following:

- Chapter 21, "TCP/IP and Internet Overview," serves as an introduction to the chapters in Part V.

- Chapter 22, "Overview of TCP/IP," helps you understand TCP/IP's importance and promise in your network, both for Internet connections and intranet connections. Chapter 22 also provides a detailed look at the TCP/IP utilities included with Windows NT.

- Chapter 23, "Using Basic TCP/IP Services," examines issues relating to configuration and application of the TCP/IP protocol. You'll learn how to configure general and advanced TCP/IP settings and options. The chapter also explores TCP/IP routing, printing through TCP/IP, and using SNMP through TCP/IP.

- Chapter 24, "Using DHCP," offers an in-depth look at Dynamic Host Configuration Protocol (DHCP), which automates assignment and management of IP addresses and other TCP/IP-related data on the LAN. You'll learn how to configure and use DHCP and explore registry settings that control DHCP's performance.

- Chapter 25, "Using DNS and WINS," explains the purpose and function of DNS and WINS under Windows NT for name resolution. You'll find tips on configuring both DNS and WINS, as well as using Hosts and Lmhost files to augment name resolution.

- Chapter 26, "Installing and Configuring Peer Web Services," explains how to install, configure, and use Windows NT Workstation's Peer Web Services, a new feature that enables your workstation to function as an Internet or intranet server. You'll also find a discussion in Chapter 26 of Java and ActiveX.

Part VI: Working with the Registry

Part VI provides a detailed look at one of Windows NT's most important components: the Registry. The chapters in Part VI include the following:

- Chapter 27, "Registry Overview," serves as an introduction to the chapters in Part VI.

- Chapter 28, "Understanding the Registry," explains the structure function of the Registry in Windows NT. In addition to learning about the Registry's structure, you'll also find a discussion of Registry size limits, diagnostics, and a comparison between the Windows 95 and Windows NT registries.

- Chapter 29, "Backing Up and Editing the Registry," explains the importance of backing up the Registry, as well as specific backup methods. You'll also learn how to modify the Registry, both indirectly and through the Registry Editor provided with Windows NT.

- Chapter 30, "Restoring and Repairing the Registry," helps you overcome problems with the registry when they occur. Chapter 30 discusses automatic Registry repair as well as techniques for restoring the Registry after a problem occurs.

Part VII: Administering a Windows NT Workstation

Even on a client workstation, some system and user management tasks are still a necessity. Part VII examines administration issues for both hardware and users through the following chapters:

- Chapter 31, "Administration Overview," serves as an introduction to system administration and the chapters included in Part VII.

- Chapter 32, "Administering Users," explains user accounts, groups and group membership, user security, and resource access. You'll find discussion in the chapter of the tools available to you to manage groups and users under Windows NT.

- Chapter 33, "Managing Server Properties," covers a wide range of topics that relate to managing the server aspects of Windows NT Workstation computers. You'll learn how to effectively manage the file system, apply directory replication, manage printers, and control system performance.

Appendixes

The appendixes to *Windows NT Workstation 4.0 Advanced Technical Reference* offer additional reference material you'll find useful when setting up, optimizing, and using Windows NT:

- Appendix A, "Registry Customization Tips," offers additional advice and tips on customizing the Registry.
- Appendix B, "The Windows NT Advanced Technical Reference CD," serves as a content overview and installation guide for the CD included with this book.
- Appendix C, "Internet and Online Resources," offers a list of resources geared toward Windows NT that you'll find on the Internet and commercial information services.
- Appendix D, "Windows NT Workstation Command Reference," explores the command-line environment in Windows NT and its most commonly used commands.
- Appendix E, "Windows NT Glossary," defines common terms relating to Windows NT.

Conventions Used in This Book

In Windows NT, you can use either the mouse or keyboard to activate commands and choose options. You can press a command's or menu's hot key, use the function keys, or click items with the mouse to make your selections. In this book, command and menu hot keys are underlined as in the following example:

Choose File, Open to display the Open dialog box.

In this book, key combinations are joined by a plus (+) sign. For example, Ctrl+C means to hold down the Ctrl key, press C, then release both keys. The following example shows a typical command:

Choose Edit, Copy, or press Ctrl+C.

Occasionally, you might need to press a key, release it, then press another key. If you need to press Alt, then F, then O, for example, the command would be similar to the following:

Press Alt, F, O to display the Open dialog box.

Names of dialog boxes and dialog box options are written as they appear on your display. Messages that appear at the command prompt are displayed `in a special font`. New terms are introduced in *italic* type. Text that you type is shown in **boldface**. If you see an instruction to "Enter **some text**," it means to type the text **some text**, then press Enter. If the instruction tells you to "Type **some text**," it means to type the text but do not press Enter.

N O T E   Notes provide additional information that might help you avoid problems or offer advice or general information related to the current topic. ■

 T I P   Tips provide extra information that supplement the current topic. Often, tips offer shortcuts or alternative methods for accomplishing a task.

CAUTION

Cautions warn you if a procedure or description in the topic could lead to unexpected results or even data loss or damage to your system. If you see a caution, proceed carefully.

TROUBLESHOOTING

I'm having a specific problem with a Windows NT feature. Look for troubleshooting elements to help you identify and resolve specific problems you might be having with Windows NT, your system, or your network.

What About Sidebars?

Sidebars are sprinkled throughout the book to give you the author's insight into a particular topic. The information in a sidebar supplements the material in the chapter.

Cross-references like the one below direct you to related information in other parts of the book.

▶ **See** "Hacking Into Government Systems," **p. 986**

Internet references such as the following point you to sites on the Internet where you can find additional information about a topic being discussed:

 MICROSOFT'S INTERNET WEB SITE
http://www.microsoft.com

Where to Go for More Information

Que offers other titles that will help you master the intricacies of Windows NT and related topics.

For more information about these titles, Que, Macmillan Computer Publishing, and other Macmillan digital services, check out the Macmillan USA Information SuperLibrary on the Internet at **www.mcp.com/que**. You'll find a wealth of information, online shopping, and more. Or, check out the **MACMILLAN** forum on CompuServe.

For other online sources of information about Microsoft Windows NT, check the WINNT forum on CompuServe or connect to the Microsoft Web site at **www.microsoft.com**. ●

Overview of Windows NT Workstation

Operating Systems Overview

by Jim Boyce

Operating system design certainly has come a long way since the development of the first mainframe operating systems, but has also evolved almost as much since the introduction of DOS in the early 1980s. Although the underlying structure of Windows NT 4.0 shares some of the characteristics of the early versions of DOS, they are by no means similar or comparable.

It certainly isn't necessary to understand the concepts behind operating system design or the intimate details of the inner workings of Windows NT to install, administer, and use Windows NT. But the more background information at your disposal, the better you'll understand the features and functions in Windows NT and how they relate to your daily use of Windows NT.

This first part of *Windows NT Workstation 4.0 Advanced Technical Reference* focuses on giving you that helpful background information. ■

Operating Systems and Windows NT Workstation

Operating systems are the soul of a computer. Without an operating system, a computer is a lifeless collection of metal, silicon, and glass. The operating system turns that hodge-podge into a useful tool, enabling your applications, and through them, enabling you to access and put to work those otherwise uncooperative bits and pieces.

The focus in personal computer operating systems has changed dramatically in the past 15 years. In DOS, for example, the focus was on providing basic core services—disk access, I/O port control, keyboard input, basic memory management, and display. Usability was not much of an issue and was left almost solely to application developers. Thus, one program usually was radically different from the next, even if both programs had the same general function.

Early work by Xerox and Apple began the conversion of the personal computer from a difficult, unruly beast only a hacker could love to a reasonably well-behaved personal data and productivity tool that anyone could at least tolerate, if not love. The introduction by Microsoft of the Windows operating environment, and later the introduction of Windows NT, have helped transform the Intel- and RISC-based PCs, as well. Windows NT 4.0 represents the latest step in Microsoft's operating system plan—bringing the ease-of-use of the Windows 95 interface to the more robust Windows NT operating system.

Operating system design is, as you might guess, a very complex process. To help understand some of the issues involved, and more fully understand and use Windows NT, Chapter 2, "Understanding Windows NT Workstation Architecture," explores the basics of what an operating system is in today's personal computer realm, how its components are important, how Windows NT compares with other operating systems, and what new wrinkles are added by including networking and connectivity into the operating system.

The Windows NT Architecture

The term *architecture* in computer software parlance refers to the design of an operating system and the way in which its components function and interact. Windows NT is different in its architectural design from Windows 95, and considerably different from the Windows 3.x (and earlier) operating environment and DOS.

As you will learn in Chapter 2, Windows NT's design provides many features that make it a stable, high-performance operating system:

- **Preemptive multitasking.** Preemptive multitasking enables Windows NT to allocate processor time to applications rather than applications seizing and holding control of the CPU. This feature makes Windows NT a more stable operating platform because poorly designed applications can't hog the CPU and degrade the performance of other applications or system performance overall.

- **Multithreaded execution.** Multithreaded applications break tasks into *execution threads*, each of which is handled independently of one another by the CPU. By supporting multithreaded execution, a program's performance and usability improves. While one thread handles printing a document, for example, you can continue working with the application while the document prints in the background.

- **Robustness.** Windows NT is a robust operating system, meaning that it is not prone to system failures due to ill-behaved or malfunctioning applications. By separating applications into their own address spaces, Windows NT keeps a failed application from affecting others and can terminate that failed application without shutting down others.

- **C2 security.** Windows NT's security model allows for flexible network design and easy user access while maintaining strict C2-level security. Windows NT includes a number of graphical utilities for managing user accounts, servers, and shared resources.

- **Networking.** Windows NT includes built-in peer-to-peer networking, enabling Windows NT to participate in a local area network (LAN) without adding the additional expense or support that would be required by adding a third-party network operating system. Windows NT integrates network functionality at the operating system level, improving network performance and usability. Its support for a variety of network protocols and services from other vendors, such as Novell, makes Windows NT both an attractive network client and server.

- **Application compatibility.** Windows NT supports applications written for Windows NT, Windows 95, Windows 3.x, DOS, and POSIX. Support for this range of application types gives you the ability to use new applications without leaving behind older applications.

- **Ease-of-use.** The addition of the new user interface patterned after Windows 95 makes Windows NT even easier to use than before. This simplified interface and consistency across platforms helps Windows NT appeal to a broader user base.

- **Multiprocessor support (scalability).** Windows NT supports multiprocessor systems, making it a good choice on servers and for intensive applications in engineering and data distribution.

In addition to learning about these features in Chapter 2, you'll learn about the core components in Windows NT, such as the kernel, hardware abstraction layer (HAL), and other components. By understanding what makes Windows NT run, you'll be able to make it run better.

Windows NT 4.0's Features

As you will learn in Chapter 3, "What's New in Windows NT 4.0," Windows NT Workstation 4.0 sports many new features and improvements to existing features. One of the most obvious changes is the introduction of an interface based on the interface in Windows 95, including the Windows Explorer. But the new features in Windows NT 4.0 go much deeper than what you see on the desktop:

■ **New interface.** Most visible of Windows NT 4.0's new features is a Windows 95-like interface, complete with Windows Explorer. This interface is in many ways easier to use than the old interface.

■ **Internet tools.** Included in this release of Windows NT is the Internet Explorer, a Microsoft-developed Web browser. Windows NT Workstation 4.0 includes a feature called Peer Web Services that enable you to create a personal Web server you can use to publish documents across your own intranet.

■ **Windows Messaging.** The Microsoft Mail client included with previous versions of Windows NT has been replaced by a Windows Messaging e-mail client. With this Messaging client, you can send and receive e-mail through a Microsoft Mail postoffice or the Internet. The addition of other Exchange service providers can expand your use of Messaging to other e-mail services, such as CompuServe. The Windows Messaging client in Windows NT is essentially the same as the Microsoft Exchange e-mail client in Windows 95.

■ **Hardware profiles.** Support for multiple hardware profiles in Windows NT 4.0 enables you to create and use different hardware configurations on a single workstation. This feature is particularly useful on notebook computers where the use of PC Card devices can change a computer's configuration with the insertion or removal of a device.

■ **486 emulator.** This new feature enables RISC-based systems to run Windows- and DOS-based applications that require 386-enhanced mode support or test for the presence of a 486 CPU.

■ **Autorun.** This feature causes CDs to start automatically when they are inserted into the CD-ROM drive.

■ **Distributed Component Object Model (DCOM).** Formerly known as Network OLE, this feature facilitates client/server applications across the network, including TCP/IP networks.

These features and others are examined in detail in Chapter 3, "What's New in Windows NT 4.0." ●

CHAPTER 2

Understanding Windows NT Workstation Architecture

by Jim Boyce

The only people who truly have to understand operating system design and architecture are the programmers and system designers who design and produce operating system. Nevertheless, understanding the inner workings of your operating system, at least on a cursory level, can help you use the operating system to best advantage. In short, it's helpful to understand at least some of the *how*, and not just the when and why.

This chapter examines Windows NT's architecture to give you an overview of Windows NT's components and how they work together to form an operating system.

First, you should have a general understanding of what an operating system is designed to do. ∎

Operating systems

An overview of general operating system concepts will help you begin to understand the Windows NT operating system.

A brief history of Windows NT

Knowing Windows NT's origins will help you understand its design and future.

Windows NT's components and features

The core Windows NT components provide a stable, easily modified operating system architecture.

Windows NT versus Windows 3.x and Windows 95

Although Windows NT might seem to have much in common with previous versions of Windows, it actually is quite different in structure and performance.

N O T E   This chapter presents the Windows NT operating system structure in increasing levels of detail. The first section presents an overview, while subsequent sections delve more deeply into the specifics of the operating system. Environment subsystems, for example, are described in broad terms in the section "The Windows NT Architecture." They are explored further in the section "Exploring the Subsystems." This chapter structure will help you derive the level of detail you need from the material, stopping after a few sections, for example, if you desire only an overview. Exploring Windows NT's architecture in technical detail would require an entire book, however, so this chapter provides an overview to familiarize you with Windows NT's structure and components. ■

Operating System Overview

Today's operating systems perform two primary functions—make the computer easy to use, and enable programs (and therefore, you) to efficiently access and take advantage of the computer's hardware. In essence, an operating system provides multiple layers of interaction between you, your programs, and the computer's hardware.

Without an operating system, a computer is a collection of lifeless and relatively useless components suitable as a doorstop or boat anchor (and a poor anchor, at that!). The computer's BIOS (Basic Input/Output System), which consists of program code stored in ROM (Read-Only Memory) in the computer, gives the computer a limited amount of functionality. For example, the system can perform a superficial hardware test to locate gross memory errors and other major malfunctions when the system is powered up.

Assuming the hardware test completes successfully, the BIOS also enables the system to begin searching for an operating system. Generally, the BIOS searches the local primary floppy disk and hard disk for an operating system. Diskless workstations, which are computers that do not contain any disk drives (either floppy or hard disk), contain a special BIOS that enables the computer to search for an operating system across the local area network (LAN). When an operating system is located, the BIOS begins booting the operating system, which takes over control of the computer.

If the CPU is the brains of the computer, the operating system is its soul. Nearly every function the computer performs is made possible and controlled by the operating system. Although the computer's hardware is capable of some special functions on its own (retrieving data from a disk, for example), the operating system must initiate those functions and process the results. In the case of disk access, for example, the operating system directs the disk controller circuitry to retrieve data from a specific area on the disk. Although the controller could retrieve the data itself, it has no "mind of its own," and must rely on the operating system to tell it to find the data.

Besides controlling hardware, an operating system also makes it possible for programs to run on the computer, and for those programs to interact with the computer's hardware. When a program needs some data from the disk, for example, it makes a call to the operating system and the operating system passes the request on to the disk controller. The data then filters back through the operating system to the program.

The operating system serves as a middleman between the programs and the computer's hardware. But why inject a layer between the programs and the hardware? Why not just let the program control the disk controller directly? There are three reasons—compatibility, simplicity, and security.

Take disk access as an example. By handing the control of the hardware over to the operating system, you eliminate the need for each program to have the ability to control the disk controller. In terms of simplicity, this means that a program developer doesn't have to concern himself with the fact that there are 50 disk controllers of various types on the market or with building support into his program for each one of those controllers. Instead, he relies on the operating system to support each of those controllers. All the programmer has to do is program the application to make the appropriate standard calls to the operating system.

When you consider that there might be seven or eight different types of devices in a typical computer (video adapter, sound card, and so on), you can see that moving the burden of hardware support from the program developer to the operating system developer (and hardware manufacturer) simplifies program development by orders of magnitude.

Placing the burden of hardware communication and control in the hands of the operating system rather than the programs also ensures compatibility. First, you can be assured that any program you buy that supports your operating system will work on your computer (barring bugs and program flaws) regardless of the type of hardware in your computer. Second, you don't have to worry that the program's developer introduced a bug into the program that would potentially cause lost data or hardware problems through incorrect handling of the hardware.

Finally, offloading the responsibility of hardware control from the application to the operating system helps ensure greater system security. By isolating and securing access to the system's hardware, the operating system protects that hardware from unauthorized access. In the case of disk access in Windows NT, for example, a program can't bypass the file system security built into the NTFS file system to access files for which it isn't authorized.

N O T E Even though NTFS and Windows NT offer good security, they still aren't bulletproof. It's possible with a specially designed driver to boot a Windows NT computer to another operating system and gain access to the otherwise secure NTFS file system, including all uncompressed files and security databases. Doing so, however, requires that you have direct access to the Windows NT computer (you can't achieve this across a network). Therefore, the computer and its files are secure as long as the computer is physically secured (behind locked doors). For more information and access to NTFS access drivers for Linux, DOS, and Windows 95, check out the *WINDOWS Magazine* Web site at **www.winmag.com.** ■

ON THE WEB

WINDOWS Magazine Enterprise Windows NTFS site:

http://www.winmag.com/ew/ntfs.htm

Just as the operating system serves as a middleman between programs and the computer's hardware, the operating system also serves as a middleman between you (the user) and the computer. You don't have to manipulate the hardware manually with cryptic commands, but instead can use a graphical interface to access the computer's hardware and your programs.

In short, an operating system provides an *abstraction layer* between you and the computer, and between your programs and the computer's hardware. This abstraction simplifies program design, improves ease of use, and ensures hardware and software compatibility. As you'll learn in the following sections, Windows NT is an excellent example of how abstraction works.

A Brief History of Windows NT

Although Microsoft doesn't tout the fact, Windows NT rose from humble beginnings in OS/2, on which Microsoft and IBM collaborated in the late 1980s. Microsoft and IBM eventually failed to see eye-to-eye on the future of OS/2, and suffered a falling-out. IBM took over OS/2 for its own development, and Microsoft opted to redesign the operating system entirely to create Windows NT, eventually capitalizing on the Windows 3.x marketing phenomena to promote Windows NT. The result is that Windows NT is radically different and improved from the OS/2 operating system.

Late in 1988, Microsoft began the task of designing what would become Microsoft's vision of the operating system for the 1990s—Windows NT. Like its bantam-weight counterpart—Windows—Windows NT enjoyed mixed success throughout its first few years of existence. Starting sometime around early 1995, however, Windows NT began to make major inroads into territory formerly held by UNIX, Novell NetWare, and even DOS.

Today, Windows NT is rapidly becoming the operating system of choice of many businesses, both large and small, for servers as well as for users. Many large companies are bypassing Windows 95 and moving to Windows NT.

The success of Windows NT has been brought about partly through creative marketing, partly through Microsoft's sheer market leverage and clout, but mostly because Windows NT is a good operating system. Why? The next few sections give you a brief overview of NT's features to answer that question and help you understand Windows NT's design and function.

Part
I

Ch
2

Windows NT Design Objectives

Windows NT is a complex operating system that required years to design and develop. Windows NT's designers had many goals for the new operating system. Understanding those design goals can help you understand not only how and why Windows NT works the way it does, but also how to take advantage of the results of those design goals. The following sections explain the features of Windows NT.

Extensibility

An *extensible* operating system is one which can be extended to include new features and enhance existing features. Extending the capabilities of some operating systems is a Herculean task, at best, because the operating system is designed such that its components are so closely intertwined as to be inseparable. Modifying one part of such an operating system requires modifying other parts and often introduces unexpected and unwanted behavior.

Windows NT's designers seriously considered future extensibility when they designed the operating system. As you will learn in the section "The Windows NT Architecture," later in this chapter, Windows NT has a very modular design. Windows NT uses a client/server model at its core, with subsystems such as security, I/O, and other basic functions carefully segregated into separate entities that interact with one another through message calls.

Because of this modular design, operating system components can be modified easily without affecting other components. If a new security feature is required, for example, it requires only that the security subsystem be modified. The new security subsystem continues to interact with the rest of the operating system as before. This modular design also means that new subsystems and their features can be added without affecting other subsystems, making it easy to extend the capabilities of the operating system.

Also figuring in the extensibility of Windows NT is the use of *objects* in the operating system. Objects are abstract data types used to represent various system resources. A *section* object, for example, is a region of shared memory. Objects are managed by the operating system and accessed by applications through standard object services, which consist of predefined API (Application Programming Interface) calls. Because objects place an abstraction "wrapper" around these data types, they can easily be changed without affecting other parts of the operating system. Thus, it's easy to modify existing object structures or add new objects to extend the capabilities of the operating system.

Also playing an important role in Windows NT's extensibility is the use of loadable drivers. This means that drivers can be added to the operating system dynamically even after the operating system is running. This enables support for new devices to be added easily to the operating system.

Lastly, the Remote Procedure Call (RPC) feature in Windows NT, which enables applications to call services independent of the location of those services, makes it possible for the operating system to access services provided by other computers on the network. These services can be made available at any time across the network, extending the capabilities of the operating system.

Portability

Another design goal for Windows NT was *portability*. A portable operating system is one which can be ported (translated) easily from one hardware platform to another. MS-DOS, for example, runs only on systems based on the Intel 80x86 architecture, limiting its appeal and market scope. Windows NT, on the other hand, runs on a variety of systems including those based on the Intel, Alpha, MIPS, and PowerPC platforms. Because of the way Windows NT is designed, it can be ported to other hardware platforms, as well.

To achieve this level of portability, Windows NT had to be written in a portable language, and Microsoft chose C as that language. Because the C language is supported on a range of platforms and is not hardware-dependent, programs (and operating systems) written in C can be ported to new platforms by recompiling the software for the new platform.

It isn't possible to write an operating system without relying on some hardware-specific code (setting registers is an example), so parts of the operating system must be very hardware-specific and non-portable. Hardware-specific code in Windows NT, such as the parts of the operating system written in assembly language (which is hardware-dependent), is carefully isolated and localized. Isolating and localizing this code made it possible to more readily change that code and port the operating system to other platforms. The hardware-specific code can be modified to suit the new platform and the operating system can be recompiled to run on that new platform.

Compatibility

At the time Windows NT was developed, many computer users still relied on MS-DOS programs, so the ability to run DOS programs under Windows NT was a design goal. During that same time period, Windows 3.0 and 3.1 were building considerable popularity for 16-bit Windows-based applications (many sold by Microsoft), so Win16 compatibility was extremely important. Because it had initially developed OS/2, Microsoft also felt obligated to enable its customers to run OS/2 applications under Windows NT. And finally, to make Windows NT attractive to government users, Microsoft decided to build in compatibility for POSIX applications.

N O T E   The acronym POSIX, taken from *Portable Operating System Interface based on uniX*, refers to a set of interface standards that simplify moving applications from one platform to another. ■

The modular nature of Windows NT figured closely in its ability to run applications written for other operating systems. Compatibility was achieved by creating separate *environment subsystems*, each of which provided an environment in which these applications could run. Environment subsystems are explained in more detail in the section "The Windows NT Architecture," later in this chapter.

C2 Security

The United States government categorizes computer security requirements for government installations into seven different levels. To expand its market to government installations, Windows NT was designed to meet level C2 security requirements, which required the following criteria:

- **Secure logon.** A C2-level system must require the user to provide a unique logon identifier (user name) and password to gain access to the system.
- **Discretionary access control.** This means that the person who owns a resource (directory, for example) can specify which other users can access the resource and what level of access they'll have over it.
- **Auditing.** This refers to the ability to identify and log several security events to identify and protect against security breaches.
- **Memory protection.** Secure memory protection prevents one process from reading another process' data without authorization, and ensures that memory is reinitialized before being reused.

Windows NT's security features not only make it salable to the United States government, but also make it an outstanding operating system for businesses that are concerned with those same security issues. You'll find not only solid security in Windows NT, but also a great deal of flexibility in how you apply that security.

Performance

Although, to a large extent, today's computers have outpaced the average user's need for speed, operating system and application performance are still vitally important. Many applications still tax the operating system and hardware's abilities, even on the fastest platforms. Performance was an even bigger issue when Windows NT was designed because the hardware of the day was less capable.

Windows NT provides excellent performance for native Windows NT applications, outperforming Windows 3.x by a factor of two or more, depending on the application. But Windows NT also provides excellent performance for running Win16 and DOS applications.

Reliability and Robustness

Another important design requirement for Windows NT was that it be a reliable and robust operating system. The operating system itself had to be reliable and as free from bugs as possible. The modular design helped ensure the operating system was reliable by isolating subsystems from one another—an errant program or subsystem might bring itself down, but not affect others. By providing each subsystem and application its own memory address space, Windows NT further ensures reliability. If a program crashes, it doesn't take others down with it. Windows NT also provides robustness, using structured exception handling to process errors and to ensure that those errors don't go undetected and are handled.

The Windows NT Architecture

As you'll learn in the following sections, Windows NT achieved its design goals in large part because of its modular client/server design. The first step in understanding how all of Windows NT's components fit together is understanding kernel mode and user mode.

Kernel Mode and User Mode

Windows NT uses two different processor modes—*kernel mode* and *user mode*. Kernel mode is a privileged processor mode in which running code has extensive access to the hardware and system data. User mode is a non-privileged processor mode in which code has only limited access to system data and must access hardware through various operating system services. Some Windows NT operating system components run in kernel mode and others run in user mode.

As explained earlier in this chapter, Windows NT uses a client/server model to separate various operating system components from one another. Object management, security, local procedure calls, process management, memory management, and I/O are low-level components that make up the Windows NT *executive*, which runs in kernel mode (see fig. 2.1). For more information about the executive, refer to the section "The Executive" later in this chapter.

Also running in kernel mode is the Hardware Abstraction Layer (HAL). The HAL provides a low-level interface between the executive and the system's hardware. For more information regarding the HAL, see the section "The Hardware Abstraction Layer (HAL)" later in this chapter.

FIG. 2.1
Windows NT's client/
server model relies on
kernel mode and user
mode to segregate
operating system
functions.

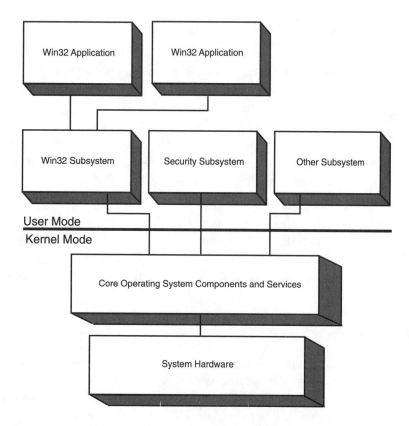

> **N O T E** Because the HAL is self-contained, it can be revised to support a different hardware
> platform. This means that the executive can remain relatively unchanged while the
> HAL is rewritten to support a different hardware platform, simplifying Windows NT's portability.
> Protected subsystems that interact with the executive conceivably could require no modification
> to work with the new platform. ▪

While the executive and HAL run in kernel mode, Windows NT's various protected subsystems run in user mode. Placing these subsystems in user mode isolates them from low-level access to the system's hardware and data. This isolation makes the operating system more reliable and secure, because these subsystems can access the system only through the executive, which controls the system. The importance of this separation will become clearer as you read more about the operating system components and how they interact.

The Hardware Abstraction Layer (HAL)

The Hardware Abstraction Layer (HAL) forms the lowest level of the Windows NT operating system. The HAL does just what its name implies—it inserts a layer of abstraction between the computer's physical hardware and the executive components. The HAL is platform-specific, containing code to enable it to communicate with and control the hardware on which Windows NT is running. Hardware-dependent functions such as I/O interfaces, interrupt controllers, and multiprocessor communication are buried deep in the HAL, isolated from the other parts of the operating system. For example, most of the code that differentiates the MIPS version of Windows NT from the Intel version resides primarily in the HAL.

The executive components communicate with the HAL to access the computer's hardware, so the HAL acts as a middleman between the hardware and the rest of the operating system. Protected subsystems and applications work through the executive to access hardware, which in turn works through the HAL, so the HAL ultimately controls all hardware access.

The Executive

The executive, as explained previously, comprises a set of components that form the core of the Windows NT operating system (see fig. 2.2). These components are of two types—*system services*, which subsystems and other executive components can call, and *internal routines*, which can be called only by other executive objects.

FIG. 2.2
The executive forms an abstraction layer between subsystems/applications and the HAL.

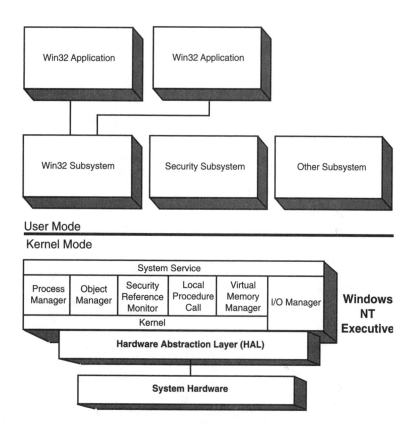

Each of the executive components provides an API-like interface through which they communicate with one another, and through which the operating system's subsystems and applications communicate with the executive components. In effect, the executive components function like servers, with the subsystems functioning as clients. The executive components also function as clients when they are communicating with other executive objects.

Each executive component is independent from the other executive objects. For this reason, an executive object can be removed and replaced by a new version to add new features to the operating system without affecting other executive components. As long as the new version of the component provides the same services and interfaces to enable the other components and subsystems to communicate with it, the operating system continues to function. For example, Windows NT's developers could write a new security reference monitor to add new security features without affecting other components. It's like replacing the engine in your car with a different one—you can't see that the engine is different, and stepping on the accelerator pedal still has the same effect. As far as you can tell, you're using the same, old engine, but the engine is running very differently under the hood.

For more detailed discussion of the executive component objects, see the section "Exploring the Executive" later in this chapter.

Protected Subsystems

The parts of Windows NT that run in user mode are its *protected subsystems* (see fig. 2.3). Protected subsystems get their name from the fact that each is a separate process that runs in its own address space, which means that each is *protected* from the others (and from errant applications) by the Windows NT virtual memory manager. If a Win32 client somehow succeeds in destabilizing the Win32 subsystem, for example, the security subsystem is unaffected.

FIG. 2.3
Protected subsystems communicate with one another through the executive.

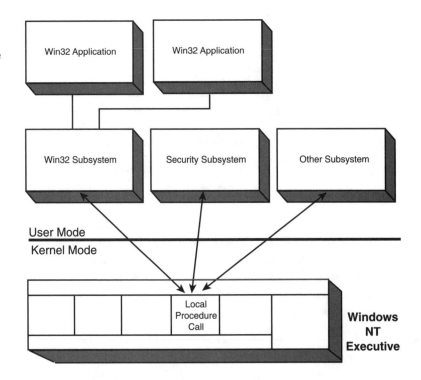

Windows NT's protected subsystems provide APIs to enable communication between subsystems and with applications, enabling subsystems to act as servers (reinforcing the client/server model). Another subsystem or application makes an API call to the executive, where the local procedure call (LPC) facility in the executive translates the call to the server. The server replies to the call, and the LPC routes the message back to the caller.

The protected subsystems are separated into two types—*environment subsystems* and *integral subsystems*. An environment subsystem essentially creates a program execution environment. The Win32 subsystem, for example, is an environment subsystem that enables Windows applications to run under Windows NT. Other environment subsystems provide program execution environments for programs designed for other operating systems: Win16, POSIX, and MS-DOS.

N O T E The Win32 subsystem handles all user/program I/O. All keyboard entry, for example, is handled by the Win32 subsystem, even if that keyboard activity occurs within a DOS console window or Win16 program. ■

Integral subsystems are those protected subsystems that provide system-wide services. An example of an integral subsystem is the security system. The security system handles all security authentication, such as logon and file access.

Included in Windows NT's protected subsystems, in addition to the integral subsystems, are *environment subsystems*. Environment subsystems, as mentioned in the previous section, are those which provide an application execution environment. The Win32 subsystem is the primary environment subsystem in Windows NT, and is the one through which all other environment subsystems process user I/O (keyboard, mouse, and video, for example). Besides the Win32 subsystem, Windows NT includes a POSIX subsystem, Win16 subsystem, and MS-DOS subsystem (see fig. 2.4).

The environment subsystems run as separate processes, each within its own private address space. Just as Windows 3.x is an application that runs on top of the DOS operating system and provides Windows applications with an operating environment in which to work, so these environment subsystems run as applications on top of the Windows NT core operating system (the kernel) and provide their own application execution environments. When a core operating system function is required, either by an end-user application or one of the environment subsystems, the subsystem in question turns control of the executing thread over to the executive. When the function is complete, the executive returns control of the thread to the subsystem. The executive schedules the subsystems' threads in the same way as for other applications, which means that the environment subsystems all multitask.

By providing self-contained execution environments, Windows NT ensures that a program failure in one environment subsystem won't affect another subsystem. If you're running a Win16 application, for example, and it fails, it won't take down any Win32 applications that are running.

FIG. 2.4

The environment subsystems serve as an abstraction layer between user applications and the kernel.

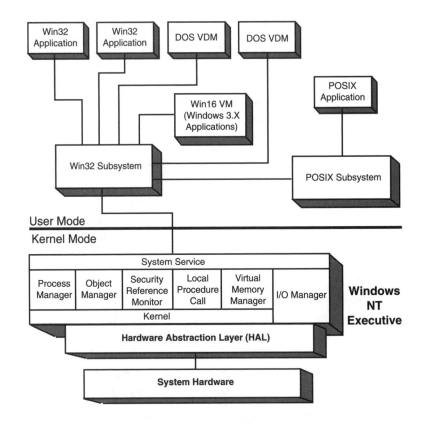

N O T E   Even though the environment subsystems are isolated from one another, they don't operate in a vacuum. Because all user I/O is processed through the Win32 subsystem, the other environment subsystems can communicate with one another and share data through the Clipboard. ▬

Structuring the environment subsystems as distinct user processes rather than incorporating their functions into the kernel is an important facet of Windows NT's reliability and extensibility. First, separating the subsystems as user processes enables Microsoft to maintain a stable base operating system (the kernel) while still providing support for multiple existing APIs. Second, the various APIs can be modified and extended without affecting the core operating system. And third, new APIs can be added to extend the capabilities of the operating system. It's possible, for example, to create a Macintosh environment subsystem, enabling Macintosh applications to run under Windows NT.

Scalability—Supporting Symmetric Multiprocessing

An important feature of Windows NT for an increasing number of users is its *scalability*, which is the ability of the operating system to run on systems with multiple processors. As hardware prices drop, the cost of systems containing multiple processors naturally drops, making them increasingly more attractive for users with very demanding applications.

A single-processor computer does not actually multitask. Instead, processes (such as user programs) share the single CPU's time on a rotating, prioritized basis. Because the CPU can switch between processes so quickly, the programs seem to run at the same time. Multitasking is a little like motion pictures—although a movie is projected as a series of still images, those images pass by so quickly they fool your eye into seeing fluid movement.

Multiprocessor systems, which contain two or more CPUs, use one of two methods—*symmetric multiprocessing* or *asymmetric multiprocessing* (see fig. 2.5). In an asymmetric multiprocessing system, one processor is dedicated to running the operating system code and user threads are handled by one or more other processors. In symmetric multiprocessor systems, processor load is distributed more evenly, with user threads and operating system threads running on any available processor.

FIG. 2.5
Windows NT uses the symmetric multiprocessing (SMP) model.

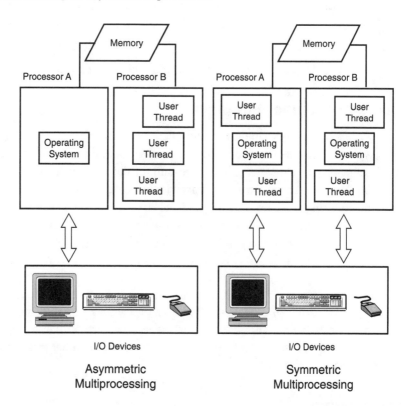

I/O Devices

Asymmetric
Multiprocessing

I/O Devices

Symmetric
Multiprocessing

Although asymmetric multiprocessing (ASMP) is easier to implement in an operating system, ASMP introduces a potential performance bottleneck by placing the burden of running the operating system on a single processor. While the CPU handling the operating system might be operating at maximum capacity, the other processors might be relatively idle, wasting their processing ability.

Symmetric multiprocessing (SMP) systems, however, allow operating system code and user threads to operate on any and all available processors. This eliminates the potential bottleneck caused by running the operating system on a single processor, increasing throughput by equalizing the burden across all processors. In addition, multiple threads of a single process can run on separate processors. A program might have a graphics-related thread running on one processor, a computationally intensive thread running on a another, while a printing thread runs on a third. This ability to schedule threads on multiple processors improves the program's performance.

Exploring the Executive

As previously explained in the section "The Executive," Windows NT's kernel consists of the Hardware Abstraction Layer (HAL) and the executive. The HAL handles hardware-specific functions, and the executive provides the set of core operating system functions that enable user-mode processes to communicate with the hardware and one another.

The executive consists of six components, which are explored in the following sections.

Objects and Object Manager

An *object* is a single runtime instance of a statically defined object type. An *object type* consists of a system-defined data type, a set of services that operate on that data type, and a set of attributes that define the object and the data it contains. In effect, objects are like black boxes. A program can interact with an object and use the data contained in it without knowing anything about the internal structure of the object type. Instead, the program (including the operating system) uses the object's attributes and services to use the object and its data. For this reason, the object can be modified and enhanced internally without affecting processes' ability to work with the object.

N O T E In Windows NT, not all data structures are encapsulated in objects. Data structures used internally by an executive component and not shared with other executive components or required by user-mode processes are not structured as objects. Only those data structures that must be named, secured, shared, or visible to other components and processes are created as objects. ■

The component of the executive that manages objects is called, appropriately, the *object manager*. The object manager creates, tracks, protects, and deletes objects. Placing the responsibility for object management in a single component of the executive achieves a variety of objectives. For example, the object manager provides a common mechanism for managing system resources (such as memory). The object manager also plays a critical role (as sole manager) in protecting objects, ensuring data security and integrity. Because access to all objects occurs through the object manager, an errant program can't corrupt an object by handling it directly, nor can a process gain access to an object without necessary security authorization.

The object manager also enables the operating system to audit the use of objects, which means that usage limits can be set on specific objects, preventing a process from taking control of a resource or using it excessively at the expense of other processes.

Windows NT supports two types of objects—*executive objects* and *kernel objects*. Executive objects are those objects maintained by the executive's components, and which are accessible by user-mode processes. Executive objects can be created and manipulated both by executive components and by user-mode protected subsystems.

Kernel objects are those which are created and manipulated only within the executive by the various executive components. Kernel objects are not visible or accessible to user-mode subsystems. Kernel objects provide low-level features and define low-level entities within the operating system.

Objects consist of two parts—an *object header* and an *object body* (see fig. 2.6). The object header stores variable data about the object, and the object body stores static data about the object. For standardization and simplicity, every object has a consistent set of object attributes that enable the object manager to manage the object. These attributes include the object's name, security descriptor, type (kernel or user), and other common information about the object. These attributes are contained in the object header. Static information that is specific to the object type, such as size, are stored in the object body.

The object manager is responsible for general object manipulation such as creating, naming, protecting, and deleting objects. Other executive components work through the object manager to define and access objects, but the object manager does not have complete control over objects. Other executive components provide services to manage objects that they define. The I/O manager, for example, provides services that enable other executive components and user-mode subsystems to handle files. The I/O manager calls the object manager to create a file object, passing it the necessary parameters to define the file object. The object manager then creates and protects the object, but the I/O manager provides the services by which other processes use the object.

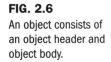

FIG. 2.6
An object consists of an object header and object body.

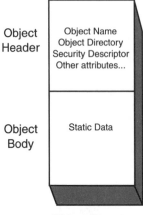

Object Structure

Security Reference Monitor

The *security reference monitor* is the kernel-mode portion of Windows NT's security system. The security reference monitor is responsible for providing security authentication and auditing for operating system resources. Consider an example in which you attempt to open a file with a program.

The first part of the whole authentication process for opening the file actually begins much earlier, when you log on. The security subsystem validates your user ID and password in the security database. If your ID and password are valid, the security subsystem creates an *access token* object and attaches it to your process. The access token contains security-related information derived from your user account. The security ID attribute in the access token object is your user ID. Other attributes in the access token object include your group IDs (memberships) and privileges.

When you attempt to open the file, your program makes an API call to the Win32 environment subsystem. Win32 calls the object manager to open the file, passing it your access token. Object manager calls the security reference monitor, which also uses the access token, comparing it with the security settings for the file to determine if you have the authority to perform the requested operation on the file. If so, the file is opened. If not, an error message is generated to inform you that you do not have the necessary access privileges.

Authenticating a user's access privileges to various objects is not the security reference monitor's only function. The security reference monitor also provides similar security functions for executive components that attempt to create, access, or modify objects. In addition, the security reference monitor is responsible for security auditing—adding security audit events to the appropriate system logs, and when configured to do so, also generating audible or visual cues to the system administrator when security events occur.

Access Control Lists   You might be wondering how the security reference monitor keeps track of the access settings for each object. When objects are created, they are assigned security descriptors (an attribute in the object's header). The security descriptor includes an *access control list* (ACL) that lists the security protections that apply to the object. When you set the access privileges for a file or directory you have created, for example, you're actually changing the object's ACL.

Entries in the ACL are called *access control entries* (ACE). Each ACE includes a security ID (such as a user or group name) and a list of access privileges that apply for that security ID (see fig. 2.7). An ACL can contain multiple ACEs, because you (and operating system components) can assign multiple levels of access for various objects.

FIG. 2.7
An access control list consists of the access control entries that define how an object can be used, and by whom.

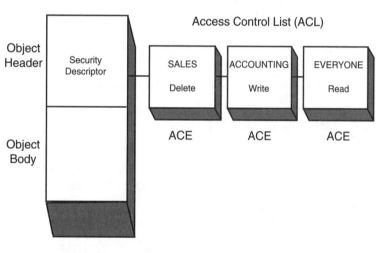

Process Manager

A process consists of an executable program with initial execution code and data, a private address space for the process' use, needed system resources such as I/O ports and files, and at least one thread. A thread is essentially a unit of execution—a logical, executable portion of a program. Printing a spreadsheet is a good example of a thread within a process. The spreadsheet program constitutes the overall process (along with address space, resources, and so on), and the task of printing the document is one thread of execution.

The process manager is the executive component that is responsible for creating and managing processes and their threads. In reality, the process manager's primary function is working through the object manager to create process and thread objects on behalf of the environment subsystems. The process manager also is responsible for destroying (through the object manager) those process and thread objects.

▶ **See** "Understanding Processes and Threads," **p. 43**

Local Procedure Call Facility

The local procedure call facility (LPC) component of the executive is responsible for handling communication between client and server processes, such as between executive components, subsystems, and user processes (programs). When the process manager is called by an environment subsystem to create a thread, for example, the call comes through the LPC to the process manager. The process manager sends a call through the LPC to the object manager to create the thread. The reply from the object manager comes back through the LPC to the process manager, which then communicates back to the environment subsystem through the LPC.

The LPC is modeled after the industry standard remote procedure call (RPC) facility that enables processes on different computers to communicate with one another. LPC is optimized specifically for processes running on the same computer.

Virtual Memory Manager

Two primary types of memory come into play in today's personal computers—physical memory and virtual memory. *Physical memory* refers to the actual memory locations in the computer's RAM and consists of 1-byte storage units. Each byte has an address to identify it uniquely, much like the numbers on a house identify its address. Each byte is numbered starting at zero and continuing incrementally to the last physical byte.

Virtual memory refers to the way in which the physical memory is structured and managed by the system and is not tied to the physical memory structure or capacity. Each process is allocated its own virtual address space, which is a range of memory addresses the process can use. The range of addresses in the virtual address space can exceed the amount of physical RAM in the computer. The computer might contain 16M of RAM, for example, but the process might be allocated as much as, say, 4G of virtual memory.

It's therefore the function of the virtual memory manager (VMM) to map sections of the process' virtual memory address space to physical address space. It's unlikely that you'll have 4G of RAM in your computer in the near future, so the VMM can obviously accommodate only a portion of the virtual address space in physical memory. The second function of the VMM is therefore to swap the contents of physical memory to disk when the amount of available physical RAM is insufficient to accommodate the amount of virtual memory needed. By swapping the contents of the virtual memory to disk, the VMM makes it seem to the process that the computer actually has 4G of physical RAM.

This swapping is like presenting an entire book to a reader using only two pages of erasable paper, one visible to the reader and one invisible. When the reader finishes with the current page (the data in memory), you copy it to the spare, invisible page (to disk). Then, you write the next requested page of data to visible page. If the reader wants to thumb back to the previous page, you swap the contents of the visible page for the invisible page. The VMM simply accomplishes a similar task with memory pages, swapping pages in memory for pages on the disk.

In addition to mapping memory address space, the VMM also enables processes to share memory. If two processes need to access the same data, the VMM copies the data into a range of physical addresses. Then, the VMM simply maps the virtual address spaces of both processes to the same range of physical memory.

Finally, the VMM is responsible for protecting memory. It's a certainty that multiple processes will always be running on your computer, each requiring its own address space. It's also a certainty that these processes will be using different ranges of physical memory at one time. It's the VMM's job to ensure that one process' virtual address space is invisible and inaccessible from another. This ensures security (an unauthorized process can't read data from another) and reliability (one process can't corrupt another process' memory).

I/O Manager

A computer processes an amazing amount of input and output (I/O). Input and output come and go to a variety of devices—the mouse, keyboard, the display, disk drives, CD-ROM drives, tape drives, redirected network resources, serial ports, parallel ports, infrared ports, and more. Something within Windows NT must manage and coordinate all this I/O, and that something is the *I/O manager*, another component of the executive.

All I/O within Windows NT is packet-based, with each I/O request represented by a structured *I/O Request Packet*, or IRP. The IRP is simply a data structure for controlling how its associated I/O operation is processed. It's the I/O manager's job to define a structured mechanism by which IRPs are created and exchanged. When an I/O request is generated (by an application, for example), the I/O manager receives the request and creates an IRP. The I/O manager then passes the IRP to the appropriate device driver. The device driver processes the IRP, performing whatever function the IRP specifies, then passes the result back to the I/O manager.

The I/O manager also provides code to support common functions that device drivers can use to process I/O requests. By implementing these common functions, the I/O manager reduces the number and types of functions that the individual device drivers must perform, simplifying the device drivers' design (and making them easier to develop).

Lastly, the I/O manager provides a set of common services that enable the environment subsystems to implement their own I/O functions.

Exploring the Subsystems

The Windows NT kernel, consisting of the executive and HAL, forms a complete operating system, though one without a user interface. The user-mode subsystems briefly described previously in this chapter provide that user interface. But paning windows on the display is just one small facet of what the subsystems do. They also provide security, application execution environments, and other features. The following sections explore the three most common Windows NT user-mode subsystems. Figure 2.8 shows the subsystems that are covered in this chapter.

FIG. 2.8
The user-mode subsystems form the upper layers of the Windows NT operating system.

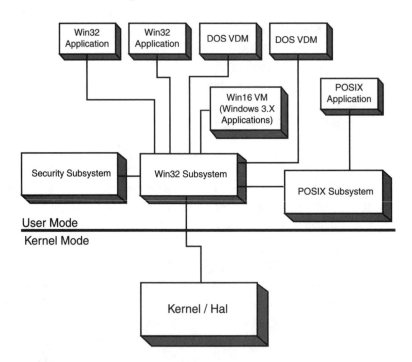

Security

The security subsystem serves as a gatekeeper between user processes (such as other subsystems and network access requests) and the resources controlled by the operating system. Local logon, for example, is processed through the security subsystem. To log on locally to a Windows NT computer, you press Ctrl+Alt+Del to display the logon dialog box. Because all I/O is handled through the Win32 subsystem, the process that monitors the system for logon requests is a Win32 program. When this process detects a logon attempt, it prompts for user name, password, and logon location (domain/workgroup). The logon process then forwards this information to the security subsystem.

The security system passes the logon information to the appropriate authentication module, which varies according to the source of the security request. In the case of local logon, the security subsystem passes the logon information to the Windows authentication module, which compares that logon information with the security account manager (SAM) database. If the logon information supplied matches an account in the SAM, the authentication module returns to the security subsystem the user's ID and a list of groups to which the user belongs.

The security subsystem then checks the local policy database for other access restrictions and privileges for that user, such as quota limits. The security subsystem uses that information to build an *access token*, which identifies the user's access privileges and rights to other processes. The security subsystem then passes that access token to the logon process, which calls the Win32 subsystem to create a user process for the user, complete with interactive shell—the Windows NT Explorer GUI.

In essence, the security subsystem serves as a high-level security monitor. In addition to processing logon requests, the security subsystem also tracks which resources are audited and works with the security reference monitor in the kernel to implement that auditing.

Win32

Without question, the most important of Windows NT's subsystems to the operating system is the Win32 subsystem. First and foremost in the Win32 subsystem's list of responsibilities is to provide an application execution environment for 32-bit Windows applications. The Win32 subsystem is therefore the environment subsystem that enables Windows NT and Windows 95 applications to run on a Windows NT system.

In addition to providing a Win32 application execution environment, the Win32 subsystem is responsible for providing the Windows NT user interface. In actuality, the part of the interface that you might typically consider to *be* Windows NT—the Explorer interface—is really just another Win32 application running on the Win32 subsystem. The core interface components that support the Explorer interface are an integral part of the Win32 subsystem. These components include:

- **Window manager.** The window manager manages the display of windows on the desktop, handles user input for applications, processes Clipboard data transfers, and other tasks such as repainting the display when you move a window or other object on the desktop.

- **Console.** The console provides windowed text support.

- **Operating system functions.** Various functions built into the Win32 subsystem enable Win32 applications to access Windows NT system services for I/O, object access and manipulation, thread synchronization, and other system-level functions.

- **Graphics device drivers.** The graphics device drivers you install in Windows NT function as part of the Win32 subsystem, performing such functions as painting the display. The GDI calls the graphics device drivers to process graphics and text, and the graphics device drivers themselves call the lower-level Windows NT device drivers to actually process the tasks on the physical hardware.

The Win32 subsystem is obviously important to your ability to run Win32 applications and access the computer through the Explorer interface. But the Win32 subsystem also is indispensable to the other environment subsystems for running non-Windows applications. For example, the Win32 subsystem processes all user I/O, so when you are running a DOS program under Windows NT, it's actually the Win32 subsystem that processes your keyboard and mouse input and translates that input to the DOS process in which the program is running.

The Win32 subsystem also processes all the output for the other environment subsystems, which means our sample DOS program's output is processed by the Win32 subsystem for display, even when the program is running full-screen. The Win32 subsystem does more than just provide a means of I/O handling for the other environment subsystems, however. Win32 also is responsible for process creation and management for the other environment subsystems, which means Win32 is an integral link between the other subsystems and the executive.

MS-DOS and Win16

One of the primary goals for Windows NT's design and success was application compatibility. The success of Windows 3.x and 16-bit Windows applications was a real incentive to Microsoft to support those applications under Windows NT. Although most Windows NT users would switch to Win32 versions of their programs over time, Microsoft had to ensure compatibility for those users' Win16 applications for the short term. And, many Win16 applications would never be rewritten for Windows NT—another incentive to support Win16 applications under Windows NT. Finally, the huge base of existing DOS applications meant that Windows NT had to support DOS programs.

Under Windows 3.x, all Windows applications run in a single virtual machine (VM) called the *system virtual machine*. This means that all running Windows applications on a Windows 3.x system cooperatively multitask in the same operating environment, sharing system resources. DOS programs running on a Windows 3.x system each have their own VM, a necessity because DOS programs by their very nature expect to have full and exclusive use of all system resources (because DOS was not designed as a multitasking operating system). Figure 2.9 illustrates VMs on a Windows 3.x system.

FIG. 2.9
Under Windows 3.x, DOS and Windows 3.x programs are accommodated in separate virtual machines.

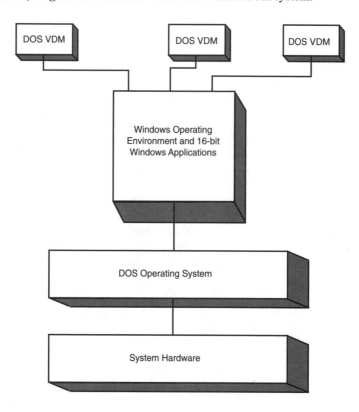

As they do under Windows 3.x, DOS applications running under Windows NT do so in a *virtual DOS machine*, or VDM. A VDM is a process created by the Win32 subsystem and is, in essence, a 32-bit Windows programs that only *looks* like a DOS environment. The VDM process provides a DOS-like environment complete with segregated address space and all other features and characteristics of a true single-tasking DOS operating system. Because the VDM duplicates a DOS operating environment, DOS programs running in a VDM perform just as they do on a computer running only the DOS operating system. The primary difference is that the VDM does not interact directly with the hardware as does DOS, but instead works through the Win32 subsystem and executive, providing isolation of VDMs from one another and other application environments to ensure system reliability.

Under Windows NT, all Win16 applications also run in a single virtual machine. Like DOS programs, the Win16 applications run in a single VDM process, sharing address space. Like the DOS VDM, the Win16 VDM simulates the DOS-based Windows 3.1 environment under which Win16 applications run. In effect, the Win16 VDM provides a Windows 3.1 operating environment, complete with its own GDI, window manager, and other Windows 3.1 components. But, the Win16 VDM works through the Win32 subsystem and executive, as do DOS VDMs.

By structuring the DOS and Win16 VDMs as Win32 user processes, Windows NT enables DOS and Win16 programs to be isolated from other programs such as Win32 programs. This isolation provides a high degree of reliability, ensuring that an errant DOS or Win16 program will not adversely affect Win32 applications by performing unsupported system calls or stepping on the address space of another program. This isolation also protects the operating system from such errant programs. Figure 2.10 illustrates the interaction between Win16 VDM, DOS VDMs, Win32 subsystem, and kernel.

FIG. 2.10
The Win16 and DOS VDMs interact with the system through the Win32 subsystem and the executive.

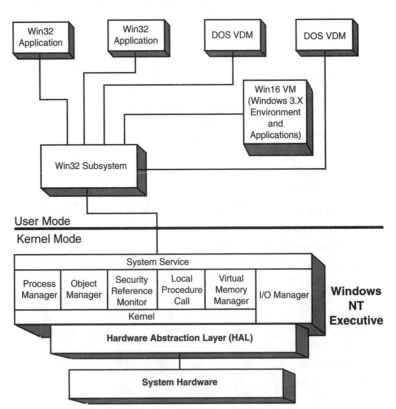

TIP By default, Win16 applications share address space. You can, however, run Win16 in separate address spaces if you prefer. In such a case, Windows NT runs the application as a separate process. This offers a means of running a potentially aberrant application without affecting other Win16 applications. To run a Win16 program as a separate process, use the Run command in the Start menu to start in the program. In the Run dialog box, enable the Run In Separate Memory Space checkbox.

Understanding Processes and Threads

Unlike its predecessors DOS and Windows 3.x, Windows NT is a multithreaded operating system. Understanding Windows NT's architecture therefore requires at least a basic understanding of processes and threads.

Overview of Processes and Threads

Programs written for single-tasking, single-processor operating systems such as DOS are very different in design from a Windows NT application. Even so, all programs, regardless of their target operating system, are similar in that all are a fixed sequence of instructions. The difference is in how the instructions are executed.

A simple BASIC language program, for example, might start execution with its first statement and execute each consecutive statement in turn until the last statement is executed. Such a program is obviously very linear in its execution. But most of today's programs are much more modular in design, owing to the structure of today's more capable programming languages such as C, which lend themselves to a more modular approach to programming. Opening a file, for example, is written as a self-contained function that can be called from any point in the program, if necessary.

The distinction between a program and a process is an important one. A *program* is the static set of instructions, whether linear or modular. A *process* is a running instance of the program, complete with address space, variables, and other resources (files, ports, and so on) needed by the program to function.

Windows 3.1 is a multiprocessing operating environment. As with Windows NT, you can run multiple programs concurrently under Windows 3.x. You might have three or four DOS programs and a handful of Win16 programs running at the same time, for example. Each one of the DOS programs is a process, and the Win16 programs function collectively as a process. One of the differences between the DOS/Windows 3.x operating environment and the Windows NT operating system is that Windows NT supports *multithreaded execution*.

A *thread* often is loosely defined as a *unit of execution*. The easiest way to envision a thread is to think of basic tasks that a typical program performs—open a file, repaginate a document, perform a database query, and print a document. Each of these tasks represent a thread of execution (although the program must be designed to structure these tasks as threads under a multithreaded operating system).

In Windows NT, threads are created as objects of type *thread*. A thread's object body attributes include a client ID that identifies the thread uniquely, a thread context (set of register values and other data that defines the execution state of the thread), and other information about the thread and its status. The object manager in the executive has the responsibility of creating, managing, and destroying threads.

The kernel schedules threads for execution on the system's CPU(s) based on the thread's priority, and changes the priority of waiting threads periodically to ensure that all waiting threads are processed. On a multiprocessor system, different threads are scheduled and execute concurrently on the system's CPUs, providing true multitasking.

Threads are typically used in a program for asynchronous operations, or those tasks that do not have to be performed linearly with other tasks in the program. Printing is a good example of such a task. If the program is designed such that printing is handled through a separate thread, you can begin printing the document (scheduling the print thread on the CPU), then continue editing the document (which uses other threads) while the printing operation takes place. On a multiprocessor system, this means that the system could be running different parts (threads) of the program at one time.

Multithreading is one of the most important reasons for upgrading your applications if you're currently running Windows 3.x versions of those applications. By upgrading to the Windows 95 or Windows NT versions, it's likely that you'll gain the advantage of multithreaded operation in those programs. Multithreading will improve the application's performance, usability, and smoothness with which it multitasks with other applications.

N O T E   Just because an application is written specifically for Windows 95 or Windows NT is not a guarantee that the program supports multithreaded execution. The program must be specifically designed to support multithreading. If you're not sure about a program, check with the publisher's tech support staff. ■

Adding a Network Layer

By definition, an operating system does not include network functionality. When Microsoft designed Windows NT, however, it did so from the point of view that Windows NT should be a complete out-of-the-box solution, including all the features necessary to enable the computer to function in a networked environment. This meant that the operating system should include its own peer-to-peer network capability and be able to interface with other network operating systems through support for a range of network clients and protocols.

In addition to wanting to provide a complete operating environment with Windows NT, Microsoft had its sights set on Novell NetWare when it designed Windows NT, hoping to take market share away from NetWare. Although it has taken quite a bit of time, Microsoft has succeeded—Windows NT is rapidly gaining market share against Novell NetWare.

Part

I

Ch

2

Network functionality can be broken into two primary functions—requesting resources stored on a remote computer, and providing access to local shared resources. These two functions are handled by the two primary networking components in Windows NT—the redirector and server.

The Redirector

Ideally, the network should be as transparent to the user as possible. When you open a remote file, for example, you should be able to do so in the same way you open a local file. A network redirector provides that transparency. A *redirector* processes local requests for network resources, redirecting those requests onto the network and to the remote server where the resource is stored. When you open a file stored on a remote computer, for example, the redirector intercepts the request, packages it, and sends it out on the network. The redirector then waits for a reply and directs the information to the application when it arrives from the remote server. The redirector also redirects printing to remote printers so the application can print to a network printer as easily (and using the same mechanisms) as printing to a local printer.

In Windows NT, the redirector is a file system driver. The redirector's primary function is to provide a layer of abstraction between you and remote network resources, making it look to you like remote network resources such as files and printers are installed right on your computer (just like local resources). When you perform an operation requesting a file, for example, the I/O manager in the executive creates an I/O Request Packet (IRP), just as it does for local I/O, and passes the IRP to the redirector. The redirector then processes the IRP, communicating with the remote server. It then passes the results to the I/O manager, which in turn passes the results to the calling process.

Besides handling network I/O, the redirector performs supporting tasks for maintaining network resource availability and reliability. For example, the redirector automatically reconnects to a remote server when the connection to the server is lost.

The Server

The second major component of the network is the *server*. Not to be confused with the generic term applied to any computer that shares its resources on the network, the Windows NT server is a file system driver that processes requests by other computers on the network to access local shared resources. When a request comes in from another computer on the network, Windows NT's security components process the request and pass it to the server. The server then processes the request, returning the results to the remote computer.

The server could have been designed as a protected subsystem, but implementing it as a file system driver (even though it processes requests for non-file resources such as printers) offers performance advantages. As a file system driver, the server becomes a part of the kernel, and therefore can access other kernel components directly rather than through NT services, as do the subsystems. A prime example is in moving large amounts of data: The server can communicate directly with the cache manager to move the requested data to the cache, and the server then moves the data directly from the cache to the network. The server therefore can bypass functions that would cause additional system overhead and reduce system throughput.

Transports (Protocols)

The server and redirector are just two components in a many-layered network mechanism in Windows NT. To ensure that network traffic can move between computers reliably, a network *transport* or *protocol* is used. The protocol defines the way in which the network data packets are structured and transmitted across the network. For one computer to communicate with another, both computers must be running the same protocol.

Windows NT implements protocols as drivers that interact with the redirector and server components to provide network access. While the redirector and server handle higher-level tasks such as receiving and processing requests for resources, the protocols convert those requests and the associated data into a standard format that the two computers can exchange reliably. Windows NT provides protocols to support a wide range of network environments. Most common are NetBEUI, TCP/IP, and IPX/SPX.

▶ **See** "Understanding Network Layers," **p. 357**

Windows NT versus Windows 3.x and Windows 95

An in-depth comparison between Windows 3.x, Windows 95, and Windows NT is beyond the scope of this book. There are some issues that warrant examination, however, beginning with DOS and Windows 3.x.

DOS and Windows 3.x

Windows 3.x provides a multitasking environment for DOS and 16-bit Windows applications. Windows 3.x is not an operating system. Instead, Windows 3.x is an application that runs on top of the DOS operating system and extends the functionality (considerably) of DOS.

Windows 3.x provides a multitasking environment for DOS and 16-bit Windows applications. Each DOS program runs in its own VDM (virtual DOS machine), and all Windows applications share a single VM called the *system virtual machine*, or system VM. Because all Windows applications share a VM, they are not isolated from one another. One ill-behaved Windows program can bring down not only the other running Windows programs, but Windows itself, bringing the whole system to its knees.

Another drawback is that Windows 3.x employs cooperative multitasking. When Windows 3.x gives control of the CPU to a Windows program, it essentially relinquishes control completely to the program. If the program chooses not to give back control of the CPU, there's nothing Windows can do to recover the system. One program can therefore hog the processor, preventing other programs from accessing the processor.

Windows 95

Windows 95 provides a step up from Windows 3.x in reliability and cooperation between programs. Windows 95 supports DOS and 16-bit Windows (Win16) applications as well as 32-bit Windows (Win32) applications. Rather than sharing a virtual machine, Win32 programs run as separate processes, which effectively isolates each Win32 program from the others. If a Win32 program crashes, it doesn't affect other running programs or the operating system. With rare exceptions, Windows 95 can shut down the program and continue running without any problems.

Another difference from Windows 3.x is that Windows 95 employs preemptive multitasking rather than cooperative multitasking. This means that Windows 95 retains control of the CPU and programs have access to it only as long as Windows 95 allows it. Windows 95 can preempt a program, suspending it to allow other programs to access the processor. This effectively prevents one program from hogging the processor. This is true for Win16 programs, because Windows 95 can preempt the process in which the Win16 programs are running (as in Windows 3.x, all Win16 programs share a VM).

In addition, Windows 95 supports multithreading, which Windows 3.x does not. As with Win32 programs running under Windows NT, Win32 programs running under Windows 95 must be specifically written as multithreaded programs.

Windows NT

Although Windows NT would seem to build on the features and capabilities of Windows 95, the reverse is actually true. Windows 95 was designed with Windows NT as the model. Like Windows 95, Windows NT provides preemptive multitasking and multithreaded execution. Windows NT also supports multiprocessor systems, which Windows 95 does not. Although you can run Windows 95 on a multiprocessor system, doing so simply shuts down all but one of the CPUs, giving you a single-processor system while Windows 95 is running.

Windows NT and Windows 95 are very different in internal structure, however, and those differences result in Windows NT being more robust, more reliable, and more secure. Although you can implement user-level security on a Windows 95 workstation (rather than share-level security), doing so requires the presence on the network of a Windows NT server to act as a security server. In short, local and remote resources are much more secure under Windows NT than is possible under Windows 95.

Performance is another important advantage offered by Windows NT. Performance naturally varies depending on the types of applications you run and how your computer is configured, but you can expect as much as a 25 percent to 50 percent increase in performance from Windows 3.x to Windows 95. Windows NT offers a similar performance jump over Windows 95, making Windows NT considerably more powerful than either Windows 3.x or Windows 95.

From Here...

You now should have a basic understanding of the core components and features of Windows NT and how those components interact. You also now have an inkling of some of Windows NT's new features. For additional information about Windows NT's components and features, refer to these chapters:

- Chapter 3, "What's New in Windows NT 4.0," offers an overview of the many new features in Windows NT 4.0.

- Chapter 9, "Optimizing Physical and Virtual Memory," explains Windows NT's memory structure and utilization in detail, with tips on how to optimize its performance.

- Chapter 10, "Optimizing the File System," provides an explanation of the FAT and NTFS file systems, which will help you understand how the operating system supports and interacts with mass media subsystems.

Part
I

Ch
2

What's New in Windows NT 4.0

by Jim Boyce

Whether you are concerned more with appearances or function, you'll find many satisfactory new features in Windows NT 4.0. From system-level features such as support for hardware profiles to user-level features such as the new Windows 95-style interface, Windows NT 4.0 is full of new features. The Program Manager interface used in previous versions of Windows NT has been replaced by the Windows 95 interface, improving ease-of-use and offering a consistent interface across the two platforms.

This chapter also discusses NDS-Aware Client/Gateway Services for NetWare; Point-to-Point Tunneling Protocol (PPTP) client, which enables a workstation to participate in a private virtual network; the 486 emulator; and autorun, which enables Windows NT to automatically launch data and audio CDs when they are inserted in the CD-ROM drive. ■

Windows Explorer

The Windows Explorer provides a means of viewing all your system's resources within the context of a single interface.

Internet Explorer and other Internet tools

Windows NT includes Microsoft's Internet Explorer Web browser and many other TCP/IP and Internet-related utilities.

Windows Messaging

The Windows Messaging client replaces the Microsoft Exchange client.

Distributed Component Object Model (DCOM)

Formerly known as Network OLE, DCOM makes it possible to create and use distributed client/server applications across the network.

DirectX

DirectX adds improved multimedia features to Windows NT.

Peer Web Services

Peer Web Services make it easy to create a personal Web server for the Internet or within an intranet.

Log on through Dial-Up Networking

Dial-Up Networking support in Windows NT enables you to log on to a domain or LAN.

Windows 95 User Interface

One of the most notable features in Windows 95 is its new interface, which most users will agree is vastly improved over the Windows 3.x interface shared by previous versions of Windows NT. First introduced for beta testing as the Shell Technology Preview, the Windows 95 interface is now firmly integrated in Windows NT 4.0 (see fig. 3.1).

FIG. 3.1
Windows NT 4.0 integrates the Windows 95 interface for improved usability.

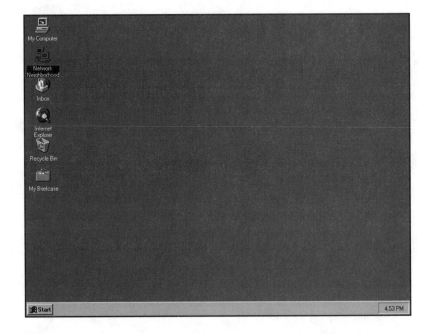

As you become comfortable with the new interface, you'll realize that it improves on many of the previous interface's shortcomings while retaining those elements that worked well. Drag-and-drop has been expanded for use in many new areas. Program Manager has been replaced by an integrated desktop. The File Manager has been replaced by Explorer, which gives you a view not only of your disks, but other resources such as the network, your e-mail inbox, the Control Panel, administrative tools, and more.

N O T E   The *Windows NT Workstation 4.0 Advanced Technical Reference* does not cover the new Windows NT interface in detail. For a comprehensive explanation, refer to *Special Edition Using Windows NT Workstation 4.0*, from Que. ■

Windows Explorer

Another key feature in the new Windows NT 4.0 interface is the Windows Explorer. Explorer is similar in function to the old Windows NT 3.x File Manager, except that Explorer gives you access to other objects in addition to your disks, including the Control Panel, inbox, and Network Neighborhood. Figure 3.2 shows the Explorer window.

FIG. 3.2
Explorer gives you a view and access to most of the resources on your system and network.

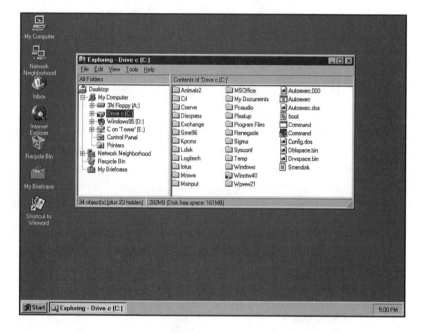

Part
I

Ch
3

The Explorer consists of a standard program window with two panes. The left pane, or *tree pane*, displays a hierarchical tree of the objects available from Explorer. The right pane, or *contents pane*, shows the contents of the currently selected object in the tree.

In general, the Explorer interface is self-explanatory for an experienced Windows user. The following are a few useful tips for features that are not obvious:

- **Using drag-and-drop.** In addition to using drag-and-drop to move and copy objects from the contents pane to another folder or the desktop, you can move and copy objects by dragging them from the contents pane to the tree pane, and vice-versa. For example, you can move a file to a network disk simply by dragging it from the contents pane to the network disk's folder in the tree.

N O T E   Unlike other types of files, dragging and dropping an EXE file copies the file, rather than moving it. To move an EXE file with drag-and-drop, hold down the Shift key while dragging the EXE file. Or, right-drag the file and choose Move Here from the context menu. ■

- **Selecting multiple items.** As in File Manager, you can select multiple items to copy, move, or delete in Explorer. To select multiple items in a series, click the first item in the series to select it, then hold down the Shift key and select the last item in the series. To select objects not in series, hold down the Ctrl key while clicking the object to select it. To select all items, press Ctrl+A.

- **Use right-click.** You can view the properties of almost any object in Explorer by right-clicking the object and selecting Properties from the context menu. The context menu also enables other tasks that vary from one object to another.

- **Activating a folder.** Explorer doesn't display the contents of a folder in the contents pane until you actually select the folder in either the tree or contents pane. This means you can select a folder to display its contents, then expand and collapse the tree to view other folder locations without opening them. This is useful when you want to move or copy objects to another folder, for example. Just open the folder, select the objects, then manipulate the tree until you can see the destination folder. Then, drag the files from the contents pane to the other folder in the tree.

- **Sort the contents pane.** When you select the Details view for the contents pane (choose View, Details or click the Details toolbar button), the pane contains four columns: Name, Size, Type, and Modified. You can sort the view on any of these four columns just by clicking the column header. Clicking the column header again switches between ascending and descending order. The current sort order is used for subsequent folders, until you specify a different sort order.

When File Manager Is Better

Explorer is useful in a number of ways, most notably because unlike File Manager, it gives you a view of a much broader range of resources. For someone who is experienced with File Manager, however, Explorer can require an adjustment in the way you do things.

For example, Explorer doesn't support MDI, so you're limited to only one window. You can, however, open multiple instances of Explorer to achieve the same effect as multiple document windows. You might prefer to continue working with File Manager, at least for some tasks. To start File Manager, choose Start, Run, and enter **winfile** in the Run dialog box.

Internet Tools

You'll find plenty of Internet client and server tools in Windows NT 4.0. On the client side, one of the most important new features is the Internet Explorer.

Internet Explorer

Internet Explorer is Microsoft's World Wide Web client software (see fig. 3.3). With Internet Explorer you can browse the Web through a dial-up connection to an Internet service provider or through a hard-wired Internet connection.

FIG. 3.3
Browse the Web with Microsoft's Internet Explorer.

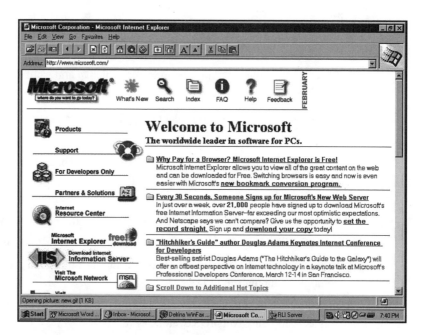

Part

I

Ch

3

Internet Explorer is designed around the new Windows NT interface. In addition to using Internet Explorer to browse remote and local Web sites, you also can view local HTML and JPEG files with Internet Explorer.

TCP/IP Utilities

Windows NT Workstation includes an impressive range of TCP/IP utilities:

■ **finger.** The finger utility displays information about a user on a system you specify.

- **ftp.** The file transfer program (ftp) enables you to transfer files between Internet nodes.

- **lpr.** This utility enables you to print to a computer running an LPD server.

- **rcp.** This utility enables you to transfer a file from a Windows NT computer to a system running rshd (remote shell daemon), such as a UNIX computer. It also can be used to transfer files between two computers running rshd.

- **rexec.** This utility enables you to execute a command on a remote computer running the REXEC service.

- **rsh.** This utility enables you to execute a command on a remote computer running the RSH service.

- **telnet.** With telnet you can log on to computers remotely to run applications and access data.

- **tftp.** The tftp utility enables you to transfer files to and from a remote computer running the tftp service.

Windows NT also includes a good selection of TCP/IP management and troubleshooting tools:

- **arp.** The arp utility modifies the IP-to-Ethernet or Token Ring address translation tables used by the Address Resolution Protocol (ARP), and is useful for overcoming routing problems.

- **hostname.** This utility displays the host name of the current computer.

- **ipconfig.** The ipconfig utility displays all current TCP/IP settings.

- **lpq.** The lpq utility enables you to determine the status of a print queue on a remote computer running the LPD service.

- **nbtstat.** This diagnostic utility displays current protocol statistics and network connections using NetBIOS over TCP/IP.

- **netstat.** This utility displays current protocol statistics and network connections.

- **ping.** This diagnostic utility tests connections to other TCP/IP nodes by sending and receiving test packets.

- **route.** The route utility enables you to manipulate network routing tables to overcome routing problems.

- **tracert.** The tracert utility enables you to trace the route to a given destination node.

You'll find extensive coverage of connectivity TCP/IP utilities in Chapter 22, "Overview of TCP/IP." Check Chapter 23, "Using Basic TCP/IP Services," for coverage of TCP/IP troubleshooting utilities.

Messaging

Like Windows 95, Windows NT 4.0 includes the Microsoft Windows Messaging Sub-system, which enables you to send and receive e-mail through Microsoft's e-mail client, Windows Messaging (see fig. 3.4). Messaging, which is also included with Windows NT, supports various service providers that enable it to communicate with a variety of message servers. Included with Windows NT 4.0 are service providers for Internet Mail and Microsoft Mail.

FIG. 3.4
The Exchange e-mail client provides an integrated messaging service.

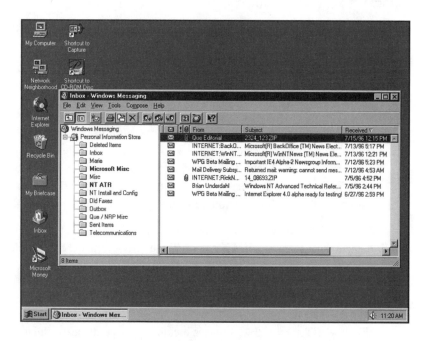

The Internet Mail provider enables you to send and receive e-mail through an Internet mail server, either through a hardwired or a dial-up connection to the Internet mail server. The Internet Mail provider supports MIME mappings to file name extensions, automating transfer of MIME attachments.

The Microsoft Mail service provider for Windows Messaging enables you to send and receive e-mail through a Microsoft Mail postoffice, including those created with other versions of Windows NT, Windows for Workgroups, and Windows 95. The Microsoft Mail provider supports remote mail, enabling you to connect to a Microsoft Mail postoffice through a Dial-Up Networking connection to send and receive mail from a remote site.

N O T E The remote capability for Microsoft Mail and Internet Mail in Windows Messaging relies on Windows NT Dial-Up Networking and requires that the mail server be supported by a Dial-Up Networking dial-in server—either the mail server itself must also serve as a Dial-Up Networking server, or a Dial-Up Networking server must be connected to the same network as, and provide access to, the mail server. Note that the CompuServe Mail provider doesn't require Dial-Up Networking to support remote mail. ■

Other New Features

In addition to the features already described, Windows NT 4.0 includes a selection of features that improve usability, networking, and hardware support. These features are described in the following sections.

Hardware Profiles

Like Windows 95, Windows NT 4.0 supports *hardware profiles*. A hardware profile is a configuration list of specific hardware. Windows NT enables you to create multiple hardware profiles and choose which profile to use in any particular Windows NT session (see fig. 3.5). For example, you might create multiple configurations for a notebook computer, using one profile when the notebook is docked and another when it is undocked.

In general, Windows NT can detect which profile it should use based on the hardware it detects during startup. If Windows NT can't detect the correct profile (because the profiles are so similar, for example), it prompts you to specify which profile to use.

486 Emulator

Windows NT 4.0 for RISC systems includes a new software emulator that enables these RISC systems to run Windows-based and MS-DOS-based applications that require 386-enhanced mode support or which look for an Intel 486 processor (or compatible). This feature broadens the available software base for Reduced Instruction Set Computer (RISC) systems, although performance of applications running under the emulator will naturally be less than that of native applications.

FIG. 3.5
Through the System icon in Control Panel you can copy, modify, and delete hardware profiles.

NDS Support

The Client/Gateway Services for Netware, which is included in previous versions of Windows NT, has been updated to support Netware Directory Services (NDS). NDS support enables you to browse an NDS tree and connect to NDS volumes, and to connect to printers on the NDS tree. The Client/Gateway Services for Netware are essentially the same as in previous versions of NT, except that NDS is now supported.

Autorun

Like Windows 95, Windows NT 4.0 supports *autorun*, which enables Windows NT to automatically start audio and application CDs as soon as the CDs are inserted into the drive. To begin playing an audio CD, for example, you simply insert it into the drive. Windows NT detects the CD, recognizes it as an audio CD, and immediately begins playing the CD.

In the case of application CDs, Windows NT can start the application contained on the CD or open a window of options for the CD (see fig. 3.6), depending on how the developer has structured the CD.

N O T E An application CD must be designed to support autorun—older CDs do not support autorun. You must manually open these types of CDs as you have with previous versions of Windows NT. ▉

FIG. 3.6
When you insert an autorun-enabled data CD, Windows NT automatically displays an application-specific menu of options for working with the CD.

 To bypass autorun, hold down the Shift key when you insert the CD in the drive. To disable Autorun, set the following Registry key:

    HKEY_LOCAL_MACHINE\System\CurrentControlSet\Services\CdRom\Autorun = 0

Distributed Component Object Model (DCOM)

In previous versions of Windows NT, Windows 95, and Windows 3.x, Object Linking and Embedding provided a mechanism for applications to work together cooperatively under a common interface. OLE is also the mechanism by which you build compound documents from data created by various applications.

The ability to use OLE across the network in these previous operating systems was very limited, at best. Microsoft has renamed OLE to Common Object Model (COM). In addition, Microsoft has expanded network support through Distributed Component Object Model (DCOM), which is a network-capable extension of COM. Through DCOM you can integrate applications and documents across a network, including the Internet.

DirectX

DirectX is a set of APIs (Application Programming Interfaces) geared toward enhancing multimedia performance. DirectX in Windows NT consists of DirectDraw 2.0, DirectSound 1.0, and DirectPlay 1.0. These APIs speed multimedia component performance by supporting hardware acceleration for graphics rendering and other new, common hardware features.

DirectDraw support has been expanded in Windows NT from previous versions of DirectDraw to include driver support for a selection of popular display adapters such as those from ATI and Matrox. You'll find more information about DirectX in Chapter 13, "Enhancing Video and I/O Performance." You'll find a sample game called Roids in the \Ddraw folder on the Windows NT Workstation CD-ROM that you can use to test DirectX performance.

Peer Web Services

Windows NT Workstation includes a set of utilities that enable you to easily set up your Windows NT Workstation computer as a personal Internet server. Peer Web Services lets your computer function as an ftp server, Web server, and news server (see fig. 3.7). Peer Web Services is an ideal solution to publishing documents and files on intranets, and turns your computer into a solid platform for authoring Web documents that you publish elsewhere. You'll find extensive coverage of Peer Web Services in Chapter 26, "Installing and Configuring Peer Web Services."

FIG. 3.7
The Microsoft Internet Service Manager provides a unified interface for managing peer Internet services.

N O T E If you need more robust or extensive Internet server support, consider the Internet Information Server IIS, which is included with Windows NT Server 4.0. IIS also is available as an add-on to Windows NT Server 3.5x. ■

Dial-Up Networking Enhancements

Dial-Up Networking in Windows NT 4.0 includes enhancements to make it a more attractive method of creating and using wide-area networking. One new feature, the Point-to-Point Tunneling Protocol (PPTP) client, enables a Dial-Up Networking client to access resources on remote servers through a secure, encrypted protocol connection. PPTP enables you to create and access private virtual networks across a WAN connection through an Internet service provider or direct connection to the Internet. PPTP supports TCP/IP, IPX/SPX, and NetBEUI.

Another enhancement to Dial-Up Networking in Windows NT 4.0 is the ability to log on to a domain through a Dial-Up Networking connection. This enables you to authenticate your logon through a remote domain controller.

From Here...

You now have an overview of the new features in Windows NT and probably are ready to put those features to work. For more information on Windows NT's new features, refer to the following chapters:

- Chapter 5, "Preparing for Installation," explores the many issues you need to consider before installing Windows NT.

- Chapter 6, "Advanced and Custom Setup Issues," helps you automate the installation process and distribute Windows NT to multiple users across a network.

Installing and Configuring Windows NT Workstation

CHAPTER 4

Installation and Configuration Overview

by Jim Boyce

Installing Windows NT Workstation is not as simple a matter as installing Windows 95 or other operating systems for personal computers. Although the installation process itself is straightforward and easy to accomplish, setting up Windows NT requires careful thought and planning—it isn't simply a matter of specifying a directory and letting Setup copy files to your hard disk.

In addition to minor considerations such as where on your hard disk you'll install Windows NT, you also have to consider many other issues. ■

Hardware and Software Compatibility

One of the first issues to consider before installing Windows NT is whether your computer's hardware is compatible with Windows NT. Now that Windows NT supports the same driver model as Windows 95, it is much more likely that your hardware is supported. Rather than dividing their development efforts, hardware manufacturers can develop a single driver to support both Windows NT and Windows 95. This means that manufacturers are able to bring their products to market more quickly.

Compatibility is not a given, however, because some manufacturers still rely on real-mode drivers that do not support Windows NT. In some cases, the lack of support for a device can prevent you from installing Windows NT. If you can't get Setup to recognize your CD-ROM drive, for example, you won't be able to install Windows NT. Chapter 5, "Preparing for Installation," addresses hardware compatibility.

Another point to consider is whether your applications will run under Windows NT 4.0. In general, most DOS applications will run under version 4.0, as will applications written for previous versions of Windows NT. Most 16-bit applications written for Windows 3.x will run under Windows NT, although some do not. In particular, 16-bit Windows applications that use private virtual device drivers (VxDs) do not run under Windows NT.

 Even if your 16-bit Windows applications run under Windows NT, you should consider upgrading to Windows NT-specific (or Windows 95) versions. Many 32-bit Windows NT and Windows 95 applications are written to support multithreaded execution, which generally means a performance increase over their 16-bit counterparts. These newer versions also are more tightly integrated with the new interface and have new features.

If you are switching from OS/2 to Windows NT 4.0, however, you need to be aware that unlike previous versions, Windows NT 4.0 doesn't support OS/2 applications. If you intend to retain your OS/2 applications, you'll need to configure your system to dual-boot between OS/2 and Windows NT. A much better solution is to switch to Windows NT versions of those applications.

If you're upgrading your system from Windows 3.x or Windows 95 to Windows NT, or you intend to dual-boot between Windows 3.x/Windows 95 and Windows NT, verify your program's compatibility. Check with the software publisher's technical support staff to determine if the version of the program you're using will run successfully under Windows NT. You can also connect to **http:// www.microsoft.com/BackOffice/infosrc.htm** to find instructions on downloading InfoSource, a directory of Windows NT-compatible hardware and software, training resources, and other Windows NT-related resources and data.

File System Choices

A question equally important as hardware and software compatibility is deciding which file system you'll use on your workstation. Windows NT 4.0 supports the DOS File Allocation Table (FAT) file system, providing backward compatibility with the file system on DOS systems (which includes computers running Windows 3.x, Windows 95, and OS/2).

In addition to supporting FAT, Windows NT also supports the NTFS file system. NTFS offers better security and auditing than FAT. Because of the method NTFS uses to allocate space on the disk, it also is more efficient than FAT. And, NTFS supports file-by-file disk compression for even greater efficiency.

N O T E Unlike previous versions, Windows NT 4.0 doesn't support the High Performance File System (HPFS) in OS/2. If your system contains an HPFS partition, you'll have to retain OS/2 on the system or convert the HPFS partition to FAT or NTFS. Also unlike previous versions of Windows NT, 4.0 doesn't include the ALLCONV.EXE utility to convert the HPFS access control list to the NTFS partition. Windows NT 4.0 does, however, include the CONVERT.EXE utility that will convert the HPFS partition to an NTFS partition. For more information on converting an HPFS file system to NTFS, refer to Chapter 5, "Preparing For Installation." ▒

▶ **See** "Evaluating and Planning the File System," **p. 88**

As you'll learn in Chapter 5, your best choice is NTFS if you need the best possible security and auditing. There can be performance tradeoffs in using NTFS, however, because the additional overhead involved versus FAT can slow down disk performance. Performance and other file system factors are explored in depth in Chapter 5.

Security Models

Before installing Windows NT, it is critical that you understand the domain and workgroup models by which Windows NT workstations interact with other computers on the network. Your choice of one over the other will depend on how many other computers are on the network, whether a particular model is already in use, and other factors. These topics are examined in detail in Chapter 5, "Preparing for Installation," and Chapter 16, "A Brief Primer on Networks."

▶ **See** "Understanding Security Issues," **p. 72**
▶ **See** "Understanding Workgroups and Domains," **p. 361**

Network Setup

Windows NT supports many network adapters, protocols, and services, making Windows NT Workstation a good client platform on all of the popular network operating systems,

Part
II

Ch
4

including Novell Netware. In fact, many users have come to view Windows NT's Netware client as better than Novell's own client. Through support for Novell Directory Services (NDS), Netware File and Print Services, and other core Netware features, Windows NT Server can mirror and even replace Netware servers without any change to the Netware clients on the network.

If you prefer a single-source network solution, you can take advantage of Windows NT Workstation's built-in peer-to-peer networking to network computers and share resources among them without any additional network operating system software. Windows NT Workstation provides a high level of security, even under its peer-to-peer model, and with the addition of a Windows NT Server node to the network, you can take advantage of additional security options and networking features.

Network setup is part of the Windows NT installation process. Or, you can skip network installation during Setup and add network functionality later. For more information on configuring network options, refer to *The Windows NT Workstation Installation and Configuration Handbook*, also from Que.

Advanced Setup Issues

It is likely that you are running Windows NT in a network environment with other users. Windows NT offers various features that simplify installation and support on multiple computers. In some situations, supporting multiple installations requires modifying Setup. You can customize Setup in many different ways to automate setup and configuration steps you would otherwise have to perform manually.

In addition to modifying Setup, you can take advantage of SNMP (Simple Network Management Protocol) to further automate distributing, installing, and supporting Windows NT. And, Windows NT offers other features that simplify installation and support across a network, reducing the amount of work you'll have to do to install and support Windows NT. For detailed discussions of these Setup issues, refer to Chapter 6, "Advanced and Custom Setup Issues." ●

CHAPTER 5

Preparing for Installation

by Christa Anderson

Before installing Windows NT Workstation 4.0, you must take some issues into account. Will your existing hardware and software work with the new operating system? What accounts do you need to set up in the User Manager, and what will you use these accounts for? How can you prepare your hardware to make the installation as trouble-free as possible? How can you protect any files that currently exist on the hard disk—and then restore them if necessary? And, finally, what file system will you use on the new system? In this chapter, we'll discuss all of these issues. ■

Addressing compatibility issues

Learn about how to best avoid compatibility problems between your existing system and NT 4.0.

Understanding security issues

What user accounts and groups do you need to create for your NT Workstation for best security?

Setting up and preparing your hardware

Learn how to avoid the installation problems that can occur even with hardware compatible with NT.

Backing up critical files

The way in which you'll need to back up and restore critical files depends on which operating system you used before upgrading to NT 4.0.

Evaluating and planning the file system

What file systems does NT 4.0 support and which is best for your needs? Find out in this section.

Addressing Compatibility Issues

As an operating system designed for security and stability, NT remains specific about the devices and software with which it will cooperate. The list of devices with which it's compatible is pretty extensive, so you should be able to find hardware for your NT machines. Software presents a little more of a problem, but as NT becomes a viable operating system, it's become much easier to find software and drivers that are NT-compatible. Microsoft revamped its "Designed for Windows 95" logo program, discussed later—at one time, some applications that passed the tests to carry the logo wouldn't run on NT, but today that shouldn't present a problem.

Hardware Compatibility

Microsoft includes a copy of the Hardware Compatibility List (HCL) when you buy NT. The fact that a piece of hardware is not on the HCL does not mean that it *won't* work with NT, but it means that Microsoft has not successfully tested the device with NT. Devices that don't have Microsoft drivers but will run under NT with third-party drivers are not supported.

Microsoft's technical support for problems involving hardware not on the HCL varies with the problem. They can still help if the problem isn't flat-out incompatibility, such as in one of the following situations:

- The hardware isn't working (that is, if you swap out the hardware the problem disappears).
- The problem only appeared when you installed a new Service Pack.
- The driver is corrupted or installed incorrectly.
- The problem you describe also occurs with hardware that *is* listed on the HCL.
- The problem has been documented in the Knowledge Base.

Bear in mind, of course, that calling Microsoft's NT technical support is a $150 investment, whether they can solve your problem or not.

ON THE WEB

If you want to check out the HCL before you buy the operating system (or save your eyes—the hard copy is a lot to get through) and you have access to the World Wide Web, you can see the list online at: **http://www.microsoft.com/backoffice/ntserver/hcl/hclintro.htm**

This is the starting point for the list—from this page, you have access to lists of the systems, SCSI adapters and devices, communications hardware, and other hardware for which Microsoft will offer technical support with Windows NT Workstation. (As of June 1996, this site applied to version 3.51 only; you can expect the information to be updated for 4.0 when the product ships.)

ON THE WEB

If you suspect that some of your hardware won't run under NT, check out **http://www.conitech.com/windows/ntwanted.html** for a frequently updated list of software and drivers without NT-compatible versions.

Software Compatibility Issues

It should be no surprise to you that some applications that worked fine with Windows or Windows 95 will not work with Windows NT. Keep three rules of thumb in mind when considering whether a device or application will work with Windows NT:

- If an application attempts to access hardware directly, it will not work with NT.
- 16-bit drivers will not work with NT—you'll need to get NT drivers for any hardware that you plan to use (such as scanners) that won't necessarily have drivers included with the operating system. Using 16-bit drivers for adapter cards can lead to strange problems, such as hard drives that won't hold a format.
- Windows NT does not support virtual device drivers (VxDs). Therefore, any applications that require VxDs (such as some multimedia applications and games) won't run under Windows NT.

NT version 4.0 does have one advantage over its predecessor in terms of software compatibility—the latest version of NT supports Telephony Application Program Interface (TAPI) version 2.0; programs that use TAPI will now run on NT. TAPI support is designed to provide developers with a standardized interface for designing telephony software incorporating data and voice mail systems, and users with ways of unifying their voice and data networks.

N O T E   Windows 95 supports TAPI version 1.4. ■

According to the rules set by Microsoft and enforced by their independent testing labs, applications that carry the "Designed for Windows 95" logo must also run under the latest current version of Windows NT (now 4.0) unless the architectural differences between the two products prevent it. In other words, you should be able to load an application designed for Windows 95 onto any computer running Windows NT Workstation unless something specific about the application demands that it run with the Windows 95 kernel.

Part

II

Ch

5

Understanding Security Issues

When installing NT, you'll automatically create an administrative account. (For better system security, it's important to assign this account a password. Do *not* assign this account a "throwaway" password—you'll need it to create any other accounts and if you forget the password you'll need to reinstall the operating system.) After installation, however, you'll have the option of using the User Manager to create some additional accounts. For reasons that we'll discuss in a minute, this is a very good idea even if you're the only one who will ever touch the computer.

Why Set Up Separate Accounts?

Why create more accounts when you've already got one? System security.

Generally speaking, it's a good idea to create a separate user account for use while working on the computer, in addition to the administrative account, even if you're the only person who will ever touch the computer. Creating a second account for those times when you're using the workstation rather than administering it is helpful for logging events (you'll always know what account you were using when you made a change because that information will be included in the system log) and also for making sure that you're thinking about what you're doing. While writing or working on a spreadsheet, for example, it might occur to you that you really ought to install that driver while you're thinking about it. If you must log off and log back on, then you'll be thinking about installing the driver, not the wording of the next paragraph, and you'll be less likely to skip a step or make a mistake.

- Separate accounts are also useful in other situations:
- Some tasks are beyond the scope of user tasks but do not require administrative privileges (such as backing up the system).
- Separate accounts are required for some automated tasks (such as directory replication).
- If the account that you use for day-to-day activities does not permit you to make drastic changes to the system, it's hard to make changes that you didn't intend when fooling around and playing "Let's see what *this* button does."

If you're not the only person to ever use the computer (or more than one person has physical access to it), there's really no question about whether you must create separate accounts on the system. It is not desirable to have people with administrative privileges using a computer. Create a user account for each person that uses the computer; if they must perform activities that require more rights than an ordinary user account, they should use one of the accounts created for that purpose. This organization of user accounts has three advantages: ease of account administration, easier tracking of events in the log, and, once again, elimination of the possibility of someone unintentionally doing something drastic to the system.

Simplifying Account Administration   With separate accounts, you'll be able to copy user account properties to create new users without having to worry as much about which user account you're creating—for example, if Terry's user account has more rights than Mary's because Terry backs up the system, then you'll have to remember which account to use as a template for new user accounts. If Terry always uses the Backup Operators account to back up, however, then his user account can have the same rights that Mary's does and either account will work well for a new user account template.

Tracking Events   If you enable logging in the User Manager and then check back in the Event Viewer, you'll notice that every user action in the log is prefaced by the account name of the person performing the action. For example, if you want to check to see whether Terry is performing backups on a regular basis, you can use the Find option in the Event Viewer to search the system event log for events with the backup account's user name, rather than sorting through all events generated by the user who performs backups.

TIP   After you identify a user name to search for in the event log, pressing F3 will highlight the next incidence of that user name in the log.

Avoiding Accidents   If you have separate accounts for ordinary use and system administration, then you're less likely to accidentally make changes to the system. Rather than idly poking around the Control Panel, you'll be thinking about what you're doing and then logging out when the task is done. Although, if you're the system administrator, it's more convenient to be able to create and delete accounts without having to log out of your Excel spreadsheet, the system is better protected if you set up one account for your "user" persona and one for your "administrator" persona.

Part
II

Ch
5

What Accounts Are Available?

NT Workstation has six types of user accounts available: administrators, backup operators, guests, power users, and users. (The directory replicator group is for use with the directory replication service—it's not for user accounts.) In brief, the group account properties are as follows:

- **Administrators**. Members of this group can do anything to the computer on which NT Workstation is running. They have all the rights of other NT groups, plus a few more: they can load and unload device drivers, set up security logging for individual file and objects, and take ownership of files and other objects.

You can make local administrators domain administrators by adding them to the Domain Administrators group on the domain's Primary Domain Controller. Domain Administrators are also administrators on all domain workstations and servers.

■ **Backup Operators.** This group's rights are specifically designed to let its members back up the system. The only rights that this group has that members of other groups (other than administrators) do not are the rights to back up and restore files and directories on the system.

■ **Guests.** Members of this group have very limited rights, even more limited than those of normal users. Members of this group only have the right to log onto the local system, shut it down, and bypass transverse checking (that is, move to directories to which they have permission via directories to which they do not have permission).

N O T E By default, the Guest account is disabled. Even when this account is enabled, however, you must log in as "Guest"—it's impossible to log onto the system using an account name not previously defined in the User Manager. ■

■ **Power Users.** As a kind of "junior administrator," members of this group have some of the same rights that the Administrators group have but that no others do. By default, they can share files and printers, change the system time, and force the system to shut down from across the network. They cannot, however, back up or restore files or directories, nor can they change share permissions assigned by the Administrator.

■ **Users.** Members of this group have the rights that most ordinary users will need. They have the same rights as those in the Guest group. Be aware, however, that members of this group cannot share files and printers with the network.

Why have both a Users and a Guest group? There's one more group that is not listed in the opening screen of the User Manager: the Everyone group, whose membership is, well, everyone. Everyone includes the Guest group, so if you have a right, normally given to Everyone, that you want to assign to the User group but keep from the guests, you can remove the Everyone group from the list of groups with that right. This will not affect the Users, but will prevent guests from doing the action permitted by that right. For example, by default Everyone can shut down the system. Guests are not listed explicitly in the list of those with this right, but as part of Everyone they still have that capability. If you re-move Everyone from the list of groups with the shutdown right, then Guests will no longer be able to shut down the system. As Users have the right explicitly, they will not be affected.

N O T E The descriptions of each group's rights list the rights that each group has *by default*. It's perfectly possible for the system administrator to employ the User Manager to add or remove rights for each of these groups. ■

If you'd like a quick cheat sheet of some of the more commonly used capabilities that each NT group has by default, take a look at table 5.1.

Table 5.1   NT Workstation User Group Capabilities (by Default)

Capability	Group
Access Computer from Network	A, E, PU
Back Up Files and Directories	A, BO
Bypass Traverse Checking	E
Change System Time	A, PU
Create User Accounts and Groups	A, PU
Force Shutdown from Remote System	A, PU
Format System Hard Disks	A
Load or Unload Device Drivers	A
Lock the Computer	A, PU, E
Log On Locally	A, BO, E, G, PU, U
Manage Audit and Security Logs	A
Manage User Accounts	A
Override the Lock of the Computer	A
Restore Files and Directories	A, BO
Share Files, Directories, and Printers	A, PU
Shut Down System	A, BO, E, PU, U
Take Ownership of Files and/or Objects	A

Note: A=Administrators, BO=Backup Operators, G=Guests, E=Everyone, PU=Power Users, U=Users

N O T E Although Power Users can create user accounts and groups, they can only edit the properties of accounts and groups that they create, not those created by a system administrator. ■

By reviewing table 5.1, you can determine which groups you must create for your particular system based on the capabilities that the people using that workstation will need. For

Part

II

Ch

5

example, if you're installing NT on a standalone computer, then you'll probably have no need to make any accounts that are members of the Power Users group because file and printer sharing won't be an issue and members of the Administrators group can take care of the administrative tasks.

Setting Up and Preparing Hardware

NT is a highly reliable operating system, and a fairly simple one to install. It's got one major requirement for trouble-free installation, however: all the hardware must work. The failed NT installations that I've seen have all come down to hardware problems, whether in the form of virus infections, compatibility problems, or damaged hardware. NT is much less forgiving of hardware problems than are DOS-based operating systems.

How do the hardware requirements for NT Workstation 4.0 differ from those of version 3.51? Overall, the requirements are similar, but there are some important differences:

- A 32-bit processor is required (386 systems are no longer supported).

- NT Workstation now requires a minimum of 117M of hard disk space (124M on RISC-based machines), up from the 90M required with version 3.51.

- The system must have either a 3.5-inch disk drive and CD-ROM or a network connection; 5.25-inch drives are no longer supported for installation.

Other than the exceptions noted here, the hardware requirements for NT Workstation version 4.0 are identical to those for version 3.51.

Under normal circumstances, if your hardware worked when running under NT version 3.5x, it should work when running under version 4.0 (except as noted above), so you may be able to avoid some of the hardware testing suggested before if you're just upgrading an NT installation and nothing about the system has changed. This is not necessarily true if you're upgrading from DOS, Windows 3.x, or Windows 95, however.

CAUTION

One of the cardinal rules in hardware testing is to make sure that the testing gets done. This means that, even if the machine is new, you should still perform the diagnostic tests and virus checks that you'd perform on any machine. This is true for two reasons. First, some computer sellers will run abbreviated versions of these diagnostics (such as short memory tests, or outdated virus scans), and second, things slip through the cracks and it's possible that the machine you've got has, in fact, *not* been tested thoroughly.

Ensuring Compatibility

The issue of hardware compatibility has already been addressed in this chapter, but checking your hardware against the HCL is an important part of making sure that the NT installation goes smoothly.

BIOS Issues

The HCL does not list compatible BIOSes, but outdated BIOS versions can cause havoc all the same. If the computer on which you're installing NT is fairly new, this shouldn't present any difficulty. However, if you run across an inexplicable problem during installation, check the BIOS version. On one occasion, I saw an outdated BIOS cause the installation to not recognize the hard disk and not find the kernel. After the BIOS was updated, however, the installation went fine. Microsoft recommends that you always have the most recent released (that is, not beta) version of your system's BIOS.

Disk Testing

In the best of all possible worlds, you should test hard disks at least once a year. Coming back to reality, you should at least test them before installing an operating system as picky about its hardware as NT is. Before beginning the installation, shut down NT, boot to DOS, and run a disk media tester such as SpinRite to make sure that the disk is working properly.

DOS handles disk errors in the following way:

Part
II

Ch
5

1. When an application requests information from the disk, DOS calls software interrupt 13 to pass the request to the system BIOS.
2. If the BIOS can't get the data from the disk, it tries again. If this attempt is successful, the BIOS passes the information to DOS without comment.
3. If the retry doesn't work, the BIOS uses error correcting code (ECC) to attempt to pull the data off the disk. If this attempt is successful, the BIOS passes the data to DOS, noting that ECC was required, but DOS does not note this.
4. If the ECC doesn't work, DOS asks the BIOS for the data again.
5. If the DOS-initiated retry doesn't work, then you see the `Error reading drive X: Abort, Retry, Ignore?` message that you're no doubt familiar with.

Notice that the BIOS retries the read three times before telling DOS that it was unsuccessful—if the read is successful after one or two retries, then the BIOS tells DOS about the problem but DOS forgets.

Not all disk media testers are created equal. The process of media testing works like this: The testing program checks the reading and writing performance of the disk by creating a series of complicated patterns and then attempting to read them from disk. The catch? DOS will cheerfully ignore reading problems that occur even if retries are necessary to retrieve the data. So long as DOS eventually gets the data, as far as it's concerned, the disk is fine. This is true even if the disk's surface is damaged. Many disk testers believe what DOS tells them about damaged disks. Some (like SpinRite) bypass the operating system and check for themselves, using software interrupt 13 to contact the BIOS rather than trusting what DOS says about it.

A couple of "gotchas" can trip you up when it comes to disk media testing. First, you'll probably notice that the thorough media testers access the hardware directly. In other words, they won't run under NT. Second, even disk testers that use interrupt 13 to contact the BIOS directly can't intercept BIOS calls—they'll never know about those multiple retries unless ECC was required to read the information from the disk. There's really nothing to be done about this. Third, any problems encountered during the test are re-corded in the disk's FAT and are erased if you format the disk. This means that if you format the disk to use NTFS so as to use all of NT's security features, then you've erased any "bad track" information that the disk tester noted about the disk. The only good part about this is that you know before installation whether the disk is all right.

The good news is that, if your disk is new, it should be in pretty good shape. Like any other technology, the science of making hard disks has improved with time.

Memory Testing

Unlike disk media testing, it's really only necessary to test memory when you first get the computer. (That is, it's only necessary to do it once assuming that you've been careful when opening it up and have not shocked the memory with static electricity.) Whatever memory test you use, be sure to use the slow memory test, rather than the fast one. The slow one may take all night, but it's a much more thorough test. You're only going to do this once, so you might as well do it right.

Network Card Testing

In the case of most adapter cards, it's fairly easy to tell when they're malfunctioning: the SCSI disk doesn't work, no music comes from the speakers that are turned on, or the video doesn't work. Network cards can be a little more difficult to notice, as you're not using them every minute that the computer is on and they don't do anything obvious when they do work.

If installing NT on a newly networked machine, it's a good idea to run a loopback routine on the network card to ensure that the card works properly. If you know that the card works, you've already eliminated one culprit if your machine can't find the domain controller or workgroup during installation.

N O T E   When running a loopback routine or any other adapter diagnostic test, run it not once but several times. Some boards don't fail until they've warmed up a little. ■

Adapter Card Installation

Adapter cards have a whole set of setup issues that you must take into account before installing NT. Although not all adapter cards use all of these settings, you must be prepared to deal with the following:

- Interrupts
- I/O address ranges
- DMA channels
- RAM addresses
- ROM addresses

T I P   The adapter card documentation should tell you which interrupts, base I/O addresses, ROM and RAM addresses, and DMA channels the adapter can use. If you've misplaced the documentation, then try checking with the card-maker's Web site, Internet newsgroup, or CompuServe forum for technical support.

Part
II

Ch
5

Interrupts   Devices external to the motherboard are assigned a number from 1 to 15 (called an interrupt request line, shortened to interrupt or IRQ) to get the CPU's attention. This interrupt is analogous to a hotline to the CPU's desk: when the CPU gets a request for data processing from a particular interrupt, it knows that a particular device has data that needs to be processed. The lower the interrupt, the higher the priority; for example, interrupt 3 has a higher priority than interrupt 5.

N O T E   Interrupt 2 is a "bridge" to the higher interrupts. Because interrupts 8–15 are linked to interrupt 2, they inherit its priority and therefore have a higher priority than interrupts 3-7. ■

The only catch to interrupts is that there are often not enough of them: as everything that contacts the CPU needs one, and all devices can only use one of a very specific range of interrupts, it's possible to have to do some fancy wheeling and dealing to sort out which devices can use which interrupt. Some other operating systems support interrupt sharing, in which more than one device uses the same interrupt to contact the CPU, but NT does not. If more than one device wants to use the same interrupt, then neither device will work, or it will work sporadically, one at a time. (In fact, this need for interrupts is one of the things pushing the implementation of the Universal Serial Bus, a card from which you will be able to cascade over a hundred devices such as joysticks, keyboards, mice, and the like.)

The only solution to the problem of sorting out your interrupts is to document them carefully. A table like the following can help you keep track of interrupts used by the adapters in your PC:

Device	Interrupt
Sound Card	7
SCSI Host Adapter	10
Network Card	5

You can also use a table like this one to establish which interrupts you can assign each adapter card, as each card will almost certainly support more than one interrupt. So, if you write in the table that the sound card will work with interrupts 2, 7, and 10, and the SCSI host adapter with 9, 10, and 11, and the network card with 5, 9, and 10, then you can see what interrupts each board will have to use to avoid conflicts.

I/O Address Ranges   When a device contacts the CPU, it has data for the CPU to process. This data must go somewhere while the device is waiting for an answer to its interrupt, and that somewhere is in most cases a spot in memory called the device's input/output (I/O) range, beginning at a point called the I/O base address. Each device's I/O range must be unique, not overlapping that of any other device. Sorting out I/O ranges can make sorting out interrupts look easy. Once again, the easiest way to do this is with a table:

Device	I/O Address Range
Sound Card; MIDI port	220h–233; 300h–331
SCSI Host Adapter	330h–333
Network Card	370h–37F

Note that the sound card requires two I/O address ranges: one for the card itself, and one for the MIDI port.

As before, you can use a table like this one not just to keep track of the address ranges each adapter card in your system uses, but also to determine how you should assign ranges. As with interrupts, most adapter cards support a range of I/O addresses; the only trick comes in identifying a collection of ranges that don't overlap each other—unfortunately, the ranges rarely start at the same point in memory.

DMA Channels CPUs are really best at processing data, not at pulling it from an adapter card and sending it to memory. Some adapter cards use Direct Memory Access (DMA) to bypass the CPU and send data directly to system memory. The mechanism used to get the data from the card to the memory is called a DMA channel. Unsurprisingly, then, it's necessary to allocate each adapter card that uses DMA, its own DMA channel.

On any machine on which you'll be installing NT, you won't be very crowded for DMA channels—not all adapter cards use them, and all DMA channels except two, which are used by the floppy controller, are free on modern PCs. Although some boards only support one or two DMA channels, the only time at which you're likely to have to think about it is if you're installing a sound card in addition to another adapter card that uses DMA. Sound cards use two DMA channels: one for the card itself, and one for the MIDI port.

ROM Addresses Some adapter cards even have ROM on them. Why would an add-in card need ROM? For the same reason that any system does: to permanently store information that the board needs.

> **CAUTION**
>
> Be careful not to overlap ROM addresses. Don't forget that your PC uses ROM addresses for more than a few adapter cards. For example, all PCs use the ROM address range F0000-FFFFF, and VGA boards use either C0000-C7FFF or E0000-E7FFF.

Part

II

Ch

5

You'll need to look at the adapter card's documentation to see whether it will need ROM addresses and which ones it will support.

SCSI IDs

As discussed earlier, one of the problems with interrupts is that it can be difficult to get enough of them—it's easy to find yourself in the situation where your sound card requires interrupt 3 or 5 but a network card is using 5 and you really wanted to keep that second serial port available, which uses interrupt 3. Few of these problems are insurmountable unless you have a lot of devices attached to your system, but it can be a headache. A workaround to this problem is to use devices that employ a middleman to handle communications with the CPU, so that only that middleman needs an interrupt.

This workaround is called SCSI, and its convenience and ease of installation contribute to SCSI's popularity with some people. (The downside is that SCSI devices tend to be more expensive than IDE devices, but if you can afford them they're great.) When setting up a SCSI system, you install a card called a *host adapter* to act as the middleman mentioned in the previous paragraph. Up to seven devices can be attached to this middleman, arranged in a bus-like physical configuration called a *SCSI chain*.

Each device in the SCSI chain, including the host adapter, needs a unique SCSI ID. Eight SCSI IDs are available. Unlike interrupts, SCSI IDs permit you a lot of latitude when it comes to assigning them, but here are some guidelines to follow:

- The higher the number, the higher the priority—SCSI ID 0 has a lower priority than ID 6. This means that it's a good idea to give fast devices (like hard disks) lower priorities than slower devices (like tape drives). Only one device can access the host adapter at the same time, so the one with the higher priority will win in case of a standoff.

- Only hard disks should use SCSI IDs 0 or 1. If you plan to boot from a SCSI hard disk, assign it ID 0. IBM PS/2s present an exception to this rule: they expect bootable hard disks to use ID 6.

- Some systems expect particular devices to be assigned a particular SCSI ID. If a device doesn't work, check the system documentation.

- Sometimes you have to fiddle with SCSI IDs to get devices to work properly. Take notes.

Other Devices

After checking all the major devices on the system, don't forget to make sure that the minor ones work:

- floppy drive
- mouse
- keyboard

These devices can create minor but annoying slowdowns in the installation process. For example, on one occasion I installed NT on a standalone PC that had been shipped from another location. Only after beginning one NT installation from the CD and floppy disks did I discover that the A: drive had been slightly damaged in transit so that its eject mechanism no longer worked. When installing NT with the CD-ROM or floppies, you boot from the Setup disk. If you abort the installation, then you must remove the disk from the

A: drive and reboot the machine—in this case, impossible. As it happens, I was able to extricate the floppy with the tweezers in my toolkit before replacing the drive, but it wasted a lot of time and caused frustration that could have been avoided if I'd checked the floppy drive with a test disk before beginning the installation, just to make sure that the drive would read, write, format, and eject properly.

Virus Checking

In the early days of NT, no virus checkers existed for the operating system as the existing ones accessed hardware and, of course, NT would not permit that. Today, several NT-compatible virus scanners and cleaners exist: Intel, McAfee, Symantec, Dr. Solomon's, and others offer these virus checkers. However, you'll still need that DOS-based virus checker (I like FPROT, myself) to scan the hard drive before installing NT.

Is virus-checking really necessary before installation? It might not be, but then there's the time that I saw NT 3.51 loaded onto a brand new machine, straight from the reseller. The installation went beautifully until the reboot. When the machine rebooted, the blue screen came up filled with hex, and then the system locked up. We started the installation over, but the same thing happened again. We checked the hardware again and it turned out to be fine, but when a copy of FPROT was run on the hard drive the Stoned virus was found there. After the drive was cleaned, the installation went as planned.

> **N O T E** Of course, when checking for viruses you must use the latest version of the scanner available. Check with the maker to see if updates to your version are available. ■

Part

II

Ch

5

NT's Hardware-Identifying Tools

Now that you're thoroughly intimidated by the idea of all the hardware documenting that you must do, it's time to introduce the tools that NT 4.0 includes to make this task easier. In the /support directory on your NT Workstation CD, you'll find the /HQTOOL and / SCSITOOL directories.

HQTOOL NT Workstation gives you the means to take an inventory of your system before installing Windows NT. (This procedure works on all computers that meet the minimum requirements for NT—12M RAM, VGA adapter 486 CPU—whether or not they have NT 4.0 installed.) To do so, follow these steps:

1. Insert a blank 1.44M floppy disk in drive A:.

> **T I P** To quickly erase a floppy in the drive, run FD144.EXE in the \HQTOOL directory.

2. Open the /HQTOOL subdirectory in the /SUPPORT directory on the NT Work-station CD and run MAKEDISK.EXE. This step will copy the following files onto the CD:

   - AUTOEXEC.BAT, COMMAND.COM, and the hidden files CONFIG.SYS, IO.SYS, and MS.SYS
   - SETRAMD.BAT
   - ZIPFILE.EXE
   - A DOS directory containing EMM386.EXE and FINDRAM.EXE and some hidden system files

3. With the disk in drive A:, reboot. SETRAM.BAT will create a 4MB RAM drive on your computer into which to runs ZIPFILE.EXE, the file that will prepare the hardware inventory.

4. When ZIPFILE is copied, it runs. You'll see a dialog box explaining the purpose of ZIPFILE and explaining how to use it. Click OK.

5. Next, you'll see a dialog box asking whether you want to run the comprehensive or safe version of the utility. If you suspect that you've got device conflicts (overlapping memory areas. duplicated interrupts, or the like) run in safe mode to run the utility without hanging your system. Otherwise, run in comprehensive mode to get the most complete picture of your system.

   ZIPFILE takes a few minutes to explore your system and then displays a dialog box describing your computer's hardware. This examination is fairly complete. When I've tried it on a couple of different computers, ZIPFILE has reported back the interrupts and I/O address ranges that correspond with my system notes. It does not report the computer name on any machine that I've tried, but this information isn't crucial unless you're keeping printouts of the results and want to be able to easily identify the computer to which each report belongs. In that case, just edit the file to include that information.

6. After you've looked at the results of the analysis, save the information to the floppy or print it out for future reference. The saved configuration information will be listed in a Notepad file called NTHQ.TXT. For example, take a look at the following excerpt from one computer's analysis:

```
System Information
Device: System board
Can't locate Computername
Machine Type: IBM PC/AT
Machine Model: fc
Machine Revision: 00
Microprocessor: Pentium
Conventional memory: 655360
```

```
Available memory: 32 MB
BIOS Name: American Megatrends
BIOS Version: AMI Plug & Play BIOS Ver. 1.0A
BIOS Date: 07/15/95
Bus Type: ISA
```

Although NTHQ.TXT is a longish file, it's pretty easy to interpret. All the DMA channels, IRQs, and I/O ranges used by your hardware are displayed. However, the report only identifies one piece of hardware—the video card—as being on the HCL, and no devices were identified by name and model type. However, this utility will tell you what hardware is in your system and identify the resources that it uses.

SCSITOOL If you have SCSI devices that you want to check for overlapping IDs, the process is much the same as for hardware detection:

1. Insert a blank 1.44MB floppy disk in drive A:.

 TIP To quickly erase a floppy in the drive, double-click FD144.EXE in the \SCSITOOL directory.

2. Open the \SCSITOOL subdirectory directory in the \SUPPORT directory on the NT Workstation CD and run MAKEDISK.EXE. This step will copy the following files onto the CD:

   ■ AUTOEXEC.BAT, COMMAND.COM, and the hidden files CONFIG.SYS, IO.SYS, and MS.SYS

   ■ SETRAMD.BAT

   ■ ZIPFILE.EXE

   ■ A DOS directory containing EMM386.EXE and FINDRAM.EXE, as well as some hidden SYS files.

3. Reboot the system with the disk in the drive. You'll see an opening menu asking whether you want to detect Adaptec or Buslogic controllers, neither, or both. If you don't make a choice in less than 30 seconds, by default the utility will attempt to detect both kinds of controllers.

4. Next, the utility will attempt to load the SCSI controllers. If it can't, and you have controllers installed, they may not be installed correctly.

5. After loading the SCSI controllers, SCSI.ZIP is copied to the RAM drive and started. You'll see an opening dialog box explaining what the utility is for and naming the log and help files. Click Yes to continue with the detection, or No to exit.

6. Detecting the SCSI adapters and devices only takes a short time. When the detection is complete, you'll see a dialog box displaying the characteristics of your system's SCSI adapters and devices. Once you're done examining the results, you can save the results to a Notepad file called SCSI.TXT for future reference.

Part

II

Ch

5

Preserving Critical Files

Unless you're installing NT on a new machine, it's probable that you'll have files on the hard disk that you'll want to preserve. Depending on what operating system you're using, however, the problem may not have as simple a solution as backing up and restoring the files.

The problem is twofold. First, it's clear that any backup application that must access system hardware, won't run under NT. That restriction effectively cuts out any DOS or Windows 3.x-based backup software. Second, NT's backup utility uses a proprietary backup system called the Microsoft Tape Format (MTF). You can back up your drive before installing NT, but unless the backups use MTF, you won't be able to restore them to the hard disk once NT is installed.

Compatible Backup Options

What are the possible solutions to this difficulty? It depends on from what operating system you're upgrading to NT 4.0. If from DOS or Windows 3.x, you've got one set of options, from Windows 95, another, and from NT 3.x, yet another. In this section, we'll describe the options available to you in each case.

> **CAUTION**
>
> No matter which backup and restore option suits your situation best, it's imperative that you always verify that the backups that you've created are restorable *before* destroying the original data. Test the restoration with the device with which the backups will be restored, not just the one on which they were created (if they're not the same one).

Upgrading from DOS or Windows 3.x   As already noted, if the computer on which you plan to install NT was previously running DOS or Windows, then you won't be able to run the backup software under NT to restore backups. However, this doesn't prevent you from backing up. The simplest method of file backup requires a network and another computer with a lot of free disk space:

1. Copy all important files to another machine on the network. If using DOS, don't forget to use **XCOPY /S** to include all subdirectories.

2. Install NT.

3. Restore the files across the network.

In the event that the computer is not connected to a network, you have a couple of other options without resorting to floppy disks. If you have a tape drive, you can back up the files, install NT *using the FAT file system*, and then boot to DOS to restore the backups with the backup utility. You can convert the partition to NTFS after the files are restored. Of course, if you deleted the previous partition you'll have to reinstall the backup utility, and if you converted it to NTFS this method won't work at all, but if you have a tape drive and no network then it's better than using floppies.

Another relatively new option is an Iomega ZIP drive, a removable drive with cartridges that hold up to 100MB of uncompressed data. The utilities that come with a Zip drive support DOS, Windows, and Windows 95; so if you're keeping any of those operating systems available on the same computer, you can reload your files after the NT installation is done. (The Windows 95 version of the utility does not work under Windows NT.) Although most tapes will hold considerably more than 100MB, ZIP drives have the advantage of being cheaper than tape drives (Zip drives run under US $200 for the parallel port version), are easily portable, and don't require you to go through the rigmarole of running the DOS-based backup utility after installing NT. For bigger drives, you can use the Jaz drive, which holds one gigabyte of data.

Upgrading from Windows 95   If you're installing NT on a computer that previously held Windows 95, your backup options depend on whether you plan to replace Windows 95 with NT or preserve both operating systems.

If you plan to replace Windows 95 with Windows NT, then you'll need to make sure that your 95 backups can be restored in Windows NT. If using tape backup, this means that you'll need to use a backup utility that supports MTF (such as Seagate's—formerly Arcada's—backup utility for Windows 95).

If you plan to keep both operating systems intact, then you'll be able to restore the backups from Windows 95, so NT/95 interoperability is not as much of an issue. (You will, however, need to use the FAT file system for any drives that must be accessible under Windows 95—NTFS-formatted volumes will be unreadable under Windows 95.) For the sake of convenience, however, it's a good idea to choose a backup utility that uses MTF, so you don't have to reboot the computer to back up and restore files.

Part II

Ch 5

NOTE   Even though Seagate's backup utility for Windows 95 supports MTF, the utility itself will not run on Windows NT. You'll need to use either NT Backup or another NT backup utility to restore files. ∎

Upgrading from Windows NT 3.x   If you're upgrading from any previous version of Windows NT, then your backup and restoration problems are simple: back up the important files (do not back up the Registry), install NT 4.0, and then restore the files. NT has supported MTF since version 3.1, so the backups should be compatible.

Evaluating and Planning the File System

NT 4.0 supports two file systems: File Allocation Table (FAT) and New Technology File System (NTFS). (The High Performance File System (HPFS) was supported in earlier versions of NT, but is not now.

During installation, your formatting choices are as follows:

- You can install NT on the existing partition without reformatting the drive, or reformatting it to FAT.

- You can install NT on the existing partition, first formatting the partition to NTFS.

- You can repartition the drive and format the installation partition to either FAT or NTFS.

N O T E Although it's certainly an option to repartition the drive and install NT on an NTFS partition, for reasons that we'll discuss shortly, this is not generally a good idea—it's better to format the system partition to FAT. ■

Over the next few sections, we'll discuss the implications of each of these choices and the situations in which each might be a good idea.

Preserve FAT Formatting on the Existing Partition

If the partition on which you're installing NT is already formatted, you don't have to reformat it during the installation. You will not want to reformat the partition to NTFS for the following reasons:

- Because you have no backup of the data on the partition. (In this case, of course, you shouldn't reformat it with FAT either.)

- Because you plan to run more than one PC operating system on the computer, and you want to maintain a single partition on the hard drive. Only Windows NT can see an NTFS-formatted partition—not Windows 3.x, Windows 95, DOS, or OS/2.

Format the Existing Partition to NTFS

If you want to take full advantage of NT's features, you'll want to format the disk to NTFS. With NTFS formatting, you can set file-level user privileges, connect to UNIX machines formatted with NFS, and more advantages that we'll discuss in Chapter 11, "Exploring NTFS," when we delve more deeply into the structure, advantages, and uses of NTFS.

N O T E The special disk configurations available through the Disk Administrator (such as volumes and stripe sets) do not need to be formatted with NTFS. ∎

NTFS does have some pitfalls, however, particularly when you're talking about only having one partition on the hard disk:

- The NTFS partition will be invisible to any other operating systems running on the same machine.
- You will not be able to boot from a DOS floppy and see the NTFS partition. This can seriously complicate the process of recovering from a bad NT installation because it eliminates the possibility of booting to DOS and retrieving data.
- On smaller disks (under 1GB), the overhead involved with NTFS formatting can impact disk access time by as much as 20 percent over access time under FAT.

Repartition the Disk and Format Partitions Separately

One of the safest compromises may be to use both FAT *and* NTFS—FAT for a small "system" partition on which you store the system files, and NTFS for another, "data," partition. This approach has the advantage of giving you NTFS advantages for system files without locking you completely out of your system should something go amiss with the NT installation. Of course, the cautions about using NTFS still apply to the data partition: the NTFS partition won't be visible to other operating systems, and its data won't be accessible to other operating systems running on the same machine, but if you back up frequently and only need to get at those files from DOS, the multiple-partition model is the best of the bunch.

As with so many things when it comes to NT, the choice between FAT and NTFS is one of compatibility versus security. If you use NTFS, you'll be able to set file-level security on your shared drives and directories, drive reads and writes should be faster (as we'll discuss in Chapter 11, "Exploring NTFS," NTFS has an organizational style superior to that of FAT), and users of other operating systems such as Macs and UNIX machines will be able to browse the NTFS-formatted drives. On the other hand, you won't be able to read any NTFS-formatted drives if you boot from a floppy, those drives will be invisible to any OS/2, Windows, or Windows 95 installations on the same computer, and DOS users will not be able to access those drives across the network.

From Here...

In this chapter, we've talked about some of the installation issues that you should really consider *before* installation. At this point, you should have a good idea of how to ensure hardware compatibility with NT and how to prepare that hardware for the installation, know what groups and user accounts you will set up when configuring the installation, know how to back up and restore any files already on the system, and have an idea of what formatting and partitioning options are open to you, and how you can use them to best suit your particular installation.

- To learn how to perform unattended installations, turn to Chapter 6, "Advanced and Custom Setup Issues."
- To learn more about NTFS and FAT, turn to Chapter 10, "Optimizing the File System," or Chapter 11, "Exploring NTFS."
- After NT is installed, turn to Chapter 23, "Using Basic TCP/IP Services" to learn how to install and use TCP/IP.

Advanced and Custom Setup Issues

by Chris Turkstra

If you consider all possible variations in hardware and software configurations, it's amazing that setup works as well as it does. In this chapter we will examine this complex process and look at some of the tools that will allow you to automate and customize the process.

Installing Windows NT Workstation 4.0 on your home computer is one matter, but installing it on 30 to 30,000 machines is another thing entirely. Unless you intend to sit in front of each one and install NT Workstation, you will need to use some of the custom setup tools available.

Lucky for you, Microsoft has reworked the automated installation tools for Windows NT 4.0. Windows NT 3.51 had a few tools that would help in the effort to automate installation, but they required some heavy tuning. These tools have been replaced with new, easier-to-use tools like "sysdiff" and "Answer Files." Unfortunately, for those of you who spent many nights perfecting the NT 3.51 "CPS" setup, your scripts aren't compatible with Windows NT 4.0. ■

How the setup process works

The setup process is quite complex. Knowing how it works can help you fix problems as they arise and will help in your planning.

How to use files and tools to customize setup

This section will describe in detail how to use the custom setup tools to customize setup. These include Answer Files, Uniqueness Database Files (UDFs), CMDLINES.TXT, and the sysdiff utility.

Installation delivery methods

This section will give you some ideas about different ways to automate the deployment of Windows NT, from login scripts to Web page links.

Installation Scenarios

We will discuss in detail an installation scenario, and how to configure the setup files accordingly.

N O T E Unfortunately, as this chapter was being written, Microsoft was re-tuning the options available for advanced setup. While the information in this chapter was correct at the time of writing, you may find a glitch or two. ■

The Setup Story

The entire setup process begins with the program winnt.exe or winnt32.exe. The winnt32 program only runs from a computer already running Windows NT, while the winnt program runs from DOS or a DOS window. The winnt(32) program will copy the Windows NT 4.0 Workstation setup files from either a network share or from a CD-ROM.

Using winnt(32) and Its Options

The syntax of winnt(32) is as follows:

```
winnt [/s:sourcepath] [/i:inf_file] [/t:drive_letter] [/x] [/b] [/o[x]]
➡[u:UDF (answer) file] [/udf:ID in UDF [UDF File]]
```

■ /s:*source path*

Tells winnt where to find the source files. If this is not specified, winnt will prompt the user for the location, even if you've run winnt directly from the source directory. You must use the /s parameter if you are performing an unattended setup.

■ /i:*inf file*

This file tells winnt what file to use for setup information. The default setup file is DOSNET.INF. This file contains information about the source and destination filenames and required disk sizes for a successful installation.

■ /t:*drive letter*

If you want setup to place the setup files on a different drive, specify the alternate drive with the /t parameter. The setup program will look for a drive with 119 Megabytes of free space on which to copy files.

■ /x

The /x option will prevent winnt(32) from creating the installation on floppy diskettes.

■ /b

Specifying the /b option tells winnt(32) to copy the contents of the boot floppies to a directory called WIN_NT.~BT and prepare the boot sector with the Windows NT loader. This means that after the boot files are copied, winnt(32) will restart your computer and load the installation from the hard disk, without ever using diskettes. You will want to use the /b parameter in most circumstances.

N O T E In the earlier versions of Windows NT, you had to boot the system with floppies in order to install, but Microsoft added a /b parameter that makes these boot floppies obsolete. While these floppies still work for installation, most people use the /b option to bypass them. Without the /b parameter, the winnt(32) program will request three diskettes from the user to create the setup boot floppies. ■

- /o[x]

  This option will create boot floppies only. If you add an "x" to the "o", winnt(32) will create floppies for a CD-ROM of floppy installation.

- /u:answer file

  /u specifies the locations of a generic answer file. Answer files (which will be covered later in this chapter) contain information that the user would normally be required to enter during the setup process.

- /udf:id[,UDF File]

  UDF files can contain different answer sets, and the /udf parameter tells winnt(32) which answer set to use for setup. If you don't specify a UDF file, winnt(32) will prompt the user to insert a diskette containing the answer file $UNIQUE$.UDF.

Major Setup Processes—Text Mode Setup

The installation of Windows NT 4.0 involves two major steps: the text mode setup and the GUI mode setup. The text mode installation is actually broken into two parts, the MS-DOS-based portion and the textual Windows NT-based portion. The text mode setup accomplishes the following tasks in preparation for GUI mode setup:

- Copies the files needed to boot Windows NT to the boot partition.

- Detects mass storage devices (SCSI Miniport Drivers) that are supported by Windows NT Workstation out of the box. You can also add more miniport drivers during this phase.

- Detects which Hardware Abstraction Layer (HAL) your computer requires, what kind of keyboard, mouse, and video card you have. It also allows you to change these options.

- Sets up the target partition (which is usually the same as the boot partition) where Windows NT will be installed. You can also select the file system to be used on the target partition.

■ Picks the directory where Windows NT will be installed.

■ Scans the partitions for corruption.

■ Copies files from the retail distribution to temporary directories (WIN_NT.~LS)

MS-DOS-Based Installation/DOSNET.INF   Windows NT setup requires that files are copied to two different places—first the boot files are installed, then the distribution files are copied. The boot mode files are copied either to diskettes or to a directory (WIN_NT.~BT) on the boot partition (if you used /b) and the rest of the files are copied to WIN_NT.~LS. The setup process gets the list of files to be copied from a text file named DOSNET.INF. Here are some of the important sections of DOSNET.INF.

The [Miscellaneous] section specifies the minimum memory required for Windows NT Workstation with the key; MinimumMemory = 12582912.

There are three [FloppyFiles.X] sections where X is 0, 1, 2. These sections specify which files are to be copied to the boot diskettes or to the win_nt.~bt directory. We'll discuss these files in detail later in this chapter. It is important to note that in these sections, there is a source and a destination specified, which may be different. For instance, in the [FloppyFiles.1] section, there is a line specifying:

```
d1,usetup.exe,system32\smss.exe
```

This specifies that the file usetup.exe should be copied to the floppy or win_nt.~bt directory as \system32\sms.exe.

The [RootBootFiles] section tells setup which four files it needs to copy onto the root directory of the boot partition. These four files are:

txtsetup.sif

setupldr.bin,LDR

ntdetect.com

ntldr

The [SpaceRequirements] section of DOSNET.INF tells setup how much free space it requires on both the boot partition and the system partition (the partition where NT will be installed). These settings are:

BootDrive = 1048576

NtDrive   = 125517824

Last, the [Files] section of DOSNET.INF lists all the files that are to be copied to the win_nt.~ls directory.

Boot Files   If you have specified the /b parameter on the command line for winnt(32), the files that would normally be copied to three diskettes are instead copied to a directory called WIN_NT.~BT on the boot partition. These files are the bare minimum 3.7M that Windows NT needs to boot the kernel and start the installation process. If you don't use the /b parameter, these files are copied to the three floppies asked for during setup.

Here is a listing of the win_nt.~bt directory:

```
Directory of C:\$WIN_NT$.~BT

.                 <DIR>         09-10-96  9:08p .
..                <DIR>         09-10-96  9:08p ..
BOOTSECT DAT          512       09-10-96  9:08p BOOTSECT.DAT
DISK103                 3       07-27-96  9:00a DISK103
CPQARRAY SYS        8,752       07-27-96  9:00a CPQARRAY.SYS
DELLDSA  SYS        5,776       07-27-96  9:00a DELLDSA.SYS
NCR53C9X SYS       11,984       07-27-96  9:00a NCR53C9X.SYS
SPOCK    SYS        5,872       07-27-96  9:00a SPOCK.SYS
OLISCSI  SYS       14,000       07-27-96  9:00a OLISCSI.SYS
NCRC700  SYS       10,704       07-27-96  9:00a NCRC700.SYS
NCRC710  SYS       11,696       07-27-96  9:00a NCRC710.SYS
AHA154X  SYS        9,392       07-27-96  9:00a AHA154X.SYS
SPARROW  SYS       20,304       07-27-96  9:00a SPARROW.SYS
AHA174X  SYS        5,648       07-27-96  9:00a AHA174X.SYS
DPTSCSI  SYS       12,336       07-27-96  9:00a DPTSCSI.SYS
ULTRA14F SYS        4,912       07-27-96  9:00a ULTRA14F.SYS
ULTRA24F SYS        4,592       07-27-96  9:00a ULTRA24F.SYS
AMI0NT   SYS        8,624       07-27-96  9:00a AMI0NT.SYS
FD7000EX SYS        5,008       07-27-96  9:00a FD7000EX.SYS
FD8XX    SYS        9,232       07-27-96  9:00a FD8XX.SYS
FD16_700 SYS       11,728       07-27-96  9:00a FD16_700.SYS
ARROW    SYS       36,976       07-27-96  9:00a ARROW.SYS
ATAPI    SYS       18,352       07-27-96  9:00a ATAPI.SYS
SYMC810  SYS       17,296       07-27-96  9:00a SYMC810.SYS
BUSLOGIC SYS        8,368       07-27-96  9:00a BUSLOGIC.SYS
SLCD32   SYS       27,248       07-27-96  9:00a SLCD32.SYS
MKECR5XX SYS       16,976       07-27-96  9:00a MKECR5XX.SYS
AIC78XX  SYS       26,992       07-27-96  9:00a AIC78XX.SYS
MITSUMI  SYS       11,472       07-27-96  9:00a MITSUMI.SYS
DAC960NT SYS       10,736       07-27-96  9:00a DAC960NT.SYS
ABIOSDSK SYS       10,000       07-27-96  9:00a ABIOSDSK.SYS
ATDISK   SYS       26,000       07-27-96  9:00a ATDISK.SYS
NTFS     SYS      366,960       07-27-96  9:00a NTFS.SYS
CDFS     SYS       61,296       07-27-96  9:00a CDFS.SYS
DISK     SYS       14,928       07-27-96  9:00a DISK.SYS
CDROM    SYS       22,128       07-27-96  9:00a CDROM.SYS
SFLOPPY  SYS        8,368       07-27-96  9:00a SFLOPPY.SYS
QL10WNT  SYS       28,720       07-27-96  9:00a QL10WNT.SYS
AMSINT   SYS       13,072       07-27-96  9:00a AMSINT.SYS
CLASS2   SYS       13,072       07-27-96  9:00a CLASS2.SYS
FLASHPNT SYS       42,672       07-27-96  9:00a FLASHPNT.SYS
CPQFWS2E SYS       41,712       07-27-96  9:00a CPQFWS2E.SYS
```

Part

II

Ch

6

```
SYSTEM32         <DIR>          09-10-96   9:08p SYSTEM32
DISK102                      3  07-27-96   9:00a DISK102
SETUPREG HIV           12,288  07-27-96   9:00a SETUPREG.HIV
SETUPDD  SYS          218,096  07-27-96   9:00a SETUPDD.SYS
SPDDLANG SYS            2,928  07-27-96   9:00a SPDDLANG.SYS
VGA      SYS           14,672  07-27-96   9:00a VGA.SYS
VIDEOPRT SYS           21,744  07-27-96   9:00a VIDEOPRT.SYS
FLOPPY   SYS           18,928  07-27-96   9:00a FLOPPY.SYS
I8042PRT SYS           25,136  07-27-96   9:00a I8042PRT.SYS
KBDCLASS SYS            9,296  07-27-96   9:00a KBDCLASS.SYS
FASTFAT  SYS          140,048  07-27-96   9:00a FASTFAT.SYS
SCSIPORT SYS           31,824  07-27-96   9:00a SCSIPORT.SYS
PCMCIA   SYS           39,056  07-27-96   9:00a PCMCIA.SYS
HALNCR   DLL           78,304  07-27-96   9:00a HALNCR.DLL
VGAOEM   FON            5,168  07-27-96   9:00a VGAOEM.FON
C_1252   NLS           66,082  07-27-96   9:00a C_1252.NLS
C_437    NLS           66,594  07-27-96   9:00a C_437.NLS
L_INTL   NLS            7,174  07-27-96   9:00a L_INTL.NLS
KBDUS    DLL            8,976  07-27-96   9:00a KBDUS.DLL
WINNT    SIF               82  09-10-96   9:08p WINNT.SIF
DISK101                      3  07-27-96   9:00a DISK101
HAL486C  DLL           47,840  07-27-96   9:00a HAL486C.DLL
HALAPIC  DLL           65,664  07-27-96   9:00a HALAPIC.DLL
HALMCA   DLL           45,952  07-27-96   9:00a HALMCA.DLL
NTDETECT COM           26,800  07-27-96   9:00a NTDETECT.COM
NTKRNLMP EXE          880,448  07-27-96   9:00a NTKRNLMP.EXE
SETUPLDR BIN          151,376  07-27-96   9:00a SETUPLDR.BIN
TXTSETUP SIF          129,352  08-11-96   7:09p TXTSETUP.SIF
NTLDR                 155,984  07-27-96   9:00a NTLDR
A        OUT                0  09-10-96   9:11p a.out
          69 file(s)     3,254,237 bytes

Directory of C:\$WIN_NT$.~BT\SYSTEM32

.                <DIR>          09-10-96   9:08p .
..               <DIR>          09-10-96   9:08p ..
NTDLL    DLL          353,552  07-27-96   9:00a NTDLL.DLL
SMSS     EXE           92,944  07-27-96   9:00a SMSS.EXE
           2 file(s)      446,496 bytes

Total files listed:
          71 file(s)     3,700,733 bytes
           5 dir(s)  8,342,833,856 bytes free
```

There are some important files here, so we'll take a closer look:

■ **Miniport drivers**. These are the drivers for devices that setup refers to as "Mass Storage Devices." They are mostly for SCSI devices like AHA154X.SYS—the driver for Adaptec AHA-154X series SCSI cards. An example of a non-SCSI miniport driver is ATAPI.SYS, the driver for Atapi CD-ROM drives.

■ **Filesystem files**. These are files that allow Windows NT to access different filesystems, such as NTFS.SYS, CDFS.SYS, and ATDISK.SYS.

- **Hardware Abstaction Layers (HALs)**. Different versions of the HAL are copied to the boot diskette. For example, HALMCA.SYS is the HAL for an IBM PS/2 Microchannel machine.

- **Other Hardware Drivers**. You will also find that PCMCIA.SYS for PCMCIA cards, floppy disk drivers, and files needed to run plain-vanilla VGA (VGA.SYS, VGAOEM.SYS) are in the boot directory.

- **SETUPREG.HIV**. Registry settings that are used in setup are in this file.

- **WINNT.SIF**. This text file contains parameters needed by setup and all the options from the answer files. The answer files & UDFs are read at the very beginning of setup and consolidated into this file. It becomes the answer file for the setup process, and its contents are later inserted into the system32\$winnt$.inf file.

- **TXTSETUP.SIF**. The txtsetup.sif file contains settings to be used during the next portion of text-mode setup—the Windows NT text-mode installation.

Distribution Files After setup has taken care of copying the boot files to either diskettes or the WIN_NT.~BT directory, it copies the files required for the next installation steps into a directory named WIN_NT.~LS. These are the files specified in the DOSNET.INF's [Files] section.

Setup copies all the files from the distribution sharepoint or the CD-ROM onto the target computer, regardless of whether you will need them. For instance, although you only have one video card, setup copies all the drivers it has to the target computer. Setup does this because until it gets through most of the GUI-mode setup, it doesn't know which options it's going to need. Since you may not have a connection to the distribution files after the setup process reboots, it may not be able to get to a driver it needs—which would hang the installation.

Rebooting After the MS-DOS-based text mode installation is over, it will reboot the computer so that it can load the Windows NT kernel for the rest of setup. Unfortunately, the reboot doesn't actually shut down a Windows 95 environment. If you are upgrading a Windows 95 computer, you will have to ask the user to shut it down or automate the process yourself.

The winnt program also creates a file called boot.ini (or alters it if it exists). BOOT.INI is a text file that describes the different boot options that the boot loader offers the user. Winnt will alter this file so that the loader starts the file WIN_NT.~BT\BOOTSECT.DAT to continue the installation.

Windows NT-Based Text Mode Installation/TXTSETUP.SIF After the drivers are loaded and you have told setup that you want to install Windows NT Workstation, setup will prompt you with a screen listing which SCSI Miniport devices (referred to as "Mass Storage Devices") it has found in your computer.

N O T E On computers with an EIDE or IDE hard drive and no SCSI adapters, the "Detected Mass Storage Devices" screen will tell you that no devices were detected. While the fact that you have no mass storage devices may seem a bit strange at first, don't worry. This screen is just telling you that you don't have a SCSI adapter. Windows NT will install on your IDE or EIDE disk without a problem. ▪

You can specify an adapter driver that doesn't come with Windows NT by pressing **S** and inserting a disk (or specifying a directory) with the drivers. Setup will look for a file named OEMSETUP.INF and display any entries it finds. If you don't have any SCSI devices, just press Enter to continue.

N O T E Just because a device isn't listed in the HCL doesn't mean you can't use it. It just means that Windows NT doesn't come with a driver for it. As Windows NT has become more popular, vendors have started distributing drivers for their devices. The Internet is a great place to look for drivers from the manufacturer. ▪

Specifying Additional Settings   You can specify different mice, keyboards, and other devices in the screen "The following list matches my computer." Very few users should have to adjust anything on this screen. The devices that are available for each setting are listed in the TXTSETUP.SIF file.

Partitions   Setup allows you to pick the partition on which you want to install Windows NT 4.0. When you select the partition, you can choose which filesystem you would like. If your computer has more than one partition, they will be listed in order. Your c: drive should be the first partition, d: will be the second partition, and so on.

T I P If you are using a Compaq computer, be careful selecting your partitions. Most Compaq computers keep a small partition at the beginning of the disk that contains the system's diagnostic programs. If you are using a Compaq and only have a c: drive, but setup displays two partitions, the second one is probably your c: drive.

After you select a target partition, you have to choose between the NTFS or FAT filesystems. If you have a FAT filesystem, you can convert it to NTFS without losing the data on it.

NTFS versus FAT on the Workstation

While NTFS is the filesystem of choice on NT Server, think carefully about what filesystem you need on the workstation. NTFS is a good choice if you have:

■ A large partition. NTFS is a bit faster on large partitions (Microsoft recommends NTFS for drives larger than 500 Megabytes, but you are probably fine with FAT up to 1 Gigabyte).

■ Security considerations. You can't delete an erased NTFS file as you can with FAT. You can't boot NT from a floppy to look at a filesystem, either.

■ Compression needs. As with 3.51, NT 4.0 can compress directories, but only on NTFS formatted file systems.

If you don't really have any of these reasons, you should probably start with FAT. FAT is easier for troubleshooting (bootable), and you can use long filenames on it. In addition, you can convert from FAT to NTFS, but you can't go back. For more information on FAT versus NTFS, see Chapter 10, "Optimizing the File System."

Choosing a Directory   You can choose a directory where Windows NT Workstation will be installed. This directory is winnt by default. If you are dual booting Windows 95, it's not a good idea to put Windows NT in the same directory as Windows 95. You will have to reinstall your Windows 95 applications under Windows NT if they are in two different directories.

System Check   After you have chosen an installation directory, setup will want to perform a check of the partition. This check is similar to DOS's chkdsk and Windows 95's scandisk.

Copying Files   The MS-DOS portion of setup copies the distribution files to a directory on your system named WIN_NT.~LS. As files are copied, they are placed in the correct directories. The setup program gets this information from the DOSNET.INF file.

Major Setup Processes—GUI Mode Setup

After you have finished the text-mode portion of setup, your system will reboot into GUI mode setup. This mode is basically a continuation of the text mode setup where you can select further settings for the software configuration.

Gathering Information   In the first part of GUI mode setup, you will get a chance to:

■ Decide the software options you want to install—Accessibility options, Accessories, Communications, Games, Exchange, and Multimedia.

■ Enter the User Name and Organization Name

■ Name this computer

■ Enter a password for the Administrator account

■ Create an Emergency Boot Floppy (EBF)

Networking Options   This is the section of setup where you choose a network adapter and configure protocols and services that you will use in networking.

Finding an Adapter   Windows NT will search the system for a network adapter that it supports. The Hardware Compatibility List has a list of all supported network cards. The files named WINNT\SYSTEM32\OEMNAD??.INF contain the network adapter setup

Part

II

Ch

6

information. For example, the file OEMNADMA.INF contains the setup information for Madge network adapters:

```
MSMDGMPISA    = "Madge Smart 16/4 AT Ringnode"
MSMDGMPATP    = "Madge Smart 16/4 AT Plus Ringnode"
MSMDGMPISAC   = "Madge Smart 16/4 ISA Client Ringnode"
MSMDGMPISACP  = "Madge Smart 16/4 ISA Client Plus Ringnode"
MSMDGMPPC     = "Madge Smart 16/4 PC Ringnode"
MSMDGMPSM16   = "Madge Smart 16 Ringnode"
MSMDGMPPNP    = "Madge Smart 16/4 ISA Client PnP Ringnode"
MSMDGMPMCA    = "Madge Smart 16/4 MC Ringnode"
MSMDGMPMC32   = "Madge Smart 16/4 MC32 Ringnode"
MSMDGMPEISA   = "Madge Smart 16/4 EISA Ringnode"
MSMDGMPPCI    = "Madge Smart 16/4 PCI Ringnode"
MSMDGMPPCIBM  = "Madge Smart 16/4 PCI Ringnode (BM)"
MSMDGMPPCMCIA = "Madge Smart 16/4 PCMCIA Ringnode"
```

The options and settings (IRQ, cable type, and more) that are available for the network adapters come from files named OEMNAD??.INF. If you have a network adapter whose driver doesn't come with Windows NT Workstation, you can tell setup to look on a disk or in a directory for an OEMSETUP.INF file for that network adapter. The Windows NT CD-ROM also comes with a directory called \I386\drvlib.nic (replace I386 with alpha, ppc, or mips if required) that contains additional drivers. Look in the drvlib.nic directory for your manufacturer if you don't have the drivers that came with the adapter.

Choosing Protocols   Setup allows you to choose any combination of network protocols: TCP/IP, IPX, NETBEUI, AppleTalk, DLC, PPTP, or Streams. The setup files for protocols are OEMNXP??.INF. See Chapter 16 for a more detailed description of the protocols and their settings. Figure 6.1 shows the protocol options.

FIG. 6.1

You can choose network protocols during setup.

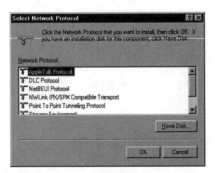

Choosing Services   After you have chosen what protocols you need to use, you can select what services you would like to have installed. If you are accustomed to Windows 95, it may be of help to think of Windows NT network services as both Clients and Services on

Windows 95. The setup information for services can be found in the files named OEMNSV??.INF. Here are the services available:

- **Network Monitor Agent.** Installs support for this workstation to be used as a network probe for Microsoft Network Monitor.
- **TCP/IP Utilities.** Installs TCP/IP programs including: finger, File Transfer Protocol (FTP), nslookup, Remote Copy (RCP), rexec, Remote Shell (RSH), Telnet, and Trivial File Transfer Protocol (TFTP).
- **Microsoft Peer Web Services.** Turns Windows NT Workstation into a Web server with Microsoft Internet Information Server 2.0.
- **NetBIOS Interface.** Creates a software interface for Microsoft networking.
- **Client Service for NetWare (CSNW).** Allows for the Workstation to log in to Novell NetWare 3.x and 4.x servers.
- **Remote Access Services (RAS).** Allows for the Workstation to dial into and accept calls from remote servers, often PPP. This service is required for most Internet Service Providers.
- **RPC Configuration.** Installing the Remote Procedure Call service enables RPC-written programs to run distributed programs.
- **RPC Services for Banyan.** RPC Services for Banyan Networking.
- **SAP Agent.** The Service Advertising Protocol broadcasts the server's availability across a network.
- **SNMP Services.** The Simple Network Management Protocol allows the computer to be managed by network monitoring tools.
- **Simple TCP/IP Services.** Simple network protocols are used mostly for testing, including Quote of the Day, Character Generator, Daytime, and Echo.
- **Server.** Installs support for the SMB (Server Message Block) protocol.
- **Microsoft TCP/IP Printing.** Creates an interface for the computer to print to and share UNIX printers.
- **Workstation.** Installs the SMB client, Network Authentication Service, Alerter, Browser, Messenger, Redirector, Directory Replicator, and the MUP Service.

Some of the services will require more questions to be answered, especially RAS. See Chapter 20, "Using Dial-Up Networking," for setting up RAS specifically.

Network Role Settings After setup starts the network, you can specify how the computer participates in the network—either in a Workgroup or in a Domain. The dialog box in figure 6.2 allows you to make this choice. If you select domain participation, you should have the account created for the computer in the domain or check the "Create computer account in domain" check box. If you check this box and enter a username and password of an account that has creation rights, the domain controller will create an account in the domain for this workstation. For more information on computer accounts and domains, see Chapter 18, "Integrating Windows NT in Microsoft Environments."

FIG. 6.2
Identify whether the computer is participating in a domain or a workgroup.

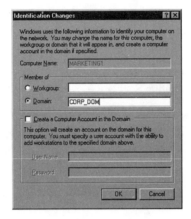

Video Mode Setup   In Video Mode Setup, you can specify a resolution and color depth setting for your video card. The dialog box in figure 6.3 will let you test the settings before they are written to disk.

FIG. 6.3
Choose resolution and color settings during Video Mode Setup.

The system will reboot itself for the third and final time, coming back up with the logon screen. You can use the administrator password you provided earlier in setup to log on.

Tools for Customizing Setup

Microsoft has built functionality into Windows NT Workstation 4.0 that allows the entire setup process discussed in the previous section to be automated.

This section will cover the different tools available for advanced and automated setup. By understanding how these tools work, you can decide which approach is best for you.

Answer Files

Answer files are the most often-used automation tool. As the name suggests, answer files are meant to automatically answer the questions that setup would normally ask the user. Microsoft has included a template file named UNATTEND.TXT on the NT 4.0 CD. The answer file you create will look like a regular INI file, with [heading] in brackets to denote a section, and keys in each section. The keys are text labels followed by values that determine how setup progresses. While NT 3.51 used the same answer file method for installation, the sections and keys have changed with NT 4.0.

The answer file setup sections affect either text mode or GUI mode portions. The sections are listed below:

Text Mode Sections   The sections of an answer file that are related to Text Mode Setup steps are listed below. Each section listed is followed with the keys and values valid for that section.

[Unattended] Section   This section details global parameters for the installation program. The keys available in this section are:

```
ConfirmHardware = yes ¦ no
```

Yes. The setup program will query the user to confirm that the list of devices it has autodetected is correct.

No. Setup will assume that the list of devices it has is correct and continue with the operation.

One of the steps in Text Mode Setup is to detect hardware installed on your machine. Setup does this by attempting to determine from a list of available drivers what hardware a machine has in it.

Sometimes it's difficult to determine the settings for this key. If you are automatically setting up machines for non-technical users and set ConfirmHardware to "no", they will be prompted with a confusing blue text screen listing the hardware devices. Imagine the quizzical phone calls that might generate. Worse, a user might modify the list, destroying the setup process. If your target workstations all have the same hardware, you can probably set this key to no. Many administrators set this key to "no" (which assumes the autodetection is correct) and deal with problems on an exception basis.

If all this sounds a bit gloomy, remember that you can specify new drivers, HALs, and other hardware settings elsewhere in this file (look in [DetectedMassStorage]). It will just require more work ahead of time to make sure you have covered all the available options.

```
NtUpgrade = no ¦ yes ¦ single ¦ manual
```

This key determines how setup deals with previous installation of Windows NT.

No. Setup will replace the installed version of Windows NT. Settings for this new installation will come from either the user, the answer file, or the UDF. Remember that if you have a previous installation and don't upgrade from it but overwrite it, the programs the user had installed will have to be reinstalled.

Yes. Setup will upgrade the previous version of Windows NT, using all the settings from that version. If you specify yes, the rest of the Answer file and UDF is ignored as settings are acquired from the previous version. If you happen to have multiple installations of Windows NT on your computer, the first one setup finds is the one used for the upgrade.

Single. If there is only one previous version of Windows NT installed, setup will upgrade it. If multiple versions are installed, setup will ask the user which one to use. If you upgrade an existing installation, all settings are derived from that installation and answer files and UDFs are ignored.

Manual. This setting will ask the user whether to replace or upgrade a previous installation. If the user chooses to replace an installation, setup will ask for a directory to use when installing Windows NT.

```
Win31Upgrade = yes ¦ no
```

This key is only valid if setup can find an existing installation of Windows 3.1 on the target computer. If you set this key to yes, setup attempts to take any valid information from the existing Windows 3.1 installation. Setting it to "no" will run setup with the defaults.

```
FileSystem = ConvertNTFS ¦ LeaveAlone
```

This section allows you to specify whether the installation partitions are converted to Microsoft's NTFS or left as they are.

ConvertNTFS. Automatically converts the partition where Windows NT Workstation is installed into the NTFS filesystem.

LeaveAlone. Installs Windows NT Workstation on whatever filesystem exists in the partition.

```
TargetPath = path ¦ manual ¦ *
```

You can specify where Windows NT will be installed.

> **Path**. Specifies the path where Windows NT should be installed. This key does not require a drive letter, just a directory. An example statement for this key is "TargetPath = WINNT."

> *****. This indicates that the setup program should generate a unique directory name for Windows NT Workstation.

> **Manual**. If the target path = manual, setup will prompt the user for an installation path.

> Path and "*" are the only two values appropriate for automated setup.
>
>   OverwriteOemFilesOnUpgrade = yes ¦ no

If this key value is yes, setup will overwrite files on the target computer with identical names.

    OemPreinstall = yes ¦ no

This key indicates that there are files in the OEM directory structure which may need to be copied as a part of setup. If this key is no, sections [DisplayDrivers], [MassStorageDrivers], [KeyboardDrivers], [PointingDeviceDrivers], and [OEMPreinstall] are all ignored.

    NoWaitAfterTextMode = 0 ¦ 1

If the OemPreinstall key is set to yes, the system will stop setup after text mode, making it possible for you to duplicate that hard drive. Copies of that hard drive will boot into GUI mode setup, allowing you to enter information specific to their situation. This option is meant for Original Equipment Manufacturers (OEMs). If you want to use the OEM features (by setting OemPreinstall = yes), but want the setup program to continue after text mode, set this key to 1. If you want the setup to stop after text mode, set this key to 0.

[DetectecdMassStorage] Section   During setup, Windows NT attempts to detect SCSI devices by loading all the Miniport drivers. If a driver can see hardware, that device is "detected" and setup will load the drivers. This section allows you to plug a driver into that "detected" list regardless of whether the device is in the system or not. You would typically use this section for devices that don't get autodetected correctly.

The drivers available to you are the ones listed in the [SCSI] section of the TXTSETUP.SIF file. If you want to make sure that all workstations on which you install Windows NT Workstation have drivers for an Adaptec 2940, put a key value of "aic78xx" in this section of your answer file.

Following is a list of standard SCSI miniport drivers from the [SCSI] section of TXTSETUP.SIF.

Part
II

Ch
6

```
[SCSI]
sparrow  = "Adaptec AHA-151X/AHA-152X or AIC-6260/AIC-6360 SCSI Host
            Adapter"
aha154x  = "Adaptec AHA-154X/AHA-164X SCSI Host Adapter"
aha174x  = "Adaptec AHA-174X EISA SCSI Host Adapter"
arrow    = "Adaptec AHA-274X/AHA-284X/AIC-777X SCSI Host Adapter"
aic78xx  = "Adaptec AHA-294X/AHA-394X or AIC-78XX PCI SCSI Controller"
amsint   = "AMD PCI SCSI Controller/Ethernet Adapter"
ami0nt   = "AMIscsi SCSI Host Adapter"
buslogic = "BusLogic SCSI Host Adapter"
flashpnt = "BusLogic FlashPoint"
cpqfws2e = "Compaq 32-Bit Fast-Wide SCSI-2/E"
cpqarray = "Compaq Drive Array"
delldsa  = "Dell Drive Array"
dptscsi  = "DPT SCSI Host Adapter"
fd7000ex = "Future Domain TMC-7000EX EISA SCSI Host Adapter"
fd8xx    = "Future Domain 8XX SCSI Host Adapter"
fd16_700 = "Adaptec AHA-2920 or Future Domain 16XX/PCI/SCSI2Go SCSI Host
            Adapt
spock    = "IBM MCA SCSI Host Adapter"
atapi    = "IDE CD-ROM (ATAPI 1.2)/Dual-channel PCI IDE Controller"
mitsumi  = "Mitsumi CD-ROM Controller"
dac960nt = "Mylex DAC960/Digital SWXCR-Ex Raid Controller"
ncr53c9x = "NCR 53C9X SCSI Host Adapter"
ncrc700  = "NCR C700 SCSI Host Adapter"
ncrc710  = "NCR 53C710 SCSI Host Adapter"
symc810  = "Symbios Logic C810 PCI SCSI Host Adapter"
oliscsi  = "Olivetti ESC-1/ESC-2 SCSI Host Adapter"
ql10wnt  = "QLogic PCI SCSI Host Adapter"
mkecr5xx = "MKEPanasonic CD-ROM Controller"
slcd32   = "Sony Proprietary CD-ROM Controller"
ultra14F = "UltraStor 14F/14FB/34F/34FA/34FB SCSI Host Adapter"
ultra24F = "UltraStor 24F/24FA SCSI Host Adapter"
```

When using this section, keep in mind that adding support for a device that isn't installed in a system is not recommended. It will at least pop up a message on system startup and at worst hang your system.

[DisplayDrivers] Section   This section allows you to specify display drivers. If you need to add a display driver that isn't included with Windows NT, you can specify it here. The syntax of this section is:

```
displaydriver = Retail ¦ OEM
```

The displaydriver key must match an entry in the [Display] section of TXTSETUP.SIF (for the "Retail" value) or TXTSETUP.OEM (for the "OEM" value).

[MassStorageDrivers] Section   This section allows you to specify SCSI Miniport drivers. In order to install a SCSI driver that isn't included with Windows NT, you must specify it in this section. The syntax of this section is as follows:

```
massstoragedriver = Retail ¦ OEM
```

The massstoragedriver key must match an entry in the [SCSI] section of TXTSETUP.SIF (for the "Retail" value) or TXTSETUP.OEM (for the "OEM" value).

[KeyboardDrivers] Section   This section allows you to specify an alternate keyboard driver. The entries in this section must have a matching entry in the [Keyboard] section of the TXTSETUP.SIF file or the TXTSETUP.OEM file.

[PointingDeviceDrivers] Section   Here you can enter any alternate mouse drivers. This section may be useful if you are using specialized drivers for a CAD workstation. The format of keys in this section follows:

```
mousedriver = Retail ¦ OEM
```

The key (mousedriver) must be present in the [Mouse] section of TXTSETUP.SIF or TXTSETUP.OEM.

[OEMBootFiles] Section   If you are using a OEM\OEMFILES\TXTSETUP.OEM file, you need to specify it in this section. You also need to specify any files that are listed in the TXTSETUP.OEM file in this section.

GUI Mode Sections
The sections below alter the setup program's behavior in the GUI portion of the setup process. GUI mode sections are available for use in a UDF file, while text mode sections only work in answer files.

[GUIUnattended] Section   This section allows you to run a program concurrently with setup and to automatically set the time zone. To run a program during setup, use the DetachedProgram key. The syntax for this key is:

```
DetachedProgram = program
```

It may be useful to run a command shell (maybe to start a game of hearts) with the following command:

```
DetachedProgram = cmd.exe
```

The TimeZone key allows you to specify a timezone without user intervention:

```
TimeZone = "timezone"
```

You must, of course, substitute "timezone" for a valid timezone. The valid timezones are listed in the timezone list box displayed during setup and as follows:

(GMT) Greenwich Mean Time; Dublin, Edinburgh, London

(GMT+01:00) Lisbon, Warsaw

(GMT+01:00) Paris, Madrid

(GMT+01:00) Berlin, Stockholm, Rome, Bern, Brussels, Vienna

(GMT+02:00) Eastern Europe

(GMT+01:00) Prague

(GMT+02:00) Athens, Helsinki, Istanbul

(GMT-03:00) Rio de Janeiro

(GMT-04:00) Atlantic Time (Canada)

(GMT-05:00) Eastern Time (US & Canada)

(GMT-06:00) Central Time (US & Canada)

(GMT-07:00) Mountain Time (US & Canada)

(GMT-08:00) Pacific Time (US & Canada); Tijuana

(GMT-09:00) Alaska

(GMT-10:00) Hawaii

(GMT-11:00) Midway Island, Samoa

(GMT+12:00) Wellington

(GMT+10:00) Brisbane, Melbourne, Sydney

(GMT+09:30) Adelaide

(GMT+09:00) Tokyo, Osaka, Sapporo, Seoul, Yakutsk

(GMT+08:00) Hong Kong, Perth, Singapore, Taipei

(GMT+07:00) Bangkok, Jakarta, Hanoi

(GMT+05:30) Bombay, Calcutta, Madras, New Delhi, Colombo

(GMT+04:00) Abu Dhabi, Muscat, Tbilisi, Kazan, Volgograd

(GMT+03:30) Tehran

(GMT+03:00) Baghdad, Kuwait, Nairobi, Riyadh

(GMT+02:00) Israel

(GMT-03:30) Newfoundland

(GMT-01:00) Azores, Cape Verde Is.

(GMT-02:00) Mid-Atlantic

(GMT) Monrovia, Casablanca

(GMT-03:00) Buenos Aires, Georgetown

(GMT-04:00) Caracas, La Paz

(GMT-05:00) Indiana (East)

(GMT-05:00) Bogota, Lima

(GMT-06:00) Saskatchewan

(GMT-06:00) Mexico City, Tegucigalpa

(GMT-07:00) Arizona

(GMT-12:00) Enewetak, Kwajalein

(GMT+12:00) Fiji, Kamchatka, Marshall Is.

(GMT+11:00) Magadan, Soloman Is., New Caledonia

(GMT+10:00) Hobart

(GMT+10:00) Guam, Port Moresby, Vladivostok

(GMT+09:30) Darwin

(GMT+08:00) Beijing, Chongqing, Urumqi

(GMT+06:00) Alma Ata, Dhaka

(GMT+05:00) Islamabad, Karachi, Sverdlovsk, Tashkent

(GMT+04:30) Kabul

(GMT+02:00) Cairo

(GMT+02:00) Harare, Pretoria

(GMT+03:00) Moscow, St. Petersburg

[Display] Section This useful section allows you to alter the way Setup acts regarding selection and setting of your video card. You need to be careful with this section—misconfiguration could at least give you a screenful of fuzz, at worst it could damage your monitor.

```
ConfigureAtLogon = 0 ¦ 1
```

The ConfigureAtLogon key allows you to skip the video detection portion of setup. If you set this key to 1, the default display resolution will be set until the first user logs on to the system. If you set it to 0, the user will be asked what video mode to use during setup, unless you use the preconfiguration keys listed below:

BitsPerPel = Color_Depth

XResolution = XRes

Yresolution = Yres

Vrefresh = Refresh_Rate

These settings, if present, will select the video mode automatically for the user. Be careful to specify a video mode that the card and monitor can both handle. The default settings for these keys are:

BitsPerPel = 8

XResolution = 640

Yresolution = 480

Vrefresh = 60

Part

II

Ch

6

The default settings would set the graphics card to 640×480×256 @ 60Hz. Windows NT will, by default, test these settings as part of the setup. If you are attempting an automated installation, you will need to set the value of the AutoConfirm key as listed here:

```
AutoConfirm = 0 ¦ 1
```

If you set AutoConfirm to 1, the setting specified in BitsPerPel, Xresolution, Yresolution, and Vrefresh will be used without being tested. If you set it to 0, setup will pause and ask the user if the settings display correctly.

[Network] Section

```
Attend = Yes ¦ No
```

If you want the Networking component of the setup process to be attended, set this key to Yes. By setting this value to yes, you will require human intervention at the keyboard to complete setup. Even though the networking section will require human intervention, the rest of the setup process can be automatic and unattended.

> **N O T E** The following adapters, protocols, and services keys of the network section all point to other sections in the text file. The existence of the key and a valid section name after it indicates that you want to install that adapter, protocol, or service—in other words, if you have DetectAdapters = AdapterSection, it implies DetectAdapters = Yes. ■

```
JoinWorkgroup = workgroup
```

This key allows you to have the computer automatically join a workgroup. Notice that there are no quotes that surround the workgroup.

```
JoinDomain = domain
```

This section allows you to automatically join a domain. In order to do this, you need to have an unused account for computername in the domain that matches this computer's name.

```
CreateComputerAccount = AccountName, password
```

The CreateComputerAccount key allows you to create an account for this computer in the domain you have specified with the JoinDomain key. The account specified must have rights to create a computer account in the domain. The three previous keys fill in the setup screen pictured earlier in figure 6.2.

> **CAUTION**
>
> The CreateComputerAccount key should be used only in secure test environments (your lab, for example). Remember that the accountname and password are stored in plain text in this file, open for reading by anyone with network privileges to the distribution sharepoint. You should not use the CreateComputerAccount key in a production environment.

User-Defined Sections

The InstallAdapters, DetectAdapters, InstallProtocols, InstallServices, RAS, and PortSections keys in the answer file are followed by values that are user-defined sections. For instance, the AdapterSection value for the InstallAdapters key is user-defined. You could call it the MyAdapters section if you like. The important idea is this: if you put a value after the InstallAdapters key, you must make a section in the answer file that corresponds with your user-defined value. For example, if you specify AdapterSection as the user-defined value for InstallAdapters or DetectAdapters, you then need to create a section in the answer file named [AdapterSection]. Although the name of the user-defined section you call is irrelevant, the keys you can place in that new section are not. We will describe the valid keys for these user-defined sections as they occur in this chapter.

```
DetectAdapters = AdapterSection
```

To detect a network adapter in the computer, specify a valid user-defined section name after the DetectAdapters key. See the sidebar "User-Defined Sections" for an explanation of this key's value.

```
InstallAdapters = AdapterSection
```

To install a network adapter (whether it is physically installed in the computer or not), specify the InstallAdapters key with a user-defined section name. See the previous sidebar "User-Defined Sections" for an explanation of this key's value.

User-Defined [AdapterSection] Section

The format of this new section is:

```
Inf_option = ParameterSection,[Path]
```

where Inf_option is the driver name out of the [Options] section of an OEMSETUP.INF file (if the driver isn't included) or OEMNAD??.INF (if you are specifying an adapter included with Windows NT). The Parameter section is another new section that contains card parameters, and the optional path value is the location and filename of the INF file. The path isn't required if you are specifying an adapter driver that is included with Windows NT Workstation.

For example, to install a 3Com Etherlink III EISA adapter (a driver that comes with Windows NT) automatically, put the line:

```
ELNK3EISA = AdapterParametersSection
```

in the [AdapterSection], and create an [AdapterParameterSection] in the unattended answer file. This section can contain no keys, but the heading needs to exist in the file for the installation to work. The ELNK3EISA driver came from the [Options] section of the system32\OEMNADEE.INF file. If you need to reference a network driver that isn't included with Windows NT Workstation, you need to reference its path and

Part
II

Ch
6

OEMSETUP.INF file. For instance, to install a Xircom CreditCard Ethernet Adapter IIps adapter (a driver for this adapter is in the drvlib.nic\xircom\ce2 directory), the following line would be appropriate:

```
CE2XPS = OEMCardParameters,drvlib.nic\xircom\ce2
```

As with the entry above, you would need to insert a [OEMCardParameters] section into the unattended answer file.

> **N O T E** Most network card OEMSETUP.INF files will cause a screen to pop up during unattended setup to confirm the IRQ, Cable Type, Base Address, and other settings. This pop up window will cause setup to halt until a button is clicked. Unfortunately, each vendor may have a different way to stop this window from pausing setup. The only way to fix this problem is to talk with your network card vendor. ■

```
InstallProtocols = ProtocolSection
```

This key of the [Network] section will allow you to install and set up options for the workstation's protocols. The key's value, ProtocolSection, is a reference to a user-defined section that will list the protocols you want installed. See the sidebar "User-Defined Sections" for an explanation of user-defined sections.

Some possible values for user-defined [ProtocolSection] are:

NBF = NetBEUIParamsSection

TC = TCPIPParamsSection

NWLNKIPX = IPXParamsSection

The values listed after the keys are user-defined sections. See the earlier sidebar "User-Defined Sections" for an explanation of user-defined sections.

```
InstallServices = ServicesSection
```

The value of this key defines a user-defined section. The user-defined [ServicesSection] section contains the actual list of services you want installed. Some possible values of this user-defined section are:

SNMP = SNMPParamsSection

CSNW = NetwareClientSection

RAS = RemoteAccessSvcsParams

The value of these keys again defines new user-defined sections. See the earlier sidebar "User-Defined Sections" for an explanation of user-defined sections. Next we will explain the keys available in the user-defined RAS section [RemoteAccessSvcsParams].

User-Defined [RemoteAccessParameters] Section

This section allows you to install the parameters for RAS. The following keys are valid in this section:

AssignSameNetworkNumber = YES | NO

AutomaticNetworkNumber = YES | NO

ClientCanRequestIPAddress = YES | NO

ClientCanRequestIPXNodeNumber = YES | NO

DialOutProtocols = TCP/IP | IPX | NETBEUI

DialInProtocols = TCP/IP | IPX | NETBEUI

ExcludeAddress = x.x.x.x-y.y.y.y

IPXClientAccess = Network | ThisComputer

NetBEUIClientAccess = Network | ThisComputer

NetworkNumbersFrom = IPXNetworkNumber

PortSections = COM1, COM2, COMX

StaticAddressBegin = x.x.x.x

StaticAddressEnd = y.y.y.y

TCPIPClientAccess = Network | ThisComputer

UseDHCP = YES | NO

The values of the PortSections key are user-defined sections. See the earlier sidebar "User-Defined Sections" for an explanation of user-defined sections. The values available in these user-defined sections are:

DeviceType = Modem

DeviceName = DeviceName

The devicename is a text string that represents a modem device.

PortName = COM2

PortUsage = DialIn | DialOut | DialInOut

[OEMAds] Section   This section allows you to customize setup with text and bitmaps you specify. This section is usually used to put your company logo on the setup screen.

```
Banner = BannerText
```

This key allows you to specify what text is displayed in the upper-left corner of the setup screen. If you want to create a multi-line banner, place an asterisk where you want line breaks. In order for this text to be displayed, it must contain "Windows NT Workstation."

```
Bitmap = BannerFile
```

Part
II

Ch
6

If you want a custom background to be displayed during setup, you can use the Bitmap key. The filename you specify will be tiled as background for the setup program.

```
Logo = LogoFile
```

This key references the bitmap that setup displays in the upper-right corner of the screen while setup is in GUI mode. This file needs to be of bitmap (.BMP) format.

```
[UserData] Section
```

This section allows you to specify the name and organization to which the workstation is registered.

```
FullName = "Name"
```

This is the username you want in the registration. The quotes are required.

```
OrgName = "Organization"
```

Put your company's name in the quotes after OrgName.

```
ComputerName = ComputerName
```

The Windows NT Workstation's network computername is identified in this setting. Note that no quotation marks are required for this key.

```
ProductID = "123-456789012345"
```

This key is the product number for Windows NT 4.0 Workstation. If this key isn't specified, setup will halt until the user enters the Product ID. This is similar to the CD Key for Windows 95.

UDF Files

If all you had were answer files, you would have to make a custom one for each user—at least the computername would need to be different from computer to computer. Wouldn't it be nice to have a file with just the *differences* from the answer file each user requires? A Uniqueness Database File (UDF) is that file. UDFs are an extension to the answer files, and use the same sections (GUI mode only) as the answer files.

The UDF file can only contain the sections and keys for GUI mode setup. The sections that are defined as text mode sections can only be in the answer file. This means that the following sections listed in the earlier Answer file section are valid in the UDF:

[Unattended]

[OEMAds]

[Display]

[GUIUnattended]

[UserData]

[Network]

[RemoteAccessParameters]

Specify a UDF filename and user within that file as an argument to the winnt or winnt32 program. Here is an example:

```
winnt /b /u:unattend.txt /udf:lindat,allusers.udf /s:i:\i386
```

This setup command line tells setup to run without using boot floppies (/b), to use the answer file "unattend.txt" for all answers except the ones duplicated or specified in the "lindat" sections of the UDF "allusers.udf."

If you were to use the command

```
winnt /b /u:unattend.txt /udf:lindat /s:i:\i386
```

without specifying a filename for the UDF, winnt will ask the user for a disk with the file named $UNIQUE%.UDF. This way, you can create a different diskette for each user. If you want to create a single command to launch the installation of Windows NT Workstation, you could create a diskette for every user that had the same UniqueID, but with different computer information. This would allow the diskette to be the differentiating key, not the launch command.

Or, if you are worried about the network load of 100 users installing Windows NT Workstation at once, you might use a few diskettes with the same UDF file (containing all the users) as "keys" for the installation. Only the computers with the "keys" can start the installation—with only a few installing at a time, your network won't become saturated.

Essentially, setup loads the values from the unattend.txt file, then loads the values for "lindat" from the allusers.udf file. This overwrites the duplicate values from un-attend.txt with the "lindat" specific values from allusers.udf, and loads any values that are not specified in unattend.txt. The resulting values are written to a file named WIN_NT.~BT\WINNT.SIF. Setup will proceed with the installation.

UDF Contents   The UDF file begins with a section that defines all the unique IDs in the file and the sections that these IDs use. This section is formatted as follows:

```
[UniqueIds]
uniqueid1 = UserData, Display
uniqueid2 = UserData,
uniqueid3 = UserData, OEMAds,  Display
```

The key values refer to sections later in the UDF. You assign unique sections to IDs by typing the ID before the section text. The resulting unique section for uniqueid1's [UserData] section looks like this:

```
[uniqueid1:UserData]
```

Part

II

Ch

6

A sample UDF follows:

```
[UniqueIds]
lindat = UserData, Display
craigw = UserData, OEMAds,  Display
davidc = UserData,

[lindat:UserData]
ComputerName = arkanoid

[davidc:UserData]
ComputerName = digdug

[lindat:UserData]
ComputerName = zaxxon

[lindat:Display]
BitsPerPel = 16
XResolution = 1024
Yresolution = 768
Vrefresh = 72

[Display]
ConfigureAtLogon = 1

[craigw:OEMAds]
Banner = "Windows NT Workstation*Setup for Corporation 2"
```

The previous UDF would create different results for each user. For instance, the command

```
winnt /b /u:unattend.txt /udf:lindat:allusers.udf
```

would have created an installation for that user with the computername of "arkanoid," a high-resolution display, and the normal banner.

The user davidc would get the normal banner and his screen resolution would be set at the time of his first logon.

The user craigw would have a special banner for his corporation and a screen resolution set at his first logon.

As you can see, the UDF file allows for some interesting configurations. Remember that the UniqueID can be anything, from users to hardware types to corporate divisions.

sysdiff Utility

The sysdiff utility is a new utility that comes with the Windows NT 4.0 resource kit that makes installing complex and custom software an easy, one command process. The utility works by taking an initial snapshot of a reference system, installing and configuring the software you want, then taking a snapshot again. The new snapshot will capture all the new files, registry, and configuration settings in one file. This file can then be distributed and applied to systems. There are specific steps you need to follow to get a valid sysdiff file.

1. Start with a fresh (Windows NT not installed) system
2. Install Windows NT 4.0 Workstation
3. Take an initial snapshot with "sysdiff /snap"
4. Install the software you will need to distribute
5. Configure the system (wallpaper, fonts, etc) with settings you need to distribute
6. Take a differential snapshot with "sysdiff /diff"

If you have followed these steps correctly, you will have a single file that contains all the changes (files, settings) you just made bundled up in it.

You can distribute this file automatically when you set up Windows NT Workstation and apply it automatically through CMDLINES.TXT (see CMDLINES.TXT section later in the chapter). If you need to install five programs that have no automated installation facility, you can install sysdiff, then install the difference file at other computers without going through the complex setup process for each piece of software.

The sysdiff.inf File   The sysdiff program's actions are controlled by editing a file named sysdiff.inf. This file will let you include and exclude directories and registry keys from sysdiff's scanning. You can use the "?," "*," and "::" entries to automatically specify different drives. The meanings of these symbols are as follows:

> * = A "*" instead of a drive letter refers to all drives available.
>
> ? = A "?" instead of a drive letter means the drive on which Windows NT Workstation is installed.
>
> :: = The double colon "::" is substituted with the drive and directory that is %systemroot%.

For example:

```
::\system32\ras
```

would translate to "c:\winnt\system32\ras" when run—if you've installed Windows NT Workstation into the c:\winnt (the default) directory. You also must have the sysdiff.inf file in the path when you run sysdiff. Following are descriptions of the sections available in sysdiff.inf.

[ExcludeDrives] Section   If you don't want to scan an entire drive, put the letter of that drive (without the semicolon) in this section. For example, if you don't want sysdiff to scan your logical d: drive, the section would look like this:

```
[ExcludeDrives]
d
```

[ExcludeDirectoryTrees] Section   This section allows you to exclude entire directory trees (the specified directory and all its subdirectories) in your scan. For example, you probably don't want to worry about the files in the \temp directories on any drives. The key value for this example exclusion would be:

```
*:\temp
```

[ExcludeSingleDirectories] Section   The excludesingledirectories section allows you to exclude a directory, but include all its subdirectories. An example of this would be:

```
c:\
```

This would cause sysdiff to ignore any changes made to files (autoexec.bat or config.sys) in the root directory of your c: drive.

[ExcludeFiles] Section   Here you can exclude single files. This section is often used to exclude any swapfiles and log files. Since a swapfile changes every time you start Windows NT, sysdiff would detect it as changed and include it in the difference file unless you would exclude it. Here are some default examples:

```
*:\pagefile.sys
system.log
```

[IncludeFilesInDir] Section   This section allows you to specify files that you want included in the difference file regardless of change. If your reference system has any files that you want to copy into the difference file, you should include that file here.

[ExcludeRegistryKeys] Section   You can enter specific registry key sections that you don't want sysdiff to scan in this section. Only all the subkeys of HKEY_LOCAL_MACHINE\System, HKEY_LOCAL_MACHINE\Software, and HKEY_CURRENT_USER are scanned by sysdiff's default. You can specify HKEY_LOCAL_MACHINE as HKLM and HKEY_CURRENT_USER as HKCU in this section. Also, there is no need to put a "\" in front of the first item after the comma. For example, Microsoft excludes the following registry key by default:

```
HKCU,Software\Microsoft\Windows\CurrentVersion\Explorer\RunMRU
```

[ExcludeRegistryTrees] Section   This section is different from ExcludeRegistryKeys in that a line specified here will cause sysdiff to skip all the items below that key during the scan. The HKLM and HKCU abbreviations from the previous sections are also available here. Following are the trees Microsoft excludes by default:

```
HKLM,SYSTEM
HKLM,SOFTWARE
HKLM,SYSTEM\ControlSet001
HKLM,SYSTEM\ControlSet002
```

```
HKLM,SYSTEM\ControlSet003
HKLM,SYSTEM\ControlSet004
HKLM,SYSTEM\ControlSet005
HKLM,SYSTEM\ControlSet006
HKLM,SYSTEM\ControlSet007
HKLM,SYSTEM\ControlSet008
HKLM,SYSTEM\ControlSet009
```

[ExcludeRegistryValues] Section   This section is similar to the previous two sections except that it allows you to exclude specific registry values from the scan.

The Reference System   Before you can use the sysdiff utility, you need to install Windows NT Workstation on a "reference system." This basically means that you need to perform a fresh installation on a machine similar to the one you will be applying to the sysdiff file. Don't use the machine after installing Windows NT, because you could make enough changes to the environment that the initial snapshot will not work on the system to which you apply the difference file.

The Initial Snapshot   After you have installed a fresh copy of Windows NT Workstation, you can take the initial snapshot with the following command:

```
sysdiff /snap [/log:LogFile] InitialFile
```

The command will launch a multithreaded program like the one in figure 6.4.

FIG. 6.4
The sysdiff program
in action.

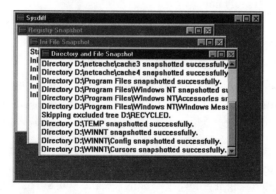

Part
II

Ch
6

When the program is done, you will have a file that contains the initial snapshot.

The Difference File   After you have created the initial snapshot, install the applications and configure the machine. When you are satisfied with the configuration, take a difference snapshot with the following command:

```
sysdiff /diff [/log:LogFile] InitialFile DifferenceFile
```

Sysdiff will again go through your system looking for differences. After it is done, the DifferenceFile will contain all the changes you've made to the system since you took the initial snapshot.

Apply the Difference File   Now that you are ready to install the difference file on a fresh computer, run the sysdiff command with the syntax:

```
sysdiff /apply /m [/log:LogFile] DifferenceFile
```

The sysdiff will unpack the difference file and install the changes for you. When you restart, the programs and settings will be in place. The /m parameter causes any files written by sysdiff in any specific user's profile directory structure to be copied instead to the default user profile. This is important because if you were the Administrator when you installed the files, sysdiff would try to install the files it found different from the snapshot in the administrator's profile directory structure. That directory doesn't exist until the administrator logs on for the first time, and no users (besides the administrator) could access those programs.

The OEM Directory

There are two potential users of unattended installation technology:

- Administrators and Users who need to install Windows NT Workstation on many client computers.

- Original Equipment Manufacturers (OEMs) who need to roll thousands of identical PCs off an assembly line.

Unfortunately, the manufacturers have it easier than us users. They only have to figure out how to perform an unattended installation on one type of system. We have to deal with all the contingencies and complexities that exist outside of a production line environment.

The OEM directory structure allows you to organize and distribute the files that don't come with Windows NT Workstation. You can use this directory as a part of installing protocols, adapters, services, software, and other files on target computers.

The OEM directory is a subdirectory that resides in the same directory from which the source files are copied. For example, if you have copied the files from the CD-ROM to a network share called \\digdug\ntworkstation\i386, the OEM directory would reside in \\digdug\ntworkstation\i386\OEM.

N O T E   In order for the OEM directory to be included in automated installation, you must be using an answer file, and in the [Unattended] section of that answer file, the OEMPreinstall key must = yes. ∎

The next sections will cover the contents of the OEM directory.

The OEM\CMDLINES.TXT File   You can think of the cmdlines.txt file as a batch file that runs at the end of the Windows NT installation. You can enter commands as they would be entered at a command prompt. This is often used for launching another product installation or a sysdiff /apply command. The syntax for each command line is the command in quotes.

```
sysdiff /apply /m diffile.dif
```

OEM\TEXTMODE This directory is where you put files that need to be copied during text mode installation. This directory is also the location for drivers that are not network related. The following are drivers that you would need to install in the OEM\TEXTMODE directory:

- Hardware Abstraction Layers (HALs)
- SCSI Miniport drivers
- Keyboard drivers
- Mouse drivers
- Video drivers

For each device or driver that you have copied into this directory, you need to follow some steps to have it installed automatically.

1. Copy the files from the vendor into this directory. Since vendors all use similarly named INF files, be sure you don't overwrite one by mistake.

2. Modify the OEMPreinstall key in the [Unattended] section of your answer file to equal "yes."

3. Copy a TXTSETUP.OEM file supplied by the vendor into the OEM\TEXTMODE directory. This file will contain the names of the vendor-supplied .INF files for each driver.

4. Modify the [OEMBootFiles] section of your answer file to include the filenames of TXTSETUP.OEM and all the INF files listed in it.

OEM\$$WINNT Files in this directory will be copied over the retail product during installation. This directory is identical in structure to the %systemroot% directory in Windows NT. If you wanted to overwrite the HOSTS file in the C:\winnt\system32\drivers\ etc directory, you would copy a HOSTS file to the OEM\$$WINNT\system32\ drivers\etc directory.

Installation Delivery Methods

A delivery method is the way that you get the setup process started on each machine. There are two main methods for deploying Windows NT Workstation.

Part
II

Ch
6

The Push Installation

The push installation is where you (the administrator) install Windows NT Workstation on the client machines when you want it to be installed as part of an automated process. The software is then "pushed" onto the computers.

This method is very appropriate for some environments, but there can be difficulties. This method of installation delivery should be entirely automated. If a machine breaks during installation, you or a technician will have to "touch" it in order to complete the installation, so your unattended installation must be robust.

Some critical things to think about before attempting a push installation:

■ **Will the automated installation work without error?**

In a push installation scenario, a technical person is probably not attending the installation unless there is a problem. Therefore, it is very important that the installation occurs automatically without errors. The thing that is most likely to cause your installation to fail is differences in machines—the more configurations you have, the less likely you are going to test every configuration. For the push installation to work well, your computing environment should be homogeneous.

■ **Can you spread the installation across users?**

Say you have the installation start when the users log in to a server, and a problem makes 20 percent of the users nonproductive all day as you fix their computers. If your target is 500 users, do you have a job at the end of that day? It's much easier to use a delivery method that allows for small groups of users to get the installation at the same time. This allows you to isolate problems and fix them with a small amount of users.

■ **Can your network handle the load?**

If you install too many users at the same time, they will saturate the network as they simultaneously copy all of Windows NT's installation files over the network. Again, spreading the installation to a small group of users or starting the installation at certain times will be the simple fix for this problem.

■ **Are your users skilled?**

If your users are power users, you probably don't want to surprise them with an unexpected upgrade. All of a sudden the applications they worked months to get working just right don't work anymore. The push installation is much more appropriate in an environment where all the PCs are the same and the users just want to be able to use their standard applications.

The push method is appropriate if:

- The computer configurations are very similar.
- You can install in smaller groups.
- The users are less skilled.
- Downtime is not absolutely critical.

The Pull Installation

You have a "pull" method of installation when the user or technician launches the setup program manually. This method is used more often than the push method because it gives more control of the installation.

Often in a pull installation, there are technicians who will attend to several machines simultaneously. They will start a computer running setup, start some more, then go back to check on the first one. Users like this because there is a person nearby to fix the computer if the installation fails, and it speeds up installation. You also gain flexibility because there is someone there who can answer setup program questions if you want each machine to be partly configured differently, and don't have time to create a complex UDF.

Here are some things to think about when designing a pull delivery:

- **Do you have enough people to cover all the computers?**

  As a part of testing, time how long it takes a technician to install Windows NT from start to stop. You can use this measure to figure out how long the entire rollout will take. If you simply don't have enough people to cover all the machines within your timeframe, consider a push installation or some extra help.

- **How geographically dispersed are your computers?**

  If you have 5,000 computers all in the same building, a pull installation may be feasible. If you have 1,000 computers in 200 locations, you may want to think of some other options.

Installation Delivery Methods

There are many very creative ways to deliver the Windows NT 4.0 Workstation to your clients, and this section will cover some popular installation methods.

All of these delivery methods utilize a *network distribution sharepoint*—a directory on the network into which installation files from the retail CD-ROM are copied. This is a network directory that the client can access at the time installation is started. This is the most common way to get the installation files to the target system.

Part
II

Ch
6

Login Script Delivery

The most common delivery vehicle is the login script installation. When the user (or the administrator) logs into a server (any server that can map a network drive), the command to start setup is a part of the script that executes as part of the user's login process. In addition, you can create a test in the login script to see if the user is a member of a group that has been assigned for installations. Here are some samples of script segments:

Sample Windows NT server script:

```
net use I: \\NT_Server1\NT4Dist
I:
cd \i386
winnt /b /s:I:\i386 /u:unattend.txt
```

 TIP If your login script allows you to identify a user as a DOS environment variable, you may be able to create a different installation for each user with a UDF. For instance, the Novell script to use a username as a UDF unique ID might look like this:

```
winnt /b /udf:%USERNAME%
```

This is a sample Novell 3.12 server script:

```
IF MEMBER OF "NT4UPGROUP" THEN
MAP ROOT I:=NOVELL_SERVER/NT40DIST
I:
cd \i386
winnt /b /s:I:\i386 /u:unattend.txt
END
```

Diskette-Based Delivery

In the diskette installation, the target is booted from an MS-DOS system diskette. This diskette loads network drivers, maps a network drive to the network distribution sharepoint, and starts the installation. If you want to use UDF files, you can give each user in your organization a diskette with their unique ID on it. Here are some sample configurations.

This is a sample Windows Networking Diskette AUTOEXEC.BAT:

```
path = a:\net
smartdrv c+ a- b- 10000
net initialize
nwlink
net start /comp:NTInstall1
net logon inst_acct /domain:NT_Install_Domain
net use i: \\NT_Install_Server\NT40Dist
i:\winnt /b /s:i:\i386 /u:i:\unattend.txt
```

This is a sample Novell Networking Diskette AUTOEXEC.BAT:

```
smartdrv c+ 10000
lsl
carddrvr
ipxodi
vlm /ps=NovellDist
login inst_acct
map root i:=NovellDist\NT40Dist
i:\winnt /b /s:i:\ /u:i:\unattend.txt
```

The diskette-based install option also has an advantage in that you know the state of the machine when setup begins. In addition, you can perform other functions, like disk optimization, before the setup process starts.

Systems Management Server (SMS) Installation

Microsoft's System Management Server (SMS) allows for operating systems to be distributed to target computers as a "package." If you have SMS installed, it would be possible to perform a query to find which computers have a certain video card installed and send them a specific installation "package" with the drivers for that video card selected. SMS also performs other functions (inventory, remote control, and so on) that may help you in supporting your network.

SMS is a sophisticated system, so you should refer to the documentation that comes with it for more information on deploying operating systems.

Other Delivery Methods

It's possible to get creative with your Windows NT delivery method. Here are some ideas:

- **E-mail link**

  If you can attach a file to your corporate e-mail system, it may be possible for your users to start an installation by clicking an install batch file icon in their e-mail.

- **Web page installation**

  If you have an intranet Web server, it is possible to launch the installation from a Web page link. If you want to start the installation from a batch file (most of you will) you will need to configure your browser to launch batch files. There are considerable security risks surrounding this, so be sure you know what you are doing. To configure Netscape Navigator 3.0 to launch batch files, you need to select Options, General settings and then the Helpers tab. Since there is no MIME type for .BAT files, you need to click the "create new type button. Enter "Application" and "DOS Batch File" in the MIME type and subtype fields, respectively. In the extensions text box, enter "bat", and enter "C:\COMMAND.COM /c" in the Launch the Application text field. Now when a user clicks a batch file, it runs.

Part
II

Ch
6

Installation Scenario

This section will give an example of how you might use the tools described previously to automate the installation of Windows NT.

Scenario Description

You are a Novell shop, but you are moving from Windows 3.1 to Windows NT on all of your desktops. You have a good technician and a single location with 200 computers. You are using IPX, TCP/IP, and SNMP but do not have DHCP services. The computers are all the same brand, but have different configurations.

For this deployment, you probably want a semi-automated installation of Windows NT. Whoever is installing the system will have the task of answering whatever questions aren't answered in the answer file during the setup process. The bulk of your work will be in the lab creating the installation answer file and the UDFs.

Since your PCs all need individual TCP/IP addresses assigned at installation, you will need to use a UDF file to specify the IP address and the user name. You would want to create a different boot diskette for each user with his/her name on it. The advantages of this are:

- All the diskettes can be identical, except for the IP address and computer name in the UDF file. The advantage to this will become clearer as we discuss the construction of the boot diskette.

- You can control the timing of the installation by having the technician or user only use the disks when you want the installation to occur.

- You know the state of the computer's environment when the installation process starts.

- You can use the autoexec.bat to perform preinstallation tasks such as defragmenting the hard disk or backing up the users' files.

Key Setup Files

The UDF file could be named a:\udf.udf and might look like this:

```
[UniqueIds]
allusers = UserData, Network

[UserData]
FullName = "User's Name"
ComputerName = "Unique Computer Name"
```

```
[TCPParams]
IPAddress = x.x.x.x
Gateway = x.x.x.x
```

The four keys in this UDF are the only items that may be different for each user. The gateway key is only important if you have a routed network. If your network is flat (not routed), the gateway parameter isn't required. You will have to either create the file on each diskette by hand or write a program to create this file as you create the boot diskette.

The unattended answer file will have a subset of the keys answered in it. Since the answer file will be the same for all the computers, you should leave it on the fileserver where the distribution files exist. We will now examine a sample answer file with commentary embedded under each key.

```
[Unattended]
OemPreinstall = no
```

Because we aren't employing the OEM directory in this installation, we set this key to no.

```
ConfirmHardware = no
```

Unless you are using devices that you know setup cannot autodetect, you don't need to confirm the hardware detected list.

```
Win31Upgrade = yes
```

Since you are upgrading the users from Windows 3.1, you will want to keep the settings they had in their previous environment.

```
TargetPath = WINNT
```

This specifies that you want Windows NT Workstation to be installed in the \WINNT directory. Not answering this simple question here will cause setup to ask during installation.

```
FileSystem = LeaveAlone
```

You could choose to convert the partition to NTFS, but if the machines used to run Windows 3.1, they probably don't need NTFS.

```
[UserData]
OrgName = "Your Company, INC."
```

Since the corporation name is the same for all of the systems here, we will put it in the answer file. If you didn't want to enter a unique username in each UDF, you could add the FullName key to this section with a username that is the same for every user.

```
[GuiUnattended]
TimeZone = "(GMT-06:00) Central Time (US & Canada)"
```

Part II

Ch 6

Since all of your systems are in the same timezone, you can safely enter the default time here.

```
[Display]
ConfigureAtLogon = 1
```

Since the users may have different requirements, you can let them select the resolution and color settings the first time they log on.

```
[OEM_Ads]
Banner = "Windows NT Workstation*Brought to you by the IS Department"
```

You can take this opportunity to display your IS department's prowess by advertising while files are copying—or you can put the boss's name here if you need a raise. Remember that you need the "Windows NT Workstation" text in there for any of the line to be displayed.

```
[Network]
Attend = no
```

Since you already know the network configuration, you will not need to have this section of setup attended.

```
DetectAdapters = " "
```

By setting this key to double quotations, setup will use the first detected network adapter.

```
InstallProtocols = ProtocolsSection
```

This key simply tells setup to look in the section named [ProtocolSection] later in the answer file for the protocols you want installed.

```
JoinWorkgroup = YOUR_DOMAIN
```

Since you don't have any NT servers to manage a domain, you should configure your computers to join a workgroup. If you had used the "JoinDomain" key, an NT server is required to validate user logons to that domain. If you want to make multiple workgroups instead of a single 200 computer workgroup, you can move this key into the UDF file and specify the workgroups there. For example, you may have 25 computers in the "Marketing" workgroup and 35 in the "Sales" workgroup. For more information on domains and workgroups, see Chapter 16, "A Brief Primer on Networks."

```
InstallServices=SelectedServiceList

[SelectedServiceList]
SNMP = SNMPParams
```

This section tells setup to look at the [SNMPParams] section for the options to use when installing SNMP.

```
NWWKSTA = CSNWParams
```

This section tells setup to look in the [CSNWParams] section for the options to use when installing the Client Service for NetWare.

```
[SNMPParams]
Send_Authentication = Yes
Any_Host = Yes
CommunityName = Public
ContactName = Contact_Person's_Name
Service = Physical, Applications, Datalink, Internet, EndToEnd
```

These keys correspond to the values available on the SNMP configurations screen. See Chapter 19, "Integrating Windows NT in UNIX Environments," for more details on the SNMP service.

```
[CSNWParams]
DefaultLocation = PreferredServer
```

This key tells setup to set the default fileserver to the value of PreferredServer. This is the server that the workstation will attach to by default. This key may also be moved into the UDF file if the users log in to different Novell servers.

```
DefaultScriptOptions = 3
```

By setting this option to 3, you instruct setup to allow the Client Service for NetWare to process both NetWare 3.x and 4.x login scripts. Setting this option to 1 allows only NetWare 3.x to be run, and 0 disables the NetWare login script processor.

```
[ProtocolsSection]
TC = TCParams
```

This key points setup to the [TCParams] section for the options to use for the TCP/IP protocol.

```
NWLNKIPX = NWLINKParams
```

This key tells setup to look at the [NWLINKParams] section for the options to use when installing the NWLNKIPX (Microsoft version of IPX) protocol.

```
[TCParams]
DHCP = no
```

This lets setup know that DHCP will not be used to obtain an IP address—one will be specified later.

```
Subnet = x.x.x.x
DNSServer = x.x.x.x y.y.y.y z.z.z.z
WINSPrimary = x.x.x.x
WINSSecondary = y.y.y.y
DNSName = your.domain.com
```

These sections set additional parameters for TCP/IP.

```
[NWLINKParams]
```

There are no options needed for the NWLink IPX/SPX-compatible protocol. This section does need to exist for setup to run unattended.

Of course, your answer files will vary, and you will need to test the installation against various computers and software setups to make sure it works correctly.

When you start setup, it will create a file called winnt.sif in the win_nt.~bt (for floppyless installations) that contains the merged settings included in the answer file and the UDF. This is the file that is actually used by the setup program, the originals are only read once at the beginning of the text-mode setup process. Here is what the winnt.sif file will look like if you used the settings listed in this section:

```
[Unattended]
OemPreinstall = no
ConfirmHardware = no
Win31Upgrade = yes
TargetPath = WINNT
FileSystem = LeaveAlone

[UserData]
OrgName = "Your Company, INC."
FullName = "User's Name"
ComputerName = "Unique Computer Name"

[GuiUnattended]
TimeZone = "(GMT-06:00) Central Time (US & Canada)"

[Display]
ConfigureAtLogon = 1

[OEM_Ads]
Banner = "Windows NT Workstation*Brought to you by the IS Department"

[Network]
Attend = no
DetectAdapters = ""
InstallProtocols = ProtocolsSection
JoinWorkgroup = YOUR_DOMAIN
InstallServices=SelectedServiceList

[SelectedServiceList]
SNMP = SNMPParams
NWWKSTA = CSNWParams

[SNMPParams]
Send_Authentication = Yes
Any_Host = Yes
CommunityName = Public
ContactName = Contact_Person's_Name
Service = Physical, Applications, Datalink, Internet, EndToEnd
```

```
[CSNWParams]
DefaultLocation = PreferredServer
DefaultScriptOptions = 3

[ProtocolsSection]
TC = TCParams
NWLNKIPX = NWLINKParams

[TCParams]
DHCP = no
IPAddress = x.x.x.x
Gateway = x.x.x.x
Subnet = x.x.x.x
DNSServer = x.x.x.x y.y.y.y z.z.z.z
WINSPrimary = x.x.x.x
WINSSecondary = y.y.y.y
DNSName = your.domain.com


[NWLINKParams]
```

We will be using a diskette-based installation here, so we need to determine how the boot disk might be arranged. Here are some steps you need to take to create the boot floppies.

1. The diskettes must be made bootable either with the DOS "format /s a:" command or the "sys a:" command.

2. Copy the files required to access the Novell server to the floppy. These will usually include: lsl.com, a card driver (like 3c5x9.com), net.cfg, ipxodi, the VLM support files, or netx.exe.

3. Copy the UDF file udf.udf to the floppy. Remember that this is the only file that is different for every diskette you create.

4. Copy other files you might want to the floppy. These might include himem.sys, smartdrv.exe, scandisk.exe, and defrag.exe.

 T I P It is very much worth the effort to run a write-behind disk cache (like smartdrv.exe) on the floppy diskette. This will dramatically reduce the amount of time it takes to copy the files from the Novell server.

Part
II

Ch
6

5. Create the config.sys and autoexec.bat files that will start the setup process.

6. Test the boot diskette on different computers.

Below are the potential listings for config.sys and autoexec.bat:

Listing: config.sys

```
device=himem.sys
```

Listing: autoexec.bat

```
smartdrv c+ a- b- 10000
lsl
3c5x9
ipxodi
vlm /ps=Novelldist
login inst_acct
map root i:=NovellDist\NT40Dist
i:\winnt /b /s:i:\ /u:i:\unattend.txt /udf:allusers,a:udf.udf
```

N O T E If you just specify a UniqueID for the UDF file and not a UDF filename, setup will prompt the user for a diskette with the file $unique$.udf on it. ■

Logistics

For a network installation, you need what is called a "distribution sharepoint." For this scenario, you would use a Novell server directory where you copy the Windows NT 4.0 Workstation contents to. All the files you need are located in the \<MachineType> directory and its subdirectories on the CD-ROM—most readers are probably using the \i386 directory. For our installation, we would also copy the unattended (unattend.txt) setup file to that same directory.

From Here...

In this chapter, you've learned how the Windows NT setup process works and how to use the tools provided by Microsoft to automate the installation. Take a look at these chapters for more information:

- Chapter 5, "Preparing for Installation," explains some of the issues you should be aware of before installing Windows NT Workstation on any computer.

- Chapter 17, "Integrating Windows NT in Novell Environments," explains in more detail how NT Workstation can be set up to work with Novell servers.

- Chapter 18, "Integrating Windows NT in Microsoft Environments," covers some of the connections to Microsoft servers you may need to set up NT Workstation.

Optimizing System and Application Performance

Performance Optimization Overview

by Jim Boyce

Because you are running Windows NT, which offers better performance than many alternatives (such as Windows 95), it's a safe bet you're concerned with the best possible performance from your workstation. Tracking and managing system performance is not a simple matter, however. Fortunately, Windows NT provides a good set of tools that enable you to monitor your system's performance and fine-tune the system.

In some cases, improving performance might be as simple as increasing the amount of memory in your system. In most cases, however, improving performance means performing a detailed examination of your system's key components to locate the source of the performance bottleneck. And, in many cases, you'll find that your system suffers from more than one bottleneck.

The Performance Monitor is your first line of defense against poor performance. As you'll learn in the other chapters in this part, you can use Performance Monitor to examine the performance of your system's CPU, disk, cache, and other system components. With the knowledge you gain from Performance Monitor, you can begin to fine-tune the system to eliminate the bottlenecks. ▪

Why Bother?

Is it really worth testing your system components to ensure that you're getting the best possible performance? In some cases, no. If you're using Windows NT "out of the box" to run productivity applications for word processing, spreadsheets, and other typical office applications, you're probably getting better-than-adequate performance. Going to the trouble of monitoring each component and attempting to fine-tune it probably will not yield an increase in performance significant enough for you to notice.

If you're running more demanding applications, such as for graphics and Computer Aided Design (CAD), testing and optimizing the system's performance could well mean a noticeable improvement. This is because these applications place a heavier burden on the disk, cache, video, and other system resources than typical office applications. A 10 percent improvement in video response would likely mean very little for a word processor, but would be significant when regenerating a large CAD drawing on the display.

Performance monitoring is also important in a networked environment. Whether you are using Windows NT Workstation or Server to make resources available to others on the network, improving disk, cache, and CPU performance can have a major impact on those users' ability to access shared resources effectively. And, eliminating bottlenecks on your workstation will lessen the impact of your use on the system by others accessing its resources.

Hardware Selection and Capacity Planning

Performance monitoring is important for ensuring optimum application performance, but it also serves other important purposes. Through monitoring and evaluating your existing hardware's performance, you can better prepare for future hardware acquisitions.

If you determine that your workstations are performing at or near maximum capacity, for example, you know you should buy more powerful workstations in the future. If you find that your servers are performing at or near maximum capacity, you can begin planning how to relieve some of the burden on those servers. You might, for example, upgrade the existing servers with more powerful models. Or, you can consider installing additional servers and off-loading some of the burden to these.

Disk Performance

As applications have become larger and more complex, they have come to rely more and more on your computer's hard disk for storage and in some cases, caching. Improving disk performance not only improves system performance overall, but can in many cases directly impact specific applications. This is particularly true for database applications and data-intensive applications such as CAD. Because Windows NT uses the disk as virtual memory, improving disk I/O has an impact on every application you run, even those that do not rely heavily on the disk.

Overall disk I/O performance really boils down to three issues: physical disk performance, cache performance, and file system. Through Performance Monitor and other tools, you can monitor the first two; through an understanding of the pros and cons of NTFS and FAT, you can evaluate the latter. Chapter 9, "Optimizing Physical and Virtual Memory," provides not only an understanding of how Windows NT uses physical and virtual memory, but also how to improve the performance of both.

When you're ready to optimize the disk subsystem itself, you can turn to Chapter 10, "Optimizing the File System." Chapter 10 explores the differences between FAT and NTFS to help you decide which file system is best for you. You'll also learn how to detect and clear cache bottlenecks, work with striped sets, and other important disk-related issues.

If you do decide to use NTFS, you'll find Chapter 11, "Exploring NTFS," indispensable. Chapter 11 not only explains the structure of NTFS, but it will help migrate from FAT to NTFS and make use of its disk compression capabilities.

Going Beyond the CPU and Disk

Naturally, many other factors besides the system's CPU and disk(s) affect performance. Video and I/O are just two of these other issues. But optimizing overall performance means more than just making sure each of the computer's subsystems is functioning as well as possible. The computer usually doesn't stand alone—other peripheral components also play a part in keeping the system running smoothly. These include an Uninterruptible Power Supply (UPS) and backup devices. The UPS keeps the system running, and backups help you prevent lost data and recover from catastrophes when they occur.

In Chapter 14, "Ensuring Data Security," you'll find topics that will help you make the most of these ancillary devices and services. Chapter 14 also explores the use of fault-tolerant volumes. ●

Part

III

Ch

7

Monitoring Performance

by Richard Neff

Monitoring the performance of a Windows NT machine is the first step in diagnosing and troubleshooting performance problems. Any computer is susceptible to performance reductions, and knowing how to find and rectify performance problems is important to keeping Windows NT running smoothly. Windows NT itself is a large program that places a heavy demand on a system, so performance maintenance is important.

Windows NT provides a tool for monitoring many different areas of the system: the Performance Monitor. Performance Monitor is a powerful and versatile tool for isolating performance trouble spots and should be considered the primary tool for this purpose. Performance Monitor is not without its faults, however, and there are other tools to help a user fill those gaps. ■

Degradation in system performance

Many factors affect system performance under Windows NT. Knowing how the different operating system components interact with one another helps in determining where performance problems are occurring.

Adding and viewing counters in Performance Monitor

Adding performance items to Performance Monitor allows you to view how the different Windows NT components are being used.

Setting Performance Monitor to use a settings or workspace file with commonly used counters

Using settings or workspace files helps the administrator use the correct counters without always adding them manually.

Changing the different views in Performance Monitor

Performance Monitor provides many different types of views, each useful for analyzing performance data in various ways.

Other tools to monitor Windows NT performance

Some tools are available to make up for Performance Monitor's shortcomings.

Why Bottlenecks Occur

Even the fastest and best-designed computers have performance limits, regardless of what type of operating system is used. These performance reductions are called *bottlenecks*, and any component of the system can be a bottleneck if that resource is being used by more items than it can handle. Performance slowdowns can occur for many reasons. Some of the more common reasons are:

- Older or inadequate hardware that isn't designed for Windows NT
- Large software applications that use many different types of resources
- Multiple applications trying to access a single resource
- Lack of sufficient memory for Windows NT and all the applications trying to run
- Multiple network users trying to access disk or printer resources of a Windows NT computer

Monitoring performance is an ongoing and long-term process. Monitoring the system over the long term helps to spotlight performance problems before they become critical. As computer technology progresses, the adequate level of performance constantly gets higher. What seems extremely fast now will be considered slow in the future. For example, 10 years ago, when 1200 bps modems were common, a 14.4 Kbps would have seemed extremely fast. Now, a 14.4 Kbps modem is considered the minimum requirement for modem connections.

Furthermore, as more applications and services are loaded on the system, the overall performance of a Windows NT machine may be reduced. If the Windows NT machine is used as a server, either as a dedicated file and print server, application server, or even a workstation with a lot of heavily used shares, the number of users connecting to the system has a major impact on the system's performance. Therefore, ongoing monitoring of the system is the first step in ensuring that a Windows NT computer runs at an acceptable speed.

Windows NT provides some tools to help monitor the performance of the Windows NT system. These tools allow a user to help pinpoint areas that are slowing down the system. The Windows NT Performance Monitor is a very powerful tool that can be used to monitor the system. The Windows NT Task Manager now has a Performance property sheet available, a new feature of Windows NT 4.0.

Overview of Performance Monitor

The most commonly used tool to monitor Windows NT and applications is the Performance Monitor. Performance Monitor enables you to track a variety of items and display information in different ways. Performance Monitor comes with the Windows NT operating system and should be the first tool used to detect and isolate performance problems. In many instances, it is the only tool needed to monitor bottlenecks.

Performance Monitor isn't restricted to viewing the local machine. It can monitor items on any other machine connected to the network, making it easier for a network administrator to monitor other Windows NT computers. Results from Performance Monitor also can be saved into log files for future reference.

Figure 8.1 shows an example of the Performance Monitor program.

FIG. 8.1

Performance Monitor enables different items to be watched and provides different ways of displaying the data obtained. In this example, the data is displayed in a chart format.

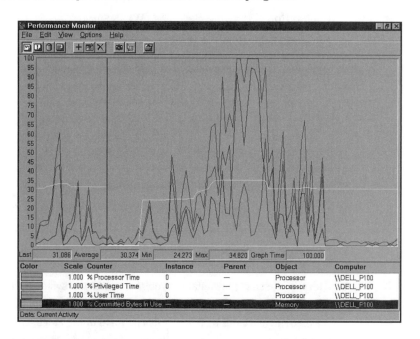

The following types of objects can be monitored using Performance Monitor (items in bold are default system objects):

AppleTalk	Gateway Service for Netware
Browser	ICMP
Cache	Image
FTP Server	IP

Logical Disk	**Process**
MacFile Server	Process Address Space
Memory	**Processor**
NBT Connection	RAS Port
NetBEUI	RAS Total
NetBEUI Resource	**Redirector**
Network Interface	**Server**
Network Segment	**System**
NWLink IPX	TCP
NWLink NetBIOS	**Thread**
Objects	UDP
Paging File	WINS Server
PhysicalDisk	

Other objects may become available as new software is installed on the Windows NT machine. For example, Microsoft SQL Server adds many other objects relating to SQL database monitoring. You will be able to monitor only the objects of items that have been installed in the Windows NT system. For example, if you do not use the Windows NT Remote Access Service (RAS), you won't see the RAS Port and RAS Total objects listed in Performance Monitor.

The following views are available in Performance Monitor:

- **Chart.** The chart view is the default view in Performance Monitor. Chart view enables objects to be graphically displayed. This view enables the user to view the monitored items over a short period of time. This view is best for actively watching the performance of a Windows NT system.

- **Alert.** The alert view enables you to monitor the system in the background while working with other applications. You can define a threshold for a counter and, if it is reached, an alert will be triggered. The form of the alert can be specified to switch to the alert view, log the event, or send an alert message directly to a user.

- **Log.** The log view enables Performance Monitor to record the selected counters into a file, known as a log file, while the user runs applications on the Windows NT system. The log file can later be examined to find potential or existing bottlenecks.

- **Report.** The report view provides a list of counters and their current values. This view is useful to see the values of multiple objects in numerical format, rather than graphed. This view is designed for active monitoring and provides a "snapshot" view of the Windows NT system.

Working with Performance Monitor

Knowing how to use Performance Monitor helps to track and analyze performance data. Performance Monitor has a variety of settings that can be used to help a user understand how the Windows NT system is operating. Performance Monitor's windows can also be arranged to better suit the needs of the user.

Starting Performance Monitor and Organizing the Layout

Performance Monitor does not require any special user privileges to be used. Any valid user of the Windows NT computer has access to Performance Monitor. The Performance Monitor program is found in the Administrative Tools folder from the Start, Programs menu. To start Performance Monitor, select it from the Administrative Tools folder or run the PERFMON.EXE file.

Use the DISKPERF command if disk monitoring is needed in Performance Monitor. Without the DISKPERF command, the Physical and Logical Disk counters do not display any values. To use the DISKPERF command, you have to log in with administrative rights. To activate these counters using the DISKPERF command, do the following:

1. Log in to the Windows NT computer as a member of the Administrators group.

2. Select Start, Programs, Command Prompt to get to the command prompt.

3. At the command prompt, type **DISKPERF** to see whether the disk performance counters have been turned on. If they are not turned on, type **DISKPERF -Y** to turn the counters on. Also, using the E switch with -Y allows performance monitoring of striped disk sets. If you do not use striped disk sets, you do not need to use the E parameter.

4. Shut down and restart the Windows NT computer. The disk counters are now available to be tracked in Performance Monitor.

NOTE Turning the disk counters on with the DISKPERF command does use system resources. However, the minimal amount that they use usually won't affect system performance. The process of manually turning on the disk counters was used to prevent 386 machines from running slowly by having to carry the extra resource burdens when Windows NT could run on that platform. In some instances, you may want to turn off the disk counters, especially if you don't intend to monitor disk performance of a particular machine. Do this by typing **DISKPERF -N** at the Windows NT command prompt. ■

For more information about the DISKPERF command-line switches, type **DISKPERF /?** at the command prompt.

You can change certain display options to better organize the Performance Monitor screen. You can perform actions such as hiding the menu and title bar, hiding the toolbar, and hiding the status bar. Hiding these items enables you to have a larger viewing area for your monitored data.

To hide or show the menu and title bar, toolbar, or status bar of Performance Monitor:

1. If it is not already started, start Performance Monitor.

2. Choose Options from the Performance Monitor menu. In the menu, items that are shown in the Performance Monitor window have a checkmark beside the menu item.

3. To hide an item that has a checkmark beside it, select that item. You can select the following menu items: Menu and Title, Toolbar, and Status Bar. You can also hide the menu and title bar by pressing Ctrl+M. You can hide the toolbar by pressing Ctrl+T and the status bar by pressing Ctrl+S.

4. To show the items after they are hidden, perform steps 2 and 3 so the item has the checkmark beside it. If the title bar and menu are hidden, you can show those items by double-clicking in a non-text area of the window. If the title bar and menu are shown, you can hide them by double-clicking in a non-text area in the Performance Monitor window.

Changing Views

Performance Monitor has four different views: Chart, Alert, Log, and Report. Each of these views is represented by icons on the toolbar. Figure 8.2 shows the four view icons on the Performance Monitor toolbar.

FIG. 8.2
The four icons on the Performance Monitor toolbar allow you to switch views.

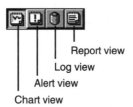

Report view
Log view
Alert view
Chart view

You also can change views by using the View menu in Performance Monitor, or by using the following keystrokes:

View	Keystrokes
Chart	Ctrl+C
Alert	Ctrl+A
Log	Ctrl+L
Report	Ctrl+R

When views are changed, menu items are automatically changed to handle the options available in each view. Some of these menu items are specific to a particular view. Other menu items will change part of the item to reflect the view. For example, the Save command from the File menu changes to Save Log Settings in log view. Also, help in Performance Monitor is context-sensitive and brings up help pertaining to the current view if the F1 key is pressed. This is consistent with other Windows NT applications that also have dynamically adjusted menus and context-sensitive help.

Using Workspace and Settings Files

Often when monitoring Windows NT systems, the same counters are often used from session to session. For example, a user may want to monitor the Total % Processor Time for one session, then six months later, monitor that same counter again. With only one or two counters, adding those counters at the beginning of each session isn't a major concern. But, if a lot of counters are being tracked, adding them each time Performance Monitor is used is inconvenient.

Performance Monitor has *settings files* that enable you to save the counters for the current view. A similar type of file called a *workspace file* saves all the counters for all of the views. Using a workspace file prevents the user from always adding counters to track for each Performance Monitor session. Instead, the settings or workspace file is opened by using the File, Open command in Performance Monitor.

To create a settings file, do the following:

1. If Performance Monitor is not already running, start the program by selecting the Start button, then Programs. Select the Administrative Tools item, and finally Performance Monitor.

2. Choose the view window for which you want to save the settings. Add any counters to the view that you want to monitor.

3. From the File menu, choose Save Settings to save a settings file or Save Workspace to save a workspace file. The Save As dialog box will appear.

4. In the File Name box of the Save As dialog box, type the file name you want for the settings or workspace file.

5. Choose the <u>S</u>ave button. The file name appears in the title bar of the Performance Monitor window.

Each settings or workspace file is saved with an extension that depends on the type of view that was saved. For example, chart view settings files are saved with the extension of .PMC. These extensions help identify the type of settings or workspace file.

Table 8.1 shows the file extensions used for view types.

Table 8.1   File Extensions and View Types

Extension	View Counters Saved
PMC	Chart view counters
PMR	Report view counters
PMA	Alert view counters
PML	Log view counters
PMW	All views counters (workspace)

After a settings or workspace file is saved, it can be loaded into Performance Monitor by using the <u>F</u>ile, <u>O</u>pen command from the menu. Additionally, the file can be copied to disk or across the network for use on other Windows NT machines that use Performance Monitor. This makes it easier to obtain the same performance data on different Windows NT systems.

Settings and workspace files can be even more convenient by specifying them on the command line of a shortcut or a menu item. This makes it easier to start Performance Monitor with the proper settings file already loaded. To load a settings file when Performance Monitor is started, type

c:\<*Windows NT directory*>\system32\perfmon.exe c:<*settings file path*>

where <*Windows NT directory*> is the location of the Windows NT 4.0 directory and <*settings file path*> is the directory location of the settings file. For example, to load PROCESS.PMA located in the WINNT4 directory, you would type **c:\winnt4\system32\perfmon.exe c:\winnt4\process.pma** in the command line box of the Run dialog box, the shortcut properties dialog box, or the menu item properties dialog box.

Adding and Monitoring Counters

Performance Monitor can monitor many items on the Windows NT system. To logically arrange these different items, Performance Monitor categorizes them into objects. These object types relate to actual devices, sections of memory, or processes. Objects contain items known as *counters*. These counters are the specific items to be measured using Performance Monitor. For example, under the Processor object, a counter called % Processor Time is used to monitor the percentage amount of total processor time that is being used by the system.

Object types also can have several *instances*. Instances do not always appear for object types, but object types such as the Processor object have an instance for each processor on the system. Instances represent any individual object out of multiple objects of the same type. Other object types, for example, the Memory object type, do not have any instances.

To begin monitoring a Windows NT system, you need to add counters to monitor. Counters are added the same way no matter which of the four views are being used. To add counters in Performance Monitor, do the following:

1. If you are not already using Performance Monitor, start the program by selecting the Start button, then Programs. Select the Administrative Tools item, and finally Performance Monitor.

2. Select the view you want to display by clicking one of the four view buttons on the toolbar.

3. From the Performance Monitor menu, select Edit. Depending on the view, you will see Add to <view type>, where <view type> is the type of view you are currently using. For example, in chart view, the menu would read Add to Chart. Select the Add to item on the menu. A window similar to figure 8.3 is displayed.

FIG. 8.3

The Add to Chart window. From this window, counters can be added to the chart for monitoring. A window similar to this one appears when adding counters to other types of Performance Monitor views.

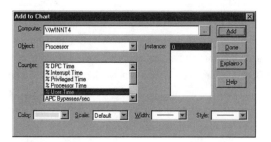

4. The Computer box displays the computer that Performance Monitor is tracking. The Object item in the dialog box is a drop-down list displaying all the object types currently available on the system. Select the object type for which you want to see counters.

5. In the Counter list, select a counter you want to track. If you are unsure of what a counter does and you would like more information, select the counter and click the Explain button. The Explain button expands the dialog box and gives a definition to explain the purpose of the counter.

6. If multiple objects exist in the Instance list, select the instance of the object you want to monitor.

7. Set any other objects specific to the view currently being used. For example, the Add to Chart dialog box enables you to select the color, scale, width, and style of the graph lines.

8. Click Add to add that counter in the display. The Add to Chart dialog box stays open to allow you to add more counters. Repeat steps 4 through 8 until you are finished adding counters.

9. Click Done after you have added all of the counters you want to monitor. This will close the Add to window.

Selecting a Different Computer to Monitor

Performance Monitor is not limited to only collecting performance information on the local Windows NT computer. Any other Windows NT computers connected to the same network can be monitored using Performance Monitor. Multiple computers, each with their own set of counters, can be monitored in the same view. This makes Performance Monitor a useful tool for network administrators who need to obtain performance data from multiple computers on the network.

N O T E While obtaining data from other computers is a useful feature, monitoring too many machines can place a heavy load on the network. Having too many network computers trying to send performance information has an impact on the Windows NT computer running Performance Monitor. Don't try to monitor too many network computers or counters at once. Also consider modifying the update intervals for the different views being used or use manual updates for counter information. This helps reduce the amount of data being transmitted across the network and to the machine running Performance Monitor. ■

To select another computer to monitor, do the following:

1. If you are not already using Performance Monitor, start the program by selecting the Start button, then Programs. Select the Administrative Tools item, and finally Performance Monitor.

2. Select the view you want to use in Performance Monitor.

3. Choose the Edit menu, and select the Add To command. This displays the Add To dialog box.

4. If you know the name and UNC path of the computer to monitor, type the UNC path and computer name in the Computer text box. If you want to browse the network, click the button with the three ellipses.

5. Select the counters you want to monitor for that machine. Also, select the options for those counters. Click Add to add those counters to the current view.

6. You can select additional computers on the network and choose counters for those machines. Repeat steps 4 and 5 to add counters for additional computers.

7. When you are finished selecting counters, click Done to close the Add To dialog box.

Clearing the Display and Deleting Selections

You can stop monitoring an individual counter in Performance Monitor by deleting that counter. If you find that you want to completely remove all the counters in the current view, you can clear the display. Clearing the display removes all the collected data for the counters in the current view, however, counters in other views are not cleared.

To clear the display of the current view, do the following:

1. If you are not already using Performance Monitor, start the program by selecting the Start button, then Programs. Select the Administrative Tools item, and finally Performance Monitor.

2. Select the view you want to clear.

3. Choose Edit, Clear Display. All the data collected for the counters in that view are removed from the view's window. However, the counters are deleted from the view.

To remove an individual counter from the current view, do the following:

1. If you are not already using Performance Monitor, start the program by selecting the Start button, then Programs. Select the Administrative Tools item, and finally Performance Monitor.

2. Select the view from which you want to remove counters.

3. Select the item to be deleted from the view by highlighting the counter or object.

4. Choose Edit, Delete. You also can select the Delete icon from the toolbar or press Del. The item is then removed from the view.

Exporting Data

Data obtained in Performance Monitor can be exported for use with other programs. For example, you may want to take the data obtained from many computers on the network and graph all the data in a program like Microsoft Excel. Also, you might want to put the exported data into a database for future reference. You can export data in any view by using the Export command. To export data, do the following:

1. If you are not already using Performance Monitor, start the program by selecting the Start button, then Programs. Select the Administrative Tools item, and finally Performance Monitor.

2. Select the view you want and add the counters for which you want to collect data.

3. Choose File, Export. The Export As dialog box displays.

4. In the Export As dialog box, use the Save As Type drop-down list box to select the type of file you want to create. You can have either a tab-delimited file, with a .TSV extension, or a comma-delimited file, with a .CSV extension. A tab-delimited file separates the data columns with tab characters. A comma-delimited file separates data with commas.

5. In the File name box, type the filename you want to use to save the exported data.

6. Click OK.

7. After the file is saved, you can open it using a database, spreadsheet, or any other programs that can import comma- or tab-delimited files.

Working with Charts

Chart view is the default view in Performance Monitor and is the most commonly used view. Chart view is useful if you are trying to monitor system performance because it displays the current counters at the exact moment and previous times throughout the system processing. Because the information is graphically displayed, it is easier to understand and compare one counter with other counters.

Because charts often monitor many different counters, you may want to select different colors or styles to help particular counters stand out. Changing the counter colors or styles is done through the Edit Chart Line dialog box. To change the color or style of a counter in chart view, do the following:

1. If you are not already using Performance Monitor, start the program by selecting the Start button, then Programs. Select the Administrative Tools item, and finally Performance Monitor.

2. Select the view you want displayed by clicking one of the four view buttons on the toolbar.

3. Choose Edit, Edit Chart Line. The Edit Chart Line dialog box appears.

4. The Color, Scale, Width, and Style boxes are drop-down list boxes. Click the down arrow to display the options available for that item. If you select an item in the Width box that is different than the default, the Style box will become unavailable. You cannot change styles of a line that is not the default width.

5. When you are finished selecting the color or style of the counter's line, click OK to close the Edit Chart Line dialog box.

You also can change options that affect the entire chart from the Options menu. Some chart items that can be changed are:

- Displaying horizontal grid lines
- Displaying vertical grid lines
- Displaying vertical labels
- Defining the number range for the vertical axis
- Displaying the legend-information area
- Displaying the value bar
- Determining the update time or setting the update time to manual
- Changing the Graph format between a line graph and a bar graph

To change options for the entire chart, do the following:

1. If you are not already using Performance Monitor, start the program by selecting the Start button, then Programs. Select the Administrative Tools item, and finally Performance Monitor.

2. Select the chart view by selecting View, Chart or by clicking the Chart View icon on the toolbar.

3. Choose Options, Chart. You also can click the Options icon, the last icon from the left, on the toolbar. The Chart Options dialog box appears (see fig. 8.4).

4. Click the appropriate item's checkbox to turn on the option. Click it again to clear the checkbox. Some options may also require the user to select the numerical value for an object.

5. When you are finished defining options for the chart, click OK to use the selected chart options.

FIG. 8.4

The Chart Options dialog box enables you to change various display options for the Performance Monitor chart.

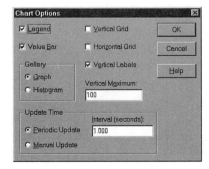

Working with Logs

Logs are extremely useful for monitoring a Windows NT computer while a user is working normally with the computer. Later, the log can be viewed and analyzed to determine if any performance bottlenecks were created. Log files can be loaded into Performance Monitor and analyzed in a different view. Because log view does not actively display data in the Performance Monitor window, log view is used only for background monitoring.

You can add objects only to a log, not individual counters. This differs from the Add command in other views. When the log is opened in another view, all of the counters are available for the objects that were recorded in the log.

Figure 8.5 shows an example of Performance Monitor using the log view.

FIG. 8.5

Log view of Performance Monitor shows important information about the logging process. Items such as the log filename, file size, and objects being recorded are displayed.

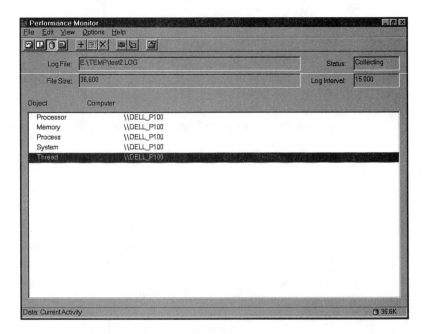

To start or stop logging in Performance Monitor, do the following:

1. If you are not already using Performance Monitor, start the program by selecting the Start button, then Programs. Select the Administrative Tools item, and finally Performance Monitor.

2. Select the log view and add the object you want to monitor.

3. Before you can start the logging process, you need to select objects to monitor. Add the object you want to log by selecting Edit, Add to Log from the menu or the Add Counter button on the toolbar.

4. Name the log file by selecting Options, then Log. In the File name box, type the filename for the log. If a log file has been created, you can add the new data to the end of that file or create a totally new log file. If needed, select update time settings for the logging process. You can choose between a manual or periodic update with a specified interval. When you are finished defining the filename and update time, click OK.

5. To start the logging process, click the Start Log button. After the logging process starts, this button changes to Stop Log. To stop the logging process, click the Stop Log button. This stops the data from being logged and changes the button back to the Start Log button.

The Log Options dialog box also enables you to select the type of update interval used by log view. You can select a periodic update with a specified time interval in seconds or choose to have the data updated manually. If the Manual Update setting is selected, you can update the collected data by clicking the Updated Counter Data icon or by selecting Options, then Update Now from the menu.

After the logging process is started, you can add bookmarks to the log file. Because logging is essentially a background process, adding bookmarks helps anyone viewing the log to better understand what was occurring at that moment. Because it is sometimes hard to tell exactly what the user of the computer was doing at an exact time in the log, a bookmark contains items that better explain what was happening. For example, if a user was running Microsoft Word on the computer, a bookmark would be added when Word is started.

Bookmarks also are automatically added if a remote computer shuts down or disconnects from the network while it is being monitored by Performance Monitor. If the computer reconnects, the Performance Monitor will start collecting data for it and add a bookmark specifying that the computer is once again being monitored.

To add a bookmark to a log file, do the following:

1. If you are not already using Performance Monitor, start the program by selecting the Start button, then Programs. Select the Administrative Tools item, and finally Performance Monitor.

2. Select the log view and add the objects you want to monitor.

3. If not already started, start the logging process following the procedure listed previously.

4. Choose Options, Bookmark. You also can use the Bookmark icon on the Performance Monitor toolbar. The Bookmark icon is the ninth icon from the left on the toolbar.

5. A bookmark dialog box is displayed. Type a comment in the Bookmark Comment box to give a description to this bookmark.

6. Click Add. This records the bookmark into the log file.

After you log data into a file, you have to load it into Performance Monitor to analyze the logged data. The logged data is best viewed in chart view, but the data can be analyzed in any view. After the log data is brought into Performance Monitor, the data is displayed until the stop time of the log. Therefore, if you are in a view that displays data for only a certain time, such as report view, you need to define the system start and stop times. You can select the start and stop times to better select the necessary information. When you are finished with the log data, you can either load other log files or switch back to current system activity.

To load a log into Performance Monitor for analyzing, do the following:

1. If you are not already using Performance Monitor, start the program by selecting the Start button, then Programs. Select the Administrative Tools item, and finally Performance Monitor.

2. Select the view you want to use to analyze the log data. Because the log view does not actively show any data in the Performance Monitor window, you will probably want to select chart, report, or alert view.

3. Choose Options, then Data From. The Data From dialog box appears.

4. In the Data From dialog box, you can select between using data collected from the current system activity or using data contained in a log file. To use a log file, select the Log File option. Then, type the log filename in the box or click the icon at the end of the box to browse for the log filename. When you are finished, click OK.

5. If needed, change the start and stop times by choosing Edit, Time Window. You can change start and stop times by dragging the gray boxes, called scroll bars, on each side of the time bar. If you have bookmarks in the log, you can choose those to be start or stop times for the Performance Monitor display. Choose OK after selecting

the desired start and stop times. The Input Log File Timeframe dialog box is shown in Figure 8.6

Part

III

Ch

8

FIG. 8.6

The Input Log File Timeframe dialog box enables you to select start and stop times for viewing counters in a log. You can drag slider bars for the start or stop times, or use existing book-marks for start or stop times.

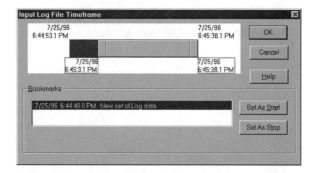

6. Add any counters you want to display from the log file. After you finish adding the counters, the information will be displayed in the view's window.

7. To switch back to monitoring the current system data, select Options, Data From. In the Data From dialog box, select the Current Activity option.

Working with Alert View

Alerts add a strong monitoring feature to Performance Monitor. The alert view is different from other views in Performance Monitor because it displays information only when a counter has actually exceeded a user-defined limit. Alert view highlights the areas that are experiencing bottlenecks and enables the user to pinpoint these trouble spots.

Figure 8.7 shows an example of Performance Monitor using the alert view.

To use alert view, you have to set alert conditions. Any counters available to any other views can be used by alert view. You can set alert events to occur either when a counter goes above a certain value, or when a counter goes below a certain value. After the alert conditions are defined, you can work on the system normally while Performance Monitor runs in the background monitoring the system.

To set alert conditions, do the following:

1. If you are not already using Performance Monitor, start the program by selecting the Start button, then Programs. Select the Administrative Tools item, and finally Performance Monitor.

2. Choose View, Alert or click the Alert View icon on the toolbar.

3. Choose Edit, Add to Alert or click the Add Counter icon on the toolbar. The Add to Alert dialog box appears (see fig. 8.8).

FIG. 8.7
The Alert view of Performance Monitor shows the interval in which data is being examined, any alerts that have been previously triggered on the system, and a legend showing the alert conditions.

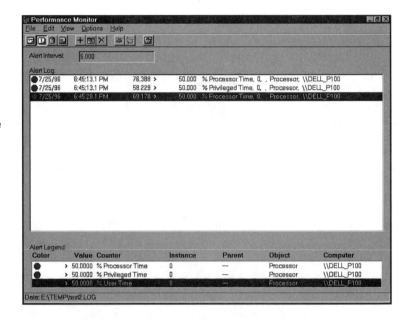

FIG. 8.8
The Add to Alert dialog box enables you to define the alert conditions in Performance Monitor. You can work on the system while Performance Monitor checks for any alert conditions.

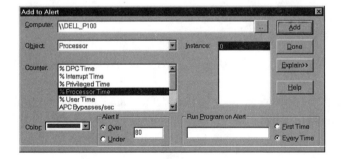

4. In the Add to Alert dialog box, select the Computer, Object, Counter, and Instance you want to monitor.

5. You can specify a color for the counter's alert icon by selecting an item from the Color drop-down list box.

6. In the Alert If box, select Over or Under to determine if you want to send an alert if a counter reaches a value either over or under the specified limit. Type the counter limit in the text box in the Alert If box.

7. If you want to run a program when an alert condition is reached, type the command line name of the program you want to execute in the Run Program on Alert box. Also, choose if you want to run the program only the first time the alert event occurs, or every time the alert event occurs.

8. Click Add to add that alert to Performance Monitor. If you want to add additional alert conditions, repeat steps 4 through 7.

9. Click Done to close the Add to Alert dialog box when you are finished adding alert conditions.

Alert view has many useful options. To open the Alert Options dialog box, choose Options, Alert from the menu. In the Alert Options dialog box, you can determine how Performance Monitor is to notify the user or administrator of an alert condition. The alert view has the following options:

- **Switch to Alert View.** Performance Monitor switches to alert view if a specified alert threshold has been reached.

- **Log Event in Application Log.** This enables the alert event to be logged in the Windows NT Application Log, which can be examined in the Event Viewer application.

- **Network Alert box.** If the Send Network Message box is checked, then the computer name or user account that is entered in the Net Name box will receive a message when an alert event occurs.

- **Update Time box.** The Update Time box enables a user to select a periodic update time or to select manual updates in Alert view.

Figure 8.9 shows the Alert Options dialog box.

FIG. 8.9

The Alert Options dialog box determines what action Performance Monitor takes when an alert condition is reached. Performance Monitor can switch to alert view, an event can be recorded in the Windows NT Application Log, or a computer or user account can receive an event message.

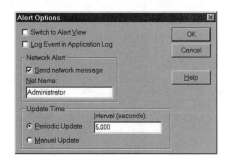

To change options for the alert view, do the following:

1. If you are not already using Performance Monitor, start the program by selecting the Start button, then Programs. Select the Administrative Tools item, and finally Performance Monitor.

2. Choose View, Alert or click the Alert View icon on the toolbar.

3. Select Options from the menu, then Alert. This displays the Alert Options dialog box.

4. Select the options you want to use for the alert view in Performance Monitor.

5. Click OK to close the Alert Options dialog box.

Working with Reports

Report view is useful when actively monitoring a system or multiple systems. Because it displays the actual numerical values, more space is available for a large number of counters. Report view also is useful for monitoring multiple instances of an object, because it enables a side-by-side layout. Report view updates counters in real time and is best for active monitoring.

Figure 8.10 shows an example of Performance Monitor in report view.

FIG. 8.10

Report view of Performance Monitor is extremely useful for seeing many different types of objects, counters, and instances. The report shows the numerical values for all of the counters at the current point in system processing.

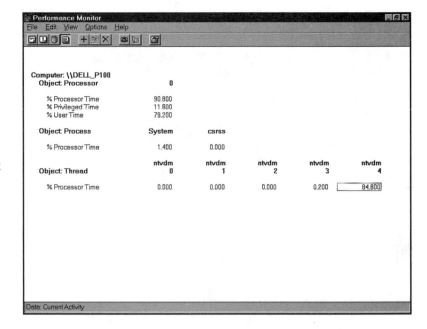

The only item that can be changed in the Options, Report command is the update time. You can select a periodic update with a specified interval or a manual update.

To change the interval options for the report, do the following:

1. If you are not already using Performance Monitor, start the program by selecting the Start button, then Programs. Select the Administrative Tools item, and finally Performance Monitor.
2. Choose View, Report or click the Report View icon on the toolbar.
3. Select Options from the menu, then Report. This displays the Report Options dialog box.
4. In the Update Time box, select either the Periodic Update option or the Manual Update option. If you select the Periodic Update option, type an update interval, in seconds, in the Interval box.
5. Click OK to close the Report Options dialog box.

Limitations of Performance Monitor

While Performance Monitor is useful as a system monitoring tool, it does have some shortcomings. For example, printing performance data directly from Performance Monitor is not possible. These limitations of Performance Monitor may not prevent it from being the primary tool for monitoring, but these limitations have created a market for products to help fill in those gaps.

Lack of Printing Functions in Performance Monitor

Probably the most noticeable limitation of Performance Monitor is its lack of direct printing functions. If you want to print the collected data, you have two options. You can use the very awkward method of hitting the Print Screen key and pasting the data into a graphics program, such as Paint. The second method is to export the recorded data and bring it into a spreadsheet or database and use that program's printing or report functions.

For more information about exporting Performance Monitor data, see the section titled "Exporting Data," earlier in this chapter.

Lack of Certain Objects and Counters

Performance Monitor also lacks some objects and counters that most users would expect to find. For example, there is no video object found in the program. Some users may want to monitor video performance and may find the lack of a video object disappointing. There is a counter that indirectly monitors video performance, using the CSRSS instance. For more information about monitoring video performance, see Chapter 13, "Enhancing Video and I/O Performance."

No Smaller Viewing Window

When actively monitoring a Windows NT system, it is often nice to be able to view the Performance Monitor window while also working with Windows NT. Unfortunately, the Performance Monitor window usually requires a large amount of screen space for all of the counters to be readable. Some other monitoring programs allow smaller sets of data to be visible on a smaller display area. The downside, however, is the inability to add many different counters to monitor.

These limitations certainly don't diminish Performance Monitor's ability to watch a Windows NT machine. Some users and administrators will never even notice the limitations of Performance Monitor. Performance Monitor is an excellent tool for monitoring a Windows NT machine and understanding how it works. However, others will want to supplement Performance Monitor with other monitoring tools.

Using Other Tools for Monitoring

Other tools exist to monitor system performance under Windows NT. Some of these tools are designed to completely replace Performance Monitor. Others are designed to provide performance information where using Performance Monitor would be unnecessary or impractical. New programs continue to be developed to monitor the performance of a Windows NT system. This section discusses the following two programs:

- The Windows NT Task Manager
- Norton NT Tools

This certainly isn't a comprehensive list of tools available to monitor Windows NT performance. These are listed to illustrate some of the more popular tools and utilities for Windows NT monitoring.

The Different Functions of the Task Manager

Under previous versions of Windows, the Task Manager had only one purpose: to display and switch to the applications currently running on the system. Under Windows NT 4.0, it takes on an expanded role. The new Windows NT 4.0 Task Manager has three tabs:

- **Applications.** This tab displays a property sheet listing all of the current user applications running on the system. This list also shows the status of an individual application under Windows NT. If the status is shown as Running, then the application is able to accept user input. If the status is displayed as Not Responding, either the application has crashed or it is busy and cannot accept user input. The bottom of the property sheet contains three buttons: End Task, Switch To, and New Task. The End Task button enables you to shut down an application on the list. The Switch To button enables you to bring that application as the topmost window on the screen. The New Task button displays a dialog box functionally identical to the Run dialog box from the Start, Run menu.

- **Processes.** The Process property sheet lists all of the processes currently running on the Windows NT system. This list is different than the application list from the Application property sheet because it lists all active programs, not just user applications. Many of these processes are started when Windows NT starts and are vital to the proper operation of Windows NT. This list also displays performance information about each process, such as the process ID (PID), the amount of CPU time currently being used, and the memory usage of the application. You also can end a process by clicking the End Process button at the bottom of the property sheet.

CAUTION

Before closing any processes on the Windows NT machine, be sure you know what they do. Many of the background processes are critical to the operation of Windows NT. Also, closing processes from the Task Manager should be considered a last resort. It is recommended that you use the Task Manager to view the processes running on the system.

- **Performance.** The Performance tab displays a property sheet similar to figure 8.11. This property sheet is a "mini" Performance Monitor. It shows the current total CPU and memory usage of the system, a graphical history of the CPU and memory usage totals, the total handles, threads, and processes, and other memory information of the Windows NT system. The Performance tab of Task Manager is ideal when you want to see an overall performance picture of the system without opening Performance Monitor and adding counters. However, the Task Manager lacks any customization and many other features found in Performance Monitor.

TIP Click any column heading in the Task Manager to sort the list. This is useful to determine which processes are using the most CPU time or the most memory. For example, clicking the MEM Usage column heading sorts the list and displays which process is using the most memory.

continues

continued

> Clicking the column heading again re-sorts the list to display the processes that are using the least memory at the top. This is useful only in the Process property sheet, but items in the Application list can also be sorted in this manner.

FIG. 8.11
The Performance property sheet of Task Manager enables you to get an overall view of system performance. This property sheet is useful for monitoring the system if you suspect an application has crashed or is overburdening the system.

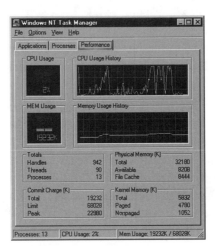

The Task Manager window displays the number of active processes, CPU usage, and memory usage of the Windows NT machine at the bottom of the window. This section of the window is displayed regardless of which property sheet is displayed. The primary purpose of Task Manager is to allow you to switch between tasks or end a crashed application. However, it is ideal to gain an overview of the Windows NT system and the different processes running on the system. While the Task Manager doesn't have as much versatility as Performance Monitor, it is especially useful if you think that an application is acting unusually or has completely stopped responding.

You can run the Task Manager by right-clicking the taskbar and selecting the Task Manager item from the shortcut menu. Other ways to display the Windows NT Task Manager include pressing Ctrl+Alt+Del and choosing the Task Manager at the bottom of the window, and running the TASKMAN.EXE program from the Run menu item or the Windows NT Explorer.

Norton NT Tools

With the popularity of Norton Utilities for MS-DOS and other Windows platforms, Symantec released Norton NT Tools to provide NT users with some Windows NT-specific utilities. The Norton NT Tools package provides items such as a virus scanner and an improved File Manager utility. One of the utilities provided with NT Tools is the Norton System Doctor. This tool enables you to monitor items on a Windows NT system.

The most significant improvement of the Norton System Doctor is the ability to view counters in a smaller area of the screen. The counters, called sensors by the program, are similar to the counters found in Performance Monitor. Each of the items can be displayed in a window that can easily be located anywhere on the screen. The display of the counters can be configured to be shown as histograms, bars, or gauges. Numerical values are also displayed under the counters. This type of display is ideal for users who want to actively monitor a system during normal use. Alarms also can be set to warn the user if a threshold has been reached.

Figure 8.12 shows an example of the Norton System Doctor on a Windows NT 4.0 screen.

FIG. 8.12

Norton System Doctor displays counters in a smaller window that is useful for active monitoring of the system. This type of display is better suited than Performance Monitor's for a user who wants to monitor a select number of counters while using the computer for everyday tasks.

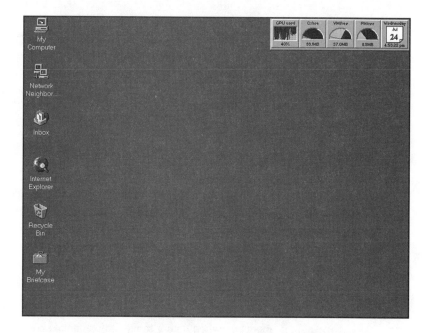

The window of the System Doctor can either have a title bar displayed, or it can be hidden from view. To add counters to the System Doctor display, choose Sensor, then Add from the menu. The following sensors can be added to the System Doctor window:

Cache Hits	Disk Space
Cache Memory Utilization	Network Reads Throughput
Cache Throughput	Network Writes Throughput
CPU Utilization	Page File Size

Page File Utilization	Virus Definition
Physical Memory	Virus Scan
Threads	Windows Up Time
Virtual Memory	

One more sensor, called Performance Data, enables all the counters used by the Performance Monitor program to be incorporated into the System Doctor display. This means that even if System Doctor doesn't have the sensor in the menu, it can be displayed if it is available to Performance Monitor. For example, if you use the NetBEUI protocol on your Windows NT computer, all of the counters listed under the NetBEUI object in Performance Monitor can be represented in System Doctor. This increases the capacity of the program dramatically.

Norton System Doctor is sometimes not as good as Performance Monitor for detailed performance troubleshooting because of its small display size. It is designed to supplement Performance Monitor by trying to provide information about certain items. It also enables non-performance related information to be displayed, such as the time/date and virus scan information. Some users will find the Norton System Doctor, as well as some of the other utilities in NT Tools, to be very useful.

Monitoring Hints

Monitoring system performance is a constantly changing task. Bottlenecks seem to occur in one area when actually they are occurring in an unrelated area. Bottlenecks also may cover bottlenecks in other areas. Even when the performance of one item is brought up to an acceptable level, it seems that another area starts slowing the system down. With this in mind, here are some hints to help you with the monitoring process:

- Always keep in mind that acceptable performance varies from one person to another. There is usually a common threshold of what is usable. Finding that threshold is important when trying to fix performance problems.

- Try to get an overview of what is occurring in the system before trying to fix a specific area. Understanding the big picture is critical to isolating specific problems.

- Be aware that what appears to be a problem in one area may, in fact, be caused by another area. A good example of this is an application that seems to be accessing the disk a lot. In reality, the application may not be accessing the disk at all; the system may be using so much physical memory that the system has to constantly access the pagefile. The symptoms are the same as an application overusing the disk system, but the causes are completely different. Be sure to monitor the right counters to understand what is occurring.

■ Bottlenecks occur depending on what is happening on the system. Sometimes modifying how the system is used will help improve performance. For example, if a user complains that Windows NT takes too long to start and you find eight major applications in the Startup folder, then the reason for the system slowdown becomes apparent. Windows NT typically takes longer to load applications than other versions of Windows because of the overhead of system protection for each application. In this case, removing applications that aren't really required in the startup group would probably solve the problem.

■ Don't try to make multiple changes at once. It is much easier to make one change, see how it affects the system, then make another. If you make a lot of changes and they don't have the desired effect, it's much harder to determine which individual items made the most difference. You may even want to write down changes and their effects for future performance tuning.

■ While optimizing performance is important, don't spend too much time on improvements that don't have much effect. Windows NT is designed to be "self-optimizing" and it usually is able to perform a certain task in the most efficient way. It is usually not worth the effort on most systems to spend an entire day to get a five percent performance increase on a system.

From Here...

Understanding what is occurring in a system is the best way to troubleshoot performance problems. Windows NT provides Performance Monitor to help the administrator of a Windows NT machine see what is happening on a system. Many different factors affect a computer's performance and being able to narrow down the source of bottlenecks is very important.

Monitoring is an ongoing process as new users and applications are added to an organization. As time progresses, new applications and hardware further push the limits of a Windows NT system and tracking the performance changes helps to identify potential bottlenecks. Knowing how to reduce the number of performance problems helps to keep the existing computer equipment running at a reasonable speed and reducing the need for constant upgrades.

For information on topics related to Windows NT performance, see the following chapters:

■ Chapter 9, "Optimizing Physical and Virtual Memory," provides more information on how Windows NT uses memory and how to optimize Windows NT's use of available system memory.

■ Chapter 10, "Optimizing the File System," describes the different types of file systems Windows NT can use and how to take full advantage of the individual features of them.

■ Chapter 12, "Optimizing CPU Performance," describes how the processor is used by Windows NT and applications and how to optimize Windows NT's processing performance.

■ Chapter 13, "Enhancing Video and I/O Performance," covers how the video and I/O subsystems can be optimized under Windows NT.

CHAPTER 9

Optimizing Physical and Virtual Memory

by Axel Larson

Optimizing a system is often described as changing bottlenecks. Relieving one resource logjam lets another take its place. Memory is perhaps the most critical resource on your computer system. Memory bottlenecks are devastating to performance because memory is the only system component that operates in the same speed range as the CPU. It's no secret that adding memory resolves many performance bottlenecks. If lack of memory is not the cause of poor performance, adding all the memory your machine can take will not yield any benefit. It may even reduce performance.

Virtual Memory is a way of maximizing the use of physical memory and fitting more progRAMs and data into memory at one time to make use of faster CPUs. NT uses sophisticated techniques to manage virtual memory. NT provides tools that you can use to check the performance of the system and identify bottlenecks. Chapter 8, "Monitoring Performance," discusses one of these tools, Performance Monitor. Later this chapter discusses its use in finding memory bottlenecks. This chapter also explores using the new Task Manager as a tool for examining system performance. ■

Optimizing physical memory

Make the best use of the physical memory on your system. You'll also learn about BIOS changes that may make your system faster.

Virtual memory and how it relates to physical memory

This section covers page tables, translation lookaside buffers, and memory organization.

How NT uses and manages memory

Examine how memory is managed as a program executes and the items you can check with performance measurement tools.

How to detect and clear memory bottlenecks

Learn which counters are important in different situations and which are merely interesting.

Optimizing virtual memory

Learn to use monitoring tools to examine NT memory usage, memory-related I/O, and other memory-related activity.

Examining System Resource issues

Compare memory solutions to other possible solutions and gain some insight on cost-benefit issues of adding memory to your system.

Understanding Memory Architecture

A thorough understanding of your system is the key to successful performance tuning. We start by examining the type of memory found in most systems.

Memory Types

There are two, and often three, kinds of memory in most machines running NT. The first is the Dynamic RAM (DRAM), which is what is usually meant when referring to memory.

DRAM comes in several types and packages, and two voltages. Most existing machines use Fast Page Mode Memory (FPM). Those built in the last year often use Extended Data Out (EDO) memory. DRAM is organized in rows and columns like a spread sheet. FPM optimizes accesses by setting the next row access while still transferring from the last few columns of the previous row.

Memory only has a portion of its total cycle time during which it can actually transfer data. A 60ns FPM DRAM has 40ns in which to transfer data. Address selection and other housekeeping activities take up the remainder of the time. EDO memory increases the data transfer portion of the cycle. This allows memory chips to work with faster CPUs. Burst EDO (BEDO) adds a pipeline and a zburst counter that allows it to transfer data even faster. FPM, EDO, and BEDO are all variations on the same basic design. This explains why EDO and BEDO are sold at or near the same price as FPM.

The longer data transfer window in EDO and BEDO means that they can run with faster CPUs without requiring a wait state. 70ns FPM can run with a 25MHz CPU with zero wait states. 70ns EDO keeps up with the CPU to 33MHz. 70ns BEDO keeps up a 50MHz system. 50ns memory pushes these speeds to 33MHz for FPM, 50MHz for EDO and 66MHz for BEDO. Dual speed systems such as those using the Intel DX2 and DX4 chips run at the base speed of 33ns or 25ns with the CPU using the faster speed internally.

Most machines today require 60 or 70 nanosecond memory. You can mix FPM and EDO or BEDO memory with certain restrictions. You will not get the advantages of the newer memory in this situation. If you mix types, each bank must use only one type.

A newer type of memory is Synchronous DRAM (SDRAM). It is quite different from the previous types because it uses an external clock to synchronize its operation with the CPU. SDRAM speed is measured in megahertz instead of nanoseconds. SDRAM runs at speeds up to 100MHz. Additionally, SDRAM has multiple internal banks so access to adjacent addresses is interleaved for even greater performance. You will probably not find SDRAM in low-end PCs due to its higher costs. We will look at new trends in memory at the end of this chapter.

Most PC DRAM sold prior to 1994 had a ninth bit to calculate parity so a failing bit could be detected. In 1994 many PCs were manufactured with non-parity memory. Memory is organized such that each byte may extend across multiple chips. Many SIMMs use one chip for each bit. The ninth bit allows them to detect when an odd number of bits have failed. If an even number of bits fail, the error may not be not detected.

Because parity requires an extra chip as well as additional circuitry, non-parity memory is cheaper to manufacture. Vendors pointed to Apple's success in using non-parity memory on the Macintoshes. They ignored the fact that Apple's forte was desktop publishing. Dropping a bit from a graphic does not have the same consequences as dropping a bit from a corporate financial database.

Part
III

Ch
9

At the same time vendors were peddling non-parity memory, they were announcing Error Checking and Correcting (ECC) memory for servers. They rationalized that a memory error on a server would affect several people while a memory error on a workstation would only affect one user. ECC memory uses standard SIMMs with a sophisticated check-sum scheme to correct single-bit errors and detect multi-bit errors. This keeps safe data that may have been corrupted by non-parity workstations.

You can mix parity and non-parity memory in a system if you follow three rules. Non-parity memory must occupy the lower banks. Each bank must contain only one type of memory. Parity checking must be disabled via motherboard jumper or BIOS setting.

DRAMs come in several packages. First there is the popular Single Inline Memory Module (SIMM) that has been the standard for the last few years. These come in 30 pin and 72 pin (double-wide) versions. Next is the Dual Inline Memory Module (DIMM). These modules have connectors on both sides of the card so they can pack memory more densely. DIMMs may have as many as 168 connector pins for machines like the Power PC RISC machine.

Two variations on this packaging are the Small Outline DIMM (SODIMM) and the "credit card" memories. These are both designed for laptop and notebook computers and differ only in form from other DRAM.

Cache Memory

High-speed Static RAM (SRAM) is used as a cache to allow fast processors to work with slower memories without adding a wait state. Not all systems include cache. SRAM is several times more expensive than DRAM, in part because it is faster and harder to manufacture.

Like DRAM, SRAM comes in various types. Three highly desirable cache features introduced with the advent of the Pentium processor are synchronous mode, pipelining and burst mode.

Synchronous mode uses the same clock as the processor to run components in lockstep and make them interoperate faster.

Pipelining is a method of speeding execution by having an operation begin when the prior operation completes its first micro-step. This is accomplished by adding an output register. More than one instruction is in the execution "pipeline" at one time.

Burst mode speeds execution by overlapping operations so each data transfer after the first one completes in one cycle.

Regardless of special features, cache generally comes as a set of three chips mounted in sockets on the motherboard. There are two data chips and one tag chip to keep track of the addresses represented by the data. Cache can function as either write-back or write-through. In write-back mode, modified data is not written back to main memory until it is replaced in the cache. This improves performance with some small risk of losing data. Write-through cache writes the data from the CPU to memory as it is received.

Finding the desired data in cache saves not only the access to the main RAM but also the time that would have been wasted by any wait states. Intel's measurements show removing a 25K Synchronous Pipeline Burst (PBSRAM) level 2 cache degrades performance of as much as 27% on a Pentium system with 16M of EDO memory. Intel recommends 512K of PBSRAM cache for a 16M (EDO) Pentium for maximum performance. The Pentium Pro chip includes Level 1 and Level 2 on the CPU chip. Level 1 is two 8K caches like the Pentium. Level 2 is 256K write back cache. The Pentium Pro can be used on motherboards that support cache which then becomes level 3.

Memory Voltage

Another difference in memory is the voltage required. CPU and memory chips operated at 5 volts until faster 3.3 volt chips were introduced. 5-volt chips will not operate on 3.3 volts. Operating 3.3-volt chips at 5 volts destroys the chips. This can be dramatic with chips popping apart and even breaking the socket.

The third kind of memory is special associative memory used for a high-speed lookup table called the Translation Lookaside Buffer (TLB). This memory is typically included on the CPU chip. We will look at it in more detail in a later section of this chapter, "Understanding Virtual Memory."

Why Adding Memory May Make Your System Slower

Adding memory can actually make your system slower in at least two situations. The first is the case where the machine has only an ISA bus (also called AT bus) and 16 megabytes of memory. The ISA bus can only directly address the first 16 megabytes due to the number of bits used for addressing. This causes the system to transfer all I/O through a dedicated buffer located in the first 16 megabytes and move it to and from the desired location.

The second case where adding memory makes things slower involves caching. Some memory caches only work with 16 megabytes of memory. Perhaps this is because they were designed to work with the ISA bus. You can adjust some caches to cache more memory by changing BIOS setup options.

The size of the cache also enters into the picture. Larger caches hold more data and usually result in a better "hit" ratio. Intel 386 and later CPU chips have a small (8K to 16K) internal cache known as the level 1 cache. The external or level 2 cache ranges in size from 64K to 512K or more.

Faster processors, larger memories, and multitasking all call for larger caches. Sixty-four kilobytes of cache is not sufficient for any system capable of running Windows NT Workstation. 128K does reasonably well for 12M. 256K will handle 16M with 512K or more cache needed for anything beyond that.

On the CD

Nucache.exe from NUTEK Memories, Inc. provides cache details on Pentium systems. Sample output follows:

```
    ©Copyright NUTEK Memories, Inc., 1995
    All rights reserved.

    NUCACHE.EXE version 1.2a - Cache detection for Pentium based systems.

    *** Thank you for using our SYNCACHE(TM) cache module ***

    Probing CPU speed... 100.0 MHz CPU detected!
    Probing L1 code cache... 8K Bytes of 2-way set associative cache detected!
    Probing L1 data cache... 8K Bytes of 2-way set associative cache detected!
    Probing L2 cache... 256K Bytes of direct mapped SYNCHRONOUS cache detected!
    Calculating bus speed... 66.7 MHz Bus!
    Measuring L1 read bus cycles and durations (within one cycle)...
        Write back to L2 before read: 14 cycles, 0.212 microseconds
                Burst read from L2:  7 cycles, 0.106 microseconds
               Burst read from DRAM: 14 cycles, 0.215 microseconds
    L2 write back to DRAM before read: 33 cycles, 0.500 microseconds
    L1 cache write policy: WRITE BACK.
    L2 cache write policy: WRITE BACK.
```

To contact NUTEK Memories, Inc., type **NUCACHE.EXE /h.**

ON THE WEB

For a research paper on cache analysis:
http://www.cs.berkeley.edu/~gribble/cs252/project.html

Intel has searchable technical documents online:
http://www-techdoc.intel.com/

ON THE WEB

Kinston Memories has a guide on memory:
http://www.spectrum-t.com/docs/mg0.htm

TechWorks' education series is online:
http://www.techwrks.com/EDSERS1.HTM

Nutek Memories can be found at:
http://www.nutekmem.com

Segmented Addressing versus Flat Addressing

Memory (DRAM) is organized in two different ways—segmented or linear. Memory accessed in linear fashion is referred to as flat memory. Segmented memory requires the program to use registers and offsets to access locations. The register is loaded with the address of a segment and the offset from the beginning of that segment is added to develop the effective address. Directly address flat memory locations by their offsets from the beginning of memory. Some processors such as the Intel 8086 only operate in segmented mode. Others operate in flat mode only or in both modes. NT uses the flat mode for all its operations.

Optimizing Physical Memory

The physical memory on your machine may not be working as hard as it can. Make sure you are getting full performance from the physical memory on your system before you begin other tuning measures.

Making Your Memory Work As Fast As it Can

One of the cheapest ways you can add performance to your system is by changing the BIOS setup that is stored in CMOS. CMOS is not part of BIOS. CMOS is part of the clock hardware used to store BIOS control information. The layout of the CMOS information varies from one BIOS maker to another. Older CMOS have 64 bytes. Newer CMOS have 128 bytes. The first 14 bytes of either are the current time and date.

Many experienced computer users avoid these changes because they are afraid a change might destroy their system. While this can happen, it is no more dangerous than testing a new program. With proper safeguards, you can make changes and undo them if they do not perform properly.

Check your motherboard manual or the BIOS setup instructions to learn how to reset the CMOS if your change causes a problem. Make only one change at a time and test by running an NT session before making the next change. If the system malfunctions, usually all you need to do is enter BIOS setup when the system is starting and reverse the last change.

First, eliminate wait states. Many BIOS's use conservative values at the expense of performance. Many specify a DRAM wait state when none is necessary. This is especially true on systems that use cache. The wait state will usually be set to one. If it is higher than two, something is drastically out of line and you should consider replacing all the memory with faster chips. You may even want to replace the motherboard. Change the wait state setting downward by one, then test to see if everything still functions properly.

Second, check the timings used for the AT bus clock if you have ISA adapter cards in your system. The standard AT bus runs at 8.33MHz. Many of the adapter cards produced in the last few years can run faster than that. You might be able to push them to 10 or 12MHz. The bus speed is specified in terms of the system clock (SCLK). Your system clock runs at bus speed. A 100MHz 486 has a 33MHz bus. The AT speed is specified as a fraction such as SCLK/3. After you change one of the bus settings, make sure you thoroughly test each adapter card. The keyboard clock is set in the same way. You can also change I/O recovery time and DMA timings. Test your disk reading and writing thoroughly after changing these two items. The changes might cause write errors. I/O recovery timing problems might not show up until a heavy load is placed on the system. DMA timing problems will show up under the first heavy I/O load.

The third item to look at is caching. Some BIOS's do not cache all of the memory, especially the area between segment addresses A000 and EFFF. These addresses are used for adapter card BIOS memory. Caching them may improve performance dramatically. If your BIOS allows you to cache each segment separately, set one segment at a time and test it. Also make sure that any memory above 16M is cached.

Shadowing takes advantage of the fact that your 32-bit DRAM is much faster than the 8-bit or 16-bit ROM on the adapter cards. Shadowing copies the ROM to faster RAM. Shadowing is counter-productive with NT. NT only uses the adapter BIOS code during startup. Shadowing the BIOS area in segments A000–EFFF prevents NT from using that memory. If you have a dual boot machine, you must choose which system you want to get the performance boost.

Part
III

Ch
9

> **CAUTION**
>
> If you have both 8-bit and 16-bit cards, make sure segments C000 and D000 do not have BIOS' from both types. If they do, either don't shadow them or move one type of card to segment E000. Otherwise you will have problems due to the way address modes are handled during the memory cycle.

> **CAUTION**
>
> If you have trouble getting NT 4.0 installed and you have an OEM version of Phoenix bios 4.50 installed, you should contact the vendor of your motherboard for an upgrade. You must provide the BIOS serial number that appears at the bottom of the screen during memory checking after the power is turned on. The PAUSE key should allow you to read your serial number.
>
> The numbers and letters in the serial number refer to the bios, the chipset and the manufacturer.

ON THE WEB

Get information directly from the manufacturer of your bios:

Award Software, Inc.
http://www.award.com/

American Megatrends Inc.
http://www.megatrends.com/

Microid Research Inc.
http://www.mrbios.com/

Phoenix Technologies Ltd
http://www.ptltd.com/phoenix.html

Look here for a page with links to many powerful search engines:
http://www.search.com/

 N O T E Yahoo is good at locating corporate home pages. AltaVista will probably return the most hits, including many that are irrelevant. The specialized searches will find information not available through the general searches. ■

Determining if You Have Enough Memory

NT Workstation requires 12 megabytes minimum. This amount of memory will run NT Workstation 4.0 but has to use paging to accommodate any application. Large applications such as CAD can require several megabytes for their own code. You also need to provide memory for your data. Large color illustrations can consume tens of megabytes of data. You can read through the vendor's literature and make an estimate of the memory you need. Make sure your cache is adequately sized for the memory you have. The only way to find out if you have sufficient memory is to determine your normal mix of programs by looking at your computer use, then measuring the impact it has on your system. Follow the performance measurement methodology used in "Detecting and Clearing Memory Bottlenecks" later in this chapter.

> **N O T E** You will see "process" used in the following pages. A process may be an application, an NT service, or a subsystem. ■

Allocating the Memory You Have

NT doesn't allow the use of third party memory managers such as Qemm. The flat addressing mode and virtual memory hardware eliminate the need for these kludges. The only real-mode memory allocation left is in your DOS-compatible Virtual DOS Machines. 16-bit Windows programs normally run in a shared VDM so they will behave just as they did in earlier versions of Windows. This saves about 2400 bytes per program, but retains all the old vulnerability to corruption from a rouge application.

You can choose to run DOS programs in a separate virtual machine by right-clicking on the icon and selecting Properties. Separate VDMs use a small amount of additional memory each but keep applications from interfering with each other.

The registry entry DefaultSeparateVDM under the key:

HKEY_LOCAL_MACHINE\SYSTEM\CurrentControlSet\Control\WOW

can be set to "yes" to automatically give each DOS session its own VDM. The worst a DOS application can do is cause its VDM to be terminated.

WOWsize under the same key can be set for RISC-based computers. It defines the amount of memory provided in a VDM when a WOW session is started. WOWsize has a 25 percent overhead so setting it to 4M causes the VDM to allocate 5M with 1M used by the system. The default size for a RISC-based machine varies with the amount of RAM on the system. You can override the defaults as long as you provide at least 3M. Defaults are 3M for less than 12M of RAM, 6M for 12 to 16M and 8M beyond that.

Understanding Virtual Memory

Segmented memory and virtual memory both extend the amount of storage available. Segmentation makes more memory available to a program, and virtual memory makes more memory available to the system. Segmentation requires real memory for all segments. Virtual memory uses disk space to extend the amount of memory available.

Pages

There are two parts to virtual memory: the memory organization and the process of moving pages in and out of memory. Virtual memory is logically organized into pages. The size of the page is restricted by the hardware. Common page sizes are 2K, 4K, and 8K. The Intel processors prior to the Pentium use 4K and the DEC Alpha uses 8K; these are the sizes used by NT on those systems. The Pentium supports 4K pages and is designed to be extended to supporting 4M pages. The Pentium Pro supports page sizes of 4K and 4M. These differences in page size are the reason virtual memory performance counters are given in bytes instead of pages.

N O T E   Swapfiles are administered with page size as the basic unit of allocation. The ability to support 4M pages implies that Intel expects huge memories to come into use before the design of the Pentium Pro becomes obsolete. This fact, plus the development of very fast memory and the ability to run many very high-speed I/O devices concurrently leads to some interesting speculation about the next generation of workstations and servers. These implications are discussed at the end of this chapter. ▪

Page Tables

Page tables are used to map virtual pages to real memory addresses so that two pages physically separate in memory appear to be contiguous and can be addressed that way by a program. At first glance, this may look like segmented memory. There are a few differences. Programs don't control their own page registers when using virtual memory, and the program is not generally concerned with the real address.

Virtual memory addressing uses special hardware to look up the address of a page and add the offset within the page to generate a real (physical) address. This hardware uses page tables which are controlled by the operating system. Some systems use two levels of tables for address resolution. Special hardware called a Translation Lookaside Buffer (TLB) is often used to speed the lookup operation.

The Translation Lookaside Buffer

The TLB is an associative memory array that holds pairs of page identifiers and the location of the corresponding pages in real memory. The TLB is used for the set of most recently used pages. Associative memory uses a special addressing scheme based on the content of memory. The processor can issue an instruction that effectively says "whichever entry has the matching page number, load your page address into a control register and let me know you did it."

TLBs are typically small due to the cost of the special hardware required. The Intel 386 TLB contains 32 entries. Pentium processors have separate 8K Level-1 caches for data and instructions. Each cache has its own TLB. Intel has not openly released information on the number of entries in these Pentium TLBs. The PowerPC 603 uses a 64-entry TLB. Since the exact implementation of virtual memory differs from one processor type to another, the code to manage pages is processor-specific.

Understanding NT Memory Use

Figure 9.1 illustrates the development of a virtual address. It also shows the role played by the Translation-Lookaside Buffer.

NT's Page Structure

NT maintains a two-level page table structure with entries in the first level, known as the page directory, pointing to page table entries in the second level table. Entries in the second-level table point to actual page locations. NT maintains a set of page tables for each process. Memory can be shared by mapping addresses for different processes to the same area. The first entry in the TLB is used to store the address of the page directory for the currently active process. NT loads that address into the TLB when activating that process. This prevents processes from accessing each other's memory unless explicitly permitted.

If the page address is not present in the TLB, NT must use page tables to locate the address. It does this by using the pointer to the page directory plus the directory offset from the virtual memory address to get to the proper page directory entry. NT then adds the address from the page directory entry and the table offset portion of the virtual address to get the proper page table entry.

The last step is the same whether the TLB contained the address of the page frame or the software had to calculate it. The page offset from the virtual address is added to the page frame address to get the real address of the data being referenced.

FIG. 9.1
The TLB provides a shortcut to the page referenced by a virtual address.

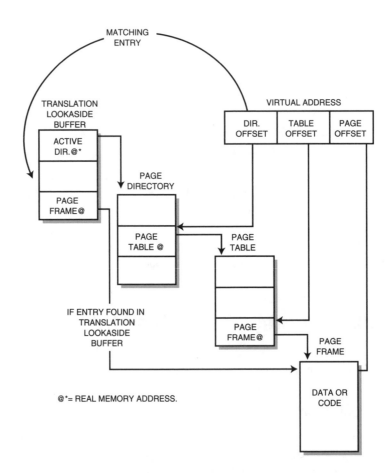

System Space

Because NT is a 32-bit system, it can address four gigabytes of memory. Virtual addressing is used to map system code and data into the upper half of this address space. Programs running in user mode and system functions running on behalf of those programs use the lower two GB. Note that these are virtual, not real, addresses.

N O T E Microsoft has announced that a version of NT that uses 64-bit addressing for data is being prepared for Digital Equipment Corporation Alpha systems "in the Windows NT 'Cairo' time frame." ■

The upper two gigabytes of the virtual address space are reserved for the operating system and divided into three regions, one for code that must always remain resident, one for a pool of memory that is never paged to disk and the last for a pool of memory that is pagable. The nonpaged pool is used for operating system tasks and data that must remain resident while active due to the nature of the functions they perform. An example of this might be memory used in gathering interrupt statistics. The paged pool is used for other system tasks. We'll use Performance Monitor to look at all three areas in "Detecting and Clearing Memory Bottlenecks" later in this chapter.

User Space

The lower two gigabytes of address space are used for user code and can always be paged. Some operating routines doing work on behalf of the user program will also use this area. An example of this would be the system component loading a memory-mapped file for a program.

Paging—Extending the Space

Paging to disk extends the address space. NT allocates pages to programs when loading them. When the memory is full, pages must be taken from temporarily inactive programs and reused. We'll take a look at this process in more detail so we can better understand the Performance Monitor counts, which we'll look at later.

Each process has a memory allocation called the "working set". Loosely, this means the amount of memory it needs to function without incurring excessive paging. When memory is plentiful NT will allow this working set to grow to an upper limit if the process is incurring a high paging rate. When memory is tight NT trims the working set until the minimum is reached. Programs can modify their working set limits via an API call. NT must load the entire working set into memory when it activates the owning process.

Memory Usage States

There is a state indicator for each virtual page. As NT uses, discards, and reuses the pages the indicator is updated.

NT can provide C2-level security. One of the requirements for this level is to never reuse a page for another program without destroying the prior content. NT does this either by writing all zeroes into the page or by loading a program into it. Pages are cleared to zero ahead of time if the system load permits. NT maintains a list of Zeroed pages. They are part of the Available Bytes count in Performance Monitor.

Pages that are in use and part of a program's "working set" are marked Valid. Valid pages are part of any of the Performance Monitor counters that reflect memory in use.

Pages removed from a working set are marked Transition if they haven't been modified. If the process needs these pages again before they are written to the paging disk, NT reclaims them by adding them back to the working set and marking them valid. These pages are also part of Available Bytes. Pages reclaimed from the transition state are reflected in Transition Faults/sec.

Pages that have been modified are marked as both Transition and Dirty. These dirty pages must be written to disk before reuse by another process. Modified pages are reflected in the counts Pages Output/sec and indirectly in Page Writes/sec.

Free pages have been written to disk (if required) and are ready to be zeroed or used to for code. They are also part of Available Bytes.

Invalid refers to pages that are paged-out to disk. A page read is required for a process to reclaim its invalid page.

A BAD page is one that generated a hardware error and has been removed from use. NT issues a `{Bad CRC}` `A cyclic redundancy check (CRC) checksum error occurred` message when the error is detected.

Detecting and Clearing Memory Bottlenecks

Tuning a system consists of gathering statistics on its performance, then trying to understand what the numbers mean. This understanding is based on knowing what tasks the system is trying to accomplish and which numbers reflect the performance of each task.

Examining Performance to Determine if a Memory Bottleneck Exists

You need to begin monitoring performance before you begin to encounter perceivable problems. This will help you establish a baseline of normal operation and make it easier to detect significant differences.

The first level of bottleneck detection is your own senses. Your time sense tells you that the machine seems to be running slower and your sense of hearing and/or sight tells you the hard disk is running continuously.

> **CAUTION**
>
> It's a well-known phenomenon that your time sense is recalibrated the moment you use a new machine that runs significantly faster than your old one. Your old machine will seem to have slowed down.

When you suspect memory is the bottleneck in your system, you should begin an organized approach to proving the fact. Use Task Manager, Performance Monitor, and optionally, PMON, to prove the existence of the bottleneck and acquire information for resolution (see fig. 9.2).

FIG. 9.2

NT's new Task Manager provides a quick look at performance.

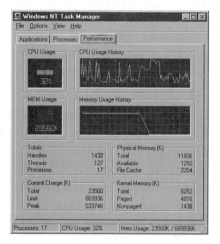

Part

III

Ch

9

Start Task Manager by right-clicking the taskbar and selecting it from the context menu. You can leave it running as an icon in the tray by checking the Hide when Minimized option.

N O T E Taskbar and tray are part of the new interface. Taskbar refers to the bar with the Start button. The tray is the recessed area at the end of the taskbar opposite the start button.

CPU Usage shows the CPU usage as of the last update. If you have two CPUs, each is considered 50% of the total. One CPU idle and one 10% busy would show 5%. You can change the update frequency from the View menu. More frequent updates will reveal momentary spikes in usage. Less frequent updates place less of a load on the system and show trends better.

CPU Usage History continuously records the total CPU usage. Note the graph moves from right to left with the most recent data at the rightmost edge. Peaks of 100% are to be expected and are of concern only if they occur frequently or last for more than a few seconds. Note that the sustained peak in figure 9.2 coincides with the decrease in memory usage. This reflects work the system is doing invalidating pages and decommitting swapfile space. The usage cluster to the right of that probably reflects NT zeroing pages to prepare them for reuse.

MEM Usage is approximately the same as Total under Commit Charge (K). It shows the memory actually in use at the time of the last update. This may exceed the amount of physical memory.

Memory Usage History is a record of Memory usage and is useful in alerting you to possible memory bottlenecks.

The counts in the Totals section fall into the "interesting" category. Handles are pointers to objects including files, instances of programs, and graphic items. Each process will have one or more Threads. The thread is the dispatchable unit of code. Processes is the count of user programs and system elements currently running on your system.

Physical Memory (K) details the real memory in your system. Total is the amount of RAM on system minus a few hundred bytes for the extended BIOS data area. Available is the memory available for both systems and user processes. If it falls below 4096K for more than a few seconds, you have a memory bottleneck. File Cache is the memory used for all files, including the paging files. The Large System Cache registry setting can change the priority NT gives to processes using this memory.

Commit Charge (K) means NT has allocated space in the paging file to guarantee the memory will be available to the requesting process. Total is the best measure available of the amount of memory currently in use. Limit is a soft limit if the page files have grown to their maximum allocation. Peak is the greatest amount of memory committed during this session.

Kernel Memory (K) refers to virtual addresses above the 2G line. It includes the paged and nonpaged pools but not NT system code. Total is just the sum of the next two items. Paged is pagable memory in use. Nonpaged is memory that must remain resident during use. It has a greater effect on performance than does Paged.

The status bar at the bottom of the Task Manager window shows key information from both the Performance page and the Processes page.

Processes shows the number of processes executing. The Processes page provides more detail on their resource consumption.

CPU Usage is a repeat of the current number on the Performance page. Mem Usage shows the Commit Charge total over the commit limit. This gives you the ratio between the memory currently in use and the amount that can be used without extending the swapfile.

Task Manager is useful for a quick look at your system performance but you'll need a more powerful tool for in-depth analysis. The tool provided with NT is Performance Monitor. Chapter 8, "Monitoring Performance", covers the usage of the tool. We will look at its application in tuning memory performance.

Performance monitor can provide a wealth of information in many areas. The number of counters may increase as you add components to your NT system. For example, adding RAS will add two sets of counters. Installing additional network protocols adds the counters needed to monitor them. There are two types of counters. Some are an instantaneous count and others are averages. Both are useful. The following discussion uses the same set of data throughout. You can relate each new counter to Available Bytes which is shown on each page as a white line. The counters are shown in the order used by Performance monitor. The first set of counters are all found in the Memory category in Performance monitor.

▶ **See** "Working with Performance Monitor," **p. 143**

Part

III

Ch

9

 TIP

Open a command-line window and enter "DISKPERF -y" to activate disk counters. Using "DISKPERF -ye" will provide detailed counts on fault-tolerant disks. The "e" will add some extra overhead and should only be used when you suspect some of your disks are slower than the others. The Diskperf setting becomes active after a shutdown/restart and remains in effect until turned off with "DISKPERF -n". You can prevent a waste of time and effort by checking that the counters are active by viewing them with the Performance Monitor chart before you record a log file.

The charts shown in figure 9.3 were created from a Performance Monitor log file so they would all show the same time frame and could be correlated. The machine used is a 486/66 with EISA bus and 32M of memory. NT was started with the "/MAXMEM=12" switch to limit memory used to 12M. The log file was generated using one-second intervals. The load was generated by the STRESS.EXE program that comes with Microsoft Visual C++ 1.5. STRESS was run using the INI file shown in the following list. STRESS. EXE is also included in the BIN directory in the Win32 SDK section of the MSDN CD.

```
[stress]
GLOBAL=-1
USER=4095
UDI=4095
DISK=20
HANDLES=50
STRESS LEVEL=1
SEED=1000
RESOURCES=global gdi user
ALLOCATIONS=random
EXECUTER ON=no
TIME INTERVAL=5
LEVEL1 = 8000 10000 40000 55000 40000 55000 100 500 150 200
LEVEL2 = 6000 8000 25000 40000 25000 40000  60 100 10 15
LEVEL3 = 4000 6000 10000 25000 10000 25000 20 60 5 10
LEVEL4 = 15000 16000 1000 10000 1000 10000 -1 -1 -1 -1
```

FIG. 9.3

Available Bytes and % Committed Bytes show two sides of the same coin.

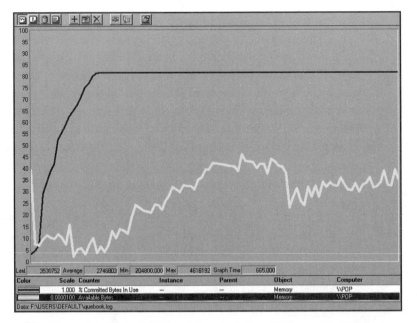

Available Bytes and % Committed Bytes In Use The black line (% Committed Bytes In Use) shows the percentage in use of memory which is reserved and allocated swapfile space. The rise corresponds to the increase in load as the Stress program gets started. This counter is useful in assessing the size of your swapfile. In this case, there is plenty of room for growth.

The white line (Available Bytes) shows the memory shortage. This figure should not fall below 4M for more than a second or two. When you look at the scaling factor for this counter, you'll see the value is divided by 10,000 so it will fit on the page. The 4M line is just above 40 on the scale. NT needs to keep some memory available to load programs. When the number drops too low, NT starts taking pages from programs' working sets. This in turn can increase the rate of paging for those programs.

A program can reserve memory and it can also commit memory which means NT must allocate space for it in the paging file. You can evaluate the size of your paging file by checking this counter. In this case, the paging file is large enough that it can accommodate quite a bit more.

Cache Bytes and Cache Bytes Peak Cache Bytes (solid black line) measure the memory used as an I/O buffer for disk and network data (see fig.9.4). It remains fairly constant here because of the particular workload. Cache Bytes Peak (dotted line) shows that once the peak was reached, the workload dropped off and did not exceed it.

FIG. 9.4
Cache bytes reached a stable peak with minor fluctuations in ongoing load.

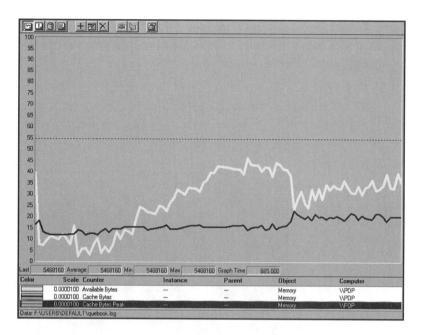

Cache Faults A cache fault occurs when the system references a file whose pages are not in memory (see fig. 9.5). The default scale divides this value by 10. The scale was changed to 1:1 to emphasize the variability. This counter doesn't relate directly to memory workload for computation-intensive programs.

FIG. 9.5
Cache Faults per second vary widely.

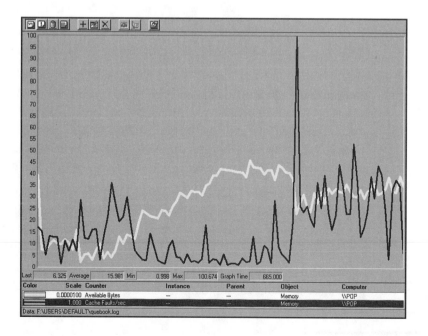

Commit Limit and Committed Bytes Commit Limit (the dotted line shown in fig. 9.6) is a "soft" limit and will grow if the swapfile size is increased. The scale was reduced to fit the values to the page.

The solid line is the ongoing count of Committed Bytes. This is memory for which swapfile space has been allocated. You can think of this number as the amount of pagable memory in use. If you wanted to run without a swapfile, you would need about this much memory.

FIG. 9.6

The Commit Limit remains constant until the swapfile is expanded.

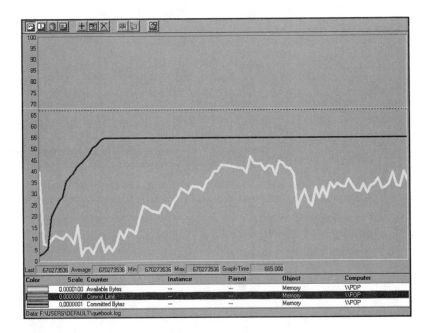

Demand Zero Faults and Free System Page Table Entries The solid black line (see fig. 9.7) is Demand Zero Faults and shows the number of times NT needed to provide a page to a program and didn't have one on the free list. Free System Page Table Entries (dotted line) is possibly an artifact of a system installed on 32M and running with only 12M. The approximately 4100 entries are enough to address about an additional 16M.

Page Faults/sec Page Faults are generated when the system accesses a page that is not in memory (see fig. 9.8). In a busy system, these can easily exceed 1000 faults per second. As working sets are adjusted to achieve the optimum balance between need and supply, this rate falls.

Page Reads/sec High paging rates are a primary symptom of a memory-constrained system (see fig. 9.9). A disk I/O operation takes thousands of times as long as execution of an instruction.

FIG. 9.7
NT runs out of zeroed pages as the workload jumps.

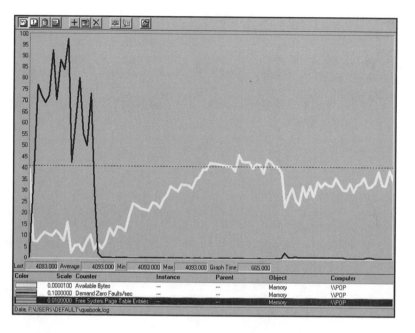

FIG. 9.8
Page Faults per second jump as the workload starts.

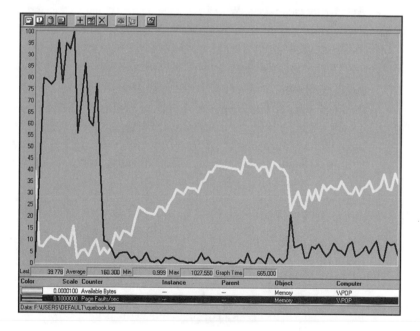

FIG. 9.9
Page Reads per
second reflect page
faults not satisfied by
reclaiming pages
from the standby list.

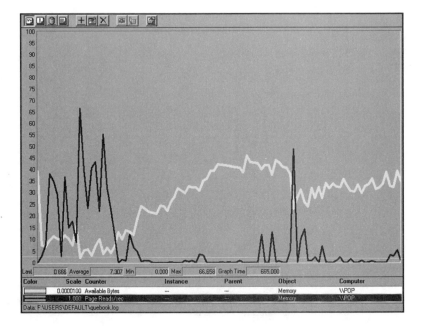

Page Writes/sec   Page Writes/sec (see fig.9.10) follows the same overall pattern as did Page Reads/sec. One write may transfer several pages so you cannot directly infer disk workload from this counter. A real workload would probably have a higher ongoing rate as records were read into memory then modified and rewritten.

Pages Input/sec   Pages Input/sec (see fig. 9.11) is a good counter to watch for signs of thrashing, that dreaded nemesis of all virtual memory operating systems. Thrashing occurs when the system spends virtually all the time getting programs ready to run and has no time left to actually run them. You may have experienced the same thing when you tried to do too many things at once. The operating system can only do what you probably did—drop some of the tasks and concentrate your priorities on the others. You can see that thrashing is not a problem in this case since the scale is 1:1 and the maximum number is a little over nine pages input per second.

Pages Output/sec   Pages output/sec (see fig. 9.12) reflects pages that have been modified and must be written to disk before they can be reused. A system actually processing data would most likely have more of an ongoing workload. A higher rate can reflect a healthy system doing lots of productive work and by itself does not indicate a memory shortage unless all the output is to the paging file.

Pages/sec   When you find Pages/sec running at a sustained high rate, you most likely have a memory bottleneck (see fig. 9.13). If you can only watch a limited number of counters, such as when monitoring several systems, make this one of them.

FIG. 9.10
Page Writes that are low during high memory use reflect programs that do little data modification.

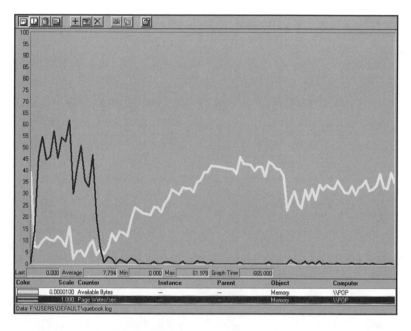

FIG. 9.11
A small amount of Page Input occurred sporadically.

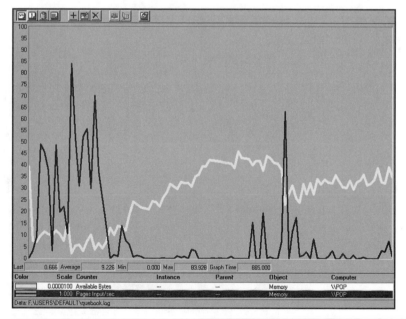

FIG. 9.12

Pages Output per second on a normal workload would not drop like this.

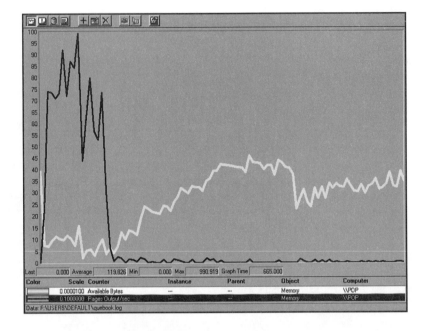

FIG. 9.13

Pages/sec is the sum of Pages input and Pages output.

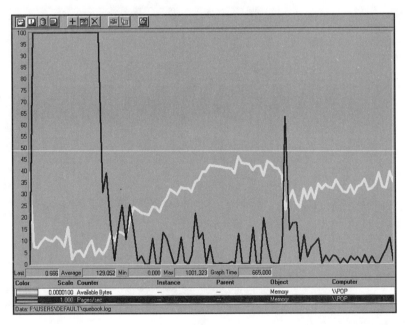

Pool Nonpaged Allocs and Pool Nonpaged Bytes   Pool Nonpaged Allocs (the solid black line shown in figure 9.14) shows the number of calls the system made to allocate nonpagable memory. It is constant in this case as programs there were not entering and leaving the system. The dotted line, Pool Nonpaged Bytes, shows the amount of memory used for file handles and other critical system objects. This memory cannot be paged and therefore represents a real drain on resources. You can't change these in any way, so they become "interesting" statistics unless they grow continuously. That would indicate a bug.

FIG. 9.14

The stability of these two counts shows an unchanging load for the operating system.

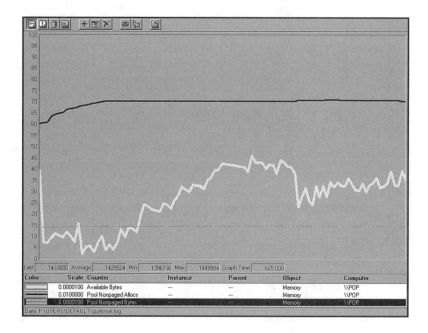

Pool Paged Allocs, Pool Paged Bytes, and Pool Paged Resident Bytes   Pool Paged Allocs (the solid black line shown in figure 9.15) show the number of times space was allocated in the system paged pool. The dashed line, Pool Paged Bytes, shows the amount of space allocated. Simple division gives you the average amount of memory allocated with each call, but be careful—they are shown at different scales. The dotted line shows the ongoing memory used by system functions. It's called Pool Paged Resident Bytes and that means memory allocated by the system that is using physical memory. This set of counters is also in the "interesting" category.

FIG. 9.15
Although NT once used a lot of space, it only occupies a small amount throughout this test.

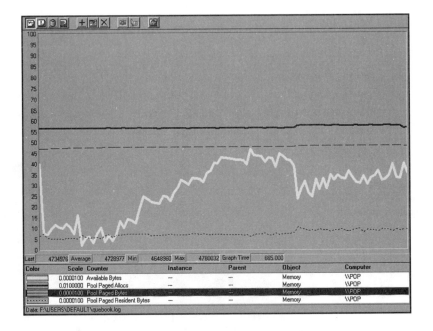

System Cache Resident Bytes, System Code Resident Bytes, and System Code Total

Bytes   The increased scale emphasizes changes in these values. System Cache Resident Bytes is the solid black line (see fig. 9.16) and shows the usage of the system I/O cache. The dashed line is System Code Resident Bytes. It correlates well with Cache Faults/sec (refer to fig. 9.5). The dotted line is System Code Total Bytes which remained constant as you would expect. System Code should only change in response to a change in system function such as starting RAS or inserting a PC Card (PCMCIA) device.

System Driver Resident Bytes and System Driver Total Bytes   System Driver Resident

Bytes (solid black line) is the pagable space occupied by device drivers (see fig. 9.17). System Driver Total Bytes (dotted line) adds the non-pagable portions of these drivers.

Transition Faults/sec and Write Copies/sec   Transition Faults/sec (the solid black line

shown in figure 9.18) indicates the number of times per second NT took a page from the outbound queue and gave it back to the owner. A rate nearing or exceeding 1,000 faults per second might indicate thrashing.

The dotted line buried at the bottom of the screen is Write Copies/sec multiplied ten fold to make it show up. Write copies occur when two or more processes share a page and one of them modifies it. Before the modification is made, NT makes a private copy for the process making the change.

FIG. 9.16
Three system
measurements are
shown at 10x the
Available Bytes scale.

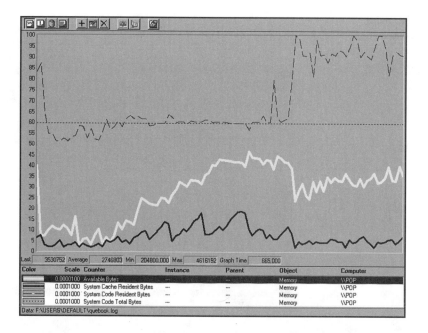

FIG. 9.17
Systems drivers are
fairly constant in their
memory use.

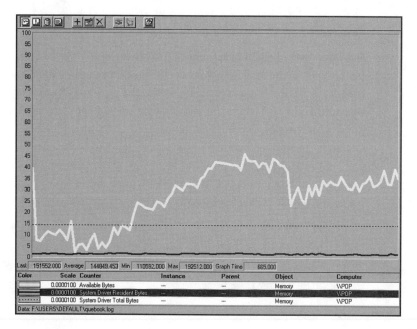

FIG. 9.18
Transition Faults
prevent unnecessary
I/O.

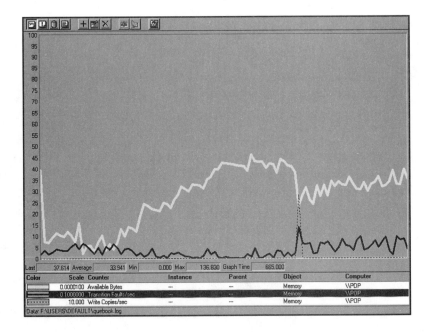

Color	Scale	Counter	Instance	Parent	Object	Computer
	0.0000100	Available Bytes	---	---	Memory	\\POP
	0.1000000	Transition Faults/sec	---	---	Memory	\\POP
	10.000	Write Copies/sec	---	---	Memory	\\POP

Data: F:\USERS\DEFAULT\quebook.log

That covers the Memory counters. Next we'll look at a three-key Physical Disk counts and then at the page file information.

Avg. Disk Queue Length (Total) and % Disk Time(Total)   Avg. Disk Queue Length (dotted line) is the total for all physical disks shown multiplied by 10 to emphasize it (see fig. 9.19). Existence of a queue means the system is waiting on the disk. In the absence of other evidence, this would point to a disk bottleneck. A memory bottleneck can easily drive disk I/O beyond the capacity of any drive made. If you are not sure if the system is constrained by memory or by I/O, look to see where the I/O is occurring. If it is all on the page file, look for other signs on memory shortages. The disk queue should never go above one for more than a second or so at a time. % Disk Time (solid black line) is also the total for all disks. It shows the percentage of the time that the disk was busy.

Disk Write Time(Total)   % Disk Write Time (see fig. 9.20) includes writes for data files and pages. Compare this to the % Disk Time to get a general sense of whether the system is thrashing. If it were thrashing heavily, programs probably wouldn't be getting control long enough to do a lot of page modification.

FIG. 9.19
Two disk counters demonstrate a side effect of a memory bottleneck.

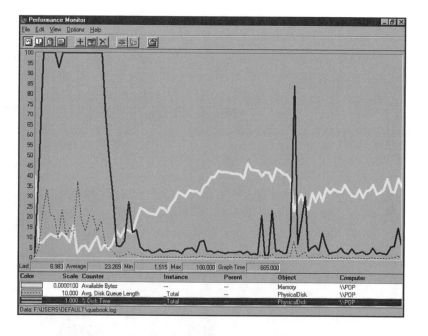

FIG. 9.20
High Disk Write Time may reflect a high rate of page modification.

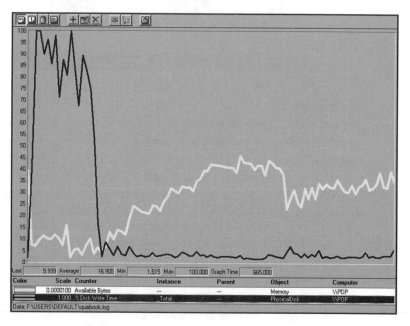

%Swapfile Usage and %Swapfile Usage Peak   The data shown in figure 9.21 is for the total
of all swapfiles. %Swapfile Usage and %Swapfile Usage Peak are identical here as the
system had not been doing much paging prior to the test. You can use the swapfile usage
peak percentage in deciding how much memory you should add to your system.

FIG. 9.21

Both swapfile counters
are identical for this
test.

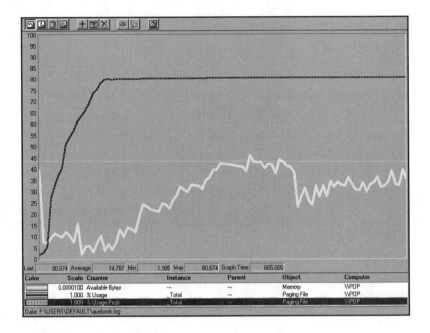

You've looked at Performance Monitor pictures until your eyes are beginning to glaze.
Before we jump into what all these nice charts add up to, we'll take a brief look at another
tool that helps you understand what is happening inside the system. PMON is a program
that came with the NT 3.51 Resource Kit and should be in either the \Support\ Debug\
<machine type> directory on your NT 4.0 CD or in the NT 4.0 Resource Kit. PMON runs
in a command-line window and provides a snapshot of the system that is updated every
five seconds. There are no command-line switches and the output cannot be redirected to
a file.

N O T E   This data in figure 9.21 does not match the data we have used throughout the
Performance monitor discussion. It was captured separately. ■

You will recognize the data in the two lines near the top of the page (see fig. 9.22). You can
identify which programs or processes are contributing the most to the workload by study-
ing the detail lines. Two columns that show new data are the Diff columns. They show the
changes since the last snapshot.

FIG. 9.22

PMON shows you what each process is using.

If you do not have PMON, you can use the page shown in figure 9.23 for the same basic purposes. You can control the rate at which the counters are updated from the View menu.

FIG. 9.23

Task Manager's Processes page shows some of the same information as PMON.

Performance tuning is part art and part science. The counters and other system information constitute the science. The art comes from understanding how the system works and relating that to the counters to gain a clear picture of what is happening.

First, let's follow a simplified scenario. We will track your session as you perform some normal activities. Think about what NT is doing at each step and note the counters that reflect that activity. The more significant counters are listed. Review their impact on memory performance.

Part III

Ch 9

1. Start your workstation and log on.

   NT checks the file structures on the disk drives and processes your login. NT creates a control entry for your user ID in the nonpaged pool. NT reads your profile from the registry and sets up your session. The counters that reflect this activity are: Available Bytes, Cache Bytes, System Cache Resident Bytes, Pool Paged Allocs, Pool Paged Bytes, Pool Nonpaged Allocs, Pool Nonpaged Bytes, Committed Bytes, and % Committed Bytes In Use.

2. Schedule+ is launched from the Start group.

   NT allocates user memory and swapfile space for Schedule's default working set and creates a control entry in the nonpaged pool. The same sets of counters are affected with the possible addition of Pages/sec, Page Writes/sec, and Pages output/sec.

3. Launch Word and type a few pages.

   NT does the same work it did for Schedule, affecting the same counters. It may also shrink Schedule's working set to the minimum. By now Pages/sec, Page Writes/ sec, and Pages output/sec are certainly relevant and some heavy disk paging activity can be expected. You would see this in Page Faults/sec, % Disk Time, % Disk Write Time, % Swapfile Usage, and possibly Avg. Disk Queue Length.

4. Start a new document and type several lines.

   NT allocates space in the nonpaged pool for the file handle. Pages to hold the data are allocated as required. These pages may replace other pages in use by Word if memory is getting short. Pages containing the material you typed are marked "dirty." Pages removed from a working set are marked "transition" and placed on the standby list.

5. Start a large graphics program to create illustrations for your new document. It takes a long time to load.

   NT may have to squeeze some more memory by paging more of Schedule to disk. Look for the paging output counters to increase.

6. Start Internet Explorer to search for some information.

   Once more NT has to find room. It trims pages from the working sets of programs that have not been actively using them. Word has just been sitting there while you work with other programs, so it will probably have more of its pages sent to disk. Again paging counters will increase and available memory will drop.

7. Word does an Autosave of your open document.

Word may use a separate thread for Autosaves. This will take nonpaged pool space to track the thread and the file handle it opens for the temporary file. It may share the pages with the data. If you enter a keystroke in the document between the time the Autosave starts and the time that page gets written to disk, NT will make a private copy of the page for the modifying process. This is invisible to the process. Write Copies/sec would reflect this although a single instance would never show on a chart.

8. You try to copy an illustration into your document but receive a message that says you'll have to close a program first as the system doesn't have enough memory to complete this operation. You save the illustrations to disk and close the graphics programs.

You may have bumped into the Commit Limit, check % Swapfile Usage Peak. If you used all the allocated swapfile, you need to allocate a higher maximum amount.

9. Switch to Schedule+ to check your appointments. This takes several seconds and the disk runs continuously.

Since Schedule has been waiting with no activity beyond keeping track of the time and the next schedule reminder, it has been paged to disk. NT must now bring it back into memory. This will be reflected in the paging input counters Page Reads/sec, Pages Input/sec, and possibly in Page Faults/sec. Less likely, but still possible is a surge in Transition Faults/sec if some of Schedule's pages hadn't been written out yet and could be given back without going to the swapfile.

10. Insert your illustrations from disk to Word, type the remainder of your new document, save it to disk, and close Word.

Cache Faults/sec may reflect pages brought back from the swapfile so they can be written to your document file. Available Bytes should increase significantly as memory used by Word is freed. NT may have to briefly bring in additional paged pool code to perform cleanup activities.

11. Add a reminder in Schedule+. It is much more responsive now.

NT may allow Schedule's working set to grow again, since memory is now plentiful.

12. Shutdown your system.

NT performs page-in activities for the logon process as it saves your profile to the registry and performs some housekeeping.

Part
III

Ch
9

The scenario we have just reviewed is a slow motion look at what happens in your system. The same things happen if the load is generated from automated processes such as compilers and linkers driven by make files. The same counters would be affected. Those affected by the passage of time, such as Transition Faults/sec would be more pronounced.

Take into account the number and frequency of monitoring samples being displayed. Too short of a sample period can give you a close-up of individual events, but prevent you from seeing the overall picture.

Compare figure 9.24 to figure 9.3. They both show the same counters taken from the same Performance Monitor log file. The sample in figure 9.24 is 185 seconds starting at the time % Committed Bytes in Use reached the peak (just under the x button in figure 9.3). It shows some brief dips that disappear when 685 seconds of data are shown on the same graph.

Log your data with as high a frequency of counts as your system will handle, then look at it using varying time scales and vertical scales. You'll see different truths.

FIG. 9.24
A different time scale reveals additional information.

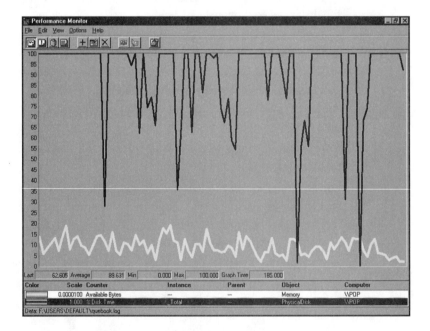

Clearing Memory Bottlenecks

NT is designed as a self-tuning system so there are not a lot of settings you can tweak manually. There are a few registry settings you can change using Regedit.exe. The usual cautions about making backups before hacking the registry apply. In addition, monitor the performance before and after each change and only make one change at a time. The following entries are found under the registry key HKEY_LOCAL_MACHINE\SYSTEM\ CurrentControlSet\Control\Session Manager\Memory Management.

The ClearPageFileAtShutdown entry is related to security, not performance. Setting it on a value of 1 will extend the shutdown time by the amount it takes to format the allocated swapfile space. It will also extend startup time as the swapfile is created.

At first glance, the very existence of DisablePagingExecutive seems contrary to the concept of a virtual memory system. This setting keeps operating system code from being paged out. It may improve performance on servers with heavily-loaded networks. Leave it alone for workstations.

The IoPageLockLimit entry limits the amount of memory that can be locked for I/O operations. When the value is 0, the default size of 512K is used. The maximum changes as the size of physical memory increases, (about 9M for a 16M system, 48M for 64M, and 448M for 512M). If you have multiple disk drives you might try setting this to 512 times the number of disk drives. You can expect an increase in disk queuing as more I/O operations are able to lock memory and proceed to the next step. Be sure to test thoroughly for any performance impact from this change.

LargeSystemCache is documented in prior NT releases with the obscure notation "Set this value by choosing the Windows NT Advanced Server installation base." Apparently this note was meant for OEM developers compiling NT. Changing the default value of 0 to a 1 means the system should favor the system cache working set over the process working set. This change favors system routines on heavily loaded systems. It gains network and I/O performance at the expense of application performance. Try this entry only if your workstation is heavily used as a peer server.

N O T E   There are four new variables whose meaning and usage were not available at the time this was written. These are PagedPoolQuota, NonPagedPoolQuota, SystemPages, and SecondLevelDataCache. Microsoft recommends leaving these unchanged. Until we can learn more about these variables and what they affect, that advice must stand. ■

If the default value of zero is present for NonPagedPoolSize, NT uses a complex algorithm at startup to calculate the values used. The calculated values are kept in memory and not written to the registry. The calculations are based on physical memory size. The minimum for this setting is 256K. The default maximum is 1M. The minimum is increased by 32K for each increase in memory over the first 4M. The maximum is increased by 400K for each megabyte beyond the first four. The maximum value approximates 80% of physical memory. The algorithm is documented in the Microsoft KnowledgeBase article

Part
III

Ch
9

Q126402 "NonPagedPoolSize and PagedPoolSize Values in Windows NT 3.5". Microsoft warns against changing the default setting.

ON THE WEB

The Microsoft KnowledgeBase can be referenced online:

http://www.microsoft.com/K/

PagedPoolSize is linked to the maximum registry size which can be changed through the Control Panel | System | Performance | Virtual Memory | Change | Maximum Registry Size screens. The maximum registry size is limited to 80% of the PagedPoolSize. The minimum is 256K and the maximum is 128M.

The PagingFiles entry is set through the Control Panel | System | Performance | Virtual Memory | Change screens. If you have multiple drives, put paging areas on all of them. This will give better paging performance, especially if the drives are on different controllers or channels. You must specify a paging file at least as large as your memory on the same drive as the system if you want the system to record a dump when it crashes.

You are restricted in memory upgrade options by the design on your motherboard. Some boards will not allow certain sizes of SIMMs. Eight megabyte and 32M SIMMs are the most common sizes where this happens. You can mix EDO and BEDO memory with Fast Page Mode memory as long as you use only one kind in each bank. Your system restricts the memory configurations to certain combinations. Often you are required to fill banks in pairs of the same size. If multiple sizes are used, the larger sizes usually must occupy the lower-numbered banks. Refer to your motherboard manual for this information.

Optimizing Virtual Memory Use

There are a few things you can adjust to make the most of the virtual memory you have. Once you have sized your memory and removed any bottlenecks, NT will automatically optimize performance within the hardware constraints. You can influence performance by your choice of paging devices.

Pagefile Size

The total minimum size of your swapfile should be the amount you normally use. You can get this number by multiplying the average % Committed Bytes In Use (refer to fig. 9.3) by the average Commit Limit (refer to fig. 9.6). If you don't have performance numbers, use the total recommended minimum size shown in the Control Panel | System | Performance | Virtual Memory screen.

Set the maximum size to 120% of your maximum swapfile usage. This provides a safety margin. Running out of swapfile space can be disruptive. If you have plenty of disk space, increase the maximum swapfile size and periodically check the percentage in use.

Paging Device

NT optimizes paging by process. You can do global optimization. Use the fastest disk drive on your system for your paging files. Paging files do not need to be recoverable in the event of a system crash. You can increase performance by using stripe sets without parity.

▶ **See** "Detecting and Clearing Disk Bottlenecks," **p. 224**

▶ **See** "Detecting and Clearing Disk Bottlenecks," **p. 224**

Disk access has three distinct components: Seek, Search and Transfer (Read or Write). Seek is the process of moving the heads to the cylinder containing the data and consumes the greatest amount of time. The average seek time is the number you see when a disk is advertised as having "10 millisecond access time." Search time is the time spent waiting for the disk to rotate the requested data to the read/write head. It averages about one half the time it takes a disk to make one rotation. The smallest figure is the transfer time. It runs from 5M per second for SCSI 1 to 40M per second for Fast Ultra Wide SCSI 3. You can't do anything about Search and Transfer time without replacing your disk drive. You can minimize seek time.

Part of performance tuning on mainframe systems and virtual memory systems is the placement of the swapfile. The swapfile is placed at the center of the physical disk to mini-mize the distance the heads would have to be moved for a given set of random seeks. You can still do this even though file location is handled by NT.

Once you have determined the maximum size of your swapfile, partition the disk into three partitions. Add 10% to the maximum size of the swapfile to get the swap partition size. Subtract the swap partition size from the total partition size. Divide the remaining partition size by two to get the size of the partitions that will not be used for swapfiles. Allocate one non-swap partition, then the swap partition, then the other non-swap parti-tion. This will place your swap partition roughly in the middle of the disk. Use the other two partitions for low activity files such as help files and historical archives.

Disk performance has a great effect on virtual memory speed once you start paging. If your disk is slower than 15 millisecond access or has a transfer rate of less than 10M per second, you should consider replacing it. Enhanced IDE mode 3 provides 11.1M per sec-ond transfer and SCSI 2 provides 20M/second.

One way to speed up swapfile activity is by placing swapfiles on physical disks that are on separate controller cards or separate channels on one card. This allows the I/O's to over-lap each other. You will also benefit from segregating heavily used program and data files

Part
III

Ch
9

from paging files. SCSI disks provide some degree of concurrent operation as they can operate simultaneously. An additional level of concurrent performance is provided by multiple controllers or controllers with multiple channels. These provide overlap for data transfer and other operations that tie up the channel.

Examining System Resource Issues

Limited resources force you to carefully look at alternatives that will make the best use of what is available. The following section discusses both current and future system considerations.

Resource Trade-offs

NT's design as a self-tuning system using flat memory mode prevents you from making the tweaks used so effectively on other systems. Since there is no distinction between the first megabyte and the remaining memory, there are no Upper Memory Blocks and no High Memory Area. Memory managers such as Himem.sys and Qemm are not needed to squeeze code and data into the crevices in the A000-EFFF area. NT just allocates another page.

You can adjust a couple of resource settings. One of these is adjusted through the Control Panel | System Properties | Performance panel (see fig. 9.25). You can bias the system towards foreground activities if you are running large compiles or other similar work. The middle setting works fine most of the time.

FIG. 9.25

This slider is the only Performance change you can make directly.

The Desktop Application heap problem mentioned in KnowledgeBase article Q126962 has been corrected by returning to the settings used in NT 3.1. This problem caused Out Of Memory errors even though plenty of physical and pagefile memory were available.

Other resource settings that you can adjust were covered under "Clearing Memory Bottlenecks".

Cost Recovery for Memory Upgrades

A memory upgrade can repay its cost in a short time. As of the time this book was written, memory prices were extremely low with 16M 70ns Fast Page Mode SIMMs selling for $150 or less.

Suppose that you have a worker earning $15 an hour using a 12M machine that constantly writes to the paging file. Assume that this person creates large documents and has to scroll back and forth 20 times an hour. If each scroll takes 30 seconds with 12M and 2 seconds with 16M, you would save 10 seconds per scroll or 40 seconds an hour. Assuming 6 hours of productive work per day, this amounts to 4 minutes a day or $1.00. If the 4M cost $40, 40 days use would pay for the upgrade. This does not even consider the fact the worker would be less likely to lose a train of thought while waiting for the scrolling.

Adjust the figures to fit your situation and current prices. You'll find that relieving memory bottlenecks usually makes good business sense.

A Look to the Future

Now that you've worked your way through a lot of tedious analysis, it's time for some fun. PC technology constantly changes at an incredibly rapid rate. Here's a look at some of the new technologies and a discussion of their impact on memory and memory performance.

In addition to the various types of DRAM discussed earlier, there are multiple kinds of video RAM and some new types of memory that are used for both main RAM and for video RAM.

Video RAM (VRAM) is memory that is dual-ported to allow multiple read and write operations to occur simultaneously on graphics cards. Windows RAM (WRAM) is also dual-ported and performs up to 50% faster than VRAM at a cost of 20% less per bit.

Rambus' DRAM (RDRAM) and MoSYS's Multibanked DRAM (MDRAM) are contenders for both video and main RAM. MDRAM contains 32 independent DRAMs with bank caching. It can deliver 800M per second at 64 bits wide and 100MHz. RDRAM can transfer a byte every 2ns at 250MHz. When organized into two 8-bit channels, it can reach 1,000M per second. These speeds exceed those provided by currently shipping cache and may eliminate the need for it.

Intel has announced the MMX extensions for the Pentium CPU series. (Intel says MMX is not an acronym for Multi-Media eXtensions or anything else.) These extensions will enhance the multimedia capabilities of future machines.

Specifications for a new ATX motherboard to replace the popular AT motherboard are available, and some vendors are building and shipping these boards. This board design rearranges components and provides better CPU cooling as well as providing a standard set of multimedia connectors.

There are also two new I/O bus designs. One of these is the Universal Serial Bus (USB) and the other is the IEEE-1394 High Performance Serial Bus. The IEEE-1394 bus standard is based on the Apple design called FireWire. The sexy name FireWire is commonly used even when the IEEE standard is meant. USB and FireWire are really complementary more than competing.

The USB bus will allow one type of connector on serial devices and allow them to be daisy-chained or connected to intermediate hub controllers in a star configuration. USB will allow up to 127 devices to be connected to a single PC.

FireWire is designed to support high performance multimedia devices such as two channels of full-motion video and CD-quality stereo audio. FireWire can directly connect up to 63 devices. Like the USB, FireWire allows the use of hubs to connect devices. Future versions of FireWire are expected to deliver up to 1.2Gb per second.

Disk drives are being made in ever larger capacities. Seagate has announced a 23Gb drive. You can expect others to follow soon.

What do all these developments mean? Look at what we have: very fast, high capacity memory; very fast CPUs that can be extended to use huge page sizes; enhanced multimedia; and lots of powerful peripherals connected via very fast buses. Obviously, we are looking at machines with huge memories, perhaps a gigabyte or more. Memory will be swapped in and out in huge quantities. Paging and memory management will become even more critical as needs jump by megabytes even as prices continue to decline. These new developments will need a powerful operating system to control everything. You'll probably see a lot of this come together with the Cairo version of NT.

ON THE WEB

Home page for Universal Serial Bus:
http://www.teleport.com/~usb/

A good write-up on FireWire:
http://www.skipstone.com/compcon.html

ATX motherboard specs:
http://www.intel.com/pc-supp/motherbd/atx.htm

From Here...

You learned about optimizing memory for performance in this chapter. Other chapters in this book cover other aspects of performance:

- Chapter 8, "Monitoring Performance," details how to best use the performance monitor.

- Chapter 10, "Optimizing the File System," covers directly-related topics such as detecting and clearing disk bottlenecks.

- Chapter 12, "Optimizing CPU Performance," lets you find out if you really need that new CPU.

- Chapter 13, "Enhancing Video and I/O Performance," helps you determine if your video card is slowing your system.

Part
III

Ch
9

Optimizing the File System

by Jim Boyce

As operating systems and applications alike have become larger, the need for quick disk access has become increasingly important. Our expanding reliance on multitasking has put an even bigger strain on disk performance—swapping between programs often means paging programs and data to disk. With all the demands on the disk, the disk can quickly become the weak link in your system's performance chain. Optimizing the disk's performance can, in many cases, have a noticeable impact on the system's performance.

This chapter examines disk performance and explains how to test for and overcome disk and cache bottlenecks. One of the first questions you'll face when beginning the process of optimizing your disk is whether to choose the FAT or NTFS file systems. ■

FAT and NTFS file systems

Choosing between these two file systems hinges on many issues, including disk size, performance, and security.

Disk performance

Several factors contribute to general file system performance, including disk and cluster size, file system type, and application.

Cache and disk bottlenecks

Testing, fine-tuning, and increasing available memory can have a marked impact on cache and disk performance.

FAT or NTFS: Which is Best for You?

You have two choices when deciding which file system you'll use on your Windows NT computer—FAT and NTFS. Each offers certain advantages and disadvantages. Although performance is an important consideration, you probably need to consider other issues, such as security. The following sections will help you understand the FAT and NTFS file systems so you can decide which is right for your situation.

A Brief Overview of Disk Structure

Before delving into the mysteries of file systems, you need to know how a disk is structured in order to understand how disk space is allocated in each file system. A hard disk, the most common storage medium, consists of multiple platters that are coated with a magnetically-sensitive material. The platters spin on a common spindle as one unit (see fig. 10.1).

FIG. 10.1
A disk consists of cylinders, tracks, and sectors.

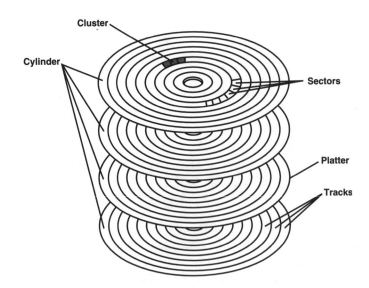

Each side of each platter has a read-write head that reads the magnetically encoded data from the disk and writes data to the disk. The heads move radially across the surface of the disk, enabling the heads to scan the entire disk surface as it spins.

As a head sits motionless over a spinning platter, the circular path it traverses is called a *track*. These circular tracks are magnetically encoded on the disk when the disk is formatted and serve as a means for organizing data on the disk. All the tracks that lie in the same location on each platter (the first track on each platter, for example) form a *cylinder*.

Each track is divided into *sectors*, with the number of sectors in each track depending on the type of disk and location of the track on the disk. Sectors are the smallest logical storage units on the disk. However, both the FAT and NTFS file systems use a *cluster* as the smallest unit of storage space.

A cluster consists of a given number of sectors. The number of sectors in a cluster depends on the drive type and partition size (see table 10.1). When the operating system allocates space for a disk, it does so by cluster, not by sector. As you'll learn in the section "Clearing Up the Bottleneck," the number of sectors in a cluster can have a significant impact on the amount of free space on the disk.

Table 10.1 Clusters and Sectors Relationships

Type of Disk	Cluster Size (in bytes)	Sectors per Cluster
3 1/2" floppy	1,024	2
1.2M floppy	512	1
0 to 15M partition*	4,096	8
16 to 127M partition*	2,048	4
128 to 255M partition*	4,096	8
256 to 511M partition*	8,192	16
512M to <1G partition*	16,384	32
1G or more*	32,768	64

Also applies to similarly sized disks consisting of a single partition and to logical drives in an extended partition.

A hard disk contains one or more *partitions*, which consist of a series of clusters. Partitions provide a means to organize the disk into logical drives represented by a drive letter, such as C or D. Each partition comprises a beginning sector and ending sector, with the number of sectors in between defining the capacity of the partition. Partitions also serve to separate one file system from another. If your system contains both the FAT and NTFS file systems, each will reside in its own partition.

Overview of the FAT File System

The FAT file system takes its name from the File Allocation Table (FAT), which is used to maintain information about disk space allocation (more on the actual FAT later in this section). The FAT file system has evolved within the DOS operating system to its present state, and is used by DOS and Windows 95 systems, as well as Windows NT.

A disk formatted with the FAT file system contains four control areas. The first of these areas is the *reserve area*, which is comprised of one or more sectors, depending on the type of disk. The boot sector is the first sector in the reserve area and contains the partition table and bootstrap program. The partition table contains information about the partitions on the disk, including the type of partition, starting and ending sector, which partition is active, and other information. The bootstrap program executes when the system starts and is responsible for booting the operating system in the active partition.

The second control area is the FAT. The FAT essentially is a reference table that maintains a list of clusters on the disk. The value of each cluster entry in the FAT records the status of the associated disk cluster. Table 10.2 lists possible FAT cluster entries.

Table 10.2   Possible FAT Cluster Entries

Entry	Meaning
0	Cluster is available
BAD	Cluster contains bad sector and can't be used
Reserved	Cluster has been set aside for use only by the operating system
EOF	Marks the last cluster of a file
### (numbers)	Number identifying the next cluster in the file

The *root directory table*, which is the third control area of the disk, works in conjunction with the FAT. The root directory table contains the names of files in the root directory, including subdirectories (which are really nothing more than files), and the starting cluster of each file.

N O T E   The fourth control area is the files area in which file data is stored. ■

Consider an example to understand how the FAT works: Assume you use WordPad to open a file named Foo.txt located in the root directory. The operating system reads the root directory table to find the starting cluster of the file, which in this example we'll assume is cluster 300. The operating system reads the data in cluster 300. Then, it reads the cluster entry in the FAT for cluster 300 and finds the value 301, which is the next cluster in the file. So, the operating system reads the data from cluster 301.

Next, the FAT entry for cluster 301 is read and the value turns out to be 320, the next cluster in the file. The operating system reads the data from cluster 320, then reads the cluster entry in the FAT for cluster 320 to find out where to go next. The entry for cluster 320 reads EOF, indicating that cluster 320 was the last cluster in the file.

> **N O T E** Originally, FAT entries consisted of 12 bits. DOS 4.0 introduced a 16-bit FAT to enable the FAT to accommodate a larger number of cluster entries, and thus, larger disks. The new FAT32 installable file system supported by the latest OEM release of Windows 95 increases the FAT to 32 bits, further increasing the number of available clusters and possible disk size.
>
> As of this writing, Microsoft has not incorporated FAT32 into Windows NT. It is very likely that FAT32 support will be made available for Windows NT in the near future. ■

Although the FAT file system can be difficult to understand at first, it's a very logical, orderly way to track data. NTFS is equally logical and orderly, but completely different in design.

Overview of NTFS

NTFS stands for New Technology File System. NTFS was designed specifically for Windows NT and provides features that make it an attractive alternative to the FAT file system.

NTFS is a *recoverable* file system. If the system fails during a file operation, NTFS reconstructs the volume and recovers from the failure. This recovery happens automatically the first time the disk is accessed after a failure, requiring no intervention from you. In addition, NTFS further secures the file system by maintaining redundant copies of critical file system data, enabling it to recover if the data becomes corrupted.

NTFS provides increased security over the FAT file system. With the FAT file system, you can apply security only at the directory level, and that level of security extends to all files and subdirectories within that directory. With Windows NT, however, you can apply security settings on a file-by-file basis. This means you can restrict access to specific files to specific users. In addition to added levels of security, NTFS also provides for detailed transaction auditing.

Another important NTFS feature is its support for fault tolerance such as mirroring drives. If one drive fails, the data is still available and secure on a redundant drive. Windows NT Server supports a full range of fault tolerance options, and Windows NT Workstation supports stripe sets.

▶ **See** "Using a Stripe Set," **p. 230**

NTFS also supports very large disk sizes. While FAT allocates clusters using 16-bit numbers (32-bit numbers for FAT32), NTFS uses 64 bits to number clusters, allowing for 2^{64} clusters—a huge number (more than 16 quintillion). NTFS uses a cluster size of 512 bytes on smaller disks and a maximum cluster size of 4K on large disks. NTFS identifies the clusters on a disk by *logical cluster number*, or LCN. The LCNs simply number the clusters sequentially from the beginning of the volume to its end.

N O T E The Disk Administrator automatically chooses a cluster size when you use it to format a disk, but you can override the default size. For more information, see the section "Using the Disk Administrator" later in this chapter. ▪

NTFS keeps track of the contents of a volume using a relational database called the *master file table*, or MFT. The MFT contains a record for each file and directory (including the MFT) with name, security descriptor, and other attributes for the file. The MFT represents an array of data, with rows in the array representing file records and columns representing attribute fields for each record (see fig. 10.2). The size of each MFT file record is constant and is set when the volume is formatted. Depending on the disk, the size is either 1K, 2K, or 4K.

FIG. 10.2

The MFT is a relational database that maintains the NTFS volume structure.

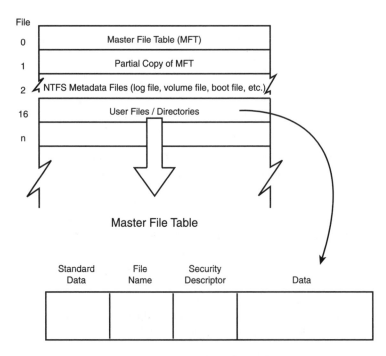

MFT Record for a Small File

One of the fields in the MFT for each file record is the Data field. For a small file, the Data field contains the file's data, which means that a small file can be contained completely within one MFT record. As a file's attributes increase in number (such as the file becoming larger) or the file becomes greatly fragmented, multiple records are needed in the MFT to contain the file. When a file spans multiple records, the primary record that stores the location of the others is called the *base file record*. In some ways, the base file record is like the directory record for a file under the FAT file system because it defines the starting point in the file's data chain.

When all of a file's attributes (including its data) resides in the MFT, the attributes are called *resident attributes*. All but the smallest files, however, will not fit in an MFT record. With these files, NTFS creates additional 2K-sized areas on the disk called *runs* to contain the additional data. (On a volume with a 4K cluster size, the run is 4K in size since a cluster is the smallest unit of storage NTFS can allocate.) Attributes stored in runs are called *nonresident attributes* because they don't reside in the MFT. As the file's attributes grow, NTFS simply adds additional runs to the file as needed.

In one way, FAT and NTFS are similar. Because NTFS stores file data in runs outside the MFT and those runs could be non-contiguous, NTFS needs some means of locating all the runs for a file in sequence. This is no different from the FAT in which the cluster entries in the FAT point to the file's subsequent clusters. The implementation in NTFS is different, however.

The clusters in a file are referenced by *virtual cluster number*, or VCN. The VCN simply numbers the clusters in the file starting with 0 and moving up to the last cluster in the file. The data attribute of the file in the MFT contains information that maps the logical cluster numbers with the virtual cluster numbers (see fig.10.3). If there are too many LCN-to-VCN cluster mappings to store in one MFT record, other MFT records are added to accommodate the additional mappings.

Part

III

Ch

10

FIG. 10.3

For large files, NTFS stores data in multiple runs with the MFT record defining the LCN-to-VCN mapping.

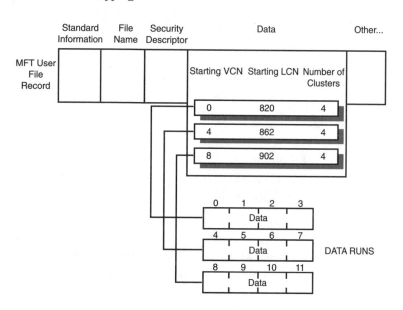

Comparing FAT and NTFS

You can see from the previous two sections that FAT and NTFS are architecturally quite different. The differences between the two file systems are most evident to the average user, however, in the features and characteristics exhibited by each (or lack thereof). In many respects, the two are identical in function. Both provide a stable, reliable file system, for example. The differences, advantages, and disadvantages in FAT and NTFS can be distilled to the following primary issues:

- Performance
- Robustness and Reliability
- Compatibility
- Security

Performance From the previous discussion about the architectural differences between the FAT and NTFS file systems, you might have come to the conclusion that the NTFS file system is more complex than FAT. Essentially, that conclusion is true. NTFS supports greater security and reliability, and these features can generate a performance overhead that on some systems can be noticeable. For the vast majority of users, however, any performance overhead caused by NTFS will be minimal and scarcely noticeable, if at all.

Performance becomes a more critical issue in large database transactions and certain other types of file I/O, including dealing with very large data files. In these situations, the performance overhead caused by NTFS can affect throughput.

Robustness and Reliability NTFS is by far more robust and reliable than FAT. NTFS' ability to recover the file system after system failures or transaction failures can be critical to many users. The fault tolerant options supported by NTFS are further reasons why NTFS is a good choice for network servers.

Compatibility Compatibility becomes an issue only on multi-boot systems that retain a DOS or Windows 95 operating system along with Windows NT. The FAT file system is usable by all three operating systems, but NTFS is usable only by Windows NT. Therefore, if you create an NTFS partition, you won't be able to access that partition when running DOS or Windows 95 on your machine.

File compression also figures into the compatibility equation on multi-boot systems. If your system contains a DriveSpace or DoubleSpace compressed volume that you use under DOS or Windows 95, you won't be able to access that volume under Windows NT because Windows NT supports neither compression utility. If Windows NT is your only operating system, or you choose to create an NTFS partition on a multi-boot system, you can use NTFS' compression mechanism on the NTFS partition.

Security Security is probably the most common reason for choosing NTFS over FAT. Although you can protect a FAT volume through Windows NT's security database on a user-by-user basis, the levels of security you can apply are not as comprehensive as with NTFS. In addition, you can apply permissions only to directories on a FAT file system, not to specific files as you can with NTFS.

Making Your Choice

The situations in which you would choose one file system over another are fairly clear:

- **Compression.** If you need to take advantage of disk compression under Windows NT to provide the most possible disk space, choose NTFS.

- **Multiple Operating Systems.** If you're running either DOS or Windows 95 on your system in addition to Windows NT, and will need to access all files on the system from either operating system, choose FAT. If you don't need to access the files in the NTFS volume when running DOS or Windows 95, use FAT and NTFS volumes, placing in the FAT volume all files you'll need to access from DOS or Windows 95. You'll be able to access all files from Windows NT.

You might decide to place Windows NT in an NTFS partition, along with any applications that run only under Windows NT. The other applications that you use under both Windows 95 (or DOS / Windows 3.x) and Windows NT can go in the FAT volume. Notice, however, that you'll have to double-install many of the applications you use in both operating systems.

Assume you're using Microsoft Office version 7.0, which runs under both Windows 95 and Windows NT. You would first install Office under Windows 95 in a FAT volume. Then, you would boot Windows NT and install Office again in the same folder on the FAT volume. You have only one copy of all the Office files, but the necessary settings to run Office have been added to both your Windows 95 and Windows NT registries. Applications that don't require registry entries typically can run on both operating systems without requiring installation under both operating systems.

- **Security.** If you need the highest degree possible of security for your file system, choose NTFS. I highly recommend NTFS for network servers. Not only will you gain additional levels of security, but you can implement security auditing of folders and files.

- **Performance.** Performance overhead really applies only to systems that require the fastest possible file system I/O, such as large databases. Unfortunately, many such systems require the additional security and robustness provided by NTFS. If performance is your greatest concern, consider using FAT on drives smaller than 1G. If you're willing to accept a small trade-off in performance, you should choose

NTFS because of its robustness and security. For drives over 1G, NTFS typically provides better performance than FAT.

■ **Reliability and Robustness**. For the most part, FAT is not a recoverable file system unless you're implementing various levels of RAID on the system and including the FAT volume(s). If reliability and recoverability are important factors, your best choice is NTFS.

Overview of File Systems and Performance

Many factors related to both hardware and software affect file system performance, and good performance doesn't include only speed. Efficient use of disk space is also a very real facet of overall file system performance. This section of the chapter examines general performance issues that include hardware options and tips for optimizing the disk's storage space.

Controller/Drive Options

Today's hard disk technology has been condensed into three primary choices: IDE, EIDE, and SCSI. Older technologies including MFT and ESDI have largely been replaced. The following sections explore the three most common options for disk technology.

IDE   IDE stands for Integrated Drive Electronics and refers to the fact that the majority of the controller hardware is incorporated directly on the hard disk, rather than residing in the system on an adapter card. Disk systems that incorporate the controller hardware on the drive are called embedded controllers. In these types of disk subsystems, a host adapter serves as an intermediary between the controller electronics on the disk and the CPU. The IDE host adapter actually does very little except provide a conduit through which the controller circuitry on the drive can access the PC's bus.

The term IDE is used generically to specify a disk interface, but technically applies to any type of embedded controller disk subsystem, including SCSI (explored later in this chapter). What the industry generally refers to as IDE drives are correctly termed AT Attachment, or ATA interface drives. The IDE term has stuck, however, and these types of drives are now known by that term.

The Case for Embedded Controllers

While you might think that adding the controller circuitry to the drive increases its complexity and would logically increase the cost for embedded controller disk subsystems, integrating the controller on the drive improves performance and actually reduces overall cost. When the controller circuitry is located on an external bus card, the controller must include additional components to handle the electrical noise to which the data signals are susceptible as they travel along the cable between the adapter and the drive. Marrying the controller to the drive also reduces the total number of components needed, which ultimately reduces costs.

Placing the controller circuitry on the drive also makes the drive more reliable, primarily because all data encoding occurs on the drive where electrical noise can be carefully controlled. The drive designers also have much more flexibility in designing how the controller and drive itself interact. This means they can incorporate new technologies and speed up the drive's performance without being constrained by supporting an external standard. As long as the drive/controller combination can communicate in a standard fashion through the host adapter to the CPU, it doesn't matter what technical wizardry goes on inside the drive's controller. Because both IDE and SCSI use embedded controller technology, these two disk subsystem types have become the most common and represent the vast majority of systems in use today.

Standard implementation of IDE is limited to support for no more than two hard disks. In systems with two drives, one drive serves as a *master* and the other as a *slave*. Contrary to its name, however, the master drive does not control the slave drive. The only function the master drive assumes for the slave is signal coding. In all other respects, the master and slave drives are equal.

Each IDE drive includes a jumper by which you configure the drive for either master or slave status. Drives generally ship from the factory configured as master drives, so if you add a second IDE drive to your system, you must change the jumper setting to configure the drive as a slave. The documentation that comes with the drive will explain how to set the jumper accordingly. IDE drives do not require termination as do SCSI drives.

N O T E IDE host adapters that support four drives are available. These host adapters essentially place two separate IDE chains on one adapter, with each chain containing a master and a slave. The host adapter's on-board BIOS handles the necessary translation between the drives and the bus to enable the four drives to be supported. ■

Each IDE drive is limited to no more than 504M because of the way the interface addresses the drives' sectors, and this is the primary limitation of IDE. Another limitation is the lack of support for devices other than hard disks (such as CD-ROM drives or tape drives) under IDE. As for performance, you can expect a throughput of from 3.3M to 8.3M per second from an IDE drive (theoretically).

EIDE Enhanced IDE (EIDE) overcomes the limitations of standard IDE. EIDE, more correctly known as the ATA-2 specification (an extension of the ATA specification), supports drives larger than 504M. It does so by using a different method to address physical disk sectors. The 504M limitation of IDE is due to the limit on the number of cylinders, sectors, and heads supported by the IDE interface. EIDE overcomes this limitation by translating physical drive geometry to virtual drive geometry. If the drive contains 2,000 cylinders and 16 heads (more than the 1,024 cylinders accommodated by IDE), the BIOS on the drive translates those numbers to 1,000 cylinders and 32 heads. The operating system is happy because it can accommodate the number of cylinders the drive appears to have. In effect, the drive fools the operating system into thinking it's dealing with a standard IDE drive.

N O T E EIDE requires support in your system BIOS, so installing an EIDE drive in your system is no guarantee it will work properly. Most BIOSes manufactured after 1994 support EIDE. Run your BIOS setup program and look for IDE settings such as LBA, CHS, ECHS, Normal, and/or Large. These settings typically indicate that the BIOS supports EIDE drive translation. If you determine that your BIOS doesn't support EIDE, you should be able to get a BIOS update from your system's manufacturer or the BIOS developer. ■

In addition to supporting larger drives, EIDE also provides potentially much higher data transfer rates. The ATA and ATA-2 (IDE and EIDE) specifications support four I/O modes called *Programmed I/O* (PIO) modes. The ATA specification supports modes 0 through 2, and ATA-2 supports modes 0 through 4. Table 10.3 lists the PIO modes and theoretical transfer rates for each.

Table 10.3   Transfer Modes Supported by ATA and ATA-2

Mode	Transfer Rate (MB/s)	Specification
0	3.3	ATA
1	5.2	ATA
2	8.3	ATA
3	11.1	ATA-2
4	16.6	ATA-2

In addition to a considerable boost in transfer rate, EIDE offers other advantages over the IDE specification. EIDE supports devices other than hard drives. You can connect IDE format CD-ROM drives and tape drives to the same interface as your hard disks. Not only does this involve fewer adapters and lower costs, but you'll enjoy better performance from an IDE interface tape drive over a drive that connects to your floppy controller. IDE CD-ROM drives typically perform at the same level as SCSI CD-ROM drives.

N O T E Most new motherboards incorporate the IDE controller directly on the motherboard, and these typically offer two IDE chains via two separate connectors on the motherboard. ■

SCSI The third option for a disk subsystem is SCSI (pronounced "scuzzy"), which stands for Small Computer System Interface. Like IDE and EIDE, SCSI uses embedded controller technology, placing the controller circuitry on the disk. SCSI actually defines a bus specification, rather than a disk interface specification.

The standard SCSI bus supports eight devices on the bus, one of which is the SCSI host adapter, which serves to translate the signals on the SCSI bus to and from the computer's bus (and the CPU). The seven other devices on the bus can be any combination of hard disks, scanners, CD-ROM or CD-R drives, tape drives, or other SCSI devices. Each device is assigned a number that identifies the device's logical location on the bus and enables the adapter to communicate with the device. Lower numbers are typically assigned to higher-priority devices such as hard disks (a boot SCSI hard drive is given LUN 0, for example).

One of the primary advantages of SCSI devices is their portability across systems. The same SCSI scanner you connect to an Intel-based PC can connect to a Macintosh, PowerPC, or Alpha system, as well as any other controlling device or system that is designed to use SCSI devices.

Part
III

Ch
10

One disadvantage to SCSI, however, is the lack of standards, even though SCSI is defined by standards. A driver for one SCSI host adapter typically won't work for another because the manufacturer has implemented the bus differently. Therefore, SCSI requires driver support on an adapter-by-adapter basis (unlike IDE, in which one driver fits all). Fortunately, Windows NT provides support for all the most commonly used SCSI host adapters, so compatibility should not be a major problem. If you don't yet have a SCSI bus in your system, check the Windows NT Hardware Compatibility List (HCL) included with Windows NT to pick a supported host adapter.

Once you get past any potential compatibility and driver support issues (usually not a problem), SCSI offers significant performance advantages over IDE and EIDE. The original SCSI specification, now called SCSI-1, was approved in 1986. SCSI-1 supports a standard data transfer rate of 5M per second; hardly a stellar performer compared to EIDE. The SCSI-2 standard, approved in 1994, provides for a fast synchronous transfer mode that doubles the transfer speed to 10M per second on 8-bit implementations. The SCSI-2 specification also provides for 16-bit and 32-bit implementations called Wide SCSI, which effectively doubles (or quadruples) the transfer rate. A Fast/Wide SCSI bus, for example, can transfer data at 20M per second—a nice performance jump beyond EIDE's fastest theoretical rate.

The SCSI-3 specification provides even further performance boosts. Products incorporating various aspects of the SCSI-3 specification are now available. The most notable feature of SCSI-3 is support for Fast-20 mode, also known as Ultra-SCSI, which provides data transfer rates of 20M per second on an 8-bit SCSI bus and a whopping 40M per second on a 16-bit SCSI bus.

Choosing a Drive Subsystem The previous three sections should have given you an idea of which disk subsystem is right for you. Most of the new systems in the mass market today incorporate EIDE drives and generally offer performance that equals most SCSI drives. In addition, the IDE drives typically are somewhat cheaper than comparably sized SCSI drives. The performance of a particular IDE drive is closely associated with the drive's design, however, so don't assume that one IDE drive will perform as well as the next.

For the fastest possible performance, you should look to SCSI-3 adapters and devices that support Fast-20 mode. Even if your system already contains an IDE host adapter and drive, you can supplement it with a SCSI bus and drive. Generally, adding a SCSI bus to a system containing an IDE adapter and devices is simply a matter of installing the SCSI host adapter and connecting the devices. Check your SCSI host adapter's installation manual for specific tips on installing the SCSI adapter and drives in a system with IDE drives.

Another reason to choose SCSI over IDE is multitasking. Each SCSI device contains its own controller, and the operating system can address multiple drives at one time. Each device can queue the commands coming from the operating system and perform them at the same time other SCSI devices are performing their queued commands. For example, a SCSI hard drive can be writing data at the same time the CD-ROM drive is reading data. IDE devices can't operate simultaneously like SCSI devices, which puts them at a disadvantage under a multitasking operating system like Windows NT.

Most new PCs will use a PCI bus, and many systems manufactured in the past few years will use a VESA local bus. You'll derive the best performance from a local bus disk adapter, which means you should choose either a VESA or PCI disk host adapter (whichever is appropriate to your system's bus type).

Cluster and Partition Size

Speed is not the only performance consideration for hard drives, particularly when using the FAT file system. The efficiency by which the drive stores data also is important to the drive's overall performance.

As you read earlier in this chapter, FAT and NTFS alike allocate space on the disk by cluster, rather than by sector. Although a sector is the smallest unit of storage space on the disk, a cluster (a group of sectors) is the smallest *allocation* unit. To understand the significance of cluster size, you need to consider an example. (You might want to refer back to table 10.1 for reference to cluster and sector relationships.)

Assume that you're using the FAT file system and store a 60 K file (61,440 bytes). You store the file on a floppy disk, which uses a cluster size of 1,024 bytes (consisting of two 512-byte sectors). Windows NT allocates 60 1K clusters, or 61,440 bytes. That's exactly how much space the file requires, and every sector is chock full of data—not a single crevice is wasted.

Now, you copy that same file to your hard disk, a monster 1G drive that contains one partition. Because you're using the FAT file system on the hard disk, the cluster size is 32,768 bytes, or 64 sectors per cluster. One cluster can't accommodate the whole file, so Windows NT allocates two clusters for a total of 65,536 bytes of storage space, which is 4,096 bytes more than the file requires. This means that eight sectors in one of the clusters are essentially empty and their potential space is wasted. This is often called *sector slack*.

What if you edit the document stored in the file and end up reducing its size to 34,000 bytes? It still won't fit in one cluster, so two are required to hold it. But now, the file is wasting 31,536 bytes of storage space. That's nearly 50 percent waste. If all your files were like that, half of your hard disk would be effectively empty but unavailable.

The actual amount of sector slack for a given file naturally varies according to the size of the file and the drive's cluster size. The first example I gave illustrated a seven percent waste of space. On that 1G drive, that amounts to about 73M wasted. If the files average 20 percent waste, you'd be losing almost 200M of space.

Sector slack and the resulting disk capacity loss are a prime reason for choosing NTFS over FAT. The maximum cluster size in an NTFS volume is 4K, or 4,096 bytes. The most you'll ever waste for any one file on an NTFS system is roughly 4,095 bytes (assuming the final added run for the file contained only one byte of data), a lot less than the potential space lost on a large FAT volume.

If you choose to retain the FAT file system on a drive, consider whether reducing the cluster size will have a positive impact on your disk's capacity. In almost every case, reducing the cluster size will have a noticeable impact on available storage space. It's better to waste half of a 8,192-byte cluster than to waste half of a 32,768-byte cluster.

The cluster size is related to logical drive size, as well as partition size. A PC's hard disk can contain up to four partitions. A primary partition can contain one logical drive. An extended partition, however, can contain multiple logical drives. Each logical drive is subject to the cluster size constraints listed in table 10.1.

N O T E A disk can contain four primary partitions, but can contain only one extended partition. So, the system might contain three primary partitions and one extended partition, for a total of four. An extended partition can, however, contain multiple logical drives. ■

Unfortunately, the only way to change cluster size is to change the size of the partition or logical drive, and the only way to accomplish that is to re-create the partition or delete the logical drive(s) in the partition and re-create them. This means backing up all of the files in the partition, removing the partition, and creating new, smaller partitions or logical drives.

One approach to take if you intend to use FAT for the entire disk is to create a primary partition sized to give you the cluster size you want for that partition, then create an extended partition using all the remaining available space on the disk. You then can create multiple logical drives of the desired size (to achieve the desired cluster size in each drive) in the extended partition. For example, assume you have a 1G drive and want the cluster size to be 4,096 bytes. Create a primary partition of 255M, then create an extended partition with the remaining space. In that extended partition, create four 255M logical drives.

The Disk Administrator is the utility you'll use to remove and create partitions, both for FAT and NTFS file systems. See the section "Using the Disk Administrator" later in this chapter for tips on creating and sizing partitions.

Detecting and Clearing Disk Bottlenecks

Performance tuning a Windows NT system often includes determining whether the disk is creating a performance bottleneck. This section of the chapter explains how to use utilities in Windows NT to monitor disk performance.

Testing Disk Performance

Testing disk performance requires that you use the diskperf utility included with Windows NT. Diskperf is a special performance statistics driver that installs between the file system driver and the disk driver, and enables performance statistics to be gathered for use by the Performance Monitor.

N O T E   Although you can test disk performance dynamically by simply opening folders and executing files, a true test requires reproducible actions. One of the best tools for testing system performance is the Response Probe, which is included with the Microsoft Windows NT Resource Kit. This section assumes you'll be using Response Probe, but because Response Probe is explained in detail in the Windows NT Resource Kit documentation, this chapter doesn't explain its use in detail. Therefore, the focus of this chapter is on the tools included with Windows NT used for disk performance testing. ■

Because the diskperf utility imposes a slight performance overhead, it does not install automatically. Instead, you must start diskperf manually from the Windows NT command prompt. To start diskperf on a local computer, log on as a member of the Administrators group, then open a command prompt and enter the following command:

```
diskperf -y
```

If you want to measure the performance of the disks in a striped set, use the following command to enable the counters:

```
diskperf -e
```

If you want to start diskperf on a remote computer, follow the command with the name of the computer on which you want the utility to start (the computer name Fred is used in this example):

```
diskperf - y \\fred
```

 TIP For a description of the diskperf command options, enter **diskperf /?** at the command prompt.

Chapter 8, "Monitoring Performance," explained how to configure and use Performance Monitor. If you have not yet read Chapter 8, you should do so, as Performance Monitor is a primary tool you can use to track a disk's performance.

The two objects you'll want to pay attention to with Performance Monitor are PhysicalDisk and LogicalDisk. These two objects appear in the Object drop-down list on the Add to Chart dialog box in Performance Monitor along with the other objects you can monitor. The following counters are available under both PhysicalDisk and LogicalDisk:

- *% Disk Read Time*. This counter tracks the percentage of time the drive is busy handling read requests.
- *% Disk Time*. This is the percentage of time the disk is busy handling read or write requests.
- *% Disk Write Time*. This counter tracks the percentage of time the disk is busy handling write requests.
- *% Free Space* (LogicalDisk only). This counter tracks the ratio of available disk space on the disk to the total usable space on the disk.
- *Avg. Disk Bytes/Read.* This counts the average number of bytes transferred during read operations from the disk.
- *Avg. Disk Bytes/Transfer.* This counter identifies the number of bytes that are transferred from the disk during read or write operations.

- *Avg. Disk Bytes/Write.* This counter tracks the number of bytes transferred to the disk during write operations.
- *Avg. Disk Queue Length.* This is the average number of write and read requests queued for the disk.
- *Avg. Disk Read Queue Length.* This counter identifies the average number of read requests queued for the disk.
- *Avg. Disk Sec/Read.* This counter tracks the average time required for a read operation to read data from the disk.
- *Avg. Disk Sec/Transfer.* This counter tracks the average time required for a disk transfer.
- *Avg. Disk Sec/Write.* This counter tracks the average time required for a write operation to write data to the disk.
- *Avg. Disk Write Queue Length.* This counter tracks the average number of write requests queued for the disk.
- *Current Disk Queue Length.* This identifies the number of requests that are waiting in the queue for execution. Any request in progress and not completed is included.
- *Disk Bytes/Sec.* This counter tracks how fast bytes are transferred to and from the disk for both read and write operations.
- *Disk Read Bytes/Sec.* This counter tracks how fast bytes are transferred from the disk during read operations.
- *Disk Reads/Sec.* This counter tracks how fast read operations are accomplished.
- *Disk Transfers/Sec.* This specifies the speed at which read and write operations are accomplished.
- *Disk Write Bytes/Sec.* This specifies the speed at which bytes are transferred to the disk during write operations.
- *Disk Writes/Sec.* This counter specifies the rate of write operations.
- *Free Megabytes* (LogicalDisk only). This counter tracks the amount of unallocated space on the disk.

A glance at the Instance list in the Add to Chart dialog box will show you that you can add a counter for a specific disk, or apply the counter to all disk operations. Adding a counter for a specific disk is appropriate when you're trying to test the performance of a specific physical or logical disk (such as testing FAT performance against NFTS, for example). Adding a counter for total disk activity is useful when testing the performance of a disk controller to which multiple drives are connected. Even in this scenario, however, you might want to track drives individually because unless the drives are identical, their performance figures will likely be different. Using Total will, however, give you an overall view of the disk subsystem's performance.

Also, rather than viewing disk data using a chart, you might find it more helpful to test disk performance with a report. This is because it can be easier to recognize specific values in numeric form rather than graphical form, particularly when the changes from one test session to another are minor.

After you've decided which items you want to track and have appropriately configured the desired chart or report in Performance Monitor, you can start the testing process. Typically, this will include creating a test file of a given size using the createfil utility included with Windows NT. The createfil utility creates a file of the length you specify containing binary zeroes. You specify the file name and size of the file in kilobytes. The following example would create a file named file.dat of 50M:

Part

III

Ch

10

```
createfil file.dat 51200
```

After you've created the test file, you can begin using Response Probe to evaluate disk performance. Response Probe is controlled by a script file that you create, or you can modify one of the sample scripts included with Response Probe.

N O T E The Windows NT 4.0 beta included the createfil utility. However, this utility might be removed from the final release version and made available only through the Windows NT Resource Kit. ■

As documented in the Resource Kit, the structure of a Response Probe script file is clearly defined, with some parameters being required and others optional. The parameters that are required are THINKTIME, CYCLEREADS, FILESEEK, CPUTIME, DATAPAGE, CODEPAGE, and FILEACCESS. The FILEATTRIBUTE, FILEACCESSMODE, RECORDSIZE, and FILEACTION parameters are optional. The following list summarizes the function of the file-related parameters:

- *FILEACCESS.* This parameter is used in the script to specify the name of the file to use for testing. Typically, this will be a file you've created with the **createfil** utility.

- *FILESEEK.* This parameter specifies the mean and standard deviation for locating the record in the file specified by FILEACCESS. In a 2,000-record file, for example, you typically would specify 1,000 to place the mean at the middle of the file.

- *FILEATTRIBUTE.* This optional parameter specifies either random or sequential access on the file specified by FILEACCESS.

■ *FILEACCESSMODE.* This parameter can be set to MAPPED, BUFFERED, or UNBUFFERED. The MAPPED option causes the file to be accessed as an array in memory. The BUFFERED option causes the file to be cached. Using UNBUF-FERED causes the cache to be bypassed.

■ *RECORDSIZE.* This parameter specifies the record size to be used when working with the test file.

■ *FILEACTION.* Use this parameter to specify either read or write actions.

The following sample is a Response Probe script file that causes Response Probe to read a 2,048-byte record from the file testfile.dat 200 times:

```
THINKTIME           0    0      (milliseconds)
CYCLEREADS          100  0      (number)
FILESEEK            0    0      (records)
CPUTIME             0    0      (milliseconds)
DATAPAGE            0    0      (pages)
CODEPAGE            0    0      (pages)
FILEACCESS          testfile.dat    (name)
RECORDSIZE          2048           (default: 4096 bytes)
FILEATTRIBUTE       RANDOM         (R ¦ S)
FILEACCESSMODE      UNBUFFERED     (B ¦ U ¦ M)
FILEACTION          R              (read / write pattern)
```

To test disk response, create your own test file and appropriate script file. Run the test and examine the results. Then, implement various changes as described in the following section, testing after each to determine whether performance is improving or degrading.

Clearing Up the Bottleneck

A number of factors can contribute to overall disk performance, including the amount of memory available. Consider the following as possible options for optimizing disk perfor-mance and eliminating the disk as a performance bottleneck.

Optimizing the Disk Controller The disk controller often is a weak link in the disk subsystem. If you read the earlier section "Overview of File Systems and Performance," you'll recall that disk controllers offer a wide range of performance possibilities. If your system currently uses IDE, a switch to EIDE or SCSI can potentially have a tremendous impact on disk subsystem performance. For example, switching from a standard IDE adapter/disk combination to a SCSI-3 adapter/disk that supports Fast-20 mode could mean a boost from 3.3M per second to as much as 40M per second, which is a truly significant performance boost.

If you're currently using SCSI, you might consider switching to a different SCSI host adapter. For example, you might currently be using an older 8-bit adapter, and could switch to a 32-bit adapter to increase transfer speeds. Before buying the new adapter, however, check with the manufacturer to see if the model of disk you're using will be capable of any increase in performance through a change in host adapter.

Additional RAM Two options are available to you for improving disk performance by adding RAM to the system. First, if your host adapter includes an on-board cache, you might be able to install additional cache RAM on the adapter, providing a larger on-board cache and corresponding performance improvement.

The second option is to increase the amount of general RAM in the system. Windows NT provides a dynamically adaptive cache, which enables the operating system to resize the cache when necessary. When Windows NT determines that a smaller cache is appropriate, it reduces the cache making additional memory available for applications and other processes. When the cache size needs to increase, Windows NT makes it larger, taking RAM away from applications and other processes. By adding more general RAM to the system, you make more memory available not only to accommodate a larger cache, but to provide increased RAM to applications. Adding RAM to the on-board cache only benefits the cache.

DMA Support Some host adapters support direct memory access (DMA) transfers. DMA support enables the host adapter to move data from the controller directly to RAM, bypassing calls to the CPU to handle the task. This not only speeds disk performance but helps reduce the load on the processor, improving overall system performance.

Fragmentation You're probably aware that a disk can become heavily fragmented, which means that files can become scattered across the disk in non-contiguous clusters. Because the files are not stored in contiguous clusters, the heads must move considerably more when reading and writing a file. This fragmentation reduces overall disk performance.

FAT volumes are susceptible to fragmentation. Contrary to common perception, so are NTFS volumes. Just because NTFS is much more efficient in its allocation of disk space (through a much smaller cluster size) doesn't mean that it won't fragment files over time, just like FAT.

Defragmentation is the process of restructuring the disk's contents to restore the contiguity of the files. In essence, defragmentation rewrites the contents of the entire disk so that files are no longer fragmented. Because fragmentation is a natural occurrence and begins to happen again as soon as the disk is defragmented, you should defragment the disk periodically.

Unlike Windows 95, Windows NT doesn't include its own disk defragmenting tool. Instead, you must rely on third-party utilities. Using such a utility on a regular basis, however, will help optimize the performance of FAT as well as NTFS volumes.

Part
III

Ch
10

N O T E Diskeeper by Executive Software is an example of an NTFS-compatible defragmentation utility. ▪

Partition and Drive Size Another issue you should consider when attempting to optimize your disk subsystem's performance is the partition and drive size the drives use, which will determine (under FAT) the cluster size of the partition or logical drive. As explained in the earlier section, "FAT or NTFS: Which is Best for You?" the size of a partition or logical disk in the FAT file system affects the cluster size. Larger cluster sizes can potentially mean considerable lost disk space due to sector slack (unused sectors in allocated clusters). By keeping the cluster size down, you reduce the amount of disk space wasted.

In addition to conserving disk space, reducing the partition or logical drive size has the added benefit of reducing the size of the physical or logical volume. This reduces the number of clusters in the drive, which indirectly reduces the amount of head movement required to access a file in the drive, particularly when the drive becomes fragmented. Searching for file fragments across a drive comprising 1,000 clusters would naturally take longer than searching for those same file fragments within a 500-cluster volume.

Naturally, you'll reach a trade-off between decreased (and more efficient) drive size and the drive's ability to contain all the files you want stored in the drive. Because the trade-off point depends entirely on the types of files with which you work and your desired method of organization, only you can determine an appropriate partition/drive size. Simply keep in mind as you evaluate your system's performance that smaller volumes typically mean better overall performance.

Distributing Disk Load As you know, Windows NT is a multitasking operating system. And as was explained in the section "Choosing a Bus" earlier in this chapter, devices on the SCSI bus can operate concurrently. One drive can perform read operations while a second drive is writing, and so on. The combination of Windows NT's multitasking and SCSI ability to multitask offers the potential for improving disk performance. If you're currently using an IDE disk subsystem, you might consider switching to SCSI and dividing the disk load among multiple disks.

You can also consider taking the idea of distributing disk load one step further by creating a stripe set.

Using a Stripe Set

Windows NT supports various levels of RAID, which stands for Redundant Array of Inexpensive Disks. RAID provides a means of extending disk capability while ensuring fault tolerance. RAID is defined in various levels. These RAID levels are described in table 10.4.

Table 10.4	RAID Levels	
Level	**Windows NT Support**	**Description**
0	Server/Workstation	Disk striping
1	Server	Disk mirroring
2	none	Bit-level striping with error correcting code (ECC)
3	none	Byte-level striping with ECC as parity
4	none	Block striping with parity blocks on a single drive
5	Server	Block striping with parity across multiple drives
6	none	Adds a second level of parity to RAID level 5
10	none	Layers together RAID levels 0 and 1
53	none	Layers together RAID levels 0 and 3

Part
III

Ch
10

Windows NT Server directly supports three levels of RAID in software, and Windows NT Workstation supports one. Other levels, however, can be supported through hardware.

RAID provides fault tolerance by distributing the file system(s) across multiple drives. The data is structured on the drives such that if one drive fails, no data is lost and the system can remain up. In many implementations, the drives are hot-swappable, which means they can be replaced without shutting down the system. So if a drive goes bad, the system administrator can replace it without shutting down the server. Users never know that anything went wrong.

Windows NT Workstation supports RAID level 0, which provides for data striping. *Striping* enables the file system to be interleaved across multiple physical disks that share the same characteristics. Each of the disks operates independently, so data can be read and written to multiple disks concurrently. Theoretically, this means that overall file system performance is directly related to the number of drives in the array. For n drives in the array, data transfers occur at $1/n$ compared to a single-drive configuration. If the system is using four drives, for example, the data can be transferred in 1/4 the time compared to a single drive. Actual performance is dependent on additional factors, but the system definitely will show a significant performance boost.

CAUTION

Windows NT Workstation supports only RAID level 0, which does not provide for fault tolerance through parity checking. RAID level 0 provides only improved file system performance, but doesn't add redundancy. Neither does a single-drive configuration for a FAT or NTFS file system. Therefore, using a stripe set does not put your file system in any more jeopardy of a hardware failure than not using a stripe set. If you need the increased data security offered by fault tolerance in other RAID levels, you need to consider either Windows NT Server or a hardware solution that will provide fault tolerance under Windows NT Workstation.

You create a stripe set using the Disk Administrator. Creating a stripe set is explained in the later section "Using the Disk Administrator."

Using a Volume Set

In addition to supporting stripe sets, Windows NT Workstation also supports *volume sets*. A volume set is a single logical volume consisting of space on as many as 32 disks. Volume sets enable you to collect scattered, unequal-sized areas of space on the disk into a single, logical drive. The primary advantages of volume sets are that they enable you to create disks larger than the largest physical disk in the system, as well as make use of sometimes small amounts of leftover space on the disk that might otherwise be too small to be of real use.

Unlike stripe sets, volume sets do not have a major impact on disk performance. Instead, they provide a means for more effective, flexible use of disk space. The disadvantage is that like stripe sets, volume sets offer no redundancy. If one drive involved in a volume set fails, the entire volume will be lost.

You create and manage volume sets with the Disk Administrator. See the section "Creating a Volume Set" later in this chapter for instructions on how to create and manage a volume set.

Using the Disk Administrator

The Disk Administrator is the utility through which most of your drive-level file system management will occur. With Disk Administrator, you can create partitions, format drives, create stripe sets, and perform other drive-related tasks. Figure 10.4 shows the Disk Administrator interface.

FIG. 10.4
Disk Administrator offers different ways to view and manage disk resources. Here, the Volumes view is used.

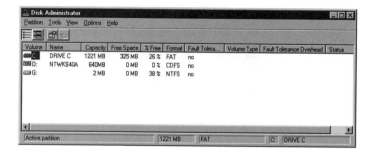

Overview of Disk Administrator

Disk Administrator is located under the Start menu in Programs/Administrative Tools (Common). When you start Disk Administrator, it displays all of the hard drives and removable drives (such as CD-ROM drives) in the system. Indicated for each drive is the capacity and type of the drive, as well as its volume label (if any) and drive letter assignment. Any free space on the drive not used by a partition appears as a shaded area (see fig. 10.5).

Part

III

Ch

10

FIG. 10.5
Disk Administrator identifies unpartitioned space as well as partitioned space on the disk.

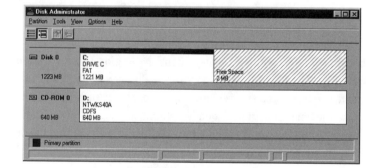

You can switch Disk Administrator between Disk Configuration view (shown in fig. 10.5) and Volumes view (see fig. 10.6). While the Disk Configuration view shows unpartitioned space, the Volume view shows only partitioned volumes, although Volume view does show unformatted partitions. Select the type of view you want from Disk Administrator's View menu. Or, you can press Ctrl+V for Volume view or Ctrl+D for Disk Configuration view.

You can further control Disk Administrator's display through the Options menu. Choosing Options, Disk Display enables you to select between having Disk Administrator display disks based on their size or sizing them equally. This selection determines the size of the box in which Disk Administrator shows the information about a drive in Disk Configuration view. It has no effect on the actual size of the drive itself. In figure 10.7, all disks have been sized equally.

FIG. 10.6
Volume view shows all
partitioned volumes,
even if the volumes
are not yet formatted.

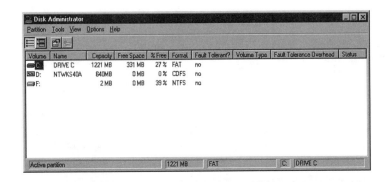

FIG. 10.7
Disk Administrator has
been configured to
show all drives the
same size.

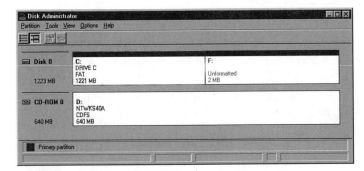

Choosing Options, Region Display opens the Region Display Options dialog box shown in figure 10.8. The Region Display Options dialog box enables you to control how Disk Administrator shows the size relationship for each partition/logical disk on a drive. If you choose the Size All Regions Equally option, each logical drive is shown using the same size box within the drive's overall box. Choosing the Size Regions Based on Actual Size option causes Disk Administrator to size the box for each logical drive proportionally to its capacity. You can apply the size selection method to a specific drive or to all drives using the two options in the Which Disk group of controls.

FIG. 10.8
Use the Region Display
Options dialog box to
control how large each
partition/logical drive
appears in the display.

N O T E If a drive contains logical disks or partitions of considerably different size, choosing the Size Regions Based on Actual Size option could cause the smaller partitions/ logical disks to effectively disappear. To make them reappear, choose the Size All Regions Equally option. Also, notice that the controls in the Disk Display Options dialog box control how the separate drives' appearances compare to one another, while the controls in the Region Display Options dialog box control how the regions within a drive appear compared to other regions in the same drive. ■

When using the Disk Configuration view, you also have the option of specifying different colors and patterns for these objects:

- ■ Primary partition
- ■ Logical drive
- ■ Stripe set
- ■ Stripe set with parity
- ■ Mirror set
- ■ Volume set

Part

III

Ch

10

To specify color or pattern preferences, choose Options, Colors and Patterns to display the Colors and Patterns dialog box (see fig. 10.9).

FIG. 10.9
Use the Colors and Patterns dialog box to control the appearance of regions and disks in the Disk Configuration view.

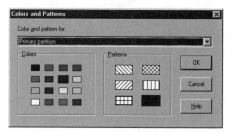

In addition to the options already explained, you can customize Disk Administrator's toolbar. To customize the toolbar to your preferences, choose Options, Customize Toolbar to display the Customize Toolbar dialog box (see fig. 10.10).

FIG. 10.10
Add, remove, and rearrange objects in the toolbar using the Customize Toolbar dialog box.

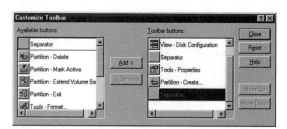

To add a button to the toolbar, select the desired button from the Available Buttons list, then click Add. To remove a button from the toolbar, select the button from the Toolbar Buttons list, then click Remove. To change the order of the buttons in the toolbar, select the button you want to move and click either the Move Up or Move Down button. When you're satisfied with the new toolbar arrangement, click Close.

Committing Disk Changes

Many of the disk changes you make with Disk Administrator are not applied immediately. Instead, you must *commit* these changes to the disk. For example, you can create or delete a partition, but until you commit the changes, the disk is unaffected. If you exit Disk Administrator without committing the changes, the disk reverts to its original state.

N O T E Disk Administrator will prompt to remind you when you exit the program if you have not committed changes. ■

To commit changes you have made to a disk, choose Partition, Commit Changes Now.

Working with Partitions

A *partition* is an area on a disk that has been designated as a logical storage area. The partition comprises a linear set of sectors, beginning at a specific sector and ending at a specific sector. A drive can contain a maximum of four partitions, although most drives can consist of only one partition. A drive can contain one to four *primary partitions*, or up to three primary partitions and one *extended partition*.

A primary partition can contain a single logical drive, which is a storage area recognized by the operating system by a drive letter, such as C or D. An extended partition can contain multiple logical drives, enabling you to break up the space in the extended partition into different logical storage areas. You might create a primary partition as drive C, for example, and then create an extended partition containing logical drives D, E, F, and G.

An extended partition is not limited to a single file system. You can create both FAT and NTFS file systems within an extended partition. You first create the extended partition, create multiple logical drives in the partition, and then format each logical drive according to the file system you want on it.

N O T E The Setup program enables you to create partitions when you install Windows NT. Disk Administrator is useful primarily when making changes to existing partitions, adding new partitions, adding new disks, and making other disk system changes after installing Windows NT. ■

Creating Primary Partitions To create a primary partition, select the region containing the free space in which you want to create the partition, then choose Partition, Create. Or, right-click in the free space and choose Create from the context menu. Figure 10.11 shows the Create Primary Partition dialog box that appears.

FIG. 10.11
You have to specify only the desired size to create a partition. This dialog box is identical to the Create Extended Partition dialog box.

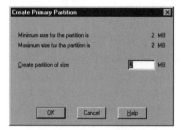

In the Create Partition of Size text box, type the size, in megabytes, of the partition you want to create. Then, click OK. Disk Administrator automatically assigns a drive letter to the partition, although the drive is not yet formatted.

▶ **See** "Formatting Drives," **p. 238**

Creating an Extended Partition and Logical Drives You can create one extended partition on a drive. The extended partition can contain multiple logical drives. To create an extended partition, select the unpartitioned free space in which you want to create the extended partition. Then, choose Partition, Create Extended. Or, right-click in the free space and choose Create Extended from the context menu. The resulting dialog box is identical to the Create Primary Partition dialog box previously shown in figure 10.11. Specify the size of the extended partition in the Create Partition of Size text box, then choose OK.

After creating the extended partition, you must create at least one logical drive in the partition. With the newly created partition selected, choose Partition, Create (or select Create from the context menu) to display the Create Logical Drive dialog box. This dialog box is identical to the Create Primary Partition and Create Extended Partition dialog boxes. Enter the desired size for the logical drive in the Create Logical Drive of Size text box, then choose OK. Repeat the process to create other logical drives in the extended partition. After creating logical drives in the extended partition, you must format the drives.

Setting the Active Partition Windows NT recognizes two special partitions—the boot partition and the system partition. These two can be, but are not required to be, the same partition. These two partitions have the following functions:

■ *Boot partition.* The boot partition contains the Windows NT operating system. This partition's boot record is responsible for booting the operating system. The boot partition can be formatted as either NTFS or FAT.

Part
III

Ch
10

■ *System partition.* The system partition contains hardware-specific files that Windows NT uses to load the operating system. The system partition must be a primary partition and marked as active (explained shortly). On RISC systems, the system partition must be formatted as FAT, but on Intel-based systems, the system partition can be either FAT or NTFS. The system partition on RISC systems is configured through setup software included with the system.

The *active* partition is the one from which the operating system will boot. You designate a partition as the active partition under Windows NT using the Disk Manager. You use other methods with other operating systems (fdisk with DOS and UNIX, for example).

N O T E   The computer can contain multiple physical disks. Only the first disk, disk 0, can be used as the boot disk. However, the boot partition doesn't have to be the first partition on disk 0. You might have Windows NT installed in the first partition and UNIX installed in another partition (or other versions of Windows NT).

Any primary partition on the disk can be designated as the active partition, enabling you to boot different operating systems. For example, if the Windows NT partition is active and you want to boot UNIX, you open Disk Administrator and set the UNIX partition to be active. Then, when you restart the system, it will boot from the newly activated partition, which contains UNIX. When it's time to return to Windows NT, you use the UNIX fdisk command to set the Windows NT partition active, then restart the system. ■

To specify the active partition on an Intel-based system, open Disk Administrator and select the partition you want to make active; then, choose Partition, Mark Active.

Formatting Drives

After you create a primary partition or logical drives in an extended partition, you must format the drive before it can be used. You have the option of formatting a drive as either FAT or NTFS. To format a drive, first select the drive you want to format, then choose Tools, Format. Or, right-click the drive and choose Format from the context menu. Either action displays the Format dialog box shown in figure 10.12.

The following controls appear in the Format dialog box:

■ *Capacity.* This drop-down list is intended for selecting the capacity at which to format a floppy disk. For hard disks, the capacity is listed as Unknown Capacity for previously unformatted disks.

■ *File System.* From this drop-down list, you can choose either FAT or NTFS.

■ *Allocation Unit Size.* This drop-down list enables you to specify the cluster size for the drive. You can choose between 512, 1,024, 2,048, and 4,096 bytes.

- *Volume Label.* Type in this text box a volume label (optional) for the disk.
- *Quick Format.* You can enable this checkbox if the disk has previously been formatted and you simply want to remove the current file system from the disk.
- *Enable Compression.* If you select NTFS from the File System drop-down list, you can enable this checkbox to have Windows NT enable compression for the volume.

Choose the desired options from the dialog box, then choose Start.

FIG. 10.12

You also can access the Format dialog box within Explorer by right-clicking a disk, then choosing Format from the context menu.

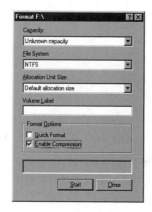

Format F:\

Capacity:
Unknown capacity

File System
NTFS

Allocation Unit Size
Default allocation size

Volume Label

Format Options
☐ Quick Format
☑ Enable Compression

Start   Close

Part
III

Ch
10

Converting FAT to NTFS

At some point, you might decide to convert an existing FAT volume to NTFS to take advantage of the additional security, compression, or other advantages offered by NTFS. Disk Manager doesn't include any mechanism to convert FAT volumes to NTFS. Instead, you must use a command-line utility called Convert to perform the conversion. The format of the convert command is:

```
CONVERT drive /FS:NTFS [/V]
```

Replace the *drive* parameter with the drive ID of the drive to be converted. Use the /V parameter to enable verbose mode, which provides additional reporting during the conversion process. To convert drive D to NTFS, for example, use the following command:

```
CONVERT D: /FS:NTFS /V
```

If you attempt to convert the boot partition, you receive a message indicating that the boot partition can't be converted while Windows NT is running. Convert asks if you want to schedule the conversion for the next time the system is restarted. If you answer yes, the drive will be converted to NTFS after you shut down and restart the system. The system will reboot several times during the conversion process, finally booting to the Windows NT GUI when the process is completed.

Creating a Stripe Set

Stripe sets were explained previously in the section "Using a Stripe Set." This section explains how to create a stripe set using Disk Administrator.

To create a stripe set, you must first select the regions of available space on the disks to be included in the stripe set. For this example, assume you're creating a stripe set from free space on drives D, E, F, and G. In the Disk Administrator, choose the Disk Configuration view. Select an area of available, unpartitioned space on drive D. Hold down the Ctrl key and select the unpartitioned space on drives E, F, and G that you want to include in the stripe set.

Next, choose Partition, Create Stripe Set to display the Create Stripe Set dialog box. With the Create Stripe Set of Total Size spin control, specify the size of volume you want to create. Disk Administrator will round up the size if the size you specify can't be distributed evenly across the disks you've selected. Next, choose OK to allow Disk Administrator to create the stripe set and apply a disk ID letter to the set.

After Disk Administrator creates the stripe set, you must format it just as you would any other volume. Still in Disk Administrator, select the partition containing the new stripe set, then choose Tools, Format. Format the stripe set as you would any other drive.

Creating a Volume Set

To create a volume set, first select various areas of free space on one or more disks. To do so, open Disk Administrator and choose the Disk Configuration view. Next, select the first area, then hold down the Ctrl key and select the other areas you want included in the volume set. When you've selected all the areas to be included in the volume set, choose Partition, Create Volume Set. Disk Administrator displays the Create Volume Set dialog box.

If you choose a size smaller than the maximum size specified in the Create Volume Set dialog box, Disk Administrator adjusts the amount of space from each selected area, potentially resulting in very small segments of unallocated free space in each region. For this reason, you should generally accept the maximum size offered by Disk Administrator, which is based on the total of all the selected regions. (See the section "Extending a Volume Set" next in this chapter for tips on extending the size of a volume set.)

After you specify the size for the volume set, choose OK to enable Disk Administrator to create the set. As with stripe sets and other disks, you must format the volume set before it can be used. Select any portion of the volume set in Disk Administrator, then choose Tools, Format, and format the disk as you would any other.

Extending a Volume Set

Unlike a stripe set that is fixed in size when you create it, you can extend a volume set by adding more free space to it. Extending an individual volume by adding space to it turns the volume into a volume set.

To extend a volume set, open Disk Administrator and select the volume set to be extended. Hold down the Ctrl key and select the areas of free space that you want to add to the volume set; then, choose Partition, Extend Volume Set to display the Extend Volume Set dialog box. Use the Create Volume Set of Total Size spin control to adjust the size of the set (the newly selected free space will already be included in the total amount); then, choose OK.

Assigning Drive Letters

Windows NT automatically assigns drive letters to drives when you create a primary partition or a logical disk in an extended partition. Disk Administrator enables you to change those drive letter assignments, giving you complete flexibility in how your drives are identified.

N O T E You assign drive letters to CD-ROM drives in the same way you do for hard drives. ■

To assign a drive letter, open Disk Administrator, select the drive in question, and choose Tools, Assign Drive Letter. Or, right-click the drive and choose Assign Drive Letter from the context menu. Either action opens the Assign Drive Letter dialog box (see fig. 10.13).

FIG. 10.13

The Assign Drive Letter dialog box gives you the option of using no drive letter for a drive.

From the Assign Drive Letter drop-down list, choose the letter you want to assign to the drive, then choose OK. Or, if you don't want to use a drive letter at all, choose the Do Not Assign a Drive Letter option button, then choose OK. If you choose this latter option, Disk Administrator removes the existing drive letter ID from the drive.

If you choose not to use a drive letter, you should apply a volume label to the volume to provide a means of distinguishing the volume. Also, the boot drive must have a drive letter assignment. Finally, use caution when you eliminate drive letters. Many applications rely on existing drive mappings to work properly, and removing a drive letter could prevent one or more applications from working properly.

Detecting and Clearing Cache Bottlenecks

The disk and controller are not the only objects that have an impact on disk performance. The cache also has a significant effect on overall disk subsystem throughput. This section examines caching and how to improve caching performance.

A Brief Overview of Caching

A *disk cache* is a buffer (an area of memory) used to store recently used data. Windows NT uses a single file system cache for all cachable devices, including the network. The cache serves as a holding area for data, both for read and write operations.

For example, when a disk read operation takes place, the data moves from the disk to the disk cache, then to the operating system so it can be used. If the operating system subsequently requests the same data, and that data is still residing in the cache, the data is copied from the cache instead of being reread from the disk. Memory transfers occur much faster than disk transfers, so the cache has a big impact on apparent disk performance. By caching network data, the cache reduces network traffic and improves local response time in the same way it improves response time for local disks.

N O T E Windows NT uses the same disk cache for CD-ROM drives and other cachable storage devices as it uses for hard disks and the network. ■

How well the cache performs naturally has an impact on overall system performance, primarily in mass storage media response and network response. Optimizing the cache's performance can therefore have a positive impact on your system.

Testing Cache Performance

You can test cache performance using the Performance Monitor included with Windows NT. As with disk performance testing, there are numerous counters provided by Performance Monitor for evaluating cache performance. These counters, which are associated with the Cache object in Performance Monitor, are as follows:

- *Async Copy Reads/sec.* This counter specifies the frequency of reads from cache pages that involve the data being copied from the cache to the application's buffer.

- *Async Data Maps/sec.* This counter indicates the frequency at which an application, through the file system, maps a page into the cache, but doesn't wait for the cache to retrieve the page if the page is not already in main memory.

- *Async Fast Reads/sec.* This indicates the frequency by which applications bypass the file system to retrieve data directly from the cache on a read operation.

- *Async MDL Reads/sec.* This counter indicates the frequency at which applications use a Memory Descriptor List (MDL) to access pages in the cache during read operations. The MDL stores the physical address of each page and enables DMA transfers.

- *Async Pin Reads/sec.* The term *pin* refers to the address of a memory page being locked (unalterable). This counter specifies the frequency at which data is read into the cache before being written back to the disk.

- *Copy Read Hits %.* This counter indicates the percentage of cache hits that returned the requested page without requiring a disk read.

- *Copy Reads/sec.* This counter specifies the frequency at which reads from the cache involve a memory copy from the cache to the application's buffer.

- *Data Flush Pages/sec.* This counter indicates the number of pages flushed from the cache to the disk caused by a write-through request or request to flush the cache.

- *Data Flushes/sec.* This counter indicates the frequency by which the cache flushes its contents to disk as a result of write-through or flush-cache requests.

- *Data Map Hits %.* This counter indicates the percentage of hits that did not require retrieval from the disk (indicating the page was already in memory).

- *Data Map Pins/sec.* This counter indicates the frequency at which data maps in the cache caused a page to be pinned in memory.

- *Data Maps/sec.* This counter indicates the frequency at which file pages are mapped into the cache during a read operation.

- *Fast Read Not Possible/sec.* This counter indicates the frequency at which applications attempted to bypass the file system to access the cache directly, but the request could not be handled without accessing the file system.

- *Fast Read Resource Misses/sec.* This counter indicates the frequency of cache misses caused by a lack of resources to handle the request.

- *Fast Reads/sec.* This counter indicates the frequency at which the file system is bypassed to access data in the cache directly.

Part
III

Ch
10

- *Lazy Write Flushes/sec.* This counter indicates the frequency at which the cache performs lazy writes.

- *Lazy Write Pages/sec.* This counter indicates the frequency in pages per second at which the cache performs lazy writes.

- *MDL Read Hits %.* This counter indicates the percentage of MDL read requests that did not require a disk access to process.

- *MDL Reads/sec.* This counter indicates the frequency at which an MDL is used to access data in the cache.

- *Pin Read Hits %.* This counter indicates the percentage of cache hits that did not require disk access to process.

- *Pin Reads/sec.* This counter indicates the frequency at which data is read into the cache prior to being written back to disk.

- *Read Aheads/sec.* This counter indicates the frequency of read operations in the cache for sequential file access.

- *Sync Copy Reads/sec.* This counter indicates the frequency at which read operations require a memory copy from the cache to the application's buffer.

- *Sync Data Maps/sec.* This counter indicates the frequency by which an application makes a request to map a page into the cache and waits for the cache to retrieve the page if it isn't already in memory.

- *Sync Fast Reads/sec.* This counter indicates the frequency at which the file system is bypassed in order to retrieve data directly from the cache.

- *Sync MDL Reads/sec.* This counter indicates the frequency of MDL reads in the cache.

- *Sync Pin Reads/sec.* This counter indicates the frequency at which data is read into the cache for writing back to the disk.

As when testing disk performance, you might need to use a combination of charts and reports to more easily identify and track the information you need to evaluate the cache's performance. Also, like disk testing, cache testing requires that you impose a load on the system under various circumstances (different amounts of cache RAM, for example). You can use the Response Probe utility included with the Windows NT Resource Kit to provide consistent testing conditions.

Clearing Up the Bottleneck

If you determine from your testing that the cache appears to be a bottleneck, the only real solutions involve adding memory or increasing the speed of the adapter/disk combination. If the host adapter supports an on-board cache, you can add more memory to the adapter's cache to improve cache performance. A better option, however, is to add more RAM to the system. Because Windows NT provides adaptive cache management, sizing the cache as needed, making more RAM available gives Windows NT more room in which to work, ultimately making more RAM available for a larger cache.

If your system contains as much memory as it will accommodate, or you're not willing to invest in more memory, your only other real option is to increase disk performance overall through the methods described earlier in this chapter. Adding RAM, however, is typically cheaper and much less of a hassle than changing adapters and/or disks. Before you foray out on a shopping spree, consider the cost difference between adding another 8M of RAM versus changing disk and host adapter hardware.

From Here...

This chapter provided an overview of file system performance and optimization. You'll find other optimization concepts and tips in these chapters.

- Chapter 11, "Exploring NTFS," offers a detailed look at NTFS and how to implement it.

- Chapter 12, "Optimizing CPU Performance," explains how to improve system performance overall through various CPU optimization techniques and the addition of multiple CPUs.

Exploring NTFS

by Christa Anderson

NTFS has a number of advantages over FAT for large volumes that require high levels of security: it uses disk space more economically, but supports larger disk sizes; it allows you to set permissions on both directories and individual files; and it supports file compression.

The previous chapter discussed how the FAT and NTFS formats worked and explored the times when each might best suit your needs. This chapter discusses NTFS itself in more detail. ■

Understanding NTFS's structure

Turn to this section to learn how NTFS organizes data on your disk.

Exploring NTFS's advantages

Learn what features of NTFS make its format superior to FAT.

Migrating to NTFS

Turn here to learn how best to change formats, either during installation or afterward.

Using and optimizing compression

Learn how NTFS's compression feature works and how to customize it for your system.

Understanding NTFS's Structure

Before getting into the details of NTFS's structure, it's necessary to briefly look at the way that a hard disk is constructed. If you know this already, you can skip ahead.

A Flying Tour of Hard Disk Geometry

The basic unit of measure on a hard disk (or floppy disk, for that matter) is the *byte*. Bytes are organized into 512-byte groups called *sectors*, and those sectors into *tracks*, or *platters*, concentric rings on the pieces of a disk that data is written on. The platters are double-sided, and each side can have thousands of tracks. Tracks are numbered from the inside out; track 0 is on the outer edge of the platter (like many other things in the computer world, track numbering starts at 0), and track 500 would be closer to the inner ring.

> **N O T E**   If your hard disk uses a technology called Zone Bit Recording (ZBR), it may have more sectors on the outside tracks of a platter than on the inside tracks. The use of ZBR means that you don't have to waste space on the outer tracks that have more room, just to match the layout of the inner tracks. ■

If this is a little hard to visualize, take a look at figure 11.1.

FIG. 11.1
Hard disk platters are organized into sectors and tracks.

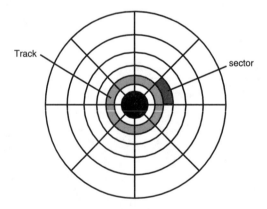

Track

sector

Hard disks have more than one platter; these platters are physically stacked on top of each other. Because they're stacked, the tracks on each platter line up. Therefore, the tracks with the same number on all platters may be grouped together and called a *cylinder*. Cylinders are a useful concept because of the way in which hard disks work.

Each platter has two reading/writing devices, called *heads*, that are roughly equivalent to the mechanism that reads records on a record player. As all the heads are attached to a bracket called an *actuator arm*, they cannot move independently of each other. There's no way to have one head on Track 3, Surface 2, and another head on Track 54, Surface 5—the second head would have to be on Track 3 as well. Thus, as the part of data retrieval that takes the most time is moving the actuator arm to the proper track, it makes sense to group data all in the same cylinder, so that head movement during reads and writes is minimized.

Yes, this is complicated; but trust me: understanding disk geometry is important to understanding how data is stored on a disk.

That's the physical organization of a disk. Logically, it's organized a little differently. As illustrated in figure 11.2, those 512-byte sectors on the disk are organized into groups called *clusters*. The number of sectors in a cluster depends on the size of the disk partition.

FIG. 11.2
The sectors on a hard disk are logically grouped into clusters.

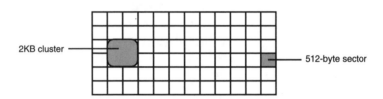

2KB cluster

512-byte sector

N O T E File systems support only a certain number of clusters. FAT, used by DOS, Windows 3.x, Windows 95, and supported by Windows NT, supports 64K clusters on a singe logical drive. As the DOS/Windows operating systems can only have clusters up to 32K in size, this limits the size of FAT logical drives used by these operating systems to about 2G. Windows NT supports clusters 64K in size, so its FAT logical drives can be as large as 4G. The theoretical limit for NTFS partitions is 2^{64} bytes. At this point, drives don't *come* that big. ■

Those who feel that real techies don't use GUIs would probably like to return to the early days of disk-based PCs. Before DOS (and the FAT disk format) was invented, you needed to know a bit more about disk geometry than what is currently the case. Rather than executing programs by name, you'd execute them by their location on the disk. So, if you had a spreadsheet package called SPREDSHT.EXE that was located at cylinder 1, head 0, sector 1, you'd run it by instructing the disk to run the program found at that location on the disk, rather than instructing it to run SPREDSHT.EXE. Once the application loaded, it could use its internal directory to find data files, so you didn't need to load data files by disk geometry.

This method works, and for small disks such as the floppies it was used with it's not terrible, but it's got one serious drawback: forget the physical location of a program, and you can't run it. Additionally, the spreadsheet's files were invisible to all other applications on the disk, meaning that not only could you not load the files into other applications (not such a big deal), but that disk space recovery for deleted files was not very efficient. How can you take over space made available in a space of which you're not even aware?

The problems associated with this method of loading applications contributed to the advent of DOS and the FAT file system, still used by most PC-based operating systems. FAT has some weaknesses, however, and those weaknesses led to the creation of another file format, NTFS.

Disk Organization Basics

In some ways, formats have been getting simpler as operating systems get more complicated. As noted previously, before the advent of FAT, you had to know the physical location, or *absolute sector*, of files on the disk to execute them. Under DOS, absolute sectors are mapped to DOS sectors, which define 512-byte sectors in terms of their relative position on the disk rather than in absolute terms. With DOS sectors, it's no longer cylinder 45, head 2, sector 0—but sector 4,354. Each of these sectors is stored in the FAT so that data can be retrieved from the disk.

The next layer of organization is made of *clusters*, or the minimum space allotted by the operating system in which data can be stored. Clusters are groups of contiguous sectors, their size depending on the size of the partition on which they exist—the larger the partition, the more sectors in the cluster. As data from only one file can be stored in each cluster, this means that the waste incurred in storing small files on a disk increases as the size of the disk increases. A file's data is not necessarily stored in contiguous clusters.

N O T E As we'll discuss later in this chapter when we talk about NTFS's advantages, one of the benefits of NTFS over FAT is that NTFS uses much smaller clusters; its largest clusters (used in partitions over 2G) are 4K, or the size of a FAT cluster used on a 128M partition. Smaller clusters mean that less room is wasted in the storage of small files. ■

The pieces of the FAT file system are:

Absolute sectors, which are mapped to

DOS or *relative sectors*, which are divided into

Clusters, which are recorded in the

File Allocation Table, or FAT

In NTFS, the pieces are similar, but they work differently in NTFS than they do in the FAT. NTFS is not interested in sectors, relative or absolute; it organizes data according to the cluster in which it is located.

The NTFS Directory Structure

NTFS uses a data structure very different from the one used by the FAT filing system. This data structure is designed to speed up the process of retrieving data (although whether it does under ordinary circumstances is a matter of some debate). Under FAT, the process of retrieving a file works like this:

1. The operating system receives an application request for a file.
2. The operating system inspects the File Allocation Table (FAT) at the top of the volume to see if the file exists.
3. The operating system notes the location of the first cluster of data as listed in the FAT, and retrieves the data.
4. Unless the file is entirely contained within one cluster, the FAT will show a pointer to the next cluster in which data for that file is contained.
5. Step 4 is repeated until all data for that file is retrieved.

This is a simple process for small directories, but it can be slow, as collecting the data to open the file is a multi-step process. NTFS takes a different approach, called *binary tree*, or *b-tree*. Rather than the flat-file database approach of FAT, NTFS uses a tree-based structure. In a b-tree environment, directory entries are stored alphabetically in a tree, but horizontally, so that it's not faster to find files beginning with A than it is files beginning with Z. Thus, the process of file-finding under NTFS goes like this:

1. The operating system receives an application request for a file.
2. The operating system checks the Master File Table (MFT) to see that such a file exists.
3. Having found the pointer in the MFT, the operating system uses the pointer to jump to the file's location on the disk and open the file.

This file system can potentially be faster on very large volumes, as the scope of the search is limited. Rather than searching the entire MFT, it's only necessary to search the part that points to the requested file name.

Part

III

Ch

11

Files on an NTFS Volume

Rather than perceiving files as data with attributes attached, NTFS sees all files as a collection of attributes, of which the data is one. The attributes that appear in all data files are as follows:

- Header (H)
- Standard Information (SI)
- File Name (FN)
- Data
- Security Descriptor (SD)

This information is organized as you see in figure 11.3.

FIG. 11.3
NTFS perceives a file as a collection of attributes, of which the data is one.

Other attributes may also be included in the file, as shown in table 11.1. There are two categories of attributes: those defined by the NTFS (called system attributes) and those defined by applications (called user-defined attributes).

N O T E Although one category of attributes is called user-defined, these attributes are, in fact, defined by the application creating the file, not the user. ■

Table 11.1 System-Defined Attributes

Attribute	Description
Attribute List	Defines the valid attributes for this particular file.
File Name	Contains the long, case-sensitive file name for the file as well as the file number of the parent directory file. If a file appears in multiple directories, then there will be a corresponding number of file name attributes. This attribute must always be resident.
MS-DOS Name	Contains the 8.3 file name created from the truncated file name, as well as the case-insensitive file name (only file names not conforming to the 8.3 format will be truncated).
Version	Specifies the update version of the file.

Attribute	Description
Security Descriptor	Contains the security information for the file. Also contains an audit field that stores the information used to determine which activities on this file will be audited.
Volume Version	Used only in volume system files.
Volume Name	Contains the volume label.
Volume Information	Used only in volume system files. Contains the major and minor version number of NTFS on the volume.
Data	Contains the normal file data as well as the normal file sizes and sizes for all attributes. This attribute may be stored in either resident (for small files) or non-resident (for large files) form.
Index Root	Used to construct the index of a particular attribute over a set of files for the purpose of indexing these files by their attribute value. Always stored in resident form.
Index Allocation	If the index stored in the Index Root attribute becomes too large, this non-resident attribute is formed to store the rest of the index information.
MFT Bitmap	Provides a map that represents the sectors in use on the volume.
External Attributes	When not all of a file's attributes will fit in its MFT record, the additional attribute(s) will be moved to a new record, i.e. stored as non-resident attributes. Not all attributes may be non-resident.
External Attribute Information	Contains information about any external attributes.

Part

III

Ch

11

The only user-defined attribute that Microsoft notes is the Standard Information Attribute (SIA), which contains the information that you see when you view a file's properties: file creation time, the last time file data was modified, the last time any attribute was modified, the last time the file was accessed, the file's standard attributes (read only, hidden, and so on), maximum file version, and the version number. SIAs must be resident in the MFT.

By default, attributes are stored in the MFT, or are resident. If a file has too many attributes to fit into the MFT, those become extended attributes (EAs) and branch, as will be discussed in a moment.

The way in which each file is stored on the NTFS volume depends on the size of the file's attributes. Generally speaking, the MFT contains a 2K pointer to each file's location on the disk. However, the smaller the file, the simpler the storage process.

Small Files   As illustrated earlier in figure 11.3, very small files (with a data attribute under 1,500 bytes) may actually be stored in the MFT, as the 2K slot reserved for that file's pointer may leave enough room for the data and its attributes. According to Microsoft, you can't count on files under a certain size being stored in the MFT (it depends on how many other attributes are in the file), but it's a possibility.

Large Files   If a file is too large to fit within the MFT, its record there takes on a slightly different appearance. Its data attribute, rather than containing data, contains a pointer to the data. This pointer is the Virtual Cluster Number (VCN) for the first cluster in each of the runs, and the number of contiguous clusters in each of the runs. Thus, the MFT entry for large files contains the information shown in figure 11.4.

FIG. 11.4

Files too big to fit into the MFT have a VCN pointing to the actual data in the data attribute of their MFT entry.

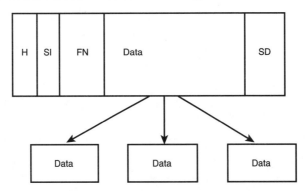

Huge Files   Without quantifying "huge," Microsoft notes that some extremely large files may have yet another kind of MFT entry, one that contains a cascade of pointers as illustrated in figure 11.5.

FIG. 11.5

Huge files may require cascading entries in the MFT, so as to contain all of the file's attributes.

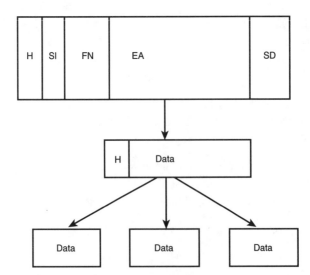

Why is this format necessary for extremely large files? Recall that each file's entry in the MFT is 2K in size. If, as discussed earlier, some files can be so small that they fit into the MFT, it stands to reason that some files could be so large that not only do they not fit, but not all of their attributes fit either. In that case, it becomes necessary to organize that file's MFT entry as shown in figure 11.5.

For even larger files, more than one branch of data pointers may be necessary. As you can see in figure 11.6, the extended attribute can point to more than one data pointer.

FIG. 11.6

The very largest files may require a few data pointers to direct NTFS to all the file's data.

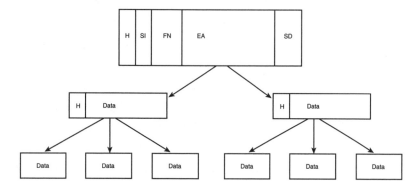

This structure, in which the only data-related attribute resident in the MFT is the extended attribute, means that a file can never be too large to fit in the directory structure.

Directory Entries   Just as every file requires an entry in the MFT, so do directories and subdirectories (or, to use NT 4.0's nomenclature, folders and subfolders) of the partition. NTFS sees directories as files just like other files, with one exception: directories are files that can contain other files. Thus, the MFT entry for a directory is similar to the MFT entry for a single data file.

The important parts of a directory's MFT entry are the entry for the directory itself, and its index, which permits the files in the directory to be sorted by any attribute criteria that are stored in the resident form of the file (that is, these criteria cannot be extended attributes).

N O T E   NTFS can only sort files by the filename attribute, but third-party sorting utilities can define other attributes by which to sort a directory's contents. ■

The placement of the index depends on the number of files in the directory. A small index, with only a few entries, is resident in the MFT. It contains the name of each file and the number of its entry in the MFT, or the file number. The contents of a small directory's MFT entry are illustrated in figure 11.7.

Part
III

Ch
11

FIG. 11.7

A small directory's MFT entry may fit entirely in the MFT.

If an index has too many entries to fit in the MFT, then it looks slightly different. (Once again, Microsoft does not define "too many," but the location of the index doesn't matter to anyone searching for files in a directory—it does not affect data retrieval time.) The root of the index remains resident in the directory's MFT entry, but the directory's entry now contains an Index Allocation (IA) attribute that points to other indexes for the data. Conceptually, an MFT entry for a larger directory looks like the one shown in figure 11.8.

FIG. 11.8

Like very large files, large directories have MFT entries that branch.

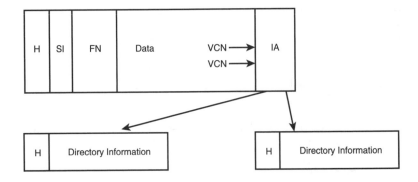

Just as indexes contain entries, indexes can contain other indexes, so index branches can get complicated.

The NTFS System Files

In addition to data, any partition formatted with NTFS has the following system files:

■ The Master File Table (MFT) records the location and attributes of each file and directory on the partition. A copy of the MFT used for recovery, called MFT2, is a mirror of the MFT and the Log File. On very large volumes, there may be several copies of the MFT so as to ensure that there is always a good copy of the MFT.

N O T E   The first 16 records of the MFT are reserved for NTFS system files, but only nine of those records are presently used. ■

■ Log File, a system file, stores boot information and is used by the Log File Service to make the volume's file system recoverable, if that should be necessary.

- The Volume File contains the information for the volume, such as its name, version, and so on.

- The Attribute Definitions Table contains the definitions of all system-defined attributes and any user-defined attributes on the volume. These definitions include the attribute name, type code, flags, display rules, indexing rules, minimum length, maximum length, and security information.

- The Cluster Allocation Bitmap maps the storage space on the volume, with one bit=one cluster. Its purpose is to make it easier to find unused space on the NTFS volume.

- The Boot File contains the volume's bootstrap in its Data attribute if the NTFS volume is bootable. This file is a file like any other data file, meaning that it may be located anywhere on the disk and protected with normal file security measures.

- The Bad Cluster File contains records of all the bad clusters on the volume. This file's Data attribute is always non-resident. If new bad clusters are found while the system is running, they are added to the Bad Cluster File instead of producing the Abort, Retry, Ignore statement familiar to those who try to read or write to bad clusters formatted with FAT.

N O T E Thinking of editing the Bad Cluster File to add the information you garnered from running SpinRite before installing? Think again; this file is not user-editable. ■

Part
III

Ch
11

- The Uppercase Table is used to convert mixed-case file names to matching uppercase Unicode characters. This table is required to support applications from environments that only use uppercase characters in their file names, such as MS-DOS.

One of the advantages to NTFS over DOS is that these NTFS system files do not have to be stored in a particular spot on the hard disk. As you may recall, all DOS system files must be stored on Track 0. If this track is inaccessible, so is the disk.

 TIP You can specify the cluster size of an NTFS partition when formatting it. To do so, format the partition from the command line using the following syntax:

```
format d: /a:xxxx
```

where xxxx may be 512, 1024, 2048, 4096, 8192, 16384, 32768, or 65536. (To specify a cluster size from 512 bytes to 4K, you can use the Format command in the Explorer, but this interface does not offer cluster sizes larger than 4K.) Specifying a cluster size larger than the default for that partition size will speed up searches and reduce external fragmentation, but will increase internal fragmentation. Data compression is not supported on volumes with a cluster size larger than 4K.

NTFS's structure is complicated, so let's finish the tour with a summary:

- NTFS perceives all files as collections of attributes, including a data attribute.
- The b-tree organizational system used by NTFS means that once the filing system has located a file on the disk, it's open.
- Like FAT, NTFS organizes data into clusters, but all other things being equal, NTFS's clusters are smaller than FAT's.
- NTFS system files do not have to reside on Track 0 of the hard disk.

Exploring NTFS's Advantages

Since NT came out in 1994, there's been a great deal of discussion about how NTFS, NT's native format, is the greatest thing since sliced bread. The reasons for NTFS's greatness are sometimes a little hard to grasp, however, as the advantages are usually couched in terms like "higher security" and "improved use of disk space." Those advantages are real, but the vague terms in which they're described sometimes make it hard to believe them. If you're interested in learning how those advantages actually work, read on.

Long File Names

One of the most well-known features of NTFS is its support for long file names. Since Windows 95 and VFAT appeared, this feature has become less unique, but it's still useful. You can create descriptive file names up to 255 characters long (including the extension), using any characters on the keyboard except the following:

> ? " / \ < > * | :

So, a file name such as **Memo.regarding.travel.regulations.txt** is acceptable, but a name such as **Memo.regarding.travel/business.regulations.txt** or **Why.do.I.have.to.do.this?txt** is not.

In most cases, NTFS file names will preserve case on NTFS volumes, but are not case-sensitive. If you create a file called C:\JUNK\THINK.TXT and later create another file called C:\JUNK\think.txt, you'll overwrite the original version of the file. The only time that NTFS file names are case-sensitive, so that Think.txt, THINK.TXT, and think.txt are *not* the same file, is when using NTFS with a POSIX-compliant application. NTFS supports POSIX, but its features are not POSIX-based.

N O T E As DOS sees all file names as uppercase, one of the attributes of an NTFS file is a case-insensitive file name that DOS can identify, even if the file name conforms to DOS's 8+3 naming convention. ■

Efficient Use of Disk Space

Your hard disk's format seriously influences how much room your data takes up on the disk. As you may know, files are not stored willy-nilly on the disk. Instead, they're organized into subdivisions of the disk called *clusters*. A cluster is the minimum unit of storage on the disk, so even if a file is smaller than the cluster size of the disk, the file will still take up the entire cluster.

If the concept of clusters is a little hard to grasp, try thinking of your disk as a room with the floor covered with cardboard boxes of a uniform size, each of which is capable of holding 100 pieces of paper. (This analogy is dear to my heart as that's the way my office tends to look after I've gotten some new equipment.) In this scenario, imagine that you're trying to organize the hard copy of your latest masterwork into chapters, putting only one chapter into each box. If a chapter is under 100 pages long, then it will fit into one box. If, however, it exceeds the box capacity by even *one page*, you'll need to use an entire box for that single page.

Although cluster size varies with the file format (as we'll see in a moment), the exact cluster size in that file format depends on the size of the hard disk partition, with bigger partitions having bigger clusters. For example, when formatted with FAT, a 250M drive has a cluster size of 4K; a 2G drive has a cluster size of 32K. As you can see, this is extremely inefficient: if you store a slew of 2K memos on the 2G drive on the server, you're using up 32K worth of disk space for each one of them. Microsoft estimates that, on average, you will waste about half of each used cluster. This is bad news for large FAT partitions.

What can you do to reduce cluster size? One option is to partition the disk. Cluster size is determined not by the size of the entire hard disk, but by the size of each partition. So, if you take that 2G disk and chop it into four 500M partitions, then you've reduced the cluster size from 32K to 8K. Partitioning has its problems, of course. Partitions can sometimes be inconveniently sized, as you realize that you've got 15M of unused space on the disk for that new application, but not on any one of the available partitions. Additonally, FAT used with NT cannot support cluster sizes larger than 64K, which translates to a 4G drive. 4G sounds like a lot, but for a file server or graphics system, you'll almost certainly need more hard disk space than that. Face it: casual users don't buy Windows NT.

N O T E As we'll discuss shortly, FAT used with DOS and Windows only supports disks 2G in size. NT supports larger clusters, which means that larger disks (up to 2^{54} bytes in size) can be supported. ◼

Thus, another solution to the problem of "cluster crunch" would be nice, and that option is NTFS. As you can see from table 11.2, this file format reduces cluster size even further than partitioning does.

Table 11.2   Cluster Sizes of Drives Formatted with NTFS

Partition Size	Cluster Size
<512M	512 bytes
513M-1024M	1K
1025M-2048M 2K>2048M	4K

Compare the cluster sizes here with those in table 11.3.

Table 11.3   Cluster Sizes of Drives Formatted with FAT

Partition Size	Cluster Size
128 M-255 M	4K
256 M-511 M	8K
512 M-1023 M	16K
1024 M-2048 M	32K

Notice that NTFS *never* requires clusters larger than 4K, the cluster size used by FAT partitions of 128M!

NTFS's better handling of space goes beyond cluster sizes. Remember how you could fill your hard drive with tiny little memos that each demanded its own cluster? NTFS's disk architecture (described earlier in this chapter) permits very small files to be stored in the Master File Table (MFT) itself, rather than just a pointer to a file. As you'll recall, the pointers in the MFT are about 2K in size. Microsoft doesn't specify an exact threshold at which tiny files will be stored in the MFT as opposed to in a cluster, but if a file is smaller than about 2K, then it may require no more room than the space required for the data, instead of both the pointer *and* the data.

N O T E   For more information on the relationship between file size and a file's entry in the MFT, turn to the previous section on NTFS's architecture. ■

Support for Large Disks

Earlier, this chapter noted how FAT drives under NT can be larger than FAT drives under DOS or Windows (4G as opposed to 2G) as DOS/Windows only support 32K clusters, and NT supports 64K clusters. It's still only the 64K clusters that FAT supports; the difference is that NT lets the clusters be bigger.

Four gigabytes is a lot, but even your system BIOS can recognize a *bootable* hard disk of 7.8G (1024 cylinders x 256 heads x 63 sectors/tracks x .5K/sector). Once NT starts running after boot time, it controls the hard disk controller without help from the BIOS (meaning that it's no longer dependent on the BIOS's ability to recognize hard disks). During operation, then, NT ignores the sections of the partition table that refer to absolute sector and cylinder numbers (which are only 6-bit and 10-bit entries), and, instead, looks in the sections that refer to the relative sector numbers and the number of sectors (both 32-bit entries). Using these entries allows NT to "see" hard disks with 2^{32} sectors, or, using the standard 512-byte sector, 2 terabytes.

NOTE NT supports sector sizes up to 4K, so if you can find a disk formatted with 4K sectors (or use an EDSI disk that you can low-level format), it can be up to 16 terabytes in size. ▓

FAT won't see those 2 terabytes, however, as its file structure only uses 32-bit fields to support file sizes. NTFS, on the other hand, uses 64-bit fields, giving it a theoretical limit of 16 exabytes. You won't find a 16-exabyte disk, but it's technically possible for NT to support an NTFS-formatted disk that big.

Of course, you have to *find* hardware that big. At this point, IDE drives are limited to .5G because of their compliance with the Western Digital standard of having only 16 heads. EIDE drives can use a kind of sector translation called Logical Block Addressing (LBA) to lie to the BIOS and tell it that a drive has more heads and fewer cylinders than it actually has. The SCSI-II command set used to address SCSI drives currently supports drives that are about 7G in size. As drives get bigger, however, NTFS should be able to keep up with them.

File Compression

As discussed in detail later in this chapter, you can compress NTFS files and volumes to save space on your hard disk. You can even format a volume to be compressed, so that every file added to that partition will be compressed without requiring you to take any extra steps.

Part
III

Ch
11

File Security

One of the primary concerns in NT's original design was security, in terms of both security from people and security from disk errors. Thus, NTFS's file security comes from a few different sources:

■ Transaction-based structure

■ Better built-in RAID support

■ File-level security for shared files and directories

Transaction-Based Structure

One of NTFS's primary goals is to preserve the integrity of the operating system. First, a little history.

Careful Writes   Before NTFS, there were essentially two schools of thought when it came to writing data to disk. *Careful writes*, used by FAT under DOS, make volume consistency the first priority. When an application requests that data be written to disk, everything stops and that data gets written, immediately. This method is useful for making sure that data is written to disk, but can be slow, as the write process grabs the CPU as soon as you request the write, and won't let go until it's done.

Lazy Writes   Another, faster, method of writing to disk is called lazy writes, or *write caching*. This method is used by FAT under NT, Windows 95, and some varieties of UNIX, and can be implemented in Windows 3.x with SmartDrive. There are several ways to implement write caching, but the basics are as follows: when an application requests that data be written to disk, the write cache program intercepts the request and stores the data in a buffer, waiting for some CPU "down-time" (or for a predetermined interval of time) to actually write the data to disk. Write caching is more or less invisible to the user, as the write cache reports to the application that the data was successfully written. The only way that you might notice write cache operations is if you notice that the hard drive light didn't come on when the computer claimed that it was writing data to disk.

Lazy writes save the CPU time and save your hard disk some wear and tear, as it can complete more than one write at the same time. The only trouble with the lazy write is that it can be caught unaware. For example, if the computer powers down unexpectedly due to a kicked cord or power outage before the cache is flushed (written to disk), then that data that you thought was written may in fact be in data heaven.

Recoverable File Systems   Volumes formatted with NTFS are designed to combine the speed of lazy writes with the security of careful writes. It works like this: when data goes to the cache, that's called a transaction. When it's actually written to the disk, that's another transaction. If the system is powered down unexpectedly, the transactions are still recorded, and any unwritten data can be found. Every I/O operation is logged by the Log File Service, along with redo and undo information. The redo information tells NTFS how to redo the transaction in case of system failure, and the undo tells it how to undo partially completed or corrupted transactions. When the transaction is successfully completed, it's listed as committed.

Every few seconds, NTFS checks the log file to see which transactions have been committed, and notes each as a checkpoint.

If the hard disk crashes, NTFS goes through three stages of data recovery:

- Analysis
- Redo
- Undo

During the analysis stage, NTFS determines what clusters need to be updated, based on the information in the Log File. In the redo stage, NTFS performs all committed transactions (recall that a committed transaction by definition has been completed successfully) that took place since the last checkpoint. Finally, NTFS looks for incomplete or corrupt transactions and rolls them back using the undo information.

The only catch to all this recoverability is that it's for *system* data, not user data. The point is to make sure that your system comes back up after a crash. This is quite important, but not a complete fix. To protect user data on the fly, you'll have to use one of the fault-tolerant RAID configurations (stripe sets with parity or mirroring) discussed in Chapter 10, "Optimizing the File System." Frequent backups, of course, are also important.

Part
III

Ch
11

CAUTION

Volumes formatted with FAT are not transaction-based; they use write caching. Therefore, if you create a system partition in which to store the operating system files and format it with FAT to make it accessible when you boot from a DOS floppy, you don't get the benefits of a recoverable file system. Back up the system Registry before making any major changes to the system, just in case something goes wrong and you need to reinstall. (See Chapters 29 and 30 on backing up and restoring the Registry to find out how.)

What NTFS *will* do for user data is avoid bad sectors on the disk. If it attempts to write to a bad sector, it will log the cluster in question in the Bad Cluster File and write the data to a good spot on the disk.

Better Fault-Tolerance Performance

Although NTFS won't save user data from system crashes on its own, it can permit you to get increased performance from fault-tolerant volumes such as stripe sets with parity or mirrored disks. If one of the disks in a fault-tolerant volume is slightly damaged, so that it still works but data can no longer be read from part of the disk, then NTFS can dynamically perform a hot fix. Rather than displaying the `Error Reading Drive C: Abort, Retry, Ignore?` message that DOS provides, NTFS will automatically go looking for the data on the other drive, or reconstruct the data using the information in the stripe set or mirror set.

File-Level Security

Although NT Workstation does not allow you to share individual files, you can set individual permissions for files stored in NTFS volumes, and then share the directories in which those files exist.

 T I P To share only a single file, create a subdirectory for that file, add the file to the subdirectory, and then share the subdirectory.

To set these permissions, right-click a file in the Explorer or in My Computer and choose Properties from the pop-up menu that appears. Once you are in the Properties folder, move to the Security tab, and then click the Permissions button to set file permissions. You'll see a dialog box like the one shown in figure 11.9.

FIG. 11.9

The File Permissions dialog box offers similar options to those available in a shared folder's Access Through Shared Permissions dialog box.

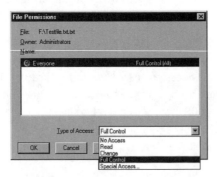

By default, Everyone has full control over files, but you can define these permissions to Read, Change, or No Access (which overrides any other access members of that group might have) based on either group membership or on an individual basis. When setting file permissions, you also have the option of adjusting a group's or user's special access to that file, defining exactly what that group or user may do to that file. You can see the Special Access options available in figure 11.10.

FIG. 11.10
You can set file permissions to define a unique set of permissions for a user or group.

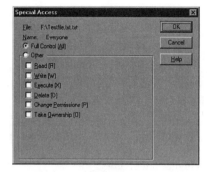

When setting file permissions, remember the following:

■ If a person is a member of more than one group, the group with the highest level of permission for a given file or directory defines that user's permission. For example, if Anna is a member of the Users group (which has Read access to a file) and the Power Users group (which has Full Control access to a file), then Anna has full control over that file. The only exception to this is the No Access permission, which overrides all other permissions.

■ The permissions granted to the group Everyone apply to all users with a local account, even if those permissions are not in one of the groups specifically assigned permission to a file or directory.

Part
III

Ch
11

Migrating to NTFS

For reasons discussed in Chapter 5, "Preparing for Installation," NTFS isn't necessarily for everyone. However, if you've been using FAT, NT's other supported file format, and have come to realize that NTFS suits you better, it's time to migrate. This section discusses some of the issues that you'll have to consider before making the change.

How Does Conversion Work?

First, how does the process of format conversion work? When you begin the process of conversion (you'll get to the mechanics in just a moment), NT sets any data in that partition aside, converts the file system from FAT's "flat file" system to NTFS's tree structure that makes it work like a relational database, then replaces the data. The only catch? You need room—perhaps as much as one-third as much as you have data—in which to store the data during the conversion.

Why is the extra room necessary? The conversion process is similar to the one you'd have to go through if you had an egg carton full of screws and you wanted to paint the inside of the egg carton red without getting paint on the screws. If you wanted to keep all the screws in the egg carton while painting it, you'd need some empty slots in the carton in which to store screws while you were doing the painting. If you didn't have the extra room, you could still paint the carton, but you'd have to remove the screws entirely from the carton first and then replace them when you were done. Similarly, you *can* reformat an FAT partition to NTFS, but you'll have to back up and replace the data on the partition.

To recap, these are the limitations on converting:

- The conversion process only goes one way; you can convert volumes from FAT to NTFS, but not from NTFS to FAT.
- You must have some unused space on the partition to be converted (as much as one-third as much as you have data).
- You cannot convert the current drive. This means that you can't convert the partition that the system files are on without rebooting.

That's how conversion works. What do you need to know before you start?

Where Are the System Files?

The first question you must ask yourself when preparing to move to NTFS is the location of the system files. Did you set aside a separate partition for them when installing the OS (a *very* good idea for reasons that will become obvious in a moment), or did you install NT onto a single partition on the hard disk?

Converting a Data Partition   If the answer is the former, then the task of conversion is simple. You'll leave the partition with the system files alone and convert only the partition with data files on it. Log on using an account with administrative privileges. Close all files stored in the partition you wish to convert, then open the command prompt (available from the Programs menu on the Task Bar), and type the following:

```
CONVERT X: /fs:ntfs
```

where *x* is the drive letter name of the partition that you wish to convert. (As you can only convert to NTFS, it's not clear why you must specify NTFS as the file system to convert to, but that's the way it is.) As this format is non-destructive, you must have enough room on the partition that you're converting to store the data while the conversion takes place.

N O T E   If you don't close all files in the partition to be converted before beginning the conversion, the conversion will not take place, but you'll have the option of scheduling the conversion to take place the next time that the system reboots. ■

Converting a System Partition   Actually, what you'll be doing here is not converting a system partition to NTFS, but repartitioning the drive so that you can format a data partition separately from the system partition. If you decide to do this, you'll have to reinstall the operating system. (Yes, it's a pain, but for purposes of recovery, it's much simpler if you have the system files on a partition separate from the data partition.)

First, back up—you're about to destroy your data by repartitioning the drive. You do not need to back up the system files, but backing up the Registry will keep you from having to recreate user accounts and set up services. See Chapters 29 and 30, "Backing Up and Editing the Registry" and "Restoring and Repairing the Registry," if you're not sure how to back up or restore the Registry.

> **CAUTION**
>
> Make sure that you can restore your data before repartitioning your hard disk! If you have any Service Packs loaded, you'll need to reload them before attempting to restore the data.

When you come to the point at which you're offered the option of installing in the current partition, delete the current partition. You'll have to confirm the deletion several times and in different ways (it is virtually impossible to delete a partition accidentally), but you'll get there eventually.

Next, create a partition big enough for all the system files (about 1G or larger, to be safe) in the free space on the disk. If you plan to install more than one operating system into this partition, of course you'll have to increase this size accordingly. By default, the partition will be a primary partition, so don't worry when you're not asked to specify what kind of partition this is. The remaining space will be free space that you can partition and format with the Disk Administrator.

Install the system files into a directory in the system partition, and complete the installation normally. When you've completed the installation, use the Disk Administrator to partition and format the remainder of the disk, then restore your data.

 TIP   After you've created the data partitions in the Disk Administrator, you'll need to commit to the changes you've made (either by exiting the Disk Administrator or choosing Commit Changes Now from the Partition menu).

Part III

Ch 11

Why Format the System Partition to FAT?

Since you've seen all the hype about how NTFS is the greatest thing since the discovery of fire, you may wonder why I don't recommend using it for the system partition. The reason is twofold and simple: first, you don't need many of the features of NTFS for a system partition, and second, you want the partition to be available when you boot from a floppy.

How is it that you don't need NTFS's features for the system partition? First of all, you don't need file-level security on the system partition: no one should be able to touch that partition except the system administrator, and you won't be sharing it. (If you decide to copy the contents of the /I386 folder from the CD to the hard disk to make it accessible to other network users, put it in a directory on the data partition.) Second, the cluster sizes on a system partition won't be large enough to really inconvenience you. On a partition smaller than 127M, they'll be 4K in size.

If you format the system partition to NTFS, you will not be able to boot from a DOS floppy to perform even the simplest of administrative tasks (such as seeing if the C: drive is visible to the operating system). You'll also be sunk when it comes to reinstalling the operating system because the installation program is FAT-based.

If this sounds alarmist, consider the following tale of woe. A government agency looking at NT Workstation to run its graphics software got two demonstration machines from the manufacturers with NT 3.51 (Service Pack 3) and the software loaded. When the demonstrator from the software company arrived, he thought that he'd be upgrading the system if he installed Service Pack 2. Instead, of course, he trashed the NT installation on one computer. (Loading Service Packs out of order is a Bad Thing.) Because the computer manufacturer had created only a single partition on the disk and formatted it to NTFS, the operating system could not be reloaded. When the installation process got to the point of loading files onto the hard disk, it could not identify the hard disk partition. The result was a lot of playing with the system's Setup utility to get it to boot even to the A: drive, repartitioning the hard disk, and much unpleasantness. *Format the partition with the system files to FAT.*

Do I Have Enough Room on the Partition?

You don't need a lot of elbow room to convert a partition from FAT to NTFS, but you do need some. It will be easy to tell if you don't have enough room. When you type **convert x: /fs:ntfs**, you'll see an error message notifying you of the space required and the space available, and saying that the drive was not converted. If you're not sure whether or not you have the room for a conversion, go ahead and try it anyway. Failure is non-destructive, and sometimes it takes a surprisingly small amount of unused disk space to complete the conversion.

All told, migrating to NTFS is a pretty simple operation, so long as you have ample space on the partition to be converted for overhead and don't attempt to convert a partition with open files on it.

Using and Optimizing Compression

DriveSpace and DoubleSpace don't work on Windows NT, but since version 3.51, Windows NT has had its own file and directory compression capabilities integrated into the operating system. These are quite simple to use, so long as you keep in mind some basic rules of thumb:

- Some files will compress more completely than others; files compressed with other compression utilities won't compress at all.

- Files moved to compressed directories will become compressed, as will directories moved into compressed directories.

- Compression may cause performance problems on NT Servers that see a great deal of write activity.

Setting Up Compression

You have two options when it comes to compressing a disk volume: compressing it when formatting, or (if it's an NTFS volume) compressing it after the fact.

Compressing While Formatting   You can't format a volume with compression in the Disk Manager. If you know when you're setting it up that you'll want to compress it, one option is to format it from the command prompt using the /C switch, instead of from the Disk Manager. The syntax of the command looks like this:

```
FORMAT X: /FS:NTFS /C
```

where X is the drive letter for the volume to be formatted and compressed.

You can also compress a volume while formatting it in Windows Explorer. Right-click the drive letter of the volume to be formatted, and choose Format from the pop-up menu that appears, as illustrated in figure 11.11.

Part
III

Ch
11

FIG. 11.11

You can choose to format a volume while in Windows Explorer.

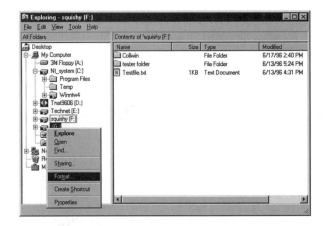

When you choose this option, you'll see a dialog box like the one shown in figure 11.12.

FIG. 11.12

To format a volume with compression automatically enabled for all files in that volume, format the disk to NTFS and check the Enable Compression box in the Format dialog box.

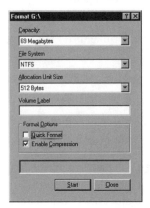

N O T E   FAT does not support compression, so this will only work on NTFS volumes. ■

Whichever method you choose, all files and directories created in those newly-formatted volumes will be compressed. If you want a particular file or directory not to be compressed, you can right-click the file or directory in question, open its Properties folder, and deselect the Compressed attribute. If you decompress a single file, it will not affect other files in the directory. If you decompress a subdirectory, the files that it contains will automatically be decompressed, but you'll be able to specify whether or not you want subdirectories within that directory to be decompressed as well.

Compression Ratios

The amount that files compress is significantly determined by their content. Text files compress fairly well, graphics files even better, and previously compressed files not at all. It's difficult to predict exactly how much a given file will compress, but you can see the compression ratios in a file's Properties folder. Right-click the file in question, and you'll see a dialog box like the one in figure 11.13.

FIG. 11.13
You can see both a file's original size and compressed size in its Properties folder.

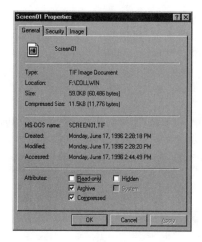

Just for comparison, note the compression ratios for these different kinds of files, as noted in table 11.4.

Table 11.4 Different Kinds of Files Compress at Different Ratios

Type of File	Original Size	Compressed Size
Text File	19.5K	12.0K
Help File	327K	177K
TIFF File	59K	12.5K
Executable File	275K	118K

Note that, proportionally, the text file compressed least and the graphics file most. These are the proportions that you should expect to see when compressing files.

When Not to Compress

File compression works quite well on a computer running NT Workstation and not acting as a server. For local processes, the read and write delay introduced by compression is not significant enough to matter.

Compression on shared volumes is another matter entirely. The delay caused by compression, in combination with the delay introduced by the network, can seriously slow down reads and writes on your computer.

What about compressing system files? If you follow my recommendations for keeping system files on a separate FAT-formatted partition, it's not really an issue—only NTFS supports compression. If you must format the system partition with NTFS and wish to compress it, however, you shouldn't see any serious performance problems.

N O T E If a volume is normally formatted with NTFS, it should compress normally. If, however, you specify a specific cluster size during the format (rather than letting NT use the default cluster size), you may run into problems. NT's file compression does not work on clusters larger than 4K. ■

From Here...

Presently, Windows NT is the only operating system that directly supports NTFS. As the filing system's benefits are more widely realized, and Windows NT increases in popularity, making interoperability more of an issue, this may change. A version of NTFS for Linux is currently (Summer 1996) in development, and other versions may follow.

- To learn more about installing NT, turn to Chapter 5, "Preparing for Installation."
- For information on more advanced installation, turn to Chapter 6, "Advanced and Custom Setup Issues."
- For more information about how NTFS and FAT compare, turn to Chapter 10, "Optimizing the File System."
- To learn more about using NT with other Microsoft clients, turn to Chapter 18, "Integrating Windows NT in Microsoft Environments."

CHAPTER 12

Optimizing CPU Performance

by Richard Neff

Windows NT is designed not only to run 32-bit Windows applications, but 16-bit and MS-DOS applications as well. These applications utilize the processor differently and are sometimes harder to monitor. 32-bit Windows applications have many different areas that can be monitored to help pinpoint the actual cause of a processor bottleneck. ■

Performance Monitor counters

There are a variety of different counters available in Performance Monitor to oversee processor performance on a computer.

Windows NT multitasking

Windows NT handles execution of multiple tasks by prioritizing and scheduling those tasks to ensure that one task does not dominiate system processing time.

User mode and Privileged mode

Windows NT has two modes of processes: User mode and Privileged mode.

16-bit Windows and MS-DOS applications

Windows NT handles 16-bit Windows and MS-DOS applications differently than 32-bit applications.

Correcting processor bottlenecks

There are steps that can be taken if a processor bottleneck is found.

Adding processors

One of the biggest advantages for using Windows NT is the support of multiple processors in a single system.

Overview of CPU Performance

Even if a Windows NT computer has the fastest hard disks, a lightning-fast video card, and massive amounts of memory, a slow processor causes the entire system performance to suffer. The processor controls, in some form, how every component works. It can be considered the grand coordinator of all the other hardware components in the computer. This is even before its primary function is served—handling all of the processing needed by the application software that the user is trying to run.

Windows NT alone is a hefty piece of software (16 million lines of code) that requires a lot of processing power. For that reason, Windows NT 4.0 requires at least an Intel 486 processor to even run. Older versions of Windows NT could run on a 386-based machine, but even then, the performance was barely acceptable for most users. Programs designed for Windows NT can place an even bigger burden on the processor. Fortunately, Windows NT allows multiple processors—something not available on Microsoft's other operating systems—to help ease the burden of running 32-bit multithreaded applications.

Creating a Processor Workspace File

When trying to monitor Windows NT performance, it is always good to have Performance Monitor running in the background with all the appropriate counters while the user goes about normal tasks. Typically, items to be monitored are added individually after Performance Monitor is started. However, after determining what items an administrator wants to monitor, a workspace or settings file can be created with the most commonly used counters.

The settings file provides a workspace of counters for monitoring in Performance Monitor. Usually, a settings file is used when many computers are being monitored or if a computer is going to be monitored at different time intervals. Rather than adding all of the counters manually, the settings file allows them to be added once. A more detailed explanation of workspace files for Performance Monitor is located in Chapter 8, "Monitoring Performance."

Settings files should have a file extension of PMW. For example, PROCESSOR.PMW would be a possible settings filename that contained counters relating to processor performance. Before we start talking about monitoring the processor in too much detail, we'll go over the process of creating a workspace file— specifically, for the creation of a workspace file of processor objects.

To create a processor workspace file, do the following:

1. Add all of the counters that you want to monitor in Performance Monitor. For this example, let's add % Processor Time, located in the System category.

2. After you have selected all of the counters, select File, Save Workspace in the Performance Monitor menu.

3. In the Save Workspace window, type PROCESSOR.PMW as the filename for the settings.

4. Now you can load the workspace file by using the File, Open command after Performance Monitor is started.

Of course, you may want to monitor processor performance every time the system is started. Do this by setting the Performance Monitor to load using the PROCESSOR.PMW file and adding it to the Windows NT Startup folder. Note that this will only work for the current user that is logged on. To start Performance Monitor with the appropriate workspace file, do the following:

1. Be sure you have a Startup folder on the system. You will have to create a Startup folder if it does not exist. If you have a Startup folder, go to step 5.

2. Choose Start, then Settings. Then, select Taskbar from the menu. When the Taskbar Properties window is displayed, select the Start Menu Programs.

3. In the Start Menu Programs property sheet, click the Advanced button to customize the Start menu.

4. After the Advanced button is pressed, an Explorer window will be displayed. In the right-hand side of the window double-click on the Programs item. This expands the tree. Look for the Startup folder in the tree. If it exists, double-click it to open it. If it does not exist, create a new folder by selecting File, New, and Folder. Give the new folder the name "Startup" and Windows NT will use this folder as the default Startup folder for the user currently logged on. Once the Startup folder is created, double-click it to open the folder.

5. Once the Startup folder is opened, choose File from the menu. Then select New, and then choose Shortcut. This opens the Windows NT Shortcut Wizard.

6. In the Shortcut Wizard, type the following in the Command Line box

    c:\\<*Windows NT directory*>\\system32\\perfmon.exe c:\\<*workspace directory*>\\processor.pmw

    where <*Windows NT directory*> is the location of the Windows NT 4.0 directory and <*workspace directory*> is the directory location of PROCESSOR.PMW. The next window asks for the name of the shortcut, let's give it "Processor Monitoring."

Part
III

Ch
12

7. Now the Windows NT Performance Monitor will start with the PROCESSOR.PMW workspace file the next time the current user logs on. However, you may want to have the Performance Monitor program minimized when Windows NT starts. To do this, select the Processor Monitoring item in the Startup folder. Then select File, Properties from the menu. Select the Shortcut tab, then select the Run: drop-down list and choose Minimized. Then, click the OK button.

8. Close the Explorer window, then choose OK in the Toolbar Properties window. When the current user next logs on to Windows NT, the Performance Monitor will start minimized with the PROCESSOR.PMW workspace file.

Charting Performance

Charting processor performance while using applications on the system gives us the best indication of how the processor is being utilized by those applications. Charting this time gives you an idea of whether a bottleneck is actually a processor-related bottleneck or whether the bottleneck is due to another part of the system. Other processor-related counters allow you to further analyze how the processor is being used by the system. With these results, you can better determine how to eliminate these processor bottlenecks.

In Performance Monitor, there are two categories that can be used to monitor processor performance: Processor and System. Both the Processor and System categories have a % Processor Time item. So, what's the difference between the two? For a single processor system, there isn't any. But, on a multiple processor system, the System object monitors all the processors on a system, while the Processor object is used to monitor an individual processor.

Now that you know how to create and use a workspace file, you need to determine what counters to include in the file. Since you want to look at processor performance on the Windows NT machine, you'll be adding some of the more important processor counters. Some of these are:

- **% Total Processor Time (System object)**. This counter shows the total percentage of processor time being used by all of the processors on the system. This object includes both the privileged and user time values. Once this counter consistently approaches 100%, the system will have to suspend some tasks in order for others to run. This condition creates a processor-related bottleneck and will cause the entire system to run more slowly.

- **% Total Privileged Time (System object)**. This counter shows the percentage of system time being spent on privileged mode operations. Privileged mode operations are operations involving the operating system applications. Examples of privileged mode operations include disk access, I/O functions, video operations, and so forth. This counter is useful in determining what processes are contributing to a processor bottleneck.

- **% Total User Time (System object).** This counter shows the amount of time the processors on the system are spending on user or application processing. This counter and the % Total Privileged Time counter make up the % Total Processor Time. If a system becomes bottlenecked and this counter value is high, then modifying the way applications are run on the system can sometimes provide a solution. If the applications are custom-developed, then optimizing the applications through coding is also possible.

- **Processor Queue Length (System object).** This counter gives an indication of the number of threads to be processed by the system. If values higher than two are consistently displayed, then the processor probably is becoming a bottleneck. In order for this counter to display anything other than zero, you must monitor at least one counter in the Thread object. Typically, you would want to monitor a thread that you think is overusing the processor and causing a slowdown in performance.

- **% Processor Time (Processor object).** This counter is typically used on multiprocessor systems. When used on a single processor system, it is the same as using the % Total Processor Time counter found in the System object. When used on a multiprocessor system, this counter shows which processors are being utilized the most and determines how the system is balancing application loads across processors: in most cases, the load should be balanced fairly evenly among the processors.

- **% Privileged Time (Processor object).** This counter is also most useful on multiprocessor systems. On a single processor system, this counter is equivalent to the % Total Privileged Time counter in the System object. On a multiprocessor system, this counter shows the % Privileged Time of an individual processor. This counter shows how much of the operating system's functions are being handled among individual processors.

- **% User Time (Processor object).** As with the other Processor object counters, this counter is usually used when monitoring multiprocessor systems. This counter is the same as the % Total User Time in the System object when used on a single processor system. This counter shows the amount of user processing or application processing being handled by an individual processor on a multiprocessor system.

Part
III

Ch
12

These counters provide a good overview of what is going on in a system when a processor bottleneck is suspected. Typically, the PROCESSOR.PMW workspace file shouldn't be used for general monitoring. Ideally, it should be used when a processor bottleneck is suspected since the counters concentrate on processor-related activity.

Analyzing CPU Performance

Now that you know which processor items can be monitored, you need to know how the processor is used by the Windows NT system. Understanding how different tasks use the processor is critical to determining which applications are causing a processor bottleneck. In fact, what at first seems to be a processor bottleneck may be something else entirely; and you need to know how to tell the difference between the different types of bottlenecks.

Windows NT can run 32-bit Windows programs designed to run under both Windows NT and Windows 95, 16-bit Windows programs, and MS-DOS programs. Each of these types of programs is handled differently under Windows NT. Understanding the differences between these various types of programs is very helpful in isolating performance problems.

N O T E   During some operations, it is common for the system to experience processor "spikes" where the processor utilization may reach 80% to 100%. These spikes do not necessarily indicate a processor bottleneck if the utilization drops back down to a reasonable level. Typically, these types of events occur when applications are first started on a Windows NT system. ■

Processor Scheduling

To better understand how Windows NT uses the processor, you have to understand how Windows NT multitasks; in other words, how Windows NT handles the apparently simultaneous running of multiple programs. Windows 3.1 uses "cooperative multitasking" to run multiple programs on the system. In this type of multitasking, a program is allowed to run until it voluntarily gives control back to the processor.

This means that programmers of applications have to explicitly code commands to give control back to the processor so that other programs can continue running. With well-written programs, this type of multitasking can work very well. However, if a program freezes or is poorly written, it may never return control back to the processor, completely halting the system.

Windows NT uses preemptive multitasking. In preemptive multitasking, the processor handles how programs—also referred to as processes—run based on the priority they have. The processor also ensures that all processes have a chance to run by giving each process running a certain amount of time to execute, regardless of the application's priority. This prevents the situation whereby a process uses the CPU indefinitely without giving other programs a chance to access the processor. For more information on multitasking, see Chapter 2, "Understanding Windows NT Workstation Architecture."

This processor control of process multitasking is known as *scheduling*. The processor schedules these processes based on a priority system. The priority of a process is based on how the user starts and interacts with it. Within processes are threads, which handle specific tasks. Each thread in the process is also assigned a priority based on the thread's processor requests, how it interacts with the user, or how it interacts with a given hardware device.

Table 12.1 shows the different interactions with the system that can cause a thread to have its priority increased or decreased.

Table 12.1   Items that Change the Priority of a Thread

Item	Priority Change
Accessing the processor	Lowers the priority of the thread.
Accessing a hardware device	Raises the priority of the thread.
Accessing a "user" hardware device	Raises the priority of the thread higher than accessing another hardware device. Examples of a "user" hardware device include the keyboard and the mouse.

Windows NT is designed to be very responsive to user requests while still trying to make sure all tasks get executed. Therefore, Windows NT gives threads that are being accessed by the user who is hitting a key on the keyboard or moving the mouse a higher priority than other threads. Windows NT also tries to allow I/O intensive threads higher priority so they don't tie up the system's hardware as long. A thread that the processor is actually executing gets its priority lowered to allow other threads a chance to execute.

On single processor systems, only one thread can be run at a time. If the system is a multiprocessor system, threads can be run on any processor when it first runs. After it is run on a processor, Windows NT tries to ensure that the thread continues to run on that processor. This allows the processor to reuse the data left in the processor's memory cache from the thread's last execution. However, this situation is not absolute, and Windows NT may change the processor that a thread uses depending on different situations.

A thread can have a priority from 1 to 31, with the higher numbers receiving more immediate processor time. Most user applications are started in the Normal Priority class which assigns a base priority of eight. If the user interacts with that application, the priority of the process is raised to nine. If the user stops interacting with the application, it drops down to a priority of seven. These priorities assume that nothing else changes in the system. As other applications receive processor time, the individual numbers may vary.

Part
III

Ch
12

However, the design of Windows NT to be immediately responsive to users can sometimes prevent certain background processes from being completed at a reasonable rate. This is especially true if a user has many foreground applications executing on a system that is constantly reaching 100% processor utilization.

If this situation occurs often, the user can reduce the foreground responsiveness to better allow background applications to run. The default setting of Windows NT Workstation is to allow the best foreground application response time. The user can change it to allow a slightly better foreground application response time than the background applications, or the user can choose to have foreground and background applications with the same response time. These options change the initial priority levels given to the applications.

Table 12.2 shows the initial priorities for the different settings.

Table 12.2 Foreground and Background Application Priorities for Different Response Settings

Performance Setting	Foreground Priority	Background Priority
Maximum	9	7
Minimum	8	7
None	7	7

To change the foreground/background application response time, do the following:

1. Open the Control Panel by clicking the Start button, then Settings, Control Panel or by double-clicking My Computer, Control Panel.

2. Double-click the System icon in the Control Panel window. The System Properties window will be displayed.

3. Click on the Performance Tab to display the Performance property sheet. Figure 12.1 shows the Performance property sheet.

4. In the Application Performance box, you should see a slider control with three settings. The control is set to Maximum by default. You can select Maximum, None, or the setting between the two.

5. After choosing the Application Performance setting you want, click the Apply or OK button. You will need to restart your computer for the changes to take effect.

FIG. 12.1

The Application Performance box, located in the Performance property sheet, allows you to change the base priority of foreground and background processes.

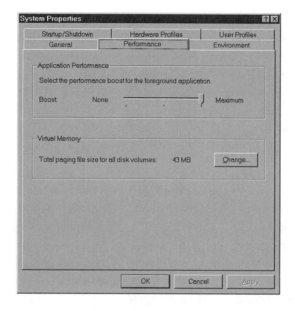

User Mode and Privileged Mode

There are two major modes of processing that can utilize processor time: user mode and privileged mode. The reason for these two modes is based on Windows NT security measures. Windows NT prevents certain programs from directly accessing hardware. Certain programs, known as privileged mode programs, handle direct communication to the hardware. Privileged mode programs have a higher level of security protection and access over other programs running on the system. Typically, privileged mode programs are item device drivers and other types of programs that need direct access to the system hardware.

User mode programs are programs, such as user applications, that need to access hardware devices by sending a request to a privileged mode program. These programs cannot directly access a hardware resource without the appropriate privileged mode program. Typically, user mode programs are applications that the user starts or other programs used by Windows NT that do not need to directly access the system hardware devices.

The purpose for having two types of program modes is to prevent a single application from incorrectly accessing a hardware device that can corrupt or freeze the entire system. Windows 3.1 did not have this level of protection, and it was fairly common for an application to freeze the entire system or cause it to become unstable by incorrectly accessing hardware devices.

Part

III

Ch

12

However, this high level of protection does have some disadvantages. First, it creates overhead that other operating systems do not have: this is one of the major reasons for Windows NT's larger hardware requirements. Second, some other applications, written for 16-bit Windows, MS-DOS, and Windows 95, try to directly access the hardware and are unable to run correctly under Windows NT. Windows NT blocks the program's attempt to directly access protected areas. These programs will not work properly under Windows NT and they should be run in the operating system that the program was designed to run under.

When trying to determine processor bottlenecks, you can analyze user mode and privileged mode processing to see how the Windows NT system is trying to run. Assume that you have a program running on the system that is causing 100% total processor utilization. The % Total Privileged Time and % Total User Time counters give you a better overview of what is going on in the system. If the % Total User Time is very high, while the % Total Privileged Time is very low, then you have an application that is using a lot of processor time without accessing a lot of system devices. Figure 12.2 shows an example of this type of application in Performance Monitor.

FIG. 12.2

This application (being monitored by the Performance Monitor) is utilizing a lot of processor time without accessing much privileged time.

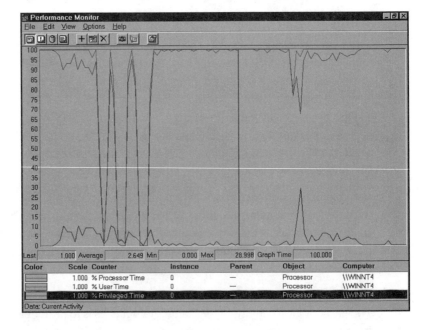

However, if you have an application that has a higher % Total Privileged Time counter, then you have an application that is using a lot of system resources to get work done. Applications of this type have to call the operating system each time they need to access a particular device. Figure 12.3 shows an example of this type of program.

FIG. 12.3

This application is making a lot of requests to the operating system to use devices on the system.

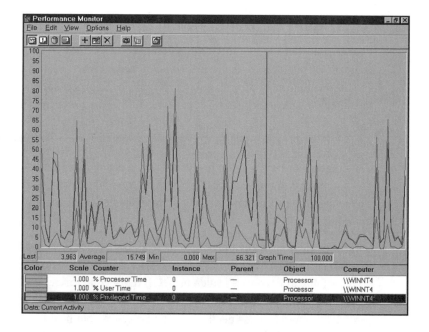

Neither of these types of programs is any better or worse than the other; they are just creating a bottleneck for various reasons and need to be handled differently. Knowing what is occurring in the system is the key to solving performance bottlenecks.

For example, assume that there a situation where the processor is reaching 80% to 100% for sustained periods of time. If Microsoft WordPad is being run on the computer, the natural instinct is that WordPad is the cause of the bottleneck. However, this may not be the case at all, and the way to find out is to see what else is occurring in the system.

If you use Performance Monitor to track the processor usage by applications, you might see that the % Privileged Time is reaching 70%. If the total processor time is at 100%, then the % User Time can only be 30%. This means that the system is spending a lot of time handling other system requests, which affects the performance of the application that is running in the foreground. It is possible that WordPad is making these requests by writing to the disk or by a similar action. But if the user is merely typing text in the document, then chances are the problem lies elsewhere.

However, if you see a situation where the % User Time is 70%, then the situation is dramatically different. This means that WordPad is the probable cause of the system slow-down if it is the only other user application running. If other user applications are running, you can determine whether WordPad is causing the problem by shutting down the other applications and seeing if the processor time drops dramatically.

Part

III

Ch

12

Lower Utilization Bottlenecks

It is possible there might be a system bottleneck even though the % Total Processor Time counter isn't at 100%. Typically, this situation occurs when a lot of threads try to access the CPU at one time or in very close intervals. Since the processor is busy with one thread, the other threads are forced to sit in a queue. The processor may not be completely utilized by the one thread, so the utilization percentage may not be excessively high, but if enough threads back up in the queue, the overall performance of the system may suffer.

The number of threads in the processor queue is not dependent on the processor utilization percentage. A processor can be 100% busy without having any items in the queue. Conversely, the processor queue can have many items backed up, while the processor utilization is low.

To further illustrate an example of a lower utilization bottleneck, assume that there are four threads that need to access the processor. The first thread uses the processor for .78 seconds for a processor utilization of 78%. If the second thread arrives .5 seconds into the processing of the first thread, then it is forced to sit in the queue. After .7 seconds have passed, two more threads need to use the processor, but it still is not available to these threads, so they also wait in the queue. While the processor utilization is at 80%, there are three threads that are sitting idle waiting to be processed.

In the preceding illustration, it is very possible on an active system, with a lot of threads running, that the queue could become quite large. This causes a system slowdown without the processor becoming overburdened. This situation arises when there are many processor requests for greatly differing amounts of time.

Monitoring the Processor Queue Length counter in Performance Monitor is the way to spot these lower utilization bottlenecks. Usually this counter doesn't have values higher than two. If you see a larger number of threads lined up in the queue, then you have a problem. This type of problem is often solved by adding processors.

16-bit Windows Applications and Processor Usage

Monitoring processor usage by 16-bit Windows applications is much different than monitoring usage by 32-Windows NT applications because of the way the two types of programs are run. Windows NT uses the Windows-16 on Windows-32 (WOW) subsystem to execute 16-bit Windows applications. This subsystem is used because 16-bit Windows applications share the same address space under Windows 3.1. However, under Windows NT, the address space used by one application is not shared with another application. The WOW subsystem allows all 16-bit Windows applications to share an address space with other 16-bit Windows applications by default.

A user can specify for a 16-bit Windows application to run in its own address space under Windows NT by checking the Run in Separate Memory Space checkbox in the Run window or by using the /separate option from the command line. You can also configure a 16-bit Windows shortcut to run in its own address space by right-clicking, choosing Properties, and then the Shortcut tab. After the Shortcut property sheet is displayed, check the Run in Separate Memory Space checkbox. Figure 12.4 displays the Shortcut property sheet.

FIG. 12.4

The Shortcut property sheet allows you to run a 16-bit Windows shortcut on the Windows NT desktop in its own memory address space.

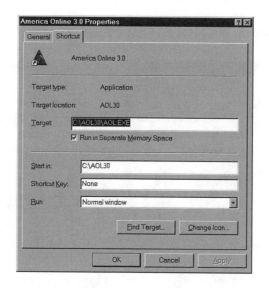

When 16-bit Windows programs are run under Windows NT, they run as separate threads but in a single process called NTVDM (or NT virtual DOS machine). Because all Windows 3.1 applications run in the NTVDM process, monitoring multiple Windows 3.1 applications can be quite tricky. The only way to identify different 16-bit Windows applications is by the NTVDM thread number.

Another hindrance in trying to monitor 16-bit Windows applications is that NTVDM starts when Windows NT starts. So, in order to monitor 16-bit Windows applications, you need to view how many threads NTVDM is using *before* you start any 16-bit applications. Then, you can start 16-bit applications and check Performance Monitor after each application starts. The step-by-step procedure is as follows:

1. Start the Windows NT Performance Monitor by selecting the Start button, Programs, Administrative Tools, and then Performance Monitor. Be sure that you start Performance Monitor *before* starting any MS-DOS or 16-bit Windows applications.

2. Change to Report view by choosing View, Report or by clicking the View Report Data button (the 4th button from the left) on the toolbar.

Part
III

Ch
12

3. Select <u>E</u>dit, <u>A</u>dd to Report from the menu or click the Add Counter button on the toolbar. The Add to Report Window is displayed.

4. In the Add to Report window, find the O<u>b</u>ject drop-drop down list. In the list, select the Thread object.

5. Once the Thread object is selected, the <u>I</u>nstance box will list all of the different threads for each process that is currently running on the system. For example, you should see something like, "ntvdm==>0" as one thread for the NTVDM process. Figure 12.5 shows an example of the Add to Report window with the Thread object selected and the threads of the NTVDM process listed.

FIG. 12.5
The Add to Report window allows you to select which thread of the NTVDM process you want to monitor. It also allows you to see how many threads are being used by the NTVDM process before any 16-bit Windows applications are started.

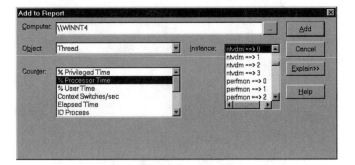

6. You can either add these items to the report by selecting a counter to use and clicking the <u>A</u>dd button or by counting how many NTVDM threads are running without any 16-bit Windows programs open.

7. Minimize Performance Monitor.

8. Start a 16-bit Windows application, then minimize it.

9. Switch back to Performance Monitor and open the Add to Report window again. Choose the Thread object and view the threads listed in the <u>I</u>nstance box. You should see one more thread of the NTVDM process running. Since you want to monitor this 16-bit Windows application, select a Counter, such as % Processor Time, and click the <u>A</u>dd button. Then, click the <u>D</u>one button.

10. Continue steps 7 through 9 until you have all the 16-bit Windows applications you want to monitor listed in the report. Figure 12.6 shows the Performance Monitor program in Report view with some 16-bit Windows applications running.

11. When you are finished, close the applications and Performance Monitor.

FIG. 12.6

This Report view of Performance Monitor shows many NTVDM threads being monitored. Each NTVDM thread is numbered and helps to determine which 16-bit application you want to monitor.

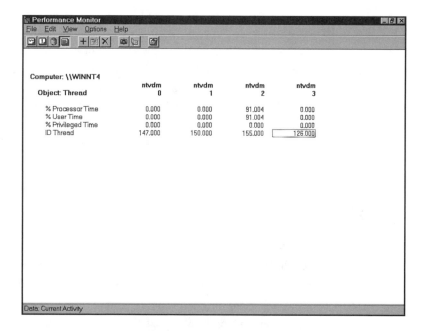

The above procedure works very well when you first start 16-bit Windows applications, but what if you close one of the applications that is listed in the middle of the threads? For example, what if there are four 16-bit applications running and the application that is being monitored by NTVDM 3 is closed? It turns out that NTVDM 4 is moved to NTVDM 3. So, how do you keep track of all of these threads when the thread labels can change? It turns out that the counter ID Thread stays constant with the application.

By adding the ID Thread counter to the Performance Monitor Report, you can keep track of the different 16-bit Windows threads. Knowing the ID Thread allows those applications to be closed in any order without causing confusion for the user monitoring the threads. Figure 12.6 shows an example of the ID Thread counters displayed for the different NTVDM threads.

Part III

Ch 12

> **N O T E** 16-bit application performance is one instance where Intel-based systems outperform most RISC-based systems. Since Intel-based processors, with the exception of the Pentium Pro, are designed to run MS-DOS and 16-bit Windows applications, these applications have pretty good performance under Windows NT. RISC-based machines cannot run these programs natively and must use emulation to run them. The overhead of the emulation process causes a reduction in performance of these applications. ■

MS-DOS Applications and Processor Usage

Trying to monitor MS-DOS applications under Windows NT becomes even more complicated than monitoring either 16-bit or 32-bit Windows applications. This complication occurs because each MS-DOS application is an NTVDM process. This situation becomes more complex if 16-bit Windows applications are used since they are all run in a single NTVDM process. Performance Monitor can only track one process of a given name at a time, and with all of these NTVDM processes being run, tracking them becomes rather interesting.

However, there is a way to track multiple MS-DOS applications using Performance Monitor, but it isn't very elegant. To monitor different MS-DOS applications using Performance Monitor, do the following:

1. Start the Windows NT Performance Monitor by selecting the Start button, Programs, Administrative Tools, and then Performance Monitor. Be sure that you start Performance Monitor *before* starting any MS-DOS or 16-bit Windows applications.

2. Change to Report view by choosing View, Report or by clicking the View Report Data button on the toolbar. Minimize Performance Monitor.

3. Start the MS-DOS application to be run under Windows NT.

4. Switch to the Windows NT Performance Monitor using the Alt+ Tab keys.

5. In Performance Monitor, start tracking the MS-DOS application. To do this, click the Add Counter button or choose Edit, Add to Chart from the menu. In the Add to Chart Window, select the Process object and any counters you want to monitor.

6. Minimize Performance Monitor again.

7. You already have one copy of NTVDM being monitored. In order to track another MS-DOS program, you have to copy NTVDM.EXE and give the copy a different name, for example: NTVDM2.EXE. Open the Windows NT Explorer and find the System32 subfolder located in the Windows NT main folder. Find and highlight NTVDM.EXE, right-click the file, and choose Copy. Copy it to the same directory, but with the filename NTVDM2.EXE. Close the Windows NT Explorer. Be sure to only copy NTVDM.EXE to another filename; do *not* rename it!

8. You now have to tell Windows NT to use NTVDM2.EXE when starting MS-DOS programs. To do this, you have to modify the Windows NT Registry. Start REGEDT32.EXE from the Start, Run, and type REGEDT32.EXE in the Run box.

9. In the Registry Editor, find and select the HKEY_LOCAL_MACHINE window. Expand the SYSTEM key, expand the CurrentControlSet key, and open the Control subkey. At the very bottom of the Control subkey, you should see the WOW subkey. Highlight the WOW subkey by clicking on it with the mouse. On the right side of

the Registry Editor screen, you should see a value called "cmdline." The complete Registry path is: HKEY_LOCAL_MACHINE\SYSTEM\ CurrentControlSet\ Control\WOW\cmdline

10. The cmdline value should contain:

%SystemRoot%\system32\ntvdm -f%SystemRoot%\system32 -a.

Double-click the cmdline value to edit the value. Add a "2" to the end of ntvdm, and then choose OK.

11. Close the Registry Editor and open a second MS-DOS session using the Windows NT command line.

12. Switch to Performance Monitor and add the NTVDM2 process. You should see both processes running in Performance Monitor. When you are finished, close both MS-DOS sessions and Performance Monitor. You should also change the cmdline Registry setting back to use the NTVDM.EXE file.

N O T E As with 16-bit Windows applications, Intel-based processors offer the best performance for MS-DOS applications. RISC-based systems require emulation for these programs to run, which slows down the applications. Some MS-DOS programs may not run at all on RISC-based machines due to hardware differences between Intel-based and RISC-based machines. ▪

"Hidden" Processes Started with Windows NT

Even when the user is not running any applications, the Windows NT system has many processes that are being handled by the processor in the background. Windows NT systems that are connected to a network have even more processes running. Windows NT Servers that are responsible for a service on the network may handle a very large number of background processes.

Windows NT has to dedicate some processor time to each of these processes. Although Windows NT tries to give user programs priority over these other processes, user applications may slow down if other processes take up too much processor time. It is also very possible for the processor queue to build up over time with all of these processes running.

Even on a non-networked Windows NT computer, here are just some of the processes you can expect to see running on a Windows NT computer:

- **clipsrv (Clipbook Server)**. The clipsrv process handles the Clipbook Server on the Windows NT computer for both local and network users. The Clipbook is the equivalent to the Clipboard of Windows 3.1, but it allows multiple items to be stored and can be shared on the network. This process may not appear until the Clipbook Viewer has been used.

- **csrss (Client Server Runtime System)**. The csrss process handles the processing of windows and other graphical components on a Windows NT system.

- **EventLog**. This process handles all of the events to be logged under Windows NT.

- **Explorer**. This process controls the presentation, interface, and tasking functions of Windows NT.

- **Idle**. When the processor is not actually executing a program thread, the idle thread is issued to that processor.

- **lsass (Local Security Administration Subsystem)**. This process handles the different security tasks for the local computer and its resources.

- **nddeagnt (Network DDE Agent)**. This process handles requests for network DDE services.

- **netdde (Network DDE)**. This process handles requests for network DDE data. It differs from nddeagnt by providing the actual DDE data rather than the handling of that data. This process may not appear unless a program is using the Network DDE process, such as the Clipbook Viewer program.

- **screg (Service Controller/Registry)**. This process handles service control functions and remote requests to the Registry.

- **spoolss (Printer Spooler)**. This process handles the moving of data from a temporary location on the hard disk to the printer device.

- **System**. This process handles a variety of system functions, such as background cache writing or virtual memory tasks.

- **winlogon**. The winlogon process handles the logging on and logging off of users on the Windows NT system.

When monitoring a Windows NT system with Performance Monitor, another process will be added: perfmon. This is the Performance Monitor program running in the background. You can also view the total processes currently running on a Windows NT machine in the Processes property sheet in the Task Manager window. Of course, if you are using Task Manager to view the processes, the process named taskmgr will be in the list.

On a networked Windows NT computer, even more processes will be running in the background. With all of these processes running, the user will run applications that use even more processor time. Most of the time, the background processes aren't very active, so they don't affect the user's application performance.

A notable difference comes when using a Windows NT computer for some sort of server on the network. For example, if a Windows NT computer is acting as a RAS server, user applications will be affected when remote users are connected to RAS. Typically, this is why Window NT Server machines are usually dedicated servers, without users running applications on them. Although it is possible to use these machines to run user applications, it often is impractical.

Even Windows NT Workstation machines that have a lot of shared files and directories may run into performance problems if those shares are accessed by a lot of network users. If such a problem occurs, the shared data is better-off transferred to a dedicated server. If no dedicated server exists, then a machine that is not heavily used can also be used to store the data.

Another way to reduce the strain on the system is to make sure that no unnecessary processes are running. To examine which processes are running, use the Windows NT Task Manager. The Processes property sheet will list all of the processes running on the system.

CAUTION

You can end processes from the Windows NT Task Manager. Before closing any processes on the Windows NT machine, be sure you know what they do. Some of the background processes are critical to the proper operation of Windows NT. Also, closing processes from the Task Manager should only be considered as a last resort. It is recommended that you use the Task Manager to simply view the processes running on the system.

Eliminating Bottlenecks

Part
III

Ch
12

Once you discover that the system is indeed running slower than it should be, you have to begin the search for which component is causing the bottleneck. After that, you must figure out how to remedy the situation. There are really only two options if the processor is determined to be the bottleneck: either upgrade the processor or add additional processors to the system.

CAUTION

Be sure that the processor is the true cause of the bottleneck before trying to upgrade to a faster processor or replacing the system. Many bottlenecks, like inadequate system memory or incorrectly configured CMOS settings, may at first appear to be processor bottlenecks. Be sure to track various items in Performance Monitor, not just processor performance. After spending hundreds or thousands of dollars, you don't want to find out that the processor wasn't the problem after all!

If the processor is found to be a bottleneck, then upgrading to a faster processor will almost always improve the overall system performance. Upgrading the processor can be accomplished three ways: installing a faster version of the current type of processor, replacing the motherboard with one that has a faster processor, or buying a completely new machine.

Certain processor types—like the Intel series of processors—have "overdrive" processors that are double or triple the clock speed of the current processor. These types of processors replace the old processor but allow the user to use the existing motherboard and its components. Be sure that any processor upgrade is compatible with Windows NT by checking the Hardware Compatibility List or by contacting the manufacturer. This option is the most practical when the bottleneck is not too severe and the user wants to keep all of the existing components.

Replacing the motherboard is another option to relieve processor bottlenecks. This option requires that the entire system be dismantled and the main system board be replaced. This is a very time-consuming and complex task and should not be done by an individual who is inexperienced with computer hardware. However, if done by a hardware-proficient individual, replacing the motherboard may provide dramatic processing improvements. Replacing the motherboard can also reduce other system bottlenecks, such as I/O bottlenecks, if the bus type or other components are faster than the older components.

The third option—to completely buy a new machine—may turn out to be the most practical. If the system is suffering numerous bottlenecks from the processor, disk system, memory, and so on, then the system is inadequate to run the current demands of the user. Buying a new machine doesn't always mean that the old machine can't be used to run Windows NT; the new machine may just handle certain tasks to reduce the load on the older machine. An example is when a replaced computer is configured to be a process server, such as an e-mail server, on a network to reduce the burden on the main file server on a network.

N O T E   If you need to replace a machine with a new one, you should consider a computer that has a processor designed for 32-bit operating systems, like Windows NT. For example, a Pentium Pro system handles 32-bit applications much better than Pentium systems, which are designed with 16-bit applications in mind. ▪

Adding Additional Processors

Adding additional processors to a Windows NT system may be the solution for some processor bottlenecks. However, other processor bottlenecks are not solved with the addition of processors to the system. Determining whether or not to add processors to the system is based on what types of programs are being run on the Windows NT system.

N O T E Multiple processors are really only useful if the Windows NT system is running 32-bit multithreaded programs. Applications designed for Windows 3.1 or MS-DOS are run as single threads under Windows NT. These programs will not gain any direct performance improvement on a multiprocessor Windows NT system. The only performance improvement that will occur is Windows NT's own ability to utilize multiple processors. ∎

Even if you run 32-bit Windows applications exclusively on your system, multiple processors still may not provide a dramatic performance increase. In order to fully utilize multiple processors, the 32-bit applications must be multi-threaded. Because Windows NT allows multiple threads to run on multiple processors, if there is only one thread used by the application, only one processor is used to execute that thread.

Also, even if you run 32-bit multithreaded applications exclusively on your system, there may be times that multiple processors don't have much of an effect on the system. If the system has many applications trying to access the same resource, only one will be able to access that resource before the other can use it. Monitor how your applications use the system when determining whether a second processor is needed.

Processing handled by multiple processors is known as *multiprocessing*. There are two types of multiprocessing: asymmetric and symmetric. Asymmetric processing assigns specific tasks to individual processors on the system. This means a process will always run on a particular processor whether or not another processor is available to handle the process. This type of multiprocessing makes it hard for applications to run on different hardware platforms. Asymmetric processing may also overwork a particular processor while leaving other processors relatively idle, if the tasks have different processing requirements.

Symmetric processing tries to even out the entire system load among all of the processors on the system. Windows NT uses symmetric multiprocessing (SMP) to handle processing with multiple processors. While Windows NT tries to keep a task running on the same processor when it can, it will move the tasks to different processors to help even out the overall system load.

Windows NT Workstation can support up to two processors by default. Windows NT Server is designed to handle up to 4 processors when using the retail version. OEM versions may allow more processors to be added. OEM versions of Windows NT can have a maximum of 32 processors, but usually it is only cost-effective to have between four to eight processors on a single system. Multiprocessor support is available for all of the processor platforms, both Intel and RISC processors, that can run Windows NT.

Part

III

Ch

12

Adding an additional processor to a Windows NT varies depending on the original number of processors in the system. If multiple processors were installed when Windows NT was installed, the additional processor can be added to the system, and Windows NT will recognize the new processor when the system starts.

However, if the system only had one processor and a second is added, then the situation is a bit more complex. The Windows NT Kernel is different for single processors and multiple processors. If a second processor is added to a single processor machine, the multiprocessor Kernel has to be installed. Microsoft recommends using the Uni- to Multi-Processor program (UPTOMP.EXE), found in the Windows NT Resource Kit, to update the Windows NT Kernel. Figure 12.7 shows the Uni- to Multi-Processor utility found in the Windows NT Resource Kit. Otherwise, you may have to reinstall Windows NT before the second processor will be utilized by Windows NT.

FIG. 12.7
The Uni- to Multi-Processor program allows the Windows NT Kernel to be changed from the uniprocessor kernel to the multiprocessor kernel, without re-installing Windows NT.

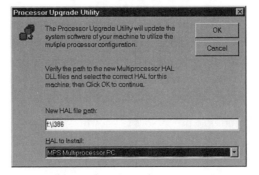

CAUTION

Before adding processors, be sure to check with the manufacturer of the system for special instructions regarding multiple processors and Windows NT. Multiprocessor systems vary on installation issues from manufacturer to manufacturer.

Monitoring and Optimizing SMP Systems

Monitoring symmetric multiprocessing systems (SMP) is very similar to monitoring uniprocessor systems, except now you have a counter for each of the processors. By monitoring individual processors, you can see which processors are being used by the different threads executing on the system. You can also monitor the overall processor performance to see an overview of how the system is handling the processing load.

To monitor individual processors, the Processor object in Performance Monitor is used. These counters allow the user to monitor the individual processors to see how they are performing. The System object counters give you an overview of the processing performance of the entire system, treating the individual processors as one larger unit.

Assume that you have an ideal multiprocessing scenario with four threads, and each thread is running on one of four processors. Since you only have four threads running, no threads are queued in the processor queue. No threads are trying to access resources that another thread is using. Under these conditions SMP works much better than a uniprocessor scenario since the system is handling four times the work with the same speed as a single processor system.

However, the ideal scenario doesn't always occur. System bottlenecks occur on multiprocessor systems that are different from single processor machines. With multiprocessor systems, one of the most common situations is the contention of resources by two separate threads. When this situation occurs, the speed advantages of multiple processors starts to diminish. The thread that is unable to use a taken resource is no longer able to execute. To make matters worse, if no other threads are available to be executed, the processor will sit idle until that resource is free.

Under the worst conditions, if all four threads want to access the same resource, then you will only have one thread actually using the resource, while the other three sit idle. A similar situation can exist on a single processor machine where four threads try to access the same resource, but monitoring it is different. With the single processor, the processor queue will build up. While under a multiprocessor system, the processor queue will be empty.

Part
III

Ch
12

Another reduction of speed can occur with multiple threads in the same process. Each new thread reduces the processor response time. Yet, multiple threads from different processes don't have the same effect. Why does this happen with multiple threads in the same process? The explanation is similar to the example above about four threads trying to access the same resource. When a process is run, a single address space is used for that process regardless of the number of threads the process has. Since each thread in the process has to use the same memory address space, the problem of resource contention occurs.

This problem of resource contention creates a slowdown when a multithreaded application is run. This helps to explain why you may not get the full advantage of multiprocessor systems that you would expect. Unfortunately, there really isn't a solution to this problem. The best you can do is realize that it occurs and not spend a lot of time trying to correct it.

From Here...

Windows NT is a very demanding operating system, and it places a very large burden on the processor. Reducing processor bottlenecks can lead to dramatic improvements in overall performance of a Windows NT system. Windows NT runs many types of applications different ways, and determining where the bottleneck occurs requires a solid knowledge of how certain applications are run.

Once processor bottlenecks are discovered, often the decision to upgrade to a faster processor or add additional processors needs to be made. Both types of hardware improvements have advantages and disadvantages and require a solid understanding of the types of applications that are being run and how the system is used by those applications.

For information on topics related to monitoring and improving Windows NT performance, see the following chapters:

- Chapter 8, "Monitoring Performance," provides more information on using the Windows NT Performance Monitor and a basic overview of monitoring Windows NT computers.
- Chapter 9, "Optimizing Physical and Virtual Memory," describes the effects of memory on a Windows NT system. It covers how both physical and virtual memory impact a Windows NT computer.
- Chapter 10, "Optimizing the File System," covers monitoring and optimizing the different file systems used by Windows NT to store data.

CHAPTER 13

Enhancing Video and I/O Performance

by Richard Neff

Because Windows NT is largely a graphical operating system, the video performance of a system is a key factor in determining how fast Windows NT will seem to the user. If the video display adapter is not designed to handle large graphic displays, the performance of Windows NT will be diminished. This is especially important when using Windows NT Workstation, because a user will be very concerned with how fast the video display performs.

Along with video performance, the I/O performance of various hardware devices is also important. Many computers use hardware devices attached to both serial and parallel ports. Devices such as network cards place higher performance demands on a Windows NT system. Ensuring adequate performance of all of the other hardware devices is very important to an administrator of a Windows NT computer. ■

Video performance factors

Many items affect the performance of video equipment under Windows NT.

Monitoring video performance

Although Windows NT does not have any type of video object that can be specifically used to monitor video performance, there is a workaround to allow some monitoring.

Optimizing video performance

There are ways, usually through hardware upgrades, to improve the video performance of Windows NT.

I/O performance factors

As with video performance, there are many items affecting the performance of I/O functions under Windows NT.

Monitoring I/O performance

The Performance Monitor allows monitoring of certain I/O performance items to see how Windows NT is utilizing I/O devices.

Optimizing I/O performance

I/O performance can be optimized in many instances.

Overview of Video Performance

The video performance of a Windows NT machine affects how fast Windows NT appears to the user. Even the fastest processor on a Windows NT machine will seem slow if the video subsystem is overburdened. Unlike a text-based command operating system, the Windows NT operating system is a graphical operating system that requires a more powerful video system.

Since Windows NT 4.0 is designed to run many of the graphics-intensive programs—most notably games—that Windows 95 is designed to run, the video performance becomes even more important than under older versions of Windows NT. However, games are not the only programs that push the video adapter to its limits; programs that handle complex drawings or programs that handle full-motion video can also burden the processor subsystem of a Windows NT computer. Even ordinary business programs are becoming more graphics intensive by including video clips and other multimedia items.

Understanding Video Bottlenecks

Video bottlenecks occur from two separate areas: the actual video controller hardware and the software drivers that interact with the Windows NT system and the video controller. One of these areas, the actual controller hardware, should be addressed before the system is even purchased.

Video Types

Before discussing video displays used by Windows NT, a brief discussion of the different video types is needed. When the IBM PC was first introduced, the color video card that was used was known as CGA (Color Graphics Adapter). The original IBM PC also had a Monochrome Graphics Adapter (MGA) for users who preferred a monochrome display. Later, EGA (Enhanced Graphics Adapter) was introduced. Earlier versions of Windows supported EGA; however, Windows NT no longer supports EGA due to its lack of popularity. Windows NT requires at least a VGA (Video Graphics Adapter) in order to work properly, although SVGA (Super VGA) is the recommended type of video adapter to be used.

However, the Windows NT VGA video mode is often used when troubleshooting displays. This video mode is universal, allowing it to be used by all adapters when Windows NT will not start properly with the current display configuration. It is used as a starting point by Windows NT to ensure that it can display the graphical user interface correctly. However, for best performance, you should try to ensure that the video driver used for normal operation is specific to your brand of video card.

Bus Types

The type of bus that the video controller uses is a critical part of the performance equation. The *bus*, when describing personal computer hardware, is the path for hardware devices to communicate with the processor. Bus types have evolved dramatically over the years, due mainly to increasing video demands by the newest generation of graphical operating systems like the Microsoft Windows family.

ISA   The Industry Standard Architecture (ISA) bus was first used by the original IBM PC computer. The original ISA bus found on the IBM PC/XT was an 8-bit expansion bus, but with the introduction of the IBM AT, it was expanded to a 16-bit bus. This 16-bit bus quickly became an industry standard for many different types of hardware adapters.

While the ISA bus proved to be adequate for many hardware devices, video requirements quickly overwhelmed the ability of the ISA standard. The ISA bus is the slowest bus available on an Intel-based computer and video cards using it are *not* recommended for adequate speed under a graphical operating system, such as Windows NT.

Ironically, while bus standards have been introduced to replace the ISA architecture, it can still be found on almost all Intel-based personal computers today, coexisting with VL-bus and PCI slots. The reason for its strong popularity has been the proliferation of hardware devices using the ISA bus. Many of these devices, such as sound cards, do not take full advantage of a faster bus architecture like video cards do. This, combined with the lower price of producing ISA cards, has kept the ISA standard very much alive to this day. However, many speed-intensive devices do not use the ISA bus.

EISA and Microchannel   When the Intel 386 processor was introduced, the ISA bus proved to be too slow for certain hardware components. To remedy this, IBM introduced the Microchannel architecture with the release of its PS/2 personal computer line in 1987. The Microchannel bus was designed to provide much faster communication speeds between the processor and the hardware devices. The Microchannel bus was a 32-bit bus that improved the speed of communication between the processor and the hardware adapter.

Part
III

Ch
13

The Microchannel bus was also designed to eliminate the complicated hassle for the user of dealing with conflicting IRQs, memory addresses, and so on, of hardware devices. Microchannel was also known as MCA; however, MCA was dropped after IBM lost a lawsuit filed by Music Corporation of America.

The Microchannel method had one major drawback: it was not backwards-compatible with the ISA hardware adapters, which had become numerous. This prevented the existing ISA-based hardware devices from working in a Microchannel machine. Also, IBM implemented a royalty structure that many manufacturers didn't agree with. A group of manufacturers decided that, instead of adopting the IBM Microchannel standard, they were going to create a new bus standard. The result of this effort was the Enhanced Industry Standard Architecture (EISA) bus.

The EISA bus was a 32-bit bus, like the Microchannel bus, but it remained backwards-compatible with existing ISA boards. It achieved this by having a special card slot where the adapter cards were connected to the computer's motherboard. The EISA card slot allowed EISA cards to seat completely into the EISA slot, while ISA cards only were allowed to seat far enough to reach the first set of connectors. EISA became the standard 32-bit bus for most non-IBM personal computers.

However, with the introduction of the 486 processor, and later the Pentium processor, even the Microchannel and EISA buses proved to be too slow for certain hardware devices, such as video cards. In addition, the growing popularity of graphical user interfaces, such as Windows and OS/2, pushed the video display speeds even further. In addition, software configuration utilities were used to set up these devices, which many users did not like. As a result, faster buses have become more prevalent, and both the Microchannel and EISA buses have been replaced.

VL-Bus and PCI   As computer processors became faster and graphical user interfaces became more common, the need for faster communication with the video adapter became necessary. To handle this need, the Video Electronics Standards Association (VESA) designed a bus known as a direct bus. This allowed "direct" communication between the processor and the video card without having to have the bus controller handling the data transfer. This bus is known as the VL-bus. This bus is very popular on most Intel 486-based personal computers.

The VL-bus also has an advantage for users who require backwards compatibility with ISA adapters, because ISA adapters can be inserted in VL-bus slots. Of course, using ISA adapters in these slots does not provide a performance advantage. VL-bus adapters are very inexpensive to implement into the motherboard, but they require more processor overhead.

Another direct bus standard was created by Intel called the Peripheral Component Interconnect (PCI) bus. The PCI bus allows the same 64-bit communications of the VL-bus but has many more speed-enhancing features to improve data communication between the PCI hardware and the processor. The PCI bus is now found on almost all Pentium-based computers. It is also found on many other platforms, such as the Apple PowerPC and DEC Alpha computers.

These direct bus standards coexist with standard ISA bus slots on a computer. A VL-bus usually has anywhere between one and three slots on a motherboard, while a PCI bus can have a maximum of four slots. The direct bus slots are primarily used by video cards, IDE or EIDE disk controller cards, SCSI controllers, and network cards. The other slots, usually ISA slots (although EISA is sometimes found), are used by other cards that don't require very fast bus speeds. These devices include sound cards, modems, and so on. This configuration allows for a good compromise of both speed and affordability. It also allows computer owners to upgrade the machine or motherboard and still be able to migrate existing ISA hardware devices.

Graphics Accelerators versus Standard Video Boards

In the earlier years of personal computing, graphical displays were considered a high-priced luxury item. Most PC's used MS-DOS, CP-M, or some other text-based operating system where graphical video functions weren't needed. Of course, as hardware became more powerful and faster, graphical operating systems became more common. With the more graphical nature of operating systems, video boards, like bus types, evolved to handle this type of system.

Older video boards that were designed with MS-DOS in mind required the computer's processor to handle most of the processing of the video display functions. This processing was handled along with the rest of the other processing functions. However, with graphical user interfaces, the display processing took up a lot more of the processor's time. This resulted in slower overall system performance.

To overcome this problem under graphically-intense programs, video boards began to contain separate video processors to handle video-related processing. These types of video adapters became known as graphic accelerator boards. This type of adapter shifted the display processing from the main processor to the video processor.

Almost all video cards sold today are graphic accelerator cards and are VGA (Video Graphics Adapter) or SVGA (Super Video Graphics Adapter) boards. Many of these boards are designed to specifically improve the performance of the Microsoft Windows family and are usually VL-bus or PCI cards.

Part
III

Ch
13

Video Memory

For video cards that contain dedicated video processors, video memory is needed to store temporary information needed by the processor. This is similar to the memory needed by the main CPU of a computer system. However, this memory is dedicated for use by the video processor, and is known as VRAM (Video Random Access Memory). Video memory requirements are based on the resolution to be displayed and the number of simultaneous colors to be shown. Without the proper amount of video memory, certain resolutions cannot be shown.

The amount of video memory that can be put on a video card depends on the manufacturer of the adapter. Most SVGA cards have at least 512K to 1M of VRAM already installed, and can allow a maximum of 2M to 8M, depending on the manufacturer. Be sure to check with the manufacturer or the adapter's documentation on the type of memory needed and the proper method of installation.

Monitoring Video Performance

One of the things you've probably noticed when using the Windows NT Performance Monitor to monitor system performance is the absence of obvious video monitoring items. While the Performance Monitor includes many items that can be watched concerning the processor, pagefile, memory, and other hardware, the video system seems to have been completely left out. This is not entirely true, even though the Performance Monitor provides no video list of items.

It is possible to get an indirect idea of the video activity of a system using Windows NT. The Process object in Performance Monitor contains an instance called CSRSS. CSRSS stands for client-server runtime system. By using the % Processor Time, % Privilege Time, and the % User Time, we can get some idea of the video performance of the system.

The CSRSS item is a subsystem of Windows NT that carries out application graphical activities. CSRSS carries all window manipulation in Windows NT, not just the graphics portion. Therefore, while measuring the CSRSS item gives an indication of video performance, not all data for that item is always related to video information. Because there is no specific video item, the CSRSS item gives us the best indication of overall video performance since a majority of its job is often the display of windows on the screen.

To monitor video performance using the CSRSS instance, do the following:

1. Open the Windows NT Performance Monitor program by clicking the Start button, then Programs. Choose the Administrative Tools item, then Performance Monitor.

2. Click the Add button to add items to be graphed in Performance Monitor. The Add button will display the dialog box shown in figure 13.1.

FIG. 13.1

The Add to Chart dialog box allows you to add the CSRSS counter items to the monitor using Performance Monitor.

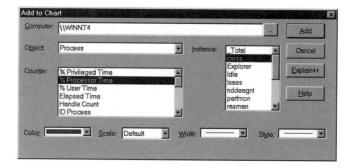

3. Click the down arrow of the O**bj**ect drop-down list box. From the list box, choose Process.

4. In the **I**nstance list, click the CSRSS item. Be sure to select this item; otherwise, the CSRSS instance will not be recorded in Performance Monitor.

5. Then in the Coun**t**er box, choose % Processor Time. This will graph the performance of the CSRSS % processor time.

6. If you want a brief explanation of what a particular counter does, click the **E**xplain button. The window will expand, and a description of the counter will be displayed.

7. You can repeat steps 3 through 6 for both the % Privilege Time and the % User Time counters.

8. When you are finished, select the Done button to close the window. Performance Monitor can then be minimized and run in the background while the computer is being used. As the computer is used, Performance Monitor can be maximized to give an indication of video performance for that computer.

Improving Video Performance

The biggest improvements in video performance occur when changes are made to the video hardware of the Windows NT system. Most new computer systems are more than adequate to handle the video requirements of Windows NT. The biggest challenge comes with older computer systems that weren't designed with a graphical user interface in mind. It has to be determined whether it is worth the expense and effort of trying to upgrade to meet the hardware requirements or whether it is more effective to buy a new machine. Many older machines are limited by the bus type that is used on the system. The bus type cannot be upgraded without a new motherboard, and without improving the bus type for the video adapter, video performance will be limited.

Part
III

Ch
13

For existing Windows NT systems, upgrading a video card to one with a faster graphics processor will also help increase the video performance of a computer system. Many video boards are designed with improving the performance of Windows in mind. For very graphics-intensive systems, higher-end video boards are the solution for slow video performance.

Adding Video Memory

Adding video memory can sometimes help improve the video performance of a video card. The biggest advantage of video memory isn't actual speed, but the amount of simultaneous colors that can be displayed at a given resolution. By default, the Windows NT VGA driver allows a maximum of 16 colors to be displayed at once. However, most graphics-oriented programs are designed for use with at least 256 total colors. It is recommended that you have at least enough video memory to display 256 colors at the resolution you are using.

The amount of video memory needed to display 256 colors depends on the resolution being used. For most adapters, 1M of video memory is needed to display 256 colors for a screen resolution of 800 x 600 or 1024 x 768. However, your adapter may allow even more colors to be displayed or a higher resolution. In these cases, 2M or 4M may be needed.

Table 13.1 helps to determine how much video memory is typically needed for the various resolutions. These figures may differ slightly depending on the manufacturer of the video card.

Table 13.1   Video Memory Needed for Different Video Resolutions

Video Memory	Resolutions Typically Available
512K	640×480 (256 colors), 800×600 (256 colors), 1020×668 (16 colors)
1M	640×480 (65K colors), 800×600 (256 colors), 1024×768 (256 colors), 1152×864 (16 colors)
2M	640×480 (16.8M colors), 800×600 (16.8M colors), 1020×668 (65K colors), 1152×864 (65K colors), 1280×1024 (256 colors), 1600×1200 (256 colors)
4M	640×480 (16.8M colors), 800×600 (16.8M colors), 1024×768 (16.8M colors), 1152×864 (16.8M colors), 1280×1024 (16.8M colors), 1600×1200 (65K colors)

Adding video memory usually requires you to purchase the memory expansion through the manufacturer of the video board. Different video boards may use different video memory types, so be sure to check with the manufacturer of the video card to determine the proper memory type used on your adapter.

Using Updated Video Drivers

The speed of the video hardware is only half of the equation. The other half consists of the video driver that determines how Windows NT handles the hardware. The default video drivers may offer very good performance for video cards, but some cards may not perform as fast as they could. Be sure to check with your video card manufacturer to see if you have the newest Windows NT driver. You can also check with Microsoft, through CompuServe or the Microsoft WWW site, for the latest video drivers from Microsoft.

ON THE WEB

http://www.microsoft.com   You can get updates to Windows NT video drivers at Microsoft's Web site.

You can also get updates to manufacturer-specific video drivers at the following Web sites:

http://www.atitech.ca   ATI Technologies Inc.

http://www.diamond.mm.com   Diamond Multimedia Systems Inc.

http://www.elsa.com   ELSA Inc.

http://www.hercules.com   Hercules Computer Technology

http://www.matrox.com   Matrox Graphics Inc.

http://www.nine.com   Number Nine Visual Technology

However, as you probably know already, video drivers from Windows 3.1, Windows 95, or Windows NT 3.1/3.5x cannot be used on a Windows NT 4.0 system. Keep in mind that some video manufacturers may not support Windows NT as well as Windows 3.1 or Windows 95. Be sure to check with the manufacturer about using a particular video card with Windows NT before purchasing that product, or check the Hardware Compatibility List to be sure the video card works properly under Windows NT.

The Windows NT 4.0 video drivers have been rewritten to improve the video performance of Windows NT. Of course, this means that video drivers used in earlier versions of Windows NT cannot be used. However, the video performance gain is dramatic in many applications. The biggest change is moving the video subsystem to a privileged mode,

Part

III

Ch

13

giving it direct access to the hardware. In older versions of Windows NT, the video drivers were user mode drivers, which did not have direct access to the video hardware and limited the speed of video performance.

Changing Resolution of the Video Driver

At higher resolutions, the graphics processor has to handle the display of many more pixels of graphical data. This increased number of pixels to be displayed may decrease the speed of graphics performance noticeably on some systems. However, some video cards are well-equipped to handle the demands of more display information. Also, the software drivers may not handle higher resolutions well, even if the graphics hardware can. Depending on the video adapter and driver, changing the resolution of the Windows NT display or the number of colors displayed may affect the video display speed.

Some adapters or drivers are much faster with different resolution or color settings, however, some drivers do not have any major performance differences between settings. If you feel that video performance is too slow, try changing to a lower resolution to see if performance is faster. You can also try reducing the number of available colors used by the driver to see if this helps improve video performance.

To modify video resolution settings or the number of colors available, use the Display item in the Windows NT Control Panel. These items are changed through the Settings property sheet in the Display Properties window. Control Panel also forces you to test the display before the settings take place to ensure that the Windows NT system can be properly viewed the next time the system is started.

The Display Properties dialog box is shown in figure 13.2.

Using the Appropriate Screen Size with a Video Resolution

Although it isn't truly performance-related, ensuring that an appropriate screen size is used with a certain video resolution helps to ensure comfortable viewing of the displayed data. Many of the advanced graphical programs that use Windows NT's video capabilities require monitors larger than the standard 14" screen. As 15", 17", and even 20"-21" monitors become more affordable, using a larger screen with higher resolutions will become more prevalent.

Keep in mind that when a monitor is said to be a 17" monitor, it is measured diagonally from one end of the *picture tube* to another end. This is not always the *viewable* screen size of the video data. For example, a typical 17" monitor has about 15" diagonal viewable inches for data, and also is about 9" high by 12" wide.

FIG. 13.2

The Settings page in the Control Panel, Display item allows you to test and modify the resolution of the Windows NT display.

The actual resolution that is usable for a certain screen size depends on the user and the applications they are using. Eye strain is a very serious situation that can be prevented by simply using the proper resolution for a certain size screen. If a user needs to use a Windows NT program at a certain resolution, then an appropriately sized monitor should be purchased for that user.

Table 13.2 helps to determine what resolution to use for a certain size monitor.

Table 13.2   Video Resolutions and Monitor Screen Size

Size	Recommended Resolutions
14" or smaller	Standard VGA (640×480), 800×600 in some cases
15"	Standard VGA (640×480), 800×600
17"	Standard VGA (640×480), 800×600, 1024×768
20"-21"	Standard VGA (640×480), 800×600, 1024×768, 1280×1024, or higher

Part

III

Ch

Many of the resolutions above 640×480 have the option of using either large screen fonts or small screen fonts. These two options should also be used to adjust resolution settings to a convertible level for a particular monitor size. For example, using the large screen font for an 800×600 resolution makes it easier to read a 14" display.

Upgrading Video Adapters

If other measures fail, upgrading the video adapter to a faster one may be the best solution. Many new video cards now support items that were originally handled by the video driver. For example, many video adapters now support items like MPEG and AVI decoding, 3-D graphics, and improved Windows NT drivers to improve video performance.

Understanding the I/O Subsystem

The I/O subsystem covers many different types of hardware: serial ports, parallel ports, disk subsystems, and so on. Chapter 10, "Optimizing the File System," covers how to optimize disk performance on a Windows NT computer. However, some items concerning disk performance will also overlap into this section.

I/O performance is based primarily on hardware design. Newer computers are better equipped to run Windows NT, not just because they usually have faster processors and more memory, but because the way they interact with hardware devices is improved. Ideally, Windows NT should be run on newer computers, with the latest hardware improvements for optimal performance. However, Windows NT may be required to run on existing systems, and this section provides some advice on how to improve I/O performance.

Overview of I/O Performance

Performance of the I/O system includes many different, often unrelated, devices. One of the original goals of the IBM PC family of computers was to be expandable, not just by IBM, but by other manufacturers of hardware components. This allowed for many different computer systems to be tailored to fit the needs of a particular individual or organization. This also allowed for many different hardware products to be developed. Even some of the original items, such as serial and parallel ports, were improved to better handle faster transfer rates and better device communication.

I/O Bus Types

Like the performance of video hardware, the bus type used also affects performance of other devices as well. Hard disk controllers often have better performance with a direct bus (VL-bus or PCI bus) adapter. However, other devices may not gain any performance improvements, regardless of the bus type. The disk controller is an example of a component that has performance improvements based on the type of bus the controller uses.

However, many I/O devices are integrated on a single hardware adapter. These types of adapters typically have one parallel port, two serial ports, a game/joystick port, a floppy controller, and an IDE disk controller. Usually an adapter is present when the computer is purchased. In some instances, these items will also be integrated into the motherboard of a particular computer. Both I/O controllers using a direct bus card or I/O controllers integrated into the motherboard typically provide better performance than I/O cards using the standard ISA bus.

Network Adapters

Other I/O devices may have improved performance when using a direct bus. A good example of this is network cards. While network cards that use the ISA bus are often suitable for network client computers, servers on the network usually need something faster. A server, whether it be a file-print server or an application server, usually receives and transmits a lot of network traffic. This high volume of traffic usually requires a faster link between the network card and the processor.

Also, with the development and introduction of many "fast" network technologies, such as Fast Ethernet (100BaseT) and 100BaseVG/AnyLAN, the need for a fast link between the processor and the network card is increasingly necessary. The PCI bus has become almost standard on all new PC's designed to be network servers. PCI network cards provide much faster network performance for these machines than ISA network cards.

Serial Ports

Serial ports were designed to handle a wide variety of external computer devices. However, because serial ports send data one bit at a time, some devices, most notably printers, were not well suited for serial port use. Serial ports are most commonly used for external modems. Other devices that use serial ports for communication with the processor include: "smart" uninterruptable power supplies (UPS's), serial mice, monitoring equipment, and so on. Because there are so many devices that can be connected to a computer using serial ports, ensuring that the devices don't conflict with each other when using these ports is important.

Part
III

Ch
13

IBM PC-compatible computers allow for a maximum of four serial ports, without an addition of a special external board. When using a special adapter board to allow more than four serial ports, Windows NT allows for 256 total serial ports on a computer. Computers often use more than four serial ports when a modem pool is configured for Windows NT Remote Access Services (RAS) or other dial-in/dial-out capabilities with multiple users.

You'll notice in table 13.3 that, by default, COM1 and COM3 share the same IRQ. The same is true for COM2 and COM4. If you have two devices attached to COM1 and COM3, or COM2 and COM4, then the two devices cannot be used at the same time. With previous versions of Windows, this was a big concern, but, fortunately, Windows NT allows you to get around this problem. Windows NT allows you to assign IRQ's to a COM port other than the default.

N O T E By assigning different IRQ settings to a port, you can have two different devices on COM1 and COM3 or COM2 and COM4 without the devices conflicting under Windows NT. On systems that dual-boot with another operating system, such as MS-DOS or Windows 95, these settings will not be operational in these other environments. These operating systems will use the default settings, shown in table 13.3, and the devices connected to the serial ports may conflict in those environments. ▇

Table 13.3 shows the default addresses and interrupt values for the four serial ports found on Intel-based computers.

Table 13.3 Default Memory Addresses and Interrupts for Serial Ports

Port	Address	Interrupt (IRQ)
COM1	03F8h	IRQ 4
COM2	02F8h	IRQ 3
COM3	03E8h	IRQ 4
COM4	02E8h	IRQ 3

In order to accommodate more than four serial ports on a computer, Windows NT requires you to manually configure serial ports on the computer before Windows NT can use them. Table 13.3 shows the default settings used when one of the default serial ports is configured. You may need to add more than four serial ports, or you may need to change the default settings of the four standard serial ports. This information is changed through the Windows NT Control Panel.

To add or change serial port settings for a Windows NT Computer, do the following:

1. Open the Windows NT Control Panel by clicking the Start button, then Settings, or by opening the My Computer icon on the desktop. Choose the Control Panel item.

2. In Control Panel, select the Ports icon. The Ports icon refers only to serial ports. Other ports, such as parallel ports, are not handled in this item.

3. Double-click the Ports icon to open; the Ports dialog box will be displayed. This window will display any ports that have been added to the Windows NT system.

4. To add port settings for a serial port, click the Add button on the right-hand side of the dialog box.

5. An Advanced Settings for New Port dialog box appears. In this dialog box you can select the new port number from a drop-down list. This drop-down list contains up to 256 possible port numbers. Select the Base I/O Port Address and the IRQ from their drop-down lists. You should ensure that the selected items do not conflict with other devices on the system. The Advanced Settings for New Port dialog box is shown in figure 13.3.

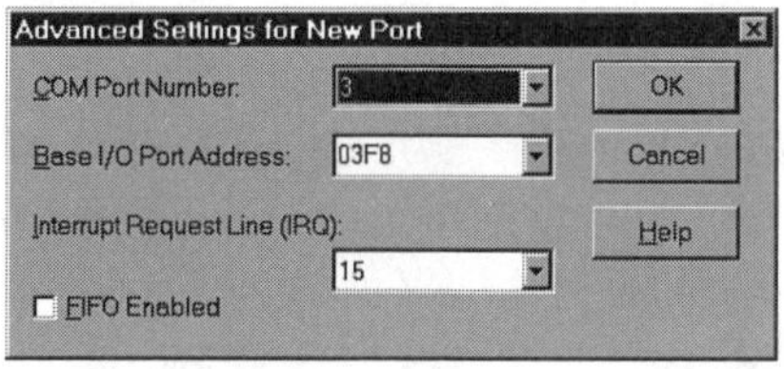

FIG. 13.3

The Advanced Settings for New Port dialog box allows you to configure settings for the new serial port to be added to the Windows NT system.

6. When you are finished, choose the OK button.

7. Once a COM port has been added, it will be displayed in the list. You can view or change the current settings of the serial port by highlighting it in the list and clicking the Settings button on the right-hand side of the Ports window. The window that is displayed, however, is not the same as the window that was displayed when the port was added.

8. Click the OK button in the Advanced Settings for New Port window. After the OK button is selected, the Windows NT system will ask you if you want to restart the Windows NT computer. You must restart the computer for the settings to take effect. To restart the computer, click the Restart Now button.

Serial ports use a chip, known as an UART chip, to control how serial communications occur with the computer. The original IBM PC used the 8250 UART and the IBM AT used the 16540 UART. However, as modem speeds became faster and faster, the 8250 or 16540 UART chips and the system processor, when used with multitasking operating systems, sometimes could not reliably transfer data. Most 486 and Pentium-based computers sold today use the 16550A series UART chip. In order to allow higher-speed communications between the serial port and the computer, the 16550A series UART offers many significant performance improvements.

Part
III

Ch
13

The 16550A series UART has two major advantages from the previous UART chips. The first advantage is that the 16550A series uses a buffer for both incoming and outgoing data. This 16-bit buffer allows data to be temporarily stored while the UART waits for interrupt requests to be handled by the processor. This prevents data from being lost while waiting on the CPU to handle interrupt requests.

The second advantage is that the 16550A sends one request to service all data in the buffer. This is an improvement over the previous UARTs used, since they had to send an interrupt request for every single character they received. By using one interrupt request for multiple characters of data, the speeds of serial communications can be dramatically increased.

Even with advances in the UART hardware, Windows 3.1 didn't take full advantage of the 16550A series UART. This allowed many third-party developers to create specialized COM port drivers to replace the default COMM.DRV used by Windows 3.1. Windows NT automatically detects 16550/16450 UART hardware. If you have the FIFO setting in Control Panel enabled and a 16450 or 8250 UART, the FIFO setting will automatically be disabled, and a message will be displayed in the Windows NT event log.

Of course, you may not be sure whether a computer has a 16550A UART. The bad news is that Windows NT 4.0 doesn't provide a way for you to find out. The Windows NT Diagnostics utility doesn't provide that information. The only way to find out the UART used on a computer is through MS-DOS or Windows 95. Using MS-DOS, you can use the MSD.EXE program.

N O T E MSD.EXE should only be run when the system is dual-booted into MS-DOS or booted from the MS-DOS boot disk. While MSD.EXE can run under a Windows NT MS-DOS prompt, it will not correctly display the UART and other COM information. ■

When using MSD.EXE, the UART will be displayed by clicking the COM Ports button. The UART Chip Used section will display the UART information. Windows 95 displays this information in Control Panel, Modems item under the Diagnostics property sheet after clicking the More Info button. If you do not have a dual-boot system and cannot use a MS-DOS boot disk because your system only uses NTFS partitions, then you should check with the manufacturer of the system to verify the type of UART chip used by the system.

Parallel Ports

The parallel port is almost universally used as the computer's printer port. However, many expansion devices, such as add-on tape drive or hard drive devices, are starting to use the parallel port to make it more convenient to users. Under Windows NT, the parallel port is used primarily for utilization by a local printer, and the use of other parallel devices is not supported by default.

While printer ports do have IRQ settings, for most printing needs, the interrupts are not needed. By default, LPT1 and LPT3 have been assigned IRQ 7. LPT2 usually is assigned to IRQ5. Since these interrupts are usually not used by the printing device, other devices, such as sound cards, use these interrupts. Windows NT isn't designed to handle communications with devices, other than printers, using the parallel port. However, some hardware manufactures may create devices that use the parallel port under Windows NT. These devices may require that the default interrupt for the parallel port be available in order to work properly.

The most significant performance improvement of parallel port performance is the introduction of bidirectional parallel ports. On the original IBM PC-series of computers, the parallel port essentially only sent data one way. Although the printer communicated to let the computer know if it was online or not, it usually didn't communicate specific errors or problems. A process known as "nibble mode" did allow standard parallel ports to send data back to the computer, but it was slow and was not usually implemented.

Bidirectional ports allow for two-way communication between the computer and the printing device. The two types of bidirectional parallel ports are the Extended Capabilities Port (ECP) and the Enhanced Parallel Port (EPP). The Extended Capabilities Port (ECP) was developed by Microsoft, Hewlett-Packard, and other manufacturers. The ECP can use direct memory access (DMA) and a small memory buffer to increase performance.

The Enhanced Parallel Port (EPP) was developed by Intel, Zenith, Xircom, and other hardware manufacturers for bidirectional communications. Most EPP ports are found on notebook or portable computers. Unlike ECP, EPP does not use any memory buffers or DMA to improve performance.

Part III

Ch 13

These types of parallel ports also require that the printer connected to these ports be able to recognized these types before bidirectional functionality can be used. Another popular use for bidirectional ports is to transfer data between portable and desktop computers via special parallel cables.

To configure bidirectional support for a parallel port, do the following:

1. Click the My Computer icon on the desktop. Choose the Printers item.

2. In order to configure bidirectional support, you need to add a local printer. To add a local printer, click the Add Printer icon.

3. The Add Printer Wizard starts. Follow the wizard to add the printer. Make sure that you select the My Computer item on the first wizard screen, *not* the Network printer server item. You will need the Windows NT CD-ROM or disks to fully set up the printer.

4. After the wizard is run, you'll see a printer icon in the Printers folder. Double-click the newly created printer icon.

5. A printer window appears showing any print jobs and the status of those jobs. You need to display the properties of the printer to configure bidirectional printing. Click Printer, then Properties to display the printer properties.

6. The printer's properties are displayed in a window. This window contains six tabs: General, Ports, Scheduling, Sharing, Security, and Device Settings. Click the Ports tab to display the Ports property sheet. The Ports property sheet is shown in figure 13.4.

FIG. 13.4

The Ports property sheet, located in the printer's properties dialog box, allows you to configure bidirectional communications between a computer and a printer. Note the printer first must be installed in order to set Windows NT to use bidirectional communications.

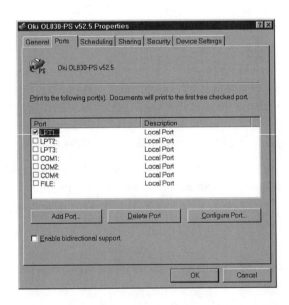

7. The Ports property sheet displays all of the available local ports, including parallel and serial ports, on the Windows NT system. At the bottom of the screen, a check box labeled Enabled bidirectional support is displayed. If your system does not have

a bidirectional parallel port, then this check box will be grayed out. If you have a bidirectional parallel port and a printer that supports bidirectional communications, check the Enabled bidirectional support check box.

8. When you are finished, click the OK button.

Other Hardware Devices

Because the IBM PC series of computers were designed to be expandable, a wide array of devices have been created for use in these computers. Many of these devices are compatible with Windows NT by using generic device drivers for Windows NT, or using a compatible driver that was designed for another, yet similar, device. Using these drivers often allows the device to work under Windows NT if a specific Windows NT driver is not available for the hardware. The performance of the device may not be as good as a driver specifically created for that device. You should always check with the manufacturer to see if a Windows NT-specific device driver has been created for any devices using generic device drivers.

There may also be times when a device has both an ISA version or direct-bus version (VL-Bus or PCI). While these devices may have the same functionality between the different bus versions, the direct-bus versions often offer much better performance than their ISA counterpart. Since Windows NT is used often in performance-critical machines, when purchasing hardware devices, the direct-bus version should primarily be considered over an ISA version. Even if the direct-bus version costs more, the performance increases are usually worth the extra money paid.

One new addition to Windows NT 4.0 is improved support for PC Cards, formerly known as PCMCIA cards. These hardware devices are found on most portable computers sold today and are used to add hardware devices to portable computers. The advantage of PC Card hardware is its small size and light weight allows it to be carried with the portable computer. Also it can be removed and replaced with other cards so the computer can be configured a variety of ways depending on the immediate need of the portable computer user.

Part
III

Ch
13

Windows NT 4.0 has a PC Card (PCMCIA) item in the Control Panel to configure and view PC Card devices attached to the system. Since so many different types of PC Card devices exist, they may also have specific configuration or monitoring programs designed for Windows NT. Of course, as with other devices on the system, be sure that the programs are designed to work specifically with Windows NT.

High Performance I/O Cards

While the serial and parallel ports used by the motherboard are adequate for most Windows NT users, users who demand higher performance should consider purchasing high performance I/O adapters. If a large number of serial ports are needed for "pools" of devices, for example modem pools, then separate adapters can be purchased to allow these devices to be attached without as much concern for conflicting IRQ or other device settings.

N O T E   Slow I/O adapters may cause bottlenecks that appear to be CPU bottlenecks and may be hard to spot. If you notice a CPU bottleneck, and the computer is using I/O devices intensively, be sure to consider the I/O adapters as a potential source of the bottleneck. ■

Monitoring I/O Performance

If you noticed a lack of video items in Performance Monitor, you've probably noticed a lack of an I/O category in Performance Monitor as well. Categories concerning I/O performance are scattered depending on the types of hardware devices being monitored. There are many items that can be monitored about disk I/O performance or network performance. Monitoring disk I/O performance is discussed in Chapter 10, "Optimizing the File System." Monitoring network performance is discussed below.

Because one of Windows NT's biggest strong points is its ability to network, it should come as no surprise that Performance Monitor allows for strong performance monitoring of network cards on a Windows NT system. The network performance monitoring is categorized based on protocol and can be used to determine the performance of the network adapter in the Windows NT machine.

You can also monitor serial port performance if you are using RAS for your serial port connection. Performance monitor has two RAS-based objects that allow you to monitor the serial port performance or modem performance of a Windows NT computer.

Some of the major network objects can be monitored using the Windows NT Performance Monitor:

   ■ **NetBEUI**. This object allows you to select items relating to network transmissions using the NetBEUI protocol. NetBEUI is typically used by Windows for Workgroups, LAN Manager, and other Microsoft-based networks. It is a small, fast protocol, but cannot be routed over a WAN.

■ **NetBEUI Resources**. This object allows you to monitor the resources made available for sharing, such as drive shares. This counter can be used to determine how often shared items are requested.

■ **NWLink IPX**. This object allows you to select items relating to network transmissions using Microsoft's NWLink protocol. NWLink is Microsoft's proprietary protocol that allows a Windows NT machine to communicate on a Novell-based network, which uses IPX/SPX. The IPX counter allows you to monitor items relating to IPX, not SPX.

■ **NWLink NetBIOS**. This object allows you to select items when NetBIOS is run on top of the NWLink protocol. NetBIOS was developed by IBM and is able to run on top of other protocols such as NWLink.

■ **NWLink SPX**. This object allows you to select items relating to SPX network transmissions using the Microsoft's NWLink protocol. NWLink is Microsoft's proprietary protocol which allows a Windows NT machine to communicate on a Novell-based network, which uses IPX/SPX.

■ **RAS Port**. This object allows you to monitor items about a computer using RAS to communicate to the network or a remote user. This object gives the current performance of a RAS port.

■ **RAS Total**. This object is similar to the RAS Port object, but allows you to display totals for the RAS port instead of the current performance.

■ **Server**. This handles items for all server-based information on the network, regardless of the protocol being used. This object allows you to see if a Windows NT computer is being over-utilized by network users. This item is used for both a Windows NT Server and Workstation computer if that computer has shared network resources and has the Server service running.

■ **Server Work Queues**. This item is similar to the Server object, but focuses strictly on the work queues of a Windows NT computer running the Server service.

■ **TCP**. This item is similar to the other protocol objects, like NetBEUI, but handles the Transmission Control Protocol when using TCP/IP. In order for this object to appear in Performance Monitor, Windows NT's SNMP services must be installed. Also, if multiple protocols are used, the TCP/IP protocol must be the highest priority protocol on the workstation in order to monitor this object. To set TCP/IP or any other protocol to have the highest priority, see the following Tip.

■ **IP**. This counter handles the Internet Protocol items when using the TCP/IP protocol. As mentioned previously, for this item to appear in Performance Monitor, SNMP must be installed on the Windows NT system and TCP/IP must be the only or highest priority protocol used.

This list displays only the major counters concerning network performance. Other counters may be available for certain systems depending on how the network is configured.

 TIP To make a protocol the highest priority protocol on a Windows NT system for monitoring, choose the Network item in Control Panel. From the Network window, choose the Bindings tab. In the Show Bindings For box, choose All Services. Then, double-click the Workstation item. The protocols will be listed in order of priority. To change the priority, select the protocol and use the Move Up and Move Down buttons to move it up or down the list.

Optimizing I/O Performance

Optimizing I/O Performance under Windows NT almost always includes modification to the hardware. This even may include completely replacing the motherboard of the system. Windows NT places a heavy load on computer hardware, and it utilizes the hardware fully.

Ideally, Windows NT should be used on a computer that was purchased with Windows NT in mind. Making sure that a computer and all of its components are listed in the Windows NT Hardware Compatibility List ensures not only compatibility, but also adequate system performance. The video hardware should be purchased with Windows NT in mind since it is a very graphically intensive operating system.

Of course, Windows NT will often be installed on systems that have already been purchased. If video or I/O performance is inadequate on these machines, then a new video card or I/O adapter is often needed. This can be further complicated if the existing computer doesn't have direct-bus expansion slots. In this case, the user is often forced to completely replace the motherboard. This is *not* a trivial task for most users, and the decision should be made about whether it is cost-effective and technically feasible to try to upgrade the existing system or buy a new computer.

Hardware Suggestions

The best suggestion to improving both video and I/O performance under Windows NT is through upgrading inadequate hardware. The following suggestions are offered to help make a slow or sluggish Windows NT system perform better:

- For better video performance, be sure that you are using a graphics accelerator board designed with the graphical needs of Windows in mind.

- If video performance is sluggish, try using a lower resolution setting for the adapter. Also, you may also want to decrease the number of colors. Depending on the video card and driver, this could have dramatic improvements on video performance.

- Be sure to use the newest Windows NT video driver for the video hardware. Often, the video manufacturer's driver will be faster than the default Windows NT driver for the same card.

- If your video card isn't allowing you to view the resolution or the color range you want, add more video memory to your graphics card. Be sure to check with the documentation or the manufacturer on the type of memory needed.

- For the best performance with internal hardware devices, be sure that you have VL-bus slots on your computer if it is a 486-based computer, or PCI slots on a Pentium-based computer. RISC-based machines can have either PCI slots or other type of expansion slots. Be sure that the most demanding hardware is used in those slots.

- Network servers and network computers that receive a lot of network requests will probably benefit from a PCI network card. Also, computers connected to networks using "fast" network technologies, such as Fast Ethernet, will probably benefit from PCI network adapters as well.

- Serial ports used from the motherboard that have high-speed modems attached should use the 16550A UART chip. This allows for use of high-speed transmissions without data loss or errors. If you have an internal modem or a high-performance card designed for high-speed serial communications, you don't need to worry about the UART chipset used by the serial ports. Be sure to configure the FIFO Enabled setting in the Ports item in Control Panel to take full advantage of the 16550A UART.

- Advanced parallel ports that support bidirectional communication allow for better management and communications between the computer and parallel port devices. Both the computer's parallel port and the printer's port must support bidirectional communications in order to take full advantage of this feature. Be sure that you check the Enabled bidirectional support check box under the Ports tab in the Printer Properties window.

- Always be sure to use the latest Windows NT device drivers for the hardware components on the system. Keep in mind that only Windows NT devices drivers can be used, not Windows 95 or MS-DOS device drivers. Contact the manufacturer for the latest Windows NT drivers. Most manufacturers have BBS systems or Internet Web pages with the latest drivers.

Part
III

Ch
13

From Here...

Video performance is very important to Windows NT since it is so graphics-intensive. Windows NT can place a lot of demands on video hardware, and if the hardware is inadequate, entire Windows NT performance will suffer. Although Performance Monitor has no direct video item, video performance can be monitored indirectly.

I/O performance consists of a variety of different hardware devices, and performance is very important to most Windows NT users. Optimizing I/O performance rounds out hardware optimization of a Windows NT system. Choosing the right hardware for Windows NT before the system is purchased will allow Windows NT to run at its best.

For information on topics related to Windows NT performance, see the following chapters:

- Chapter 8, "Monitoring Performance," provides more information on monitoring the Windows NT system and includes a more detailed discussion of how to use the Windows NT Performance Monitor.
- Chapter 9, "Optimizing Physical and Virtual Memory," handles how to use memory more effectively under Windows NT.
- Chapter 10, "Optimizing the File System," describes how to optimize the Windows NT file system, including FAT and NTFS.
- Chapter 12, "Optimizing CPU Performance," covers how to optimize the processor performance on a Windows NT computer.

CHAPTER 14

Ensuring Data Security

by Christa Anderson

Because Microsoft has been promoting Windows NT Workstation as the operating system for power users, you might expect them to include all the features that a power user would need in this OS—including data security options. To a point, this is true, but not entirely. You don't have a full array of data security functions in this OS, and they may be somewhat dependent on other products.

This chapter discusses the data-security features of Windows NT Workstation 4.0, and where NT falls short, how you can get these features. ■

Optimizing and Automating Backup Services

Learn how to use NT Backup for the best data protection.

Using Fault-Tolerant Volumes

This section discusses RAID as it does—and doesn't—apply to NT Workstation.

Employing and Managing a UPS

Learn how to set up the built-in power protection features of your workstation.

Optimizing and Automating Backup Services

Like NT Server, NT Workstation comes with NT Backup, a utility that you can use to back up your data and system Registry. Although this utility does not have all the features of some backup programs (for example, it will not back up files that are in use at the time), it's still very handy to have and will be all that most people need to back up a standalone workstation. (NT Workstation machines that are acting as network servers may be a different matter—in that case, you may want to consider one of the more elaborate backup utilities.)

A Brief Introduction to NT Backup

Once you've installed the tape device that you want to use from the Control Panel, the mechanics of using NT Backup are pretty simple.

> **N O T E** To use NT Backup, you first must install a tape device—this utility does not work with other backup options such as removable drives or optical drives. ■

To use NT Backup, follow these steps:

1. Start NT Backup, located with the rest of the Administrative Tools. You'll see all the available drives.

2. Click the checkbox to the left of a drive to select it for backup. You can select more than one drive at a time.

3. Click the Backup button on the left end of the toolbar, or choose Backup from the Operations menu.

4. Name the backup tape, adjust the options as necessary (for example, deciding whether to add data to any already on the tape or replace it, and how detailed to make the log), and click OK.

It's very simple. If all that you want to do is back up the system when you think about it, you can probably skip the rest of this section and go on to the discussion of RAID. The more complex aspect of using NT Backup is figuring out how to use it best, and how to use some extra utilities to advantage.

Creating a Backup Schedule

If you are generating files of any importance (and, if you've bought Windows NT and are reading this book, I imagine that you do), then you should back up on a daily basis. If backing up every day strikes you as inconvenient or unnecessary, just think about having to recreate a week's or month's worth of data.

NT gives you several different backup options:

- **Full backups** ("normal" to NT). All selected files are copied to the tape and the archive bit set.

- **Copied backups**. All selected files are copied to the tape but the archive bit is not changed.

- **Daily backups**. All selected files that have changed that day are copied to the tape but the archive bit is not affected.

- **Incremental backups**. All selected files that have changed since the last full backup are copied to the tape, but the archive bit is not affected.

- **Differential backups**. All selected files that have changed since the last backup of any kind are copied to the tape, and the archive bit set.

I find that combining weekly full backups with daily incremental or differential ones works quite well. Doing full backups is quite time-consuming, and the more inconvenient it is to do backups the less likely it is that you'll ever get around to it. Better to keep a full backup as a base and then add the newer files from the less comprehensive backups. If you plan to do backups each night after you're done for the day, then you should never have to worry about losing more than a day's worth of material.

Once you've established how often you intend to back up, it's a good idea to reinforce your routine with a written schedule. If you create a table with the date and type of each backup and sign off each one as it's completed, then you'll always know at a glance where you stand.

Your daily backups should always include both your data and a copy of the system Registry. Ordinarily, it's not necessary to back up other system files—if things have gotten to the point at which you'd need to restore the operating system files, you've already reinstalled NT anyway. But the Registry information is vital for restoring your system to the point at which you left it. Although these files are not backed up by default (odd, that), it's a very good idea to select that option in the Backup dialog box.

N O T E Backing up the Registry doesn't mean that it will be automatically restored if you should restore files. You must explicitly tell NT Backup to restore the Registry. ▦

Using WinAt to Schedule Backups

You can't back up in the middle of the day because it takes too long and NT Backup won't back up files that are in use.

Part
III

Ch
14

T I P   One backup utility that will back up files currently in use is Seagate's (formerly Arcada's) NT Backup, the full-blown version of the software that comes with NT.

Sometimes you forget to start the backup program when you're leaving for the day. Given all this, how can you make sure that you back up regularly?

NT Backup can run from the command line, so one way to do this is to create a batch file and set it to run at a certain hour with the AT command-line utility that comes with Windows NT.

The syntax of AT that's relevant to scheduling automated backups is shown in table 14.1.

N O T E   Although AT has a switch that you can use to run a process that requires user input, since we're talking here about running a backup without user input, it's not really relevant. ▤

Table 14.1   AT Syntax for Scheduling Backups

Switch	Description
\\computername	Use this switch to specify a remote computer on which to run NT Backup. By default, the operation will take place on the local computer.
id	Specifies an identification number for the scheduled command. You'll need an ID number to manipulate the command scheduler should that become necessary.
/delete	Cancels a scheduled command. If you don't supply an ID number, then all scheduled commands on the computer are canceled.
/yes	Use with the /delete switch to cancel all jobs without confirming the cancellation.
time	Specifies the time at which the command is to run.
/every:date[,...]	Runs the command on each specified day(s) of the week or month. If you don't specify a date, AT assumes that you mean the current day.
/next:date[,...]	Runs the specified command on the next occurrence of the day (for example, next Tuesday). If you don't specify a date, AT assumes that you mean the current day.
"command"	Specifies the Windows NT command or batch program to be run—in this case, NTBACKUP.

As a command scheduler, AT works, but it can be confusing to set up the switches not only for the command that you want to run but for the scheduler running it. Unless you're a hard-core type who really enjoys working from the command line, you may prefer using a slightly more Windows-based version of it, called WinAt. If you've got the NT Resource Kit, then on the accompanying CD you've got WinAt. It's also on the CD included with this book. The only catch to this utility is that you still must know the command-line parameters of the program that you want to schedule—it doesn't work with dialog boxes. Then again, you don't need to know the utility switches, just those of the application to schedule.

ON THE WEB

If you've got Web access, you can download WinAt from:

http://rmm.com/nt

To start WinAt, make sure that the Workstation and Scheduler services are running and run WINAT.EXE. If the Scheduler service is not already started, you'll see a dialog box telling you so and asking if you want to start it. You do. Once you've started up WinAt, you'll see a dialog box like the one shown in figure 14.1.

N O T E The Workstation service must be running for WinAt to work; so even if you're running Windows NT on a standalone computer, you'll still have to install networking. ■

FIG. 14.1
Use WinAt to schedule automatic backups for a time when you won't be using any files.

To add an event to the Scheduler, click the <u>A</u>dd button and enter the command in the dialog box shown in figure 14.2, using the necessary switches. NTBACKUP's command-line switches are shown in table 14.2.

Part
III

Ch
14

Table 14.2   NTBACKUP Switches

Switch	Description
/a	Changes the backup mode to append, so that files are added to the data already on the tape, rather than replacing what's there. By default, existing data will be overwritten, so you must use this switch if you want to keep the other data.
/v	Turns on data verification, so that once the backup is complete the files on the tape are compared with those on the disk to ensure that the data was written correctly.
/r	Restricts access to the tape to the tape's owner and the administrator.
/d	Lets you describe the backup, such as "Full backup done on 08/01/96" (you must enclose the description in quotation marks). This can help you keep your backups straight.
/b	Backs up the local Registry. Always use this switch.
/hc	Turns hardware compression on or off, depending on which you specify.
/t	Lets you specify the backup type: Normal (full), Copy, Incremental, Daily, or Differential. By default, you'll do a Normal backup.
/tape: (n)	Lets you specify which tape drive the backup should be made to, if you have more than one.
/l	Creates a summary log of the backup process. You must specify a location in which to write the log and enclose that destination in quotation marks, like this: "c:\ntwork4\logs\daylog.txt".
/e	Specifies that the backup log should contain exceptions only.

FIG. 14.2

You must set the backup options from the command line to schedule an automatic backup.

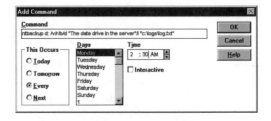

To perform two types of backups at different intervals, you'll need to create two entries. For example, as I perform weekly full backups and daily incremental backups, I'll create two entries: one to be performed every night at 2:00 A.M., the other every Monday at 2:30 A.M.

N O T E   When you create a WinAt event, it's assigned a number. That number belongs to that
event for good—if you delete event #0 of 4, for example, then the next event you create
will be event #4 (they're numbered from 0), not event #0.   ■

Once the backups are set up in WinAt, all that you need to do is swap out the tapes you
use every morning. Using this utility simplifies the backup process considerably. For the
first day or so after you set up the backups, it's a good idea to make sure that they took
when you come in the morning. It's also a good idea to check the backup log to ensure
that nothing went wrong with the process, or to note where problems occurred.

Ensuring Backup Integrity

Just plugging the tape in on a regular basis isn't enough for protecting your data. The time
to find out that the backups aren't working or that something else is going wrong is when
the original data is still on the drive, not when you're trying to restore it.

Keep More Than One Generation of Backups   Never trust that the current set of data is
all that you'll need. It's perfectly possible that one day you'll delete a file and then realize
two weeks later that you really did need it after all. Therefore, make it a rule to keep a
couple of generations of full backups, keeping more or fewer depending on how far back
you want to be able to keep data. Two months is as long as most people will need, but you
can adjust that time for your situation. It might not be a bad idea to make a full backup for
your archives every six months, just as a precaution.

Use the Verify Option   NT Backup will verify that the data written to the tape matches
the data on the hard disk. Although this option increases the time it takes to back up, use
it. Any discrepancies will be noted in the backup log, and it's a lot better to know about
problems now than when you need to restore.

N O T E   Don't panic if you open the backup log and see that some files failed the verification
process. Some system files (such as event logs) may change between the time that
they get backed up and when they're verified.   ■

Practice Restoring Data   Before removing the tape after a backup, try restoring a
couple of files just to be sure that the hardware is working properly. I've seen a misaligned
tape drive refuse to catalog or restore files on a tape that it backed up (don't ask), and it's
better to know about problems like this before you need to restore the data.

Part

III

Ch

14

Using Fault-Tolerant Volumes

Over the years, hard disks have become increasingly reliable. In one of my systems, I have one that's been running nearly non-stop for three years, has moved twice, and has traveled hundreds of miles. It's working wonderfully, and I have no reason to doubt that it will continue to do so.

No reason, that is, except Murphy's Law. At the worst possible time, I *expect* this hard disk to crash. After all, even the most reliable disk media fails eventually, and the longer it survives, the greater the chance that it will fail. (In fact, as I write this, I'm glancing down at the computer, half expecting the disk to fail now just to prove me right.)

Now, I back it up—as we discussed in the previous section, that's only common sense. To expedite data recovery, however, I could combine my backups with fault-tolerant volumes that can recover from the loss of a disk. Doing this would be an especially good idea for a computer that's any kind of network server because it takes a much shorter time to recover data using fault-tolerant volumes than it does using backups—sometimes, almost no time at all. The idea of fault-tolerant volumes, after all, is that you should be able to access your data even after one of the hard disks has gone to data heaven.

NT and Fault Tolerance

In Windows NT in general, fault tolerance is achieved via software-based RAID (Redundant Array of Inexpensive Drives). NT supports three RAID levels:

- Disk Striping without Parity (Level 0)
- Disk Mirroring/Duplexing (Level 1)
- Disk Striping with Parity (Level 5)

N O T E Although the various paradigms of RAID are termed "levels," they're not levels in the sense that level 5 is more secure or quicker to recover than level 1. Not all RAID levels contribute to fault tolerance. ▪

Disk Striping Without Parity   This RAID level links partitions of equal size on two or more physical hard disks. These linked partitions share a single drive letter, such as G:. When you write data to drive G:, the data is written in stripes across all the linked partitions. For example, if you had a string of data that consisted of the numbers from one to eight and a two-disk stripe set, then the distribution of data might look like this:

- Disk 1: 1,3,5,7
- Disk 2: 2,4,6,8

If this method of data storage doesn't look very secure to you (after all, if Disk 1 dies, you've lost half the data set, and you can't get to the other half because the drives operate in tandem), you're right: this RAID level is designed to increase data retrieval performance, not contribute to data integrity.

The more disks that you stripe, the greater the chance that one of them will fail and bring the others down with it. You can calculate the likelihood of a failure by dividing the manufacturer's *mean time to failure* (MTF) by the number of drives used. If one drive has an MTF of 30,000 hours, then three drives of that kind have an MTF value of 10,000 hours. If you use disk striping, it is imperative that you back up on a regular basis—if one disk goes, all of the data in the stripe set is unavailable.

Disk Mirroring/Duplexing   Another two-disk RAID approach does provide data integrity, however. In disk mirroring, the contents of one disk partition are copied to a partition of the same size on another physical disk. Should one of the disks fail, the data is still on the other disk, so once you break the mirror set and treat the drive like a single unit again, you'll be able to retrieve the data. For example, the same eight-number string of data described in the previous section would be distributed in a mirror set like this:

- Disk 1: 1,2,3,4,5,6,7,8
- Disk 2: 1,2,3,4,5,6,7,8

Mirroring is pretty fail-safe due to the low possibility that both drives will fail at once, but for further security, you can mirror two drives on separate drive controllers. That way, you're protected from controller failures as well. The two-controller method of mirroring is called disk duplexing, but it works just like disk mirroring.

Disk mirroring does increase the time required for disk writes, but disk reads can be completed more quickly as data can be pulled from both disks at once.

Although disk mirroring provides data security, it's very inefficient in terms of disk space—for every megabyte of data that you store, you'll need two megabytes of space.

Disk Striping with Parity   It's possible to combine some of the improved performance of disk striping with the data security of disk mirroring. Disk striping with parity is similar to disk striping, with two exceptions. First, it requires a minimum of three physical disks, not two. Second, in addition to the data written to each disk, this RAID level writes parity information as well, so that if one of the disks in the stripe set dies, the data on that disk can be recreated from the parity information. To return to our eight-number data string:

Part
III

Ch
14

- Disk 1: 1,4,7,P
- Disk 2: 2,5,8,P
- Disk 3: 3,6,P

The P in each set stands for "parity."

Disk striping with parity takes a little longer to write data than does writing to a single disk, but reads are faster as data can be read into memory from more than one disk at a time. Its overhead is lower than disk mirroring, too. Whereas disk mirroring "wastes" 50 percent of the space it requires with redundant information, disk striping with parity "wastes" 1/3 of the space it uses with the parity information, and the more disks that are involved in the stripe set the more efficient it is.

RAID and NT Workstation

OK, that's RAID. How do the fault-tolerant aspects of it apply to NT Workstation? They don't.

Unfortunately, NT Workstation only supports disk striping (not disk striping with parity) and volume sets, which allow you to combine areas of free space on separate physical hard disks to create logical drives. (Volumes are not fault-tolerant—they have the same vulnerabilities to disk failure that disk striping does and for the same reason.) Although the help files and some visual options in the Disk Administrator (where you set up disk configurations) seem to imply that you can set up fault-tolerant volumes in NT Workstation, they're incorrect. For illustration, compare the NT Workstation Disk Administrator in figure 14.3 with the NT Server Disk Administrator shown in figure 14.4.

FIG. 14.3
The NT Work-station Disk Administrator does not support the creation of fault-tolerant volumes.

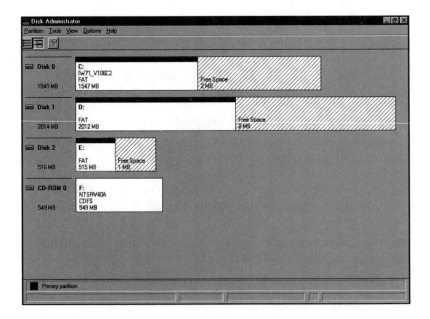

FIG. 14.4
The NT Server Disk Administrator.

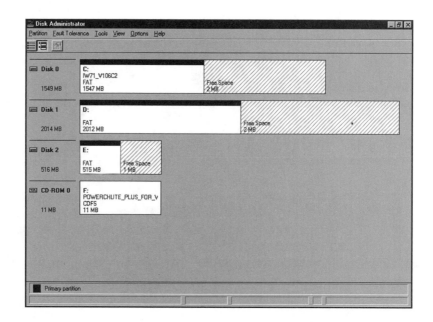

How, then, can you get fault tolerance for the disks accessible from your NT Workstation? You've got two options: keep all important data on a computer running NT Server and use its fault tolerance, or get a hardware RAID solution for your NT Workstation. Given Microsoft's advocacy of NT Workstation as the OS of the power user, I would have thought that support for fault tolerance went without saying, but evidently Microsoft didn't see it that way.

N O T E For those running NT Server and NT Workstation on the same computer, you can't set up fault-tolerant volumes in NT Server and expect them to translate to NT Workstation. When you start up the Disk Administrator under NT Workstation, you'll see a message box telling you that the volumes are corrupt and unreadable. It's not—it's just not in a format that NT Workstation can understand. ■

Although NT Workstation doesn't include support for fault tolerance, the issue is important enough that I'd like to go over the basics here.

Fault-Tolerant Volumes with NT Server

Once you've got an OS with built-in fault tolerance, setting it up is easy. Start up the Disk Administrator, found in the Administrative Tools folder. You'll see a screen that looks like the one in figure 14.5.

Part
III

Ch
14

FIG. 14.5

The Fault Tolerance menu in the NT Server Disk Administrator contains the options for setting up disk mirroring and striping with parity.

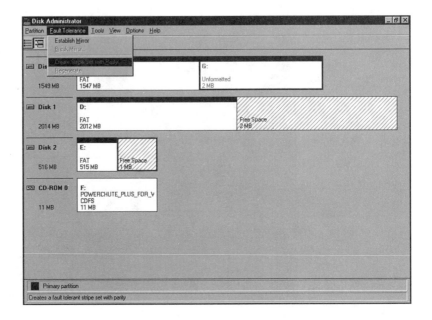

The tools that you'll be using are found in the Fault Tolerance menu. You can see the contents of this menu in figure 14.5.

CAUTION

To establish a stripe set or mirror set, you must reboot the computer. Don't do this during working hours, or you'll disconnect everyone currently logged on to the computer.

Establishing a Mirror Set   To establish a mirror set, select the partition that you want to mirror, and then Ctrl+click an area of free space the same size or larger than the first partition. Both areas should have a heavy black line around each of their borders.

N O T E   "Free space" to NT is not unused disk space, but rather an unpartitioned area on the disk. All fault-tolerant disk configurations require free space. If you don't have any, you'll have to repartition your hard disks. ■

From the Fault Tolerance menu, choose Establish Mirror. When you do, the mirror set will be created without any further action on your part, and the area of free space will be color-coded magenta and linked to the partition that you originally selected. The changes will not take effect until you confirm the changes, exit the Disk Administrator, and reboot the system.

From this point on, any data that you save to the original partition's drive letter will be saved in both locations.

Should one of the disks in the mirror set fail, the data is instantly recoverable. You'll know if one of the disks fails when you try to write to that drive letter, as you'll see an error message. Additionally, when you start up the Disk Administrator, you'll see a message box informing you that a disk has been removed since the last time that you ran the Disk Administrator.

As read and write operations apply to both drives, you won't be able to access the data on the good drive while it's still part of the mirror set. To access the data, follow these steps:

1. Open the Disk Administrator and select the mirror set.

2. Choose Break Mirror from the Fault Tolerance menu. You see the message shown in figure 14.6.

FIG. 14.6
You'll see a warning message if you attempt to break a mirror set, whether or not one of the drives in the set has failed.

3. Click OK.

The mirror set will be broken, and you'll be able to access the data. After you reboot, the dead disk will disappear from the Disk Administrator.

Once you've fixed or replaced the other drive, you'll be able to reestablish the mirror set for fault tolerance.

Disk Striping with Parity Establishing a stripe set with parity requires little more work than establishing a mirror set. Just follow these steps:

1. Start up the Disk Administrator.

2. Choose at least three areas of free space on three separate physical disks. You can Ctrl+click to choose more than one at a time.

    A thick black border will appear around each selected area of free space.

3. From the Fault Tolerance menu, choose Create Stripe Set With Parity.

4. In the dialog box that appears, select the size of the stripe set. Note that the set can be no larger than three times the smallest area of free space in the set, but can be smaller than that.

Part
III

Ch
14

After you've specified the size of the stripe set, the newly created volume will appear in the Disk Administrator in light blue.

5. You need to reboot the system for the change to take effect.

6. Open the Disk Administrator and format the new stripe set. At this point, the stripe set will look something like the one shown in figure 14.7.

FIG. 14.7
The status of a stripe set with parity is shown on the status bar at the bottom of the Disk Administrator.

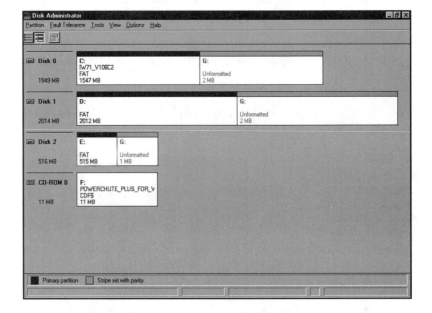

Recovering data from a stripe set is a little more involved than recovering mirrored data. Whereas you can simply break the mirror set and use the good drive on its own, when striping you must regenerate the lost data on a new drive. Shut down the system, insert the new drive, restart and select an area of free space on the new drive that's at least as large as the areas on the other disks, and then choose Regenerate from the Fault Tolerance menu. While the data is being recreated on the new drive, you can use the computer for other operations.

That's the abbreviated guide to fault tolerance with NT. For more information, take a look at Que's *Special Edition Using Windows NT Server 4.0*, by Roger Jennings.

Other RAID Solutions

If storing files on an NT Server machine isn't an option for you (perhaps if your computer isn't networked), then you might be interested in third-party RAID solutions. They're out there, but be warned: the reason why it was so terrific when NT Server had RAID built into it is because most options are quite expensive—possibly many thousands of dollars.

Software   Even NT Server doesn't offer a full range of fault-tolerant configurations. For example, you can't use the Disk Administrator to switch from one server to another. For high-powered systems, some third-party vendors have created software RAID solutions that support some RAID levels but also have capabilities not built into NT.

For example, Sunbelt Software offers the Octopus for NT Server and NT Workstation. This is not your father's fault-tolerant package: It supports disk and system mirroring either locally or across the network, but does not support disk striping with parity. At $999, it's a little pricier than I'd be prepared to pay for single-station fault tolerance, but if you're prepared to go to the expense of a hot-swappable workstation for applications that cannot go down, then it might be worth it. A demo version of this software is on the companion CD to this book.

Hardware   Hardware-based fault tolerance has been around for quite a while. These days, it's normally based on a RAID controller that's hooked up to several SCSI disks (many packages come with three disks) and then writes and regenerates the information on the disks. It's said that hardware RAID systems see more speed benefits from speedy RAID levels than do their software-based counterparts.

The biggest drawback to hardware-based RAID, however, is that it's incredibly expensive. You'll pay thousands of dollars for a Windows NT-compatible RAID system. For an NT Server computer running a network, this might be worth it if you simply cannot have the system fail, but if you're running NT Workstation, it hardly seems worth it. It would be cheaper to buy a second machine, load NT and your other applications on it, and then stick it in a corner to be loaded with backups if necessary.

I hate to sound defeatist about hardware RAID, but in the context of this book, it's overkill. One of the first things to define when it comes to data protection is the point at which the protection is worth more than the data, and that point comes long before the tens of thousands of dollars mark, particularly considering that NT Workstation comes with backup capabilities.

Employing and Managing a UPS

You're probably familiar with the idea of having an uninterruptible power supply (UPS) on the network server. Should the power fail, it's important to make sure that you give the network time to shut down gracefully. Although you can plan for scheduled outages (such as when the power company is working on the lines in your area), you can't plan for thunderstorms, downed telephone lines, or the semi that ran into a power pole. Protecting the server goes almost without saying for most organizations that have networks at all.

However, it's less common to use a UPS with client workstations or standalone machines. First, UPSes aren't cheap—at least a couple of hundred dollars. Second, they don't do anything obvious like improve your display or speed up your disk access time. If you've got some extra money for hardware and you want both power protection and a new CD-ROM drive, then the CD-ROM may win just because it has an immediate impact on how your computer works. Under normal circumstances, you shouldn't notice that you have power protection at all. However, they are very necessary pieces of equipment. After all, if you don't have power, you won't be using the new CD-ROM drive.

Why Use a UPS?

It's those *abnormal* circumstances that you have to plan for, however, and those abnormal circumstances can affect a workstation almost as much as they can a server. The obvious ones are power outages: in many areas of the east coast, power outages are almost as common as the near-daily thunderstorms. But blackouts aren't the only power problems that can impact computers: noisy power and power fluctuations can be just as dangerous in the long run as can blackouts, because they can damage your system's hardware. Then too, even if you're working on a network client and saving data to a protected server, if you don't save, then the power protection on the server can't help you at all when the power goes out.

In short, if you're doing something high-powered enough to require an operating system such as Windows NT on your workstation in the first place, you should be thinking about how to protect your data and hardware from power fluctuations, and plugging in a UPS is the most effective way of doing so. Surge-protected power strips are a handy way of plugging a number of components into one outlet, but don't confuse them with power protection. First, in the case of power surges, most surge protectors have far too high a tolerance for high voltage—by the time they stop the voltage coming through the line from reaching your computer, the levels are already unacceptable. Second, they don't offer power conditioning that can protect your system from noisy power (such as that produced from running heavy equipment off the same circuit).

About UPSes

UPSes filter the building current through a battery. When you plug the UPS into the wall, the power goes to the battery, not to the computer's power supply. While in the battery, the power is "evened out" to eliminate any voltage spikes or sags that could damage your equipment. From there, most of the power is directed to the computer's power supply, with a little siphoned off to charge the battery.

These days, most devices that you see advertised as UPSes are in fact SPSes, or Switched Power Supplies. The difference is that in a UPS there is no point at which the power source changes, whereas in an SPS there is a point at which the power stops coming directly from the outlet (with conditioning) and starts coming from the battery. This used to be more of a concern than it is now because of the switching time involved, but these days most SPSes can switch so fast that the computer has no time to realize that it's temporarily unpowered. It must go without power for about 80ms to notice, and most good devices can switch in 4ms or less. It's not a UPS exactly, but it can fake it convincingly. I've been using devices that were technically SPSes for years without experiencing any problems.

 T I P For best results, when choosing a UPS (that is, an SPS sold as a UPS), look for one with a switching time of less than 14ms.

What Should You Look for in a UPS?

We've touched on some of the reasons why you need a UPS. In brief, these are the things you should look for while you're shopping:

- Power conditioning to eliminate or reduce power surges and sags
- Sufficient power (the more devices you have in your computer, the more power the UPS must have to keep them running long enough to shut down gracefully)
- A switching time of under 4ms
- Serial interface so that you can use NT's UPS Service

N O T E You don't need to run the UPS Service to benefit from having a UPS—you don't even need to have it plugged into a serial port. However, if you use the UPS service then you can get diagnostic information about the power to your system and can control some aspects of it with software.

Personally, I live in an area with lots of thunderstorms and fairly frequent power outages, and I've had good luck with my American Power Conversion (APC) UPSes. In one case, I've been using the same UPS for three years without changing the batteries, and have yet to lose data due to power loss or experience fried components. In particular, the SmartUPS is designed to work with NT (APC is an official Microsoft Solution Provider), even coming with PowerChute, a software package that lets you monitor the quality of the power coming into your system.

Part
III

Ch
14

Installing a UPS

The process of installing a UPS is pretty straightforward. First, shut down the system entirely. Place the UPS near your computer in an adequately ventilated area. Plug all devices for which you want power protection into the plugs at the back of the device. The sole exception to this is a laser printer: do *not* plug a laser printer into a UPS unless it's specifically designed for that purpose. Laser printers demand as much power as some kitchens, and if you try to run one off a UPS you'll overload it immediately. In fact, that's worth a warning for those who are skimming.

CAUTION

Do not plug a laser printer into a UPS. Laser printers pull so much power that they'll cause the battery to overload immediately.

If you're planning to use the UPS service, don't forget to plug the serial cable into one of the COM ports. Note which one you're using. You'll need this information when setting up the UPS service.

When you've got everything plugged in, plug the UPS into a grounded outlet. You should see status lights indicating the normal functioning of the UPS. Although it hasn't had a chance to charge yet, there's probably enough juice in the battery that the system should be able to cope with power outages from the time you plug it in. If not, then plug it in on its own and let the battery charge for about two hours.

The UPS Outlet

Choosing an outlet for your UPS may not just be a matter of plugging it into the nearest outlet. First, the outlet cannot be switched (i.e., connected to a light switch). Second, it must be grounded properly. If it's not a grounded outlet (with space for a three-pronged plug) don't just plug an adapter into it—rewire the plug. If it is a grounded outlet, test it with a voltage meter, available at most hardware stores for around $5, to determine whether it's wired correctly. Fourth, avoid plugging the UPS into a circuit shared with heavy equipment or coffee makers.

If this seems like a fair amount of work, you're right. But since you've gone to the trouble of getting a UPS, you might as well set it up properly.

When the UPS is ready and all components are plugged in, power up the devices. They should all start up normally—if they don't, check to make sure that all power cords are fully plugged in. Sometimes the plugs on the back of a UPS are a little less receptive than those in the wall.

Now that the hardware setup is taken care of, it's time for the software part. (That is, it's time for the software part if you bought a UPS with a serial interface. If not, then you can skip to the next chapter now.) When NT starts up, open the Control Panel and choose UPS Service, as shown in figure 14.8.

FIG. 14.8
The UPS Service configuration icon is located in the Control Panel.

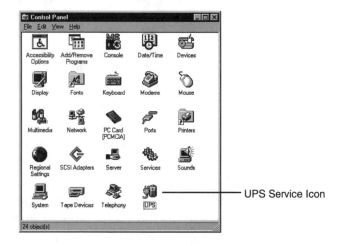

UPS Service Icon

When you click the icon, you'll see a dialog box like the one shown in figure 14.9.

FIG. 14.9
NT won't automatically detect a UPS, so the first step in configuration is to tell the system that a UPS is connected.

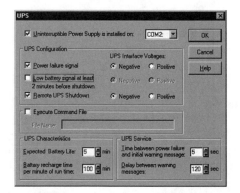

To complete this dialog box, you'll need your UPS documentation. This dialog box is pretty straightforward—just make sure that you get the voltages positive or negative as necessary.

Part
III

Ch
14

Managing a UPS

In most cases, there's little to be done in terms of managing a UPS if you set it up properly in the first place. Ideally, you should be able to plug it in and forget about it until the next power outage, when you should be patting yourself on the back for having installed it.

To get to that point of nirvana:

■ Keep track of the age of your UPS's batteries. First, they do wear out eventually. Second, if your UPS is not working properly and you know that the batteries are new, then that can be an indicator of something else wrong.

■ If your UPS comes with additional software, use it. (One example is discussed in the next section.) You can use this software to configure your UPS for remote shut-down, to notify you via e-mail or paging in case of emergency, and to get information about the quality of the power going to your computer.

■ Keep your system documentation handy so that you know what the status lights on the front mean. Some UPSes are more complicated than others. For example, one of my UPSes has a single "Yes, I'm alive" status light; another, smarter one has four arrays of lights that provide information about the power getting to your system, the charge on the battery, and the like.

■ Make sure that the UPS is properly ventilated. UPSes like the same environmental conditions that computers do.

■ Don't overload your UPS. Some units are more capable of complaining about overwork than others, but putting too many devices on a UPS not equipped to handle them will shorten the useful life of the system battery.

PowerChute Plus

If you get APC's Smart UPS, then you'll also get a software package called PowerChute Plus, complete with serial cable. With this package, you can do more power-related moni-toring than you'll probably ever want to.

The PowerChute manual is quite good, and if you've any use for this information there's not much need to rehash it here. These are just a few points for those intending to set it up who aren't in the practice of reading manuals first. (Normally, I'm not either, but this information is important):

■ Of the two serial cables in the box, use the black one for working with a SmartUPS. This is the "smart signaling" one that you'll use to let the UPS and PowerChute talk to each other.

- You must be logged on as an administrator to install PowerChute, and you must install it on the local machine.

- After you install PowerChute, the icon for the UPS Services will disappear from the Control Panel because it's incompatible with PowerChute. To get it back, you must uninstall PowerChute.

- Once you've installed PowerChute, you're not done until you start up the UPS Service (from the Service utility in the Control Panel). Set it for Automatic startup.

Other than that, installing PowerChute is easy: insert the CD-ROM in the drive, and choose Setup. The setup program will ask you for some information about your UPS (what kind it is, what port it's on), how you want messaging to work, and how long the UPS should run while on battery power.

 To keep from running your battery dry or being caught unawares at system shutdown, choose to shut down your system after a fixed time period of battery use. If the battery runs low before that time is up, then the system will shut down automatically.

Once it's installed, you've rebooted the system, and the UPS service is running, you can start PowerChute from the Start menu to open a control panel. From there, you can test the UPS's battery by simulating a power shutdown, choose to monitor another networked NT computer, shut down the server (or schedule a future shutdown), set up system power logging, or configure other UPS settings.

From Here...

In this chapter, we've discussed some of the ways in which you can protect your data with backups, fault-tolerant drives, and UPSes. With the exception of fault tolerance, NT Workstation makes it easy for you to protect your data. If you're generating work of any importance, you should take advantage of NT's features to help you protect it.

- For more information about the Disk Administrator, turn to Chapter 10, "Optimizing the File System."

- For more information on backups, turn to Chapter 29, "Backing Up and Editing the Registry."

Part
III

Ch
14

Optimizing Network Performance

Networking Overview

by Jim Boyce

Ten years ago, local area networks (LANs) were few and far between in the personal computer world. Adding network capability to an office required the addition not only of the network hardware, but third-party network software. Setting up and managing the network often was more difficult than the average office worker could handle. Over the years, networking has become the norm, rather than the exception, and much easier to implement. Even small businesses see the advantages of networking their computers to share data, peripherals, and other resources. Operating systems like Windows NT and Windows 95 make it possible.

As the Internet continues to increase in popularity and users and companies find new ways of communicating with one another, networking becomes even more important. Where network capability was once a third-party add-on, it now is built into the operating system. Windows NT includes built-in peer-to-peer networking as well as network client software to support other network operating environments, such as Novell Netware. In addition, you'll find good Internet support in Windows NT Workstation, from its TCP/IP protocol and utilities to the Peer Web Services with which you can build a personal Internet web server.

More demanding Internet users can rely on the Internet Information Server included with Windows NT Server as a platform for their Internet servers. ■

Integrating with Other Environments

Because of its support for many protocols, Windows NT is an excellent network client. If you're creating a new network (networking your computers for the first time), your best option is to use Windows NT's built-in, peer-to-peer network capability. You can choose among the NetBEUI, IPX/SPX, and TCP/IP protocols, because the Microsoft network client supports all three. With the addition of Windows NT Server to the network, you can create a network domain to simplify security authentication.

Instead of creating a new network, however, you might be migrating to Windows NT from DOS, Windows 3.x, or Windows 95, and already have another network operating system in place. For example, you might be using Netware client software to access Netware servers. If this is your situation, one option is to retain your existing Netware servers and continue to use Netware clients. The workstations on which you install Windows NT can use the Netware client included with Windows NT to access the network's servers. Other workstations can continue to use their existing Netware clients. By retaining your existing servers and clients, you minimize the disruption to the network's users and reduce the cost associated with switching to a new network operating system. You can make the transition gradually while continuing to use the existing servers.

At some point, however, you might decide to switch to Windows NT Workstation on all client computers and Windows NT Server on your network's servers. Windows NT Server can provide the same functions as a Netware server, and can replace a Netware server without the need to change network clients. So, you might switch over your servers to Windows NT Server and continue to use the Netware clients on the workstations until you can gradually switch over the workstations, also.

This type of network integration is an important issue for many businesses. For that reason, *Windows NT Workstation 4.0 Advanced Technical Reference* provides coverage of network integration. After an introduction to network technology in Chapter 16, you'll find tips in Chapter 18, "Integrating Windows NT in Microsoft Environments," to help you integrate Windows NT with systems based on DOS, Windows 3.x, and Windows 95.

In Chapter 17, "Integrating Windows NT in Novell Environments," you learn how to take advantage of the Netware client software and utilities included with Windows NT to connect to Netware servers and share resources on a peer-to-peer basis. You'll also learn how to replace a Netware server with Windows NT.

To round out the coverage of network integration, Chapter 19, "Integrating Windows NT in UNIX Environments," shows how to connect your Windows NT workstations to computers running UNIX. You'll learn shows how to access shared resources, use X-Windows to run UNIX applications, print to UNIX printers, and transfer data.

Dial-Up Networking

You might want to take advantage of another important networking feature in Windows NT—Dial-Up Networking, known in previous versions of Windows NT as Remote Access Services (RAS). Windows NT Workstation includes both client and server software, enabling you to use Dial-Up Networking to dial into a remote dial-up server or turn your computer into a dial-up server.

For example, you can use Dial-Up Networking to connect to your office LAN when you're traveling, enabling you to continue to access files, printers, and e-mail outside the office. Or, Dial-Up Networking might be the mechanism you use to connect different branches of your company. Dial-Up Networking also is the mechanism used by Microsoft Exchange to enable you to connect to a remote Exchange e-mail server.

Another use for Dial-Up Networking that might be important to you is Internet connectivity. If your office LAN is connected to the Internet, you can add a Dial-Up Networking server to the LAN and enable users in your organization to dial into the network to connect to the Internet. Because the Dial-Up Networking server relies on Windows NT's security, you are assured that your dial-up connection to the LAN and Internet is safe from unwanted intrusion.

You'll find Dial-Up Networking explored in detail in Chapter 20, "Using Dial-Up Networking." Chapter 20 discusses how to set up Dial-Up Networking, use scripting to automate connections, and use the PPP, SLIP, and CSLIP connection protocols. ●

CHAPTER 16

A Brief Primer on Networks

by Jim Boyce

Many of the chapters in this book deal with networking in one way or another. Having an understanding of today's networking concepts is important to understanding Windows NT's networking features. This chapter examines general network topics as they relate to Windows NT to give you an understanding of network features and capabilities in Windows NT.

First, let's put the network in perspective. ■

Overview of general LAN concepts

You learn about various types of networks and the difference between a server and a workstation.

Understanding the physical network components

You learn about LANs, network interface cards, adapters, and media.

Understanding network layers

This section examines the standard network layer structure defined by the OSI network reference model.

Understanding domain and workgroup models

You learn about using domains to centralize user accounts to simplify system administration.

Understanding network security models

You can protect shared resources from unauthorized access and specify different levels of security.

LAN Overview

You're probably familiar with networks, at least in general terms. Traditionally, networks have been used primarily to share disk and printer resources. This is true of both dedicated and peer-to-peer networks. A *dedicated network* is one in which one or more computers are designated as servers and perform no other function but to share their resources. These dedicated *servers* often are relegated to very specific tasks. A server that is used to store applications, data files, and other reference data is called a *file server*. A server that acts as a print resource, sharing its printers with other computers on the network, is called a *print server*. A server that shares a large database with the network is often called a *database server*. And in many dedicated networks, servers perform multiple roles. A server might share its disks as well as its printers, for example.

In a peer-to-peer network, the distinction between workstation and server becomes blurred. In a *peer-to-peer network*, any computer on the network can act as a server while continuing to act as a workstation. You might share a local document directory with the entire network or a selection of other users, for example. While you use the computer as a workstation, other users can access the files in your shared folder.

Today's typical network often incorporates both dedicated servers and peer-to-peer networking. Furthermore, the network has grown to encompass more than just file and print sharing. The network's primary purpose is still information sharing, but the means by which information is shared has evolved. In addition to sharing files and printers, users share information with one another through e-mail. In many networks, sharing information through Web documents is becoming common. As network speed has increased, other methods for sharing information and communicating have become more popular. Many networks are adding desktop conferencing, which allows users to share and edit documents dynamically. Video conferencing, which effectively turns the network into a video phone system, is also becoming more popular.

Windows NT offers an excellent platform for all of these network uses. Windows NT Server is an excellent network operating system for sharing resources as a dedicated server. Windows NT Workstation's peer-to-peer capability makes it a good tool in small networks for sharing files and printers and for messaging. And, Windows NT Workstation computers can rely on a Windows NT Server node to act as a security server, placing an additional layer of security on the workstation's peer-to-peer sharing. Support for a wide variety of protocols, particularly TCP/IP, makes both Windows NT Workstation and Windows NT Server good choices for building intranets and expanding the network. The inclusion of PPTP (Point-to-Point Tunneling Protocol) provides a means for extending intranets outside traditional physical limitations. You might build an intranet with segments of the network located on different continents, with each segment blending with the rest to create a widely distributed LAN.

Even though the manner in which networks are applied has changed in recent years, the underlying technology has not changed that much. The physical components of the network, for example, have changed little although they have increased in speed and performance.

Understanding the Physical Network

A Local Area Network (LAN) generally consists of a given number of computers connected together by cables or wireless connections such as infrared or RF (Radio Frequency). On the network, each computer is called a *node*. A network comprises many different physical components besides the computers themselves, some inside the computers and some outside. These components are loosely termed the *physical network*. The following sections offer an overview of the physical components found in typical networks.

The Network Interface Card (NIC)

The *network interface card*, or NIC, is the one piece of network hardware you'll find in every networked computer. The *NIC* is an adapter card physically similar to the video adapter, disk controller, and other adapter cards in the computer, though obviously different in function. The NIC serves as the link between the cable that connects the computer to the network and the operating system. It's primary function is to receive, process, and pass to the operating system incoming network traffic, as well as the reverse: receiving data from the operating system and translating the data onto the network. Data moving across the network is often called a *data packet*. A data packet is a collection of data that has been encapsulated for transmission.

N O T E   Computers that connect to a network through a dial-up connection do not require a NIC. ■

Each NIC uses a unique network address to enable network data packets to be directed specifically to the NIC, much like the way you direct a letter to a specific house by the house's address. The NIC monitors the packets coming from the network, and if the packet is meant for the computer, the NIC processes the packet and transmits it up the chain to the operating system. If the packet is meant for another node, the NIC simply passes on the packet. The NIC doesn't perform this function by itself, however. The various layers of the network operating system serve as a sort of operating system for the

NIC, enabling it to perform its job. You'll learn more about network layers and their functions later in this chapter in the section "Understanding Network Layers."

The network card determines in large part the efficiency of the network. Because data can be transmitted on the network faster than the NIC can process the data, the packets must be buffered until the NIC can process them. A slow network card can become a performance bottleneck, and a fast network card can improve network performance considerably.

Like other types of adapters, NICs typically require the use of an Interrupt Request line (IRQ) to enable communication with the CPU. Except on systems that enable IRQ sharing, this IRQ assignment must be unique to the NIC. Many NICs default to IRQ2, while others default to IRQ10. All, however, provide a means for selecting an IRQ that does not conflict with other IRQ assignments in the computer. Some require that you set jumpers or DIP switches on the NIC to set the IRQ, but others enable the operating system to automatically configure the IRQ setting. This latter type of NIC is said to be *software configurable*.

In addition to requiring an IRQ, NICs also require an *I/O base address*, also referred to as the *I/O port address* (referred to in the rest of the chapter as simply the base address). The NIC's base address specifies a memory address, and this memory address serves as a port through which the NIC and operating system communicate. Network adapters typically use a base address somewhere in the range from 0×200 through 0×300, although a NIC can use a different base address.

If you already have a network adapter installed and functioning under Windows NT, you can easily view and change the IRQ and base address settings for the NIC. To do so, open the Control Panel and double-click the Network icon to display the Network property sheet. Click the Adapters tab to display the Adapters page. The Network Adapters list shows all the NICs installed in the computer. Select the adapter whose settings you want to view or change, then click Properties. A dialog box similar to the one shown in figure 16.1 will appear. Use the controls on the dialog box to change settings as desired.

N O T E   The configuration dialog box for one NIC will likely be at least somewhat different from another. Therefore, the dialog box you see on your system will probably be slightly different from the one shown here. ▪

You'll be prompted to restart Windows NT after making a change to network settings to enable those settings to be applied.

N O T E   If you need help installing and configuring NICs or network services under Windows NT, refer to the *Windows NT Installation and Configuration Handbook* (Que, 1996) ▪

FIG. 16.1
The property page for an adapter often includes settings other than IRQ and base address.

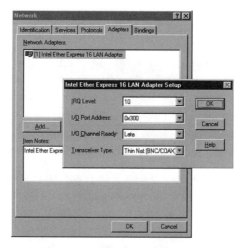

Media

A LAN requires some mechanism to move packets from one node to another. The term *media* refers to the type of connection used between nodes on the network. Typically, media is synonymous with *cable*, though wireless mechanisms such as infrared technology are becoming more popular. Commonly used media include *twisted pair, coaxial cable* (also called *coax*), *fiber optic cable*, and *free space*.

Physical media such as twisted pair, coax, and fiber optic cable are often referred to as *bounded media*. Wireless connections such as infrared and radio are referred to as *un-bounded media*.

Twisted Pair Cable Twisted pair cable currently is the most commonly used type of network media. Twisted pair cable is similar to the cable used for telephone lines. The twisted pair cable used for network connections, however, is considerably sturdier than typical phone cable. More expensive twisted pair cable contains pairs of wires enclosed by metallic-foil sheathing, with the entire bundle shielded by a metallic braid. Other types of twisted pair wire contain additional twisted pairs, fiber optic cable, and voice/data lines in the same bundle. Less expensive unshielded twisted pair wire can be used in some installations.

N O T E Twisted pair cable gets its name from the fact that pairs of wire in the cable are twisted around one another. The twists reduce or eliminate electromagnetic fields generated by current flow in the wire, improving signal propagation and quality. ■

Twisted pair wire that has a shield around it to help reduce interference and improve data transmission is called *shielded twisted pair*, or STP. Wire that is not shielded is called *unshielded twisted pair*, or UTP.

Coaxial Cable (Coax)   Coaxial cable is another commonly used network medium. The cable is similar, though not identical, to the cable used for cable television. Coax typically offers higher data-transfer rates over longer distances than does twisted pair wire due to lower signal loss and interference. Standard BNC (twist on/off) connectors are used to connect coax cable to the NIC and to other devices, such as routers.

Fiber Optic   Fiber optic cable consists of a light-carrying material core (usually glass) encased in a protective jacket. Unlike copper-based media (twisted pair and coax), fiber optic cable transmits data as pulses of light. Fiber optic cable offers many advantages over other media, including signal propagation over very long distances without amplification, relative immunity to electrical noise, high bandwidth, and difficulty in tapping (offering greater security).

Fiber optic cable is considerably more expensive than copper media, however, which limits its use primarily to connections in which speed is extremely important or cable length must be very long.

Unbounded Media   Wireless connections are becoming more common, and enable network connections where physical bounded media connections are not possible or feasible. Current wireless technology includes radio and infrared implementations. In such a wireless network, transceivers send network packets without a cabled connection. The primary benefit of wireless networking is the cable planning and installation, making it a good choice in old buildings in which installing cable could be difficult.

However, unbounded media can be more susceptible to interference, although proper installation and adherence to distance limitations will eliminate this problem. Security could be a factor—it is possible to "tap in" to an unbounded network because there are no set connection points as there are in a wired network. If the utmost security is required, either use a wired network or verify with the wireless network's manufacturer that it is not susceptible to unauthorized access. Finally, you need to consider the cost of adding cabling versus installing a wireless network. Typically, the adapters and other hardware required to implement a wireless network are more expensive than for a conventional wired network.

Topology

The term *network topology* refers to the way in which the nodes on a network are connected to one another. The three common topologies in use today are *star*, *ring*, and *bus* topologies.

A simple star topology network consists of nodes connected to a central hub, much like the points of a star connect to its hub. In a distributed star topology network, multiple stars are connected together through the hubs. Figure 16.2 shows two simple stars connected together to form a distributed star network. Star topology networks offer the advantage of easy fault detection; it's relatively easy to locate faulty cables and other components because the fault typically lies between the failed system and the hub. The star topology also lends itself to easy expansion across multiple floors because you can simply run cables from the hub to the additional computers or to a new hub on the next floor.

FIG. 16.2
Bus and star topology networks are different in structure.

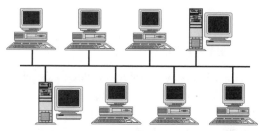

Bus-based LAN

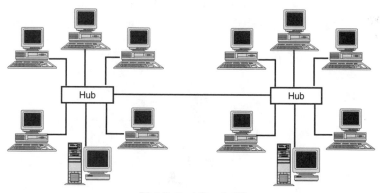

Distributed Star LAN

The hubs control network communication by routing data packets, boosting the signal, and controlling transmission errors. Although you might think that all hubs perform the same functions, they do not—sometimes even within the same LAN. A passive hub, for example, simply routes data packets without performing any additional processing. Active hubs also perform other tasks, including amplifying and retiming the signals.

A bus topology network consists of one or more linear bus segments to which the network's nodes are connected in a series (refer to fig. 16.2). The primary cable is called the *backbone* cable, and the nodes often are connected to the backbone by drop cables. In a simple bus network, the backbone is the sole cable, running from one node's NIC to the next. The cable is connected to the NIC by a BNC T-connector, rather than a drop cable.

The primary advantage of a bus topology is the relative ease with which you can connect nodes, usually without the need for other hardware (such as a concentrator or repeater). The disadvantage is that if one segment of the bus fails, the entire network is affected.

In a ring topology network, the network nodes are connected in a continuous ring. Ring topology works well in small networks where the nodes can be connected easily to the ring, but is not suited to networks in which the nodes are separated by long distances or located on different floors.

Bridges and Routers

LANs have distinct distance limitations due to signal loss. An Ethernet LAN, for example, has a limit of 2,500 meters using multiple segments and repeaters (that amplify the signal), with a limit of no more than four repeaters. Devices such as *bridges* and *routers* enable you to extend the reach of a network.

A bridge connects two separate physical networks to form one logical network, such as connecting a bus-topology Ethernet LAN and a Token Ring network (see fig. 16.3). In this example, the bridge contains two network cards—an Ethernet card and a Token Ring card. The Ethernet card connects the bridge to the Ethernet LAN, and the Token Ring card connects the bridge to the Token Ring LAN.

FIG. 16.3
A bridge connects
dissimilar LANs.

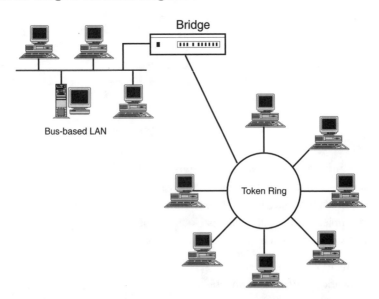

The bridge functions as a node on both LANs, serving as a "double agent" of sorts. When network traffic is directed from node A on the Ethernet LAN to node B on the Token Ring LAN, for example, the bridge removes the Ethernet header from the packet and replaces it with a Token Ring header. The bridge then waits for a free token and places the packet on the network when one is available.

Bridges not only enable you to connect together dissimilar networks, but they also help overcome distance limitations. Once a packet has passed the bridge, it is subject only to the limitations of the local network, and not to the limitations of the network from which it came.

Part
IV

Ch
16

Routers perform a function similar to that of a bridge because they route packets from one node to another. Routers not only maintain information about different routes between destinations, but also which path is the most optimum. The router bases its decision on which route is the best based on a variety of criteria, including how many hops between the router and the destination, the transmission time to reach the destination, the cost of transmission, and other points. Therefore, rather than just passing on a packet like a bridge, a router makes an intelligent decision on how best to transmit the packet.

N O T E A *hop* is the link between two store-and-forward devices. A store-and-forward device is any network device that stores and forwards network packets (such as a router). ■

Understanding Network Layers

The physical network components described in the previous section form the lowest layer in the network. Figure 16.4 illustrates the standard network layer structure defined by the OSI (Open Systems Integration) reference model.

The first two layers (physical and link) define the way data is physically transferred on the network. The network, transport, and session layers define the way data is processed before being passed to the operating system (or processed before being passed to the lower layers). The presentation layer represents the operating system, and the application layer represents the workstation's network software. Above the application layer are the user interface and general applications that use network resources.

By breaking the network model into different layers, it's much easier to accommodate different network technologies. For example, the network protocols (TCP/IP, NetBEUI, and so on) are not dependent on the NIC or cabling, but instead can work on any hardware because the intervening layers translate and process the network traffic into the proper format. Layering also helps make the network transparent to the user interface and applications. Because the layers hide the protocols and physical hardware from the interface and applications, you can change protocols and hardware without making any changes to the interface or your programs to enable them to access network resources.

FIG. 16.4
The OSI layer model segregates network functions into specific layers.

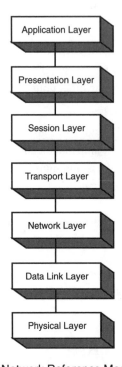

Network Reference Model

The following sections examine the seven network layers, beginning at the bottom-most layer.

Physical Layer

The physical layer defines the physical connection to the network. At this layer, network transmission consists of individual bits, with upper layers of the network processing and packaging the bits into packet form. The physical layer does not define the media used, but defines the way data is transmitted.

Data Link Layer

The data link layer is responsible for processing *frames*, which are the units of data by which the layer communicates. A frame comprises a string of bits grouped into various fields. In addition to the actual data bits, the frame includes fields to identify the source and destination of the frame and an error control field that enables the receiving node to determine when transmission errors occur.

The data link layer strips outgoing frames into individual bits for transmission, and reassembles incoming bits back into frames. In addition, this layer establishes node-to-node connections and manages the transmission of data between nodes, as well as checking for transmission errors.

Network Layer

The network layer is primarily responsible for routing data packets efficiently on the network. The two network protocols included with Windows NT that are most commonly used in networks where routing is required are TCP/IP and IPX/SPX. The IP protocol, which is part of the TCP/IP protocol, is responsible for routing at the network layer. IPX, which typically is used in NetWare environments, serves the same purpose.

In addition to TCP/IP and IPX/SPX, Windows NT also includes the NetBEUI protocol. NetBEUI was designed to provide efficient transport in small networks and works well in such networks. NetBEUI can't be routed, however, which eliminates its use in large, complex networks where routing is often necessary. If you have a small, self-contained network, NetBEUI should be your protocol of choice. Otherwise, you should consider either TCP/IP or IPX/SPX.

Transport Layer

Although the network layer is responsible for routing, it doesn't perform error checking: it simply passes the packets back and forth. There is no guarantee that a packet will arrive at the destination or that it will arrive in the correct order. Some level of error checking is therefore required, and the transport layer provides this reliability. The transport layer checks for errors and causes the packets to be retransmitted when an error occurs.

Windows NT's two primary routable protocols, TCP/IP and IPX/SPX, provide reliable transmission. The TCP portion of the TCP/IP protocol is responsible for error checking and placing packets in the correct order. SPX performs the same function in the IPX/SPX protocol.

Session Layer

The session layer is responsible for reliable and secure communication between nodes. When two network nodes communicate, it's called a *session*. The session layer is responsible for establishing the communication link and the rules by which the session will be accomplished, including the transport protocol to be used. This layer also involves security authentication—the server node authenticates the client node's request through the security subsystem, validating what the client can and can't access.

Presentation Layer

The presentation layer serves as an intermediary between the session layer and the application layer. The presentation layer translates the data from one format to another if required for the session and application layers to communicate. The presentation layer also can perform such tasks as data compression and encryption.

Application Layer

The application layer does not, as you might think, represent the network abilities of your day-to-day applications (word processor, and so on). Instead, the application layer provides an interface between the network and the user interface and applications. In general, the application layer provides a layer of abstraction between you and the network, making the network essentially transparent. Because of the application layer, a program you're using to open a file can do so as easily across the network as it does locally.

Bringing Together the Layers

While it isn't terribly important to understand the exact function of each layer, understanding the layers and their general purpose helps you understand how network capability can be implemented in Windows NT. The different levels of the operating system provide layers of abstraction between you and programs at the top, and the computer's hardware at the bottom. A program doesn't have to "know" how to access the computer's hard disk, because intervening layers in the operating system translate the access requests. For this reason, you can easily add new types of hardware to the system without changing the program to be able to access it. Instead, the hardware manufacturer (or Microsoft) creates a device driver that resides at the lower levels of the operating system and serves as an intermediary between the upper levels and the new hardware.

The network layers offer the same type of abstraction. When you're browsing the network for shared resources, you don't need to know anything about the protocols in use, what type of cabling is used, or any other technical information about the network. You simply double-click icons in the Network Neighborhood folder, and their resources appear on the desktop. The various network layers translate the data from the highest level (you) to the lowest level (the physical network).

This layered mechanism also makes it much easier to change and expand the network. If you have been using NetBEUI and now are expanding to the Internet, or simply want to create your own intranet, you can do so simply by changing from the NetBEUI protocol to the TCP/IP protocol. Your applications see no change; they still access network resources in the same way as before. And there is no change in the way you use the interface to browse for resources. This is because the applications and interface are dealing with the application layer, and the transport protocol(s) are isolated deeper in the stack at the network, transport, and session layers. This flexibility extends all the way to the physical layers: you can install a different NIC without having to install a different version of the protocol you're using.

Understanding Network Relationships in Windows NT

As a network grows, keeping track of and supporting resources and users can become quite complex. Even on smaller networks, distributed resources can be difficult to manage. Under Windows NT, *domains* enable you to centralize user accounts while still enabling users to access the network and its resources from any point in the network. To administer servers effectively, you need to understand domains and their relationship to the network.

Understanding Workgroups and Domains

In Windows NT, as well as in Windows for Workgroups and Windows 95, a *workgroup* is a collection of computers on a network that are grouped together by a logical workgroup name. When you browse for resources on the network, you first see those computers on the LAN that are part of your workgroup. In Windows NT, for example, the Network Neighborhood displays an icon for each of the computers in your workgroup (see fig. 16.5) if you're using a workgroup model.

A computer can belong to any workgroup on the network. In fact, it's very simple to change from one workgroup to another. Just open the Control Panel, double-click the Network icon, click Change on the Identification page of the Network property sheet, and specify a workgroup name. If the workgroup doesn't exist, you effectively create a new workgroup. Note, however, that a computer can belong to only one workgroup at a time.

Workgroups simplify network browsing by providing a means by which a system administrator can group together users who share common resources and goals. If you're a member of the Accounting department, for example, you probably work most with resources shared by other users in the same department. When you browse the network for resources, you first want to see what's available in your department (workgroup). Then, if necessary, you want to be able to browse the network for resources outside your workgroup. Because the network could be quite complex in sheer numbers, the use of workgroups simplifies browsing the entire network. Rather than browse through 200 unrelated workstations, for example, you can browse through only those workgroups that you know offer resources of use to you.

FIG. 16.5

Workgroups provide a means of organizing computers into logical groups.

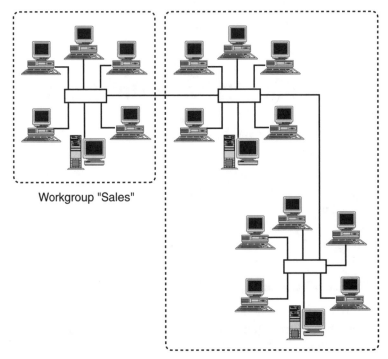

Workgroup "Sales"

Workgroup "Production"

Although workgroups considerably simplify network browsing, they do little, if anything, to simplify system administration. However, domains do simplify system administration. A *domain* is a group of computers and users who share common security and user account data. Domains enable centralization of account access and account management. Unlike a workgroup, in which a user must have an account on the computer he is logging onto, a domain user can log on from any workstation in the domain. More important for the administrator, however, is that you can administer accounts in one central location, which simplifies administration. The user has one domain account, and can log onto any server or workstation in the domain with that one account.

Domains are not a geographical entity, but rather a logical one. Therefore, domain members need not be located within the same physical area. Any mechanism that enables a computer to connect to the domain server to access the account data can be used to add that computer to the domain. Domain members can therefore be located in different buildings or even in different countries. Users who telecommute can connect to the domain through a Dial-Up Networking connection, or if they have local Internet access, can connect through the Internet to the domain using PPTP (Point-to-Point Tunneling Protocol).

In addition to simplifying network administration, domains provide the same organization of resources to the network as workgroups. When a domain user browses the network for resources, he sees the resources organized by domain. The Network Neighborhood, for example, displays an icon for each computer in the user's domain. If the user needs to access a resource outside his domain, he double-clicks the Entire Network icon from the Network Neighborhood folder, and sees icons for each of the other domains in the network.

Part
IV

Ch
16

The security and user account information are stored in the *directory database*, which also is referred to as the Security Accounts Manager (SAM) database. The SAM is stored on the primary domain controller (PDC) and is replicated to backup domain controllers (BDCs) for reliability and to reduce security authentication load on the PDC.

Primary and Backup Domain Controllers

Each domain includes one primary domain controller (PDC), and can optionally include one or more backup domain controllers (BDCs). The PDC stores the account and security database, and responds to access requests from workstations and servers in the domain. The PDC checks the validity of the account and password provided by the remote process, then approves or disapproves the access request. When you administer user accounts and privileges, you do so on the PDC. You do not, however, have to be logged on physically to the PDC. Instead, you can log on from any computer in the workgroup, including through a dial-up networking connection.

The backup domain controller (BDC) provides a backup to the PDC. The PDC replicates the user account database and related information to all BDCs on the network. If the PDC is unable to respond to an access request, the BDC handles the request. Although it isn't necessary to have a BDC on the network, you should create at least one.

Understanding Trust Relationships

A *trust relationship* is a special logical relationship between domains. In a trust relationship, one domain trusts another domain's users. The *trusting domain* allows users who have accounts in the *trusted domain* to access resources in its domain. For example, assume that domain A is the trusting domain, and domain B is the trusted domain. A user from domain B can access resources in domain A.

A trust relationship can be unidirectional or bidirectional. Just because domain A trusts domain B doesn't mean that domain B trusts domain A. You must explicitly set up the trust relationship to be bi-directional between the two domains if that is the way you want it. Figure 16.6 illustrates the concept of trust relationships.

FIG. 16.6
You can create nontransitive, unidirectional and bidirectional trust relationships.

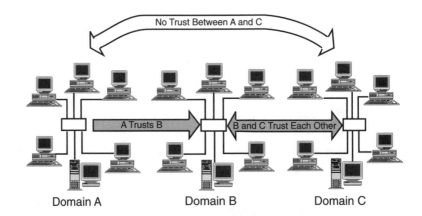

Domain A   Domain B   Domain C

Domain trust relationships are not *transitive*. This means that trusts do not pass from one domain to another. For example, if domain A trusts domain B and domain B trusts domain C, that doesn't mean that domain A trusts domain C. If you want domain A to trust domain C, you must explicitly set up the relationship between domain A and domain C.

Understanding Groups

User accounts enable an administrator to apply resource access on a user-by-user basis. For example, the administrator can grant directory access to a user and deny access to other users. On an NTFS volume, this user-by-user access control can extend to individual files in the directory.

Granting access on a user-by-user basis can become very tedious, however. If you have 200 users on a network, you don't want to have to individually allow or disallow access to each resource. *Groups* overcome this problem.

Each user account can be a member of one or more groups. Groups enable an administrator to grant access to resources not on an individual basis, but on a collective basis. The administrator grants access to a resource to a group. Then, the administrator makes a member of that group each user who must have access to the resource. When a new resource must be made available to the group, the administrator simply grants to the group the ability to access the resource. Members of the group then automatically have access to the resource.

Windows NT supports two types of groups: *global* and *local*. A global group comprises user accounts only from a single domain—the domain in which the group was created. The global group can contain user accounts but not other groups. A local group comprises user accounts and global groups from one or more domains. Users and groups from a trusted domain can be added to a local domain to grant those trusted users and groups access to resources in the local domain. Although local groups can contain global groups, they cannot contain other local groups.

▶ **See** "Creating and Modifying User Accounts," **p. 704**

Windows NT includes many predefined local groups and user rights. These groups are defined in Table 16.1. For a more detailed explanation of groups, see Chapter 32, "Administering Users."

Part
IV

Ch
16

Table 16.1   Built-In Groups

Group	Type	Automatic Contents
Administrators	Local	Domain Admins
Domain Admins	Global	Adminstrator
Backup Operators	Local	None
Server Operators	Local	None
Account Operators	Local	None
Print Operators	Local	None
Power Users	Local	Setup user
Users	Local	Domain Users
Domain Users	Global	Adminstrators
Guests	Local	Domain Guests, Guest
Domain Guests	Global	Guest
Replicator	Local	None

Integrating Existing Workgroups in Domains

Windows for Workgroups and Windows 95 clients on the network can enjoy the benefit of domains along with Windows NT clients. Setting the workgroup name of a Windows for Workgroups client to the name of a domain on the network adds that client to the domain.

When the user browses for network resources, she sees the computers and other re-sources in the domain. If the user account and password supplied by the Windows for Workgroups user is a valid account in the domain, the user is automatically logged on to the domain when she logs on to Windows for Workgroups.

You also can configure Windows 95 clients to log on to and become part of a domain. As with Windows for Workgroups clients, Windows 95 clients see the other computers in their domain when they browse for resources. To control Windows 95 domain logon, double-click the Network icon in the Control Panel. Click the Identification tab in the Network property sheet, and then enter the desired domain name in the Workgroup text box.

To enable domain logon for a Windows 95 client, authenticating the Windows 95 workstation's logon through the user account database on the domain, double-click the Network icon in the Control Panel on the Windows 95 client. Double-click the Client for Microsoft Networks to display the General property page for the client (see fig. 16.7). Enable the Log On To Windows NT Domain check box, then enter the domain name in the Windows NT Domain text box, and click OK. Close the Network property sheet and restart the Windows 95 client for the change to take effect.

FIG. 16.7
Windows 95 client logon can be authenticated on a domain, ensuring added security for the client.

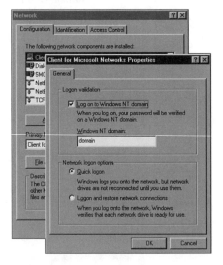

Choosing a Domain Model

The number and relationship among domains in the network is called a *domain model*. The way in which you structure your network (which domain model you choose) is going to depend in large part on the size of the network. A single domain can accommodate roughly 26,000 users with individual workstations and 250 groups (based on a maximum recommended SAM database size of 40M). Those numbers will satisfy all but the largest networks, so a single domain can accommodate nearly any network. You should consider creating multiple domains, however, if your network encompasses multiple departments or accommodates a large number of users. Breaking up the network into multiple domains can simplify management and improve performance.

A domain's SAM database naturally grows as more users are added to a domain. As the SAM database grows, it takes longer for the domain controller to search the database and more overhead to manage it. Microsoft recommends a maximum size of 40M for the SAM database. A user account requires about 1K of space in the database. A computer account requires about 0.5K. A group account requires about 4K assuming an average group size of 300 members. You can use these numbers to determine the approximate size of the SAM database for your network under different domain models.

For example, if your network consists of one-user workstations, the SAM will contain one user account and one computer account for each user, for a total of 1.5K per user. Then, you can add the amount of space required for group accounts (however many you think you'll need) to determine a target SAM database size. As the number of users per workstations changes, you'll have to adjust your numbers accordingly. For example, if you average two users per workstation, you'll need half as many computer accounts as user accounts, or about 2.5K per computer.

In most cases, however, the size of the SAM database won't be the deciding factor in how you configure your domain(s). Because you can accommodate a very large number of users and computers with a single domain, the key factors in how you structure the network will be ease-of-access for users and ease-of-management for yourself. The following sections explore different domain models to help you decide which one is right for your network.

Using a Single Domain Model

As its name implies, the single domain model comprises a single domain for the entire network. All users have accounts in this domain, but also can have local accounts at various workstations (see fig. 16.8). The single domain model is not suited only to small, single-department networks, but can be used for practically any network and any number of departments. Because of administration considerations, however, the single domain model is best suited to relatively small networks in which few departments are involved.

FIG. 16.8
A single domain model can comprise a large number of nodes.

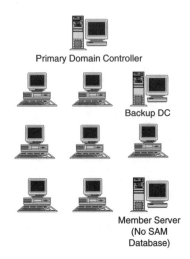

Primary Domain Controller

Backup DC

Member Server
(No SAM
Database)

Single Domain Model

In a single domain model, a member of the Administrators group can administer any server on the network. When the network is small, one administrator can generally handle administration for multiple departments. In some situations, however, you might want to separate administrative duties for security reasons. The easiest way to do that is to use a single master domain model.

Using a Single Master Domain Model

In a single master domain model, the network is split into multiple domains, with one domain serving as the *master domain* (see fig. 16.9). Each of the secondary, or *resource*, domains trusts the master domain, which means that these resource domains recognize the user and global groups defined in the master domain. The master domain, however, does not trust the secondary domains.

All user accounts reside in the master domain, and users log on to the master domain, regardless of the domain in which their computer resides. Since each of the resource domains trusts the master domain, any user can access resources in any of the other domains, subject to the restrictions of his account. This simplifies resource access by enabling all users to access resources throughout the network, but still retains the security of restricting access through group membership methods.

The primary advantage to this model is flexibility in network management. The system administrator can manage all user accounts for the entire network by administering a single domain. If desired, the network administrator can manage resources in each of the resource domains, or can offload that responsibility to local administrators in each resource domain. And last, resources are organized and browsed by their domain, which means that users in a particular domain will see the resources in their own domain listed in the Network Neighborhood folder. When they need to go outside of their own domain, they can open the Entire Network folder to browse for other domains.

FIG. 16.9
Domains in a single master domain model have a unidirectional trust relationship with the master domain.

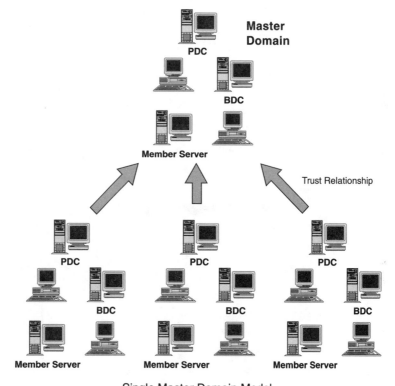

Single Master Domain Model

 TIP It's important to include a backup domain controller for the master domain in each resource domain, primarily because the domains will probably be separated from one another by different network segments. If a segment fails and cuts off a resource domain, its users still can work through the BDC to log on and access resources in the local domain.

Using a Multiple Master Domain Model

As its name implies, the multiple master domain model relies on multiple master domains, each servicing a number of secondary resource domains. The master domains store the user accounts and groups, and the resource domains contain the majority of the network's shared resources.

Within the multiple master domain model, the master domains enjoy bidirectional trust relationships with one another (see fig. 16.10). The resource domains have a unidirectional trust relationship with the master domains. Because the master domains share bidirectional trust, a user can log on to the network from any domain and gain access to resources throughout the network, subject to the restrictions of his account. A user temporarily assigned to a European subsidiary, for example, could still log on to his home domain in the USA. If his account is configured for roaming profiles, he enjoys the same desktop and working environment regardless of his logon location.

▶ **See** "Managing User Profiles," **p. 727**

FIG. 16.10
Each master domain contains a PDC and at least one BDC.

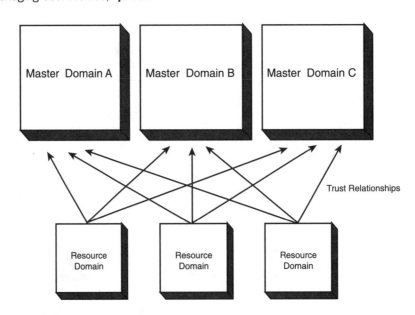

Multiple Master Domain Model

Depending on the connections between master domains and the reliability of those connections, you might consider adding a BDC in each master domain for neighboring master domains. If a connection between two domains is severed for some reason, the BDC can continue to process requests for the disconnected domain.

Creating and Managing Domains

Creating a domain includes creating a primary domain controller for each domain, and (optionally) backup domain controllers.

You can create a domain in two ways:

- Create a new primary domain controller when you install Windows NT Server. This is explained in the section "Creating a Domain During Setup," later in this chapter.

- Use the Network property sheet (accessed from the Network icon in the Control Panel) to change the name of the domain on a primary domain controller to a new domain name. This is explained in the section "Moving a Domain Controller to a New Domain," later in this chapter.

Before you begin creating and moving domains, however, you should understand how Security IDs (SIDs) work, because SIDs affect how and when you can create and move domains.

Understanding Security IDs

Windows NT Server assigns a Security ID (SID) to a PDC when you create the PDC. The SID then becomes a key component of the domain's security mechanism. As you add BDCs and computers to the domain, the PDC's SID is prefixed to those computers' names. When those other computers connect to the domain, they do so using the SID.

If you perform a new installation of Windows NT Server on an existing PDC, Setup will assign a new SID to the PDC—even if you specify the old domain name. Because the SID will be different, any BDCs or workstations that previously were members of the domain will not be able to find the new PDC. Therefore, you should never perform a new installation of Windows NT Server on an existing PDC. If the PDC is damaged in some way, you should allow the BDCs to handle security until you can get the PDC back up. If you are unable to do so, promote a BDC to be the PDC in the domain (see the section "Promoting a BDC to a PDC," later in this chapter). Then, reinstall Windows NT Server on the old BDC, making it a PDC.

N O T E Performing an upgrade on the PDC retains the SID and doesn't cause a loss of domain identity. ■

You also should never install a domain controller when the PDC is unavailable. Doing so will cause the server to become a PDC, which creates a second SID for the domain. Because the SID doesn't match the old PDC's SID, the new domain controller won't be able to function as a domain controller in the domain. To create a new domain controller in an existing domain, install the new domain controller while the existing PDC is available. This will cause the new controller to be installed as a BDC. Then, promote the BDC to a PDC while both domain controllers are active. This will automatically demote the existing PDC to a BDC.

Creating a Domain During Setup

When you install Windows NT Server, Setup prompts you to specify the security role of the computer. You can choose domain controller (primary or backup) or server. If you specify that the computer is to be a PDC, enter the name of the domain that the server will control. Setup then searches the network to verify that the domain name you have specified does not already exist. Setup proceeds only if you have specified a new domain name.

Moving a Domain Controller to a New Domain

You can create a new domain by moving an existing domain controller to a new domain. To do so, follow these steps:

CAUTION

If you intend to rename a domain, remember that you'll have to change the configuration of every existing workstation in the domain that you want to access the new domain. You also must reinstall the BDCs for the domain—you can't move them as you can a PDC. In addition, any trust relationships will have to be reconfigured. Finally, you'll have to change at the workstations all persistent connections to resources on the server to reflect the new name.

---

1. Open the Control Panel and double-click the Network icon.

2. Click the Identification tab of the Network property sheet to display the Identification page.

3. Click the Change button to open the Identification Changes dialog box (see fig. 16.11).

FIG. 16.11

Enter the new domain name in the Identification Changes dialog box.

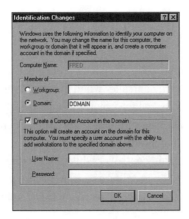

4. In the Domain Name text box, type the name for the new domain.

5. If you want to change the server's computer name, type a new name in the Computer Name text box.

6. Choose OK.

When you choose OK, Windows NT Server checks the network to determine if the domain name you specified is already in use. If the name is available, Windows NT Server displays a dialog box informing you of the consequences of changing domain names. Choose Yes if you want to continue with the name change, or choose No to cancel the process.

Managing Domain Controllers

In addition to creating and moving domains, you might have to perform additional domain administration tasks, such as the following:

- Creating a Backup Domain Controller (BDC)
- Promoting a BDC to a PDC
- Demoting a PDC to a BDC
- Synchronizing domains

Creating a Backup Domain Controller (BDC) A BDC receives a copy of the user account database from the PDC, and handles requests for authentication when the PDC is unavailable. For example, if you must take down the PDC for maintenance, the BDC can handle logon authentication for the domain. Therefore, it is important that your network contain at least one BDC.

You can only create a BDC when you install Windows NT Server. Therefore, to promote a server to BDC status, you must reinstall Windows NT Server on it.

Promoting a BDC to a PDC Occasionally, you will need to promote a BDC to PDC. For example, if you're going to shut down the PDC for maintenance, you should promote a BDC on the network to PDC. Doing so with the PDC online automatically causes the PDC to be demoted to a BDC.

N O T E If at all possible, you should promote the BDC when the existing PDC is online. Promoting the BDC while the PDC is online causes the PDC to be automatically demoted to a BDC. Also, very recent changes to the user database might not be incorporated in the BDC's database.

To promote a BDC to PDC, follow these steps:

1. Open the Start menu and choose Programs, Administrative Tools, Server Manager. The Server Manager opens.
2. Verify that no users are logged on to the system, or broadcast a message to all users that the system will be shut down temporarily.
3. When you're ready to proceed (when all users have logged off), choose View, Servers to view only servers on the network.
4. In the list of servers, select the BDC you want to promote to a PDC.
5. Choose Computer, Promote to Primary Domain Controller.
6. Server Manager warns you that promoting the BDC will close all client connections to the BDC and current PDC. If you're ready to proceed, choose Yes. Choose No if you want to cancel the task.

Demoting a PDC to a BDC   If you are unable to demote a PDC automatically by promoting a BDC to PDC, you can do so manually. For example, your PDC might suffer a hardware failure that takes it offline. You then can promote a BDC on the network to serve as PDC.

When you restart the original PDC, however, Windows NT Server displays a message that at least one service or driver failed during system startup. A little exploring in the Event Viewer will turn up a message that a PDC is already running in the domain. After you start the original PDC, follow these steps to demote it to a BDC:

1. Open the Start menu and choose Programs, Administrative Tools, Server Manager. The Server Manager appears.
2. Choose View, Servers to restrict the view to servers.
3. Select the server you want to demote.
4. Choose Computer, Demote to Backup Domain Controller.

Synchronizing Domains   In most cases, your network's BDCs will remain synchronized with the PDC. It is possible, however, for a BDC to become desynchronized from the PDC. To synchronize a BDC with a PDC, follow these steps:

1. Open the Server Manager.
2. Select the server you want to synchronize with the PDC.
3. Choose Computer, Synchronize with Primary Domain Controller (or choose Synchronize Entire Domain if you want to synchronize all domain controllers in the domain).

Creating and Removing Trust Relationships

If your network is large, it probably contains multiple domains. In many situations, creating trust relationships between domains can simplify administration and user access. Through trust relationships between domains, a user only needs an account in one domain to access other domains and their resources.

▶ **See** "Understanding Trust Relationships," **p. 363**

▶ **See** "Understanding Trust Relationships," **p. 363**

Creating a trust relationship requires two steps. First, the trusted domain must be configured to allow the other domain to trust it. Second, the trusting domain must be configured to trust the trusted domain. If each domain is managed by a different administrator, you'll have to coordinate setting up the relationship with the other administrator.

Use the following steps to create a trust relationship:

1. On the domain to be trusted, choose Start, Programs, Administrative Tools, User Manager for Domains.

2. In the User Manager, choose Policies, Trust Relationships to open the Trust Relationships dialog box (see fig. 16.12).

FIG. 16.12
Create trust relationships through the Trust Relationships dialog box in User Manager.

3. Choose the Add button next to the Permitted to Trust this Domain list. The Permit Domain to Trust dialog box opens (see fig. 16.13).

FIG. 16.13
Specify a domain name and optional password to enable another domain to trust the current domain.

4. In the Domain to Permit text box, type the name of the domain that will be permitted to trust the current domain.

5. (Optional) In the Initial Password and Confirm Password text boxes, enter a password that the administrator of the trusting domain must provide when she sets up the trust relationship from her domain.

6. Choose OK, then repeat steps 3 through 5 for additional domains you want to trust the current domain. When you're through adding domains, choose Close.

7. Acquire a password for the trust relationship from the trusted domain's administrator (refer to step 5).

8. Log on to the trusting domain as administrator and start the User Manager.

9. Choose Policies, Trust Relationships to open the Trust Relationships dialog box.

10. Choose the Add button next to the Trusted Domains list. The Add Trusted Domain dialog box opens (see fig. 16.14).

FIG. 16.14
Enter the domain and password for the trusted domain.

11. Type the name of the trusted domain in the Domain text box, and type the password for the domain acquired in step 7 in the Password text box. Choose OK.

12. The User Manager attempts to locate the domain on the network and validates the request to establish the relationship. If successful, the domain name will be added to the Trusted Domains list. If unsuccessful, User Manager displays an error message that the specified domain controller can't be found.

Adding and Removing Computers in a Domain

The PDC and BDC are naturally members of a domain because they control the domain. Computers running Windows NT Workstation also can function as members of a workgroup or of a domain. If the computer is physically connected to a domain, you should configure the computer as a member of the domain to gain the administrative advantages that domain membership offers over workgroup membership.

To add a Windows NT Workstation node to a domain, log on to the workstation as a member of the Administrators group. Open the Control Panel and double-click the Network icon. On the Identification page of the Network property sheet, click the Change button to display the Identification Changes dialog box (see fig. 16.15). Select the Domain option, then enter the domain's name in the associated text box.

FIG. 16.15

Choose between
workgroup and
domain membership
in the Identification
Changes dialog box.

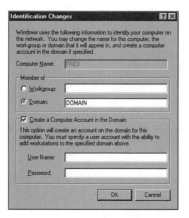

If the computer does not already have an account on the domain controller, enable the Create a Computer Account in the Domain check box. In the User Name and Password text boxes, provide a user account and corresponding password on the domain that has the right to create accounts and add computers to the domain.

To instead create an account at the domain controller, log on to the PDC as a member of the Administrators group. Start the Server Manager and choose Computer, Add to Domain. The resulting dialog box and required information will be self-explanatory.

Computers running Windows NT Server that are not functioning as a PDC or BDC (called a *member server*) also can belong to a domain. Member servers typically perform specific tasks, such as acting as file, print, and remote access servers. Not turning these servers into PDCs or BDCs optimizes their performance by not adding the overhead of user authentication and SAM database replication.

Member servers that belong to a domain, like workstations in the domain, do not maintain a copy of the SAM database. However, you can assign permissions to the server's resources by individual user or by group. The member server maintains a trust relationship with the domain. You therefore can apply resource access permissions to resources on the member server using both local and group memberships, as well as individual user accounts.

To further increase security on the member server, you can create accounts on the member server, rather than on the domain controller. Because the member server doesn't share account information with domain controllers, using local member server accounts adds another layer of security to the server's resources.

In addition to Windows NT Workstation and Server computers, LAN Manager 2.x servers can belong to a domain. A LAN Manager 2.x server can function as a BDC, but it can't function as a PDC.

N O T E   Members of the domain administrator's and server operators' groups always have the permission to add workstations to the domain, even if that right is not explicitly assigned to those groups. However, if you want to enable users to add their computers to domains by themselves, you can explicitly assign that right to a group or specific user account. ■

Whether you use the workgroup or the domain model, you need to consider how you will apply network security. The options become more complex as you add different types of clients to the network. If the network includes Windows 95 clients as well as Windows NT clients, for example, you should consider bringing the Windows 95 clients under the Windows NT security umbrella. The following section examines the different security models you can employ in a Windows NT environment.

Understanding Network Security Models

The primary purpose of a network is to share resources such as disks and printers, and a good network makes those resources easily available while still protecting those resources from unauthorized access. The first line of defense for resources in a Windows NT network is the user account. In a workgroup environment, a user must have a user account on the computer where he's logging on. In addition, he must have a user account at each server (including peer Windows NT Workstation servers) from which he wants to access resources.

In a domain, the user only needs one account in the domain, which enables him to log on from any computer in the domain and access any shared resource in the domain, subject to his account's restrictions. Without a user account, you can't log on, and are therefore prevented from accessing *any* resources, whether local or on the network.

Two types of logon are possible with Windows NT, the first of which is an *interactive* logon. With an interactive logon, the user provides the account name and password in the Logon Information dialog box. If the computer is part of a domain, the user can specify either the name of a domain or the name of the computer at which he's logging on, depending on where his user account is stored. If the computer name specified is not the name of the local computer, *pass-through authentication* begins.

The local computer forwards the logon request to the domain controller for the domain in which the computer belongs. The domain controller checks the provided domain name, and if it matches its own domain name, authenticates the account through its SAM database. The domain controller then returns a security access token that enables the user to log on and access user resources on the local computer and in the domain, subject to the user's account restrictions.

If the domain provided in the Logon Information dialog box doesn't match the domain name in which the logon computer resides, the domain controller determines if the specified domain is a trusted domain. If the specified domain is not a trusted domain, the domain controller refuses the logon. If the specified domain is a trusted domain, the domain controller forwards the logon request to the domain controller of the trusted domain. The trusted domain controller authenticates the logon request, passing the security access token back to the local domain controller, which passes it to the logon computer.

The second type of logon is a *remote* logon. This type of logon occurs when the user is already logged onto the computer or domain, and attempts to connect to a remote resource. When you attempt to connect to a remote disk resource, for example, your user account information is passed to the computer containing the resource. That computer authenticates the request against its SAM database.

Although the logon process uses your user ID and password by default to log on to remote computers, you can override that information and specify different account information for logon to the remote computer. To log on with a different account name for a disk resource, locate the resource in the Network Neighborhood folder, then right-click the resource and choose Map Network Drive from the context menu. (Or, you can simply right-click the Network Neighborhood icon and choose Map Network Drive, then specify or browse to the resource's path.) In the Connect As text box on the Map Network Drive dialog box, type the name of the account under which you want to log on to the remote resource. If the account is stored in a different domain, specify the domain name, a forward slash, and the resource name, as in *domain\name* (such as Accounting\Fred).

Part
IV
Ch
16

Controlling Guest Logon

Just because a domain is untrusted doesn't mean you can't log on to that domain. If you attempt to connect to a domain account or a computer in an untrusted domain, the computer (PDC in the case of a domain account) authenticates your logon request against its local SAM database. If you specify a valid account and password, you will be logged on. You probably assume that if the account you specify doesn't exist, you'll be denied access. However that isn't necessarily the case.

If the Guest account is enabled on the remote computer or domain, and that Guest account has no password (a common practice), you'll be logged onto the remote domain or computer as a guest, subject to all the privileges and restrictions that apply to that account.

Because a Guest account that is unprotected by a password allows logon from virtually any point in the network, you should consider disabling the Guest account on all computers and domains if access to that account would pose a security risk. At the very least, carefully examine the rights assigned to the Guest account to ensure that network security can't be compromised.

User-Level Security versus Share-Level Security

In a Windows NT environment, all resources are shared with *user-level security*. This means that the share is protected by the SAM database, either on the computer itself or on the domain. You can access the share only if the share has been set up to allow access to your user account or to a group to which you belong.

In Windows for Workgroups and Windows 95 environments, shared resources are protected using *share-level security*. Each share is protected by a combination of two passwords, one controlling read-only access and the other controlling full access (see fig. 16.16). If you specify the read-only password, you can only read from the resource (such as reading files in a directory). If you specify the full access password, you have full access to the share (in the case of a directory, this means you can delete and copy files in the directory).

FIG. 16.16

Windows 95 computers use share-level security by default to protect shared resources.

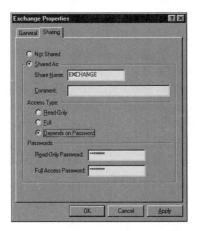

N O T E Although you can protect a share using two different passwords, you don't have to use both. If you want a resource to have only read access and not allow full access to anyone, use the Read-Only option. To use both read-only and full levels of access, use the Depends on Password option and specify two different passwords. ▇

Any user can access a resource protected by share-level security regardless of his logon account, domain, and so on, as long as he provides the correct password. While this method is acceptable in many situations, it provides little security flexibility—it is possible to restrict specific users only by not giving them the appropriate password. Share-level access also requires that you maintain and administer resource passwords outside of the SAM database, decentralizing administration.

If your network contains only Windows NT computers, the question of share-level versus user-level security is irrelevant. If your network includes Windows 95 workstations, however, you should understand that you can take advantage of user-level security on those Windows 95 workstations. This means that instead of protecting resources with a read-only and a full-access password on these nodes, you can use the same type of user and group access control you use on your Windows NT computers.

Setting Up User-Level Security

Enabling user-level security on a Windows 95 workstation is simple. It first requires that a Windows NT computer be available on the network to act as a security server, authenticating access requests for the resource. This Windows NT computer can be running Windows NT Workstation or Server, and doesn't have to be a PDC or BDC. It simply needs to contain a list of the users and groups you want to use to manage access to the resource.

To enable user-level security on a Windows 95 workstation, log on to the Windows 95 computer and open the Control Panel. Double-click the Network icon, then click the Access Control tab to display the Access Control page (see fig. 16.17).

FIG. 16.17

Share-level security is the default security mechanism for Windows 95 computers.

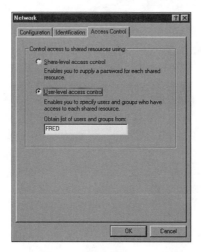

Choose the <u>U</u>ser-Level Access Control option button, then specify the name of the computer or domain that will act as the security server for the computer. Choose OK and restart Windows 95 to make the change take effect.

 TIP In addition to using a Windows NT computer for security authentication, a Windows 95 computer can rely on a NetWare server running bindery emulation to process security requests. The Windows 95 computer must be running the File and Printer Sharing for NetWare Networks service, however.

The list of users and groups that can access a share on a Windows 95 computer is stored on the Windows 95 computer, and not on the security server. The accounts and groups themselves are located on the security server. Although you can view the accounts and groups from the Windows 95 computer and assign various accounts and groups to a re-source, you can't manage accounts directly. You can, however, run the User Manager for Domains client on a Windows 95 computer to manage accounts remotely.

Sharing Resources with User-Level Security

After you have configured the Windows 95 computer for user-level access and restarted the computer, all previous shares are removed from sharing. You must then reshare any resources you want to make available on the network and apply user account and groups accordingly.

To share a resource on a Windows 95 computer with user-level security, first locate the resource you want to share. Right-click the resource and choose Sharing to display the Sharing page of the resource's property sheet (see fig. 16.18).

FIG. 16.18
The user-level security
Sharing page is
different from the
share-level security
Sharing page.

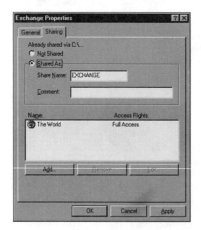

Specify a share name for the resource, just as you would when sharing a resource on a Windows NT computer. Then, click the Add button to add users and groups to the list of accounts that can access the resource. Choosing Add displays the Add Users dialog box (see fig. 16.19), which lists the users and groups on the security server.

The Read-Only and Full Access rights behave just as they do with share-level security. For the most control over access, assign custom access to a user or group by selecting the user or group from the Name list, then clicking the Custom button. After you choose OK to close the Add Users dialog box, select the custom user from the Sharing page and click the Edit button to display the Change Access Rights dialog box (see fig. 16.20).

FIG. 16.19
You can grant three levels of access using the Add Users dialog box.

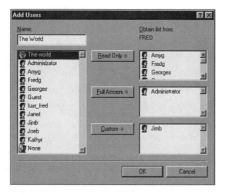

FIG. 16.20
Using Custom Access Rights allows much greater flexibility than Read-Only or Full access.

If you examine the rights listed in table 16.2, you'll notice that the rights extend beyond those normally available on a FAT file system, the only file system supported on Windows 95 computers. This additional flexibility in controlling resource access can be extremely valuable and worth the addition of a single Windows NT computer in an otherwise all-Windows 95 network.

Table 16.2   File Operations and Access Rights

File Operation	Access Rights Required
Change access rights	Change access control
Change directory or file attributes	Change file attributes
Copy files from a directory	Read, list files
Copy files to a directory	Write, create, list files
Create and write to a file	Create files

continues

Table 16.2   Continued

File Operation	Access Rights Required
Delete a file	Delete files
Make a new directory	Create files
Read from a closed file	Read files
Remove a directory	Delete files
Rename a file or directory	Change file attributes
Run an executable file	Read, list files
Search a directory for files	List files
See a file name	List files
Write to a closed file	Write, create, delete, change file attributes

Because Windows 95 computers support only the FAT file system, you can't assign rights to specific files, but only to directories. Access rights for a shared directory pass down to its subdirectories.

From Here...

This chapter provided a brief refresher of network concepts to help lead into the following chapters:

- Chapter 17, "Integrating Windows NT in Novell Environments," provides tips on incorporating Windows NT with Novell NetWare clients and servers.
- Chapter 18, "Integrating Windows NT in Microsoft Environments," offers a detailed look at using Windows NT with other Microsoft operating systems.
- Chapter 19, "Integrating Windows NT in UNIX Environments," explores methods and tips for connecting Windows NT workstations and servers to UNIX-based networks and services.

CHAPTER 17

Integrating Windows NT in Novell Environments

by Sue Plumley

Windows NT Workstation is quickly becoming the standard in clients, not only for Windows NT Server networks but for Novell NetWare networks as well. Windows NT Workstation integrates smoothly into the NetWare network, providing the user with all of Windows NT's and NetWare's advantages. A Windows NT Workstation user can share resources with the network—including files, directories, printers, and so on—besides accessing resources over the NetWare network.

Microsoft has had plenty of practice at making clients work with Novell; Windows for Workgroups and Windows 95 both integrate completely with Novell networks and Windows NT is no exception. ∎

Using NetWare clients

Learn which NetWare clients to use, how to install them and how to choose protocols and services for your Windows NT Workstation.

Configuring the client service for NetWare

Decide whether to use a preferred server or default tree and context in Windows NT Workstation.

Using logon scripts in Windows NT and NetWare

See the difference between login scripts in NetWare and logon scripts in Windows NT and learn how to create scripts that perform the functions you need.

Sharing resources in NetWare environments

View the available resources and access them from Windows NT; also, learn to share your own resources across the network.

Using NetWare file and print services

Take advantage of NetWare's file and print services by mapping drives and capturing printers within Windows NT.

Integrating NetWare print queues with Windows NT

Control printing using either the Windows NT and NetWare network print queues.

Using NetWare Services and Protocols

When attaching a computer that's running Windows NT Workstation to a Novell NetWare network, you must first install a client service and a compatible protocol so the workstation can access and communicate with the NetWare server. Windows NT provides everything you need to prepare the workstation for NetWare. After configuring the workstation, you can access the NetWare network resources the same way you access any Microsoft network: through the Network Neighborhood.

Using Microsoft versus Novell

You can use Novell's NetWare Client for Windows NT, available from the Novell Forum library on CompuServe, or you can use Microsoft's Client Service for NetWare. There are less problems with consistency in connecting, fewer crashes, and response time across the network is quicker using Microsoft's Client Service. Programs from the workstation seem to work more efficiently with NetWare.

Windows NT Workstation includes a Client Service for NetWare that enables workstations to connect to resources on NetWare servers 2.x or later. Additionally, Windows NT's Client Service for NetWare supports NetWare 4.x servers running either NetWare Directory Services (NDS) or bindery services. Finally, logon scripts are also supported.

In the past, Novell's client for Windows required no other client be installed; therefore, you could not use a Microsoft client at the same time. You either belonged to a Novell network or a Microsoft network. If you use Microsoft's client for NetWare, you can be members of both networks with no problem whatsoever.

ON THE WEB

Get updated client software from Novell's World Wide Web site: **http://www.novell.com** or FTP server at **ftp.novell.com.**

You should, however, install the Novell client if you use any of the following:

- NetWare NCP Packet Signature
- NetWare (Internet Protocol)
- 3270 emulators that require a DOS TSR
- Custom VLM components

If none of the preceding examples apply to your site, you can safely and successfully use Microsoft's client for NetWare. Microsoft's client for NetWare uses the NWLink IPX/SPX Compatible Transport protocol, which works well with NetWare.

N O T E At the time this book was written, the only Novell Windows NT client available was for
Windows NT 3.5. Novell will upgrade that client, but how they choose to build the new
client for Windows NT 4 is still a mystery. ▪

▶ **See** "Integrating with Windows for Workgroups Clients," **p. 416**

▶ **See** "Integrating with Windows 95 Systems," **p. 420**

No matter which client you choose to install, the procedure is the same: you use the Network dialog box, Services tab to install client services for NetWare, as described in the
section "Installing NetWare Services and Protocols," later in this chapter.

Protocol Issues

Part
IV
Ch
17

Windows NT installs the NetBEUI protocol by default; however, you can install the
NWLink IPX/SPX-Compatible Transport to enable your workstation to access a NetWare
server and network. IPX/SPX stands for Internetwork Packet Exchange/Sequenced
Packet Exchange and it is a protocol that Novell built for NetWare. IPX/SPX is based on
a Xerox protocol called Xerox Networking Services, or XNS. Microsoft first added the
IPX/SPX-compatible protocol to Windows NT as part of Windows NT 3.5 for compatibility
with the most popular local network type in the world: Novell NetWare.

Part of Windows NT's IPX/SPX protocol is NWLink, a transport protocol that's compatible with IPX/SPX. NWLink supports the sockets application program interface (API),
that some NetWare-based applications servers, or NetWare Loadable Modules (NLMs),
use to communicate with client computers. Because of NWLink, Windows NT can connect to computers running NetWare as well as to other Windows NT Workstations and
Windows NT Servers.

N O T E NWLink, by itself, is worthless as a protocol because it doesn't include a NetWare-
compatible redirector. Using NWLink, however, with IPX/SPX takes care of that
problem. ▪

Besides the NWLink IPX/SPX-Compatible Transport, Microsoft also includes an NWLink
NetBIOS protocol to maintain compatibility with Novell's version of NetBIOS protocol that
many users often load.

N O T E If there are other workstations using Microsoft operating systems—Windows for
Workgroups, Windows 95, Windows NT Workstation or Server—attached to your
network, make sure you keep your NetBEUI protocol so you can still attach to those workstations
over the Microsoft network. Windows NT Workstation enables you to be a member of both
networks and take full advantage of all resources available. ▪

Installing NetWare Services and Protocols

Use the Network dialog box to add services and protocols to your Windows NT Workstation. If you already belong to a Microsoft network—Windows NT Server, Windows 95, or Windows for Workgroups—you do not need to remove your Microsoft services to install NetWare services if you use the Windows NT-supplied Client Service for NetWare.

To install NetWare service, follow these steps:

1. Double-click the Network icon in the Control Panel and click the Services tab in the Network dialog box.

2. Click the <u>A</u>dd button. The Select Network Service dialog box appears (see fig. 17.1).

FIG. 17.1
Windows NT's client service for NetWare is the most efficient client.

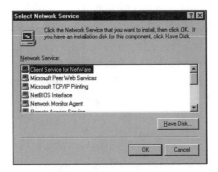

3. Choose Client Service for NetWare from the list of <u>N</u>etwork Services or choose <u>H</u>ave Disk to install Novell's Client for Windows NT.

4. Click OK; you can now choose the protocol for NetWare.

To install the protocol if it's not already installed, choose the Protocols tab of the Network dialog box and follow these steps:

1. Click <u>A</u>dd to display the Select Network Protocol dialog box (see fig. 17.2).

FIG. 17.2
When you choose the NWLink IPX/SPX Compatible Transport, you're actually adding two protocols that work together to perform efficiently.

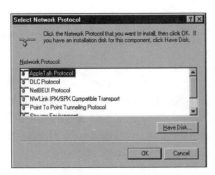

2. Select the NWLink IPX/SPX Compatible Transport and click OK.

3. To configure the protocol, select it in the Network Protocol list box in the Network dialog box and click the Properties button. The NWLink IPX/SPX Properties dialog box appears, as shown in figure 17.3.

FIG. 17.3
Set the frame type for your NetWare version; choose AutoDetect to let NT set the frame type.

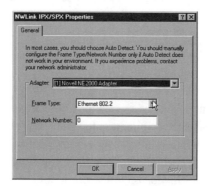

Part
IV
Ch
17

4. In Frame Type, choose either the Ethernet 802.2 (the default frame type for NetWare versions 3.12 and 4.0) or 802.3 (the default for NetWare versions 3.11 and lower).

N O T E If your network is running on a multinet host, set the network number (in hexadecimal form) to make it easier for the NetWare file server to be identified. ■

5. Click OK to close the Network dialog box and restart the computer for the settings to take effect.

TROUBLESHOOTING

I cannot get my Microsoft Client for NetWare to start. The client services uses NWLink, a protocol that enables your Windows NT workstation to communicate with NetWare file and print servers. To make sure the NWLink is enabled, click the Services icon in the Control Panel. In the list of services, find Client Service for NetWare. If it is not started, select the service and click the Start button.

If the client service is started, check the Event Viewer, System Log for any errors or problems that might be keeping the client from starting.

continues

continued

I chose my preferred server but Windows displayed a message saying I cannot be authenticated on that server. Is there anything I can do? Yes, if you have permission from the system administrator, you can click Start, Programs, Administrative Tools, User Manager. In the User Manager, choose your name from the list of usernames and choose User, Rename. Change your Windows NT username to your NetWare username. If you do not know your NetWare username or you cannot access the Rename dialog box in the User Manager, see your system administrator.

Checking Your Bindings

Before closing the Network dialog box and restarting your computer, you may want to check your bindings to make sure everything is connected properly. The Bindings tab of the Network dialog box shows bindings for network cards, protocols, and services installed to your computer. Besides checking the bindings, you can arrange the order in which the computer accesses information on the network; for example, you can put the protocol you use most often first to reduce connection time.

When checking the bindings, double-click the service or protocol to view its contents. Any binding with a red circle and line passing through it is disabled. If you are having trouble connecting to the network, check the bindings to make sure they are all enabled. Click the Enable button for the selected binding. To move a binding up or down in the list, click the Move Up or Move Down button after selecting the binding you want to move.

Using a Gateway Service Instead of Client Services

If your office has both a Windows NT Server and a NetWare server running parallel, you can attach to both networks from a Windows NT Workstation and get the benefits of two networks instead of one. All you do is install the Gateway Service for NetWare to the Windows NT Server computer and all workstations connected to the Windows NT Server can see the NetWare server without any further installation of services.

To install the Gateway, follow these steps:

1. Click the Services tab in the Network dialog box.

2. Click the Add button and select the Gateway Service [and Client] for NetWare in the Select Network Service dialog box.

3. Enter the path to the setup files (generally to the CD). Windows NT copies files and then adds the Gateway Service for NetWare to the list of Network Services.

4. Click OK to close the Select Network Service dialog box. When Windows NT returns to the Network Properties sheet, choose OK. Windows NT notifies you to shut the computer down for the new settings to take effect. Click Yes. While the computer boots, you should prepare the NetWare server as described in the next section.

To create the user in NetWare, follow these steps:

1. Run SYSCON, NETADMIN, or NWADMIN from the NetWare-attached workstation and create a user on the NetWare server that matches the user that will log on from the Windows NT computer. Set the password for the user.

2. Create a NetWare group called NTGATEWAY and place the newly created user in that group.

   Now you can go back to the Windows NT Server to complete the process.

3. When the Windows NT Server has rebooted, the Select Preferred Server for NetWare dialog box appears. Click Cancel and confirm that you want to continue.

4. Open the Control Panel and double-click the icon labeled GSNW; the Gateway Service for NetWare dialog box appears. Choose your preferred server.

5. Click the Gateway button. The Configure Gateway dialog box appears.

6. Choose the Enable Gateway check box and enter the user's name in the Gateway Account text box; fill in the user's Password, Confirm the Password, and click OK.

Configuring Client Service for NetWare

After you install the NetWare service and protocol to your Windows NT Workstation, the CSNW (Client Service for NetWare) icon appears in the Control Panel as shown in figure 17.4.

FIG. 17.4
The CSNW icon is where you set the preferred server.

The preferred server is the default server you log on to when you log on to Windows NT. The preferred server checks your username and password to make sure you have permission to log on to the network; the preferred server also provides access to resources, such as files and printers.

N O T E If your network is not an NDS (Network Directory Services for NetWare) environment,
you should set a preferred server; if your network uses NDS, you'll use a default tree
and context. Although NetWare enables you to use both a preferred server and default tree and
context, Windows NT limits you to using one or the other; you cannot use both in the Windows NT
environment. ■

CAUTION

You can specify None as a preferred server and Windows NT will log you on to the nearest available
NetWare server; however, you should specify a preferred server to avoid crowding a server that may be
limited to a specific number of users or a server on which you are not a user.

To specify a preferred server, follow these steps:

1. Open the CSNW icon to display the Client Service for NetWare dialog box, as
   shown in figure 17.5.

FIG. 17.5
Configure the client
service for NetWare.

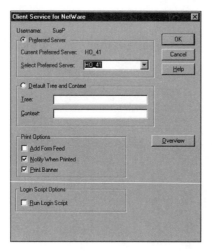

2. Choose either the Preferred Server or the Default Tree and Context option.

Using Login Scripts

You cannot use the NetWare login scripts with Windows NT, because it does not support
that scripting language. You can, however, assign a logon script in the User Manager
using the User Environment Profile dialog box (see fig. 17.6). NetWare uses the term
"login" and Windows NT uses the term "logon"; both terms refer to the same process.

FIG. 17.6
Create a login script and then assign it to one or multiple users.

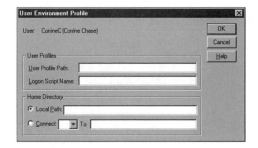

You create the script file and store it in the login script path:

C:\SYSTEM32\REPL\IMPORT\SCRIPTS.

If you use a login script, you must select the Run Login Script check box in the Client Service for NetWare dialog box (see fig. 17.7).

FIG. 17.7
Make sure you check the Login Script option in the CSNW dialog box if you're using a script file.

Part
IV

Ch
17

Use a text editor to create your login script. Generally, login scripts are created on the Windows NT Server using the parameters listed in Table 17.1; however, if you're using a Windows NT Workstation as a client/server and you have User Manager for Domains loaded to the workstation, you can use the following parameters to set login scripts for other users on the domain.

▶ **See** "Managing Users and Groups with the User Manager," **p. 411**

Table 17.1   Login Script Parameters

Parameter	Description
%HOMEDRIVE%	Specifies the user's local workstation driver letter connected to the user's home directory
%HOMEPATH%	Refers to the full path to the user's home directory
%HOMESHARE%	Refers to the share name that contains the user's home directory
%OS%	Refers to the operating system of the user's workstation
%PROCESSOR_ARCHITECTURE%	Refers to the processor type of the workstation
%PROCESSOR_LEVEL%	Refers to the processor level of the workstation
%USERDOMAIN%	Refers to the domain that contains the user's account
%USERNAME%	Refers to the user's name

TIP If your login scripts consist mainly of drive mappings in NetWare, delete the script and map your drives through Windows NT, as described in a later section of this chapter.

Attaching to a NetWare Network

Attaching to a NetWare network is similar to attaching to a Microsoft network; you use the Network Neighborhood or the Find command. After you locate the server, you may need to attach or log in, depending on your preferred server selection.

Finding a Server

Using the Find command, you can locate the NetWare server and open the server's window to access or view resources. Additionally, after you've searched for a server one time, its name remains in the drop-down list of Named servers.

Choose the Start button, Find command, and then choose Computer. In the Named text box, enter the name of the NetWare server you want to find preceded by two back slashes to indicate a network drive (\\HO_41, for instance). Choose the Find Now button. Figure 17.8 shows the NetWare server found in the Find Computer window.

FIG. 17.8
Use the Find command to locate a NetWare server.

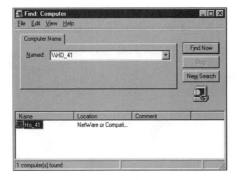

Double-click the server in the Find window to open the drive. If you are not logged on to the NetWare network, Windows NT will display the Enter Network Password dialog box in which you enter your username and password.

Part

IV

Ch

17

Using the Network Neighborhood

Use the Network Neighborhood to attach to the NetWare network if you are unsure of the server's name. Open the Network Neighborhood. If you are only attached to a NetWare network, the server appears immediately in the Network Neighborhood. However, if you are attached to a Microsoft network in addition to a NetWare network, you may need to go a little deeper to get to the NetWare server.

If the NetWare server is not displayed, double-click the Entire Network icon. Next, double-click the NetWare or Compatible Network and then choose the NetWare server that you want to attach to. Again, you may need to enter a password and username to identify yourself to the network. Figure 17.9 shows the progression from the Network Neighborhood, to the Entire Network, to the NetWare Network, and then to the server.

Attaching to the Network

When you first log on to Windows NT Workstation, you enter a username and a password. If these are not the same as your username and password on the NetWare server, you will be prompted to log on to the NetWare server, using the dialog box shown in figure 17.10.

In addition, you can log off of a network and on to another at any time; and if you are in doubt as to which network you are on, you can easily find out in the Network Neighborhood.

To log off of a network, select the server to which you are attached in the Network Neighborhood dialog box. Choose File, Log Out. Windows NT displays a message dialog box to confirm; choose Yes. Windows NT displays another message telling you that you have detached from the server.

FIG. 17.9
Work your way through
the layers to get to the
NetWare server.

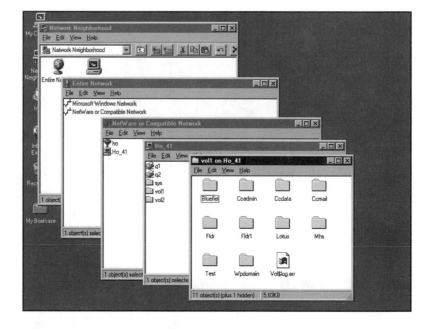

FIG. 17.10
Enter your username
and password as it is
recorded on the
NetWare server.

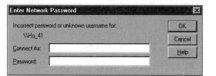

To log on to that network or another, you can choose File, Attach As to display the Enter
Network Password dialog box (refer to fig. 17.10).

To find out which server you are attached to, choose the File, Who Am I command in the
Network Neighborhood window. Figure 17.11 shows the resulting dialog box.

FIG. 17.11
Who Am I identifies
your server, username,
and the connection
type.

Sharing Resources in NetWare Environments

You can use any of the resources on the NetWare network that you have been assigned
rights and permissions for by the NetWare administrator. Files, directories, printers, and

other resources available to the NetWare network can also be made available to a Windows NT Workstation.

View the available resources in the Network Neighborhood. Generally, NetWare resources are made available in the Public directory on the NetWare server; but ask your network administrator if you cannot find what you need on the server. Figure 17.12 shows the progression from the server to the SYS volume, to the Public directory. You can also use the Windows NT Find command to locate files and directories on the NetWare server.

FIG. 17.12
Browse the NetWare server from the Network Neighborhood.

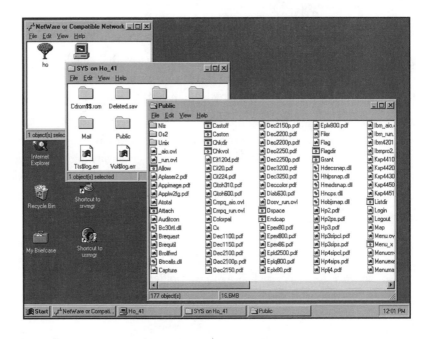

Part
IV

Ch
17

To use the resources, you can capture the printer, open folders, and copy, read, or edit files as you would on your own computers. Not only can you view and connect to servers on the network, you also can connect to other computers on the network and share their resources.

You can view connections to your computer at any time from the My Computer window. Open My Computer and from the drop-down list of drives and directories (from the toolbar), choose Network Neighborhood. Figure 17.13 shows a NetWare server and two computers attached to the Windows NT Workstation.

FIG. 17.13
View the network
connections through
the My Computer
window.

Using NetWare File and Print Services

NetWare supplies its own file and print services that enable you to access resources on
the NetWare server using utilities at your Windows NT Workstation; however, an easier
way to use drives and printers through NetWare is to use Windows NT features for mapping drives and capturing printers.

Mapping a drive through Windows NT is easier than using NetWare's MAP command.
The map command enables you to quickly access any folder or directory on the server.
Additionally, you can add any network printer to use from Windows NT quickly and easily.

Mapping Drives

You can avoid using NetWare's MAP command by mapping your drives through the Network Neighborhood in Windows NT. When you map a drive, you assign a drive letter to a
network resource, such as a drive or folder. Mapping drives makes access to network
resources faster and easier than opening several layers of windows to find the resource on
the server or the network.

You might choose to connect a map as a root of the drive to help keep path statements
from getting too long; for example, map to directory \\HO_41\VOL2\USERS\SUE so you
use the mapped drive of J instead of the entire path.

To map a drive, follow these steps:

1. Open the Network Neighborhood and select the folder representing the shared
   directory to which you want to map.

2. Choose File, Map Network Drive. The Map Network Drive dialog box appears
   (see fig. 17.14).

3. In the Drive drop-down list, select an unassigned drive letter.

4. In Connect As, enter a username if you do not want to connect to the server using
   your logon name. Choose the Reconnect at Logon check box if you want to reestablish the connection each time you logon to the network.

FIG. 17.14
Map a drive to make access faster and easier.

5. Click OK to close the dialog box and map the drive. Figure 17.15 shows the mapped drive connection in the My Computer window.

FIG. 17.15
Map a drive so you don't have to open layer upon layer of windows and folders.

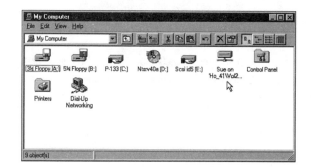

Capturing Printers

To use a printer on the network, you must connect to a NetWare print queue. You don't actually connect to a printer on the network; you connect to the print queue, and the server configuration determines which printer to send your job to. If one printer is busy, for example, the NetWare print queue may hold your print job or send it to another printer.

You capture a NetWare printer in Windows NT by using the Add Printer wizard. After adding the network printer, you can print to the NetWare print queue just as you would to a Windows NT printer.

To capture a printer, follow these steps:

1. In the Printers folder, double-click the Add Printer icon. The first Add Printer Wizard dialog box appears (see fig. 17.16).

2. Choose the Network Printer Server option and click Next. The Connect to Printer dialog box appears.

3. In the Shared Printers list, double-click the server to expand the list. Select the network printer you want to use and the printer's name appears in the Printer text box. Install the printer driver, if necessary, and supply the Windows NT CD required for installation.

FIG. 17.16

Choose to install a network printer to your workstation so you can print as if the printer were directly attached to your computer.

 T I P You might need to double-click the tree in the Shared Printers list to see additional servers or computers on the network; and then continue to expand those elements until you find the printer you want to use.

4. Click OK to close the dialog box. Follow any instructions until the final Add Printer Wizard dialog box appears, telling you the printer was successfully installed.

5. Click the Finish button. The printer appears in the Printers window (see fig. 17.17).

FIG. 17.17

The network printer is permanently installed to your system.

N O T E You can set the print options: Add Form Feed, Notify When Printed, and Print Banner in the Client Service for NetWare dialog box (refer to fig. 17.5); double-click the CSNW icon in the Control Panel. These options are similar to those available directly on the NetWare server using the capture utility. ▪

N O T E A Windows NT Server add-on product, File and Print Services for NetWare, enables a computer running Windows NT Server to provide file and print services directly to NetWare client computers; the Windows NT Server appears just like any other NetWare server to the NetWare clients and the clients can access files and printers at the server. ▪

TROUBLESHOOTING

When I try to map using the NetWare MAP utility, I get a memory allocation error. Is it something I'm doing wrong? The mapping table created by the NetWare MAP utility needs a default environment size in the Command Prompt window of at least 4,096 bytes. You can designate COMMAND.COM as the command interpreter for the Command Prompt window and reset the environment size by entering this command in the CONFIG.NT file:

```
shell=%systemroot%\system32\command.com /e:4096
```

Alternatively, you can use the Windows NT feature for mapping drives instead of using the NetWare MAP utility.

When I print to the captured network printer, no queues show up in the Print Manager. What's wrong? If the print job is not showing up in your Print Manager, your Windows NT username and password don't match the username and password for the preferred server. The server validates your user credentials before it sends the jobs to the print queue. First, you should check the Network Neighborhood to verify you can see the NetWare file server; if you cannot see the server, verify that your Client Service has started.

If the service has started and you have already logged in, you can use the SETPASS command at the MS-DOS Command Prompt to change your username and password on the NetWare servers. If you still have problems, see your network administrator.

Integrating NetWare and Windows NT Print Queues

The print queues you want to use depend on the system you're most familiar and comfortable with. You can use Windows NT's print queue or NetWare's print queue.

▶ **See** "Managing Printers," **p. 749**

Windows NT's Print Queue

Windows NT's print queue enables you to view documents in the print queue, pause printing, cancel printing, and rearrange the documents in the print queue. Figure 17.18 shows a typical print queue connected to a network printer.

To control the printer, use the Printer menu; you can pause printing, delete all documents from the queue, share the printer with others on the network, and set properties for the printer.

FIG. 17.18
With several jobs in the Windows NT queue, you can control the order of printing.

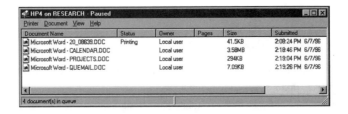

To control a print job, select the job and click the Document menu, which lets you pause and resume a job, as well as cancel the job. You also can view the properties of a print job, which include the size, pages, owner, and priority setting.

Once again, you must have access rights to control print jobs other than your own in a Windows NT print queue.

▶ **See** "Setting Account Policies," **p. 738**

NetWare's Print Queue

NetWare provides a command you can use to control printing services and queues in a NetWare network: PCONSOLE. You must run the command from a DOS prompt, such as the Command Prompt window or the Run dialog box in Windows NT. The PCONSOLE command enables you to check the status of a print job and rearrange jobs in the queue (if you have the rights to do so).

To run NetWare's PCONSOLE command in Windows NT, first map the drive that contains the PCONSOLE command. This saves time if you use it a lot. The PCONSOLE file is found in the PUBLIC directory of the NetWare server. Next, open the Run command box and enter the drive or path and the command name: such as G:\PCONSOLE (mapped) or \\HO_41\VOL2\USER\PUBLIC\PCONSOLE.EXE. Figure 17.19 shows the command window with the PCONSOLE program running.

In the list of Available Options, choose one of the following:

■ **Print Queues.** To view available print queues on the network

■ **Print Servers.** To view available print servers on the NetWare network

■ **Quick Setup.** To add another print queue to the list

■ **Change Current NetWare Server.** To view or choose an available server

Choose Print Queues to view available print queues on the NetWare network. Select the print queue you want to view and press Enter; the Print Queue Information box appears (see fig. 17.20).

FIG. 17.19
The PCONSOLE command enables you to control printers.

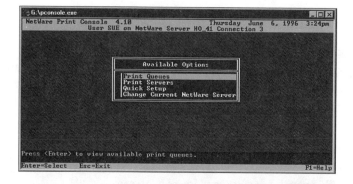

FIG. 17.20
View the status and jobs in the print queue.

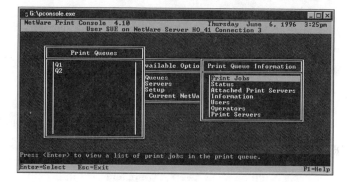

Part
IV

Ch

17

To check and control the print queue, choose any of the following options in the Print Queue Information box:

- **Print Jobs.** Displays a list of current jobs in the queue
- **Status.** Displays the current number of print jobs in queue, number of active print servers, and the operator flags for that queue
- **Attached Print Servers.** Displays a list of print servers actively servicing the selected queue
- **Information.** Displays the print queue identification number
- **Users.** Displays the users and groups that can submit print jobs to the selected queue
- **Operators.** Displays the users and groups that manage this queue's status and print job entries
- **Print Servers.** Displays a list of print servers that are assigned to service the selected queue

Press Esc to close any open box in PCONSOLE; press Esc to exit PCONSOLE and then choose Yes when prompted to Exit.

NetWare 3.1x versus 4.x Issues

The primary differences between versions 3.1x and 4.x of NetWare is in the database user, group, and how server information is stored. Version 3.1x of NetWare uses a database called a bindery and in version 4.x, the bindery is replaced by Network Directory Services (NDS).

The bindery manages one server; whereas NDS supports the whole network, including every resource on the network: users, groups, printers, volumes, and servers. Additionally, version 4.x of NetWare supplies what is called bindery emulation which provides compatibility with previous versions of NetWare.

 T I P When you're using the Microsoft Client for NetWare networks, you're connected to the NetWare server and network under a binder connection, even if the NetWare version is 4.x.

Version 3.1x

You can view users and groups, and other network information, from a Windows NT Workstation using NetWare tools. SYSCON is a DOS Utility you can run in a Windows NT Workstation Command Prompt window if your NetWare version is 3.1x. SYSCON enables you to control accounting, file servers, group, and user information.

The following are some additional Novell utilities you can use in a Windows NT Workstation Command Prompt window:

Utility	Description
FCONSOLE	Monitors the file server and lets you perform such functions as broadcast, console messages, down (prepare the server for shut down) the file server, check file server status, and so on.
RCONSOLE	Gives you access to the file server console from a workstation
FILER	Determines file creation date, last access date, size, owner, and so on, of a file
SALVAGE	Undeletes files from a NetWare volume
SESSION	Maps network drives with a menu
SLIST	Displays all NetWare servers on the network

Version 4.x

Some utilities cannot run under Windows NT when you use the Microsoft Client for NetWare rather than the Novell VLM network drivers. You use these commands in

NetWare 4.x that employs the Network Directory Services to manage a multiserver network. Following are the utilities that operate under Windows NT only when the Novell VLM network drivers are used:

Utility	Description
NWADMIN	Administers the NDS directory tree under Windows
CX	Changes contexts within the NDS directory tree
NETADMIN	Administers the NDS directory tree under DOS

Changing Your Password

One handy NetWare command you can use, no matter which version of NetWare you're using, is SETPASS. SETPASS lets you change your NetWare password. You must be attached to the server to use the command.

To change your password, follow these steps:

1. Open the Start menu and choose the Run command.

2. In the Open text box, enter the path to the server and then the SETPASS command; for example: \\HO_41\SYS\PUBLIC\SETPASS.

3. Click OK and Windows NT opens a Command Prompt window. You'll be prompted for your old password; enter it.

4. Next, you'll be prompted for the new password and to enter a confirmation of the new password. Enter those. The server sets the password and closes the Command Prompt window. The next time you log on to the network, you must use your new password.

You can use other NetWare commands at a Command Prompt and Windows NT provides numerous networking commands, as well. See Appendix D, "Windows NT Workstation Command Reference," for some of the network commands you can use at the Command Prompt.

From Here...

In this chapter, you've learned about integrating your Windows NT Workstation computer with a NetWare network and server. Take a look at other networking chapters in this book:

Part
IV
Ch
17

- Chapter 15, "Networking Overview," introduces networking.

- Chapter 16, "A Brief Primer on Networks," covers some networking basics, such as network layers, domains and workgroups, security, LANs, and WANs.

- Chapter 18, "Integrating Windows NT in Microsoft Environments," covers using Windows NT Workstation as a client/server in a network, and sharing resources with other workstations running Windows for Workgroups, Windows 95, and Windows NT.

Integrating Windows NT in Microsoft Environments

by Sue Plumley

Windows NT Workstation is flexible and easy to use in a networking environment. You can set up a network using Windows NT exclusively as a workstation or as a client/server on your network. As a client/server (or in a peer-to-peer model), computers running Windows NT Workstation can share their resources—printers, directories, files, and so on—with other users while limiting access and maintaining workstation security.

You also can attach a computer running Windows NT Workstation to many other workstation computers—including other Windows NT Workstations, Windows for Workgroups, Windows 95, and MS-DOS computers—for sharing information and resources. Naturally, you also can use NT Workstation as a client only on an NT Server or NetWare network. ■

Use Windows NT Workstation as a client/server

Share your resources while maintaining security by assigning rights to other users and permissions that govern which of your files and directories you share.

Attach to MS-DOS workstations

Share the resources of workstations using the Microsoft Network Client for MS-DOS version 3.0.

Access Windows for Workgroups computers

You can attach to any Windows for Workgroups computer on the network to share data and resources from your Windows NT Workstation.

Windows 95 workstations offer resources

The similarity between Windows 95 and Windows NT architecture enables you to take full advantage of Windows 95 workstation resources.

Using Windows NT Workstation as a Client/Server

Windows NT Workstation is useful as client software, enabling users to control many of the elements of his or her own computer—for example, files and folders, applications, customization of the environment, security, resources, and so on. Additionally, the Windows NT Workstation client can be used as a client/server, thus letting other computers on the network use its resources and data.

I've found it to be extremely useful for most, if not all, Windows NT Workstation clients to function as a client/server. As an administrator, I can choose which resources from each workstation I want to share with the other clients or I can let any individual workstation user control her own resources. As long as we're all in agreement, the latter method works the best, freeing my time for other administrative duties.

You can control who has access to your workstation with the User Manager, setting passwords for individuals and groups who use your resources, creating users and groups, and setting rights for those users and groups. Additionally, certain administration tools can be added to a Windows NT Workstation from the Windows NT Server by the network administrator for use in controlling clients and servers on the network, in particular, the User Manager for Domains enables the workstation user to control various users and groups across domains.

Domain versus Workgroup

When networking in a small company, a workgroup system may be the best solution. In a workgroup, all workstations can share all resources with each other. You can use a client/server system to manage a workgroup; I often suggest to my clients they use the Windows NT Workstation computers within the workgroup as client/servers.

Workstation users often share all of their resources because the group is small and everyone knows everyone else; however, Windows NT Workstation software lets each user control rights and permissions to their own resources. If you prefer not to share a printer, folder, or file, you can change the permissions attached to that resource. If you want to limit the access of certain users or groups to your workstation, you can set the rights that control your own workstation.

A workgroup system is acceptable until the company, and the network, begin to grow. As more computers are added to the network, security and identification problems start gumming up the works. For example, with more computers attached to a network, file and folder security becomes more important. Additionally, the more computers and printers on a network, the harder it is to identify each one; it may become difficult to find the computer you want to gather files from or the laser printer you want to print to.

Using domains in place of workgroups can help with this problem. Domains separate workstations into manageable groups that can easily be supervised and controlled individually or as a collection of domains. Windows NT Workstation works well in a domain organization because the user can still control permissions to resources.

N O T E Naturally, if you're a member of multiple domains, trust relationships may enable users from other domains to access your resources. You do, of course, still have control over your own workstation; you can select a domain from within User Manager and choose individual users or groups from other domains to whom you'll grant the rights to use your resources. ■

▶ **See** "Understanding Workgroups and Domains," **p. 361**

Workgroups The simplest of Microsoft's networks is a workgroup. This is a network in which all computers can share hard disks, printers, files, and other resources. In a workgroup, a computer can be either a workstation or a client/server. A workstation is a computer that doesn't share any of its resources, whereas a client/server shares its files, programs, printer, or other resources.

In a Microsoft workgroup, the following operating systems can be used as client/servers:

- Windows for Workgroups 3.11
- Windows NT Workstation 3.51 or 4.0
- Windows NT Server 3.51 or 4.0 (not Windows NT Advanced Server 3.1)

You can also add any Windows 3.x or DOS machine that uses the supplied client as a workstation-only computer on your workgroup network. NT Server software includes a Network Client Administrator from which you can create the client software for Windows 3.x and MS-DOS computers.

Each user of a Windows NT Workstation computer can assign passwords to other users and/or groups to limit or stop others from accessing his computer and its resources through the User Manager.

Domains The domain system provides more security and less administration across the network. A domain is a group of servers and computers that share user account information and security features. Whereas with the workgroup system, you use a password to secure each resource, the domain system filters all requests for resources through one computer called the primary domain controller, usually a Windows NT Server. This controller computer monitors and assigns resources when they're requested.

Part **IV**

Ch **18**

In a domain, you have one password that enables you to access resources in the domain. The network administrator assigns specific permissions to you under this one password. When you log onto the network, Windows NT makes available the resources for which you have permission.

As a Windows NT Workstation user, you can assign passwords to other users or groups, whether in that domain or in a trusting domain, to control access to your workstation and its resources.

N O T E If you have the User Manager for Domains loaded onto your workstation, you can manage users and groups from other domains. User Manager for Domains can be installed to any Windows NT Workstation computer from the Network Client Administrator program on the Windows NT Server by a member of the Administrators group. ∎

Users and Groups

Users of a workstation and the network are assigned certain rights that enable them to use or limit use of available resources. The system administrator can assign rights to users, as can a user of a Windows NT Workstation client/server. The rights assigned from a Windows NT Workstation govern the user's use of that workstation from the network.

Groups   In addition to user's rights, group rights can be assigned from a Windows NT Workstation. It saves time to assign rights to a group and then assign users to a group instead of trying to outline each user's rights. Windows NT's predefined groups include:

- **Administrators.** Members have full rights to administer the workstation.
- **Power Users.** Members share directories and printers.
- **Replicator.** Members perform file replication within a domain.
- **Backup Operators.** Members back up files and directories on the workstation regardless of file security.
- **Database.** Members have the right to collect and compile data from the workstation.
- **Everyone.** All users are members.
- **Users.** Members are ordinary users.
- **Guests.** Members are granted access to the workstation but have read-only rights.

Each predefined group has specific rights allotted to it; however, rights can be changed and added. You can, of course, create your own groups and assign rights to them as needed.

To save time when creating groups, I often copy the predefined group that has rights assigned that I want to start with; then I name the group and change options to suit my network and domain setup.

Rights   You can assign rights from a Windows NT Workstation to users and/or groups. If the workstation participates in a domain, the rights of users from the local and trusted domains can also be set.

The rights that can be assigned from a Windows NT Workstation are as follows:

- Access this computer from the network.
- Back up files and directories (this right supersedes files and directory permissions).
- Change the system time.
- Force shutdown from a remote system (this right is not currently implemented but reserved for future use).
- Load and unload device drivers.
- Log on locally.
- Manage auditing and security log.
- Restore files and directories.
- Shut down the system.
- Take ownership of files or other objects.
- Advanced right: Bypass traverse checking (enables user to travel through directory trees and change directories).
- Advanced right: Log on as a service.

N O T E   Users can be members of multiple groups, and therefore accumulate the various permissions of each group. ■

Managing Users and Groups with the User Manager

The User Manager is available on all Windows NT Workstation machines and is used to manage rights and passwords of individual users and groups. Figure 18.1 shows the User Manager in Windows NT. Open the User Manager by choosing the Start button, then Programs, Administrative Tools, and User Manager. Chapter 32 explains how to use the User Manager.

▶ **See** "Creating and Modifying User Accounts," **p. 704**

▶ **See** "Managing User Profiles," **p. 727**

Part
IV
Ch
18

FIG. 18.1

Manage individual users or groups by setting passwords and rights.

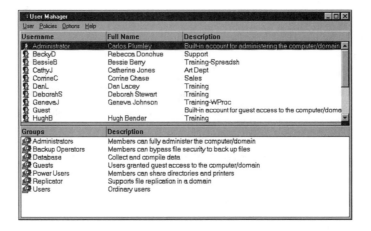

Using the Network Client Administrator

Windows NT's Network Client Administrator, an administrative tool included with Windows NT Server 4, enables you to create Client-Based Network Administration Tools. You can use this option to install the User Manager for Domains to workstations running Windows NT Server, Windows NT Workstation, and Windows 95.

With the Network Client Administrator (NCA), you can create installation disks and start-up disks for both MS-DOS and Windows for Workgroups. Although Windows for Workgroups machines can attach to and access computers running Windows NT Servers and Workstations without an additional client, you can create a TCP/IP client for Windows for Workgroups computers using the NCA.

Additionally, using the NCA, you can install the following tools to a Windows NT Workstation computer: DHCP Manager, Remote Access Admin, Remoteboot Manager, Server Manager User Manager for Domains, WINS Manager, and so on. You can install the following tools to a Windows 95 computer: Event Viewer, Server Manager, and User Manager for Domains.

To start the Network Client Administrator, choose Start, Programs, Administrative Tools, and Network Client Administrator. Choose the Client-based Network Administration Tools option and choose OK; follow the steps for copying the installation files to a shared folder on the Windows NT Server or Windows NT Workstation or copy the files to a new folder and then share the files. The workstations then install the administrative tools by connecting to the share.

The User Manager for Domains looks and behaves just like the User Manager except the domain name precedes the user names, such as SALES\HughB.

Sharing Objects

In addition to assigning rights to certain users to control their use of your workstation, you can limit others' use of your resources by setting permissions on your objects.

Objects are printers, modems, CD-ROMs, directories, files, and so on and you set permissions through the Windows NT Explorer. You can even set permissions for individual files within a directory.

The theory here is you can allow others to access your Windows NT Workstation; however, you might not want them to access specific directories or other resources.

When you share a file, directory, or printer, you assign it a *share name* that other users of the network see. Windows NT Workstation and Windows 95 users can see share names by double-clicking the names of computers on the network in the Network Neighborhood. MS-DOS users use the Net View command to see share names and Windows for Workgroups users can see share names in the File Manager when they connect to a network drive.

To connect to shared directories from Windows NT Workstation, use either the Network Neighborhood or the Find, Computers command from the Start menu. To view shared printers, use the Printers dialog box.

Consider mapping network drives to quickly access another workstation's resources and create shortcuts on your desktop to quickly access directories, files, and so on.

Part

IV

Setting Permissions   Set sharing by selecting the resource—file, directory, or printer, for example—and then choosing File, Sharing. All resources have a Properties dialog box. Figure 18.2 shows the Sharing tab in an HP4 Properties dialog box.

Ch

18

FIG. 18.2

When you choose to share a printer, you enter the shared name that all those with rights will see.

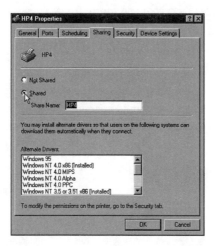

Customize the permissions by choosing the Security tab in a Properties dialog box and choosing the Permissions button. Figure 18.3 shows the Printer Permissions dialog box.

FIG. 18.3

Set permissions for individual objects on the workstation.

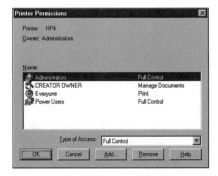

> **N O T E**   Permissions are cumulative across groups; but the No Access permission overrides all others. ■

Special Identities   You can grant permissions to any user or group on the network, including Windows NT's predefined groups and special identities. The predefined groups are Administrators, Backup Operators, Database, and so on. Following is a list of Special Identities in Windows NT:

- **Creator Owner.** Represents users who create files and directories in the current directory; the creator of a file or directory gains the Creator Owner permissions you set for the directory containing the new addition. Creator Owner permissions can only be set on directories.

- **Interactive.** Represents all current and future users accessing a file from the local drive only.

- **Network.** Represents all current and future users accessing a directory over the network.

- **System.** Represents the operating system of the local workstation. Windows NT sets system permissions and you should not cancel these. You can, however, set system permissions if a system service needs to access them.

Default Permissions   Windows NT Workstation installs with certain default permissions assigned to its directories. You should not revoke these default permissions because you could cause parts of the operating system to stop working. Following is a list of the directories and the groups for which you should not change default permissions:

Table 18.1   Default Permissions

Directory	Group
\Root directory	Administrators, Everyone, CREATOR OWNER
\SYSTEM32	Administrators, Everyone, CREATOR OWNER

Directory	Group
\SYSTEM32\CONFIG	Administrators, Everyone, CREATOR OWNER
\SYSTEM32\DRIVERS	Administrators, Everyone, CREATOR OWNER
\SYSTEM32\SPOOL	Administrators, Power Users, Everyone, CREATOR OWNER
\SYSTEM32\REPL	Administrators, Everyone, CREATOR OWNER
\SYSTEM32\REPL\IMPORT	Administrators, Everyone, CREATOR OWNER, Replicator, NETWORK
\USERS	Administrators, Everyone
\USERS\DEFAULT	Everyone, CREATOR OWNER
\WIN32APP	Administrators, CREATOR OWNER, Everyone
\TEMP	Administrators, CREATOR OWNER, Everyone

CAUTION

Never view or examine permissions using the Explorer on the SYSTEM32\REPL\IMPORT directory, which contains permissions that enable directory replication. The slightest disturbance of these permissions can cancel them and prevent the operating system from working correctly.

Part
IV

Ch

18

Integrating DOS Systems

A DOS client and a computer running Windows NT Workstation can share data across the network if the DOS client is running Microsoft's Network Client version 3.0 for MS-DOS. Additionally, the DOS client can use printers, applications, and data stored on the Windows NT Workstation and the Windows NT Workstation can access applications from the DOS client.

 TIP

The Network Client for MS-DOS can be installed from the Windows NT Server to the DOS workstation; additionally, you can create installation or startup disks for the DOS client using the Network Client Administrator.

Applications

Windows NT can run most MS-DOS applications, even if they're not designed for Windows NT, although sometimes a device driver designed to run with Windows NT is required. If you have an application that doesn't include the device driver for Windows

NT, contact the manufacturer of the application to see if they have developed a version of the software that is compatible with Windows NT.

Some applications that require either a Windows NT-compatible device driver or an application upgrade include applications that directly communicate with hardware (scanner or fax cards, for example), applications that directly communicate with disk drivers (like disk maintenance software), and applications that use their own graphics device drivers to communicate with the hardware (such as software that uses a private printer driver).

NT supplies a default PIF (Program Information File) that your DOS applications can use if the PIF supplied with the application doesn't work with NT. The PIF is named _DEFAULT.PIF and is located in the system's root directory. Additionally, you can create and modify PIFs by right-clicking the file in the Explorer and choosing the Properties command.

NT also supports TSR (terminate-and-stay-resident) programs running in a command-prompt window. You should start the TSR in the same command-prompt window in which you started the application requiring it. You could, on the other hand, create a custom startup file that starts the TSR but does not add the memory-resident program to the AUTOEXEC.NT or CONFIG.NT files. When added to one of the configuration files, additional copies of the program start every time you open another command-prompt window.

Printing

You can use a printer attached to an MS-DOS workstation by making the printer accessible to your applications. Remember, though, that MS-DOS workstations have their own locally installed printer drivers instead of using printer drivers from the network; so if the client's driver has not been updated, you may have problems printing from some applications.

> **CAUTION**
> Any shared directories on an MS-DOS client are going to use the 8+3 characters naming convention; keep this in mind when accessing an MS-DOS client.

Integrating with Windows for Workgroups Clients

Microsoft has made Windows NT Workstation compatible with other Windows versions so you can share data and resources between them. Windows for Workgroups,

Microsoft's workgroup network solution, works well within a Windows NT network. Using the Network Neighborhood, you can view and access resources on a Windows for Workgroups computer, as shown in figure 18.4. Naturally, the Windows for Workgroups computer must enable the file and printer sharing options before you can access these resources.

FIG. 18.4
Access folders, files, printers, and programs from a Windows for Workgroups workstation.

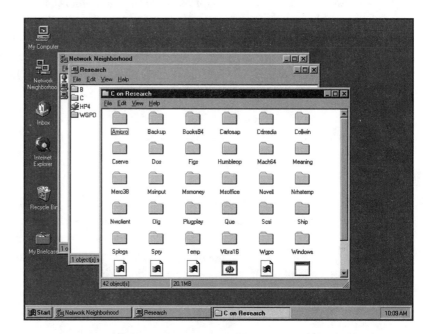

N O T E The easiest way to integrate with Windows 3.0 or 3.1 is to upgrade these clients to Windows for Workgroups; however, if you cannot upgrade, try setting up the client with the LAN Manager options. You will need a redirector (like the Workgroup Connection) loaded when you install Windows so setup can sense the network and load the drivers. ■

If the user logged on to the Windows for Workgroups computer that has the same workgroup name as the Windows NT domain, neither you nor the user will be able to browse the network. Suppose that you have several computers running Windows for Workgroups in the SALES domain, along with several computers running Windows 95 and Windows NT Workstation. The Windows for Workgroups computers also see each other in a workgroup and have identified themselves as members of a workgroup called SALES. Identification of workgroups and domains takes place in the Network dialog box, Identification tab.

When one of the Windows for Workgroups computers logs on to the network, the network identifies it as a member of the SALES workgroup instead of the SALES domain.

Part
IV

Ch
18

Therefore, the WFW computer cannot see or access the domain and no one on the domain can see or access the workgroup.

Files and Directories

You can open and use any directories or files on the Windows for Workgroups computer if the user has designated them as shared. The Windows for Workgroups user can share files and directories as read-only, full, or as protected by a password that it sets. You will not see a directory in the Network Neighborhood if it isn't shared by the Windows for Workgroups computer. You can run any shared programs on the Windows for Workgroups computer as well.

Keep in mind that Windows for Workgroups is installed on a DOS machine and therefore follows the 8+3 character naming convention with files and directories.

Applications

You can run Windows 3.11-based applications on a Windows NT Workstation computer with few problems; however, if you run several Windows 3.11-based applications at the same time and one crashes, all of the applications crash. You could run each application in a separate memory space to prevent problems, but that uses more memory and may slow the system. Additionally, running an application in its own memory space prevents it from sharing memory and therefore working with other applications. The OLE and DDE features still work with an application running in its own memory space.

In addition to sharing the resources of the Windows for Workgroups computer, you can communicate with the user of that computer in numerous ways. Because both operating systems are Microsoft Windows, you both share the Microsoft Mail, Schedule +, WinPopup, and Chat applications that enable you to communicate with each other over the network.

N O T E If you use NT's Network Client Administrator to create a Windows for Workgroups TCP/IP client for the network, you can take full advantage of NT's security, resources, and 32-bit architecture. You must install and configure TCP/IP, however, on both the server and the workstations. For more information, see the online help in NT Server or for the Network Client Administrator. ▪

Printing

You can print to any printer attached to a Windows for Workgroups workstation. The easiest method of using the printer is to drag the printer icon to your desktop to create a shortcut; then you can drag your documents to that icon to print them. Figure 18.5 shows the shortcut icon to a Windows for Workgroups printer.

FIG. 18.5

Create a shortcut to the Windows for Workgroups printer.

Shortcut to HP4 on Research

To make the Windows for Workgroups printer available to your applications on the Windows NT Workstation, you must install the printer to your Printers folder. Using the Add Printer Wizard, choose the N̲etwork printer server option in the first wizard dialog box. When you choose the Next button, the Connect to Printer dialog box appears. Choose Microsoft Windows Network and then double-click the Windows for Workgroups computer to which the printer is connected (see fig. 18.6).

FIG. 18.6

Locate the printer on the Windows for Workgroups computer.

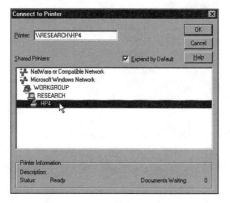

Part

IV

Ch

18

Windows NT may display a dialog box saying the printer driver is not installed and asking if you want to install it to your machine; choose Y̲es to continue. Select the manufacturer and the printer, or insert a disk if necessary. Windows NT may also request you insert the Windows NT Workstation CD-ROM for needed files.

Next, you're given the option to set up the device settings for the printer, as shown in figure 18.7. Personally, I'm always hesitant to alter device settings for someone else's printer; I usually accept the defaults.

When the installation is complete, the printer is added to your Printers folder and is available to your programs (see fig. 18.8). You can also open the print queue for the printer and control your print job as you would any other printer in Windows NT.

FIG. 18.7
Modify device settings
for the printer.

FIG. 18.8
Print to the Windows
for Workgroups printer
just like any other
printer on the
network.

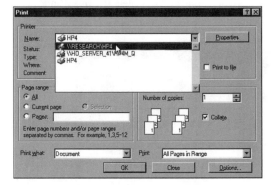

Integrating with Windows 95 Systems

Using Windows NT Workstation in conjunction with a Windows 95 system is almost like using two Windows NT Workstation computers. The architecture and interfaces of the two are almost identical. Using a Windows 95 client is similar to using a Windows for Workgroups client with Windows NT, as well.

You attach to a Windows 95 computer on the network by using the Windows NT Network Neighborhood or the Explorer. Figure 18.9 shows the Windows 95 computer's shared hard drive.

N O T E Windows NT Server 4.0 includes the Network Client Administrator, which you can install to a computer running NT Workstation. With the Network Client Administrator and the NT Server CD, you can install Windows 95 as a client and configure it to any computer on the network. The entire Windows 95 program is on the NT Server CD. Naturally, you must purchase an additional license for each installation of Windows 95 to the network. ■

FIG. 18.9
Open the Windows 95
computer's shared
drive to view available
resources.

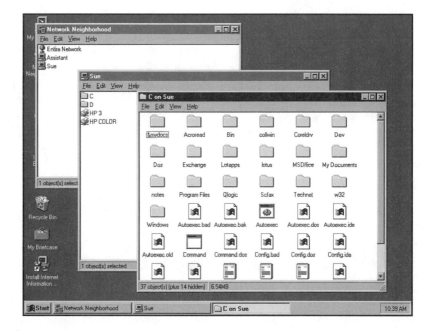

Files and Directories

Just like a Windows for Workgroups share, Windows 95 can share folders (directories)
and files as read-only, full, or dependent on a password. In Windows 95, however, the user
can set two passwords: one as read-only and one as full access. Depending on the settings
of the Windows 95 client, you may be limited in your access to its resources.

If files and directories are marked as full-access share on the Windows 95 computer, you
can create, modify, add, and delete files and directories on that computer.

You also can run applications from the Windows 95 client, if the files are shared. Additionally, you can use chat and mail programs between a Windows 95 computer and a Windows
NT computer if those programs are installed to both. Unlike Windows for Workgroups
and Windows NT Workstation computers, Windows 95 does not include such programs as
Chat, Schedule+, and Mail but you could install those or similar programs for communication purposes.

Printing

Windows 95 clients can share their printer with other network workstations. Windows NT
Workstation can take advantage of a local printer on a Windows 95 client in either of two
ways. You can drag the printer icon to your Windows NT desktop to create a shortcut or

you can install the printer driver to your Windows NT computer. Figure 18.10 shows a list of shared printers in the Windows 95 client window.

FIG. 18.10

Install the printer drivers for the shared printers to make use of the Windows 95 computer's resources.

To install the printer driver so your applications have full access to the printer attached to a Windows 95 computer, follow the directions in the "Printing" section of "Integrating with Windows for Workgroups Clients," earlier in this chapter.

Integrating with Windows NT Workstations

You can quickly and easily access any of the resources on another Windows NT Workstation from your own Windows NT Workstation client. As long as rights and permissions are set for you to use the client, you can access files, directories, programs, printers, and other resources. Attach to another Windows NT Workstation using the Network Neighborhood and use the resources as you would within your own workstation.

N O T E   To use a printer connected to another Windows NT Workstation, you must first install that printer to your workstation using the method described earlier in the "Printing" section of "Integrating with Windows for Workgroups Clients." ■

From Here...

In this chapter, you've learned to integrate the Windows NT Workstation with clients running MS-DOS and other Windows versions. Additionally, you've learned to share the resources of the Windows NT Workstation and to limit access to your resources. Take a look at the following chapters for related information:

- Chapter 17, "Integrating Windows NT in Novell Environments," explains NetWare clients, file and print services, print queues, NDS, and shared resources with a NetWare environment.

- Chapter 19, "Integrating Windows NT in UNIX Environments," shows you how to use Windows clients under Windows NT, print to UNIX printers, transfer data, and use NFS.

- Chapter 32, "Administering Users," discusses creating and modifying user accounts, controlling resource access, managing user profiles, and setting account policies.

Part
IV

Ch
18

Integrating Windows NT in UNIX Environments

by Chris Turkstra

Windows NT Workstation has become a great platform to use in the company of UNIX. Microsoft has spent a large amount of time making Windows NT interoperable with UNIX, especially in the areas of TCP/IP and Internet services. Two drivers have made UNIX integration more important than ever for Microsoft: the explosion of the Internet and TCP/IP.

Connecting to the Internet means speaking TCP/IP, and speaking TCP/IP originally meant running UNIX. Many of the systems on the Internet today still run some form of UNIX. Because of this, the importance of DNS, NFS, and many other TCP/IP connectivity mainstays has increased tremendously since the release of Windows NT 3.51.

Many companies have a sizable installation of UNIX systems. These systems often run mission-critical applications that need to be accessed from corporate desktops. In order for companies using UNIX to effectively implement Windows NT Workstation as the desktop operating system, Microsoft needed to provide UNIX Interoperability.

Operating system comparison

We will take a look at some of the key differences between UNIX and Windows NT. Understanding these differences will allow you to integrate the two more effectively.

File services

File transfer is often considered one of the most important and basic aspects of system interoperability, and this section will address the installation and configuration of both Windows NT and third-party file transfer programs.

Print services

Everything you need to print to a UNIX printer comes with Windows NT 4.0. This section will cover how to get the most out of UNIX print services.

Application interoperability

You can use Telnet and X Windows to run most UNIX applications on Windows NT.

Other UNIX tools

We will discuss SNMP and expanded use of some UNIX derived Windows NT commands such as: finger, nslookup, simple TCP/IP services as well as third-party tools.

This chapter will give you a good understanding of the options available to you should you need to integrate Windows NT with a UNIX environment.

UNIX is a network operating system by design, and TCP/IP is the language UNIX networks speak. Thus, the central part of connecting your Windows NT systems with UNIX is the TCP/IP protocol. The TCP/IP Protocol must be installed before any of the programs in this chapter will run. See Chapter 23, "Using Basic TCP/IP Services," for the details of installing TCP/IP.   ■

Operating System Comparison

Windows NT and UNIX share some commonalities as well as some differences. In general, the design of Windows NT capitalizes on the many strengths of UNIX while avoiding the weaknesses. In order to properly integrate the two environments, you should know some of the differences between the two operating systems. While explaining all the differences and similarities would fill volumes that only a true geek would love, this section will attempt to provide an overview of how the two operating systems compare.

Please note that the many different flavors of UNIX will allow some readers to find specific instances where the statements in this section can be proven incorrect. This section is meant to characterize the two operating systems with generalities, not to speak in absolutes.

System Architecture

When UNIX was created, the "personal computer" didn't exist. The systems available were large systems with dumb terminals that had no intelligence or CPU. They simply echoed the interactions between the main computer and the user. As a result, UNIX was originally developed as a "host based" or "multi-user" system, where the processing is done on one computer. Even though some UNIX systems are a part of a larger client/ server system, the "host based" design has stayed with UNIX. Windows NT has been designed from the ground up as a client/server system. The client is no longer a terminal, but a complex and powerful computer running its own operating system.

Subsystems

UNIX administrators sometimes (possibly often) have to "recompile the kernel" and reboot the UNIX system. This is because operating system functionality (for example, subsystems) and critical parameters are compiled into the *kernel*. The kernel is conceptually similar to the MSDOS COMMAND.COM. As you know, Windows NT also has a kernel but it is designed as a "microkernel." Only the most low level and vital functions are performed by the microkernel, keeping it as small as possible. This means that protected systems in Windows NT can be added or removed, without changing the base operating system or the other subsystems. In comparison, the UNIX kernel itself usually must be different for different processors, hardware architectures, and even software options.

Login Scripts

The traditional UNIX user environment is actually controlled and defined within the UNIX computer. Login scripts such as .login, .profile, .cshrc, and .kshrc are automatically run to set up the UNIX environment when the user logs on to a UNIX system. While these scripts are syntactically similar to Windows NT login scripts, the NT login script executes on a workstation and affects its environment, whereas the UNIX script executes on the environment created on the host system. The upshot is that the scripts themselves are entirely incompatible. There is no way to run a UNIX login script on Windows NT the way you can run Novell login scripts.

Virtual Memory (Swap)

Providing virtual memory is the process of simulating real memory (RAM) with disk space. When Windows NT or UNIX runs out of real memory, it "swaps" the least frequently used memory blocks with disk space. While NT and UNIX share a 4K memory page size, NT's design calls for less user upkeep. UNIX requires the administrator to manage swap space as a separate physical disk partition. Windows NT keeps the swap space within a local filesystem (as a file: pagefile.sys), and manages its size according to how much it needs.

Part
IV

Ch
19

Network Utilities

Microsoft originally offered some basic UNIX networking utilities as part of the Windows NT resource kit. In version 4.0, Microsoft has included most of these utilities in Peer Web Services or as part of the operating system itself. DNS, for example, is included with NT 4.0 and is now integrated with WINS.

File Systems

UNIX names physical devices as files. The system and users actually interface with a device such as a tape drive through a file named /dev/tape. Windows NT does not share this file metaphor for devices, but does create "objects" for devices. Also, the UNIX and

Windows NT filesystems are both journaling filesystems, meaning that they can keep track of additional statistics about a file, such as who used it last.

File Services

File sharing is simply the ability to transfer data between systems. Windows NT comes with several text-based client programs (ftp, tftp, rcp) that can transfer data back and forth with UNIX systems, and a simple service (FTP server) to allow UNIX systems the same capability. Third-party products enhance these capabilities.

FTP: File Transfer Protocol

FTP is probably the tool most often used for UNIX file transfer. The FTP client allows you to "get" and "put" files on remote systems, and is installed with the TCP/IP protocol.

> **CAUTION**
>
> Because the File Transfer Protocol was devised primarily for academic use, security was not a huge issue. As a result, FTP transfers user names and passwords over the network as unencrypted "cleartext." A hacker attached to the network along the route your data flows could use a sniffer to capture your FTP user names and passwords.

The commands supported in the text mode FTP program are rudimentary, but have been enough to get the job done on UNIX systems for quite some time. Chapter 22 has a detailed description of the command line FTP utility, so I won't cover its usage in detail here. You've probably used FTP (maybe through a World Wide Web Browser) to transfer files to and from systems on the Internet.

> **N O T E** Many third-party versions of FTP are available that give you graphical interfaces, quick file viewing, and drag-and-drop functionality. After using one of these programs, you probably won't use the text program again. A popular one is called WS_FTP, and is free to home users. It is also available on the CD-ROM included with this book. ■

The text-based FTP client (FTP.EXE) allows you to transfer files back and forth to UNIX systems running the FTP server daemon called "ftpd." Windows NT Workstation has an FTP service equivalent to the ftpd daemon. In previous versions of Windows NT, you installed this FTP server by adding Simple TCP/IP Services to your network configuration. In Windows NT 4.0, FTP server is installed as a part of Microsoft Peer Web Services and is no longer installed with Simple TCP/IP Services. See Chapter 26, "Installing and Configuring Peer Web Services," for more information.

TROUBLESHOOTING

My company has a firewall to the Internet. I can use my Web browser to get through it, but when I click an FTP site, I get errors. I can FTP to other computers on my company network, so why can't I get to a site past the firewall? FTP uses TCP port 20 to send data and port 21 to send control information (the commands). If you are behind a firewall to the Internet, check with the firewall administrator to see if these ports are allowed passage. There may also be additional steps you need to take (like sending quoted commands) to get through.

rcp: Remote Copy Program

rcp is a file transfer program that allows you to exchange files with systems running the rshd (Remote SHell Daemon) program. rcp works somewhat like a DOS copy command, with the addition of source and destination computers and some security. If you need to, you could even copy a file from one computer to another from a third computer. This capability is useful if you are managing two systems remotely and don't wish to copy the file to your local computer first. You may find it useful to think of rcp as a single line FTP session.

N O T E A daemon is a UNIX program that is always running, waiting for a request for service or connection, servicing that request, and shutting down the connection. Daemons are similar to the Windows NT services. ■

The parameters to use rcp are as follows:

rcp [-a | -b] [-h] [-r] [host][.user:]source [host][.user:] path\destination

<table>
<tr><td>-a</td><td>Specifies ASCII transfer mode for files. This mode is identical to the FTP ASCII transfer mode and is only used for text files. This mode converts the EOL characters to a CR for UNIX systems. If you don't specify a binary transfer mode, ASCII will be used.</td></tr>
<tr><td>-b</td><td>Specifies binary image transfer mode. This mode puts and gets files without translation.</td></tr>
<tr><td>-h</td><td>Specifies that hidden files should be transferred.</td></tr>
<tr><td>-r</td><td>Recursive copy. This will copy all files in all directories below the directory specified in the command line. Both source and destination must be directories, not files.</td></tr>
<tr><td>host</td><td>Specifies the host computer to copy to or from.</td></tr>
<tr><td>.user:</td><td>If you want to use a user name different from your current login, or if you specify the host as an IP address, you must specify the user.</td></tr>
</table>

       path\   Specifies the path to copy from or to. This path is relative to the speci-fied user's logon directory.

A sample rcp command to copy a binary file named /tmp/msg1.dat from a computer named "landshark" to a computer named "candygram" with the user name "joe" and name it /tmp/newmsg.dat is:

```
rcp -b landshark:\tmp\msg1.dat candygram.joe:\tmp\newmsg.dat
```

N O T E   In order to use the rcp command, both computers must contain their partner computer in a file called .rmhosts, .rhosts, or hosts.eqiv. You can find out the syntax of .rhosts by typing "man rhosts" at the UNIX shell. Be sure to read the man page—there are severe security implications surrounding the .rhosts file. ■

tftp: Trivial File Transfer Protocol

The trivial file transfer protocol is a less secure version of FTP; it is primarily used for booting X Terminals or other devices that need to download an operating system or configuration at power-up. There is no user authentication with tftp, and no file browsing capability.

While Windows NT does not come with a tftp server, the client (TFTP.EXE) is installed when you install TCP/IP. It has the following options:

tftp [-i] host [GET | PUT] source [dest]

    -i   Specifies binary image transfer mode. This mode should be used for transfers of binary (non-ASCII text) files.

    host   The name or address of the tftp server.

    GET | PUT   You can specify either GET to transfer a file from the tftp server to your computer or PUT to send a file to the tftp server.

    source   Specifies the name of the file to transfer.

    dest   Specifies where to transfer the file to.

NFS: Network File System

NFS is probably the most useful tool for sharing data with a UNIX system. NFS allows you to mount a UNIX filesystem as a logical drive. For instance, using NFS you can map your U: drive to /mount/shared on the UNIX system. The only bad thing about NFS is that it doesn't come with Windows NT—you have to acquire an NFS client from a third party in order to use NFS.

T I P A free tool named SAMBA is available that allows for NFS-like filesystem access without buying an NFS client. While the software is not supported by a corporation, SAMBA provides bidirectional disk mounting without modification to Windows NT.

There are two parts to setting up an NFS directory. The first step is to set up the UNIX system to share the NFS directory you need. You need root equivalent access (root is the UNIX administrator) to export a directory.

Start by using Telnet to connect to the UNIX system from Windows NT either by entering **start telnet <hostname or IP address>** from a command prompt or from a run dialog box. Log on to the system with a root (or equivalent) account.

The UNIX command exportfs is used to setup shared directories. Running exportfs by itself will produce a list of currently exported directories. To export a directory on a UNIX system, you can do one of two things.

1. Edit the /etc/exports file and run exportfs -a on the UNIX system. The -a parameter tells the NFS server to export all directories in the /etc/exports file.

2. Use the exportfs -i <filesystem> command. The -i parameter for exportfs translates roughly to "ignore the /etc/exports file and share this directory anyway."

For example, to export the /usr/bin directory on a UNIX system, the command

```
exportfs -i -o ro /usr/bin
```

grants any system on the network read-only access to the /usr/bin directory.

Directories exported with the -i parameter will not be automatically re-exported after a UNIX system reboots. Only directories listed in the /etc/exports file will be re-exported at system startup.

For more information on the exportfs command, including security options, read the manual page by entering the command **man exportfs** at the UNIX prompt.

Part
IV

Ch
19

NFS Exports

An NFS export on a UNIX system is conceptually identical to sharing a directory on a Windows NT computer. The information about which directories are currently shared on the UNIX platform is kept in the /etc/xtab file, and the file /etc/exports contains the directories that are exported with the exportfs -a command, a command usually run at the UNIX system startup.

> **CAUTION**
>
> NFS is unfortunately both powerful and insecure. If misconfigured (something that can happen quite easily), NFS can allow any user on any system access to the entire UNIX filesystem. Many popular hacks on UNIX systems use NFS for breaking in. Please make sure you know exactly what the ramifications are of each command you enter. Consult your local UNIX guru!

Print Service Interoperability

When it comes to UNIX printing, Windows NT Workstation includes just about everything you need. You can print to UNIX printers, share UNIX printers, and even print from UNIX to Windows NT Workstation.

Printing from Windows NT to UNIX Printers

Windows NT is capable of printing to most lpd (Line Printer Daemon) printers—a UNIX standard for remote printing that has aged incredibly well. The generic UNIX printing mechanism is specified in RFC 1179, and includes communications specifications for lpd (the print server portion) and lpr (Line Printer Remote)—the client portion. This includes printers attached directly to a UNIX machine and lpd compatible print servers such as Hewlett Packard "Jet Direct" cards. Before you can print to a UNIX printer, you have to install the Microsoft TCP/IP Printing Service.

Installing the Microsoft TCP/IP Printing Service

Microsoft TCP/IP printing can be installed from the Windows NT Control Panel. You install this service the same way you install any Windows NT service—through the Services tab in networking. To start the setup process, follow these steps:

1. Launch the Control Panel, and double-click the network icon.
2. Select the Services tab, then choose the Add button. Windows NT displays a Select Service dialog box.
3. Select the Microsoft TCP/IP Printing service from the list.

When you select OK, the service will be installed and you will have to restart your machine for the service to take effect.

Installing the UNIX Printer

In order to print to a UNIX printer, you will need to set up a printer port. To add the port, follow these steps:

1. Select Settings, then Printers from the Start Menu.

2. Double-click the Add Printer icon as if you were installing a regular printer.

3. Even though you are printing to a network printer, keep the My Computer button selected—you are actually adding a virtual printer port to your system that you can assign printer drivers to.

4. Select Add Port to bring up the available port types. Windows NT will display an Add lpr compatible printer dialog box like the one shown in figure 19.1.

FIG. 19.1
The lpd printer port dialog box allows you to create a virtual printer port.

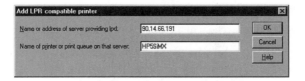

Add LPR compatible printer

Name or address of server providing lpd.   90.14.66.191   OK

Name of printer or print queue on that server: HP5SiMX   Cancel

Help

5. Fill out the first box with the DNS name or IP address of the print server, and the second box with the printer name.

T I P If you are using a hardware print server (such as a HP JetDirect Card), or you don't have the exact print queue name, it is usually possible to enter any text into the print queue name box—the default printer will be used.

At this point, Windows NT will attempt to send a test command to the UNIX Printer. A message box will pop up only if this command failed. If you are connected to the network and you get this message, you have probably entered something incorrectly. You'll need to check your settings and enter it again.

You should see your lpd printer listed in the printer port similar to the one in figure 19.2.

Part
IV
Ch
19

FIG. 19.2
The Printer Ports
dialog box with lpd
highlighted.

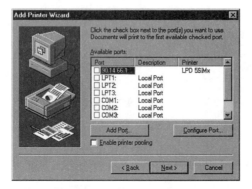

To assign a printer to your new port, follow these steps:

1. Make sure the box next to the UNIX printer port is selected and click Next.

2. From here, select the manufacturer and model of the printer that you are printing to. Windows NT will probably need to copy some drivers from the NT CD-ROM at this point.

3. In the next window type a name that you would like to see from your applications, such as "lpd Printer on HP box."

4. Now you have the opportunity to share this printer with other computers. If you choose to share the printer, you will need to enter a share name and select all the platforms that will be printing to it.

5. You should try to print a test page to test your setup. If you can successfully print the test page, you will be able to select this printer in your applications.

Sharing Your UNIX Printer with other Workstations

You can share a UNIX printer as a Windows NT printer with other Microsoft network machines as long as you have a protocol (and security) in common with that machine. This means that you can set up one NT workstation with both TCP/IP and IPX/SPX to act as a print UNIX printer server/gateway for an IPX/SPX-only network.

There are no special steps to sharing a UNIX printer. You can follow the steps outlined in Chapter 32, "Administering Users," to create a printer share.

Printing from UNIX to Windows NT

Not only can you print to UNIX printers, you can let UNIX computers print to a printer connected to your Windows NT computer. The process of printing from UNIX to Windows NT involves starting the Windows NT lpdsvc and the UNIX command lpr. In the beginning of this section, we stated that Windows NT can print to any lpd compatible print server—starting the lpdsvc basically turns your NT computer into an lpd-compatible print server. Of course you must have a printer that you can print to (either networked or local) before you can share it with UNIX systems.

> **N O T E** Any printer that you can print to from your Windows NT workstation can be shared with UNIX systems. This allows for many new configuration possibilities—including printing to a Netware printer from a UNIX system through Windows NT. ■

To start the lpdsvc, either type:

```
net start lpdsvc
```

at the command prompt; or open the control panel, double-click Services, select TCP/IP Print Services, and click Start.

When you start the TCP/IP Print Service, printers that you have shared on your computer become separate print queues on an lpd print server. For example, if you have an HP LaserJet attached to your LPT1 port shared as "Local4Si" and your machine is named "Landshark," starting lpdsvc creates a printer named "Local4Si" on an lpd print server named "Landshark." You would print to this queue from UNIX with the command:

```
lpr -S landshark -P local4si <filename>
```

You will need to substitute an IP address for "landshark" if you don't have a DNS or an entry for "landshark" in the UNIX file /etc/hosts. See Chapter 25 for more information on DNS and the hosts file.

If you want the lpdsvc to start automatically, do the following:

1. Open Services from the Control Panel.
2. Select TCP/IP Print Services from the service list and click the Startup button.
3. Change the startup type to Automatic and click OK.

When you reboot, the service will start without user intervention.

Part
IV

Ch

19

Printing Utilities

The UNIX command lpq allows you to check the status of a print queue in a UNIX (lpd) print queue. The command syntax is:

```
lpq -S <server> -P <printer> [-l]
```

The -S option is used to specify an lpd server name, and is a required parameter. The server name can be an IP address, a UNIX host name, or a Windows NT computer with the TCP/IP print server (lpdsvc) started.

The -P option specifies a printer queue, and is a required parameter. Since it is possible to have more than one computer at each lpd server, you must name the printer you need status for.

The -l option tells lpq to give verbose output about print jobs currently running. In practice, the -l option doesn't appear to actually add any information to the Windows NT report, but it may make you feel better when your jobs aren't printing.

The default information returned by the Windows NT TCP/IP print service is: Owner, Status, Job Name (the filename), Job ID, Size, Pages, and Priority.

Application Interoperability

Microsoft has included the simplest UNIX application interface with Windows NT—Telnet. Telnet allows you to access the UNIX shell (command prompt) from a remote location. Because UNIX was designed to use a command line interface, most UNIX applications and virtually all UNIX administration chores can be accessed from a simple Telnet session. Many UNIX gurus do 99 percent of their work from a Telnet session. The basic command syntax for Telnet is:

```
telnet <Hostname or IP address> <port>
```

You normally leave the port parameter out so Telnet will use TCP port 23, the designated Telnet port. Take a look in Chapter 22, "Overview of TCP/IP," for detailed information on Telnet.

X Windows

Like Windows NT, UNIX has a GUI called "X Windows." In X terminology, the server software runs on the computer that displays the program output, and the client software runs on the computer that does the processing. This means that when you talk about an X/server, you are referring to software running on the desktop computer. This GUI was only able to run on specialized X/Terminal hardware until software companies came out with Windows-based X/servers that turn your PC into an X/Terminal.

ON THE WEB

Microsoft does not offer an X/server, but there is X/Server software available from several vendors—here are some:

X/Servers for Windows NT

Hummingbird Communications, Ltd.	eXceed/NT	(416) 496-2200	**www.hummingbird.com**
Digital Equipment Corp. for NT	eXcursion	(800) 344-4825	**www.dec.com**
Network Computing Devices, Inc.	PC Xware	(415) 694-0650	**www.ncd.com**
WRQ Corporation	Reflection	(206) 217-7500	**www.wrq.com**

Configuring eXceed for Windows NT

Part
IV
Ch
19

One of the popular X/servers is eXceed for Windows NT. Because this isn't an X Windows book, we won't cover how to install eXceed, but we will touch on how to use it.

N O T E   When installing eXceed, make sure you select Windows Sockets TCP/IP stack. Installing the stack supplied by Hummingbird (SuperTCP) may cause problems as Windows NT 4.0 uses Winsock 2.0. ■

To start using eXceed:

- Start up the local X/Server on your computer by running one of the Local X demos like Ico. This will allow you to see that the server is running.
- Use the Telnet application to connect and log on to the UNIX system.
- Run your application by entering its command and specifying your machine as the display parameter. The syntax for xclock (a simple graphical clock program) is:

```
xclock -display <your IP Address or hostname>:0
```

If the path to xclock is present in your environment, an X window displaying your application should appear.

TIP

To run a UNIX command in the background (on most systems), add a "&" symbol to the end of the command. For example, entering:

```
xclock -display <your IP Address or hostname>:0 &
```

will give you the UNIX prompt back in your Telnet session.

TROUBLESHOOTING

Can I run X applications over a modem connection? You can, but it will be painfully slow. Be prepared to wait several minutes for your first window to open. X applications are designed to be run over a LAN.

When I run an X program on the UNIX system, I get the error message "cannot connect to display." What am I doing wrong? This error message could mean several things, and you have to track down the problem manually. First, try to run X applications locally. If that works, your X/Server is working correctly, and the remote X application is having trouble connecting to it. If it doesn't, you probably have the X/Server software misconfigured or not started.

Because you are successfully using Telnet to access the UNIX system, your TCP/IP routing is working correctly. Some things to try:

- If you used a hostname in your command, try using your machine's IP address instead. Unless you have a DNS server that knows your Windows NT workstation's name or has an entry for it in /etc/hosts, the X application will have problems finding your machine.

- Attempt to remove the :0 from the X application command line or change it to a :1 or :01. An example:

```
xclock -display 90.12.100.2 &
```

I have Windows NT Workstations that run X applications and use DHCP. Their IP addresses are changing, and I want to know how I can figure out how to launch X applications to a dynamic IP address without finding out my new IP with ipconfig and actually typing it into the shell command? The easiest way around this problem is to reserve an IP address for each machine. For information on DHCP, look in Chapter 24, "Using DHCP." Another approach to solving this problem is to use a Windows NT server as your DNS server. With the new WINS lookup through DNS feature in NT 4.0, a UNIX system can translate the NT workstations netbios hostname to an IP address using regular DNS queries. See Chapter 25, "Using DNS and WINS," for information on setting up a DNS server.

Other UNIX Tools

There are many useful tools derived from UNIX that are included with Windows NT Workstation. This section will cover some of the most useful of these tools.

Simple Network Management Protocol (SNMP)

SNMP is a protocol that provides basic administration information about devices attached to a network. SNMP is typically used by SNMP management software (Openview, Netview, SNMPc, and more) that enables system administrators to get information on network connected devices ranging from power conditioners to multiprocessor UNIX systems. In order to get information from a device, that device must be capable of broadcasting information or responding to SNMP queries. Windows NT 4.0 includes SNMP services that provide this functionality to SNMP management systems. This section will cover the installation and configuration of SNMP services on Windows NT.

 TIP Even if you don't use an SNMP manager, installing SNMP will give you some new capabilities. Performance Monitor will allow you to view and capture additional information about the TCP/IP protocol after you install the SNMP service.

You install the SNMP service the same way you install any Windows NT service—through the network windows services tab. Just follow these steps:

1. Launch the Control Panel, and double-click the network icon.
2. Select the Services tab, then choose the Add button. Windows NT displays a Select Service dialog box.
3. Select the SNMP Service service from the list.
4. Click OK. The service will be installed and you will have to restart your machine for it to start.

Configuring SNMP   SNMP transfers information either as alerts (broadcasts) or as responses to queries. With so many different devices offering SNMP services, you can imagine how quickly a network can fill up with broadcast messages. Instead of flooding your network with messages indicating that all your devices are healthy, you should probably have important SNMP devices (servers or routers, for example) send traps but have less important devices respond only to queries. If you choose not to send traps, a system could fail without you knowing it between the times your SNMP manager polls it.

SNMP uses the concept of communities and destinations (hosts) as a method to help group your machines. A destination is a machine within a community. If you are familiar with TCP/IP, a community is like a network, and a destination is like a host—except there

Part
IV

Ch
19

is no routing between communities. The Windows NT SNMP service automatically responds to queries from a community called "public" by default, but doesn't send traps to any community by default.

Agent Tab   The Agent tab tells the SNMP agent what information you want to make available to SNMP management software (see fig. 19.3).

FIG. 19.3
The SNMP Agent tab.

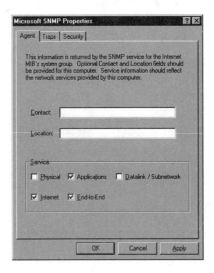

You should type the name of the system administrator in the contact box and the machine's physical location or other identifying information in the location box. The Service group box allows you to specify what level of information you want to provide to SNMP queries or broadcasts. If you are broadcasting traps, minimize the number of boxes checked. You can select from the following checkboxes:

- **Physical**. Checking this box will enable physical media network statistics.
- **Internet**. This box only applies if this workstation is an IP router. If so, this box will enable errors from higher level network software.
- **Applications**. Checking this box enables information and statistics from TCP/IP applications like WWW Services, FTP, and SMTP services.
- **End-to-End**. This box applies to computers that are end nodes on a network. If you are running TCP/IP, you should probably have this box checked.
- **Datalink/Subnetwork**. This check box only applies if your NT workstation is acting as a part of a logical network, as a bridge for example.

Traps Tab   Traps are broadcast messages your SNMP service sends. This tab will allow
you to specify which community and destination to send traps to (see fig. 19.4). If you
leave the community box blank, the SNMP service will only respond to queries. After you
have put in a community name or names, you can input a trap destination as a host name,
IP address, or IPX address. If you specify a community or a host that doesn't exist, your
SNMP traps will go unnoticed.

FIG 19.4

The SNMP Traps tab.

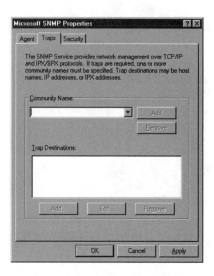

Security Tab   The check box at the top of figure 19.5 labeled Send Authentication Trap
directs the SNMP service to send an alert to the community and destination specified if
unauthorized access is attempted. Unauthorized access is defined as a query coming from
any community not listed in the Accepted Community Names list, or a host not listed in
the Only Accept SNMP Packets from These Hosts list. To add communities or hosts, click
the Add button and type in the desired name.

Part
IV

Ch
19

Finger

While strangely named, finger is actually a useful tool. It allows you to find out information
about a user or a domain from Windows NT Workstation. The basic finger syntax is:

```
finger [-l] [user]@host
```

What information gets returned depends on the OS policies at the computer you are contacting. Usually finger will return the last time the user logged in, their office and phone
number, and the text in the users .plan or .project file in their home directories—if these
files exist. Some users have programs set up that will tell you some constantly updated

information in their .project or .plan file. Finger can be a valuable tool for finding information from an e-mail address. If you finger with just an @host command, you may get information back about that computer system.

FIG 19.5

The SNMP Security tab.

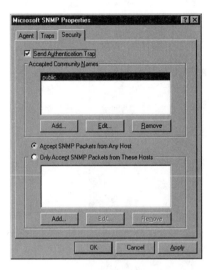

Nslookup

Nslookup is a diagnostic utility that gives you information culled from DNS servers. If you want to read more about DNS, take a look at Chapter 25. Nslookup basically allows you to convert IP addresses to host names and vice versa.

The basic nslookup syntax is:

```
nslookup [-option ...] [computer-to-find ¦ - [server]]
```

Although nslookup has an array of options, most people use it to test their DNS and convert IP addresses to DNS names. For the first argument, type the host name or IP address of the computer you want to look up. For the second argument, type the host name or IP address of a DNS name server. If you omit the second argument, the default DNS name server will be used.

Below is sample output from nslookup:

```
C:\>nslookup 133.145.224.3 199.28.12.3
(null)   amerigo-fddi.mycorp.com
Address:  199.28.12.3
(null)   hitiij.hitachi.co.jp
Address:  133.145.224.3
```

Simple TCP/IP Services

Windows NT supports Simple TCP/IP Services. These services truly are simple. The TCP/IP services are installed from the networks services tab in control panel. These services are:

- *Echo (RFC 862)*. Immediately returns characters.
- *Discard (RFC 863)*. Discards sent characters.
- *Character Generator (RFC 864)*. Returns a repeating pattern of characters.
- *Daytime (RFC 867)*. Returns the system date and time.
- *Quote of the Day (RFC 865)*. Returns a specified string.

These services each have a port assigned that you can look up in the services file. While these services may be of use in advanced TCP/IP testing, they should normally not be installed.

Other Tools

If you just can't get enough UNIX, it is possible to buy toolkits that are essentially Windows NT versions of popular UNIX programs. The MKS Toolkit from Mortice Kern Systems, Inc. includes almost 200 popular UNIX commands. Contact Information: Phone: (800)265-2797, Internet: **www.mks.com**.

From Here...

Part
IV

Ch
19

This chapter has shown you how to integrate Windows NT with UNIX environments by using both Microsoft and third-party applications. Related chapters in this book are:

- Chapter 22, "Overview of TCP/IP," for an introduction to TCP/IP networking in Windows NT 4.0.
- Chapter 23, "Using Basic TCP/IP Services," for expanded coverage of FTP, Telnet, and other TCP/IP programs.
- Chapter 25, "Using DNS and WINS," for information on WWW, Gopher, and FTP servers.

CHAPTER 20

Using Dial-Up Networking

by Craig Zacker

Networking is an integral part of Windows NT, even when the computer is not physically attached to a local area network. Remote network access has been a priority of the operating system since its initial release, but what began as a basic extension of a Windows NT network to a remote computer has evolved into a remote access solution that can accommodate virtually any function of a heterogeneous internetwork, providing distance users with access not only to files and printers, but to client/server applications and even Internet resources as well.

This chapter covers many different aspects of the remote access capabilities provided by the Windows NT 4.0 operating system. ■

Remote access and multi-protocol routing

Windows NT provides complete network access to the remote user with only a single transport protocol.

Remote access scenarios

The ways in which Windows NT's remote access capabilities can be used for much more than transferring files between home and office.

Remote access security

Windows NT security mechanisms can be extended to the remote user.

Installing the Windows NT Dial-Up Networking features

Learn to configure Windows NT workstations and servers for remote access.

What Is Dial-Up Networking?

As the local area network became an ever more indispensable business tool, the difficulties of employees who work at home or on the road were compounded. Increased reliance on e-mail and mission critical client/server applications made a data connection to the home office essential, but many of the solutions available were technically demanding, insecure, expensive, and frustratingly slow.

Windows NT addresses all of these shortcomings with the Remote Access Service (RAS) included in version 4.0. Networking is so well integrated into the Windows NT infrastructure that a computer accessing a network from a remote location uses what is essentially the same network client as a LAN-connected machine, substituting a modem, ISDN (Integrated Services Digital Network) link, or X.25 PAD for a network interface card. Once the connection has been established, the user interface functions no differently than it would with a direct network connection, albeit at a slower speed.

An RAS client connecting to a network uses a Windows NT user account that is no different from that of a local user. Additional measures can be applied, as well, that can ensure the network against unauthorized access. Windows NT 4.0 also introduces PPTP, the Point-to-Point Tunneling Protocol, a new transport mechanism that allows remote users to establish efficient, secure, and inexpensive network connections over the Internet. Also, multi-line connections allow multiple modem connections to be combined to increase available bandwidth.

Routing versus Remote Control

Many people are confused by the claims made by the different remote access products on the market today. There are, in fact, two basic philosophies of remote computer access, both of which can provide network access, and both of which have uses in the computing world. The differences between the two center around the nature of the data that is passed over the modem connection and where the actual application processing takes place.

Remote control services are provided by software products marketed by a number of different manufacturers, among them Symantec's Norton PCAnywhere and Microcom's Carbon Copy. Products like these allow you to take control of a computer from a remote location, using a modem, LAN, or Internet link to pass keyboard, mouse, and display data between the two machines.

When you launch a program using a remote control connection, it is the host machine's processor that actually runs the application. The remote computer is used only for communications tasks, such as passing keystrokes and mouse movements to the host. The advantage to this technique is that it allows the remote user access to all resources available to the host. Thus, if the host is connected to the network, so is the remote user. What's more, remote control can be used to perform network administration tasks from another location; tasks that can only be performed using the processor on the host machine.

The drawbacks to remote control are numerous, however. First and foremost, it is a single-user solution. Each remote computer must connect to a different host machine, which cannot be used for any other purpose while the remote user is connected. Remote control may therefore be suitable for office employees who wish to connect to their machines from home, but it is not practical for a sales force that travels on a semi-permanent basis.

N O T E There are products on the market, such as Cytrix's Winframe, that provide remote control services for multiple users on a single machine. For remote user environments that must support hundreds of users, however, remote node access is generally preferable to remote control. ▦

Remote control is also relatively slow. When these products were first developed, DOS was the environment of choice, and their performance was deemed acceptable in a character-based environment. Today's Windows applications, however, generate a great deal more display data that must be transmitted, and mouse movements must be added as well. Even using the fastest modems available, screen redraws can be painfully slow.

The other form of remote access, used by Windows NT's RAS, addresses these problems in most cases. Instead of using the remote computer to control a host system, Windows NT allows it to function as an independent and fully functional network client of its own. In essence, the telecommunications link between the remote and the host machine forms a subnet, with the host system functioning as a router between the internal network and the remote system.

Part

IV

Ch

20

In this way, the remote computer can log on to the network as a client unto itself, independent from the host machine. While a remote control client would use the access rights and IP address of the host, an RAS client is assigned its own IP address and may have wholly different rights than those of the host.

When an RAS client runs a program, the processing is performed within the remote computer itself. This will nearly always provide the remote user with better performance, as long as the application files are actually installed on the remote machine. This is a crucial point. A remote user who dials into the corporate network to run an application that is stored on a network drive is not going to get very good performance, especially with a

Windows application. So many large files will have to be transmitted over the modem (or other) connection that performance will actually be worse than that of a remote control connection.

A remote access computer, to be truly useful, must be equipped with the appropriate software at the client end, even if this means additional expenditure for software licenses. As a case in point, let's assume that a remote user wants to check her e-mail from abroad. If the mail client software is not installed on the remote computer, her remote session will have to begin with the transmission of several megabytes of program files before the application will even start. This defeats the entire purpose of client/server computing.

If the client has been installed on the remote machine, the application is launched locally, and the only data that must pass through the telecommunications link is the actual e-mail traffic itself. When suitably configured and equipped, therefore, RAS is ideal for accessing network resources like e-mail and other client/server applications. Unlike remote control, in which every new screen must be serially transmitted over a slow link, only the data itself is transmitted by RAS.

Of course, it is possible that remote access may be desired in a non-client/server environment. For a user who works from home and requires access to network resources, the possible additional cost of equipping the remote system with the software needed to make this practice practical must be balanced against the cost of remote control access, which may be a preferable solution, in this case.

Dial-Up Networking versus RAS

When implementing remote access on a large scale, however, the primary advantage of RAS is that a single Windows NT server machine can host up to 256 users at one time. RAS runs as a network service on Windows NT, and ships with both the Server and Workstation versions of the product. Windows NT Workstation, however, is not intended to be used as a host server for an entire network, and can only accommodate a single RAS client.

The RAS client in the NT Workstation operating system is referred to as Dial-Up Networking, and it includes a wizard that allows a user to easily configure the system to access an office workstation or server on which RAS has been installed (as well as the network to which it is connected) from a remote location, with no additional equipment required other than a modem and a phone line.

On a server designed to provide RAS access to multiple users, the hardware requirements obviously will be greater. Windows NT supports a wide range of the multi-port devices that allow multiple modems to be attached to a single computer without requiring individual COM ports for each one. Both the Server and Workstation products can also utilize ISDN or X.25 connections for access at higher speeds.

Because Windows NT uses industry standard protocols for its Remote Access Service, the Dial-Up Networking phonebook can be used to connect to any host system that uses the Point-to-Point Protocol (PPP). This means that Windows NT is not limited to dial-up communications with other Windows NT machines, or even other Microsoft clients. It can be used, for example, to connect to any Internet Service Provider (ISP) that uses PPP, no matter what platform it is running, and allows the Windows NT machine to gain access to the Internet. In fact, Windows NT's ability to function as a router allows a single computer connected in this manner to provide Internet access to the entire local network (connected using traditional network interface adapters).

In fact, a Windows NT server with a high-speed Internet connection that is running the Remote Access Service can function as an ISP itself, allowing hundreds of users to dial in and access Internet resources.

On an individual level, users can run RAS on their personal workstations at the office and connect to them from home using the Dial-Up Networking client, gaining access to local area network services as well as the Internet, at the same time.

RAS Scenarios

The degree of flexibility designed into the Windows NT RAS modules should allow the network administrator to envision a number of different situations in which RAS may be put to use on the corporate network.

The most basic scenario is that of a worker running Windows NT Workstation on his office computer who wants to connect from his or her home machine. This may be for the purpose of simply transferring files from the office to the home, or the user may require access to higher-level network resources like corporate databases or even the company's Internet connection. As long as both computers are equipped with modems, it is a simple matter to install the RAS service on the office machine and the Dial-Up Networking client on the home computer. In fact, the home machine can even be running Windows 95 instead of Windows NT and still gain full access. This arrangement would typically be managed by the worker himself, as the configuration of individual computers for remote access would be impractical on a large scale.

If an organization requires RAS services for a large number of users, it makes sense to centralize the operation by installing a RAS server that is maintained by the network administrator. A single Windows NT server can support up to 256 RAS users simultaneously, supporting not only the occasional home user but telecommuters and traveling employees as well. In this scenario, there is no need for each user to have a computer in the office; the server can act as a gateway to any of the resources available on the network.

Obviously, the hardware requirements for a remote access server on this scale involve quite a bit more than a modem and a phone line. To use more than four normal asynchronous modems on a single server, it has to be equipped with a multi-port device that allows multiple modems to be run using a single COM port. The device may be realized as a spider-like cable that connects four or eight modems to the computer, or as separate boxes providing jacks for 16 or more serial cables. The boxes may be daisy-chained so that hundreds of modems can be used. On large installations, the modems themselves would typically be rack-mounted, to save space and so that the modems could share power supplies (for purposes of fault tolerance). A multi-port device can also, when used in a roll-over, prevent excessive ringing by making the phone line busy whenever the application is not ready to answer a call.

The computer used as the RAS server would also have to have sufficient memory and processing power to accommodate the needs of a large number of simultaneous users. Windows NT's RAS solution is well-suited to this role, because it can be scaled up gradually as RAS demand increases. Additional modems and multi-port devices can be added any time that additional facilities are needed.

Many manufacturers now market self-contained RAS servers that incorporate all of this hardware into a single package. Some use Windows NT as their operating system, while others may not. In many cases, Windows NT clients can connect to a RAS server that is using other software. However, always be sure to check the standards compliance and interoperability of the products that you select before purchasing.

As mentioned earlier, Windows NT's RAS is not limited to modems for its communications links. ISDN and X.25 are supported also, providing sufficient speed for a WAN connection between a small branch site and the home office. Two Windows NT computers (even running NT Workstation) connected with such a link could each function as the gateway to the remote network for the other, providing sufficient bandwidth for the exchange of e-mail and other critical services at a very low cost.

As ISDN continues to make inroads into the home, RAS can provide the means for more efficient telecommuting. Although ISDN's 128Kb/sec doesn't approach the speed of the average LAN, the improvement in performance over a 28.8K modem is remarkable. As this technology becomes more affordable, the many economical and environmental benefits of an off-site work force will make telecommuting a practical alternative for many organizations.

The Point-to-Point Protocol

On a normal LAN, the Windows NT network client allows multiple protocols to be transmitted over the same network by providing a buffer—called the NDIS interface—between the various network layer protocols and the network interface adapter. The NDIS interface allows traffic using any protocol to pass through to any network adapter, as long as both are written to the same common interface.

NDIS is not used by RAS, however. Instead of providing an interface by which multiple protocols can be transmitted over the same medium, RAS provides a single common protocol that is used to encapsulate the traffic generated by all of the other network protocols. It is called the Point-to-Point Protocol, or PPP, and is based on open standards published as RFCs 1661 and 1662 by the Internet Engineering Task Force (IETF).

As the name implies, the PPP is used to create a dedicated connection between two computers. Unlike traditional network protocols, it is not capable of multicast or broadcast transmissions. PPP is a connection-oriented protocol. A session is established between two computers before any data is sent, and remains in effect for as long as the computers communicate. While other connection-oriented transport protocols like TCP and SPX might establish many separate connections in the course of performing a computing task, the PPP is geared towards the media over which it is used. When computers are connected by modem, a single PPP session remains open as long as the telephone connection remains intact.

The PPP specification consists of the following elements:

- A frame within which packets generated by different network protocols are encapsulated for transmission.
- A separate Link Control Protocol that is used to send the control traffic that establishes, maintains, and breaks down the PPP connection.
- Individual Network Control Protocols for use in packaging each of the network protocols supported by PPP for transmission.

Part
IV

Ch
20

The PPP is designed to multiplex data from different sources over a single connection, with a minimum of control overhead. Multiplexing is the process of sending different kinds of signals over a single connection. In this case, packets generated by the TCP/IP, IPX/SPX and NetBEUI protocols can all be encased in PPP frames and sent over a single phone line. Within the PPP connection, protocols can be mixed indiscriminately; the protocols that are transmitted at any particular moment depend on the amount of traffic being generated by each network process at that specific time. On arriving at their destination, the packets are separated into their individual protocols, with each being directed to the appropriate protocol stack in the receiving computer.

The PPP Frame

As with any other network protocol, the PPP receives existing packets and adds its own header to them before transmission. In a PPP connection, these packets consist of the normal frames created by the individual protocols at the Network layer and above. TCP/IP traffic, for example, arrives at the PPP client as normal IP datagrams. Instead of being framed by a Datalink protocol such as Ethernet or Token Ring for transmission over a local area network, each datagram becomes the data field of a PPP packet that is then transmitted to the computer at the other end of the link via modem (or other device).

Because the PPP connection functions as a Datalink protocol for what is effectively a two-node network segment, there is no place for the transmitted packets to go other than the destination computer. For this reason, it is not necessary to add additional fields to the PPP header containing information like the network address of the destination computer, as a Data Link layer protocol would. The connection has been established, both computers know where the data is going; what's important is that the data gets there promptly and reliably. For this reason, the PPP frame that is added to each packet is very small, consisting only of a single field that is used to identify the protocol being carried within.

The general problem with connection-oriented protocols is that they require an inordinately large percentage of control traffic in order to provide reliable service. This control traffic can take the form of additional bits that are added to each packet before it is transmitted, or it can be concentrated in the process by which the connection is established. Because PPP relies upon the use of connections that remain open for relatively long periods of time, it is more efficient for it to devote a greater amount of time and traffic to the establishment and testing of a reliable connection than to include additional reliability mechanisms in each packet.

To illustrate this concept, consider the traffic needed to transmit a typical World Wide Web page over the Internet. The HyperText Transfer Protocol (HTTP) that is used on the Web requires an individual TCP connection for each text and graphic file that is transmitted. Thus, for an average Web page, there might have to be 5 or 10 individual TCP connections established, utilized, and then broken down. Compare this to a PPP connection used to transmit the IP packets that make up the same Web page. A user dials into a service provider and establishes a single PPP connection that might remain open for minutes, or even hours. Because the PPP connection is only established once, it makes sense to devote a greater amount of traffic to setting up the connection, in order to reduce the burden on the individual packets. Meanwhile, that single PPP session may be used for thousands of individual TCP connections. Performing an elaborate connection routine for each of those would be far less efficient than adding mechanisms like checksums and packet numbers to the individual datagrams, which is what TCP does.

Establishing a PPP Connection

In order to establish a stable and reliable PPP connection, each of the two computers transmits packets containing Link Control Protocol (LCP) messages that inform the other machine of its capabilities and provide authentication services. This is followed by individual Network Control Protocol (NCP) exchanges for each of the protocols to be transmitted over the link. Once the link has been established, the transfer of data begins. To terminate the session, another exchange of LCP packets occurs, which breaks down the connection in an orderly manner.

This sequence of events is illustrated in figure 20.1.

FIG. 20.1
A PPP connection is established, maintained, and terminated by the Link Control Protocol.

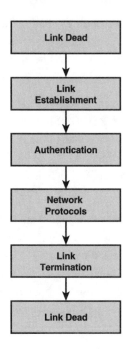

An LCP packet utilizes the same frame as a PPP data packet, with a protocol identifier that declares it to be LCP traffic, and not one of the data protocols to be carried. (The appropriate protocol identification numbers are included as part of the Assigned Numbers RFC.) Inside the frame is a simple LCP header that includes fields that describe the function of the packet and specify an identification number by which the exchange of specific requests and replies can be identified. LCP packets fall into three distinct categories, whose functions are self-explanatory:

- Link Establishment
- Link Maintenance
- Link Termination

The LCP is used to perform all of the link establishment, maintenance, and termination tasks for a PPP connection that are not specific to a particular network protocol. The LCP exchanges that occur during the life of a connection proceed in phases, described in the following sections.

The Link Dead Phase This is the beginning and ending phase of all PPP connections, in which no communications are occurring between the two computers.

The Link Establishment Phase The remote computer initiating the connection (the PPP client) sends a CONFIGURATION REQUEST packet that specifies the PPP configuration options desired by the client, such as the maximum allowable packet size, the authentication protocol to be used and/or the quality protocol to use.

If the receiving or host computer (the PPP server) is able to establish a connection with all of the options specified by the client, it returns a CONFIGURATION ACK packet. If the server recognizes all of the options, but cannot satisfy all of them, it returns a CONFIGURATION NACK packet containing the options that must be changed. If the server fails to recognize one or more of the options, it returns a CONFIGURATION REJECT packet containing the unrecognized options.

The Authentication Phase Once the link has been established, authentication of the remote computer's identity may be required. The IETF documents define several different authentication protocols that may be used. Windows NT supports two that are defined in RFC 1334: the Password Authentication Protocol (PAP) and the Challenge-Handshake Authentication Protocol (CHAP). Message exchanges for these two protocols are described in the "RAS Security" section, later in this chapter. RAS also supports several other protocols in order to provide compatibility with third-party PPP products.

The authentication process required by the host computer must be completed satisfactorily before the Network Control Protocol exchanges can begin (although link quality testing can proceed during authentication). A failed authentication causes the connection to proceed immediately to the Link Termination phase.

The Network-Layer Protocols Phase Once the remote computer has been successfully authenticated, the negotiations for the individual network protocols to be transported within PPP packets can commence. Windows NT supports the use of the NetBEUI, IPX/SPX, and TCP/IP protocols over its RAS service, either individually or simultaneously.

IPX/SPX support is initialized using IPXCP (the Internetwork Packet Exchange Control Protocol), as defined in RFC 1552, and TCP/IP with IPCP (the Internet Protocol Control Protocol), defined in RFC 1332. Windows NT's support for NetBEUI is not standardized by the IETF.

Any of the supported network protocols can be initialized at any time during a PPP connection, but that initialization must be completed before any traffic using that protocol is transmitted. The NCPs are similar to LCP in their message types and packet formations, differing primarily in the options offered by each one.

IPCP's options allow the remote computer to request a specific IP address or request that the host supply one. The two computers can also negotiate the use of the Van Jacobson IP header compression algorithm, which can help to reduce control traffic over slow links. IPXCP includes similar options that allow the assignment of network and node addresses, and the configuration of compression and router options. Using the same CONFIGURATION packet types as LCP, each NCP reaches an OPEN state upon successful completion of its negotiations. Traffic using that network protocol may then proceed.

The Link Open Phase   At this time, traffic over the PPP link may include any combination of LCP, NCP and network protocol traffic. Additional NCP initializations may occur during this phase, as can the termination of any currently open network protocol.

The Link Termination Phase   Once a link has been established, it can be terminated at any time due to authentication failure, quality testing failure, or at the deliberate request of the remote user. Link termination is negotiated separately from the termination of the individual network protocols. The termination of the PPP connection (obviously) terminates the network protocols as well, but termination of the network protocols does not force the termination of the PPP connection, even if all of the network protocols are inactive.

The Link Termination process uses simple LCP packets that contain little more than a protocol field (to signify the purpose of the message) and a unique identifier that is used to match requests with acknowledgments. The remote computer sends a series of TERMINATE REQUEST messages to the host, which responds with one or more TERMINATE ACK packets. This returns the two computers to the Link Dead phase, at which time the remote system terminates the physical connection.

This procedure describes the process by which a PPP connection is terminated in an orderly manner. Appropriate time-outs are also in place to terminate and reset the connection state, should an interruption occur in the Physical layer.

Part
IV

Ch
20

The Serial Line Internet Protocol (SLIP)

The Serial Line Internet Protocol, or SLIP, is the progenitor of the PPP. It is an extremely simple mechanism that was designed to carry IP datagrams over a serial connection, such as those between modems. Although it has largely been replaced by PPP, SLIP is still used today by a few dial-up systems and Internet Service Providers, so it is still supported by the Windows NT RAS client. It is not supported by the Windows NT RAS server, however, because in comparison with PPP, SLIP is woefully inadequate.

SLIP can be most accurately described by listing its shortcomings. It provides a simplistic framing mechanism for the IP datagrams coming from the network layer, but it has no packet addressing capabilities, supports no authentication protocols of any kind, uses only a single packet type, and is limited to the transmission of TCP/IP traffic only. It also adds no additional capabilities for error checking/correcting, data compression, or data encryption.

A SLIP client allows a user to log on to a remote system by presenting a terminal window that provides an interface to the host system. A user specifies a login name by hand and furnishes the correct password before being allowed access. This process can be automated in a Windows NT client by the creation of a script, but the password information is still transmitted without any sort of security encryption.

The user must also supply IP address information to the SLIP client manually, as there is no facility for the transmission of control traffic of any kind. A SLIP client simply begins sending data packets over the serial link, and appends a single control character to the end of each packet. That's all there is to it. As a result of these limitations, the use of SLIP for RAS communications that require even the most rudimentary network security is strongly discouraged.

RAS Security

When implementing a remote access solution on a corporate network, security is naturally a major concern of the system's administrator. Windows NT's RAS architecture provides a multileveled security system that can be customized to the needs of the organization as well as the requirements of specific users. The security mechanisms available to the administrator fall into the following categories:

- PPP Authentication
- RAS Options
- Third-Party Security Products

- Native Windows NT Security
- Encrypted Data Communications

The following sections examine each of these types of security. They can be used in any combination to provide virtually any degree of protection required.

PPP Authentication

As described earlier in this chapter, the Point-to-Point Protocol provides the capacity for an authentication protocol to be used before a remote computer can gain access to an RAS server. Because Windows NT's RAS modules are designed to be interoperable with other manufacturer's products, several different authentication protocols are supported. The protocol to be used is agreed upon by the two computers during the Link Establishment phase of the PPP negotiation.

The Challenge-Handshake Authentication Protocol (CHAP)   When a Windows NT RAS client contacts a Windows NT RAS host, the Challenge-Handshake Authentication Protocol (CHAP)is used by default. This is a highly secure authentication protocol, based on a three-way challenge and response mechanism, that is defined in RFC 1334.

The first CHAP exchange occurs immediately after the Link Establishment phase of the PPP negotiation. The host computer sends a CHALLENGE packet to the remote system. The packet contains a field that indicates the encryption algorithm to be used for the transmission of password information, as well as a unique identifier for the packet and a challenge value. The remote system must then reply with a RESPONSE packet containing the same identifier, and an appropriate password that has been encrypted using the same challenge value. The host then returns a SUCCESS message, which allows the next phase of the PPP negotiation to begin, or a FAILURE message, which forces a Link Termination.

As an additional measure of security, CHAP challenges are also issued at repeated intervals during the PPP session. Each challenge uses a different identifier and challenge value, so that a static response packet that might have been furnished by a potential intruder will cease to be valid at the next iteration. A failure to successfully respond to a challenge at any time will cause the termination of the link.

Aside from agreeing on the use of CHAP as the authentication protocol, the two computers must also agree on a common encryption algorithm. The Windows NT default is DES, which is the encryption standard used by the U.S. government. The windows NT RAS client also supports RSA Security Inc.'s MD5, which is another algorithm that is used by other manufacturers of RAS products.

Part
IV

Ch
20

The Shiva Password Authentication Protocol (SPAP)   CHAP also provides a mechanism that allows the two computers to negotiate down a scale of progressively less secure protocols until a common one is found. If the two connected computers cannot agree on the use of CHAP with any of the available algorithms, the second choice is SPAP, the Shiva Password Authentication Protocol. Shiva is a manufacturer of RAS clients and servers, and SPAP is its own proprietary protocol. It is not as secure as CHAP, but Windows NT supports it in both its RAS client and server, when trying to connect to a Shiva counter-part. (That is, a Windows NT client will use SPAP when connecting to a Shiva LAN Rover RAS server, and a Shiva client will use SPAP when connecting to a Windows NT server, but a Windows NT client will never use it to connect to a Windows NT server.)

The Password Authentication Protocol (PAP)   The last resort, if permitted by the network administrator, is PAP, the Password Authentication Protocol, as defined in RFC 1334. PAP uses an AUTHENTICATE REQUEST packet to send a user name and password from the remote to the host in clear text, with no encryption. The host responds with either an AUTHENTICATE ACK or AUTHENTICATE NACK message, that results in a continued PPP negotiation or termination of the link, respectively.

PPP Authentication Passwords   Although it is possible to regulate a Windows NT user's remote access privileges, as we shall see, it is nevertheless the same Windows NT user name and password that provide local network access that are used for RAS authenti-cation. This greatly increases the danger inherent in allowing the use of clear text authentication.

An intruder on the internal network has only to monitor the traffic on the segment where the RAS server is located to see the names and passwords of all remote users logging in using PAP. The intruder would then have access to any of that user's resources, from either the internal network, or by connecting remotely at a later time, using any authenti-cation protocol.

 Although it is by no means a foolproof measure, locating the RAS server on its own network segment will complicate the task of capturing the RAS users' traffic from other locations on the local internetwork. Another technique is to make the RAS server a backup domain controller, so that the users would always be authenticated by the local machine.

After the detection of such an incident, simply eliminating PAP access would not be suffi-cient to plug the security leak. The passwords of any users that have ever logged in using PAP must be considered suspect, and changed immediately.

Fortunately, if you are using the Windows NT RAS server and you restrict your users to the various Microsoft RAS clients, authentication will be performed in a secure manner.

You can remove the option that allows unencrypted passwords to be transmitted, preventing unsecured access without inconveniencing your users.

> **N O T E** See the section "Configuring RAS Authentication Options," later in this chapter, for instructions on how to restrict the authentication protocols that can be used by RAS clients. ▪

RAS Options

Although Windows NT's RAS uses the standard NT user accounts for RAS authentication, this does not mean that all of your users with valid local accounts must be allowed remote access. The Windows NT Remote Access Administrator is an application that allows you to select users or groups of users that are to be allowed remote access. You can also perform these same tasks using the standard Windows NT User Manager utility.

Once a user is granted remote access privileges, additional protection can also be provided. By default, RAS clients are allowed access to all of the resources that would normally be available to them from the local network. The administrator, however, can restrict their remote access only to those resources located on the host computer, if desired. This way, a user dialing into his office computer from home can be restricted to the resources on his own computer, and prevented from accessing the network.

Another way to limit users' access is to restrict the use of certain protocols over the RAS connection. You may wish to allow users to access the Internet through your RAS server using TCP/IP, but deny the use of IPX, so that access to the NetWare resources would be limited.

One of the most foolproof security mechanisms of Windows NT's RAS is the callback feature. To use this, the network administrator enters into the Remote Access Administrator the phone number from which a remote user will be dialing into the system, as shown in figure 20.2. When the user connects to the RAS server and is successfully authenticated, the server disconnects and redials the user at the specified number. This not only helps to prevent unauthorized access, but allows company phone lines to be used for the bulk of the communications, usually providing cost savings through lower rates and reduced expense accounts. Callback requests can also be configured by client. This function is accessed by clicking the More button in the Dial-Up Networking dialog box, selecting Logon Preferences, and then choosing the Callback tab in the Logon Preferences dialog box.

FIG. 20.2

Remote Access to the network can be secured by configuring the server to call the remote computer at a pre-designated number.

Native Windows NT Security

Of course, the most fundamental means of providing secure RAS access is the same as that used to control LAN access: the standard Windows NT network access control mechanisms found in the User Manager and in the Permissions dialog boxes for specific shares and directories.

Windows NT's auditing features also allow the administrator to track RAS usage, as well as any and all attempts to access protected resources by RAS users.

Third-Party Security Products

In addition to the security measures provided by the Windows NT operating system and the PPP standards, support is also provided for external security products that require a remote client to have a hardware or software "key" in order to gain access to an RAS server. This provides an added level of protection that is wholly independent of the operating system and the network.

Data Encryption

When RAS is used in industries that require the most extreme security measures, such as financial and government institutions, administrators may opt to encrypt all of the data that passes over the RAS connection, and not just the user names and passwords. While adding a significant amount of processing overhead that will degrade performance to some degree, this process ensures that even an intruder tapping a telephone line will be unable to access the data carried over the PPP connection.

Virtual Private Networks

With the Internet having become a ubiquitous part of the business world, one of the biggest hurdles facing network administrators and Internet developers is the fundamental lack of security that hampers the medium. As vendors scramble to define a commerce standard, and mechanisms are developed to provide secure Internet transactions, the possibility of running corporate network traffic over the Internet has quietly become a reality with Windows NT 4.0. A new protocol included with the package allows for the creation of secure Virtual Private Networks (VPNs).

A VPN is essentially a wide area network link that uses the Internet instead of a dedicated phone line or dial-up connection. A host computer in the home office is outfitted with a dedicated Internet connection, and a filter is applied that allows only traffic using the new Point-to-Point Tunneling Protocol (PPTP) to pass through the host machine to the Internet. This protocol takes the packets containing TCP/IP, IPX/SPX and NetBEUI traffic that have already been encapsulated by the PPP, encrypts them, and adds an IP header to create datagrams that are delivered to the ISP and sent out over the Internet. This additional IP header forms a "tunnel" across the Internet that insulates the contents from exposure to unauthorized users.

On the remote side, a computer running Windows NT creates its own PPP link to a local Internet service provider, and can thereby log on to his company's private network through the Internet, by providing the appropriate authentication codes. However, the server can be configured so that even the right access codes will not function unless the PPTP is used. RAS on the host server functions as a firewall for network traffic, allowing PPTP packets in and rejecting all others. This technique can produce enormous savings, both in hardware (no modems or multi-port devices needed) and in telephone costs (no long distance charges, 800 numbers, or leased lines).

Because the network traffic is encapsulated by the PPTP, it is possible for remote users to contact computers on the corporate network that do not have IP addresses that are registered on the Internet. Local subnet traffic is insulated from the actual Internet by the PPTP frame, which is created by a computer that does have a registered address. This insulation also allows the data within the PPTP datagrams to be secured from unauthorized access by any of the means available to the PPP, including CHAP password protection and data encryption.

Part
IV

Ch
20

PPTP is defined in a specification that is the work of several major players in the remote access field, including Microsoft, 3Com, U.S. Robotics, and Ascend Technologies. To allow any PPP client to connect to a Windows NT RAS server using PPTP, ISPs must install a minor software upgrade, but any Windows NT 4.0 PPP client capable of accessing a particular NT 4.0 RAS server through a dial-up can also access it through the Internet using PPTP, with no modifications on the part of the service provider. Support for the protocol in the hardware industry seems strong, but it remains to be seen what effect a large amount of private traffic will have on the Internet itself. Those who believe that the

Internet's infrastructure has already been overburdened by the meteoric growth of the World Wide Web over the past two years will have to modify their predictions as to when the eventual collapse will occur.

Installing the Windows NT RAS Server

In order for remote computers to be able to dial into a Windows NT machine, it must have the Remote Access Service installed. This is a network service that installs like any other, from the Network Control Panel. The Remote Access Service is included with both Windows NT Server and Workstation. The versions in the two products are virtually identical, except that NT Server supports up to 256 simultaneous remote users, while NT Workstation only supports one.

Before you add the RAS the service, it is a good idea to install the communications hardware that the system will be using to host remote users. This is not required, but if modems, ISDN links, or X.25 pads and their required drivers are tested and fully functional before using them for RAS, a major troubleshooting step can be eliminated if a problem should occur later.

Once the hardware has been installed, open the Network Control Panel, select the Services tab and click the Add button. Select Remote Access Service from the list presented and click OK. You may then be prompted to insert your Windows NT CD-ROM so that files can be copied. Once the service has been installed, the Remote Access Setup dialog box will be displayed, as shown in figure 20.3.

FIG. 20.3

The Remote Access Setup screen allows you to designate which hardware devices are to be used with RAS.

Select the modem on the COM port that you wish to use for RAS in the dialog box (if you have more than one modem installed) and click the Configure button. Indicate whether the system should be able to dial out only, receive calls only, or both, and click OK.

Then click the Network button, and you will see the Network Configuration screen shown in figure 20.4.

FIG. 20.4

The Network Configuration screen is used to indicate which network protocols are to be transmitted over the computer's RAS connections.

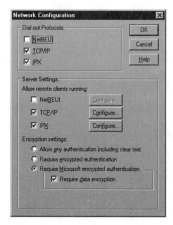

The Dial out Protocols section at the top of the dialog box allows you to choose what network protocols should be allowed when the computer is used as a RAS client. If the computer will be used for receiving calls only, this field can be ignored.

The Server Settings field is for incoming traffic. Click the appropriate check boxes next to the protocols—NetBEUI, TCP/IP or IPX—that you want RAS clients to be able to use when accessing your system. The incoming protocols that you choose can depend on what services you want to provide to your users, what security measures you may wish to implement, and what protocols are in use on your network.

N O T E See Chapters 17, 18, and 19 for more information on the Windows NT networking architecture. ■

If, for example, the Windows NT machine is to be used to provide Internet services to dial-in users only, you should be sure to disable the NetBEUI and IPX protocols, even if you are not running them on your network. The reason for this is that they can affect the performance of the RAS client computer, if it is connected to its own network. If a user on a NetWare network were to dial in to your server and IPX services have been allowed, the PPP would begin an IPXCP negotiation at the proper time, informing the remote user that all regular NetWare services will be lost while the PPP connection is active. If, on the other hand, you wanted users to be able to access NetWare traffic, it would be prevented by the failure to allow IPX services in this dialog box.

Part
IV

Ch
20

Each of the three protocols has its own configuration dialog box, ranging in complexity according to the protocol. The RAS Server NetBEUI Configuration dialog box is the simplest. It provides only a single option: whether the remote user should have access to the entire network or only to the local machine. This option is provided in all of the other protocol dialog boxes as well. NetBEUI requires no other configuration settings because it relies on broadcasts to locate other machines on the network. The remote machine can log on to the host network with just a NetBIOS name (entered during the operating system installation), and locate any other machine by asking it to identify itself.

N O T E   See Chapter 25, "Using DNS and WINS," for more information on broadcasts and other name resolution techniques. ■

Of course, because NetBEUI is non-routable, it is generally limited to use on a relatively small network. IPX and TCP/IP are internetwork protocols, and their dialog boxes are understandably more complex. The other options in both of these are primarily concerned with the assignment of a unique address to the remote computer as it dials in.

Configuring TCP/IP for RAS Clients

The RAS Server TCP/IP Configuration dialog box (shown in fig. 20.5) allows three possible means of assigning an IP address to the remote computer. One way is to use an existing DHCP server on the network to assign IP addresses from its already configured scopes. To do this, simply click the radio button for the Use DHCP to assign remote TCP/IP client addresses option, and the configuration is completed. Each client that dials in to the RAS server will be assigned an IP address (and other TCP/IP settings) according to the same terms and conditions as a local DHCP client.

N O T E   See Chapter 24, "Using DHCP," for more information on setting up a DHCP server. ■

FIG. 20.5

A RAS server can assign static IP addresses to dial-up clients or use the network's existing DHCP services.

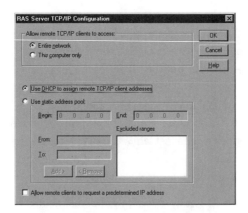

The second method for assigning IP addresses is to create a pool of static addresses in this dialog box, which will be assigned only to RAS users as they connect to the server. To do this, click the Use Static Address Pool radio button and enter the beginning and ending IP addresses of the range you wish to use, in the fields provided.

If you do not have a range of contiguous addresses that can be used, enter the highest and lowest numerical addresses that are available and use the Excluded Ranges fields to exclude whatever addresses between the two are already in use. Entering a range in the From and To fields and clicking the Add button will exclude that range from the address pool. (You can also enter the same address in both the From and To fields to exclude a single address.) This process is very much like that used to create a scope with the DHCP Manager.

The third method for assigning IP addresses to RAS clients is to click the Allow remote clients to request a predetermined IP address check box. This will cause an IP address already configured on the client's computer to be used instead of one assigned by the server. Use this option when you wish to ensure that your RAS clients are each assigned the same IP address whenever they log on to the network.

 TIP It is not a good idea to allow remote users to specify their own IP addresses, unless a specific application absolutely requires it. Typographic errors or inexperienced users could easily cause IP address conflicts, resulting in failed access or interruption of other services.

The selection of IP addresses for your RAS clients should be based on the same criteria as for your internal network. Treat RAS clients no differently than local TCP/IP clients in this respect. If your network users have direct access to the Internet, for example, then the IP addresses used for RAS must be registered, just like those for other users.

Configuring IPX for RAS Clients

If you want your RAS clients to be able to access NetWare resources, you must enable the IPX protocol, and configure it using the RAS Server IPX Configuration screen shown in figure 20.6.

FIG. 20.6
The RAS Server IPX Configuration dialog box allows you to choose whether RAS clients should be assigned individual addresses.

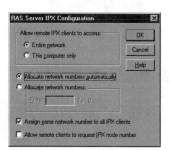

NOTE Novell markets a product called NetWare/IP that allows IPX traffic to be carried within IP datagrams. When this product is used, you don't have to configure RAS to support the IPX protocol. ■

Part
IV

Ch
20

As with TCP/IP, all computers running IPX must have an address. IPX addresses are hexadecimal, and identify the network on which the computer is located, as well as the node itself. Normal LAN clients have their node address hardcoded into the network interface adapter, while the network number is assigned by the administrator. Since an RAS client need not have a traditional network interface adapter, one is emulated by the RAS software through the assignment of an address.

You can allow RAS to allocate available network addresses to dial-up clients automatically, by clicking the appropriate check box, or select Allocate Network Numbers, instead, and specify the first of the network address that you want to use in the From field. The To field will be computed automatically, based on the addresses available.

If you click the Assign Same Network Number to All IPX Clients check box, a single address will be used for all dial-up clients. This can serve to reduce the amount of RIP (Routing Information Protocol) traffic generated by the addition of RAS clients. If each client is assigned its own address, then each must have its own routing table entry. If one address is used, then only one entry is needed.

Whether or not you should use this option depends on what NetWare services you will be providing to your remote users. If all that is required is file and printer access, then you can safely use a single address. If dial-up users will be accessing client/server applications running on NetWare servers, however, individual addresses will probably be required.

Click the Allow Remote Clients to Request IPX Node Number check box if you want to allow the use of a node number specified by the remote user in the RAS client software.

> **CAUTION**
>
> The option to allow RAS clients to specify their own IPX addresses is one that should be exercised with great care, as it poses a potential security risk. This feature can allow a dial-up client to utilize the address of another user on the local network, and possibly intercept traffic that was destined for that user. In most cases, the use of this option should not be necessary.

Configuring RAS Authentication Options

Having configured the desired network protocols, you must now consider what means of client authentication you plan to use. The Encryption Settings area of the Network Configuration dialog box allows you to choose among the authentication protocols described in the "PPP Authentication" section, earlier in this chapter.

Three radio buttons are available, providing the following options:

- **Require Microsoft Encrypted Authentication**. Uses CHAP with DES encryption
- **Require Encrypted Authentication.** Uses CHAP with MD5 encryption or SPAP
- **Allow Any Authentication Including Clear Text**. Allows the use of PAP

The options are listed here in reverse order from how they appear in the dialog box because Windows NT's RAS server will attempt to negotiate for the use of the most secure authentication protocol, and proceed downwards to the less secure options, if allowable.

The option you choose should attempt to impose the highest level of security based on the RAS client software that your remote users are running. If all of your RAS clients will be running Windows NT or Windows 95, you can require Microsoft encrypted authentication, for the highest level of password security. If you choose this option, you can also choose to Require Data Encryption, which will force all of the traffic carried by the PPP to be encrypted, and not just the authentication messages. This provides a greater level of security, but also imposes a significant additional load on the RAS server's system resources.

PPP clients by manufacturers other than Microsoft (whether or not they run on Microsoft operating systems) do not support Microsoft encryption, but they may utilize another encryption protocol that is supported by Windows NT. Choosing the Require Encrypted Authorization option will allow RAS access to these clients while still maintaining a high level of security.

If you choose to allow the use of any authentication protocol by selecting the third option, you are endangering the security of your user and password information. The use of this option may be required in some situations, such as when an ISP uses Windows NT to provide dial-up Internet services to customers, in which case other means should be used to insulate RAS users from sensitive systems.

Once you have made your selections, you can click OK to close the Network Configuration dialog box and click the Continue button in the Remote Access Setup dialog box.

Part
IV

Ch

20

Starting the Remote Access Service

After installing and configuring the Remote Access Service, it is ready for use, once you start the service and grant remote access rights to your users. The RAS installation process does not configure the service to start up automatically. You can change this behavior from the Services Control Panel by selecting the Remote Access Service, clicking the Startup button and selecting Automatic. You can also manually start and stop the service from this dialog box.

RAS can also be started, stopped, and paused from the Remote Access Administrator, an application that is installed with the service. Like most Windows NT administration programs, the Remote Access Administrator allows you to control any RAS server on the network. With it, you can also grant user rights and monitor the current RAS activity.

After launching the Remote Access Administrator, the service on the current machine is displayed, if it is running. To start or stop the service, select the appropriate command from the Server menu. You can also choose Select Domain or Server to specify the name of a different RAS server on the network for display.

N O T E   In this context, the term RAS server refers to any Windows NT machine with the Remote Access Service installed, whether it is running the Windows NT Server or Workstation operating system. Both versions of the service can be administered from this same interface. ■

Before a user can gain remote access to the network, she must have a Windows NT user account that is created in the normal manner with the User Manager. Just like an internal user, the account must include the appropriate rights to all of the resources that the user will access from a remote location. In addition, the account must be explicitly granted the right to access those resources via RAS.

RAS rights can be granted to existing users from the User Manager, or from the Remote Access administrator, by selecting Permissions from the Users menu in order to display the Remote Access Permissions dialog box shown in figure 20.7. Select a user from the list provided and click the Grant Dial-In Permission To User check box, or click the Grant All button to allow access to all users.

FIG. 20.7
Windows NT users must have explicit permission to access the network using RAS.

In this same dialog box, you can specify whether the callback option should be enabled for each user. When enabled, the callback feature causes the RAS server to disconnect a dial-up user immediately after authentication, and dial the remote computer using the number provided. To enable this feature, Preset To radio button and fill in the telephone number of the remote user's computer (including any dialing codes needed to reach an outside line). You can also choose the Set by Caller radio button, to allow the RAS client software to supply the call back number.

This dialog box can also be displayed in the Windows NT User Manager, by clicking the Dialin button that appears on each user's Properties screen.

The callback feature can serve two purposes. First, it causes the majority of the RAS telephone charges to be incurred by the home office. This will usually result in lower long distance rates and better tracking of RAS costs.

N O T E Tracking the true cost of an organization's remote access program has traditionally been a difficult task because mobile users will typically include the long distance telephone costs in personal expense reports that do not distinguish between voice and data calls. The use of Windows NT's callback feature cannot only allow a more accurate estimation of RAS costs, but can also allow traveling personnel to avoid excessive long distance telephone rates. ■

The second advantage, when the callback phone number is specified at the server, is the security of knowing that RAS sessions will be limited only to the telephone numbers supplied to the network administrator in advance. Even if the client software is allowed to supply the callback phone number, the server can maintain a log of activity that includes all of the numbers used, possibly allowing unauthorized usage to be traced.

As a safety measure, this feature obviously is only as secure as the telephone system itself. A person with sufficient knowledge and access could conceivably spoof the system by usurping a user's phone number, but this feature can repel most casual attempts to hack into a Windows NT RAS system.

Installing the Windows NT RAS Client

Part
IV
Ch
20

The influence of Windows 95 on Windows NT 4.0 is particularly evident in the RAS client. A wizard has been added that makes the task of configuring the remote client very simple. As with the RAS server installation, the modem (or other hardware) that will be used for remote access should be installed first, in the normal manner.

Then, choose Dial-Up Networking from the Start Menu's Accessories group. If RAS has not been installed on the machine, Dial-Up Networking will require access to the Windows NT CD-ROM in order to copy files. Once this has been done, you can create an entry in the Dial-Up Networking phonebook by entering an identifying name for the RAS server in the New Phonebook Entry Wizard screen. If you click the Next button, the wizard will ask a series of simple questions to determine the correct configuration needed to establish a connection with your RAS server. Users that are unfamiliar with the RAS process can easily configure the RAS client in this way.

However, because you have already learned about the RAS client options from this chapter, select the check box that says "I know all about phonebook entries and would rather edit the properties directly," and click the Finish button. This will present the New Phonebook Entry dialog box. This dialog box contains all of the RAS client settings. Once you have created a phonebook entry, you can return to this dialog box by clicking the More button on the main Dial-Up Networking screen and selecting Edit Entry and Modem Properties.

The following sections cover the individual pages of the dialog box, and all of the settings that are needed to connect to an RAS server. In many cases, the settings of the client must match the features enabled at the server. You may have to consult your network administrator to find out what the proper settings should be for your environment.

The Basic Screen

When the Edit Phonebook Entry dialog box is opened, the Basic tab is selected by default, as shown in figure 20.8. Here you can specify the name by which the entry will be identified in the phonebook, as well as a comment that you can use for any descriptive information that you wish. Enter the phone number of the RAS server in the field provided. Be sure to include any additional codes needed to place the call from your current location.

FIG. 20.8

The Basic tab is used to specify the phone number and modem to be used to contact a particular RAS server.

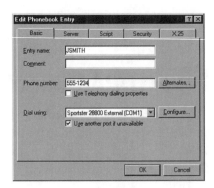

Click the Alternates button to specify multiple phone numbers for the RAS server, or click the Use Telephony Dialing Properties check box to use the dialing parameters you have previously set using the Telephony Control Panel. The Alternates button opens the Phone

Numbers dialog box, in which you can enter additional numbers. Type each number in the New phone number field and click the Add button to insert it into the Phone numbers list. You can then modify the order in which the numbers are dialed using the Up and Down buttons or have the list order automatically modified by filling the Move Successful Number To The Top Of The List On Connection check box. Click OK to return to the Edit Phonebook Entry dialog box.

N O T E The Alternates feature can allow Windows NT RAS clients to access any one of multiple modems on a server without the need to create a hunt group at the host location. The Telephony Control Panel allows the traveling user to associate special dialing codes, calling card numbers, or call waiting codes with a particular phonebook entry. ■

In the Dial Using field, you can select the modem or other device that you wish to use to connect to the RAS server (if you have more than one installed). Click the configure button to modify modem settings for the RAS session. You can also elect to use more than one modem connection by selecting the Multiple Lines option. If you select this option, click the Configure button to open the Multiple Line Configuration dialog box.

This dialog box displays all of the modems available on your computer. Click the check boxes for all of the modems that you would like to use to access your RAS host, using the Phone numbers and Configure buttons to access the Phone Numbers and Modem Configuration dialog boxes, if necessary. Enabling this option allows you to use multiple modems to connect to your RAS server. The bandwidth of the individual connections is combined in your computer by a process called *demultiplexing*. This is a simple, portable, and relatively inexpensive way to increase the bandwidth of your connection without the need for ISDN or other high-speed communications technologies.

The Server Screen

The Server page of the dialog box (see fig. 20.9) is used to specify what type of connection is to be established to the server as well as the protocols to be used.

FIG. 20.9
The Server screen is used to configure the protocols that will be needed to connect to the RAS server.

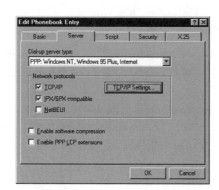

Part
IV

Ch
20

The Dial-Up Server Type field provides the following options. For reasons of security and efficiency, a PPP connection should be used whenever possible (see "The Point-to-Point Protocol," earlier in this chapter).

■ **PPP: Windows NT, Windows 95 Plus, Internet**. Creates a standard Point-to-Point Protocol connection that can carry TCP/IP, IPX and/or NetBEUI traffic; supported by Windows NT version 3.5 RAS servers and above, the Windows 95 Dial-Up Networking host (requires the Microsoft Plus Pack), and most Internet Service Providers.

■ **SLIP: Internet**. Implements a TCP/IP-only connection using the Serial Line Internet Protocol, an all but obsolete protocol (having been replaced by the PPP) that is still used by a few Internet Service Providers.

■ **Windows NT 3.1, Windows for Workgroups 3.11**. The RAS server in Windows NT 3.1 supports neither PPP nor SLIP, but does allow a connection to be established using only the NetBEUI protocol.

N O T E   Although the Windows 3.1 version of RAS was limited to the use of the NetBEUI protocol, access to NetWare resources can be granted to remote users via the Gateway Services for NetWare module that shipped as an add-on to the original Windows NT 3.1 release. This service allows a Windows NT server to log in to a NetWare server (as a client) and make its volumes appear to other Windows NT users as though they are standard Windows NT shares. ▦

Two check boxes at the bottom of the dialog box allow you to enable the use of software compression during a PPP connection and to enable the PPP LCP extensions.

Because most modems will enable some form of hardware-based compression by default, you may not need to use software compression. Data can only be compressed once, and the addition of a second compression mechanism would be redundant. The delays imposed by the additional compression algorithm are very slight, but for peak performance, check the properties of your modem and select one compression method only. (Generally, hardware compression is preferable to software compression, as it imposes no additional burden on the system processor.)

The LCP extensions are additional elements of PPP's Link Control Protocol that are defined in a separate standard document (RFC 1570). They define additional LCP function codes that can be used by one computer to identify its PPP implementation or transmit a Time Remaining value to the other computer. The document also codifies the callback feature used by Windows NT and other RAS products. Check this box if your RAS server supports these extensions (as Windows NT does).

Network Protocol Configuration   While the SLIP and Windows 3.1 server options support only a single protocol, if you are using a PPP connection, be sure to specify which protocols will be used during your connection to the RAS server in the Network Protocols box. If you are using TCP/IP with a PPP connection, click the TCP/IP Settings button to display the dialog box shown in figure 20.10.

FIG. 20.10

To use the TCP/IP protocol during an RAS session, you must specify the means by which your computer is to be assigned an IP address.

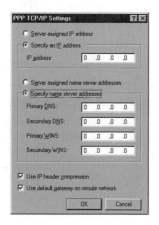

PPP TCP/IP Configuration   As shown earlier in this chapter, the means by which TCP/IP settings are assigned to RAS clients is also configured in the Windows NT RAS server, and obviously the settings here in the client must conform to any limitations imposed by the server. If, for example, the server has been configured to assign IP addresses to RAS clients automatically (either from a static pool or using DHCP), check the Server Assigned IP Address radio button. If DHCP is also being used to provide the addresses of DNS and WINS servers, you can also click the Server Assigned Name Server Addresses radio button.

If the server is not configured to assign IP addresses and other settings, however, you must specify values for the IP address and name server fields after selecting the appropriate check boxes. The correct settings should be supplied to you by the network administrator.

Part

IV

Ch

20

N O T E   Depending on whether you are connecting to a private network or an Internet Service Provider (ISP), you may be given settings only for DNS servers, only for WINS servers, or for both. The client can even function with no name resolution at all, but every client (remote or local) that is using the TCP/IP protocol requires an IP address. ▪

TIP The use of DHCP (the Dynamic Host Configuration Protocol) simplifies the whole IP configuration process by automatically supplying a client with all of the settings needed. See Chapter 24, "Using DHCP," for more information.

The Use IP header Compression check box should be enabled if your RAS server supports the Van Jacobson compression algorithm (as Windows NT does). The Use Default Gateway on Remote Network check box allows the RAS client to gain access to other network segments using the same default gateway as the RAS server.

SLIP TCP/IP Configuration   If you are using a SLIP connection to an ISP, the TCP/IP Configuration dialog box is slightly different, as shown in figure 20.11. On a SLIP connection, the IP address and name server addresses must be provided by the client, so there are no automatic assignment options to be found here. You can elect to Force IP Header Compression by filling the appropriate check box, and elect to Use the Default Gateway on the Remote Network or not, in the same way as with a PPP connection. Because SLIP does not support the automatic negotiation of the frame size as PPP does, you can select the size is supported by your server.

FIG. 20.11
TCP/IP configuration settings for a SLIP connection must be specified by the RAS client.

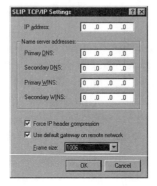

The Script Screen

When a Windows NT RAS client attaches to a Windows NT RAS server, the entire connection and logon process is negotiated automatically. If an NT RAS client is used to connect to a different server, however, there may be additional steps required to gain access that the client software cannot account for.

After the client dials in to the server and the modem connection is established, the server may present additional prompts to which the NT client has no replies. You can handle this problem in two different ways, using the options provided on the Script page of the Edit Phonebook Entry dialog box (see fig. 20.12).

FIG. 20.12

The Script page allows you to specify scripts to be used both before and after dialing into a server.

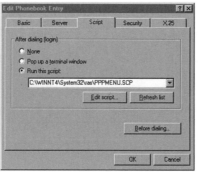

If you select the Pop Up a Terminal Window radio button, you will be able to interactively supply the correct information needed to log in to the server. This can become a tedious chore, however, and Windows NT provides a scripting language that you can use to automate the process. Click the Run This Script radio button, and specify the full path to a script file in the field provided. Clicking the Edit script button will load the default script file into Notepad, allowing you to review or edit its contents.

N O T E The default script file is called SWITCH.INF and is stored in the \WINNT\SYSTEM32\ RAS directory. ■

Clicking the Before Dialing button opens a similar dialog box that allows you to select a script to be run before dialing in to the server. This can be used to automate the commands needed to use a modem pool or make other adjustments before a modem can be activated.

RAS scripts are plain ASCII files, either with an extension of SCP, or located in the default SWITCH.INF file. In most cases, they will be needed when dialing in to RAS networks or ISPs that offer multiple services over the same telephone lines. You could also use a script to automate a network login using a name and password that are different from those registered by the operating system.

Windows NT includes sample script files that demonstrate the techniques for connecting to the most common RAS scenarios. The CompuServe script (CIS.SCP, shown in the directory listing below) is an excellent example of what occurs when connecting to a dial-up service that uses prompts during the logon process, with the added wrinkle of the need to change the port settings from 8 databits and no parity to 7 databits and even parity during the logon process.

Part
IV

Ch
20

```
proc main
    set port databits 7
    set port parity even
    transmit "^M"
    waitfor "Host Name:"
    transmit "CIS^M"
    waitfor "User ID:"
    transmit $USERID, raw
    transmit "/go:pppconnect^M"
    waitfor "Password: "
    transmit $PASSWORD, raw
    transmit "^M"
    waitfor "One moment please..."
    set port databits 8
    set port parity none
endproc
```

The waitfor commands indicate the text that is expected from the host, and the transmit commands specify text to be sent to the service by the client. $USERID and $PASSWORD are variables whose values are taken from the dialog box that is displayed before the service is actually dialed.

Thus, if you normally log on to a service interactively using a terminal window, you could automate the process by making notes of the exact prompts sent by the host and your exact responses to them. Then take one of the sample scripts provided with Windows NT and modify it to suit your particular prompts. It is almost always easier to work with an existing script than it is to write one from scratch.

The Security Screen

The options presented in the Security page of the Edit Phonebook Entry dialog box (see fig. 20.13) are nearly identical to those encountered during the configuration of the RAS server, in the "Configuring RAS Authentication Options" section, earlier in this chapter.

FIG. 20.13
The authentication options selected on the Security page must agree with those configured on the RAS server.

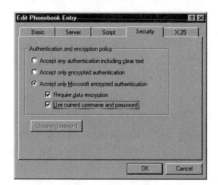

The authentication option that you select on this screen must be in agreement with the settings of the RAS server to which you will be connecting. If, for example, you were to require Microsoft encrypted authentication, you would not be able to connect to your ISP, unless they were running Windows NT as well. Check with the administrator of the RAS server to find out which are the proper authentication and encryption settings. If you are using a script to supply your user name and password, then selecting an option in this dialog box is unnecessary.

The Use Current User Name and Password check box indicates whether you wish to use the name by which you logged on to the Windows NT machine while connecting to the RAS server. Your ISP may provide you with a user ID that is different from that which you use locally, or you may log on to Windows NT as Administrator, and not have those same rights to the RAS server.

The X.25 Screen

RAS and the Point-to-Point Protocol are not limited to the use of asynchronous modems for their connections. RAS can also be used to establish WAN links between offices. X.25 is a nearly obsolete packet-switching protocol that has long been used for WAN connectivity. It traditionally requires a hardware device called a PAD (packet assembler/disassembler) to establish a connection, but dial-up X.25 connections are now available through most major telephone networks, such as CompuServe, MCI, Sprint and AT&T.

In order to establish an X.25 connection using RAS, values must be supplied for the fields in the X.25 page of the Edit Phonebook Entry dialog box, shown in figure 20.14. Select the Network to be used from the drop-down list and enter the X.25 Address of the RAS server to which you will connect in the field provided.

FIG. 20.14
Parameters for the use of X.25 connections through commercial telephone networks are entered in the X.25 screen of the Phonebook Entry dialog box.

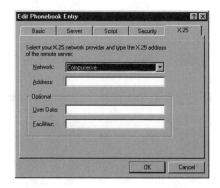

Initiating a RAS Session

Once you have created a phonebook entry, click the Dial button to connect to the remote server. Unless you have elected to use your current user name and password for the remote logon, you will be presented with a dialog box like that shown in figure 20.15, where you can specify the user name and password to be used during the authentication procedure. (These are also the values that will be assigned to the $USERID and $PASSWORD variables used in RAS scripts.)

FIG. 20.15

Enter your user name and password in the Connect to Office dialog box.

Once you are connected to the RAS server, you will be logged on to the network just like any local user. You can then access any network resources (to which you have rights) in the usual manner. If you are connecting to an ISP, or if your private network is connected to the Internet, you will be able to use Windows Sockets applications like Web browsers, Telnet, and FTP without any further adjustments. The installation of the Dial-Up Networking modules in Windows NT Workstation even adds a Dial-Up option to the standard NT logon dialog box, so that you can use RAS to connect to the network immediately upon starting the computer.

From Here...

Because Windows NT's RAS capabilities are a natural extension of its networking architecture, it is important to understand the ways in which the RAS modules fit in the Windows networking model. See the following chapters for more information:

■ Chapter 16, "A Brief Primer on Networks," provides a basic introduction to Windows networking.

■ Chapter 22, "Overview of TCP/IP," and Chapter 23, "Using Basic TCP/IP Services," cover the protocol most often used to establish RAS connections.

■ Chapter 32, "Administering Users," covers the process of creating accounts for your RAS users and controlling their access to network resources.

Using TCP/IP and Internet Features

CHAPTER 21

TCP/IP and Internet Overview

by Jim Boyce

The Internet, since its inception, has been an important research and communication tool for education and government. For the average business user, however, the Internet has been more hype than reality because of limited content and the fact that it was generally not very useful. Only a few years ago, there was very little on the Internet that was of use to the business person. Today's business users enjoy a broad range of useful Internet resources. Business use of the Internet has therefore experienced explosive growth in the past few years.

The vehicle through which Internet traffic happens is Transfer Control Protocol/Internet Protocol (TCP/IP)—the network protocol used for all Internet traffic. Generally, TCP/IP is most commonly used to connect computers to the Internet. Many companies, however, are coming to view TCP/IP as an excellent in-house protocol for their LANs. TCP/IP is a stable, efficient network protocol, and the TCP/IP utilities included with Windows NT are as useful for troubleshooting and management on a LAN as they are for the Internet. ∎

TCP/IP Support in Windows NT

Recognizing the importance of TCP/IP and Internet connectivity to today's personal computer users, Microsoft has built excellent TCP/IP and Internet support into Windows NT. In addition to the TCP/IP protocol itself, Windows NT Workstation includes a selection of TCP/IP connectivity utilities:

- **finger.** The finger utility displays information about a user on a system you specify.
- **ftp.** The file transfer program (ftp) enables you to transfer files between Internet nodes.
- **lpr.** This utility enables you to print to a computer running an LPD server.
- **rcp.** This utility enables you to transfer a file from a Windows NT computer to a system running rshd (remote shell daemon), such as a UNIX computer. It also can be used to transfer files between two computers running rshd.
- **REXEC.** This utility enables you to execute a command on a remote computer running the REXEC service.
- **RSH.** This utility enables you to execute a command on a remote computer running the RSH service.
- **telnet.** With telnet you can log on to computers remotely to run applications and access data.
- **tftp.** The tftp utility enables you to transfer files to and from a remote computer running the tftp service.

Windows NT also includes a good selection of management and troubleshooting tools:

- **arp.** The arp utility modifies the IP-to-Ethernet or Token Ring address translation tables used by the Address Resolution Protocol (ARP), and is useful for overcoming routing problems.
- **hostname.** This utility displays the host name of the current computer.
- **ipconfig.** The ipconfig utility displays all current TCP/IP settings.
- **lpq.** The lpq utility enables you to determine the status of a print queue on a remote computer running the LPD service.
- **nbtstat.** This diagnostic utility displays current protocol statistics and network connections using NetBIOS over TCP/IP.
- **netstat.** This utility displays current protocol statistics and network connections.
- **ping.** This diagnostic utility tests connections to other TCP/IP nodes by sending and receiving test packets.

- **route.** The route utility enables you to manipulate network routing tables to overcome routing problems.

- **tracert.** The tracert utility enables you to trace the route to a given destination node.

Each of these TCP/IP utilities can be very useful in transferring data and troubleshooting connections. Those of you who are familiar with UNIX and the corresponding UNIX equivalents of these utilities will have no trouble using them under Windows NT. If you're new to TCP/IP or these utilities, you'll find complete coverage of them in Chapter 22, "Overview of TCP/IP."

DHCP

DHCP (Dynamic Host Control Protocol) is a mechanism by which a DHCP server manages and assigns IP addresses to computers within its IP domain. DHCP is an important tool for efficiently managing IP address in an intranet, particularly for dial-up users. If you have 200 users who dial into your TCP/IP network, but only have 50 connections available (through modems, for example), it is much more efficient to allocate only 50 IP addresses for those dial-up users, rather than 200. Because only 50 can connect at a time, allocating 200 IP addresses would be a waste of 150 addresses you could use internally. Through DHCP, however, dial-up users would automatically be assigned an IP address when they connect to the network. Their IP addresses would therefore vary from one connection to another.

 DHCP is also useful for allocating IP addresses locally on a network because it simplifies IP address management. Rather than assigning addresses manually and having to keep track of them, you can allow a DHCP server to assign them automatically.

Windows NT Workstation fully supports DHCP, as you will learn in Chapter 24, "Using DHCP."

DNS and WINS

Another important TCP/IP issue is host name resolution—resolving IP domain names into IP addresses. Through support for Domain Name Service (DNS) and Windows Internet Name Service (WINS), Windows NT enables you to use easy-to-remember domain names rather than cryptic IP addresses when establishing network connections.

DNS is the standard name resolution mechanism on the Internet, and the one supported by UNIX systems. Windows NT provides full support for DNS, both as a client and server.

WINS provides a more dynamic name resolution mechanism and relies on a Windows NT WINS server to resolve host names. In addition to resolving IP host names, a WINS server also can resolve NetBIOS names into their IP addresses. Your computer's NetBIOS name is its name on your LAN, and can be different from your computer's TCP/IP host name. By also resolving NetBIOS names, WINS makes it even easier to connect to resources on your network.

You'll find complete coverage of both DNS and WINS in Chapter 25, "Using DNS and WINS."

Peer Web Services

Windows NT includes a set of features collectively called Peer Web Services that enable you to turn a Windows NT workstation into a peer Web server on an intranet or the Internet. In addition, application developers are beginning to take advantage of ActiveX and Java to integrate advanced features into their Internet-aware applications. But using ActiveX or Java is not without pitfalls. You'll find in-depth coverage of both in Chapter 26, "Installing and Configuring Peer Web Services," along with specific tips on setting up and using Peer Web Services. ●

CHAPTER 22

Overview of TCP/IP

by Craig Zacker

As the Internet explosion consumes the computer industry, an increasing amount of attention is being paid to one of the oldest networking protocol suites still in general use. TCP/IP is the *lingua franca* of the Internet, and all but universal on UNIX networks, but it is only recently that mainstream network operating systems like NetWare and Windows NT have begun to use it.

Many administrators of heterogeneous networks are realizing that network traffic can be reduced and efficiency increased by selecting a single set of protocols for use with all of their network operating systems, instead of having two or three proprietary protocol suites that share the same medium. In most cases, TCP/IP is the only candidate that fits the bill for all of their hardware and software. ■

The history of TCP/IP

The unique requirements imposed on its developers led to the qualities praised in TCP/IP today.

Understanding TCP/IP communications

Understand how the different protocols fit into the OSI reference model, and how the functions of the protocols combine to produce the efficiency for which they are known.

Integrating TCP/IP into a Windows NT network

You learn how the protocols integrate with the Windows NT network communications stack, and how you can use TCP/IP as your sole Windows NT networking protocol.

Using TCP/IP utilities

Windows NT ships with its own versions of many standard TCP/IP utilities. This section covers their purpose and use.

A Brief History of TCP/IP

TCP/IP is the common name given to a suite of protocols that was developed during the 1970s for use on a large-scale military internetworking project called the ARPANET. In 1969, under the auspices of DARPA (Defense Advanced Research Projects Agency), computers of all different types were joined in an experimental attempt to create a universal packet-switching network environment.

The computer networks that existed at this time were mostly of proprietary design turnkey solutions devised and marketed by a single manufacturer. The ARPANET was designed from the start to be a research platform aimed toward greater networking compatibility, and was kept free from the influence of any one particular vendor of computer products.

Development of a Standard

This experimental network quickly came to be more than a research platform. It was relied on by many of its users for everyday traffic, as it provided an avenue of communication that was not available before. In 1975, it became an operational network, and development of the protocols that were to become TCP/IP began around this time. TCP/IP is a shorthand expression for Transport Control Protocol/Internet Protocol, which are the two most commonly used protocols in the suite.

The protocols became ratified military standards in 1983, and all computers connected to ARPANET were required to use them. It was about this time that the term *Internet* began to be used to refer to the combined network that was now composed of two entities: ARPANET and its military adjunct, MILNET. With DARPA's help, the TCP/IP protocols were incorporated into the Berkeley (BSD) UNIX operating system, beginning the association of TCP/IP and UNIX.

Founding Concepts

The TCP/IP protocols were designed with several concepts in mind that were innovative at the time, and are still the primary reasons for the protocols' continued popularity today. These are:

- **Hardware Independence.** The protocols are not bound or limited to any specific hardware or software platform.
- **Standardized Addressing.** Any host computer on any TCP/IP network can be individually and specifically addressed, even when connected to a network as large as the Internet.

■ **Open Standards.** The TCP/IP protocols are based on standards documents that are publicly available and may be used freely for any hardware or software development project.

■ **Application-level Protocols.** The standards include protocols functioning at the highest levels of the networking model (for example, FTP, SMTP), providing unified access between diverse environments and operating systems.

These features merit further discussion, as they are crucial to the implementation of TCP/IP on a Windows NT network.

Hardware Independence   From its inception, it was understood that the Internet would consist of computers of all different types. It was therefore imperative that protocols be developed that did not rely on the computer's hardware or its operating system in any way for the accomplishment of their stated functions. The protocols must have clearly defined interfaces, both at the top (for interaction with various applications) and at the bottom (for use with many kinds of different hardware).

TCP/IP successfully achieves all of these goals. Its protocols are used on computers ranging from micros to mainframes and on networks of all types.

Host Addresses   For organized network communication to take place, there must be a method by which each machine on the network is uniquely identified. This is usually accomplished by the assignment of two different addresses: one unique identifier for the network on which a group of computers is located, and then another unique identifier for each node on that network. Both of these addresses can cause problems for a potential Internet protocol.

On local area networks, each node has a unique number assigned to its network interface adapter, either at the factory or by the administrator. Many protocols rely on this interface node address as a means of identifying each computer on a network. TCP/IP, however, was not to be limited to LANs or to any particular kind of network, nor could it rely on any other computer resource for any of its functions. It had to supply an address of its own.

Unlike node addresses, network addresses are usually defined by the network administrators themselves. For use on a corporate internetwork, this is perfectly acceptable, as long as the administrator gives each network a unique address. For a protocol used on the Internet, however, which would link hundreds and eventually thousands of different networks together, there had to be a way of centrally assigning network addresses, so as to allow no duplication. This central assignment of network addresses must also be organized in such a way as to minimize the administrative overhead. Keeping track of network address assignments for a worldwide internetwork would be an administrative nightmare.

The TCP/IP protocols, along with some high-level organizational bodies, accomplish this end, providing every computer on the Internet with its own unique address.

Open Standards   The TCP/IP protocols are based on standards documents that are freely available to anyone, both for consumption and for criticism. While many networking standards are developed by mysterious, elite, international organizations with long acronyms, proposed changes to the TCP/IP specifications can be submitted by anyone. Indeed, the standards documents themselves are known as Requests for Comment (RFCs). While some RFCs admittedly stray well into the technological stratosphere, a great many of them are actually useful, readable documents that can help you understand the more detailed or obscure aspects of TCP/IP and the Internet.

ON THE WEB

Internet Requests for Comment (RFCs) are available on many anonymous FTP servers, worldwide. Some are listed here:

> **DS.INTERNIC.NET**
> **NIS.NSF.NET**
> **NISC.JVNC.NET**
> **FTP.ISI.EDU**
> **WUARCHIVE.WUSTL.EDU**
> **SRC.DOC.IC.AC.UK**
> **FTP.NCREN.NET**
> **FTP.SESQUI.NET**
> **NIS.GARR.IT**

Most of the sites place the documents in a top-level directory called RFC. Most of the files are ASCII text, but PostScript is used for documents containing graphics or illustrations.

Application Protocols   Many of the programs that are commonly associated with TCP/IP networks and with the Internet are actually application-layer protocols that are defined in the Internet RFCs. When TCP/IP is used to link different types of computers, third-party products are often used to facilitate the interface between machines. Even without such products, native TCP/IP utilities like Telnet and FTP provide a unified (albeit rudimentary) access between unlike systems. When you sit at your Windows NT workstation and download an RFC document from one of the anonymous FTP servers listed here, you might be accessing a UNIX machine, a mainframe, or another Windows NT box, but it won't make any difference. You might be lost if you sat in front of that remote machine's console, but with a few simple FTP commands, you can traverse its directory structure and access its files, thanks to TCP/IP.

Fitting TCP/IP into the OSI Reference Model

As with most of the protocols used in the real world, it is difficult to fit TCP/IP neatly into the networking layers defined by the OSI reference model. The suite consists of many protocols, most of which are used for specific purposes. However, the basic operational functionality of the OSI model, in which successive protocols each adds its own header to a data packet as it travels down the stack, is in place.

The two OSI layers that are most obviously represented, however, even in the name of the suite, are the Transport and Network layers. TCP, the Transport Control Protocol, and IP, the Internet Protocol, fit into the functions of these two layers perfectly.

As discussed in Chapter 16, "A Brief Primer on Networks," the Network and Transport layers are responsible for the transmission of data packets from their source to their destination. IP functions at the Network layer, and is the only protocol that is used by all TCP/IP transmissions. In TCP/IP parlance, the individual packets are called *datagrams*. Datagrams are the fundamental data units of a TCP/IP network, created by the IP protocol and passed down to the layers below, where they are packaged for their introduction to the physical network medium.

Beneath the Network layer are a large number of specialized network access protocols used to facilitate the interface of IP with whatever network type is represented in the Data Link and Physical layers. In Windows NT, the network interface is controlled by the NDIS (Network Driver Interface Specification) driver, which is not part of the TCP/IP suite. When datagrams are passed down through the NDIS layer, they must be adapted to the needs of the physical network.

Above the Network layer, the two protocols most often used are TCP and UDP, the User Datagram Protocol. Together with IP, these protocols account for nearly all of the end-to-end TCP/IP traffic across the internetwork. Above the Transport layer are many of the protocols that are known to users, such as FTP, Telnet, and SMTP. Several others are designed to be all but invisible to the average user, such as RIP, DNS, and NFS.

The higher level protocols tend to overlap the top three layers of the OSI model in various ways. Elements of Session and Presentation layer functionality are often present, but these are most often referred to as Application layer protocols.

As you can see in figure 22.1, the TCP/IP protocols comprise their own four-layer protocol stack within the overall stack that represents the entire computer system. The Network and Transport layers correspond with their OSI model equivalents. The Application layer protocols perform various upper layer functions, and the Network Access protocols furnish any part of typical Data Link or Physical layer functionality.

FIG. 22.1

The protocols of the TCP/IP suite operate on four levels within the OSI reference model.

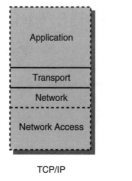

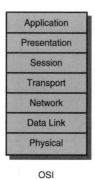

TCP/IP   OSI

The following sections examine these four layers in detail, as well as the major protocols that can run in them on Windows NT systems.

The Network Access Layer

As the name implies, TCP/IP's Network Access layer protocols are used to prepare IP datagrams for introduction onto the network medium, whatever that may be.

As explained earlier, TCP/IP provides its own host addressing system, used to identify each of the host computers on an IP network. The header that is added to the datagram by IP as it passes through the Network layer specifies the IP addresses of the datagram's source and destination. However, once the datagram is passed from the Network layer to the next layer below, the datagram must be packaged for transmission over the network. Another header and footer are added to the datagram to accommodate whatever network type is being used to send the packet, be it Ethernet, Token Ring, X.25, or any other.

Obviously, for the packet to reach its destination successfully there must a protocol for the conversion of the IP address to whatever addressing mechanism is used at the Data Link layer. This is the primary function of the Network Access protocols in the TCP/IP suite. Because the network's Data Link protocol is unaware of TCP/IP's addressing scheme, TCP/IP must be made aware of the network's scheme.

Probably the best known of the TCP/IP Network Access protocols is called the Address Resolution Protocol, or ARP. The primary function of ARP is to translate the IP addresses of computers on the network to Ethernet addresses and back again, allowing a properly formulated Ethernet frame to be created.

When IP finishes packaging a datagram and passes it down to ARP, the datagram's destination IP address is looked up in a table of IP addresses and their equivalent Ethernet addresses that ARP maintains. If the address is not found, ARP broadcasts an ARP request packet containing the new IP address over the network. The computer to which that IP address belongs responds with an ARP reply packet containing the Ethernet address of the host. The sending computer then updates its table with the new entry for future use. The reply packet also can be broadcast over the network so that all machines running TCP/IP can update their ARP tables. In Windows NT, the ARP utility is used to view the contents of the computer's ARP table.

N O T E See Chapter 23 "Using Basic TCP/IP Services" for more information on using Windows NT's ARP utility. The ARP protocol is defined in RFC 826, *Address Resolution Protocol*. ▨

ARP is only one of many Network Access protocols that are used to prepare IP datagrams for transmission. Remember that TCP/IP is used to transmit data over many radically different types of networks. There are as many protocols as there are network types, and new protocols must be developed whenever a new network type comes into general use. Windows NT is compliant with only a relatively small number of network types, however (when compared to the entire world of computing), so only a few of the network access protocols are provided with the operating system.

The Network Layer

Functioning at the Network layer, IP, the Internet Protocol (defined in RFC 791), is the most important, most heavily used protocol of the suite. All of the higher-level protocols use IP as the transport vehicle for their network communications. Among the functions performed by IP are:

- The packaging of upper layer data into datagrams
- The implementation of the TCP/IP host addressing system
- The routing of datagrams between different networks
- The fragmentation and defragmentation of datagrams to accommodate the requirements of different network types
- The passing of data between the Transport and Network Access layers in both directions

IP is what's known as an unreliable, connectionless protocol. Far from reflecting on its efficiency, these terms define the nature of IP's communications capabilities. A *connectionless* protocol is one that transmits packets without having previously ascertained the availability of the destination computer. A *connection-oriented* protocol exchanges a series of packets (called a handshake) with the destination node, establishing a connection before any user data is actually transmitted. IP packets may therefore be sent out over the network, even when the receiving node is unavailable. Packets may also arrive at the destination by different routes, and consequently, in a different order than they were sent.

IP is also called an *unreliable* protocol, in a technical sense, because it has no mechanisms of its own for error detection and correction. If used by itself, therefore, no guarantee is given that datagrams will arrive at their destination in the order in which they were sent, or even that they will arrive at all. Packets sent to an unavailable destination may be lost, without any indication to the sender that a failure has taken place.

Fortunately, IP is rarely, if ever, used alone. It functions instead as the carrier for other protocols. IP is the envelope providing basic packet delivery functions, while the mechanisms for guaranteeing delivery are supplied by higher layer protocols. One of the basic measures of a network's efficiency is the ratio of control information to actual user data in network communications. A connection-oriented transmission with full error detection adds a significant amount of overhead (in the form of extra control bits) to a transmission. By implementing these additional functions at the higher layers, they can be supplied only for the transmissions that require them. IP works hand-in-hand with the upper layer protocols to provide only the reliability that is needed, when it is needed.

The IP Header   A request from an application is passed down through the layers of the protocol stack, with each protocol adding its own header (and sometimes footer as well) to the existing packet. By the time the packet reaches the Physical layer, it consists of several headers, with the original request encapsulated in the center. It is the addition of the IP header that establishes a packet's identity as a datagram.

The IP header consists of as many as 24 octets (which is the term for bytes, in TCP/IP-speak) of control information, usually broken down into 32-bit words, that provide all the information that is needed to transmit the datagram to its ultimate destination. This header is attached to the beginning of every packet received from the Transport layer before it is passed to the Network Access layer below. The layout of the IP header is shown in figure 22.2.

The IP header is composed of the following fields:

First Word

- **Version (4 bits)**. Indicates the version of the IP header being used (this is version 4).

- **Internet Header Length (IHL) (4 bits)**. Accounts for the optional sixth word by specifying the overall length of the IP header (in 32-bit words).

- **Type of Service (8 bits)**. Used to indicate the network service priority desired for this datagram, based on current network traffic levels and predetermined transmission parameters.

FIG. 22.2
The IP protocol header contains all of the information needed to deliver a datagram to its destination.

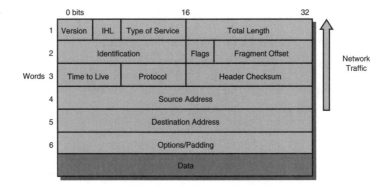

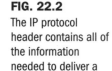

- **Total Length (16 bits).** Indicates the overall length of the datagram in octets (bytes); used to determine whether or not datagrams must be fragmented for transmission over a particular network.

Second Word

- **Identification (16 bits).** Used in the fragmentation/defragmentation process to identify the datagram to which a fragment belongs.

- **Flags (3 bits).** Used in the fragmentation/defragmentation process to indicate whether the given datagram may be fragmented, and whether or not all of the fragments composing the original datagram have been received.

- **Fragmentation Offset (13 bits).** Used in the fragmentation/defragmentation process to define the starting point of this fragment in the reassembled datagram (measured in units of 64 bits).

Third Word

- **Time to Live (8 bits).** Indicates the amount of time (in seconds) that the datagram may remain in the internet system, providing a means for the automatic removal of undeliverable datagrams from the network. This value is decremented by at least one second every module processing the datagram (even if the process has taken less than a second).

- **Protocol (8 bits).** Specifies the Transport layer protocol for which the datagram is destined at the receiving node.

- **Header Checksum (16 bits).** Used to verify the correct transmission of the IP header only; no error detection or correction of the user data is performed by IP. This value is recomputed and verified each time any field in the header (such as Time to Live) is modified.

Fourth Word

■ **Source Address (32 bits).** The IP address of the computer sending the datagram.

Fifth Word

■ **Destination Address (32 bits).** The IP address of the computer that will ulti-mately receive the datagram.

Sixth Word (optional)

■ **Options (variable).** Used to enable certain routing, security, or time stamp options in a particular datagram. The options and the option field may or may not appear in a particular datagram, but they must be supported by all IP modules.

■ **Padding (variable).** Additional bits used to pad the option field into a 32-bit word.

IP Routing   As with the Network layer protocols, IP is responsible for routing datagrams between different networks. Computers on a TCP/IP network are said to be either *end systems* or *intermediate systems*. End systems are attached only to a single network and are typically called *hosts*, while intermediate systems are connected to two or more net-works. Intermediate systems on TCP/IP networks are also referred to as *gateways*.

> **N O T E**   The term *gateway* is often used in networking to refer to an interface between unlike protocols. This is not necessarily the case in TCP/IP. An IP gateway functions solely at the Network layer, performing the function of what is more often called a router, exchanging datagrams between networks that may be of the same type. ■

When the IP protocol on an end system receives a packet from an upper layer protocol, it examines the packet's destination address to determine the network on which the destina-tion system is located. If the destination is on the local network, then the datagram is sent directly to that address. If the destination address is on another network, then the datagram is sent to the IP layer of a gateway, an intermediate system where the same decision is made for the next leg of the journey. IP is not aware of the entire trip that will be made by the datagram from source to destination. It is only aware of its own network, and the gateways to other immediately adjacent networks.

As shown in figure 22.3, datagrams that pass through the entire protocol stack on host systems only reach as high as the IP layer on gateways.

On your company's internal network, packets may pass through three or four different networks on their trip from source to destination. When an IP datagram is sent over the Internet, however, it may wind its way through dozens of gateways and many different physical network types before reaching its destination. TCP/IP provides the means to traverse these distances efficiently, and most of the primary tools are provided by IP and its helper protocol, ICMP.

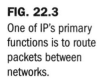

FIG. 22.3
One of IP's primary functions is to route packets between networks.

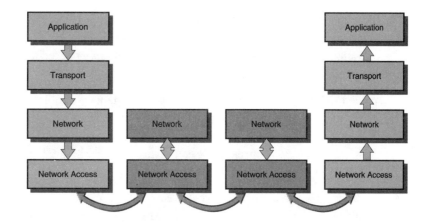

Datagram Fragmentation When datagrams pass through multiple gateways to reach their destinations, they may also have to pass through unlike networks. A typical example of this may be a system or router that is used to connect a corporate network to the Internet. Such a gateway will have one host interface for the internal network (an Ethernet adapter, for example), and a second interface connecting to an Internet service provider using, say, a T-1 connection.

When routing datagrams from the internal network to the Internet, IP compares the maximum transmission units (MTU) for both networks to determine if the datagrams can be sent as is. In this example, it is likely to be found that the Internet connection cannot handle packets as large as those sent over the Ethernet network. It is then the responsibility of the IP implementation in the gateway to begin a process called *fragmentation*, by which each of the larger datagrams are split into several smaller datagrams for transmission.

The process is then reversed at the receiving system; the fragments are reassembled into their original form using the information furnished in the second word of the IP header, described above. After a Flag informs the recipient that all of the fragments comprising a particular datagram have been sent, IP compares the Identification numbers to gather all the fragments of that datagram, and then assembles them in the order specified in the Fragmentation Offset field.

Fragmentation is one of the features of TCP/IP that allows it to be used on so many diverse network types, while adapting to the capabilities of each.

The Internet Control Message Protocol As defined in RFC 792, the Internet Control Message Protocol (or ICMP) provides additional control functions for IP that help it to achieve greater efficiency. It is the only other TCP/IP protocol that operates at the Network layer. Encapsulated with IP datagrams themselves, ICMP messages can provide several additional functions to the IP service.

If you have ever used the TCP/IP PING utility, then you have explicitly used an ICMP function. PING sends an ICMP *echo request* packet to a designated host. If the host is operating properly, it responds with an ICMP *echo reply* packet of its own, thus assuring the sender of its availability.

While PING uses ICMP packets to ascertain the status of another host at the user's request, a similar function can be performed during regular processing, without an explicit command. ICMP packets are often sent to inform a sending computer that a datagram's destination address is unreachable, specifying further whether it is the destination's network, host, protocol, or port that is unavailable.

ICMP packets also are used to provide flow control. When a system receiving datagrams from a particular sender starts to be overwhelmed by too many packets, it directs ICMP Source Quench messages at the sender, which slows down its transmission rate until the messages are no longer received.

ICMP is also used to inform a host that its datagrams must be fragmented to reach their destination, or that datagrams have been discarded by an intermediate or end system due to corruption having been detected in the header. It should be emphasized that the use of ICMP for these functions does not guarantee the reliability of IP transmissions. Datagrams may still fail to reach their destination without the host being informed, unless a higher level protocol is used to provide this function.

Another important function of ICMP is that it is used to help sending hosts make the most efficient routing decisions possible. The IP layer of any host is only directly aware of computers on the networks to which it is attached. When a host computer is located on the same network as two or more gateways, it has a choice as to which gateway it should use to access other networks.

Having no way of knowing which gateway is the more efficient route to the destination, the host will send its datagrams to the default gateway defined in the TCP/IP configuration. This gateway, knowing of the computers located on two or more networks, may be able to determine that the host's datagrams could be routed more efficiently if they were sent through a different gateway. It will then generate an ICMP Redirect message to inform the host of this fact.

ICMP is only used, in this respect, when a gateway supplies routing information to a host. A different protocol is used when two gateways must communicate, called (not surprisingly) the Gateway to Gateway Protocol (GGP).

The Transport Layer

Two protocols operate at the Transport layer of the TCP/IP stack. One is TCP, the Transport Control Protocol itself, and the other is the User Datagram Protocol (UDP). These two protocols provide different levels of service to a transmission, but they share one common function: to deliver datagrams to the appropriate port on the host system.

N O T E Port numbers are used to identify the upper layer processes for which transmissions are intended. Port numbers are discussed later in this chapter. ▓

The User Datagram Protocol UDP (defined in RFC 768), like IP, is a connectionless, unreliable protocol that allows applications to exchange messages with a minimum of control overhead. It is not generally used for the transmission of user data, which requires a greater degree of reliability. UDP adds only a two-word header to a datagram, as shown in figure 22.4.

FIG. 22.4
The UDP frame header adds a minimum of overhead to the datagram.

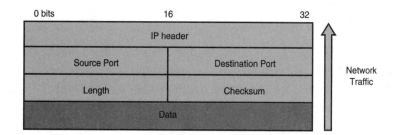

The UDP header is composed of the following fields:

First Word

- ▪ **Source Port (16 bits)**. An optional value indicating the location of the sending process in the host computer (padded with zeroes if omitted).

- ▪ **Destination Port (16 bits)**. Used in combination with the IP address (furnished by the IP header) to identify the process in the destination system for which the datagram is intended.

Second word

- ▪ **Length (16 bits)**. Specifies the length of the datagram, in octets, including this header and the enclosed data (but not including the IP header and other outer frames).

- ▪ **Checksum (16 bits)**. This is a checksum value computed on the UDP header and data, plus a pseudo-header composed of the Source Address, Destination Address and Protocol fields from the IP header.

UDP is not used as much as TCP. It adds little or no value to the protocol stack, except for the port number of the destination process. It is used in situations when application layer protocols supply the mechanisms for transmission reliability, or when the datagrams are so small that a complete retransmission of the packet uses less overhead than would the addition of error detection capability.

An application might use a UDP transmission when it is sending a query to another computer, from which it expects an immediate reply. The failure to receive a reply causes the application to resend the query. Two of the application protocols in the TCP/IP suite that do rely on UDP are the Internet Name Server Protocol (INSP) and the Trivial File Transfer Protocol (TFTP).

The Transport Control Protocol   The most commonly used protocol combination, as the name of the suite implies, is TCP over IP. TCP (defined in RFC 793) is the perfect counterpart to IP in that it supplies the connection-oriented, reliable delivery service that IP lacks. Most of the commonly used TCP/IP applications, including FTP, Telnet, and HTTP, all rely on TCP for accurate transmission of data. Like UDP, TCP also supplies the port number of the process at the destination system for which the transmission is intended.

Before any user data is transmitted, TCP contacts the destination host and exchanges what is known as a three-way handshake. This is used to ensure that the destination is ready to receive data and to exchange sequencing information so that both systems can verify that all packets are received in the correct order. This is what is meant by a connection-oriented protocol. After the connection is established between source and destination, a TCP transmission is no longer thought of in terms of discrete datagrams. Instead, each packet is considered to be a *segment* of the overall transmission.

TCP uses a system called *positive acknowledgment with retransmission* to guarantee the reliable delivery of each segment. The sending host transmits its segments; those that are not acknowledged by the destination within a certain time-out period are automatically retransmitted. The header for each segment includes a checksum computed on the segment's data field as well as the header information. This is recomputed at the destination to verify that the segment is undamaged.

The TCP header is necessarily more complex than those of UDP and even IP, because it must provide the means for control information to pass in both directions. The layout of the TCP segment header is shown in figure 22.5.

The TCP header is composed of the following fields:

First Word

- **Source Port (16 bits)**. The port number of the process at the source computer that is generating the transmission.

FIG. 22.5

The TCP segment header includes fields that are used to provide guaranteed, reliable delivery of data.

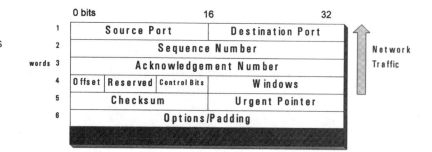

- **Destination Port (16 bits).** The port number of the process at the destination computer that is to receive the transmission.

Second Word

- **Sequence Number (32 bits).** Specifies the number of the first octet in this segment out of the entire sequence; used to maintain the correct order of the segments.

Third Word

- **Acknowledgment Number (32 bits).** Specifies the sequence number of the next segment that the destination computer expects to receive.

Fourth Word

- **Data Offset (4 bits).** Specifies the length of the TCP segment header in 32-bit words, indicating the beginning of the data field.

- **Reserved (6 bits).** For future use; value must be zero.

- **Control Bits (6 bits).** Six binary flags used to indicate the function or purpose of the segment:

URG:	Urgent Pointer field significant
ACK:	Acknowledgment field significant
PSH:	Push Function
RST:	Reset the connection
SYN:	Synchronize sequence numbers
FIN:	No more data from sender

- **Window (16 bits).** The number of octets (beginning at the sequence number specified in the Acknowledgment field) which the destination computer is able to accept from the source; used for flow control.

Fifth Word

- **Checksum (16 bits).** Computed on the TCP header and data fields, plus a pseudo-header composed of the Source Address, Destination Address, and Protocol fields from the IP header as well as the combined length of the TCP header and data fields. The pseudo-header protects against TCP segment misrouting by reverifying the IP fields.

- **Urgent Pointer (16 bits)**. Specifies the location of urgent data relative to the Sequence Number of this segment; only used when the URG control bit is set.

  Sixth Word (optional)

- **Options (variable)**. Used to supply various optional values. The only actively used option is a specification of the maximum segment size allowed at the computer sending this segment; this option is only used during a TCP connection handshake (when the SYN control bit is set).

- **Padding (variable)**. Used to pad the option field with zeroes in order to fill the 32-bit word.

When a computer seeks to initiate a TCP transmission, it sends an initial packet to the destination with the SYN control bit set. This packet contains no user data, but it does specify the beginning sequence number that is used by the source. The destination computer then responds with its own packet, with the ACK bit set and its own beginning sequence number. Each computer uses its own sequence numbers, but each maintains a track of the others' numbering.

After the handshake is completed, the actual transmission of data begins. In a TCP/IP transmission, the term sequence refers to the entire data stream sent during the connection; however, many segments are required. The source computer includes a sequence number in every segment that specifies the number of the first byte included in that segment, out of the total number of bytes for the entire sequence. This number, therefore, can be used by the destination computer to verify that the segments have been received in the proper order.

The destination computer also sends segments back to the source, the purpose of these being to supply positive acknowledgment of receipt and provide flow control. The Acknowledgment Number in such a packet indicates to the source that all of the bytes in the sequence prior to that number have been received undamaged. It is therefore unnecessary for an acknowledgment to be sent for every individual segment. If no acknowledgments are received by the source in a given period of time, it begins retransmitting segments from the last positively acknowledged sequence number. If retransmissions are not acknowledged either, the sending computer will eventually time out and consider the connection to be broken.

The Window field in an acknowledgment segment informs the source computer of the maximum number of octets (beyond the octet number specified in the Acknowledgment Number field) that can be accepted by the destination. This allows the source computer to adjust its transmission rate accordingly.

After all of the user data has been transmitted, a segment with the FIN control bit is sent, informing the destination that there is no more data and begins breaking down the logical connection between the two computers.

TCP provides an extremely reliable medium for the transfer of data, but the cost in terms of control traffic is high, as you can see by comparing the TCP and UDP headers. This is one of the reasons why reliability services are usually provided in higher level protocols. This way, they can be selectively applied only to the data that requires them.

The Application Layer

At the Application layer of the TCP/IP stack are all of the protocols that make use of the underlying Transport and Network protocols for their transmissions. TCP/IP includes many different application protocols, some of which the user interacts with directly, and others that function all but invisibly to the user. Windows NT supports many of these protocols, but you should be aware even of those that are not supported, especially if you are going to use TCP/IP to connect to the Internet.

The best known of the TCP/IP Application layer protocols are:

- **FTP.** This is the File Transfer Protocol that allows you to access the file system of remote computers using a standardized interface that is irrespective of either computer's native file system.
- **Telnet.** The Network Terminal Protocol allows you remote access to another TCP/IP system on the network using a standardized interface.
- **SMTP.** Simple Mail Transfer Protocol is used by many e-mail server programs to deliver electronic mail both internally and over the Internet.
- **DNS.** The Domain Name Service is used to associate numerical IP addresses with their host and domain names.
- **RIP.** This is the Routing Information Protocol that is used to exchange data between computers that helps them to make more efficient routing decisions and bypass non-functioning routers.
- **NFS.** A Network File System that can be used by different types of computers to provide a common file system that is fully accessible over a network.

FTP and Telnet are examined in detail later in this chapter. Windows NT also provides its own additional modules to supplement the application protocols defined by the TCP/IP standards. For example, while Windows NT uses the DNS for IP name resolution, it also supplies WINS, the Windows Internet Naming Service, which improves on the DNS concept by performing a similar function for NetBIOS names.

▶ **See** "WINS Name Resolution," **p. 588**

Understanding TCP/IP Communications

For TCP/IP communications to take place, the datagrams generated by the source computer must find their way to the destination network, and then to the destination host computer, and then to the destination transport protocol, and then to the destination application port. There are three TCP/IP processes responsible for the accomplishment of these tasks:

- **Addressing.** The process by which each network and host computer on an internetwork is uniquely identified.

- **Routing.** The process by which datagrams pass through gateways to reach the destination network.

- **Multiplexing.** The process by which data is forwarded to the correct protocol and port, out of many that may be running on the computer.

IP Addressing

The IP address is the single most innovative aspect of the TCP/IP protocol suite. It can identify any single host computer on an internetwork, even on the Internet. An IP address consists of 32 bits, notated as four decimal values representing one octet each, separated by periods. An octet can have any value from 0 to 255, although certain address values are not used, having been reserved for other purposes.

An IP address identifies both a particular network and the individual host on that network.

N O T E The term host is not synonymous with computer or system. A single computer can interface with more than one network, and consequently can have more than one host. Each host, however, must have its own IP address. ■

If you are running TCP/IP on an internal network (that is, one that is not linked to the Internet), then you can assign any valid IP address values that you want to your networks and hosts. Any computers that you will be connecting directly to the Internet, however, must be on a network with an address that has been registered with InterNIC, the Internet Network Information Center. InterNIC is the clearinghouse for all Internet IP addresses, ensuring that every host's address is unique.

InterNIC does not register individual hosts, only networks. Host addresses are assigned by the administrators of the individual networks. The network address is part of the 32-bit

IP address. Which part of the address represents the network and which part represents the host is determined by the address class and the subnet mask.

IP Address Classes   InterNIC registers three different classes of IP address that theoretically are assigned depending on the needs of the organizations receiving them. The class is identified by the values of the first three bits of the address.

N O T E   Remember that although IP addresses are always notated using decimal values, they are actually 32-bit binary numbers. There are times when the binary values of the individual bits are more easily understood than their equivalent decimal values. This is particularly true in matters of address classification and subnet masking. ■

- **Class A**. The first bit of a class A address is always 0, meaning that the first octet of the address can have a value between 1 and 126. Only the first octet is used to represent the network, leaving the final three octets to identify 16,777,214 possible hosts.

- **Class B**. The first two bits of a class B network are always 1 and 0, meaning that the first octet can have a value between 128 and 191. The first two octets are used to identify 16,384 possible networks, leaving the final two octets to identify 65,534 possible hosts.

- **Class C**. The first three bits of a class C network are always 1, 1, and 0, meaning that the first octet can have a value between 192 and 223. The first three octets are used to identify 2,097,151 possible networks, leaving the final octet to identify 254 possible hosts.

CAUTION

There are also certain IP addresses that should never be assigned to networks or hosts:

- The value 127 in the first octet is reserved for loopback testing of local computer operations. It allows a host, essentially, to ping itself.

- The values 0 and 255 should not be used for any octet, as these are the accepted values for broadcast addresses (addresses that transmit to every station on the network).

- The values 224-254 in the first octet (representing an address with 1, 1, and 1 as its first three bits and sometimes referred to as a class D address) are reserved for special use by other protocols as multicast addresses (addresses representing groups of hosts).

Subnet Masking   If you have a network address registered with InterNIC, this does not mean that you are forced to run all of your computers on a single network. You can use a subnet mask to divide your assigned network into subnetworks and assign IP addresses based on the physical layout of your internetwork.

A *subnet mask* is a filter registered in your TCP/IP stack that tells the system which bits of the IP address represent the network and which represent the host. The mask is expressed in the form of a normal decimal IP address, but it is easier to think of it in its binary equivalent. A subnet mask is 32 bits in which 1s indicate the part of the address representing the network and 0s represent the host.

For example, if you have a small one-segment network and you obtain a class C address, then you can use it without modification. You would enter a subnet mask of 255.255.255.0 in all of your computers, and assign individual host addresses using the values 1 to 254 in the last octet of the IP address. The 255s represent binary octet values of 11111111, meaning that all of the first three octets are used to identify the network.

A more complicated example would be when you are assigned a class B address and you have an internetwork of your own that is composed of many individual segments. It would be impractical to use the class B address as it is (with a subnet of 255.255.0.0), and number the hosts in a single sequence from 1 to 65,534, using the last two octets. Instead, you would rather establish subnets that represent the physical segments on your internetwork. You would do this by applying a subnet mask of 255.255.255.0 on all of your hosts. The first two octets of their IP addresses would be the values assigned by InterNIC. The third octet, however, would now represent part of the network address instead of the host. You can assign values to this third octet representing each of the segments on your network, and then use only the fourth octet to address as many as 254 hosts on each subnet.

Subnet masking can be more complicated still, when a mask is applied only to certain bits of an octet. Careful conversion between binary and decimal values is then necessary to prevent improper configurations.

Subnet masking is something that must be organized on a internetwork-wide basis. The individual TCP/IP user should consult the network administrator to find out how the network addresses are formed before manually assigning a subnet mask. Fortunately for users and administrators alike, the subnet mask is one of the many TCP/IP parameters that can be automatically furnished to a workstation using the Windows NT DHCP (Dynamic Host Configuration Protocol) service.

▶ **See** "Advantages of Windows NT's DHCP Server," **p. 554**

ON THE WEB

InterNIC can be contacted by phone at (800) 444-4345 in the United States, (619) 455-4600 in Canada, or by electronic mail at info@internic.net. Requests for Internet registration can be sent to hostmaster@internic.net. More information about the registration process is available from the anonymous FTP server: is.internic.net, in the /INFOSOURCE/FAQ directory.

IP Routing

Before IP datagrams can be delivered to the correct host, they must be delivered to the correct network. When the source and destination computers are not on the same network, then one or more gateways are used to route packets to the correct network.

Every TCP/IP system maintains an internal routing table that helps it to make routing decisions. For the average host computer, located on a network segment with only a single gateway, the routing decisions are simple: either a packet is sent to a destination host on the same network, or it is sent to the gateway. As stated earlier, IP is aware only of the computers on the networks to which it is directly attached. It is up to each individual gateway to route the packets on their next leg of the journey to the destination.

It may be the case that a host computer is located on a network segment with more than one gateway. Initially, packets addressed to other networks are all sent to the default gateway that is set as part of the host configuration. However, the default gateway may be party to routing information that is unavailable to the host, and send an ICMP Redirect packet instructing the host to use another gateway when sending to a particular IP address. This information is stored in the host's routing table. Whenever the host attempts to send packets to that same IP address again, it consults its routing table first and sends the packets to the alternate gateway.

A host's routing table can be viewed from the command line by using the NETSTAT -NR or the ROUTE PRINT command. This displays the IP addresses found in the table, the gateway that should be used when sending to each, and other information defining the nature and source of the routing information.

▶ **See** "Basic Troubleshooting Techniques," **p. 539**

After you get beyond the host system, and particularly when you are dealing with Internet communications, this routing process can be very elaborate. There are several TCP/IP protocols that are designed for use only by gateways to exchange routing information that allows them to make the most efficient routing decisions possible, such as the Gateway to Gateway Protocol (GGP) and the Exterior Gateway Protocol (EGP). This prevents the traffic of each individual host from flooding the entire Internet in search of a single network.

Suffice it to say that most of the routing done in TCP/IP is table-based. Hosts and gateways each maintain their own routing tables and perform lookups of the destination address found in incoming packets. While the Internet at one time relied on a collection of central *core gateways* as the ultimate source of routing information for the entire network, this became impractical due to the tremendous growth of the Internet in recent years. Routing is now based on collections of autonomous systems called *routing domains*, that share information with each other using the Border Gateway Protocol (BGP). Fortunately, most of this functionality is transparent to the average user, but isn't it exciting to imagine the routing through innumerable gateways that must take place when you FTP to a server on the other side of the world?

IP Multiplexing

After the transmitted IP datagrams have been received at the host computer, they must then be delivered to the appropriate Transport layer protocol, and then to the appropriate application service. On the sending computer, the process of combining the requests made by several different applications into traffic for a few Transport protocols, and then combining the Transport protocol traffic into a single IP data stream, is called *multiplexing*. Multiplexing is literally a process by which several messages are sent using one signal. At the receiving computer, the process is reversed, and is called *demultiplexing*.

As seen in the IP header, the Protocol field in word three indicates which Transport protocol is to receive that datagram. In the same manner, the Destination Port fields in the UDP and TCP headers indicate the application service for which the packet is destined.

The numerical values assigned to specific protocols and application services are defined on the host computer in text files named Protocol and Services, respectively. These are located in the \Windows\System32\drivers\etc folder on a Windows NT workstation. Many of the values assigned to particular services are standardized numbers found in the Assigned Services. RFC. FTP, for example, traditionally uses a port number of 20, on all types of host systems.

Port numbers are individually defined for each Transport protocol. In other words, TCP and UDP can both have different assignments for the same port number. The combination of an IP address and a port number (notated as 123.45.67.89:20) is known as a *socket*.

> **CAUTION**
> Do not confuse the TCP/IP term *socket* (with a lowercase s) with the Windows Sockets application development standard created by Microsoft, even though the Windows NT TCP/IP utilities were developed using this standard.

Also, the Services file (which is capitalized) should not be confused with Windows NT services, even though some of the Services are indeed services.

Using TCP/IP on the Corporate Network

The two networking phenomena that have led to the increased use of TCP/IP on corporate networks are the growth of the Internet and the rise of the heterogeneous network.

Many business networks today are running more than one network operating system at the same time. There are several different scenarios that lead to this condition. One may be that internal networks that were previously separated are now being joined together to pool resources (such as Internet connections). Another is that the use of a particular client/server application that runs only on a certain platform may be desired.

Many networks today are combining Windows NT with NetWare on the same network. NT has proven to be an excellent application server platform, but many users are unwilling to give up NetWare, and so retain it for their core file and print services. UNIX workstations are also being attached to the general corporate network. The network management capabilities provided by UNIX platforms, and the expense of UNIX equipment make it practical to maximize the use of all corporate computing resources.

Finally, every user on every platform would like a connection to the Internet. For most corporate installations, this means installing a T-1 or other high-speed link to an Internet Service Provider and connecting it to a router that provides access to LAN users.

As a result of this kind of growth, administrators may suddenly find themselves running two or even three separate sets of protocols on the same network. This situation creates a good deal of redundant traffic and makes it difficult to troubleshoot transmission problems. Administrators seeking to consolidate their traffic into a single protocol suite usually find that there is one set of protocols that best supports all of these different platforms and needs. That, of course, is TCP/IP.

UNIX and the Internet were designed around the TCP/IP protocols, so that is not a problem. The NetWare/IP product, while not as seamless as it might be, allows NetWare to use TCP/IP to completely replace its native IPX/SPC protocols. The following section examines the way in which TCP/IP fits into the Windows NT networking architecture, thus making it possible for TCP/IP to be used as the sole protocol on nearly any corporate network, if desired.

Fitting TCP/IP into the Windows NT Networking Stack

Chapter 16, "A Brief Primer on Networks," examines the Windows NT networking model. There, you learned that the protocol stack for the operating system uses two multipurpose interfaces to contain whatever transport protocols are selected for use. At the boundary between the Transport and Session layers of the OSI model is the Transport Device Interface (TDI), and beneath the Network layer is the NDIS (Network Device Interface Specification) 3.0 Interface.

The TDI allows Windows NT applications and services operating at the Session layer and above to gain access to the network regardless of the protocols being used, as long as the protocol drivers are written to the interface.

The NDIS interface, at the juncture of the Network and Data Link layers, operates in the same way. The NDIS drivers are the interface to the network hardware below, and they also work with the TCP/IP Network Access protocols to create an interface with IP at the Network layer, above. Thus, the bulk of the TCP/IP protocol suite can be slipped neatly between the TDI and NDIS interfaces, as shown in figure 22.6.

FIG. 22.6
The TCP/IP protocols are bounded by the TDI at the top and the NDIS interface at the bottom.

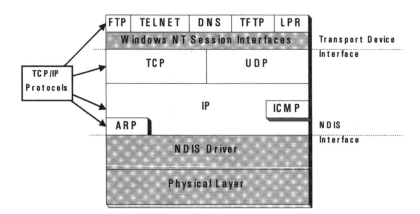

There are gray areas in the layering of the TCP/IP protocols within the Windows NT stack. Chief among these are some of the TCP/IP utilities that really are fully realized applications in themselves. FTP and Telnet, for example, are realized as executable files in Windows NT, that clearly operate in the Application layer.

These are not like native NT applications, however, that can be used with any compatible networking protocol. They are only used with TCP/IP, so although they operate above the TDI and are written to the Windows Sockets standard, they remain part of the TCP/IP suite. This is explainable by the fact that Windows NT was designed to accommodate TCP/IP, rather than the other way around. Microsoft is wholly responsible for the implementation of TCP/IP that is used by the Windows NT operating system. There was nothing to stop them from designing the protocol drivers however they wished, as long as what went out over the network cable conformed to the published standards.

The other area of overlap is at the Network Access layer. Because the different TCP/IP Network Access protocols are designed to accommodate the needs of different network types, they may extend into territory that is traditionally thought of as belonging to the Data Link or Physical layer. TCP/IP should theoretically be insulated from considerations specific to Ethernet, for example, but ARP is an essential part of the stack. That its place in the hierarchy should more rightly be below or alongside the NDIS driver, rather than above it, is just another example of the ways that networking practice does not conform to networking theory.

Overview of TCP/IP Utilities

TCP/IP affirms its commitment to being a platform-independent protocol suite by including in its specifications a number of powerful application protocols. Windows NT includes its own versions of many of the standard TCP/IP utilities based on these protocols.

These utilities can be separated into two categories of functionality. One is composed of diagnostic utilities used to monitor and troubleshoot the TCP/IP client itself. These are covered in Chapter 23, "Using Basic TCP/IP Services." The other consists of the connectivity utilities, the functions and uses of which are covered in the following sections.

Finger

Finger is a command line utility that displays information about a user or users on a remote system. The remote system must be running the Finger service for the command to function. The output varies depending on the remote system being addressed.

Syntax: `finger [-l] [username] @hostname`

Parameters:

`-l`	Displays information in long list (verbose) format.
`username`	Replace with the name of the user on the remote system about whom you want information. When no username is specified, information on all users is displayed.
`@hostname`	Replace with the hostname or IP address of the system you want to query.

FTP

Probably the most well known of the application protocols, File Transfer Protocol (FTP) uses a TCP connection to transfer files to and from remote computers regardless of the file systems being used at either end. FTP represents the epitome of TCP/IP's platform independent philosophy, because it provides the user with the same interface on any computer where it is used. The command syntax is based on UNIX, but even users to whom UNIX is completely alien are able to rapidly familiarize themselves with the few simple commands needed to upload and download files.

To connect to a remote system using FTP, the remote system must be running an FTP server program. The FTP client is installed as part of the normal Windows NT protocol installation. An FTP server for Windows NT is included as part of the Microsoft Peer Web Services package that ships with the Windows NT Workstation product. It also is a part of the Internet Information Server that ships with the Windows NT Server product. The FTP server runs as a network service, and allows multiple users to connect to the machine simultaneously. Nearly all UNIX operating systems run an FTP server daemon by default; FTP is often used for file transfers between UNIX systems, even when they are on the same network.

N O T E A *daemon* is the UNIX equivalent of what is called a *service* by Windows NT. It is a program that runs all of the time, and provides resources that are available to any process that requests them. ▪

After you have used the FTP utility to connect to a remote system, you are prompted to enter a username and a password. The user account is maintained only on the remote system; it is in no way related to the local Windows NT security system. Familiarity with FTP is most evident in Internet users because of the thousands of FTP servers that support anonymous access. This means that these servers offer collections of files free for the downloading to anyone who logs in with the username "anonymous." Internet etiquette decrees that you identify yourself by supplying your e-mail address in the password field. Some systems check the password field for a valid e-mail address (usually by searching for the @ character); others do not.

CAUTION
The FTP, Telnet, and REXEC utilities all rely on unencrypted passwords that are sent over the network to the remote system. An intruder could conceivably tap your network using a protocol analyzer and retrieve the passwords used. Windows NT, on the other hand, never transmits an unencrypted password. Microsoft therefore recommends that you use passwords with the TCP/IP utilities that are different from those used with your Windows network accounts.

After logging in, you are granted access to part of the remote system's directory structure. You traverse the directories using basic UNIX commands, locate the files that you wish to download, and then use the GET command to retrieve them. You also can use the PUT command to upload files, if you have been permitted to do so by the host. Note that file names on FTP servers are case-sensitive. You must always type the name exactly as you see it. The files in a particular directory are identified only by file name, size, and date. Descriptions of the files in each directory may sometimes be found in a file called 00index or README.

If your network has a high-speed connection to the Internet, FTP will make you want to throw away your modem forever. Enormous files are transferred in seconds and empty hard drives are filled in a matter of hours. The standard interface provided by the FTP command line utility is designed for basic functionality. It is not user-friendly. Many third party FTP client programs for Windows NT are available that provide GUI interfaces, file icons, drag and drop, and other associated file management functions. After you have TCP/IP installed on your Windows NT workstation, you can run any of these programs without the need for any system modifications.

Syntax: `ftp [-v] [-n] [-i] [-d] [-g] [hostname] [-s:filename]`

Parameters:

`-v`	Prevents the display of remote server responses to client commands
`-n`	Prevents autologon upon connection
`-i`	Prevents individual file verifications during mass file transfers
`-d`	Displays debugging messages
`-g`	Allows wildcard characters to be used in file and directory names
`hostname`	Replaces with host name or IP address of the remote system to be accessed
`-s:filename`	Allows you to specify a text file containing a series of FTP commands to be executed in sequence

Table 22.1 lists the major commands used during an FTP session. A complete listing is available through the Windows NT Help system.

Table 22.1 FTP Session Commands

Command	Function
open *hostname*	Initiates a session with a remote FTP host
close	Terminates the current session (without closing the FTP program)
exit	Closes the FTP program, returning you to the command prompt
ls	Lists the files in the current directory
ls -l	Lists full information for the files in the current directory
cd /*dirname*	Changes to a different directory
cd ..	Moves up one level in the directory tree
pwd	Displays the current directory name
binary	Specifies that the file to be transferred is a binary file
ascii	Specifies that the file to be transferred is an ASCII file
get *filename*	Transfers the specified file to the local system
recv *filename*	Transfers the specified file to the local system (same as get)
mget *filemask*	Transfers multiple files to the local system (using wildcards)
put *filename*	Transfers the specified file to the remote system
send *filename*	Transfers the specified file to the remote system (same as put)
mput *filemask*	Transfers multiple files to the remote system (using wildcards)
hash	Displays status of the current operation as files are transferred
prompt	Toggles the use of prompts for each individual file during multiple file transfers
help	Displays an FTP command summary

TFTP

TFTP is the Trivial File Transfer Protocol. It is a simplified version of FTP that provides less reliability, less functionality, and less security. TFTP uses UDP as its transport protocol, as while FTP uses TCP. There are also no user authentication services with TFTP.

Because it does not use a connection-oriented protocol, there is no browsing of directories permitted with TFTP. You must know the filename that you want to retrieve and include it as part of the command line.

Syntax: `tftp [-i]` *host* `[get] [put]` *source [destination]*

Parameters:

`-i`	Specifies that the file be transferred in binary mode
host	Replaces with the hostname or IP address of the remote system
`get`	Specifies that the file is to be transferred from the remote system to the local system
`put`	Specifies that the file is to be transferred from the local system to the remote system
source	Specifies the name of the file to be transferred
destination	Specifies the location where the file is to be transferred

Telnet

Telnet is a terminal emulation program that allows you to access and operate a remote system that is running the Telnet server (not included with Windows NT) and on which you have a valid user account, using a TCP session. Telnet can emulate a DEC VT 100, DEC VT 52, or TTY terminal.

The Windows NT implementation of Telnet uses a GUI interface to establish the connection to the remote system and set terminal and display preferences. Terminal emulation then occurs within a window. Once connected, you log on to the remote system just as though you were sitting in front of it, and you are then granted access to the command line.

Syntax: `telnet [host] [port]`

Parameters:

`host`	Specifies the host name or IP address of the remote system to be addressed
`port`	Specifies the port number in the remote system to which you will connect. When omitted, the value specified in the remote system's services file is used. If no value is specified in services, then port 23 is used.

RCP

RCP is a utility that allows you to copy files between the local system and a remote system that is running the remote shell server, rshd. Alternatively, you can direct two remote systems running rshd to exchange files among themselves.

A text file on the remote system, called .rhosts, must contain the host name and user name of the local system for file transfers to take place.

Syntax: `rcp [-a] [-b] [-h] [-r] source1 source2 ... sourceN destination`

Parameters:

`-a`	Specifies that the file(s) be transferred in ASCII mode
`-b`	Specifies that the file(s) be transferred in binary mode
`-h`	Allows files on a Windows NT system with the hidden attribute to be transferred
`-r`	Copies the contents of all of the source's subdirectories to the destination (when both source and destination are directories)
`source`	Specifies the name of the file to be transferred (and optionally its host and user names, in the format *host.user:filename*)
`destination`	Specifies the name of the file to be created at the destination (and optionally its host and user names, in the format *host.user:filename*)

REXEC

The REXEC utility allows noninteractive commands to be executed on a remote system that is running the rexecd service. Redirection symbols can be used to refer output to files on the local system (using normal redirection syntax) or on the remote system (by enclosing the redirection symbols in quotation marks, for example, ">>").

> Syntax: `rexec hostname [-l user] [-n] command`
>
> Parameters:

`hostname`	Specifies the host name of the system on which the command is to be run
`-l user`	Specifies a user name under whose account the command is to be executed on the remote system (a prompt for a user password will be generated at the local machine)
`-n`	Redirects rexec input to NUL
`command`	Specifies the command to be executed at the remote system

RSH

RSH is used to execute commands on remote systems that are running the rsh service. It has the same redirection capabilities as REXEC and the same .rhosts requirement as RCP.

> Syntax: `rsh hostname [-l user] [-n] command`
>
> Parameters:

`hostname`	Specifies the host name of the system on which the command is to be run
`-l user`	Specifies a user name under whose account the command is to be executed on the remote system (a prompt for a user password will be generated at the local machine)
`-n`	Redirects rsh input to NUL
`command`	Specifies the command to be executed at the remote system

LPR

The LPR utility allows you to print a file on a printer connected to a remote BSD type printer subsystem that is running an LPD server.

> Syntax: `lpr -Sserver -Pprinter [-Jjobname] [-ol] filename`
>
> Parameters:

`-Sserver`	Specifies the host name of the system to which the printer is connected
`-Pprinter`	Specifies the name of the printer to be used

`-Jjobname`	Specifies the name of this print job
`-ol`	Used when printing a non-text (Postscript) file from a Windows NT system to a UNIX printer
`-l`	Used when printing a non-text (Postscript) file from a UNIX system to a Windows NT printer
`filename`	Specifies the name of the file to be printed

From Here...

■ For more information on the Windows NT networking architecture, see Chapter 16, "A Brief Primer on Networks."

■ For more information on using the TCP/IP services provided by Windows NT, see Chapter 23, "Using Basic TCP/IP Services."

■ For information on automatically configuring Windows NT TCP/IP clients, see Chapter 24, "Using DHCP."

■ For more information on IP name resolution, see Chapter 25, "Using DNS and WINS."

CHAPTER 23

Using Basic TCP/IP Services

by Craig Zacker

The manner in which TCP/IP and Windows NT work together is not a matter of chance. The operating system's evolution centers around the protocols and is the leading choice among administrators of large networks. This is due to the large-scale project started in 1985 in which Microsoft migrated their 35,000 node worldwide network to the TCP/IP protocols under Windows NT.

It was their experiences in planning such an enormous project that led Microsoft to recognize the administrative shortcomings of the protocols. As a result, they set out to develop new modules for their own use, such as DHCP and WINS, that eventually became an integral part of the Windows NT TCP/IP implementation. Not satisfied to market a proprietary solution, however, the specifications for these modules have been submitted as RFCs to the Internet Engineering Task Force in the traditional manner, so that other hardware and software manufacturers can adapt their products to the new standards.

Windows NT implements the IETF TCP/IP standards

Windows NT's implementation of TCP/IP both exemplifies and expands on the body of specifications that make up the protocols.

TCP/IP fits into the Windows NT networking architecture

Above the Transport Device Interface, Windows NT provides several programming interfaces that are used by TCP/IP to provide network services.

Windows NT fits into the TCP/IP internetworking routing mechanisms

Windows NT traffic can be routed using TCP/IP, and the operating system can perform the routing itself.

Install and configure the Windows NT TCP/IP services

Configuring TCP/IP at the client level can be simple or complex. Understanding all of the options provided can make even the workstation version of the OS a powerful networking tool.

Test and troubleshoot your TCP/IP installation

Windows NT includes many utilities that can help you to understand how TCP/IP is communicating, or why it's not.

Chapter 22, "Overview of TCP/IP," examined the protocol suite. Most of the concepts presented there can be applied to any implementation of TCP/IP, on any platform. This chapter deals with TCP/IP as it is specifically realized in the Windows NT 4.0 environment. ■

Using TCP/IP on a Windows NT Network

In the release of Windows NT, version 3.1, NetBEUI was the native Windows networking protocol. For small single-segment networks, it was quite satisfactory and offered performance levels that rivaled the competing products. NetBEUI has no networking layer, however, and relies solely on network broadcasts for its name resolution. As a result, NetBEUI cannot be routed between network segments, and prevents broadcasts from being sent outside the local network. This makes the protocol unsatisfactory even for medium-sized organizations.

The alternative was the IPX/SPX protocols that are native to Novell NetWare. These are realized in the Windows NT NWLink protocol. Interoperability with NetWare would be a major factor affecting Windows NT's acceptance in the marketplace. NWLink is routable, but Microsoft did not want to commit themselves to what is essentially a proprietary set of protocols (particularly when Novell is the proprietor).

Several other protocols were considered for use in Microsoft's network rollout project, but when they examined TCP/IP, they found several factors working in its favor. TCP/IP was:

■ A tried and proven technology for large scale network integration, having been developed in coordination with the Internet project.

■ Based on published standards that were not only freely available, but were open to suggestion, as well.

■ Widely implemented. TCP/IP is supported in some way by nearly every operating system.

The use of TCP/IP did pose some difficulties for Microsoft's engineers. The prospect of assigning and maintaining IP addresses and host names for 35,000 users, in over 50 countries, was daunting.

Thus, the modules that Microsoft developed to dynamically assign TCP/IP parameters and perform name resolution on their own network became a part of the Windows NT product and Microsoft's contribution to the TCP/IP standards.

Windows NT Standards Compliance

The standards on which the TCP/IP protocols are based are published by the Internet Engineering Task Force (IETF), a body composed of representatives of over 100 organizations. The documents are known as Requests for Comments (RFCs), this name serving as an indication of the unusual flexibility with which this organization maintains the standards.

Part

V

Ch

23

Microsoft's implementation of TCP/IP (which is found in Windows NT as well as the other Windows network client operating systems) fully supports many of the RFCs. Microsoft has also contributed to the development of several of the documents through its own efforts in the development of the DHCP and WINS modules. DHCP and WINS are covered in-depth in Chapter 24, "Using DHCP," and Chapter 25, "Using DNS and WINS."

Publishing the specifications of their TCP/IP modules was beneficial to Microsoft and to the rest of the networking community. For technologies like DHCP and WINS to be effective on a large internetwork, they must be compatible with the hardware used to connect the different networks. While a computer running Windows NT can be used to route traffic between networks, this is not recommended for high volume network interfaces. Most large sites use a dedicated router, and that router must recognize and support the protocols used on the networks to operate effectively.

Therefore, by submitting their standards documents as RFCs, Microsoft makes it easier for other companies to manufacture compatible hardware and software. To aid in this process, Microsoft also holds events called "bakeoffs," where manufacturers are invited to test the interoperability of their products with Microsoft's products and with each other's products. This sort of environment can often provide more realistic and comprehensive testing scenarios than would otherwise be possible.

TCP/IP and the Windows NT Networking Architecture

In Chapter 22 "Overview of TCP/IP," you learned how the TCP/IP protocols responsible for the transport of data over the network operate between two interfaces in the Windows NT networking stack: the NDIS interface and the Transport Device Interface (TDI). Windows NT can effectively use several different sets of protocols simultaneously because of a driver that implements a modular environment used in many UNIX operating systems called *Streams*.

Streams creates a boundary layer just below the TDI and above the NDIS interface. Within those boundaries are the Network and Transport layer protocols for TCP/IP and IPX/SPX, as shown in figure 23.1. Any other Streams-compatible protocols can be used in the same way. Among the protocols that ship with the Windows NT product, only

NetBEUI functions outside of the Streams environment, communicating directly with the TDI and the NDIS interface.

FIG. 23.1

The Streams environment enables Windows NT users to choose from a variety of network protocols.

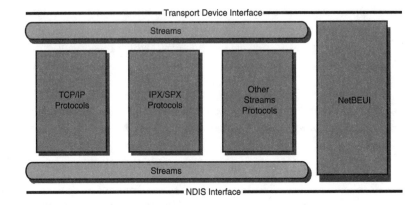

Above the TDI are the user-mode interfaces (also known as application programming interfaces, or APIs) that provide the tools with which programmers can develop applications that access the transport protocols. The fundamental upper-layer network access modules in Windows NT are the *server* and the *redirector*, which allows basic file and print communications between computers on a Windows network. As the names imply, these modules redirect local resource requests generated by applications out to the network, and respond to the requests from other computers by providing file and print services. These modules are displayed in the Windows NT Network control panel as the Server and Workstation services, and are installed with the basic Windows network client. Because any Windows NT machine can both share and access shared resources, all versions of the operating system contain both server and workstation capabilities.

The Windows NT implementation of TCP/IP supports these and several other APIs, such as Windows Sockets and NetBIOS, to varying degrees. Programmers generally use one or more of these other interfaces for an application's more complicated networking tasks, those that require more functionality than simple commands. Using these interfaces, distributed applications can be developed that connect remote computers at a high level.

The user-mode interfaces are not a part of the TCP/IP or any other protocol standard; in fact, they are not protocols at all. They are architectural elements of the operating system that allow upper-layer processes to communicate with a network protocol stack in a standardized manner. They also demultiplex the communications generated by many different application processes into a single stream that can be packaged and sent by each transport layer protocol.

Demultiplexing is the process of sending more than one message using only one signal. From a network communications perspective, the user-mode interfaces are part of a complex process that allows a multitasking operating system like Windows NT to reduce the messages generated by several applications into a single stream of IP datagrams, as shown in figure 23.2.

FIG. 23.2
The user-level interfaces are an interim step in the demultiplexing of the TCP/IP communications process.

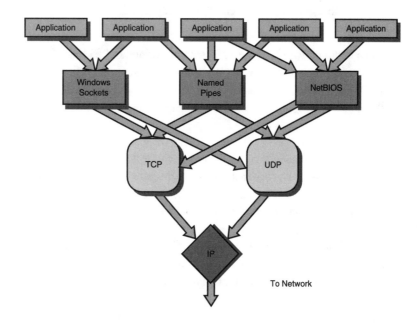

Part
V

Ch
23

The sections that follow describe the user-mode interfaces supported by Windows NT's TCP/IP stack.

Windows Sockets   Based on the Berkeley sockets interface (well-known in UNIX circles), Windows Sockets is an open standard developed through the collaboration of more than 30 vendors of TCP/IP software as part of the Microsoft Windows Open System Architecture (WOSA) program. The goal of the project was to create a standardized application programming interface that could be used by any implementation of the TCP/IP protocols in the Windows environment. This would obviate the need for applications developers to modify their code to comply with the peculiarities of different TCP/IP stacks.

ON THE WEB

Version 2.2 of the Windows Sockets standard was ratified in May 1996. The document can by downloaded via anonymous FTP from:

ftp.microsoft.com/bussys/WinSock/winsock2.

The term *socket* refers to a connection between two high-level processes on remote computers. In TCP/IP terms, a socket connection includes the IP addresses of both machines, the transport protocol (TCP or UDP) used to connect them, and the port numbers of the communicating applications. Applications using Windows Sockets establish a reliable connection between a client and a server (usually with TCP) to transfer large amounts of data with a guarantee of accurate delivery and timely service.

Windows Sockets is the most used TCP/IP API standard today. Many of the TCP/IP utilities included with Windows NT, such as Telnet and FTP, are Windows Sockets applications, as are nearly all World Wide Web browsers and other Internet programs. Windows NT supports all 16-bit, as well as 32-bit Windows Sockets applications, so most third-party products written to the specification can be used.

N O T E Although users of Windows NT and Windows 95 may be quick to forget the fact, there is a significant market for third-party TCP/IP clients for Windows 3.1 and other operating systems that does not include an integrated TCP/IP stack. The third-party products using the Windows Sockets standard can usually be identified by the inclusion of a WINSOCK.DLL file, which is the first library called by a Windows Sockets application. ■

NetBIOS The Network Basic Input/Output System (NetBIOS) is one of the original interfaces used in Microsoft networking products. The original Windows NT release (version 3.1) relied on a simplified networking stack that consisted of the NDIS driver, the NetBEUI protocol, and the NetBIOS API. This combination can still be used, but as stated earlier, it is not practical for large and segmented networks. The Windows NT redirector, in fact, uses the NetBIOS interface.

The limitations of this arrangement are a result of the NetBEUI protocol, however, not the NetBIOS interface. NetBIOS can also be used with TCP/IP, thanks to standards published as RFCs 1001 and 1002, which define the NetBIOS over TCP/IP interface (sometimes called NetBT). Despite this inclusion as part of an IETF standard, however, NetBIOS is still not a protocol, nor is it to be considered part of the TCP/IP suite. The standard defines a specification for the transport of NetBIOS application traffic over an internetwork using the TCP/IP protocols. By extending the reach of NetBIOS applications beyond the local network, it becomes a robust programming interface that is used by many of Windows NT's basic functions, including the server, workstation, browser, messenger, and netlogon services. Windows NT also provides compatibility with older NetBIOS applications by supplying an emulator that allows the applications to traverse the Transport Device Interface.

Many of the functions performed by NetBIOS resolve to the Session layer of the OSI reference model. NetBIOS is often responsible for establishing the connection between two computers that will be used by an application running through another interface.

As part of the Session-layer functionality, and in addition to providing an application programming interface, NetBIOS also defines the naming convention used to identify machines on a Windows network. Your Windows network machine name (which may be different from your IP host name) can be as many as 15 characters, plus a sixteenth character used to indicate certain network resource types, such as machines that have been designated as browsers or domain controllers. NetBIOS names can also define groups of machines for multicast addressing.

When used with NetBEUI, computers on a Windows network can be located only through network broadcasts. The sending machine transmits a query for a particular name, and that computer is responsible for responding to the query. On a large network, the needless traffic caused by this process is enormous, slowing down all other communications. The same is true with NetBIOS over TCP/IP, if broadcasts are still relied on for identification. The NetBIOS queries have to propagate over the entire internetwork, causing even more severe traffic problems.

This is one of the major obstacles to Microsoft TCP/IP rollout program. Their solution to the problem is the Windows Internet Naming Service (WINS): a database that associates the NetBIOS names of computers with their IP addresses. Like a NetBIOS DNS for a private network, it is the resource that all of the network's computers look to for name resolution.

WINS goes beyond the functionality of a DNS by being dynamically updated. The IP address and host name of a TCP/IP machine must be manually added to a DNS table, which can then be propagated to other DNSs. When using a system like DHCP that automatically allocates IP addresses, however, it would be all but impossible to keep up with the ever-changing IP assignments. On a Windows NT *rhino* server (that is, a server running both DHCP and WINS), each IP address that is assigned by DHCP is immediately added to the WINS server. Multiple WINS servers on a network can then replicate their information amongst themselves, keeping everyone current with no administrator intervention. The theory and practice of using DNS and WINS are examined in depth in Chapter 25, "Using DNS and WINS."

Other APIs   Windows NT also supports a number of other user-mode interfaces under TCP/IP. Some, such as Named Pipes and Mailslots, are supported for reasons of backward compatibility with older applications designed for use with Microsoft LAN Manager. Both of these interfaces take the form of file systems in the Windows NT networking stack. As such, they can allow an application to communicate directly with other processes on the same machine, as well as with those on remote systems. Mailslots, for example, provide a low overhead messaging service using User Datagram Protocol. Network communications for these interfaces go through the Windows NT redirector. The redirector uses four command types provided by the Server Message Blocks (SMB) protocol (session control, file, printer, and message), to communicate with other computers on the network. SMBs enable Windows NT machines to exchange files and other services with computers running other Microsoft networking products like LAN Manager, Windows 95, and Windows for Workgroups.

Windows NT also supports Remote Procedure Calls (RPCs), which is an interface that makes use of the other interfaces covered earlier to facilitate network communications. All of these APIs coexist on every Windows NT machine, providing a library of functions that programmers can utilize at will. In the upper layers of the networking stack, the boundaries between the layered processes defined by the OSI reference model become increasingly obscure, and it is not unusual to see these interfaces used for communications tasks that span the Session, Presentation, and Application layers.

Installing the Windows NT TCP/IP Services

Because Windows NT 4.0 has the Windows Explorer shell, the installation of the TCP/IP protocol is simple. The Network dialog box in the Control Panel now uses tabs, providing easy access to all options and a greater segregation of the different networking modules.

As in Windows 95, the networking components of Windows NT are broken down into three types: adapters, protocols, and services. These types form a stack corresponding to the overall networking architecture; the services run on top, passing application data through the protocols, which code it for transmission via the adapter.

A minimal Windows NT network installation consists of an adapter driver, the NWLink IPX/SPX Compatible Transport protocol, and the Server, Workstation, and Computer Browser services. The NetBIOS Interface and the RPC Name Service Provider services are also installed. These modules enable the Windows NT workstation to connect to other Windows network machines as peers or to Windows NT servers as a client. When networking is installed as part of the operating system setup, you are prompted to indicate which of the three protocols supported by Windows NT you want to install. You can select any combination of the NetBEUI, NWLink IPX/SPX, and TCP/IP protocols, and the appropriate services for each are installed as the result of your selection. Many of the other network services are optional, and must be explicitly installed from the Control Panel. Some Windows NT services can be run with different protocols, while others are designed for use with a specific one.

After the networking modules are installed, they must be bound to provide an unbroken communications channel extending from the application processes at the top of the networking stack to the network adapter driver at the bottom. Services are bound to protocols and protocols are bound to adapters. By default, Windows NT binds together all of the modules that are capable of working with each other. It does not bind the NetWare client service to the TCP/IP protocol, for example, because the two are not compatible. (The NetWare/IP product enables the NetWare operating system to use TCP/IP as a transport protocol, but it is not supported by the Microsoft TCP/IP stack. You must use a third-party product.)

You may have to remove some of the bindings that Windows NT creates by default. For example, you may use TCP/IP to connect to an Internet Service Provider through a dial-up connection, but not on your local network. In that case, you would have two adapters installed, a regular network interface card and the Remote Access WAN Wrapper, which enables your modem to be treated like a network adapter. You would want to unbind TCP/IP from the network card, and any other protocols from the Remote Access adapter. The hierarchical display in Windows NT 4.0 makes it much easier to manage network bindings than in previous versions of the operating system, as discussed later in this chapter.

Assuming that the basic networking modules listed previously have already been installed on your Windows NT workstation, you can add the TCP/IP protocol by opening the Network Control Panel and selecting the Protocols tab, as shown in figure 23.3. The currently installed protocols are displayed on this screen. Click the Add button and in the Select Network Protocol dialog box highlight the TCP/IP Protocol and click OK.

You are prompted to specify if you want to use a DHCP server on the network to configure your TCP/IP parameters. If your network does use DHCP, then you can run TCP/IP at your workstation without being familiar with any of the material in this chapter. All of your settings will probably be automatically assigned, relieving you of any manual configuration tasks. After the DHCP prompt, Windows NT then copies files to your workstation drive, and prompts you to insert the Windows NT CD-ROM or specify a location for the installation files, if necessary.

When you install the protocol, Windows NT also copies the native TCP/IP applications and utilities (examined later in this chapter and in Chapter 22) to your local drive. These are considered to be part of the protocol suite and require no separate installations.

After the files have been copied and the Windows NT Registry modified, you are returned to the Protocols screen of the Network dialog box. TCP/IP has been added to the list.

Configuring TCP/IP Properties

Depending on the configuration of your network and what you expect from your workstation, configuring the TCP/IP client in Windows NT Workstation 4.0 can be simple or

Part
V

Ch
23

difficult. If you elected to use DHCP, then you can click the Close button and restart your machine, because you're finished. If your DHCP server is configured properly, it will supply you with all of the settings that you need.

If you're not using DHCP, however, then highlight TCP/IP in the Network Protocols listing and click the Properties button. This opens the Microsoft TCP/IP Properties dialog box, that contains all of the settings needed for TCP/IP to operate.

The IP Address Page

The first tab on the dialog box displays the IP Address screen, into which you enter the three basic TCP/IP parameters, as shown in figure 23.3. Any changes made to the IP Address parameters will not take effect until you close the Network dialog box and restart your computer.

FIG. 23.3
The settings on the IP Address tab identify you to the other computers on the network.

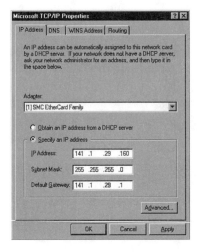

The three parameters required in the IP Address screen are as follows:

- **IP Address**. Identifies the host adapter in your computer to the IP protocol layer on all of the other computers on the network.

- **Subnet Mask**. Indicates what part of the IP address represents the network on which the host is located, and what part represents the host itself.

- **Default Gateway**. Specifies the IP address of another computer on the same network segment; a computer that is also connected to one or more other networks. When your workstation generates a data packet destined for a computer on another network, the packet is sent to the Default Gateway machine, which then becomes responsible for passing it along on the next leg of its journey.

If you select the <u>O</u>btain an IP Address from a DHCP Server option button, then the other settings are grayed out. While DHCP servers can optionally assign values for many different TCP/IP parameters, these three are basic, and are so interrelated that they are usually supplied together.

CAUTION

If you have values specified anywhere in the TCP/IP Properties dialog box, and later elect to use DHCP to obtain configuration values, you must remove any explicit settings for parameters that are to be supplied by DHCP. Any values appearing in the dialog box (including those appearing in grayed-out fields) override the settings provided by a DHCP server.

Part
V

Ch
23

For a typical, non-DHCP workstation configuration, the values for these three fields would have to be supplied to you by your network administrator. You could then simply type the values into the fields (whether you understand them or not) and proceed to the next screen. Setting these parameters can sometimes be considerably more complex, however, and in those cases, it is very useful to know what the numbers actually represent.

CAUTION

It is often difficult to resist the temptation to enter any IP address into the field provided, "just to see if it works." This practice is not recommended. If someone else is currently using the address when you boot your machine, Windows NT will reject it and fail to log on. However, the other person may boot his computer after you have begun to use the address, in which case his logon will fail. This person then angrily calls the network administrator, who traces it back to you, and informs you that you've just usurped the CEO's IP address.

Identifying Network Hosts   You learned about the structure and formation of IP addresses and subnet masks in Chapter 22. The IP address is only one of four unique identifiers used by various network processes to send data to a Windows NT machine running TCP/IP. The other identifiers are the MAC address, the host name, and the NetBIOS name. Each of these other three names, however, is resolved with the IP address at some point during routine use. By understanding the relationships between these identifiers, you can more easily see how TCP/IP and Windows NT mesh together to resolve most of the problems inherent in communications over a large internetwork.

The MAC address is the 6-byte hexadecimal node address that is hardcoded into all Ethernet and Token Ring network interface cards by the manufacturer. Other types of network cards, such as ARCnet, have the MAC addresses assigned by the network administrator. In either case, the value assigned must be unique to that network. The datagrams prepared by the TCP/IP Network layer protocol contain only an IP address, which is meaningless to the Data Link layer process that controls access to the network medium. Therefore, the equivalent MAC address for each IP address is determined using the TCP/IP Address Resolution Protocol (ARP), and cached in the local machine.

The host name is assigned to each IP interface for ease of use on the Internet. The host name is composed of one or more unique words followed by the domain name of the network on which the machine is located, with a period between each word (as in jsmith.mycorp.com). Host names are resolved into IP addresses through the use of either a host table on the local machine (in the form of a text file called HOSTS) or a domain name service (DNS).

The NetBIOS name (often called the machine name in Windows NT circles) is the unique name assigned to each computer on a Windows network. It can be different from the host name. When a Windows network uses the TCP/IP protocols, NetBIOS names are re-solved into IP addresses using either a host table (called LMHOSTS, and different from that used for Internet host names), network broadcasts, or the Windows Internet Name Service (WINS).

Duplicate Address Detection IP addresses on a TCP/IP network must all be unique, and Windows NT uses ARP packets to ensure that no two network hosts are using the same IP address. Whenever the protocol stack is initialized, Windows NT transmits an ARP request, specifying the IP address it is configured to use. If another machine on the net responds to the ARP, then Windows NT will continue the logon without enabling IP, generating a pop-up message and a log entry that specifies the MAC address of the conflicting machine.

If the other machine is also running Windows NT, it will receive the message as well, but will continue to function normally after sending out its own ARP request (so that the other machines on the network will have the correct MAC address in their ARP caches). If the other machine is not running Windows NT, it most likely will not know that the conflict occurred and will not advertise its presence to the network using ARP. Traffic destined for that machine maybe sent to the wrong place.

Configuring Multiple Host Adapters It is important to know that an IP address does not identify a computer, it identifies a host. A host can be a network interface card, an asynchronous or ISDN modem, or any other communications device that connects the computer to a network. A system can therefore be connected to two networks at the same time, but each host device must be assigned its own unique IP address, as well as an additional subnet mask and default gateway.

Notice that the IP Address page in the Microsoft TCP/IP Properties dialog box contains an Adapter selector that enables you to switch between the various adapters installed on your computer. Each adapter receives its own settings for all of the parameters, even down to the use of DHCP. (Many Internet Service Providers provide IP addresses through DHCP, while you may be assigned a static IP address on your local network.)

A computer connected to two or more networks through the use of multiple TCP/IP hosts is known as a *multi-homed* system. Windows NT provides the ability to route TCP/IP traffic between the networks, but this feature is disabled by default. While a Windows NT workstation is not recommended for use as a high-volume router, it can effectively allow different networks to communicate. The configuration parameters that control the routing process will be discussed later in this chapter.

Part
V

Ch
23

Advanced IP Address Configuration Options   If you click the Advanced button on the IP Address tab, an Advanced IP Addressing dialog box opens (see fig. 23.4), allowing you to further elaborate on the values for the parameters on the main screen. These options can benefit users working on a more complex network, or those requiring special services from this Windows NT workstation.

FIG. 23.4
The Advanced IP Addressing dialog box provides more options for the configuration of the IP addresses, subnet masks, and default gateways.

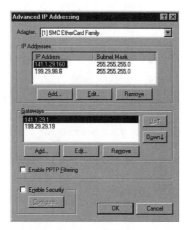

The Advanced IP Addressing dialog box is a superset of the previous screen. Any parameters that you have entered in the IP Address tab are reflected here, and any changes made here display on the other screen when you return to it. As before, you can make a selection from the Adapter selector to configure multiple hosts. For each adapter, this dialog box lets you specify multiple IP addresses and multiple default gateways.

A single host may require more than one IP address in situations where a single physical network segment is broken up into multiple logical IP subnets. To send IP packets to all of the other machines on the physical network, it is necessary to have an address on each of the logical networks. You can specify as many as five IP addresses and subnet masks in this dialog box.

While multiple IP addresses can be used simultaneously, multiple default gateways are used only as a fault tolerance measure. If your computer is located on an IP network with more than one gateway system, then you can specify both gateways in this dialog box, and adjust the order in which the gateway addresses are used. If the first gateway listed is not reachable for any reason, the packets destined for other networks will be sent to the second gateway system. You can specify as many as five default gateway systems using this dialog box.

N O T E   The multiple default gateways feature of Windows NT does not in any way affect the normal function of the TCP/IP protocols. The order in which the default gateways are listed does not indicate an order of preference that is observed by the gateway systems involved. Any default gateway may still send an ICMP Redirect packet to the sending node to inform it of a more efficacious route for its datagrams. Secondary default gateways are only used by a sending node when it receives an ICMP packet indicating that the current default gateway is unreachable. ■

Click the Enable PPTP Filtering checkbox in the Advanced IP Addressing dialog box if you will be using one of the adapters on your system to connect to the Internet and you want to allow remote users to access your internal network through the Internet using the Point to Point Tunneling Protocol (PPTP). This option prevents any protocols other than PPTP from entering your system through the specified adapter. Use this option when you want your machine to function as a Internet gateway for remote access. With PPTP, a user anywhere in the world can securely access your corporate network by logging in to a local Internet Service Provider and connecting to your workstation via the Internet. The remote user's traffic is packaged as PPTP traffic, and once inside your machine, it is routed to the appropriate internal network resource.

▶ **See** "Virtual Private Networks," **p. 460**

Windows NT also enables you to limit the types of TCP/IP traffic accepted by a particular host adapter in your system. Click the Enable Security checkbox and then click the Configure button, and the TCP/IP Security dialog box is displayed (as shown in fig. 23.5).

FIG. 23.5
The TCP/IP Security dialog box enables you to restrict the types of traffic that can reach a particular host.

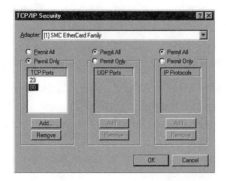

Once again, be sure that the proper host adapter is selected before enabling any new settings. You can restrict the TCP/IP traffic allowed by a host adapter by specifying either ports or protocols. A *port* is an indicator of the application process to which a packet is to be delivered. Every datagram entering the TCP/IP protocol stack from the network specifies (in the IP header) the Transport protocol to which it should be delivered. The TCP or UDP header then specifies the port to which the data in the packet should be sent.

▶ **See** "Fitting TCP/IP into the OSI Reference Model," **p. 489**

Part

V

Ch

23

Using the three sections of the TCP/IP Security dialog box, you can restrict an adapter to the use of certain TCP ports, certain UDP ports, and certain IP protocols. (TCP ports and UDP ports are treated separately because these two Transport protocols each maintain their own port number designations.) To enable one of the filters, click its Permit Only radio button and click the Add button to specify the numeric value of the port or protocol that you want to permit.

Port and protocol values for the standard TCP/IP modules are published in the *Assigned Numbers* document (RFC 1060). These assignments are listed in two files located in your workstation's \Windows\System32\Drivers\Etc directory. The SERVICES file lists the port numbers of common TCP and UDP processes and the PROTOCOL file lists the numeric values for the various TCP/IP protocols. You may use custom or proprietary applications on your network that specify other port assignments for their processes. This is why SERVICES is a plain text file, so that it can easily be modified with additional entries. Any port assignment listed in SERVICES can be specified in the TCP/IP security dialog box. (It is not likely that you are using a proprietary TCP/IP protocol on your network, but any module listed in the PROTOCOL file can be used in the same way.)

These security options enable Windows NT to function as a rudimentary Internet firewall, protecting users on your internal network from outside intrusion, or limiting their access to certain Internet services. You may, for example, want to allow your users to GET files from FTP sites, but prevent them from participating in some of the more dubious Internet activities. Windows NT Workstation 4.0 also ships with Microsoft Peer Web Services, which enables the workstation to host World Wide Web, FTP, and Gopher sites. These security options prevent outside Internet users from accessing your machine in any way other than those you specify.

The DNS Page

Clicking the DNS tab of the TCP/IP Properties dialog box displays the screen shown in figure 23.6. As mentioned previously, the Domain Name System is used to translate between IP addresses and their equivalent host names. If your network is not connected to the Internet, you might not use a DNS at all, and you can safely leave this dialog box blank. If you are on the Internet, however, it is important to know that DNS and WINS are not functional equivalents. They provide similar services, but WINS equates NetBIOS names with IP addresses and is usually limited to an internal network, while a DNS allows you to resolve any of the millions of host names on the Internet to its IP address. A Windows NT network that is also connected to the Internet probably uses both DNS and WINS servers.

FIG. 23.6

In the DNS screen, you specify your host and domain names and the addresses of the DNS servers that you wish to use.

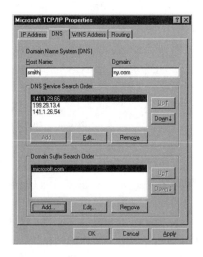

N O T E   Some sources use the term Domain Name Service for the initials DNS, but RFCs 1034 and 1035 refer to the mechanism as a Domain Name System. ■

A single DNS is not a complicated mechanism when considered by itself, but in conjunction with the huge network of other DNS servers throughout the Internet, its capabilities are extraordinary. There is no mechanism in a DNS that queries a particular IP address to find out its host name, or vice versa. It is simply a lookup table, manually edited by the network administrator whenever an entry concerning his network must be added or modified. As such, it is little more than a server-based equivalent of a HOSTS file, which is a lookup table stored on the workstation's local hard drive.

The strength of a DNS lies in the fact that when it is queried for the IP address of a host name not in its table, it passes the request up to its default gateway system's specified DNS. An unresolved query can travel upstream in this manner through many different servers, eventually reaching one of the core servers that is updated with the domain information registered with the Internet Network Information Center (InterNIC).

As explained in Chapter 22, "Overview of TCP/IP," a network must register a domain name (for example, microsoft.com) before it can place computers directly on the Internet. This is so that there is an ultimate source for accurate DNS information concerning each connected network. A query for a host name that is not found in many successive DNS tables will ultimately reach a core server that can refer the machines down the line to the DNS that is registered as the authoritative source for address information concerning a specific domain.

After a host name has been resolved in this manner, it is saved in the local DNS table so that it will not be necessary to go through the whole process again for the same address. This distributed system allows any machine on the Internet to retrieve information on any other machine, without the need for a central table containing every single host name.

The host name is purely a tool of convenience for Internet users and has no real relationship to the Windows NT network or to the TCP/IP protocols, outside of the DNS. Whenever you use a remote site's hostname in a TCP/IP application or command, the first step in processing your request is to resolve the name into an IP address using a DNS. Only the IP address is used by the protocols to identify the host after that.

The host name does not even have to be specified in Windows NT for it to be used effectively. The first two fields in the DNS screen of the TCP/IP Properties dialog box call for you to specify your Host Name and your Domain name, but these fields are optional, and can be omitted with no effect.

You must then enter the addresses of the DNS servers that you will use to resolve the host names specified in your TCP/IP applications. You can add up to five DNS addresses in this field, and use the Up and Down buttons to arrange them into the order you want them to be searched.

The DNS servers that you specify don't have to be located on your network. If you are connected to the Internet, then the address of any functional DNS server can be used. Of course, response times will be greater when the DNS is running on a local network machine. The specification of multiple DNSs is not required; the option is provided so that you can minimize the delays that may be caused by host name lookup requests that are passed through many different Internet servers. If you regularly connect to various hosts on a particular remote site, you can improve your access times by specifying the authoritative DNS for that site in you workstation configuration.

N O T E   The Windows NT Server product now includes an optional DNS service. See Chapter 25, "Using DNS and WINS," for more information on this and other name resolution concepts. ■

The Domain Suffix Search Order field allows you to further simplify your hostname requests. Any suffixes entered here will automatically be appended to hostnames as they are looked up in the DNSs. For example, entering microsoft.com as a suffix would allow you to type "FTP rhino" at the command line and be connected to the ftp server at rhino.microsoft.com. You can specify up to five suffixes, which will be searched in the order listed. Again, use the Up and Down buttons to arrange the entries to your satisfaction.

The WINS Address Page

The Windows Internet Name Service performs the same name resolution function for the NetBIOS names of the Windows computers on your internal network as a DNS does for IP hostnames. Easy to remember computer names are automatically converted to IP addresses by reference to a server database.

Windows NT can use other means for resolving NetBIOS names into IP addresses. The LMHOSTS file, located on a server or a local drive, functions just like a HOST file. It is a plain ASCII text table of NetBIOS names and their accompanying IP addresses. Network broadcasts can also be used (which is how the NetBEUI protocol operates); a NetBIOS name is announced to the entire network and the computer using that name is expected to reply with its IP address. WINS eliminates the need for manually editing the LMHOSTS file, and reduces network traffic by using fewer broadcasts. These other methods usually are still used, however, as fallbacks when WINS fails to perform effectively.

Unlike a DNS, WINS has its own information gathering capabilities that allow it to track the computers on your network without the need to manually update a lookup table. WINS has also been designed to be the natural partner of DHCP. It would be impossible to manually maintain the DNS entries for a large network with dynamically assigned IP addresses for its hosts. Whenever DHCP assigns an address to a machine, the configuration information is used to update the WINS database.

To use WINS, click the WINS Address tab in the Microsoft TCP/IP Properties dialog box to display the screen shown in figure 23.7. As on the IP Address page, you are given the capability to define different WINS server addresses for each of the network host adapters installed in your computer. Although a WINS server on a nonlocal network can be accessed and used, it is preferable to specify a server on the local segment, if one is available. You may also use one adapter for TCP/IP access to an internal network, and another adapter to access the Internet through a dial-up connection, in which cases your WINS selections will almost certainly differ. A secondary WINS server address can also be supplied, in the event the primary server is unreachable.

FIG. 23.7
The WINS Address
page allows you to
specify the server that
will provide NetBIOS
over TCP/IP name
resolution for your
network.

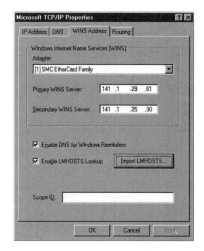

You may think it odd to find a checkbox labeled Enable DNS for Windows Resolution on this page, when it seemingly should be found on the DNS screen. This function allows you to substitute IP host names for NetBIOS names when you are specifying Windows network paths using the Universal Naming Convention (UNC). While you might normally enter the path name \\SMITHJ\FILES when trying to open a drive window for a share on another user's machine, this feature allows you to use his host name or IP address in the same syntax, as in \\john.mycorp.com\files or \\199.124.165.14\files.

The default Windows NT installation can also use network broadcasts (on the local segment only) and the local LMHOSTS file (located in the \Windows\System32\Drivers\Etc directory) for name resolution. If you want to import a centrally maintained LMHOSTS file from a network drive, click the Enable LMHOSTS Lookup checkbox and select the Import LMHOSTS button to open a standard browser window that you can use to locate the file you want to import.

A Scope ID is a value that can be used to create a group of computers on a NetBIOS over TCP/IP network that can only communicate with each other. No outside machines can address the group, nor can the group address outside machines. The Scope ID field is used to identify the members of such a group by entering their assigned Scope ID. This option is rarely used.

CAUTION
A multihomed computer can only use one Scope ID, no matter how many network adapters are installed or how many different networks the machine connects to. The Scope ID field in the WINS

continues

continued

Address screen does not change when a different adapter is selected, but if you use DHCP to assign TCP/IP settings, it is possible for the IP addresses of different adapters to include different Scope IDs. In this case, each host adapter will write its assigned Scope ID to the same registry key in turn, and the ID for the adapter that is configured last will remain the operative setting. This prevents the computer from accessing one or more of the networks to which it is connected.

The Routing Page

There is one final tab on the TCP/IP Properties dialog box, labeled Routing. This tab contains a single option—a checkbox used to Enable IP Routing. By default, a multihomed Windows NT system will not route IP traffic between networks. Earlier versions of Windows NT required you to manually edit the Registry to enable IP routing, but now this checkbox is provided.

Routing is an optional process whenever two or more adapters are installed in a single Windows NT machine, connecting it to two or more different networks. It does not matter what type of adapter is used; when you connect to your network from an outside computer with the Windows NT Remote Access Service (RAS), the network machine that you are connecting to is functioning as a router.

Two types of IP routing are possible on Windows NT: static routing and dynamic routing. Static routing involves the manual creation of a routing table (using the ROUTE utility) that is stored on the computer and used as a reference for the system's routing decisions. Depending on the complexity of your network, a packet arriving at your new router could conceivably take several different paths to its destination. Efficient routing is achieved when the path is chosen that involves the fewest number of intermediate systems, or hops. Each instance in which a packet is transferred from one network segment to another is called a *hop*.

On a large internetwork, it can be difficult to maintain static routing tables on each of the network's routers. That is why there is a protocol that allows routers to communicate amongst themselves, so that updated routing information can be shared by all of the routers on the network. This is called *dynamic routing*, and the protocol is called the Routing Information Protocol (RIP for Internet Protocol).

RIP is a standard supported by many of the routing software and hardware products on the market today. Using RIP allows the Windows NT router to communicate with other routers on the network, to share information about changing conditions and optimum routing paths. Using Windows NT as a router also allows DHCP traffic to be relayed from one network segment to another. Without this capability, it would be necessary to have a DHCP server on each network segment.

The RIP for Internet Protocol and the DHCP Relay agent only ship with the Windows NT 4.0 Server product. You can only route using static tables with Windows NT Workstation. On a small network, however, static routing would very likely be preferable. If you have only a few network segments the routing chores are relatively simple, and efficient route selection is not an issue. Static routing will provide good performance without the additional network traffic incurred by using RIP.

Larger networks use Windows NT routing for RAS and Internet connection environments. For high-volume internetwork routing within a single site, a dedicated routing device is usually recommended.

Part
V

Ch
23

Bindings

Another tab in the Network Control Panel is the Bindings tab (see fig. 23.8). The Bindings screen displays a graphical representation of the networking modules that you have installed in your system. As explained earlier, services use protocols for transport and protocols use adapters for network access.

FIG. 23.8
The Bindings tab shows the relationships between the Windows NT networking modules.

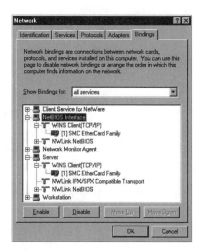

The bindings display is more improved than previous Windows NT versions. You can now select whether to view the bindings in the context of either services, protocols, and adapters. The collapsible tree structure enables you to concentrate on a particular area of interest.

You can also manipulate network binding from this screen. Individual bindings can be enabled or disabled, allowing you to minimize the amount of unnecessary traffic on your network. For example, an adapter used to connect to an Internet service provider need not be bound to the NWLink IPX/SPX protocol. This capability also is good for troubleshooting purposes, as it allows you to disable network modules without having to uninstall them.

On multihomed systems, you also can prioritize network access by controlling the order in which the bindings appear. Because Windows network traffic can use either NWLink or TCP/IP for transport services, the first protocol bound to the Workstation service, for example, will be the first one used. You modify the order of the bindings by dragging and dropping them within the list.

Simple TCP/IP Services

Windows NT also includes support for some of the minor debugging services that are specified in the TCP/IP standards. These are bundled together into a single network service module called Simple TCP/IP Services.

The Simple TCP/IP Services are installed, like any other Windows NT service, from the Network Control Panel by selecting the Services tab and clicking the Add button. After the service is installed, the Windows NT machine can respond to requests from other TCP/IP systems for the Echo (RFC 862), Discard (RFC 863), Character Generator (RFC 864), Daytime (RFC 867) and Quote of the Day (RFC 865) services.

Each of these services operates over either TCP or UDP, using standard port numbers found in the SERVICES file and the *Assigned Numbers* document (RFC 1060). As the names imply, packets sent to the Echo service are immediately returned to the sender and those sent to the Discard service are dropped without any response. A request to the Character Generator service returns a repeating pattern of ASCII characters, just for the purpose of generating data traffic. A daytime request returns the current date and time on the remote system, and Quote of the Day returns a specified text string.

These services are used as system debugging tools and, aside from the Daytime service, which can be used to synchronize the clocks of networked computers, serve little productive purpose once the system is functioning properly.

TCP/IP Troubleshooting

Networking with Windows NT is a complex process, and a failure to communicate with another machine on the network can be caused by any number of different problems. The TCP/IP protocols are as likely to be a cause of problems as any other part of the networking stack; even more so because of the large amount of manual configuration that is often required.

To aid in the resolution of TCP/IP networking problems, Windows NT includes a collection of diagnostic and configuration utilities that are ported from UNIX utilities of the same or similar names. The following sections examine these utilities, as well as some of the ways in which they can be used to test your TCP/IP installation, locate problem areas, and let you get a better idea of what's actually happening on your network.

Basic Troubleshooting Techniques

As with any troubleshooting process, the aim is to isolate the cause of the problem by eliminating the elements of the process that are functioning properly. This is particularly true when TCP/IP communications are involved. If you are unable to connect to an FTP site on the Internet, the problem can lie anywhere between your FTP client application and the remote site's FTP server application.

Thus, your FTP program itself may be malfunctioning, or there may be trouble with the TCP protocol that carries the FTP packets, the IP protocol that carries the TCP segments, the Ethernet frame that carries the IP datagrams, or the corresponding processes in the destination computer. There might also be a hardware problem at any point in the connection. This means that it could be in your machine, your network, your service provider's network, any of the interim gateways used, or any of the hardware at the destination site, and this is only an abbreviated list.

TIP If your TCP/IP settings have been manually configured, the most common cause of problems is an incorrect value in the TCP/IP Properties dialog box. If a newly configured machine is not functioning properly, check and double-check the settings. If a connection that previously functioned (and has not been changed) is no longer operative, then the problem probably lies in the hardware or outside of your machine.

Therefore, the first order of business in troubleshooting a problem of this type is to begin eliminating potential causes by repeating the same process in different ways. If you can't connect to one FTP site, try connecting to a different one. If you are successful, then it becomes far more likely that the problem is at the remote site.

If you are unable to connect to any site on the Internet, the next step would be to determine if the problem is in your network or in your machine. If, for example, you can connect to another machine on your corporate internetwork, then you know that the problem lies in the Internet connection.

If necessary, you can then proceed to try to connect to a machine on your local network segment (as opposed to another segment on your internetwork). If this is possible, then you know that the problem concerns your gateway to the other network segments. If you cannot connect to any other system at all, it is then time to begin looking at your own system.

Duplicating the same process at another workstation can help in this end, but it can also complicate things if the problem is in your local network. A different machine may be on a different segment, use different gateways, DNSs, WINS servers, and so on.

Another way to narrow down the possible causes of a problem is to address the networking stack vertically. For example, if you cannot connect to another machine using FTP, then try to connect to the same machine using just IP (with PING). If this works, then the problem lies somewhere in the upper layers of the stack. If IP fails, then try communicating with another protocol stack, if possible. This can tell you if there is a problem in the Physical layer.

This process, however, does not isolate the physical location of the problem as the first technique does. If you can access a site with PING, but not FTP, the problem could still be in your system, the remote system, or anywhere in between.

Using both of these techniques can eliminate the great majority of a problem's potential causes, but it is important in any troubleshooting process to be logical and grindingly methodical. If you try to combine the two techniques—such as when failing to connect to a remote site using FTP, you try using PING to contact a local system—you will only end up confusing yourself and possibly making the situation worse instead of better.

PING

The most useful TCP/IP utility is PING, which is used to determine whether a remote system can receive and reply to IP communications from the local host. PING sends a series of IP packets containing ICMP Echo Request messages to the address or host name specified on the command line. When everything is operating normally, the remote system returns an ICMP Echo Response packet for each request received. The responses are displayed as they are received back at the source computer, along with the number of bytes sent, the round trip time for the transmission, and the Time-to-Live value, as shown here:

```
Pinging 199.29.133.199 with 32 bytes of data:

Reply from 198.29.133.169: bytes=32 time=540ms TTL=115
Reply from 198.29.133.169: bytes=32 time=518ms TTL=117
Reply from 198.29.133.169: bytes=32 time=678ms TTL=117
Reply from 198.29.133.169: bytes=32 time=524ms TTL=117
```

PING is the fundamental tool for determining whether a TCP/IP system can communicate with another. When used correctly, it can help to diagnose many different types of problems, both in a computer's networking stack itself and in the link to another machine.

Syntax: `PING` `[-a]` `[-n count]` `[-l length]` `[-t]` `[-f]` `[-w timeout]` `destination`

Parameters:

`-a`	Resolves IP addresses of destination systems into host names
`-n count`	Transmits the number of Echo Request packets specified by *count* (default is 4)
`-l length`	Sends Echo Request packets containing length amount of data (default is 64 bytes; maximum is 8192 bytes)
`-t`	Causes PING to send continuous Echo Request packets until interrupted
`-f`	Prevents the Echo packets from being fragmented by gateways
`-w timeout`	Sets the timeout interval in milliseconds
`destination`	Specifies the Echo Request destination by IP address or host name

Part
V

Ch
23

PING's ability to use either IP addresses or host names allows you to use it for one of the most fundamental TCP/IP troubleshooting techniques. If you are unable to connect to a remote site using its host name, try using its IP address. If you are able to connect, then the problem is one of name resolution.

You can also test a TCP/IP installation with PING, even when it is not connected to the network. The network address 127 has always been reserved for use as a loopback address, that is, any transmission sent to the IP address 127.0.0.1 is returned immediately to the same stack that generated it, without it reaching the Physical layer. The PING 127.0.0.1 command should generate the same results as any other PING, if the stack is functioning properly. Obviously, this procedure can't speak for the efficacy of your network or most of your TCP/IP settings, but it will tell you that the protocol has been installed correctly and is functional.

You can also use the loopback address with other TCP/IP programs. For example, you can test your FTP server by using the FTP 127.0.0.1 command. This allows your FTP client program to connect to your FTP server, when both are located on the same machine.

TRACERT

While PING can tell you whether an IP connection to a remote system can be established, it cannot tell you how it is established. When troubleshooting TCP/IP routing problems, how the packets arrive at their destination is as important as whether they arrive at all.

TRACERT is a useful and entertaining command line utility that displays the route taken by IP packets from their source to their destination. It is derived from an equivalent UNIX utility called traceroute. The route is traced by sending a series of ICMP packets to the destination with steadily incrementing Time-to-Live (TTL) values. The first packet sent has a TTL value of 1. Because the TTL value is decremented by every gateway that the packet passes through, that 1 is changed to a 0 by the first gateway receiving it. The TTL value, having expired, causes an ICMP Time Exceeded packet to be sent back to the sender, along with the amount of time, in milliseconds. The second packet has a TTL value of two, and is therefore stopped by the second gateway it reaches. Each subsequent packet gets one step farther until one reaches the destination. All of the packets returned to the sending computer are then ordered using the time delay figures, and displayed.

TRACERT is useful for determining whether IP gateways on your network are functioning properly. If, for example, on a large internetwork you have a multi-homed machine that is connected to two network segments, A and B, you may be able to PING systems on both segments without being certain that both adapters are functioning. The system on network B that you are pinging may in fact be reached through network A, using another gateway. If you run a TRACERT to a system on each of the two networks, you can be certain that your packets are reaching their destination.

Syntax: TRACERT [-d] [-h *max_hops*] [-w *timeout*] *hostname*

Parameters:

-d	Prevents display of the resolved names of interim systems
-h *max_hops*	Specifies the maximum number of hops to be traced
-w *timeout*	Specifies the maximum waiting period for a reply (in milliseconds)
hostname	Specifies the full host name or IP address of the destination system

N O T E   Some routers filter out Time Exceeded packets, causing them to be discarded before they return to your workstation. TRACERT cannot create a trace to any system on the far side of such a router. ▪

TRACERT is a useful tool on your local network, but on the Internet it becomes a fascinating behind-the-scenes look at the path that your Web or FTP connection takes to its destination. The trace shown here tracks the route taken from a dial-up connection to a large service provider in New York, to a World Wide Web server located on the outskirts of Paris.

```
Tracing route to www.mycorp.fr [192.7.79.30]over a maximum of 30 hops:
1    368 ms    343 ms    342 ms    arl-dial-33.comp.com [145.174.210.52]
2    346 ms    342 ms    336 ms    145.174.5.129
3    351 ms    379 ms    344 ms    fddi0-core.arl.comp.net [206.156.223.54]
4    341 ms    365 ms    349 ms    atm1-02-core.dub.comp.net [206.156.223.98]
5    435 ms    352 ms    332 ms    fddi4-border2.dub.comp.net [206.156.223.67]
6    361 ms    380 ms    336 ms    border4-hssi1-0.NorthRoyalton.mci.net
➥[204.70.102.5]
7    347 ms    347 ms    439 ms    core1-fddi-1.NorthRoyalton.mci.net
➥[204.70.98.33]
8    511 ms    367 ms    340 ms    core1-hssi-3.WestOrange.mci.net
➥[204.70.1.102]
9    361 ms    363 ms    354 ms    core2.Washington.mci.net [204.70.4.189]
10   365 ms    359 ms    360 ms    mae-east-plusplus.Washington.mci.net
➥[204.70.74.102]
11   362 ms    380 ms    363 ms    was-gw3.pipex.net [192.41.177.190]
12   487 ms    479 ms    475 ms    Vincennes2-S0.2.OLEANE.NET [193.128.43.34]
13   488 ms    457 ms    462 ms    Vincennes4-E0.OLEANE.NET [194.2.3.251]
14   477 ms    497 ms    493 ms    Alben-GW.OLEANE.NET [193.28.24.202]
15   515 ms    515 ms    523 ms    www.mycorp.fr [193.57.78.30]
Trace complete.
```

The number in the left column indicates the TTL value for that hop. The next three columns are the round trip times for three transmission attempts using that TTL. The column on the right displays the IP address (and the host name, if possible) of that gateway. In this example, notice the jump in the access times between hops 11 and 12 as the signal crosses the Atlantic.

HOSTNAME

HOSTNAME is a command line utility with no parameters. It displays the IP host name of the local machine as registered by the DNS specified in the TCP/IP Properties dialog box.

IPCONFIG

Syntax: IPCONFIG [/all] [/renew adapter] [/release adapter]

Parameters:

/all	Displays all TCP/IP configuration settings for all host adapters
/renew adapter	On a system using DHCP, causes reassignment of the assigned parameters
/release adapter	On a system using DHCP, causes all assigned parameters to be released, disabling TCP/IP on that adapter

Part
V

Ch
23

IPCONFIG is used to display the current operating TCP/IP parameters for each adapter installed in a Windows NT machine. When DHCP is used to assign IP addresses and other settings, IPCONFIG is the most convenient way of determining exactly what settings have been assigned to your machine. When used with no parameters, it displays only the IP address, subnet mask, and default gateway for each adapter. The /all parameters displays all settings, as shown in this example.

```
Windows NT IP Configuration
        Host Name . . . . . . . . . : smithj.mycorp.com
        DNS Servers . . . . . . . . : 179.69.173.9
                                      179.69.173.14
        Node Type . . . . . . . . . : Hybrid
        NetBIOS Scope ID. . . . . . :
        IP Routing Enabled. . . . . : Yes
        WINS Proxy Enabled. . . . . : No
        NetBIOS Resolution Uses DNS : Yes
Ethernet adapter SMCISA1:
        Description . . . . . . . . : SMC Adapter.
        Physical Address. . . . . . : 00-00-C0-EA-D2-99
        DHCP Enabled. . . . . . . . : No
        IP Address. . . . . . . . . : 131.1.29.50
        Subnet Mask . . . . . . . . : 255.255.255.0
        Default Gateway . . . . . . : 131.1.29.1
        Primary WINS Server . . . . : 131.1.25.30
        Secondary WINS Server . . . : 131.1.29.61
Ethernet adapter SMCISA2:
        Description . . . . . . . . : SMC Adapter.
        Physical Address. . . . . . : 00-00-C1-DA-D3-97
        DHCP Enabled. . . . . . . . : Yes
        IP Address. . . . . . . . . : 131.1.43.52
        Subnet Mask . . . . . . . . : 255.255.255.0
        Default Gateway . . . . . . : 131.1.43.1
        Primary WINS Server . . . . : 131.1.25.30
        Secondary WINS Server . . . : 131.1.29.61
```

ARP

The Address Resolution Protocol (ARP) functions at the bottom of the TCP/IP protocol stack. It is used to ascertain the node address of an Ethernet or Token Ring workstation to which IP datagrams are to be transmitted. IP datagrams must be enclosed in a Data Link layer frame before transmission. The only way for IP to know the Data Link layer address of the system that it wants to transmit to is to broadcast that system's IP address in an ARP Request packet. The system using that IP address then returns an ARP Reply packet containing the MAC address assigned to the network host adapter.

N O T E   ARP only functions on the local network segment. While the destination address in an IP datagram's header indicates the ultimate receiver of the packet and never changes, an Ethernet or Token Ring frame header contains the address only of the next network interface to which it will be sent. In the case of an IP packet, this is the sending system's default gateway. The gateway system then changes the MAC address to that of the next system on the route to the destination. As a result, if all of your IP packets are sent to computers on other networks, your ARP table will be empty. ■

After the reply is received, the IP packets are transmitted and the destination's IP address and associated MAC address are stored in the workstation's ARP cache for later use. The ARP cache is purged on a regular basis. The ARP Reply packet is also broadcast to the rest of the network, so that other workstations can maintain their own ARP tables.

The Windows NT ARP utility allows you to view and modify the contents of your workstation's ARP table. You can remove entries from the table and add new entries that will be retained permanently, and never purged.

Syntax: `ARP [-a] [-d ipaddress] [-s ipaddress macaddress] [hostaddress]`

Parameters:

`-a`	Displays all ARP table information for all hosts
`-d ipaddress`	Removes the entry for the specified IP address from the ARP table
`-s ipaddress macaddress`	Creates a new permanent table entry associating the IP address specified with the MAC address specified.
`hostaddress`	Specifies the IP address of the host adapter whose table should be modified

ROUTE

The ROUTE command enables you to view, modify, add, or delete entries in the workstation's static routing table. You can override the use of the default gateway when transmitting to a particular network by adding an entry to the routing table. The ROUTE PRINT command displays the current contents of the routing table, as shown here.

```
Active Routes:
Network Address    Netmask            Gateway Address    Interface      Metric
0.0.0.0            0.0.0.0            120.110.10.100     120.110.10.1   1
120.110.10.0       255.255.255.0      120.110.10.1       120.110.10.1   1
120.110.10.1       255.255.255.255    127.0.0.1          127.0.0.1      1
120.255.255.255    255.255.255.255    120.110.10.1       120.110.10.1   1
127.0.0.0          255.0.0.0          127.0.0.1          127.0.0.1      1
224.0.0.0          224.0.0.0          120.110.10.1       120.110.10.1   1
225.255.255.255    255.255.255.255    120.110.10.1       120.110.10.1   1
```

Part
V

Ch
23

Syntax: `ROUTE [-f] [[print] [add] [delete] [change] [`*`destination`*`] [MASK`
`netmask``] [`*`gateway`*`] [METRIC `*`costmetric`*`]`

Parameters:

`-f`	Clears all gateway entries from the routing table (before any other commands are executed)
`print`	Displays a routing table entry (with no parameters, displays all entries)
`add`	Creates a new routing table entry
`delete`	Removes an entry from the routing table
change	Modifies an existing routing table entry
`destination`	Specifies the host to which the command should be addressed
`MASK `*`netmask`*	Specifies the subnet mask value for the routing table entry
`gateway`	Specifies the gateway for the routing table entry
`METRIC `*`costmetric`*	Specifies an integer cost metric (from 1 to 9999) used to calculate the best route to a specific network.

NETSTAT

The NETSTAT utility displays the workstation's TCP/IP connections currently in use as well as packet statistics for the network interface and for the individual protocols, as shown here.

```
Active Connections
   Proto  Local Address            Foreign Address            State
   TCP    smithj:1372              ftp.mycorp.com:ftp         TIME_WAIT
   TCP    smithj:1390              www.mycorp.com:80          ESTABLISHED
   UDP    smithj:nbname            *:*
   UDP    smithj:nbdatagram      *:*
   UDP    smithj:nbname            *:*
   UDP    smithj:nbdatagram      *:*
Interface Statistics
                                Received            Sent
Bytes                           4441152             86989
Unicast packets                 1230                902
Non-unicast packets             4087                80
Discards                        0                   0
Errors                          0                   0
Unknown protocols               9456

IP Statistics
  Packets Received              = 3705
  Received Header Errors        = 0
  Received Address Errors       = 14
```

```
       Datagrams Forwarded                  = 0
       Unknown Protocols Received           = 0
       Received Packets Discarded           = 0
       Received Packets Delivered           = 3691
       Output Requests                      = 961
       Routing Discards                     = 0
       Discarded Output Packets             = 0
       Output Packet No Route               = 0
       Reassembly Required                  = 0
       Reassembly Successful                = 0
       Reassembly Failures                  = 0
       Datagrams Successfully Fragmented    = 0
       Datagrams Failing Fragmentation      = 0
       Fragments Created                    = 0
TCP Statistics
       Active Opens                         = 28
       Passive Opens                        = 11
       Failed Connection Attempts           = 0
       Reset Connections                    = 17
       Current Connections                  = 0
       Segments Received                    = 1160
       Segments Sent                        = 846
       Segments Retransmitted               = 4

UDP Statistics
       Datagrams Received                   = 232
       No Ports                             = 2299
       Receive Errors                       = 0
       Datagrams Sent                       = 101
```

NETSTAT allows you to see what type of connection is used by a particular application and to determine whether it is currently transmitting or receiving data. The *interval* parameter allows you to examine protocol statistics over a period of time as other processes continue to function.

Syntax: NETSTAT [-a] [-e] [-n] [-s] [-r] [-p *protocol*] [*interval*]

Parameters:

-a	Displays all active TCP/IP connections and their state (TCP only)
-e	Displays transmission statistics for the network interface
-n	Displays active TCP/IP connections using IP addresses
-s	Displays individual protocol statistics for IP, ICMP, TCP and UDP
-r	Displays the routing table
-p *protocol*	Displays active connections for the specified protocol. With the -s switch, displays statistics for the specified protocol
interval	Continually redisplays protocol statistics, with a delay of *interval* seconds between displays

Part

V

Ch

23

NBTSTAT

The NBTSTAT command displays statistics and connections for NetBIOS over TCP communications. It can also be used to make changes to the LMHOSTS file immediately active by purging the name cache and reloading it from LMHOSTS.

Syntax: NBTSTAT [-a *remotename*] [-A *remoteaddress*] [-c] [-n] [-R][-r] [-S] [-s] *interval*

Parameters:

-a *remotename*	Displays the NetBIOS name table for the machine name specified
-A *remoteaddress*	Displays the NetBIOS name table for the IP address specified
-c	Displays the contents of the NetBIOS name cache
-n	Displays NetBIOS names for the local machine
-R	Purges the NetBIOS name cache and reloads the LMHOSTS file
-r	Displays NetBIOS name resolution statistics
-S	Displays current NetBIOS workstation and server sessions,listing remote hosts by IP address
-s	Displays current NetBIOS workstation and server sessions,listing remote hosts by name
interval	Redisplays protocol statistics continually, with a delay of *interval* seconds between displays

Windows NT Performance Monitor

Utilities like NETSTAT can give you some idea of the TCP/IP traffic patterns of your network, but the most comprehensive picture of all of its processes is provided by the Network Monitor application that ships with Windows NT 4.0 Server product, as well as the Microsoft Systems Management Server (SMS). Network Monitor intercepts and captures every packet that passes by a particular network host adapter. Windows NT Workstation includes an agent for the Network Monitor that allows the application (running on another machine) to capture the packets from an adapter on your workstation.

Normally, a network adapter monitors the passing traffic and only processes the packets destined for its own node address. Network Monitor puts an adapter into *promiscuous mode*, forcing it to process all of the packets transmitted on the network segment. (You must be using a network adapter that is capable of promiscuous mode operations.) Packets can be selectively captured and displayed using filters to isolate specific hosts or protocols (see fig. 23.9).

FIG. 23.9
Network Monitor provides a detailed view of every packet's header information and contents.

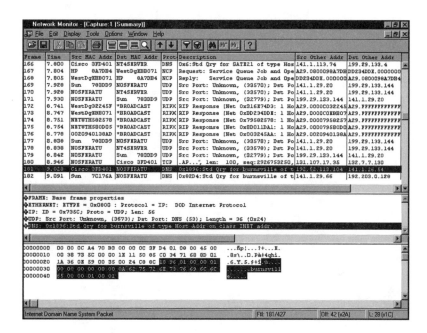

With Network Monitor, you can examine a network connection in minute detail, seeing every exchange of data that takes place between two computers. As a troubleshooting tool, it presupposes the existence of a functioning connection, but for diagnosing problems in higher level functions, it is unparalleled.

From Here…

In this chapter, you learned how to install and configure the components of the Windows NT TCP/IP stack, as well as some of the underlying theory behind their design.

- For more information on the fundamental concepts of TCP/IP transport, see Chapter 22, "Overview of TCP/IP."

- For more information on the installation, configuration, and use of the Windows NT DHCP service, see Chapter 24, "Using DHCP."

- For more information on the name resolution services that can be used with Windows NT, see Chapter 25, "Using DNS and WINS."

Part
V

Ch
23

CHAPTER 24

Using DHCP

by Craig Zacker

The Dynamic Host Configuration Protocol, or DHCP, is an element of the TCP/IP protocol suite that allows vital TCP/IP configuration parameters such as IP addresses, subnet masks, and default gateways, to be assigned to network workstations by a centralized computer functioning as a DHCP server. The protocol was created by the Microsoft Corporation, in conjunction with many other organizations, as a means to alleviate the inherent administration difficulties associated with the assignment of IP addresses to workstations on large internetworks.

A DHCP server consists of two components: a mechanism for tracking and allocating TCP/IP configuration parameters, and a protocol with which these parameters are delivered to and acknowledged by the client. The DHCP standard, published in the Internet Engineering Task Force's RFC (Request for Comment) 1541, is based on the BOOTP protocol defined in RFC 951, with which it remains backward-compatible.

BOOTP is a protocol that was designed for use by servers to deliver TCP/IP configuration settings, and then to facilitate the TFTP transfer of an executable operating system boot file to diskless workstations. While BOOTP is capable of assigning statically

Simplify the administration of a Windows NT network

DHCP can prevent the need for manual configuration of workstation TCP/IP settings as well as work together with WINS (the Windows Internet Naming System) to provide network name resolution services.

How DHCP servers and clients cooperate

The process by which workstations request and renew their TCP/IP settings demonstrates the ways in which DHCP can resolve many of the common configuration problems that afflict IP networks.

Install and configure a DHCP server

The DHCP server module that ships with Windows NT can help to furnish a workstation with many other settings and services in addition to an IP address.

Configure your server using the DHCP Manager

Windows NT includes a DHCP Manager application that allows network administrators to monitor and configure DHCP servers anywhere on the enterprise network.

configured IP addresses to workstations from a central server, DHCP can dynamically assign and renew workstation configurations from a pool of IP addresses, solving many of the problems that have hampered the utility of BOOTP. Windows NT Server ships with an integrated DHCP server module that allows many different types of TCP/IP clients to request configuration parameters from a central source, preventing the duplication of addresses and simplifying network administration tasks.

By definition, the user of a workstation that is a DHCP client is absolved from any involvement with the TCP/IP configuration process. The whole DHCP mechanism is designed to obviate the need for the user training or administrative intervention that has plagued the use of TCP/IP in the past. ■

The Origins of DHCP

The design of the TCP/IP protocols was based on the need to solve a number of problems endemic to the creation of the large-scale, cross-platform, packet-switching network now known as the Internet. Chief among these problems was the need to devise a method for addressing any individual computer on this network of networks; a method that was not based on factors specific to any particular hardware platform or operating system.

Different types of computer networks have different ways of identifying the machines that comprise them. An Ethernet or Token Ring LAN will have a unique MAC (Media Access Control) address hardcoded into each network interface card by the manufacturer. Because each manufacturer numbers its cards sequentially, and because part of that MAC address consists of a code identifying the manufacturer itself, the device's address is unique not only on the local network where it is used, but on all networks everywhere. No other adapter exists that uses that exact same address.

This convention would be quite sufficient for use on an open network such as the Internet, except that not all networked computers use it. On some network types, the identifying hardware address is assigned by the network administrator. Other computers (such as stand-alone machines using a dial-up Internet connection) have no identifying hardware address at all. Chapter 22, "Overview of TCP/IP," discusses the IETF standards call for the use of a completely separate address by which IP networks and hosts can be identified.

Administrative Problems of TCP/IP

Because the IP address has no inherent association with the computer's hardware or software configuration, it could not practically be assigned by any product manufacturer except through a massive administrative effort that would require more cooperation among vendors than has ever been dreamed possible. The task of supplying unique IP addresses to individual hosts has therefore been left to the network administrator.

When dealing with a relatively small number of computers, the configuration of individual machines is not a significant problem. However, the increasing popularity of TCP/IP as an all-purpose LAN protocol and the incredible growth of the Internet have suddenly placed network administrators in a position where they are responsible for the configuration of hundreds or thousands of TCP/IP-equipped computers.

This leaves the administrators with two choices: either they allocate the manpower needed to have trained personnel manually configure each workstation, or they develop a documented procedure by which users can configure their own TCP/IP settings.

The first solution is expensive, possibly requiring temporary personnel to assist in configuration chores on a large TCP/IP network rollout. The second solution holds a great potential for configuration error, as users would be following instructions by rote, unaware of the nature or significance of the parameters they are adjusting. There would also be a tendency for one unsophisticated user to supply another with his or her machine settings, with the assurance that "this is a configuration that works," resulting in the single most common TCP/IP configuration problem: duplication of IP addresses.

In either case, it is necessary for someone to manually maintain a listing of the IP addresses assigned to specific machines to avoid duplication. Every time that a workstation is moved, or a new one installed, an IP address must be assigned and the listing updated.

Microsoft itself faced this problem while planning the conversion of its 35,000-node global internetwork to TCP/IP, and it set about developing a mechanism for its own use that could also be added to its commercial network operating system products and published as an open Internet standard.

Part V

Ch 24

BOOTP and DHCP

When the development of DHCP began, a standard already existed for delivery of IP addresses (as well as boot files) from a central server to individual workstations. It was defined in RFC 951 as the Bootstrap Protocol, or BOOTP. BOOTP is a protocol that allows a workstation to receive static IP address information from a server as it loads its TCP/IP stack. It was designed for use on diskless workstations that had no nonvolatile storage medium for semi-permanent configuration settings. The configuration data delivered by BOOTP is not intelligently derived; it is manually entered by the administrator into a table that equates specific MAC addresses with specific IP addresses (and other basic configuration settings).

As a result, BOOTP is no more than a means of storing the TCP/IP settings for all of a network's workstations in a single place and delivering them as needed. The administrators of the network are still responsible for seeing that the computers are configured properly, that there are no duplicate IP addresses assigned, and so on. BOOTP only relieves them of the need to travel to each individual workstation.

This in itself is not an insignificant achievement. The number of administrative manhours that can be saved by the use of BOOTP on a large network makes it a most useful alternative to manual configuration. However, when dealing with tens of thousands of nodes located in more than 50 countries, as Microsoft was, even the maintenance and replication of the required BOOTP servers would be a Herculean task.

What Microsoft needed was a means of dynamically assigning IP address settings to workstations as they were needed. This would allow new workstations to be added to the network without reconfiguring either the workstation or the server. DHCP was the result of Microsoft's efforts.

Advantages of Windows NT's DHCP Server

The DHCP server module that ships with Windows NT Server conforms with the standards defined in Internet Engineering Task Force's Requests for Comment documents 1531, 1532, 1541, and 1542. Among the features defined by the standards and implemented by Windows NT are:

- Manual, automatic, or dynamic IP address allocation
- Allocation of additional TCP/IP configuration parameters
- Automatic name resolution with WINS
- Internetwork routability using BOOTP relay agents

ON THE WEB

The IETF Request for Comments documents are available from many FTP and World Wide Web servers, including

ftp://ftp.internic.net/rfc

IP Address Allocation   Windows NT's implementation of DHCP is capable of furnishing TCP/IP configuration settings to workstations using three different allocation methods: manual, automatic, and dynamic.

Manual allocation is the equivalent of the service provided by BOOTP. Settings defined by the network administrator are stored on the DHCP server and delivered to the workstation whenever its TCP/IP stack is initialized.

In the *automatic allocation* process, the settings delivered to the workstation are selected by the server from a pool of valid addresses. The values selected during a workstation's first DHCP negotiation become the permanent settings for that computer.

Dynamic allocation is the same as automatic allocation, except that the settings delivered to the workstation are only leased for a limited amount of time. Periodically, the negotiation process between the DHCP client and server must be repeated in order to renew the lease on a particular IP address.

Dynamic allocation resolves one of the most persistent problems addressed by the protocol's developers: the roving user. When a computer is moved from one subnet to another (as in the case of a laptop or a demonstration machine), it requires different IP address, subnet mask, and default gateway values. Dynamic allocation allows the workstation to automatically acquire the new settings that it needs without leaving its previous settings permanently allocated and yet unused.

Part
V

Ch
24

Windows NT's DHCP server allows you to use all of these different allocation methods simultaneously. IP addresses can be automatically allocated from a designated range of addresses called a *scope*, with or without a lease. At the same time, you can designate permanent IP address assignments for specific machines, excluding the addresses from the scope and associating them with specific hardware addresses.

However useful the dynamic allocation of IP addresses is, there are times when you will want to assign a permanent IP address to a computer, such as for a machine used as a World Wide Web or FTP server on the Internet. In a case like this, regularly changing IP addresses would confuse users and especially DNSs. You could assign a static IP address to such a machine in the normal manner, eschewing DHCP entirely, but using the manual allocation capabilities of the Windows NT DHCP server allows you to keep the records of all of your address assignments in one central location. This way, there is no chance of accidentally reassigning that static address to another machine.

Extended TCP/IP Parameter Allocation   Windows NT's DHCP server can furnish a client with far more than an IP address and subnet mask. Over 50 additional predefined parameters can be supplied as well, many of which are intended for use with DHCP clients other than that supplied with the Microsoft Windows operating systems. You also can define additional parameters yourself, making the Windows NT DHCP server suitable for use with many different workstation platforms.

The Microsoft DHCP client can be assigned the following parameters by the Windows NT DHCP server. All of the other parameters listed in the Windows NT DHCP Manager are intended for use with third-party clients.

- **IP address.** The 32-bit dotted decimal address used to identify a particular host on a particular IP network.

- **Subnet mask.** The 32-bit dotted decimal value used to specify which bits of the IP address identify the network where the host is located, and which bits identify the host itself.

- **Router.** The IP addresses of gateway systems on the host's local network, through which IP packets are sent to remote networks (accessed in the order they are listed).

- **DNS servers.** The IP addresses of computers running a DNS service or daemon (accessed in the order they are listed).

- **Domain name.** The name of the Internet domain to which the client belongs.

- **WINS/NBNS (NetBIOS name server) addresses.** The IP addresses of WINS servers used for name resolution on the local network.

- **WINS/NBT (NetBIOS over TCP/IP) node type.** A code indicating the NetBIOS name resolution mechanisms to be used by the client, and the order in which they should be used.

- **NetBIOS scope ID.** A string used to identify a group of NetBIOS machines that can communicate only with each other.

DHCP and Name Resolution   Another problem created by the dynamic allocation process is that of name resolution. Domain name systems (DNSs) and HOST files, the traditional mechanisms that allow host names to be used instead of IP addresses when addressing other computers, both rely on static lookup tables manually maintained by users or network administrators. Obviously, the advantages of DHCP would be completely negated if administrators had to manually register every dynamic IP address change in a name resolution table.

Windows NT overcomes this limitation by including the Windows Internet Naming System (or WINS) with the NT Server product. WINS is a name resolution database that works together with DHCP to automatically update itself whenever a computer's IP address changes. Unlike a HOSTS file or a DNS, WINS does not track the computer's Internet host name. Instead, it tracks the machine's NetBIOS name. This is the 15-character (maximum) computer name that you select during the Windows NT installation process. With a properly configured WINS server (which can run on the same machine as the DHCP server), users can specify a computer's NetBIOS name in any application that would otherwise call for an IP address.

N O T E See Chapter 25, "Using DNS and WINS," for information about the WINS to DNS interface in NT 4.0 and how it can be used to provide DHCP for hosts needing IP name resolution. ■

NetBIOS names and WINS are intended for internal network use, because there is no central administrative body that registers computer names, as InterNIC does domain names. If your machines are connected directly to the Internet, you can run a DNS as well, to maintain standard Internet host name equivalents for your computers' IP addresses. For more information on WINS and name resolution, see Chapter 25, "Using DNS and WINS."

DHCP Routability DHCP was designed to be a resource for the entire enterprise network. It is therefore necessary for the protocol to be routable, so that DHCP clients can communicate with DHCP servers across IP gateways or routers. Otherwise, it would be necessary to have a DHCP server on each network segment. This was one of the advantages of designing DHCP to be backward-compatible with BOOTP. Many existing routers already comply with the BOOTP standard, and DHCP traffic uses the same packet structure as BOOTP. You also can configure any Windows NT server to function as a DHCP relay agent, which eliminates the need for explicit BOOTP or DHCP support in a router.

Part
V

Ch
24

Understanding DHCP Communications

When a client computer is configured to use DHCP to acquire its IP configuration settings, it will attempt to communicate with the DHCP servers on its local network each time that it is rebooted or the TCP/IP stack is reinitialized. This communication may be for the purpose of requesting new configuration settings or confirming the continued use of settings that it has already been allocated.

DHCP clients and servers utilize the User Datagram Protocol (UDP) for their communications, with clients transmitting to the *DHCP Server* port (67) and servers to the *DHCP Client* port (68), as defined in the *Assigned Numbers* RFC. Windows NT's DHCP communications are channeled through the Remote Procedure Calls (RPC) application programming interface. All DHCP communications use the same packet format, as shown in figure 24.1. This is the same packet that is used for BOOTP, defined in RFC 951, with additional options defined in other standards.

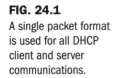

FIG. 24.1

A single packet format is used for all DHCP client and server communications.

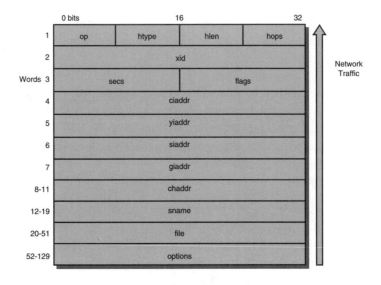

The fields that comprise the DHCP packet are as follows:

- **op** (1 octet). Specifies the message type. 1 = BOOTREQUEST, indicating a packet sent from client to server; 2 = BOOTREPLY, indicating a packet sent from server to client.

- **htype** (1 octet). Indicates the type of hardware address specified in the chaddr field, using the ARP codes defined in the Assigned Numbers RFC.

- **hlen** (1 octet). Indicates the length (in octets) of the hardware address specified in the chaddr field.

- **hops** (1 octet). Set to zero by the client, optionally incremented by relay-agents to indicate the number of intermediate subnets between client and server.

- **xid** (4 octets). A randomly selected transaction ID number chosen by the client and used by the server to identify all subsequent packets in a particular DHCP negotiation.

- **secs** (2 octets). Specifies the amount of time (in seconds) since the client started the TCP/IP initialization process; used to distinguish multiple messages of the same type sent during a single DHCP negotiation.

- **flags** (2 octets). The first bit is used for the broadcast flag, which when set to "1" by the client, instructs all DHCP servers and relay agents to broadcast their replies rather than unicast them. All other bits are unused at this time, must be set to zero by the client, and must remain unchanged throughout the DHCP negotiation process.

- **ciaddr** (4 octets). Specifies the current workstation IP address when a client is requesting the continued use of an already assigned configuration with a DHCPREQUEST message; otherwise it is set to "0."

- **yiaddr** (4 octets). Specifies the IP address being offered or assigned to a client by a DHCP server in a DHCPOFFER or DHCPACK message; otherwise it is set to "0."

- **siaddr** (4 octets). Specifies the IP address of the next server to be used during a client's bootstrap sequence; used only when a boot file transfer is required by the client, and the boot files for different machine types (specified by the "class identifier" option) are stored on different servers.

- **giaddr** (4 octets). Specifies the IP address of the DHCP relay agent to which a server should send its replies when the client is located on a different network segment or subnet; set to "0" when client and server are located on the same network.

Part V

Ch 24

- **chaddr** (16 octets). Specifies the hardware address of the client, according to the type and length specified in the htype and hlen fields; furnished by the client in DHCPDISCOVER and DHCPREQUEST messages and used by the server to address unicast replies.

- **sname** (64 octets). Specifies the host name of the DHCP server (optional); may also be used for overflow from the options field (if the "options overload" option is set).

- **file** (128 octets). On diskless workstations requiring full BOOTP services, specifies the name of the boot file required by the client; may also be used for overflow from the options field (if the "options overload" option is set).

- **options** (variable, minimum 312 octets). The first four octets of this field contain the values 99, 130, 83, and 99, the so-called "magic cookie" (defined in RFC 1497) which defines how data that follows is to be interpreted. Succeeding fields may contain any of the options defined in RFC 1533 "DHCP Options and BOOTP Vendor Extensions." Individual options are of variable length, and consist of a "tag" octet, which identifies the option, and a "length" octet, followed by the number of octets specified in the "length" octet, containing the option value itself. Available options include all of the additional configuration parameters that can be furnished by BOOTP (as specified in RFC 1497) plus specific DHCP extensions. Options not fitting in the maximum length field (as determined by the network type being used) can be inserted into the file and sname fields, if they are unused.

All DHCP message packets must include the "DHCP Message Type" option, which identifies the packet as performing one of the following basic DHCP functions:

Value	Message Type	Purpose
1	DHCPDISCOVER	Used by clients to locate DHCP servers
2	DHCPOFFER	Used by servers to offer IP addresses to clients
3	DHCPREQUEST	Used by clients to request a specific IP address
4	DHCPDECLINE	Used by clients to reject an offered IP address
5	DHCPACK	Used by servers to acknowledge a client's acceptance of an IP address
6	DHCPNAK	Used by servers to reject a client's acceptance of an IP address
7	DHCPRELEASE	Used by clients to terminate the lease of an IP address

The initial DHCP message sent by a client during the TCP/IP initialization process is always intended for broadcast to all of the DHCP servers on the internetwork. It is the responsibility of the routers or computers functioning as DHCP relay agents on the local network to propagate the traffic generated by a client to other networks.

If the client fails to contact any DHCP server, it may continue to utilize any settings that have already been assigned to it until the client's previously negotiated lease has expired. After the lease has expired, or if the client has not yet been assigned any configuration settings, the initialization of the TCP/IP stack will fail, preventing any further IP communications from taking place and generating an error message at the client. The Windows NT client will, in this instance, repeat its attempts to contact a DHCP server until an appropriate response is received, generating an error each time the predetermined timeout values are reached.

A DHCP client that has no current configuration settings assigned to it by a server must begin the client configuration sequence from the beginning. There are several different circumstances that can leave a DHCP client in an unconfigured state:

- The workstation may be a new DHCP client.
- The workstation may be a previous DHCP client whose lease has expired.

- The workstation may have been moved to a different subnet, causing its previous settings to be declared invalid.
- The workstation may have explicitly released its hold on its previous settings.

The process by which a DHCP client negotiates the lease of its configuration settings with a server follows the sequence shown in figure 24.2, and described in the following section.

FIG. 24.2
A DHCP client is assigned an IP address only after a 4-step negotiation with a DHCP server.

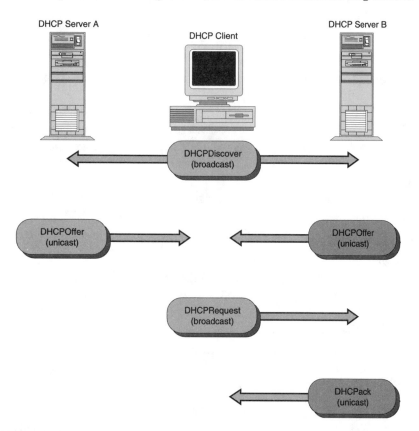

Part
V
Ch
24

The DHCP Negotiation Process

Any client beginning a new DHCP negotiation sequence is, by definition, operating without a valid IP address. Therefore, the DHCP client software allows it to send only a broadcast message to the local network containing a DHCPDISCOVER message.

DHCPDISCOVER is a generalized request for TCP/IP configuration settings from the client to all DHCP servers on the internetwork. The client furnishes its hardware type (htype), the length of its hardware address (hlen) and the hardware address itself (chaddr). On a typical Ethernet or Token Ring network, this will be the MAC address assigned to the network interface card. The client also selects a transaction ID (xid) that is used by all replying servers to identify their packets as pertaining to this particular DHCP negotiation.

The hardware address information allows the DHCP server to address a unicast reply to the client and allows it to maintain its own records equating the hardware address with the proposed IP address.

N O T E The DHCP service allocates addresses to network hosts, not necessarily to computers. On a multi-homed machine, each host adapter can be (but need not be) a DHCP client. Each client conducts its own independent DHCP negotiations and maintains its own lease on an IP address. ▪

The client may request the assignment of a particular IP address and/or lease time duration by specifying these values using the Requested IP Address and IP Address Lease Time options. (The ciaddr field is not used for this purpose in a DHCPDISCOVER packet.)

On receiving the DHCPDISCOVER message, each DHCP server contacted responds to the client with a DHCPOFFER packet that contains an IP address and other settings for the client's consideration. The DHCPOFFER message is usually sent as a unicast transmission to the hardware address supplied in the DHCPDISCOVER packet. However, the client may not be able to receive a unicast message before it has been assigned an IP address. In these instances, the client sets the broadcast flag (the first bit in the flags field) to "1," forcing the server to send its DHCPOFFER message as a broadcast.

The DHCP specifications do not require that the server reserve the offered settings for use by the client until a DHCPREQUEST message is received, indicating that the client will accept the offer. Such a reservation allows for a more efficient process from a network traffic standpoint, but there are circumstances (such as a shortage of IP addresses) in which the offered address might be allocated to another client while the acceptance message is still pending. This forces the server to return a DHCPNACK message to the client, forcing the entire negotiation process to begin again.

The DHCP negotiation process is deliberately designed so that the client might receive DHCPOFFER messages from more than one server. After the client's timeout period has elapsed, it selects one of the servers based on the configuration values offered and transmits a DHCPREQUEST packet, specifying the selected server's IP address in the Server Identifier option. If no DHCPOFFER packets are received by the client, it times out, generates an error message, and sends a new DHCPDISCOVER packet.

The DHCPREQUEST packet is sent as a broadcast message. This is because it is used not only to notify the selected server that its offer is being accepted, but to notify all of the other servers that their offers are being declined. Towards this end, the secs field of the DHCPREQUEST packet must be the same as that of the DHCPDISCOVER packet, to ensure that the same servers receive the follow-up message.

When a server receives a DHCPREQUEST packet indicating that its offer has been accepted, it writes the offered configuration settings to its database, associating them with the client's hardware address and creating what is known as a *bound client*. The server then sends a DHCPACK message to the client, signaling that the settings have been registered for the client's use. If the server is no longer able to honor its previous offer (having allocated the offered IP address to another client, for example), it sends a DHCPNACK packet to the client, terminating the negotiation and forcing the client to begin again with a new DHCPDISCOVER message.

Finally, on receiving the DHCPACK message, the client performs a final check on the offered IP address by using the Address Resolution Protocol (ARP) to make sure that no other host on the network is using that address. If the IP address is found to be acceptable, the TCP/IP client is configured using the settings supplied by the server, completing the negotiation process. If the IP address cannot be used, the client sends a DHCPDECLINE packet to the server, and then waits a minimum of 10 seconds before beginning the negotiation process again with a new DHCPDISCOVER message.

If the client fails to receive either a DHCPACK or DHCPNACK reply from the server, it will retransmit the DHCPREQUEST packet as many as 10 times before terminating the negotiation.

Releasing an IP Address Assignment

After a lease has been negotiated, all communications between a client and its designated DHCP server use the combination of the host's IP address (carried in the ciaddr field) and its hardware address (carried in the chaddr field) to uniquely identify that lease. This is known as the "lease identification cookie." If a client wants to terminate its lease with the server, it sends a DHCPRELEASE packet containing these two values, at which time the server returns the IP address back to its available state.

Renewing an IP Address Assignment

Each time that a DHCP client computer is rebooted, or the TCP/IP stack reinitialized, it must contact its DHCP server to renew its IP address assignment. This is done to ensure that address is still usable by the client. Fortunately, on these occasions, the DHCP negotiation process is abbreviated, eliminating the need for the DHCPDISCOVER and DHCPOFFER packets.

When the workstation already has an IP address that it wants to continue using, it broadcasts a DHCPREQUEST packet to the local network. As before, the DHCP relay agents on the local network are responsible for routing the packet to the DHCP servers on other subnets. The DHCPREQUEST packet contains the client's current IP address (which it wants to continue using) in the ciaddr field, and its hardware address in the chaddr field, forming the cookie that identifies the client lease to the server.

The server evaluates the request from the client and grants or denies the continued use of the IP address with a DHCPACK or DHCPNACK message, respectively. It is by this process that DHCP's dynamic allocation process solves the roving user problem. If, during the address renewal, the server detects that the client has moved to a different subnet, the entire configuration is voided and the lease terminated, forcing the client to negotiate a new lease by issuing a new DHCPDISCOVER packet.

The client's treatment of a DHCPACK message is the same as during an initial lease negotiation. The client ARPs the network to check for a duplicate IP address in use and issues a DHCPDECLINE message if it finds one.

If the client receives no response to its DHCPREQUEST message, it will retry 10 times and then attempt to negotiate a new lease with a DHCPDISCOVER message. If the client does not receive a response from any DHCP server, it will continue to use its current configuration settings until its lease expires. Once the lease has expired, no further IP communications (except for DHCPDISCOVER broadcasts) are possible until a new lease is negotiated.

Lease Expiration and Renewal

The primary advantage of DHCP over its predecessor, BOOTP, is its capability for dynamic allocation of IP addresses. Configuration settings are not permanently assigned to clients unless the network administrator configures the server to assign them that way.

By default, the Windows NT DHCP server dynamically allocates IP addresses. The length of the standard lease is defined for each scope during its creation (it defaults to three days). A DHCP client can be said to always be in one of three states, regarding its current lease. The initial state, on successful negotiation of a lease, is the BOUND state, as mentioned earlier. The DHCP standard calls for the specification of two lease time periods, called T1 and T2. T1 is 50 percent of the total lease period, and T2 is 87.5 percent of the total lease period.

The aim of establishing these two interim periods in the lease is to allow the client sufficient time to negotiate a lease extension before it actually expires. When a DHCP client reaches the T1 interval (as defined in the DHCP packet's Renewal [T1] Time Value option), it is changed from being in the BOUND state to the RENEWING state. The client, at this time, attempts to renew its lease with its DHCP server by sending it a DHCPREQUEST message.

This DHCPREQUEST packet, however, is different from those discussed thus far. First, it is a unicast message directed solely at the client's designated DHCP server, rather than a broadcast. Second, it must not include the "Server Identifier" in its options field. The lack of this option distinguishes the packet from the other DHCPREQUEST messages generated by the client.

The server replies to the client's renewal request with a standard DHCPACK or DHCPNACK packet containing the unique xid value selected by the client for this renewal negotiation. This either allows the client to continue using its current parameters for another full lease period, or forces it to negotiate a completely new lease. If no reply is received from the server, the client continues to retransmit DHCPREQUEST packets whenever half of the time remaining in the T1 interval is expended.

If the client reaches the T2 interval (87.5 percent of the total lease period, as defined in the DHCP packet's Rebinding [T2] Time Value option), it enters the REBINDING state. At this time, the client begins to broadcast its DHCPREQUEST messages, in the hope of contacting any DHCP server. These DHCPREQUEST packets include the client's current IP address in the ciaddr field and, as before, must not include a Server Identifier.

While a client is in the RENEWING or REBINDING state, other TCP/IP communications proceed normally, but on expiration of the lease the client enters the UNBOUND state, and all TCP/IP communications other than those needed for a DHCP renegotiation are halted. A belated DHCPACK message that arrives after the expiration of the lease and before the negotiation of the new lease will allow communications to be resumed, however.

Running a Windows NT DHCP Server

DHCP runs on a Windows NT server as a network service, and is installed much like any other Windows NT service. First, however, the computer must have the Microsoft TCP/IP stack installed and configured.

A DHCP server cannot itself use DHCP (even running on another server) to obtain its configuration settings. It must be manually configured with a static IP address and all of the other required parameters. This is so that its clients can always be assured of locating the server (under normal conditions).

Because DHCP can be relayed to other networks by routers that comply with the published DHCP standards or by Windows NT machines that have been configured as DHCP relay agents, it is not necessary to have a DHCP server on every segment of an internetwork. However, many large networks run the DHCP service on several machines, both to cut down on excess internetwork traffic and to provide fault tolerance.

It is particularly recommended that, in a WAN environment, you run a separate DHCP server at each physical location and configure your routers to prevent DHCP traffic from being propagated across the WAN links. This prevents the DHCP traffic (which, as you have seen, makes frequent use of network broadcasts and multiple packet exchanges) from saturating your WAN connections needlessly.

Installing the Windows NT DHCP Service

To install the DHCP service, open the Network Control Panel on your Windows NT server and select the Services tab. Click the Add button and select Microsoft DHCP server from the list presented. Windows NT copies the necessary files (prompting you to insert your source CD-ROM if necessary), installs the DHCP Manager application, and activates the DHCP service.

The DHCP service itself is configured to start whenever Windows NT boots. You can manually start, stop, pause, or continue the service from the Services Control Panel, as well as modify its Startup options. You also can control the DHCP service from the command line, using the following NET commands:

- NET START DHCPSERVER
- NET STOP DHCPSERVER
- NET PAUSE DHCPSERVER
- NET CONTINUE DHCPSERVER

All other DHCP maintenance and configuration tasks are performed from the DHCP Manager, as covered in the next section.

Configuring the DHCP Service

The DHCP Manager is a Windows NT application that allows you to monitor and configure all of the DHCP servers on your enterprise network. It ships only with the Windows NT server product (as does the DHCP service), but you can run it remotely from a Windows NT workstation as well. By default, the manager lists only the local machine, with its scopes arrayed hierarchically in a collapsible tree display, as shown in figure 24.3. When you highlight a scope in the left pane, the right pane displays the DHCP options that have been configured for that scope.

FIG. 24.3
The DHCP Manager screen displays the scopes and options for all of the DHCP servers on your internetwork.

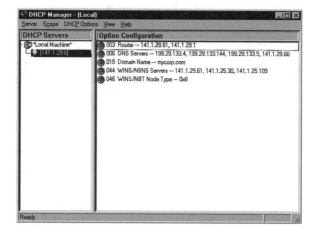

To add another DHCP server to the display, choose Server, Add and enter the desired DHCP server's IP address or host name or NetBIOS name. Click OK, and the new server and its scopes are added to the screen.

Creating a New Scope On a newly installed DHCP server, only the local machine is displayed, and the first order of business is to define a scope, that is, a range of IP addresses that are to be allocated to clients. To do this, highlight the Local Machine entry in the left pane and select Create from the Scope menu to display the Scope Properties dialog box, as shown in figure 24.4. This screen is used to specify what IP addresses on a particular subnet are to be assigned to DHCP clients.

You can only create a single DHCP scope on a given subnet. If you are planning to use DHCP to assign client IP addresses on a subnet that already has statically configured clients, you must create a large scope and then exclude the addresses that have already been assigned. If your DHCP server will have clients on several different networks or subnets, create one scope for each network, excluding static addresses as needed.

FIG. 24.4

In the Scope Properties dialog box, you define the IP addresses that are to be assigned to your DHCP clients.

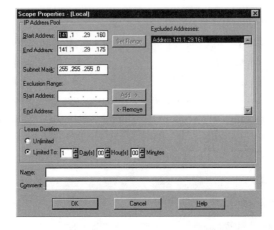

> **CAUTION**
>
> Be sure to exclude the IP address of the DHCP server itself from the scope you create for its subnet. The server must have a static address; attempts to allocate that same address with DHCP can cause severe problems on your network.

To create a scope, enter the starting and ending IP addresses and the appropriate subnet mask in the IP Address Pool box. In the Exclusion Range fields, you can then enter the addresses within the new scope that you want to exclude from allocation. You can exclude a range of addresses, or a single address by entering the same value for the start and end addresses.

In the Lease Duration box, you define the length of time that your clients will be able to use the IP addresses allotted to them before a renewal of the lease is required. The default period is three days. If the computers on your network are not often moved or reconfigured, then you can cut down on DHCP traffic by extending the lease period. On a constantly changing network (in a demonstration or laboratory environment, for example), or on a network where IP addresses are in short supply, you can reduce the lease time as needed.

Selecting the Unlimited radio button causes IP addresses to be automatically allocated to clients on a permanent basis. The addresses of machines that are removed from the network are never returned to the scope for reallocation, and must be released manually by the administrator.

You can enter any text that you want to in the Name and Comment fields, to identify the scope that you are creating. The name of the scope will appear in the left pane of the DHCP Manager, along with its subnet address.

After you click OK in the Create Scope dialog box, you are asked if you want to activate the scope for immediate use. In most cases, you should respond No to this prompt, as you still must configure the options that you want to supply to clients along with an IP address.

Configuring DHCP Options   As discussed earlier, you can deliver many additional options to DHCP clients aside from an IP address. Windows NT allows you to configure these options globally, or for each scope. If you are serving clients on more than one network segment, it will obviously be necessary to configure certain options (such as Routers) differently for each subnet's scope. Other options, such as your organization's Domain Name, lend themselves to global definition. If you are using DHCP only on a single network segment, you can safely configure all of your options globally. You also can combine global and scope options to make the DHCP administration process as easy as possible.

To configure these options, choose DHCP Options, Scope, or Global in the DHCP Manager. The dialog boxes for these two options are all but identical (see fig. 24.5). All of the DHCP options are available in both dialog boxes, allowing you to select the most convenient configuration.

FIG. 24.5
The many options available for delivery to DHCP clients can be configured globally or by scope.

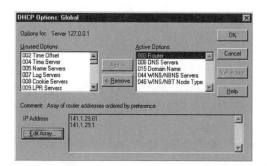

To specify that an option be delivered to clients, highlight it in the Unused Options pane of the DHCP Options dialog box, and click the Add button. The option then appears in the Active Options pane on the right. To configure the value of the option, click the Value button and the dialog box expands to display the current value for the highlighted option as well as a means to edit that value. The format of the display depends on the nature of the option being viewed.

Of the many options available in this dialog box, remember that only a handful of them can be utilized by computers running the Microsoft TCP/IP Client. These options are listed in the "Extended TCP/IP Parameter Allocation" section, earlier in this chapter. The other options are defined in RFC 1533, and are used by non-Microsoft clients.

Typically, you will want to add options to specify your clients' routers (that is, default gateways), DNS servers and a domain name (if your clients are connected to the Internet), and WINS servers and a WINS node type (if you will be using WINS for name resolution on your internal network).

Activating a Scope   After you have configured all of the desired options for a particular scope, you must activate it before those addresses can be allocated to clients by the service. Choose Scope, Activate, and the light bulb icon next to the scope in the main Manager display should be lit. You can deactivate a selected scope from the same menu.

Creating a Client Reservation   As mentioned earlier, DHCP also can be used to manually allocate IP addresses. This is done by creating a client reservation that associates a particular IP address with a particular hardware address in the DHCP database. To create a reservation, choose Scope, Add Reservations, and fill in the dialog box shown in figure 24.6.

FIG. 24.6
Specific IP addresses can be permanently allocated using the Add Reserved Clients dialog box.

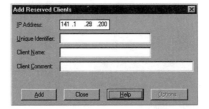

Enter the IP address that you want to assign, and the hardware address of the host adapter in the Unique Identifier field. For an Ethernet or Token Ring adapter, you enter the node address, but this field also can hold whatever other name or address is appropriate for the computer being used. The Client Name and Client Comment fields are for identification purposes only.

After you have created the reservation, you can configure options for it in the same way that you did for a scope.

Viewing DHCP Activities

To view the clients that currently have IP addresses allocated by a DHCP server, choose Scope, Active Leases from the Manager's menu to display the dialog box shown in figure 24.7.

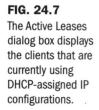

FIG. 24.7

The Active Leases dialog box displays the clients that are currently using DHCP-assigned IP configurations.

Select a client in the Active Leases dialog box and click the Properties button to display the client's Unique Identifier, and the Name and Comment fields specified during the configuration process.

Part
V
Ch
24

Installing the DHCP Relay Agent

The DHCP Relay Agent is another Windows NT service, that allows DHCP traffic to be routed to servers on other subnets, even when the routers or gateways connecting them are not compliant with the BOOTP relay standard defined in RFC 1542. The relay agent service can run on any Windows NT server, from which it can service all of the DHCP clients on the local network.

The IP addresses of the DHCP servers on other networks are specified in the DHCP Relay properties screen. The agent then intercepts all DHCP client traffic generated on the local network and sends it to the DHCP servers that have been specified. In the same way, server traffic is sent to the agent, which propagates it over the local segment.

The DHCP Relay Agent is installed from the same Services screen in the Network Control Panel as the DHCP service itself. Click the Add button, and select DHCP Relay Agent from the list presented. After the required files have been copied to the local machine, the service will start. If the agent has not yet been configured with the IP addresses of remote DHCP servers, you will be prompted to do so, and presented with the dialog box shown in figure 24.8. After the agent has been configured, you are prompted to restart your machine so the agent can be started.

The DHCP Relay properties screen is also accessible from the Microsoft TCP/IP Properties dialog box, whether or not the agent service is actually installed. You therefore can configure the agent before you install it, and have it be fully functional after you restart the machine. You must restart the computer when you first install the service, but any configuration changes that you make later take effect as soon as you close the TCP/IP Properties dialog box or click the Apply button.

FIG. 24.8

The DHCP Relay Agent properties dialog box is where you specify the addresses of the DHCP servers that you want local DHCP clients to use.

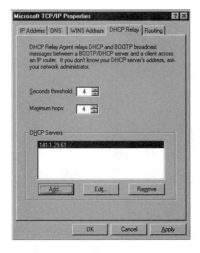

To specify a DHCP server to which local client traffic is to be relayed, click Add in the DHCP Servers box and enter the desired server's IP address. Repeat the process for each server you want to add.

Careful configuration of DHCP relay agents is a good method of controlling the propagation of DHCP traffic on your internetwork without having to reconfigure or upgrade your routers. By specifying only the DHCP servers at the local site, you can preserve the bandwidth of expensive WAN links. You also can limit the propagation of DHCP traffic by adjusting the number of routers or gateways that DHCP packets are allowed to pass through (with the Maximum Hops setting) or by limiting the amount of time that a DHCP packet can take to reach a server (with the Seconds Threshold setting).

Installing a DHCP Client

Because DHCP is designed to remove the burden of TCP/IP configuration chores from the user, designating a Windows NT machine to be a DHCP client is a simple process even for the most novice computer user. When you first install the TCP/IP protocol in Windows NT, you are asked if you want to use DHCP. If you respond Yes, the task is done. Restarting the computer initializes the TCP/IP stack and generates the first DHCPDISCOVER message.

On a computer that already has the TCP/IP protocol installed, switching to a DHCP-supplied configuration is simply a matter of filling the appropriate checkbox in the IP Address screen of the Microsoft TCP/IP Properties dialog box.

N O T E When you are converting a Windows NT machine from a static TCP/IP configuration to a DHCP-supplied one, be sure to remove the values from all of the settings that will be supplied by DHCP. Any values left in the TCP/IP Properties dialog box (even in grayed-out fields) will override the settings furnished by DHCP. ▪

From Here...

In this chapter, you learned how the Windows NT DHCP server service can be used to simplify the administration of a network's TCP/IP clients. For more information on Windows NT's implementation of TCP/IP, consult the following chapters:

- For more information on the fundamental concepts of TCP/IP transport, see Chapter 22, "Overview of TCP/IP."

- For more information on installating and configuring the Windows NT TCP/IP client, see Chapter 23, "Using Basic TCP/IP Services."

- For more information on the name resolution services that can be used with Windows NT, see Chapter 25, "Using DNS and WINS."

Part
V

Ch
24

CHAPTER 25

Using DNS and WINS

by Craig Zacker

As demonstrated in the previous chapters, the assignment of an IP address to each host on a network is critical to the establishment of reliable TCP/IP communications. For an IP transmission to reach its intended destination, it must be able to locate the machine using that address. Computers have other mechanisms for identifying themselves, as well. At a lower level, each host adapter has a unique hardware identifier, which a service like DHCP equates with a specific IP address. This allows a centralized database of identifying information to be maintained by eliminating the need for manual configuration of each computer.

Computers can have identifying names at higher levels, as well. The average user has difficulty dealing with the numeric IP addresses of many machines, so various systems have been developed to assign names to individual hosts. The standardized naming of Internet services and the registration of computer names on internal networks create working environments that are more friendly to the user. However, there must be a mechanism by which host names or computer names are converted into the equivalent IP addresses required by the TCP/IP protocols. ∎

The name resolution mechanisms provided in Windows NT

Windows NT can resolve each type of name into an IP address in several ways. Various combinations of these methods provide efficient coverage for virtually any type of network.

The Windows Internet Name Service (WINS)

WINS is the Windows NT NetBIOS naming system. It provides automated name registration and resolution services for private networks of any size.

The Domain Name System (DNS)

The traditional name resolution mechanism for the Internet, a DNS server allows users to address millions of nodes on the Internet.

HOSTS and LMHOSTS files

On smaller networks, simple text files can be used to resolve names into addresses, allowing internetwork communications between hosts.

Understanding Name Resolution and TCP/IP

Whenever an application uses TCP/IP protocols to communicate with another computer, the IP datagrams are delivered to the destination machine using its IP address. Host names are never carried in an IP header (the "envelope" in which data is carried from one computer to another). The computer names that are supplied by users while working in their applications are always resolved into IP addresses before any communication with the remote system is initiated.

Thus, when you open a Web browser and enter the host name **www.microsoft.com** as your intended destination, that name is resolved into an IP address before a single byte of data is sent to the Microsoft Web server. If, for whatever reason, the name cannot be resolved, activity will cease and an error message will be generated.

N O T E   Computers are provided with names solely for the ease of their users. Remember that an IP address can always be used in place of a host name in any TCP/IP application. This is why it's a good idea to substitute a valid IP address for the host name as one step in the troubleshooting process when you have a problem connecting to a remote site using TCP/IP. If a connection is made with an IP address, then the problem is solely one of name resolution. This can be an annoyance, but is far less drastic than a complete service interruption. ■

For names to be converted into addresses accurately and efficiently, two mechanisms are required. First, there must be a method of ensuring that computers' names, like their IP addresses, are unique. Obviously, if there were two Web servers on the Internet with the same name, users' results would be unpredictable, to say the least. The process of ensuring that a computer's name is unique to its network is called *name registration*.

Name registration can be a technological or an administrative process, depending on the naming system in use. There is no technology that can stop me from setting up a Web server and configuring its Internet name as **www.microsoft.com**. I would, however, be immediately pounced upon by several hundred lawyers, and rightly so. Trademark and copyright issues aside, **microsoft.com** is a domain name that has been legally registered as belonging to the Microsoft Corporation. This is an example of the administrative name registration that is used on the Internet.

The sheer number of computers on the Internet makes a distributed, administrative name registration mechanism the only practical solution. On a private network, however, it is possible to implement a system by which the name of each computer is registered as it boots, and an attempt by any machine to use a duplicate name is rejected. This is how WINS (covered later in this chapter) functions.

The second required mechanism is a means by which any computer on a network can determine the IP address of any other computer from its name alone. This process is called *name resolution*. There are several methods that can be used for name resolution. They offer varying degrees of performance and accommodate the needs of different types of networks. The factors that are used to determine which is the optimum name resolution method for your network are usually the network traffic generated by the process versus the ease of administration.

There are two basic ways of resolving names on a network. Either you look up the names in a table that lists the appropriate IP addresses, or you query the machines on the network to ask the holder of a particular name to identify itself. In general, the lookup table requires more administrative effort while the query method generates more network traffic.

Each method can be realized in different ways. Lookup tables can be stored on a local drive or on a server. Queries can be sent directly to the machine being addressed via network broadcasts, or to another machine responsible for handling them.

Windows NT supports several name resolution methods, which can be combined to provide fault tolerance in different network situations. First, however, it is necessary to examine the computers' names themselves.

Node Names

Windows NT supports two types of computer names: the IP host name and the NetBIOS machine name. Each naming system uses its own independent mechanisms for name registration and resolution. In a simple world, you could say that computers on the Internet use host names and computers on private Microsoft Windows networks use NetBIOS names—but the world is rarely simple.

Many of today's Windows networks combine both of the naming systems. It is quite possible for a single computer (even one with a single host adapter) to have both an IP host name and a NetBIOS name. What's more, these names may or may not be different.

The *host name* is the standard computer naming system of the Internet, as defined in the Internet Engineering Task Force's RFCs (Requests for Comments) 1034 and 1035. A company or organization registers a unique domain name with the registrar of one of the root domains (such as com, edu, net, or one of the domains representing countries, such as fr, de, uk, and so on). The domain name combined with the root domain results in a unique identifier for that internetwork, such as **mycorp.com**.

Part

V

Ch

25

Each individual host on the network is assigned a unique name by its administrator. The domain name is appended to this name to create an identifier for that individual computer that is unique on the Internet, such as **smithj.mycorp.com**.

The host name assigned to the individual machine can be as simple or as complex as is needed to keep it unique. A computer on a small or medium-size network might be called **smithj.mycorp.com**, while large networks might create one or more layers of subdomains to indicate the department or geographical location of a group of hosts, as in **smithj.marketing.mycorp.com**.

The motivating factor behind the design of the Internet host naming system was for it to be used with the Domain Name System (DNS), defined in the same RFC documents. Although it can be used on a private network, the DNS is designed to allow name resolution for computers at remote Internet locations to occur without the need to maintain a massive database of every machine name on the Internet. This is explained in the section "DNS Name Resolution," later in this chapter.

The second type of computer name used on Windows NT networks is the NetBIOS name. NetBIOS is a software interface that has been used for many years by applications that require controlled communications between networked computers. NetBIOS has its own naming system that it uses to identify the network's computers. A NetBIOS name has 16 characters, but Windows NT reserves the last character to identify special network resources, such as browsers and domain controllers. The NetBIOS name may also be followed by a scope ID that defines a group of computers on the network.

The NetBIOS name is the computer name that you specify during an installation of Windows NT (or Windows 95 or Windows for Workgroups). It has been a Microsoft networking convention since the earliest days of the LAN Manager product.

Name Resolution Methods

As mentioned, Windows NT supports several mechanisms for name resolution, for both NetBIOS and IP host names. The simplest method for resolving names into IP addresses is an obvious one: create a table containing each computer name on a network and its IP address. When a name is furnished to an application by a user, the name is located in the table and its corresponding IP address is substituted in any TCP or UDP communications that may be needed.

The use of a lookup table for name resolution raises several important questions:

■ *How is the table to be updated?* The task of manually editing the lookup table would be very time-consuming on a large network.

- *Where is the table to be located?* If the table is located on a computer's local hard drive, the task of modifying its contents is compounded by the number of machines, as is the possibility of error due to improper data entry.

- *How large can such a table be?* On a network composed of hundreds or thousands of nodes, the huge tables required would impose significant delays on communications processes as the table is read.

Windows NT does, in fact, support the use of locally stored, manually edited lookup tables for both IP host names and NetBIOS names. The table of host names and their IP addresses is stored in a file called HOSTS, located in the \WINNT\System32\Drivers\Etc directory on a Windows NT machine. NetBIOS names are stored in a separate table called LMHOSTS, in the same directory.

The use of a locally stored table becomes increasingly impractical as networks grow larger, for reasons of both maintenance and performance, but there are alternatives. Instead of looking up a name in a table, it is also possible to locate the machine in questions by querying the network using a broadcast.

In the broadcast method of name resolution that can be used by NetBIOS, a packet is sent to all of the workstations on a network. The packet contains the name that is to be resolved. It is the responsibility of the computer using that name to reply to the broadcasting node and to furnish its IP address in the reply packet. All of the other nodes receiving the broadcast simply discard it.

The broadcast method is effective, and it does not require the maintenance that a static table does, but it is subject to two severe limitations. First, it generates large amounts of network traffic. Each time one computer wants to communicate with another, a broadcast is required. A large number of machines, all generating broadcasts in the same way, could saturate a network with mostly wasted traffic.

The other problem inherent in using broadcasts for name resolution is that the broadcasts are limited to the local subnet. Machines located on the other side of routers or gateways cannot be contacted in this manner.

On some networks, these problems may not be too severe. If the majority of users' transmissions are limited to computers on their local network segment, and that segment is not overly populated, an effective name resolution system can be created through the combined use of broadcasts for local traffic and LMHOSTS file entries for the occasional internetwork transmissions.

On large private networks or on the Internet, these name resolution methods are obviously impractical. Just imagine how large a HOSTS file containing every name and address on the Internet would be, or how the process of broadcasting to every single host would affect Internet traffic and performance levels.

Part
V

Ch
25

To address these problems, the Domain Name System (DNS) was developed to provide name resolution services for the Internet. The DNS is designed to be an open-ended system that can accommodate a virtually unlimited amount of growth on the Internet. Administrative chores are divided between organizations (such as InterNIC, the Internet Network Information Center), which maintain the listings of domain names, and the individual network administrators themselves, each of whom is responsible for maintaining the list of the machine names and addresses on his or her own network.

A DNS can be used on a private network, whether it is connected to the Internet or not, but its primary drawback is that the listings of the network's host names and IP addresses are static. Its information must be manually updated by an administrator when a change in the network occurs. When you remove the domain-based functionality that a DNS acquires from the Internet, it becomes little more than a server-based host table—it's effective but impractical on a large private internetwork. As demonstrated later, WINS fits the bill for this environment more completely, providing a wholly automated administrative solution.

As described in Chapter 24, "Using DHCP," the Microsoft Corporation encountered these same name resolution problems as they planned the conversion of their own 35,000-node worldwide internetwork to the TCP/IP protocols. For the protocols to be practical, a network of this size requires automated processes to accomplish the name registration tasks that have traditionally been performed manually.

What was required was a means of providing NetBIOS services over TCP/IP in such a way that each computer's name and address automatically registered in a central database as the machine booted. This was particularly essential in Microsoft's case, not only because of the sheer size of their network, but because they were developing DHCP, a service that assigns IP addresses automatically.

Services like DHCP (and its predecessor, BOOTP), because they do not provide name resolution, make the automatic registration of names and IP addresses into a lookup table more of a necessity than a convenience. It would be all but impossible for administrators to manually edit a name listing to keep up with the changing IP addresses on a large network using DHCP.

WINS (Windows Internet Name Service) is the result of Microsoft's development efforts. It is a distributed, replicated database of NetBIOS names and addresses that is automatically updated by DHCP servers. Its name registration feature also prevents two computers on a network from using the same name, and its data replication capability allows for the browsing of network resources across routers.

The rest of this chapter is dedicated to the examination of these name resolution mechanisms and how they are implemented, installed, and configured in the Windows NT environment.

Understanding the NetBIOS Name Service

On a Microsoft Windows network, the NetBIOS name is the basic identifier used to locate resources on the network. It is the first element in the standard UNC (Universal Naming Convention) system used to specify the name of a share that a user wants to access.

NetBIOS is not a protocol, nor is it defined by an official standard like so many other networking systems. It is, instead, a programming interface—such as Windows Sockets or Remote Procedure Calls—used by application developers to provide services to their programs that allow for the identification and location of network resources and the orderly establishment and breakdown of communications to those resources.

There is no single standard on which all NetBIOS implementations are based. The closest thing to a NetBIOS specification is generally considered to be a document called "Technical Reference PC Network" from the IBM PC Network Technical Reference Manual, first published in 1984.

Because it is used for core networking functions, like file transfers between machines, NetBIOS is a crucial element of the Windows NT networking model. The Workstation and Server services that run on all NT machines are completely reliant on NetBIOS for their communications with the other computers on the network.

Part
V

Ch
25

N O T E Remember that regardless of whether you are running the Windows NT Server or Workstation product, your machine runs both the Server and Workstation services. This makes it capable of functioning as both a client and a server, which is the definition of peer-to-peer networking. ■

Because it is a software interface that operates between the application and Windows NT's Transport Device Interface (TDI), NetBIOS can use different protocols to carry its messages over the network. The original protocol used by Windows NT and its predecessor, LAN Manager, was *NetBEUI*. NetBEUI stands for NetBIOS Extended User Interface, and was designed for the transport of NetBIOS data.

NetBEUI is not a practical alternative for large, multi-segment networks, however, because it relies on broadcasts for the location of network resources and has no network layer capabilities, which makes it non-routable. Microsoft's own corporate network and the Windows NT project required a default protocol that could transport NetBIOS traffic across large internetworks efficiently.

Fundamentals of NetBIOS over TCP/IP

TCP/IP was chosen as an internetwork protocol, and the result was a series of IETF documents that define a standard for the provision of NetBIOS services using the TCP/IP protocols. Because both NetBIOS and TCP/IP provide unique identifiers for each machine on the network, the standard describes the mechanisms by which the NetBIOS name and the IP address can be reconciled.

RFCs 1001 and 1002 outline the name registration and resolution methods that are to be used when NetBIOS traffic is carried by the TCP/IP protocols. In Windows NT parlance, this is referred to as NetBIOS over TCP/IP, or *NetBT*.

The NetBT standards define both session and datagram services for NetBIOS traffic. The session services use TCP (the Transport Control Protocol) to provided connection-oriented, reliable, full-duplex transmissions between computers. This means that a communications session is established between the two computers before any data is sent; that all transmissions are checked for errors (and resent, if necessary) at the destination; and that traffic can travel in both directions during the session. The NetBIOS data is transmitted in units that are referred to as *messages*, each of which can be no larger than 131,071 bytes.

NetBIOS' datagram service uses *UDP* (the User Datagram Protocol) to transmit its traffic over the network. As described in Chapter 22, "Overview of TCP/IP," UDP is a much simpler protocol that does not provide the extensive connection and error-checking features found in TCP. Its transmissions are therefore described technically as being connectionless and unreliable, but this is not really the case, in the literal sense of those terms.

The datagram service is used when precise and timely service is not absolutely required of the transport protocol, or when other mechanisms are present that protect against the effects of data corruption or loss. Most of the NetBIOS control traffic, especially that which is dedicated to name resolution tasks, uses the datagram service. Only the datagram service can be used to send broadcasts to an entire network.

NetBT Node Types

The NetBT specifications define several types of NetBIOS nodes based on the mechanisms they use to perform their name registration and resolution tasks. NetBIOS nodes can utilize either *broadcast* or *unicast* transmissions for these purposes. When broadcasts are used, machines are located by the general transmission of a request specifying a NetBIOS name to which only the holder of that name is expected to reply.

Nodes that use unicast transmissions, however, send their requests to a specific IP address on the network. This is not the address of the intended recipient (which is as yet undetermined), but of an intermediate system called a NetBIOS Name Server, or *NBNS*. The standards allow a good deal of latitude regarding the specific functions of an NBNS. It can be as simple as a server-based repository for the names and IP addresses submitted by NetBIOS clients, or it can provide additional name management services, such as the defense of registered names against duplication. WINS is a NetBIOS Name Server that provides full management services, with additional enhancements not defined in the RFCs.

N O T E The IETF standard does not cover the use of a locally-stored host table (such as an LMHOSTS file) in its node types because the process occurs wholly within the computer and does not require the use of network communications. Windows NT allows for the optional use of the LMHOSTS file, however, as well as HOSTS files and DNS servers for NetBIOS name resolution. ■

NetBIOS nodes can be configured as any one of the following types:

Part

V

Ch

25

- **B-node**. NetBIOS machines that rely on network broadcasts for name registration and resolution.

- **P-node**. NetBIOS machines that rely on point-to-point (unicast) communications with a NetBIOS Name Server for name registration and resolution.

- **M-node**. NetBIOS machines that rely on broadcasts for name registration. Name resolution activities first use broadcasts and, if unsuccessful, use point-to-point communications with a NetBIOS Name Server.

- **H-node**. NetBIOS machines that use a NetBIOS name server for both name registration and resolution (the Windows NT default), unless an NBNS cannot be located, in which case broadcasts are used until contact with an NBNS can be established.

- **Microsoft-Enhanced**. Same as H-node with the addition of optional services that allow the use of LMHOSTS files, WINS proxies and/or DNS servers, and HOSTS files through Windows Sockets calls.

WINS clients on a Microsoft Windows network are configured as H-nodes by default. Clients not configured to use WINS are designated as B-nodes. The LMHOSTS and DNS options can be enabled on manually-configured clients by selecting the Enable DNS for Windows Resolution and Enable LMHOSTS Lookup check boxes in the WINS Address tab of the TCP/IP Properties dialog box (see fig. 25.1). A DHCP scope can be configured to assign any node type to clients, as well as the additional options.

FIG. 25.1
WINS clients can be configured to use LMHOSTS files and DNS servers for name resolution, if the designated WINS servers are unavailable.

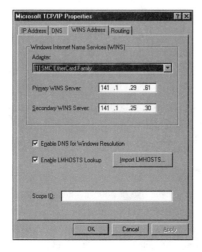

When all possible options are enabled, the name resolution mechanisms in a WINS client are accessed in the sequence shown in figure 25.2.

FIG. 25.2
Windows NT provides many fallback mechanisms for name resolution, each of which must fail for a name to remain unresolved.

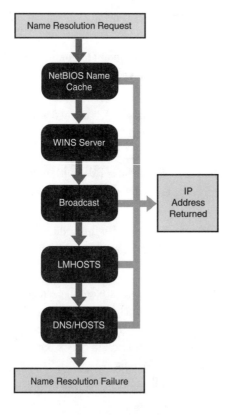

NetBT Name Registration

As mentioned earlier, the NetBIOS name is supplied during the installation of the Windows NT operating system. The NetBT specifications call for each NetBIOS name to undergo a registration process each time it logs on to the network. This is often referred to as *claiming* a NetBIOS name. The process ensures that the name is associated with the correct IP address and that no other computer is using the same name.

CAUTION

A Windows NT machine can only register a single NetBIOS name. On a multi-homed system, the NetBIOS name can only be registered with one of the installed adapters. On a machine that is functioning as a gateway to the Internet, for example, you would want to associate the NetBIOS name with the adapter connected to the internal network.

Registering NetBIOS Names Using Broadcasts

On a B- or M-node system (or a P- or H-node system that has failed to connect with a WINS server), a NAME REGISTRATION REQUEST containing the proposed machine name is broadcast over the local subnet using a UDP datagram as the system boots. If any other computer on the network is already using that same name, it responds with a NEGATIVE NAME REGISTRATION RESPONSE unicast, and the registration of the name is denied. If no responses are received after a specified time-out period and a specified number of retransmissions of the request, then the requesting node transmits a NAME OVERWRITE DEMAND packet and the registration is granted.

This procedure is, of course, only a registration in the sense that the node has checked for the existence of a duplicate name and has assumed the responsibility for defending the name that it has registered. There is no central resource where this new name and its IP address are stored. For future NetBT communications to take place, the workstation must respond to any broadcasts containing its name by returning its IP address to the sender.

CAUTION

When name registration packets are broadcast, they are sent only to the nodes on the local subnet. This makes it possible for two nodes on different subnets to utilize the same name. If you're using other mechanisms (such as LMHOSTS files) to allow nodes to contact machines on other subnets, don't let duplicate names come into conflict.

For the same reason, you shouldn't mix node types on an internetwork. If you do, the situation may arise in which a WINS client is capable of detecting a name conflict with a B-node client on another subnet, but the B-node client is not capable of detecting that same conflict.

Part
V

Ch
25

Registering NetBIOS Names Using WINS

On a P- or H-node, the same NAME REGISTRATION REQUEST is generated, but it is sent as a unicast to the designated WINS server rather than as a broadcast. If no other computer has registered the desired name, the WINS server returns a POSITIVE NAME REGISTRATION RESPONSE to the sender and enters the new name and its IP address into the WINS database.

If, on receipt of the request, the WINS server finds an entry for the requested name in its database, it performs a name challenge by sending a NAME QUERY REQUEST to the machine already using the name. If a POSITIVE NAME QUERY RESPONSE is returned, then the other machine has successfully defended the name and a NEGATIVE NAME REGISTRATION RESPONSE is transmitted to the new registrant. If the challenged machine does not reply after several attempts, or sends a NEGATIVE NAME QUERY RESPONSE, then the name is reassigned to the new registrant and a POSITIVE NAME REGISTRATION RESPONSE is returned.

N O T E   An M-node system begins its name registration with the broadcast method. If it receives no negative responses to its claim, it must then begin the WINS name registration process. A NetBIOS name is only registered to an M-node if both procedures are successful. ■

When a name is successfully registered with a WINS server, the response packet sent to the registrant contains a *time-to-live* (TTL) field that indicates how long the registration will remain valid. Each time the WINS client logs onto the network, the TTL value is renewed. If the time period expires while the computer is still logged onto the network, the WINS client software automatically begins another registration sequence with the server. Usually, this process is transparent to the user at the client computer.

When the TTL period expires without a renewal, or when the client shuts down the system in an orderly manner, the NetBIOS name registration is released. After a designated period of inactivity, the name is pronounced by WINS to be extinct. When a name has been released, it can be immediately reassigned to a different computer without the need for a challenge. If the name is no longer used, but has not been released properly (due to a system reset, for example), the WINS server will challenge any attempt to register the same name. If there is no response to the challenge, then the name is reassigned.

NetBT Name Resolution

Once a computer has registered its NetBIOS name, it can receive transmissions from any other computer registered on the network. It can also send data to other computers after first determining the intended recipient's IP address. For example, each time you browse the Network Neighborhood in the Windows NT Explorer and click to display the shares on a particular computer, your system must first resolve the NetBIOS name you see in the display to an IP address that it can use to establish a TCP connection. This process is also referred to as *name discovery*.

Windows NT supports several name resolution methods, which are used in an order that is defined by the node type selected for each computer. Should any of the mechanisms fail to resolve a name, the next one is tried until all possible avenues have been exhausted.

On nearly all networks, the use of WINS and the designation of the computers as H-nodes (with or without the additional options) is strongly recommended. It is only on the smallest single-segment networks that the broadcast method of name resolution is practical, and in those cases, the use of NetBEUI as a transport protocol may be preferable to TCP/IP.

The following sections describe each of the name resolution mechanisms and the circumstances under which they are used. They are presented in the order used by an H-node using WINS with all of the additional resolution options enabled. Other node types omit certain methods and vary the order in which they are used, but the mechanisms themselves are unchanged.

Part
V

Ch
25

The NetBIOS Name Cache

The NetBIOS *cache* is the simplest and most efficient form of name resolution. It is simply a listing, stored in the local machine, of the names that have already been resolved during that Windows NT session, along with their IP addresses. The cache, unfortunately, is volatile. It is deleted each time the user logs out or shuts down the Windows NT machine. This is done to ensure that the information contained there remains current.

The contents of the cache can be displayed by issuing the nbtstat -c command from a DOS command prompt, as shown:

```
c:\>nbtstat -c
Node IpAddress: [120.110.10.1] Scope Id: []

              NetBIOS Remote Cache Name Table
     Name            Type      Host Address     Life [sec]
     _____
FTP.MICROSOFT.C<03>  UNIQUE    198.105.232.1        -1
FTP.MICROSOFT.C<00>  UNIQUE    198.105.232.1        -1
FTP.MICROSOFT.C<20>  UNIQUE    198.105.232.1        -1
NT4SERVER      <03>  UNIQUE    141.1.29.61          -1
NT4SERVER      <00>  UNIQUE    141.1.29.61          -1
NT4SERVER      <20>  UNIQUE    141.1.29.61          -1
CHRONOS        <03>  UNIQUE    141.1.25.30          -1
CHRONOS        <00>  UNIQUE    141.1.25.30          -1
```

```
CHRONOS        <20>  UNIQUE     141.1.25.30       -1
NOSFERATU      <03>  UNIQUE     141.1.25.109      -1
NOSFERATU      <00>  UNIQUE     141.1.25.109      -1
NOSFERATU      <20>  UNIQUE     141.1.25.109      -1
```

The `nbtstat -r` command will display the number of NetBIOS names that have been resolved using broadcasts and WINS respectively.

N O T E   See Chapter 23, "Using Basic TCP/IP Services," for more information on the use and syntax of the `nbtstat` utility. ■

The NetBIOS name cache is always the first resource checked in the name resolution process for any node type. This allows repeated connections to the same machine to be established with a minimum amount of delay.

WINS Name Resolution

The Windows Internet Name Service (WINS) is a database that can store the NetBIOS names and IP addresses of computers anywhere on an internetwork. When multiple WINS servers are used, their data can be replicated so that each server maintains a complete record of all registered computers. The replication process can be scheduled to occur at specified times or specified intervals, thus allowing even networks connected by slow WAN links to maintain a complete picture of the entire enterprise network in the most efficient possible manner.

WINS is also the only name registration and resolution resource used by Windows NT that automatically maintains its own non-volatile records of NetBIOS names and IP addresses. DHCP clients, for example, are automatically re-registered each time they attach to the network. Even if they are assigned a different IP address at each logon, the WINS database remains current with no manual intervention.

When WINS is used to register all of the computers on the network, the name registration process is usually very simple. A computer sends a NAME QUERY REQUEST containing the name whose address is to be discovered in a UDP datagram to a WINS server. This is the server whose address is specified in the WINS tab of the TCP/IP Properties dialog box. The server consults its database and responds with another unicast containing either a POSITIVE NAME QUERY RESPONSE packet that contains the IP address of the requested name (and any other available information), or a NEGATIVE NAME QUERY RESPONSE indicating that it has no registration record of that name.

While it is processing the request, the WINS server may send interim WAIT FOR ACKNOWLEDGMENT RESPONSE (or WACK) packets to the requester, so that it does not time-out and proceed to the next resolution option.

If the requesting system receives a negative response, or if the WINS server does not respond at all, it proceeds to send a request to the alternate WINS server address specified in the Microsoft TCP/IP Properties dialog box.

If the second WINS resolution attempt fails, the computer then proceeds to use its next designated resolution mechanism. P-node and M-node systems will proceed to access the LMHOSTS file, if they have been configured to do so. H-node systems will proceed to the broadcast name resolution method, allowing continued access to computers on the local subnet. If an H-node system has been unable to establish contact with a WINS server, it will continue to poll for a WINS presence, even after it has begun to use broadcasts or other name resolution methods. When the WINS server comes back online, the system will immediately revert back to WINS resolution.

Notice that the WINS name resolution process uses no broadcast messages, and that whether the NetBIOS name being resolved is on the local or a remote subnet is irrelevant. WINS name resolution affords the greatest possible efficiency with the least amount of administrative effort.

WINS and Internetwork Browsing WINS provides other services in addition to name registration and resolution: it also allows clients to browse the machines located on subnets all over the enterprise. A network composed of only B-nodes (such as non-WINS clients) must be carefully configured to allow such internetwork browsing to take place.

Part
V

Ch
25

N O T E Browsing is the process by which the NetBIOS names of all networked computers are displayed in a user interface, such as the Windows NT Explorer. The user can select any machine and examine its shares, and can even display files and directories (if assigned the appropriate rights). Browsing is a function that is distinctly separate from actual network access. It is a great convenience to the network user, but it is by no means a necessity. It is sometimes possible to access a computer on another subnet by specifying an exact UNC path name, even when the user cannot browse the machines on that subnet. ■

Browsing is a function that is based on the election of a Master Browser for each subnet containing Windows computers. The Master Browser maintains the list of all the NetBIOS machines on the subnet. It is refreshed every 12 minutes, and replicated to selected Backup Browsers, that can take over if the Master should fail. The Browser service runs on all Windows NT computers, and allows any machine to fulfill the role as a Master or Backup Browser. When a Master Browser cannot be found on a particular subnet, an election process is begun to designate a new Master.

The Primary Domain Controller (PDC) is always designated as the Domain Master Browser, which replicates the browse list to all the Master Browsers in that particular domain. There must be a Master Browser on each subnet containing machines in that domain.

On a network using WINS, communications between browsers on different subnets are simplified by the use of an enterprise name resolution resource. The browsing of other subnets is also provided automatically and transparently by WINS. When a network relies on broadcasts for name resolution, a domain must have a Master Browser on every subnet that its users are able to browse.

Further, because the computers on other subnets cannot be contacted by broadcasts (and therefore cannot have their names resolved into IP addresses), manual entries in the LMHOSTS files of all the computers involved will be needed for proper browser communications to take place.

A properly configured entry in the LMHOSTS file can allow a user to access the shares on a machine in another subnet, but that machine will still not appear in the Network Neighborhood or the Entire Network displays unless the browsers are functioning correctly.

WINS and the Internet   As noted previously, WINS automatically provides clients with the ability to access computers anywhere on an internetwork. This is done without the need for concern about the subnet limitations of broadcast transmissions or the proper distribution of browsers. Amazingly, this same principle holds true even when the internetwork in question is the Internet itself.

If you create a WINS server on a Windows NT machine with direct access to the Internet, you'll be able to connect to your internal network from any location in the world by using the services of a local Internet Service Provider (ISP) with a Windows NT or Windows 95 workstation. By specifying your network's WINS server in the client configuration of the remote computer, access will be granted to shared drives on network machines by specifying the NetBIOS name in the Run dialog box or by connecting a network drive in the Windows NT (or Windows 95) Explorer.

Passwords will have to be provided, when necessary, and browsing the network will not be possible from the remote site. However, a connection that is sufficient for basic file management tasks can be achieved through a dial-up modem connection. Obviously, the faster the Internet connections on both sides of the equation, the better the performance will be.

> **CAUTION**
> Although this drive sharing technique utilizes the standard Windows NT security system, it still transmits data through unencrypted links. For better security, use the Point to Point Tunneling Protocol, which is discussed in Chapter 20, "Using Dial-up Networking."

Broadcast Name Resolution

When a NetBIOS name is registered using broadcasts, the registrant itself becomes responsible for defending the name against duplication and responding to any queries. This is unlike a WINS registration when the WINS server assumes these responsibilities.

An attempt to resolve a NetBIOS name via broadcasts begins with a computer generating the same NAME QUERY REQUEST packet that would be used for WINS name resolution, except that the UDP packet is sent out to all of the computers on the local subnet. Each computer receiving the request examines the packet for its own name. Failing to find it, the packet is discarded, but a computer receiving a query for its own name must generate a POSITIVE NAME QUERY RESPONSE and transmit it back to the original sender as a unicast.

When a name is successfully resolved using the broadcast method, its IP address is stored in the system's name cache for future use, but a new set of broadcasts must be generated for each new name resolution.

Because the UDP broadcasts cannot pass through routers, the broadcast method can only be used to resolve the names of computers on the local subnet. On a B-node computer, the failure of a broadcast name resolution will cause the system to resort next to consulting the local LMHOSTS file. This modified B-node service was the default name resolution mechanism in the original Windows NT 3.1 release, and is still used if a computer is not configured to use WINS.

An M-node system, after failing to resolve a name using broadcasts, will revert to the use of a NetBIOS name server. This design was intended for networks on which the majority of transmissions are restricted to machines on the same subnet and on which the NBNS is not as capable as WINS. For this reason, M-node is rarely used.

An H-node system will pronounce the name resolution process a failure after both the WINS and broadcast methods are unsuccessful, unless the additional name resolution options are enabled in the WINS configuration screen.

LMHOSTS Name Resolution

LMHOSTS is an ASCII text file that, in its simplest form, contains NetBIOS names and their IP addresses. It allows computers to resolve names without generating network traffic. As a result, it can resolve names anywhere on the internetwork without regard to subnet barriers.

The unfortunate drawback of the LMHOSTS file is that it must be manually created and maintained on every computer where it is used. When a new machine is added to the network, the administrator must edit the file to add a new entry, and then see that the change is propagated to every machine on the network.

The use of LMHOSTS is not defined in the NetBIOS over TCP/IP specifications because it requires no network communications. However, Microsoft networks have made use of it ever since the LAN Manager product.

Unlike a HOSTS file, which is searched for an IP host name before a DNS is used, the LMHOSTS file is consulted by Windows NT only after the available cache, WINS, and broadcast options have been unsuccessful in resolving a NetBIOS name. The exception to this rule is that any entries in the LMHOSTS file that are accompanied by a #PRE notation are automatically loaded into the NetBIOS name cache at system startup. This provides these names with the fastest possible name resolution service.

N O T E On a Windows NT system, the LMHOSTS file is located in the \WINNT\System32\ Drivers\Etc directory. There is also a file called LMHOSTS.SAM that provides heavily annotated sample entries as an aid to creating your own LMHOSTS file. See the section, "LMHOSTS Files," later in this chapter for more information on LMHOSTS syntax. ■

Using DNS for Windows Name Resolution

If all of the name resolution mechanisms on an H-node system fail, another alternative is possible. Selecting the Enable DNS for Windows Resolution check box in the WINS Address page of the client properties dialog box will cause the client's designated DNS servers to be accessed in search of the desired NetBIOS name. For this purpose, all of the domain identifiers in the DNS's host names after the first period are dropped. Thus, a DNS listing that provides an IP address for **smithj.mycorp.com**, will be delivered to a NetBIOS requester seeking a connection with SMITHJ.

CAUTION

While it is possible for a computer to have a host name that matches its NetBIOS name, this need not be the case. A single Windows NT machine can fulfill several roles, such as functioning as an FTP, World Wide Web, and DNS server at the same time. This can cause it to have several names, all entered in the DNS server as pointing to the same IP address. Do not use this option if you have host names in your DNS that point to different addresses than their NetBIOS counterparts.

This option also allows you to specify DNS identifiers (either host names or IP addresses) in UNC paths. \\smithj.mycorp.com\cdrive will therefore identify the shared C drive on the computer with the IP address specified in the DNS as belonging to **smithj.mycorp.com**.

Understanding Domain Name System Services

The Domain Name System (DNS) was created in the 1980s to accommodate the name resolution needs of the Internet. Originally a relatively small collection of computers, the network that was then called ARPAnet relied on a host table to resolve computer names into IP addresses. At that time, it was possible for every connected computer to have a complete listing of all the computers on the internetwork. Changes were e-mailed to the Network Information Center at the Stanford Research Institute, which maintained the list and made it available to all users. One had only to download the latest version every so often to keep current.

As the volume of new entries grew, this arrangement quickly became unwieldy for the administrators of the list and its consumers. Today, of course, a complete listing of the millions of computers on the Internet would be enormous, and resolving each host name would impose unacceptable delays as the list was parsed. The DNS is a distributed name service and database system that was designed to spread the administration tasks around the network by dividing it into domains. Now, only domains are registered in the central repository, not individual hosts. The assignment of a host name to each computer is performed by the network administrator. As long as the administrator avoids creating duplicate names within the domain, the combination of the host name (such as smithj) and the domain name (such as **mycorp.com**) forms a fully qualified domain name, or FQDN (**smithj.mycorp.com**), that is unique on the Internet.

Part

V

Ch

25

N O T E Do not confuse the term *domain* when used in connection with the Internet with a Windows NT domain. Although both represent groups of computers, an Internet domain is a name registered with InterNIC to identify the computers belonging to a particular company or organization. A Windows NT domain is a collection of computers located on a single internetwork that have been grouped for administrative reasons. ■

A DNS server, like a WINS server, is a database of computer names (in this case, IP host names), but the comparison ends there. Compared to WINS, a DNS server by itself is surprisingly unintelligent. Its host table has no automatic name registration capabilities, and must be manually updated each time a change is made to the network.

DNS Name Registration

Name registration for the DNS is an administrative process, not a technological one. It is the authoritative DNS servers for a particular domain that are responsible for the ultimate equation of host names and IP addresses. Because domain names must be unique, they are registered with an administrative body (in most cases, InterNIC). InterNIC prevents the duplicate registration of domain names and associates the name with the IP address of its DNS servers.

As far as the names of individual computers within a given domain are concerned, it is the act of manually editing the DNS tables that registers the name with a particular IP address. Even though the DNS page of the Microsoft TCP/IP Properties dialog box provides fields for users to enter their host and domain names, these entries are optional. The names entered in these fields are not delivered to the DNS, nor need the host name of a particular computer appear anywhere in the client software configuration. The maintenance of host names, all name registration, and name resolution activities can be performed by the DNS server.

DNS Name Resolution

For the resolution of names representing computers within the local domain, a DNS server functions as a centrally located host table. Requests containing host names are sent to the DNS server, which looks them up in its tables and returns a response containing the appropriate IP address. Its underlying strength is evident only when users try to resolve the names of computers located at remote Internet sites.

In the distributed architecture of the DNS, there is no single repository that contains a complete listing of all Internet computers. There is, instead, a collection of computers known as *root servers* that contain a complete listing of the domain names registered by individual networks. The individual domains and subdomains branch out from the root servers in a hierarchical, inverted-tree fashion—just like a giant file system. The listing in a root server for each domain includes the IP addresses of the DNS machines that have been designated as the authoritative sources for information on the hosts in that domain.

This way, the administrators of each domain only have to maintain host tables for their own machines. Every DNS server has the addresses of the root servers in its tables, so they can always be located. By beginning at the root of the Internet tree, any host on any computer can be located by parsing the FQDN from its root domain down to its host name and consulting the authoritative sources for each level.

For example, when John Smith issues a query for **ftp.mycorp.com** by entering the name in his FTP client program, John's local DNS server consults its own host tables and fails to resolve the name. The server then passes the request to a root DNS server that is responsible for maintaining the com domain listings. The root server locates the domain called **mycorp.com** in its tables and returns the IP address of **mycorp.com**'s authoritative DNS server (called **ns.mycorp.com**) to John's DNS server. John's DNS server then sends the resolution request to **ns.mycorp.com**, which maintains the listings for the computers in the mycorp domain, including **ftp.mycorp.com**. The IP address for **ftp.mycorp.com** is then supplied to John's DNS server, which passes it to John's workstation. John's workstation can then initiate a TCP connection with the destination.

This may seem like a complex series of transactions, but the DNS server on John's network caches the information that it receives from other DNS servers, thus maintaining a library of the hosts and domains accessed by the network users. If John, or any other user on his network, was to then open his Web browser and access **www.mycorp.com**, his DNS would know enough to send the query request directly to **ns.mycorp.com**, rather than the root server again.

Using a HOSTS File

The HOSTS file, the original name resolution mechanism for TCP/IP and the Internet, is not dead, even though it no longer contains host names and IP addresses for every computer on the Internet. Stored on a local hard drive (in the \Windows\System32\Drivers\etc directory on a Windows NT machine, by default), it provides the fastest possible host name resolution because it avoids network communications entirely, and because it is consulted before communications with the DNS server begin.

Windows NT uses the LMHOSTS file for NetBIOS name resolution as a last resort because it is more likely to provide outdated information than the other methods. However, because the data in both HOSTS files and DNSes is updated manually, it is assumed that their records are less volatile and more likely to be concurrent.

If you have a few Internet hosts that you access on a regular basis, you can minimize your connection delays by adding them to your computer's HOSTS file. Of course, if you go overboard and add 52 names, you may find that parsing the file imposes a greater delay than accessing the DNS server. Stick to the half-dozen or so most often used sites, and prioritize them if you want. The first entry will take slightly less time than the last.

Part
V

Ch
25

Installing a WINS Server

The WINS server for Windows NT ships as part of the Windows NT Server product only. It runs as a service and is installed through the Network Control Panel, like any other network service. To begin the installation, select the Services tab, and click the Add button. From the list of installable services that appears, select Windows Internet Name Service and click OK. Windows NT will then copy the required files for the WINS service and the WINS Administrator program, after prompting you for the location of the NT source media.

For what it does, WINS is designed to be all but transparent to the network. As soon as the service is started, clients can begin to access its services. The default configuration settings will provide immediate functionality to nearly all types of networks.

You can start, stop, and pause the WINS service in the Services Control Panel, where you can also modify its startup parameters. You can use the following commands from the DOS prompt to perform the same functions:

- ■ `net start wins`
- ■ `net stop wins`
- ■ `net pause wins`
- ■ `net continue wins`

Using the WINS Manager

The WINS Manager utility that is installed with the WINS service allows you to manage, monitor, and configure all of the WINS servers on your network from a central location. Although the manager ships only with the Windows NT Server product, it will run effectively on a Windows NT Workstation when launched from a shortcut to the WINSADMN.EXE file in the \WINNT\System\32 directory of a server running the WINS service.

The WINS Servers pane of the WINS Manager window displays the servers you can manage (see fig. 25.3). By default, only the local machine is displayed (if it is running WINS). Choose Server, Add WINS Server to display the Add WINS Server dialog box, that allows you to specify additional servers to be managed. The IP addresses of your WINS servers are displayed by default. When you select a server from the list, its current statistics appear in Statistics pane of the WINS Manager window.

FIG. 25.3

The WINS Manager allows you to administer to all of the WINS servers on your network from one location.

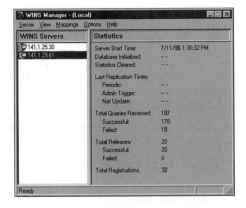

You can also display the contents of a server's database at any time by choosing Mappings, Show Database. The Show Database dialog box appears (see fig. 25.4), allowing you to see the machines that have been registered.

FIG. 25.4

The WINS database contains the NetBIOS name and IP address of every registered computer, as well as the date and time that the registration will expire.

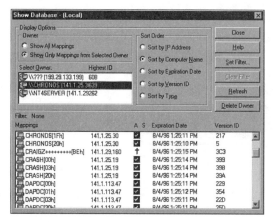

The Preferences dialog box, shown in figure 25.5, also allows you to access the following options:

- **Server Statistics**. These options allow you to specify whether the statistics displayed in the WINS Manager should be automatically updated, as well as the number of seconds that should occur between updates.

- **Computer Names**. Selecting the LAN Manager-Compatible check box allows WINS to recognize the 15 character NetBIOS names used by Microsoft networking products, including LAN Manager and Windows NT. NetBIOS names are actually 16 characters, but the last byte is reserved for other uses on Windows network clients. Deselect this check box if you will be using WINS to service non-Windows clients with 16 character names.

- **Miscellaneous**. Selecting the Validate Cache of "Known" WINS Servers at Startup Time check box causes each of the servers listed in the WINS Servers pane of the Manager window to be verified as running an active WINS server each time you load the manager. If the WINS service is not detected, you are asked if you want to remove that server from the list. Selecting the Confirm Deletion of Static Mappings & Cached WINS Servers check box simply affords you an additional measure of security against the inadvertent deletion of WINS entries.

Click the Partners button to display these additional options:

- **New Pull Partner Default Configuration**. This option allows you to specify the time that your WINS server should begin to replicate the entries of its new partners into its own database, as well as the time period between replications.

Part V
Ch 25

■ **New Push Partner Default Configuration**. This option allows you to specify the default number of modifications that are to be made to your WINS database before it signals its partners to inform them that a replication is necessary.

FIG. 25.5

The Preferences dialog box allows you to set defaults for the WINS Manager's display, verification, and replication options.

The configuration tasks performed in the WINS Manager fall roughly into three areas:

■ Adjustment of name registration parameters

■ Manual addition of database entries

■ Configuration of database replication parameters

Adjusting Name Registration Parameters   As described earlier, the WINS server applies a preset time-to-live interval to all NetBIOS name registrations. On most networks, the default values set by the software are satisfactory. However, you can adjust the intervals at which a renewal of the registration is required and at which it is declared extinct in the WINS Server Configuration dialog box, shown in figure 25.6. These are global settings; they affect all WINS database records except for those that are manually added by the administrator.

FIG. 25.6

You can adjust the intervals at which NetBIOS names registered in the WINS database expire in this dialog box.

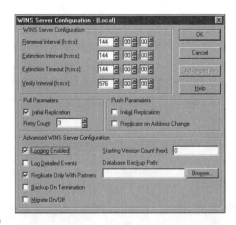

Adding Database Entries NetBIOS name registration records can be manually added to the WINS database by the administrator. These are called static mappings and are not subject to the renewal and extinction intervals of automatically created entries. To add a static mapping, choose Mappings, Static Mappings and click the Add Mappings button. After entering a NetBIOS name and IP address, you can choose from five different types of mappings:

- **Unique.** A standard, single-user mapping that associates a given NetBIOS name with a single IP address.

- **Group.** A container for multiple NetBIOS users that are identified using the Windows NT User Manager. The addresses of the individual group members are not stored in the group mapping.

- **Domain Name.** A Windows NT container that is identified by the inclusion of the hex character 1C in the sixteenth position of the NetBIOS name. Selecting this option modifies the dialog box to allow for the specification of multiple IP addresses to be assigned to the domain name mapping.

- **Internet Group.** Another container mapping in which up to 25 IP addresses can be specified as belonging to the group. By default, the Internet group is identified by the inclusion of a space (hex character 20) in the sixteenth position of the NetBIOS name.

- **Multihomed.** Allows the specification of multiple IP addresses for a single NetBIOS user name. Used on systems containing two or more network interface adapters.

After you have entered the desired information, click the Add button to save your new static mapping to the WINS database. You can also click the Import Mappings button to create batches of static mappings using a text file configured just like an LMHOSTS file.

Replicating WINS Databases For reasons of fault tolerance, it is usually recommended that the WINS server service be run on at least two Windows NT machines. This allows clients to access an alternate server, should their primary server not be available. WINS servers can be automatically replicated so that names registered on one server are copied to the databases of the other WINS servers on the network at regular intervals.

To enable database replication, you must designate the servers that will be the replication partners of the server you are currently managing. You can create partnerships for each of your WINS servers from the same WINS Manager interface, so be sure to remain aware of what server you are working on.

WINS allows you to designate a server as a push partner, a pull partner, or both. A *push partner* delivers its information to another server, while a *pull partner* receives information. It is recommended that every WINS server have at least one push and one pull partner on the network, but these do not have to be the same machine. If you have more than two WINS servers on your network, you can establish a ring of partnerships in which each server pushes to its upstream neighbor and pulls from its downstream one. The arrangement of the partnerships is not important to WINS, as long as every WINS server has access to all of the registration data generated on the network.

To configure the WINS server's replication behavior, highlight the server in the WINS Servers pane of the WINS Manager window, and choose Server, Replication Partners to display the Replication Partners dialog box (see fig. 25.7).

FIG. 25.7
The Replication
Partners dialog box
allows you to configure
the way in which WINS
database information
is propagated
throughout the
network.

To add a server to the display, click the Add button and specify the desired server. When it is displayed in the dialog box, you can specify whether you want it to be a push or pull partner, and configure the replication properties. You can also initiate unscheduled replication events by clicking the Push and Pull buttons in the Send Replication Trigger Now area to signal selected partner servers to begin the replication process. You can also click the Replicate Now button to initiate replication in the current server.

LMHOST Files

Windows NT can revert to the use of an LMHOSTS file for name resolution when the normal mechanisms fail to resolve a name or are unavailable. On B-node systems, it will automatically be consulted when the broadcast name resolution method fails. It is, therefore, an essential element of internetwork communications on a network not using WINS. On the other node types, the option to use LMHOSTS is available on the WINS page of the Microsoft TCP/IP Properties dialog box. When WINS fails to resolve a name, either because it has not been registered or because the WINS servers are unreachable, broadcasts may allow the resolution of local names to continue, but the LMHOSTS file is likely to be the client's primary means of resolving names on other subnets.

Your LMHOSTS file should be in the \Windows\System32\Drivers\Etc directory on your Windows NT machine. Like a HOSTS file, the basic syntax of LMHOSTS calls for each IP address and its associated NetBIOS name to be entered on a single line of a plain text file, with at least one space between name and address. When it is accessed, the file is parsed in the order that the entries are listed. It can be beneficial to place your most commonly used entries at the top of the list.

N O T E Windows NT provides a sample LMHOSTS file with examples of the various extensions. It is called LMHOSTS.SAM and is located in the \Windows\System32\Drivers\Etc directory of every Windows NT machine that has had the TCP/IP protocols installed. ■

Unlike a HOSTS file, however, LMHOSTS provides additional capabilities through the use of extensions that identify certain entries as having added meaning. These extensions are as follows:

- **#PRE**. The #PRE tag causes the entries to which it is affixed to be preloaded into the Windows NT computer's NetBIOS name cache when the system is booted. Because the cache is accessed before any other name resolution resource, this provides the quickest possible name resolution performance. #PRE entries should be placed at the end of the LMHOSTS file because they're pre-loaded and would only cause needless delays in parsing the other entries if they were listed first. To use the #PRE tag, add it to the end of a standard LMHOSTS entry, leaving at least one space after the NetBIOS name, as follows:

  ```
  141.1.29.61   smithj    #PRE
  ```

- **#DOM:<*domain name*>**. The #DOM tag causes the entry to which it is affixed to be associated with the Windows NT domain specified by <*domain name*>. When the computer specified in this entry is elected a Master Browser, it will receive the domain browse list from the Primary Domain Controller, no matter where it is located. This process allows non-WINS clients to browse the machines that are located on other subnets within their domain. To use the #DOM tag, add it to the end of a standard LMHOSTS entry, leaving at least one space after the NetBIOS name, as follows:

  ```
  141.1.29.61   smithj    #DOM
  ```

- **#INCLUDE <*file name*>**. The #INCLUDE tag allows an LMHOSTS file located on another computer to be read as though it was on the local drive. This allows an administrator to create a single LMHOSTS file and store it on a server drive. Modifications made to the server file will then be read by each machine accessing it in this manner. Replace <*file name*> with a fully qualified UNC path name to the desired file. A path name pointing to a computer on another subnet must have its

Part
V

Ch
25

NetBIOS name pre-loaded by a separate #PRE-tagged entry in the LMHOSTS file, so that the name can be resolved before access to the remote file is allowed.

```
#INCLUDE \\nt4server\share\etc\lmhosts
```

- **#BEGIN_ALTERNATE**. This tag is used to offset a group of #INCLUDE statements to provide fault tolerance for server-based LMHOSTS files. Place the #BEGIN_ALTERNATE tag on a separate line by itself, and follow it with at least two #INCLUDE entries. The #INCLUDEd files are accessed in order until one loads successfully, at which time the focus jumps to the next #END_ALTERNATE tag found, allowing processing to proceed from there.

- **#END_ALTERNATE**. This tag, placed on a line of its own, signals the end of an array of #INCLUDE tags that commenced with a #BEGIN_ALTERNATE entry. In the following example, the ALTERNATE tags will cause the LMHOSTS file on nt4server to be read first. If LMHOSTS cannot be found on nt4server, the server2 file will then be accessed. If the LMHOSTS file on nt4server is accessed successfully, however, processing will jump to the #END_ALTERNATE tag and proceed from there.

```
#BEGIN_ALTERNATE
#INCLUDE \\nt4server\share\etc\lmhosts
#INCLUDE \\server2\cdrive\tcpip\lmhosts
#END_ALTERNATE
```

- **\0xhh**. This tag allows special characters to be included in NetBIOS names by specifying them in hexadecimal form. Some applications require a particular character in the 16th position of the NetBIOS name, which can be supplied by placing the name in quotes and inserting \0xhh (where hh is the hexadecimal value of the desired character) in place of the special character. Note that the variable only replaces a single character of the NetBIOS name. You must pad out 15 characters with spaces to place the special character in the 16th position, as shown:

```
141.1.29.61  "application     \ox14"
```

Installing a Windows NT DNS Server

The Windows NT DNS server was supplied as beta software with the Windows NT Resource Kits for versions 3.5 and 3.51. As of Windows NT 4.0, it is a fully integrated component of the Server product and includes a graphical DNS Manager application to aid in the maintenance of the often-cryptic DNS configuration files.

Like WINS, the DNS server runs as a Windows NT service and is installed from the Network Control Panel. Select the Services tab, click the Add button and choose Microsoft DNS Server from the list provided. When Windows NT has prompted you for the location of the source files and has completed the necessary copies, the service is started, and the DNS Manager is added to the Start menu.

At this point, if you are not hosting your own domain on the Internet, the DNS is fully functional. Name resolution requests sent to the DNS server will be passed to the root server and any additional referred servers using the settings provided, and the responses will be returned to the user's computer. To host a domain, you must create the ASCII database files that the DNS uses as the source of its information. Windows NT includes sample files in the \Windows\System32\Dns\Samples directory that can help you do this.

The process essentially involves the creation of database entries that contain host names, their related IP addresses, and codes indicating the role of that host. Entries specifying the host names and addresses of the domain's DNS servers are required, as are entries for each of the computers that are to be accessible from the Internet using a host name.

Using the DNS Manager

Configuring a DNS server is a complex process that requires more knowledge of the inner workings of the DNS than can be provided in this book. Fortunately, Windows NT provides a tool that can help administrators avoid the most common problem affecting DNS configurations—mistakes in the syntax of the configuration files.

Part V
Ch
25

The DNS Manager, like the WINS Manager, allows you to control multiple DNS servers located anywhere on your network from a central location. Although the program only ships with the NT Server product, it can be run on a Windows NT Workstation system by creating a shortcut to the executable file on the server drive. You specify the addresses of the servers you want to manage by choosing DNS, New Server.

The Windows NT DNS manager provides a graphical interface to the DNS configuration. It allows you to create new configuration files as needed and enter new records into existing files through standard Windows dialog boxes. The files or modifications are then written to the DNS configuration files on command, using the correct syntax. The Domain Name Service Manager window allows you to view basic DNS statistics, as well as the cached information recorded by the DNS server during its previous name resolution activities (see fig. 25.8). This information can be very helpful in determining whether a name resolution failure was caused by the local DNS server or by one of the many others it might have contacted.

Configuration files are created and edited by highlighting the appropriate item in the DNS hierarchy (shown in the left pane of the manager) and then choosing DNS, Properties to edit the parameters of the chosen item or then choosing another option on the DNS menu. Appropriate dialog boxes appear for each item, such as the New Resource Record dialog box, shown in figure 25.9, in which you can specify the required information for the entry. When you complete the desired changes, you must choose <u>D</u>NS, <u>U</u>pdate Server Data Files to commit your changes to the DNS's configuration files.

FIG. 25.8

The Domain Name Service Manager allows you to view the contents of a DNS server's cache in a graphical format much like that of a file system.

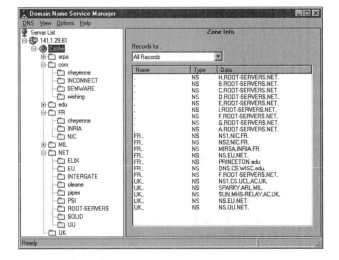

FIG. 25.9

The DNS Manager prevents syntax errors in the DNS configuration files by providing users with standard Windows dialog boxes.

Using WINS for DNS Lookups

There are other DNS server products that can be used on Windows NT, but the Microsoft version is unique in that it can utilize WINS to resolve names that could not be discovered in the traditional way. If a DNS lookup of a host name fails, and the DNS server is configured to use WINS, the domain (and subdomain) names are stripped from the host name, and the DNS server sends a standard NAME QUERY REQUEST to the designated WINS server. The request contains only the part of the host name preceding the first period; **smithj.mycorp.com** would therefore become smithj.

Manually configuring the DNS server to use WINS was a matter of creating an entry beginning with $WINS and then specifying the IP addresses of the WINS server to be contacted. The DNS Manager, though, simplified the process further by providing a WINS Lookup page in the Zone Properties dialog box for every DNS zone (see fig. 25.10).

FIG. 25.10
WINS lookups for failed DNS name resolutions can easily be enabled for any domain simply by specifying the WINS server to be used.

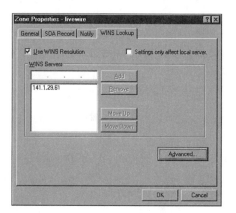

Enabling Name Resolution at Windows Network Client Workstations

Part
V
Ch
25

After all of this material concerning the complex processes that allow Windows NT users to specify names in their applications instead of IP addresses, you may be surprised at how incredibly easy it is to make use of the services covered in this chapter. The configuration pages for both DNS and WINS clients are part of the Windows NT TCP/IP Properties dialog box, which you open from the Network Control Panel. Detailed instructions for the configuration process are provided in Chapter 23, "Using Basic TCP/IP Services," but once you understand the concepts, they really are little more than a matter of typing the correct IP addresses in the right places.

A properly configured Windows NT workstation using WINS and a DNS should be able to contact any other computer on an internal network or on the Internet without difficulty. If you take advantage of the alternative methods described in this chapter, you can even survive a failure of one or more of your name resolution methods and still continue to work normally.

Choosing the Best Name Resolution Method for Your Network

After examining the various name resolution methods available to Windows NT networks, you may be concerned about making a decision as to which methods to use for your network. Obviously, each network has its own requirements, but this is by no means an either/or decision. You can use any or all of the methods described in this chapter simultaneously. The decision breaks down this way:

- If you are connected to the Internet, you should definitely use a DNS.
- If you have a private network with Windows NT machines on more than one subnet or segment, you should definitely run WINS.
- If you qualify in both of the above, you should have both DNS and WINS capabilities.

Broadcasts, HOSTS, and LMHOSTS files can be largely relegated to fall-back status. They can provide continued connectivity during a failure of either a WINS or DNS server and slightly enhanced performance levels to savvy users.

For a typical medium-sized business network that has a serious commitment to Windows networking, the recommendation would be, in fact, to use all of the name resolution methods covered in this chapter. A single, reasonably-equipped Windows NT server could easily run all of the TCP/IP services provided by the operating system at the same time, including DHCP, WINS, DNS, and even the Web, FTP, and Gopher services provided in the Internet Information Server.

This is certainly not the optimum configuration from a fault tolerance perspective, but it serves to show that using these services does not mean a major investment in additional computers for each one. What's more, even if budgetary concerns are paramount, using these services does not necessarily entail running them on your own servers. Your ISP should be able to supply you with access to their DNS servers for a monthly fee, and there are even companies providing private WINS service over the Internet.

ON THE WEB

WINS, and other Windows networking services, can be obtained from Winserve. See their World Wide Web site at **http://www.winserve.com**.

From Here...

DNS and WINS are elements of the Windows NT TCP/IP architecture that allow simplified access to resources that are fundamentally identified by IP addresses. For more information on TCP/IP and its related Windows NT modules and services, see the following chapters:

- Chapter 22, "Overview of TCP/IP," covers the basic structure of the protocol suite and the usage of the TCP/IP applications included with Windows NT.

- Chapter 23, "Using Basic TCP/IP Services," describes how the TCP/IP protocols fit into the Windows NT networking architecture and covers troubleshooting techniques and the use of Windows NT's TCP/IP diagnostic utilities.

- Chapter 24, "Using DHCP," covers the Windows NT service that can be used to automatically configure the TCP/IP settings on users' workstations as they log on to the network.

Part
V

Ch
25

CHAPTER 26

Installing and Configuring Peer Web Services

by Serdar Yegulalp

Microsoft's Peer Web Services (PWS), which are provided with Windows NT, let you host simple World Wide Web (WWW) services from your Windows NT system. PWS also let you host ftp and gopher services, and with the provided tools you can administer the site remotely and establish connections between HTML documents and ODBC data sources.

PWS is also small—no more than 3.8 megabytes in its full installation—and requires less effort to install and configure than most other products in its category. It's also on the Windows NT CD-ROM, making it that much less expensive to obtain and use. The downside is that its power and configurability are limited compared to other programs. ∎

Installing PWS from the Windows NT CD-ROM

Learn to select and deselect various components of PWS.

Configuring specific Web services

Examine the configuration of the WWW, gopher, and ftp servers.

Using the Internet Service Manager program to get the most out of Peer Web Services

Set up virtual directories or domains, control access to specific pages, and set up your own custom login messages for FTP sites, just to name a few.

Setting up your Internet Server for proper security

With Internet security a hot topic and an important subject, some of the more important tips are listed here.

Installing PWS from the CD-ROM

Peer Web Services are provided on the Windows NT Workstation 4.0 CD-ROM. Different versions of PWS have been provided for the different types of processors supported by NT.

Installing the Correct Processor Version

To find the correct version of PWS for your system's processor, look in the subdirectory that you loaded Windows NT from for a subdirectory labeled Inetsrv. For instance, if you installed the Intel x86 version of NT, look in the \I386\ INETSRV directory.

To begin installing PWS, run the program in that directory entitled INETSTP.

 You can also launch the Peer Web Services installation routine through the Network applet in the Control Panel by selecting the Services tab and clicking Add. This brings up a list of network services to be installed. Click Microsoft Peer Web Services in the list and click OK. Make sure you have the Windows NT distribution CD-ROM available in the drive you installed Windows NT from.

The INETSTP Program

When you first execute the INETSTP program, you're greeted with a copyright and licensing notice that also warns you to close all other running applications. Click OK to continue, and the Peer Web Services Setup window will open (see fig. 26.1).

There are seven main configuration options in the Peer Web Services Setup window, all initially selected. To deselect an option, click the checkbox to the left of the option to clear it.

The Internet Service Manager is not checked by default. You will want to check it because configuring the Peer Web Services without it is difficult at best.

The initial directory into which the PWS programs are to be installed is **\%SystemRoot%\System32\Inetsrv**. To change this, click the Change Directory button and either point to a new directory in the file dialog box that comes up, or type the name of a new directory in the text box at the top of the file dialog box.

If the directory you're specifying doesn't exist, you'll be prompted if you want to create it. Responding "yes" will create the directory. Responding "no" will return you to the file dialog box.

FIG. 26.1
The main configuration window of the INETSTP program lets you choose which program options to install or remove.

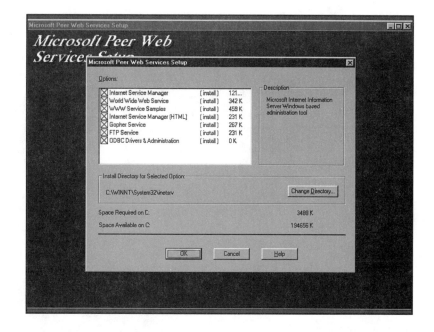

The seven options listed in the menu are:

- **Internet Service Manager**. This is the program from which all the Internet services are configured, stopped and started. You will need to install this in order to make any real use of the Peer Web Services.

- **World Wide Web Service**. The WWW server itself, which allows your computer to operate as an HTTP server.

- **WWW Service Samples**. An example Web site that demonstrates most of the functions of the PWS, with code that can be analyzed and studied.

- **Internet Service Manager (HTML)**. A secure, HTML-based remote configuration system that lets you use any Web browser to remotely administer PWS.

- **Gopher Service**. A server that allows the computer to operate as a gopher server.

- **FTP Service**. Allows your computer to publish file directories for access through anonymous or password-secured FTP.

- **ODBC Drivers and Administration**. These drivers allow access to ODBC databases from the server(s).

When you finish selecting which components of PWS to install, click OK.

The INETSTP program next presents you with a list of directories (see fig. 26.2) that the various services will get their publishing information from—in other words, where they will look for the data that they will make available to outside users.

Part
V

Ch
26

FIG. 26.2

The INETSTP program lists the directories to host data from.

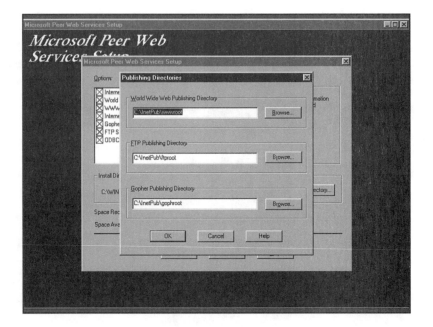

If you want to change the names of the directories, you are free to do so by clicking the text box containing the name of the directory and typing in the new directory name. If you want to browse for a particular directory, click the Browse button next to the directory name you want to change, and a directory browsing window will open. From there you can either navigate to the directory you want to use or type a new one in the text box at the top of the directory browsing window.

When you are finished making changes to the publishing directory names, click OK to continue. If any new directories need to be created, the program will prompt you to choose Yes or No. Clicking No will send you back to the publishing directories windows.

At this point the INETSTP program will copy the selected files to your system. When it has finished, the program will let you know that installation has completed successfully. You do not need to reboot the system in order to make use of PWS.

When installation is finished, click the Start button and look under the Programs submenu. A new common folder, named Microsoft Peer Web Services, has been installed. If you expand that folder as well, you'll see that several objects have been placed in the directory:

- **Internet Service Manager.** This is the heart of Peer Web Services.
- **Internet Service Manager (HTML).** Selecting this brings up an HTML page in whatever browser is selected as the default for HTML. This page lets you remotely administer most of the PWS options. This option will be explained in detail later.
- **Peer Web Services Setup.** This option brings you to the PWS Setup program.

Internet Service Manager

The Internet Service Manager lets a user administer settings for each of the installed Internet services (see fig. 26.3). It can also be used to connect to another computer on which PWS are running and administer changes there if the user is allowed to do so.

FIG. 26.3
Internet Service Manager shows the three installed services—WWW, gopher, and FTP—up and running.

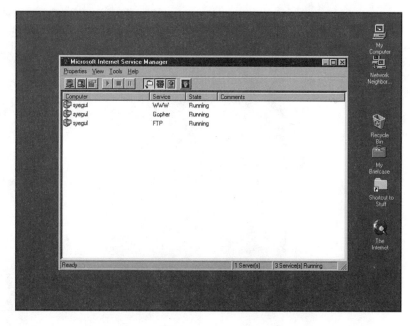

N O T E All of the services listed in the Internet Service Manager are also listed in the Services window available from the Control Panel. They can be stopped and started there as well, but they cannot be configured. ■

The WWW Service

The World Wide Web (WWW) Service allows you to publish HTML documents that reside in any directory available to the computer. It does not inherently support

Secure Sockets Layers (SSL) connections; you will have to purchase a separate SSL server in order to accomplish that. It does, however, host any conventional http-compatible document, including ActiveX and Java applications.

To configure the WWW Service properties, double-click the WWW Service entry in the Internet Service Manager's list of services, or right-click the entry in the list and select Properties. You can also select the service and use the Properties, Service Properties selection from the main program menu.

The Properties window for the WWW Service has three tabs: Service, Directories, and Logging.

Service Tab   The Service tab (see fig. 26.4) holds the most commonly edited options for the WWW Service.

FIG. 26.4
The most common service options, like port number and connection timeout, are kept here.

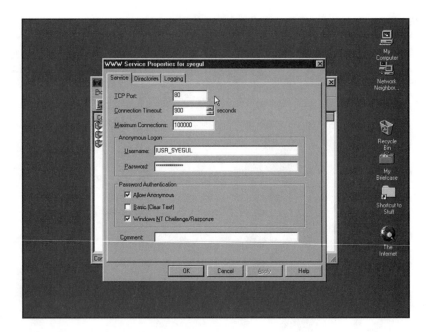

The main options listed on the Service tab are:

- **TCP Port**. This is the virtual port number on which the WWW Service listens for requests. This defaults to 80, the standard for the http protocol, and will not need to be changed unless you are deliberately hosting the WWW Service on another port. After changing this value, you will have to shut down the system and restart.

- **Connection Timeout**. This is the length of time, in seconds, that the server waits before pulling the plug on an inactive user. This value ensures that all inactive users, including ones who attempted to close a connection and failed, are eventually disconnected. The default setting for this is 900 seconds, but you may want to decrease it if your site is only hit for one page at a time by a given user.

- **Maximum Connections**. This is the maximum number of simultaneous connections the service supports. The default is 100,000, which should be more than enough. If you have a narrow-bandwidth Internet connection (such as a 28.8 dialup connection) or a machine that isn't very powerful, you may want to reduce this number to something more realistic to prevent having your connection overloaded.

The Anonymous Logon section of the Service tab holds two options that pertain to anonymous connections to the server. (The vast majority of the connections to the server will be anonymous, since standard http connections all work in an anonymous fashion anyway.) A description of these options is listed above, in the section that describes the Service tab of the WWW Service Properties sheet.

The Allow Anonymous checkbox will allow only anonymous connections to this particular ftp service.

Finally, the Comment field lets you type in whatever comment you wish to make about this particular server. This comment is visible in the main window of the Service Manager. For instance, you could make mention of what kind of documents are in the given directory, whether or not they are sensitive, and so forth.

Directories Tab   The Directories Tab (see fig. 26.5) holds a list of the directories which the WWW Service uses to find HTML documents and other material to be published on the Internet.

Part
V

Ch
26

When the WWW Service is installed, it creates three directories that are used with the Web server. There's no realistic limit to the number of directories you can have installed for use with the Web server. The small house icon next to a given directory entry means that this directory is the "home" directory, or the default directory that will be presented when someone logs on to the Web server without specifying a document or a path.

The controls in the Directories Tab are as follows:

- **Add**. Clicking this button creates a new, blank directory entry, the details of which are described in the later section "Directory Properties".
- **Remove**. Clicking this button removes the highlighted directory entry.
- **Edit Properties**. Clicking this button lets you bring up a window containing the properties of the highlighted directory entry, the details of which are described in the later section "WWW Service Directory Properties."

■ **Enable Default Document.** Checking this box ensures that when a user logs into a directory that you specify in the directory list and does not specify a document, the user is automatically provided with a default document. This option is enabled by default. The default document is Default.html and is specified in the Default Document text box.

■ **Directory Browsing Allowed.** Checking this box allows a user to obtain an ftp-style list of all files in a directory if they log into a directory without specifying a document. This option is initially disabled and should be kept off for security reasons unless you are specifically providing a directory that should be browsed ftp-style.

FIG. 26.5
The "publishing directories" referred to here will in the future contain the data that you will want to make available to each service.

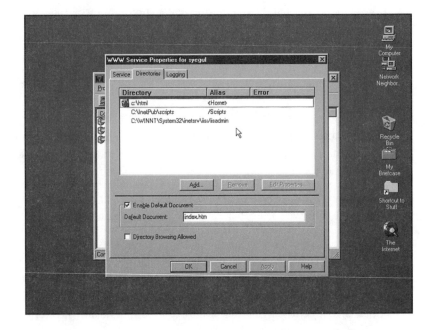

The Logging Tab   The Logging tab on the WWW Service Properties sheet (see fig. 26.6) contains information about how transactions posted to and from the WWW server are logged. Information logged about each hit contains the time and date, the directory and document transferred, and the IP address and registered machine name of the connected user.

FIG. 26.6
Hits can be logged
to either plain-text
files or to an SQL
database.

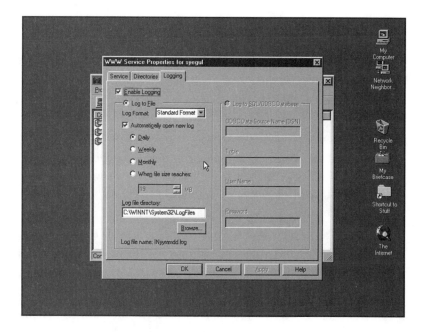

Here are the controls on the Logging tab:

- **Enable Logging**. Checking this box turns on logging, and enables the rest of the logging options on the Logging tab. Unchecking the box turns off logging and grays out the other logging options. This option is checked by default.

- **Log to File**. When this radio button is selected, the log is written to a plain-text ASCII file (as opposed to an ODBC database). This option is selected by default.

- **Log Format**. There are two options for the way the log is formatted: Standard and NCSA Format. Standard is the default setting; NCSA Format doesn't need to be used unless you are more comfortable with reading files in that format, or if you are using a third-party log analysis utility that requires the logs to be in NCSA format.

- **Automatically Open New Log**. Checking this box generates new logs at a specified interval. If this option is not selected, the same log file will grow indefinitely until you run out of disk space (not a good idea). This option is checked by default.

- **Daily/Weekly/Monthly**. Choosing one of these options causes a new log file to be created in the interval specified.

- **When File Size Reaches**. Choosing this option lets you specify how large (in megabytes) the log file size has to be before a new one is created. You can use either the spinner controls on the text box to raise or lower the value, or you can type one in directly.

Part
V

Ch
26

- **Log File Directory**. This text box holds the pathname for the directory where the log files are kept. You can change this option by clicking the text box and typing in a new pathname. Click the Browse button to browse for an existing path to use as a log file directory.

- **Log to SQL/ODBC Database**. Selecting this option causes the log to be written to a specified ODBC-connected database. This option is unchecked by default and is disabled unless you have ODBC drivers installed in Windows NT.

- ODBC Data Source Name. This field holds the file pathname and file name of the ODBC database that the log information will be written to. This field, like the other ODBC database information fields, is grayed out unless you have selected the Log to SQL/ODBC Database option.

- **Table/User Name/Password**. These fields let you specify which table to use in the specified database, and what user name and password to use when logging into the specified database to make changes.

WWW Service Directory Properties   When you edit the properties of a directory listing in the WWW Service, you are presented with the following options (see fig. 26.7):

- **Directory**. This is the physical directory on the system that contains HTML documents you want to publish on the Internet. Click the Browse button to browse for an existing path to use as a document directory.

- **Home Directory**. Clicking this option makes the current directory entry into the home directory—the default directory for when someone logs on to your domain without specifying a pathname or document. Only one directory entry can be specified as the home directory.

- **Virtual Directory**. Clicking this option lets you turn the current directory entry into a virtual directory. With this you can assign a path to the directory entry that is used by users logging into the site, but which doesn't correspond to where the documents are actually stored on the server.

N O T E   If you create a virtual directory on a network drive, the directory must be on a computer in the same Windows NT domain as the Peer Web Services. ■

- **Alias**. The Alias text box holds the alias under which the virtual directory will be presented. For instance, if your domain name was whatever.com and you registered a virtual directory as /etc, it would be accessed by using the URL http://www.whatever.com/etc.

CAUTION

Virtual directories do not automatically appear in WWW directory listings. You must make explicit references to the virtual directory in whatever URL links you create that are meant to access it.

- **User Name/Password**. These text boxes are used only when the directory specified in Directory uses a Universal Naming Convention (UNC) name, such as \\Bigmachine\Webdocs. When this type of naming is used, the directory will be available under a user name and password that the user provides in the appropriate text boxes. The user must be a valid Windows NT user. Using this method allows you to use user permissions to more precisely control access to certain directories and their contents.

- **Virtual Server**. Checking this option lets you publish this directory entry under its own individual IP address. Click the IP address fields to type in the 32-bit dotted decimal address that you wish to use as the virtual server name for this directory.

CAUTION

Don't use the Virtual Server option unless you are registered to use the IP address you are specifying. Conflicts with existing addresses, whether on- or off-site, can be troublesome (or can get you *into* trouble).

- **Read**. The Read Access checkbox indicates that the contents of this directory are readable. This option is checked by default. Do not enable this option for directories that are to contain programs.

- **Execute**. This checkbox indicates that the contents of this directory can be executed remotely by clients. Scripts and executables should be the only items placed in a directory with this option enabled.

- **Require Secure SSL Channel**. Enabling this option requires a connection through a Secure Sockets Layer (SSL) in order to access it. You need to have Secure Sockets installed to make use of this option.

Part
V

Ch
26

FIG. 26.7
The properties for
each directory entry
in the WWW service
include the physical
path to the data
hosted and the virtual
path name on the
WWW server, if any.

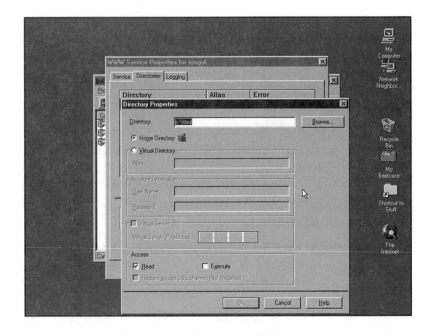

The FTP Service

The FTP Service allows you to publish remotely browsable directories of files that can be
viewed, downloaded, or contributed to, depending on the access granted to an individual
user.

To configure the FTP Service properties, double-click the FTP Service entry in the
Internet Service Manager's list of services, or right-click the entry in the list and select
Properties. You can also select the service and use the Properties, Service Properties
selection from the main program menu.

Service Tab   The Service tab (see fig. 26.8) holds the most commonly edited options for
the FTP Service. Very few of these options will need to be changed from their default
settings, with the possible exception of the virtual port.

The main options in the Service tab for the FTP Service are:

- **TCP Port.** This is the virtual port number on which the FTP Service listens for
requests. This defaults to 21, the standard for the ftp protocol, and will not need to
be changed unless you are deliberately hosting the FTP Service on another port.
After changing this value, you will have to shut down the system and restart.

- **Connection Timeout.** This is the length of time, in seconds, that the server waits
before pulling the plug on an inactive user. This value ensures that all inactive users,

including ones who attempted to close a connection and failed, are eventually disconnected. With the FTP service, it's not recommended that you decrease this value below 100 seconds, since browsing ftp directories can be slow for the user.

■ **Maximum Connections**. This is the maximum number of simultaneous connections the service supports. The default is 100,000. If you have a narrow-bandwidth Internet connection (such as a 26.8 dialup connection) or a machine that isn't very powerful, you may want to reduce this number to something more realistic to prevent having your server or your connection overloaded.

FIG. 26.8
The most common service options, like port number and connection timeout, are kept here.

Anonymous Logon   The Allow Anonymous Connections section of the Service tab holds two options that pertain to anonymous connections to the ftp server. Whether or not you choose to allow anonymous connections to your ftp server is up to you, depending on the nature of the data you want to host.

The Anonymous Logon options are Username and Password. Both of these refer to a Windows NT user account, created when you installed Peer Web Services, which holds the security information and permissions for anonymous Web users. This password is only used within Windows NT, since anonymous users do not provide a valid name and password to log on. The name for the account is IUSR, plus whatever the local computer name is.

The password has been assigned randomly, but it can be changed. If you do change it, it must be changed both here and in the entry for the same user in the User Manager. Blank passwords are not allowed for this user.

By default, the IUSR_*computername* account can log on locally; this option is enabled or disabled in the Dialin section of the User Properties sheet for a user account. You must have this option enabled for this account as long as you want anonymous logons to be possible.

Password Authentication   The Password Authentication section of the Service tab governs how passwords, used for non-anonymous logons, are handled:

- **Allow Anonymous**. Checking this box allows users to log in anonymously. Deselecting it forces users to log in with a valid username and password. This option is checked by default.

- **Basic (Clear Text)**. Checking this option causes passwords to be sent over the Internet in clear text format. While most browsers support clear text, it's not recommended to use this format without working through a Secure Sockets Layer, since clear text sent over the Internet can be easily intercepted. For obvious reasons, this option is not checked by default.

- **Windows NT Challenge/Response**. Checking this option forces the server to authenticate all passwords using the Windows NT Challenge/Response protocol, which is encrypted and can be sent without the need for a Secure Socket Layer. At this point, Microsoft Internet Explorer is the only browser that supports Challenge/ Response; even Microsoft's FrontPage doesn't (yet) support Challenge/Response. This option is checked by default.

Finally, the Comment field lets you type in whatever comment you wish to make about this particular server. This comment is visible in the main window of the Service Manager.

FTP User Sessions Window   Clicking the Current Sessions button in the Service tab displays the FTP User Sessions window, which shows all the currently connected users of the ftp service (see fig. 26.9). The user list contains the user name (provided in lieu of a password if they are logged on anonymously), their 32-bit Internet address, and the total time they have been logged on.

FIG. 26.9
Each unique IP address currently accessing the service is listed here.

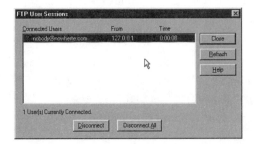

Here are the commands associated with this window:

- **Disconnect**. To disconnect a given user from the ftp service, click their name in the Connected Users list to highlight it and then click the Disconnect button.

- **Disconnect All**. Clicking this button disconnects all connected ftp users. A dialog box will appear before the users are disconnected, to confirm that you really want to do this.

- **Refresh**. Clicking this button updates the ftp user list.

To close the FTP User Sessions window and return to the Service tab, click Close.

Messages Tab   The Messages tab holds messages that the ftp server broadcasts to users when they connect or disconnect from the service (see fig. 26.10).

- **Welcome message**. Type here the message that is first presented to users when they first log on to the ftp service. This can be a description of what's new, a statement about what's available (or not available) at this site, or anything else you wish.

- **Exit message**. This field contains the message sent to the remote user when they log off.

- **Maximum Connections Message**. This field contains the message sent to users who attempt to connect when the maximum number of users (specified in the Service tab) has been reached.

FIG. 26.10
Each field in the Messages tab holds a different context message to be sent to a connected user.

Part
V

Ch

26

Directories Tab   The Directories Tab (see fig. 26.11) holds a list of the directories which the FTP Service uses to find files to be published in ftp directories.

FIG. 26.11

The list of ftp directories also lists comments (if any) and which directory is shown by default upon login.

When the ftp Service is installed, it creates one directory that is used with the ftp server. There's no realistic limit to the number of directories you can have installed for use with the ftp server.

The small house icon next to a given directory entry means that this directory is the "home" directory, or the default directory that will be presented when someone logs on to the Web server without specifying a document or a path.

When you create folders in this home directory, they are automatically visible via ftp. You do not need to make discrete ftp directory listings for every subdirectory.

The Logging Tab   The Logging tab on the FTP Service Properties sheet contains information about how transactions posted to and from the FTP server are logged. Information logged about each hit contains the time and date, the directory and document transferred, and the IP address and registered machine name of the connected user. For details on the workings of the Logging tab, see the section entitled "Logging Tab" under the description of the WWW Service.

FTP Service Directory Properties   When you edit the properties of a directory listing in the FTP Service, you are presented with the following options (see fig. 26.12):

- **Directory**. This is the physical directory on the system that contains HTML documents you want to publish on the Internet. Click the Browse button to browse for an existing path to use as a document directory.

- **Home Directory**. Clicking this option makes the current directory entry into the home directory—the default directory for when someone logs on to your domain without specifying a pathname or document. Only one directory entry can be specified as the home directory.

- **Virtual Directory**. Clicking this option lets you turn the current directory entry into a virtual directory. With this you can assign a path to the directory entry that is used by users logging into the site, but which doesn't correspond to where the documents are actually stored.

- **Alias**. The Alias text box holds the alias under which the virtual directory will be presented. For instance, if your domain name was whatever.com and you registered a virtual directory as /etc, it would be accessed by using the URL http:// ftp.whatever.com/etc.

> **CAUTION**
>
> As with WWW virtual directories, ftp virtual directories do not automatically appear in ftp directory listings. You must make explicit references to the virtual directory in whatever URL links you create that are meant to access it.

- **User Name/Password**. These text boxes are used only when the directory specified in Directory uses a Universal Naming Convention (UNC) name, such as \\Bigmachine\Webdocs. When this type of naming is used, the directory will be available under a user name and password that the user provides in the appropriate text boxes. The user must be a valid Windows NT user. Using this method allows you to use user permissions to more precisely control access to certain directories and their contents.

- **Access**. Check the appropriate boxes to control the types of access available to the ftp directory. Check Read to enable read access and Write to enable write access.

> **CAUTION**
>
> Be careful with the way you set read and write permissions. Read and write permissions set through the ftp server have nothing to do with the permissions conventionally given to a directory through Windows NT. Make sure that you are not accidentally exposing a directory to some kind of attack!

Part
V

Ch
26

FIG. 26.12
The FTP Service
Directory Properties
sheet contains details
about a specific ftp
directory entry.

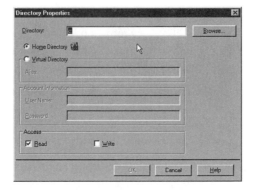

The Gopher Service

The Gopher Service allows you to publish remotely browsable and searchable directories of topically organized documents. Most Web browsers support the gopher protocol, making it possible to browse gopher archives with the same ease as browsing the Web.

Gopher is different from ftp in that the server allows the client to perform searches and finds with documents. Up until the invention of the Web, gopher was the preferred way to store documents that were searched and indexed, and to a great degree it still is.

To configure the Gopher Service properties, double-click the Gopher Service entry in the Internet Service Manager's list of services, or right-click the entry in the list and select Properties. You can also select the service and use the Properties, Service Properties selection from the main program menu.

Service Tab   The Service tab (see fig. 26.13) holds the most commonly edited options for the Gopher Service. The main options are:

■ **TCP Port**. This is the virtual port number on which the gopher Service listens for requests. This defaults to 70, the standard for the gopher protocol, and will not need to be changed unless you are deliberately hosting the Gopher Service on another port. After changing this value, you will have to shut down the system and restart.

■ **Connection Timeout**. This is the length of time, in seconds, that the gopher server waits before pulling the plug on an inactive user. This value ensures that all inactive users, including ones who attempted to close a connection and failed, are eventually disconnected. With the Gopher Service, it's not recommended that you decrease this value below 100 seconds, since browsing gopher directories can be slow for the user—not as slow as with ftp, but slow enough (because of the user needing to digest everything he sees) to make anything less than 100 problematic.

- **Maximum Connections**. This is the maximum number of simultaneous connections the service supports. The default is 100,000. If you have a narrow-bandwidth Internet connection (such as a 28.8 dial-up connection) or a machine that isn't very powerful, you may want to reduce this number to something more realistic to prevent having your server overload.

- **Service Administrator**. The Service Administrator fields hold the name and e-mail address of the user who administrates the Gopher Service. Click the text boxes and type in the appropriate name and e-mail address. Most system administrators will create a specific e-mail account for the receipt of complaints for gopher and ftp services, such as "ftp-master@whatever.com"

- **Anonymous Logon**. The Anonymous Logon section of the Service tab holds two options that pertain to anonymous connections to the gopher server. Since all connections to the gopher server are anonymous by nature, these options must be configured correctly. They are given default settings when Peer Web Services are installed, and do not need to be changed. For more details on the Anonymous Login settings, see the section "Anonymous Login" under the description of the Service tab for the WWW Service and FTP Service.

- **Comment**. Type here any one-line comment you wish to make about this service. The comment will be displayed in the main Internet Service Manager screen.

FIG. 26.13
The Gopher Service Properties contains all the main configuration options for the Gopher Service.

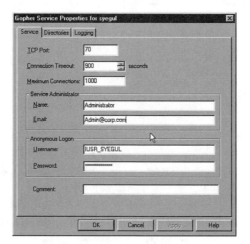

Part
V

Ch
26

The Logging Tab   The Logging tab on the Gopher Service Properties sheet contains information about how transactions posted to and from the gopher server are logged. Information logged about each hit contains the time and date, the directory and document transferred, and the IP address and registered machine name of the connected user. For examples and details on the workings of the Logging tab, see the section entitled "Logging Tab" under the description of the WWW Service.

Gopher Service Directory Properties   When you edit the properties of a directory listing in the Gopher Service, you are presented with the following options:

- **Directory**. This is the physical directory on the system that contains HTML documents you want to publish on the Internet. Click the <u>B</u>rowse button to browse for an existing path to use as a document directory.

- **Home Directory**. Clicking this option makes the current directory entry into the home directory—the default directory for when someone logs on to your domain without specifying a pathname or document. Only one directory entry can be specified as the home directory.

- **Virtual Directory**. Clicking this option lets you turn the current directory entry into a virtual directory. With this you can assign a path to the directory entry that is used by users logging into the site, but which doesn't correspond to where the documents are actually stored.

- **Alias**. The Alias text box holds the alias under which the virtual directory will be presented. For instance, if your domain name was whatever.com and you registered a virtual directory as /etc, it would be accessed by using the URL http:// ftp.whatever.com/etc.

> **CAUTION**
>
> As with WWW and FTP virtual directories, gopher virtual directories do not automatically appear in gopher directory listings. You must make explicit references to the virtual directory in whatever URL links you create that are meant to access it.

- **User Name/Password**. These text boxes are used only when the directory specified in Directory uses a Universal Naming Convention (UNC) name, such as \\Bigmachine\Webdocs. When this type of naming is used, the directory will be available under a user name and password that the user provides in the appropriate text boxes. The user must be a valid Windows NT user. Using this method allows you to use user permissions to more precisely control access to certain directories and their contents.

Stopping, Starting, and Pausing Services

Sometimes it's necessary to take a service offline to make changes to its settings. Under Peer Web Services, there are two ways you can take a service offline: *stopping* and *pausing*.

There are important differences between stopping and pausing a service:

■ Stopping a service turns it off completely and unloads it from memory. If you stop a service, then close and reopen the Service Manager, you will find that the service is no longer visible. You will have to manually restart the service through the Services window, available from the Control Panel.

■ Pausing a service is the same as stopping it, except that the service is not unloaded. It is still available in memory, just inactive, and can be easily un-paused to resume normal activities. It does not disconnect existing users, nor does it permit new users to log in.

Generally, when you need to take a service offline to make changes, pausing it will be sufficient. You will not need to stop and restart a service unless there is some reason it needs to be unloaded and reloaded.

Stopping a Service   Stopping a service can be done one of two ways: through the Internet Service Manager program, or the Services window of the Control Panel.

If you are using Internet Service Manager, follow these steps:

1. In the main Internet Service Manager window, click the name of the service you want to stop. This will highlight it.

2. Click the Stop button on the toolbar (see fig. 26.14).

3. Also, you can select the Properties, Stop Service menu option to accomplish the same thing.

If you are using the Services window of the Control panel, follow these steps:

1. Select the name of the service to stop (in fig. 26.15, it's the World Wide Web Publishing Service) and click it to highlight it.

2. Click the Stop button to stop the service.

Part
V

Ch
26

FIG. 26.14
The toolbar control to stop a service resembles the stop button on a VCR.

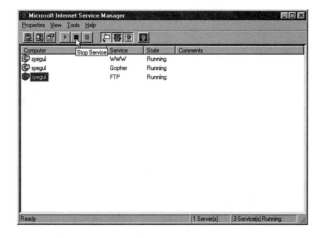

FIG. 26.15
Clicking the Stop button to stop a service may take several seconds to take effect.

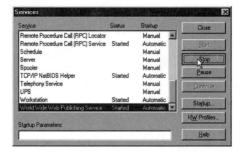

Pausing a Service   Pausing a service can also be done one of two ways: through the Internet Service Manager program, or the Services window of the Control Panel.

If you are using Internet Service Manager, follow these steps:

1. In the main Internet Service Manager window, click the name of the service you want to stop. This will highlight it.

2. Click the Pause button on the toolbar (see fig. 26.16).

3. Also, you can select the Properties, Pause Service menu option to accomplish the same thing.

If you are using the Services window of the Control panel, follow these steps:

1. Select the name of the service to pause (in fig. 26.17, it's the World Wide Web Publishing Service) and click it to highlight it.

2. Click the Pause button to stop the service.

FIG. 26.16
The Pause button on the toolbar resembles the pause button on a VCR.

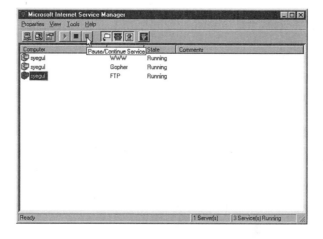

FIG. 26.17
Clicking the Pause button to stop a service may take several seconds to take effect.

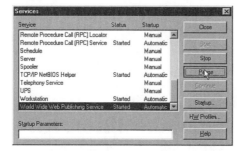

Connecting to and Viewing Other Servers

The Internet Service Manager program lets you connect to Windows NT machines elsewhere on the network that are also running Internet services, and view and configure them remotely.

If you know the name of another Windows NT computer on the network you want to connect to, select the Properties, Connect to Server option from the Internet Service Manager's main menu. You can also press Ctrl-O to achieve the same effect.

A dialog box will appear, asking you for the computer name (see fig. 26.18). Type in the name of the computer you want to connect to and click OK.

FIG. 26.18
Type in the name of another computer on the network that has PWS running.

If the computer you've specified is a valid Windows NT computer name and is accessible from the network and is running Internet services, the updated list will display the newly connected computer.

Another option lets you connect to and view *all* Windows NT computers on the network that are running Internet services. To run a search for these computers, select the Properties, Find all Servers option from the Internet Service Manager's main menu. You can also press Ctrl-F to start the search. A dialog box will appear to inform you that the search for other NT Internet services is under way (see fig.26.19). When the search is finished, the Internet Service Manager display will be updated to show the Internet services running on other computers it has found (if it's found any).

FIG. 26.19
The search for the other computer should not take more than a few seconds.

Service View Options

Since the Internet Service Manager lets you examine Internet services on more than one machine, there are several display organization options that let you sort and filter the views of the available services. All of these options are contained in the View menu on the Internet Service Manager's main menu.

- **FTP, Gopher, WWW**. Toggling these options on and off will show or hide all ftp, gopher or WWW services.

- **All**. Toggling this option shows all running services, regardless of previous selections.

- **Sort by Server, Sort By Service, Sort By Comment, Sort By State**. These options let you sort the display by the selected criterion: server, service, comment, or state (running/paused/stopped).

N O T E   The Sort By options are only available when the Report View option has also been selected. ■

- **Server View**. Selecting this option changes the Internet Service Manager display to a tree diagram with the servers as the highest-level branches, and their services as sub-branches.

- **Services View**. Selecting this option changes the Internet Service Manager display to a tree diagram with the services as the highest-level branches, and the servers they are running on as their sub-branches.
- **Report View**. This is the default view that Internet Service Manager presents.

Securing Peer Web Services

Running an information server of any kind can pose a security risk. Warnings about the general lack of security on the Internet appear constantly in the media. While some of this kind of news is alarmism, there are some very valid concerns for information security mixed in with the hype. Here is a list of suggestions, from the general to the specific, that will allow you to tighten security on a Peer Web Server system.

- Use a proxy server or firewall to heighten protection against attacks. A proxy server screens out unwanted inbound packets and insures that outbound traffic is from authorized locations and on authorized ports only. Windows NT Server's TCP/IP routing can be configured to work as a proxy server by disallowing certain kinds of traffic, but this is a fairly advanced exercise and a commercial product is really recommended for the best results.

- Use secure sockets for all commercial transactions. Never allow a situation to exist where a user could unwittingly send credit card numbers or other sensitive personal information across a plaintext connection. Users should be warned against sending such information in a standard plaintext mail message, and a secure server channel should be set up and dedicated to any kind of Internet commerce. Don't be held liable for a very avoidable mistake.

- When using secured servers, make sure you are using valid forms of security for your locale. Some types of secured-server software are not permitted for export. For instance, software that uses 40-bit cryptography keys are approved for export by the U.S. government. Software that uses anything stronger (anywhere from 128- to 1024-bit keys) cannot be exported to other countries.

- Have a reliable and workable way of reading and evaluating access logs to the site. SQL databases, with the right tools (such as Microsoft Access or FoxPro), are easier to work with than text files when the number of hits per day is in the hundreds or thousands. Data are much easier to sort, search, and analyze when they're already in some systematized form.

- Be careful with the way you share out directories. Don't casually allow anonymous ftp or anonymous logins in general, unless you're certain that the information you're hosting isn't crucial. Be extra careful with network-shared directories, since a

Part

V

Ch

26

mistyped pathname can expose whole hierarchies of data that you may not want to reveal to the public.

■ Leave the IUSR_ password alone. When you install PWS, the IUSR_ password is set randomly and is next to impossible to crack. Don't change this password unless you have a good reason to, and definitely don't change it to something that would compromise your machine's security.

■ Don't use the PWS machine to hold truly sensitive data. The best possible protection against accidentally publishing sensitive information is not to provide it in the first place. If you are dedicating a machine as a Web server, see that it gets used for just that and nothing else. Also make sure that there are no unsecured routes from the PWS machine to any other machine on your network that could hold sensitive data as well.

■ Use NTFS to properly set permissions on all directories. Take the trouble to make sure that the NT system and root directories are not accessible to anyone except administrators.

■ Even though the Internet services don't directly rely on NTFS security for read/write permissions to hosted directories, it's still important to maintain routine security on these directories in the event someone finds a way to login as a local user.

Remotely Configuring Peer Web Services

When you install Peer Web Services, you are given the option to install a remote HTML administration utility. This utility—a series of HTML pages that allows you to change many of the options available in the Peer Web Services Manager program—is placed in a virtual directory named /iisadmin (see fig. 26.20).

Using the HTML administration utility is not all that dissimilar from using the PWS program, except that you cannot stop or start the services remotely. You must have administrator access at the local console to be able to do that.

N O T E   By default, PWS is not set to accept clear-text logins, but rather to work with Windows NT Challenge/Response protocol. Netscape Navigator does not support this protocol. If you are going to use the remote HTML PWS configuration utilities, turn on the Challenge/Response protocol and use Microsoft Internet Explorer version 2.0 or higher to remotely administer your Internet services. Using cleartext authentication over an open network—especially when sending your administrator password—is *dangerous*. ■

FIG. 26.20
The look and feel of the remote PWS HTML utility is designed to replicate the layout of the tabbed controls in the PWS Manager.

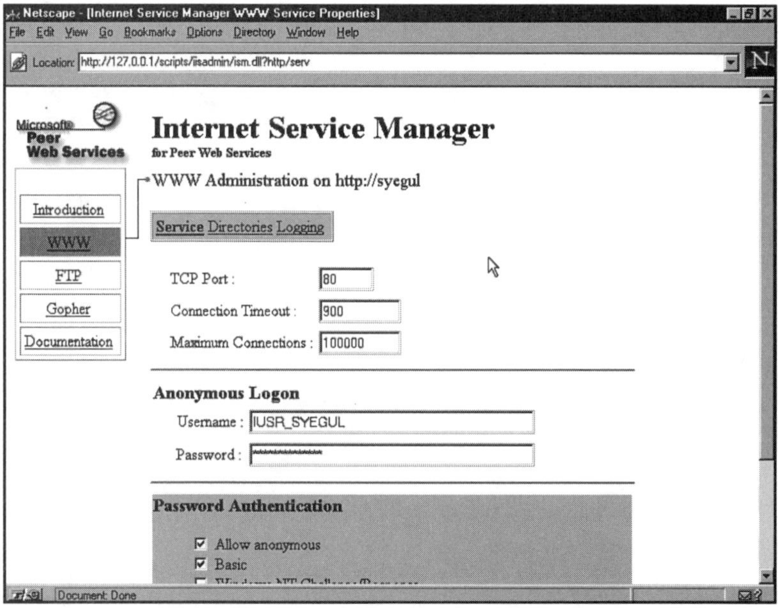

From Here...

The Peer Web Services aren't by any means the most complete solution to everyone's Internet serving needs, but they provide a strong foundation upon which a user can gain some experience. You may also want to do further research in the following sections of the book:

- Part IV, "Optimizing Network Performance." You'll want to get the most throughput you can, no matter what server software you use.

- Chapter 19, "Integrating Windows NT in UNIX Environments." The vast majority of Web serving is done through UNIX or UNIX-like operating systems. If you don't know much about UNIX at this point, now's a good time to start.

- Chapter 20, "Using Dial-Up Networking." The quickest way to get on the Internet is usually through a phone line, and you may want to get the basics of DUN down pat while you're at it.

- Part V, "Using TCP/IP and Internet Features." Learning the basics of the TCP/IP protocols, such as how to configure firewalls and packet routing, is critical knowledge for any Web administrator.

Part
V

Ch
26

P A R T

VI

Working with the Registry

CHAPTER 27

Registry Overview

by Jim Boyce

The Windows NT Registry is a complex and often hard-to-fathom database that your computer uses to maintain hardware and software configuration settings. For the most part, the Registry replaces INI, SYS, and COM files used in Windows, DOS, and LAN Manager, although some Windows applications still continue to use INI files rather than store their settings in the Registry. The Registry also helps eliminate CFG files by incorporating their settings into the Registry. Moving these configuration settings from their multiple sources into a single database eases administration.

In brief, the Windows NT Registry is structured as a hierarchical database. The Registry contains five main subtrees, which simply are branches in the Registry's hierarchical structure:

■ **HKEY_LOCAL_MACHINE.** This branch contains information about the local computer, such as bus type, amount of memory installed, device drivers, and other system data.

- **HKEY_CLASSES_ROOT.** This branch contains OLE and file-class associations.
- **HKEY_CURRENT_USER.** This branch stores settings about the current user's configuration, such as desktop settings, network connections, and environment variables.
- **HKEY_CURRENT_CONFIG**. This branch stores configuration information about the current hardware profile.
- **HKEY_USERS.** This branch stores all currently loaded user profiles.

Each of these branches is further divided into *hives*, which are discrete bodies of *keys* and *subkeys*. These keys and subkeys contain values for the various settings that apply to the hive.

Working with the Registry

By understanding the Registry and how to edit it, you gain absolute control over every aspect of your computer's function. But with such power comes the potential for catastrophe. It's possible—even easy—to change a few Registry settings and corrupt your system's configuration so badly that it will not boot. Understanding the ramifications of editing the Registry is therefore as important as understanding how to make those changes.

In addition, it's important to understand that you can accomplish most configuration changes without editing the Registry directly. Instead, you can use the icons in the Control Panel to change hardware and software settings that affect Windows NT's operation. Application settings generally can be changed from within the application. So, the average user seldom needs to even view the contents of the Registry, much less actually modify it directly. Some settings, however, can be changed only by directly modifying the Registry.

The Registry Editors

Windows NT includes two tools that enable you to view and modify the Registry. Both tools are called the Registry Editor. The first of these tools, REGEDT32.EXE, is located in the \WINNT\SYSTEM32 folder. If you've worked with the Registry in previous versions of Windows NT, REGEDT32 will look familiar to you (see fig. 27.1), because it is the same Registry editor included with previous versions of Windows NT.

The other Registry Editor included with Windows NT 4.0 is REGEDIT.EXE, located in the \WINNT directory. This Registry Editor takes advantage of the new Windows NT interface, providing an Explorer view of the Registry (see fig. 27.2). By bringing all of the Registry branches together into a single tree, this new editor makes it easier to switch from one tree to another.

Other than the fact that REGEDIT provides a more cohesive interface for all the Registry branches, there are no real advantages of using one editor over the other.

FIG. 27.1
REGEDT32 uses the MDI child window interface to enable you to view and modify Registry settings.

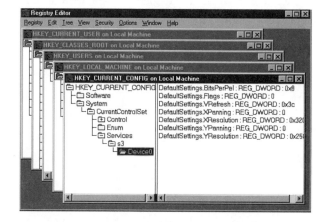

FIG. 27.2
REGEDIT uses an Explorer-like interface to provide a view of the Registry that is consistent with views of other resources, such as disks.

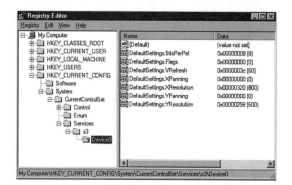

Focusing on the Registry

The chapters in this part focus on all aspects of working with the Registry. In Chapter 28, "Understanding the Registry," you learn how the Registry is structured and functions. It's particularly important that you read the section "Registry Cautions" in Chapter 28 to help avoid potential problems as you move into the chapters that follow.

Chapter 29, "Backing Up and Editing the Registry," explains the process you should use as you begin editing the Registry. One of the most important steps is to back up the Registry so you'll have a clean working copy, should something go wrong during editing. With the Registry backed up, you can use the two Registry editors provided with Windows NT to begin modifying your Registry.

Part
VI

Ch
27

Chapter 30, "Restoring and Repairing the Registry," examines common problems that can lead to a corrupted Registry. In Chapter 30, you'll also learn about the ways in which Windows NT can automatically repair the Registry. For times when automatic repair won't work, you can turn to Chapter 29 to restore the Registry from a backup copy. ●

CHAPTER 28

Understanding the Registry

by Richard Neff

One of the key differences about administration and configuration of a Windows NT machine over a Windows 3.1 system is the Windows NT Registry. Windows NT uses the Registry in a similar manner that Windows 3.1 uses INI files, the AUTOEXEC.BAT file, and CONFIG.SYS file. The Windows NT Registry handles configuration settings for both hardware and software and is a key component for the correct operation of Windows NT.

Unlike INI files, the Registry is not a text file and it is more complex than the INI file structure. Extra care is needed to configure the Registry properly, and in many instances, direct editing of the Registry is not needed for a Windows NT system to be configured properly. However, knowledge of the Registry is important in understanding how Windows NT works. ■

Windows NT Registry structure

The Windows NT Registry structure is very complex and understanding how it is laid out can be useful for troubleshooting.

Registry comparisons

The Windows NT Registry is different from the Windows 3.1 INI structure and even the Windows 95 Registry structure.

Using INI files

On some systems, INI files should still be kept on systems using Windows NT.

Keys, Subkeys, Hives, and Values

The Windows NT Registry uses items such as keys, subkeys, hives, and values to keep important information available to Windows NT.

The five Registry keys

Each of the five keys of the Registry has a distinct purpose for controlling the Windows NT system.

Overview of the Registry

The Windows NT Registry is a central database containing most of the settings for the Windows NT environment. This database handles most of the configuration options available under Windows NT. It contains configuration information for the hardware used as well as the settings for software run under Windows NT. The Registry is designed to replace the INI file structure used under Windows 3.1 with a more streamlined and hierarchical database structure.

Registry Cautions

Before even discussing the Windows NT Registry in any detail, you should be completely aware that the Registry is central to the correct operation of Windows NT. Without a correct Registry, Windows NT will not operate properly, and in some instances, may not even allow Windows NT to run. The Windows NT Resource Kit lists all of the Registry entries and values. The Resource Kit is the only way, short of complete reinstallation, to manually return the Registry values back to their default values.

In short, do *not* make changes to the Registry unless you are sure that what you are modifying is correct. Also, be very careful when typing entries into the Registry. Some of the entries may be very cryptic or complex, but they must be typed correctly. Always double-check the typing of any entry you modify in the Registry. It is also a good idea to have backed up the Registry files to tape to ensure that you can recover the original Registry should the modified one be corrupted beyond repair. Additionally, you should run RDISK from the Command Prompt or the Windows NT Explorer to update the Emergency Repair Disk.

Also, keep in mind that in most cases, hardware and software configuration is easier when using the Windows NT Control Panel. Most configuration options are designed to be set under Control Panel, rather than through direct modification of the Registry. Using Control Panel helps to insure that all of the necessary information is added to the Registry in the proper format. However, there are certain options that can only be configured through direct modifications of the Windows NT Registry.

Advantages of the Registry

The biggest advantage of the Registry is the consolidation of system settings into a central database file. It is a true database for configuration settings and is laid out in a tree structure, making it easier to find and modify related information. The database also uses a common structure throughout the Registry, making it easier for the administrator of the Windows NT machine to modify the Registry correctly.

Another advantage is that a copy of the Registry is always on the hard disk, making it a bit easier to repair if the Registry gets corrupted. The Emergency Disk, created with the Windows NT installation or created using the RDISK command, makes it easier to repair damaged Registry files of a Windows NT machine. Furthermore, the Registry can be modified from another computer, making remote administration and configuration of many Windows NT machines easier.

Disadvantages of the Registry

Despite all the positive attributes of the Registry, there are still some disadvantages. First, if you've ever looked at the Registry using the Windows NT Registry Editor, you've probably been overwhelmed by the size and complexity of it all. It certainly doesn't look like the familiar INI structure used with Windows 3.1! However, this can be overcome with a little patience and, hopefully, you'll feel a lot more comfortable after reading this chapter.

Another potential disadvantage is the relative ease with which you can disrupt the operation of Windows NT by incorrectly modifying the Registry. Although Windows NT does a good job of backing up Registry files and is reasonably good at trying to repair the Registry, if you make certain modifications you can keep Windows NT from working at all. So, once again, don't modify Registry values unless you are sure of what that entry does!

How the Registry Is Used by Windows NT

Many items in Windows NT use the Registry for information. Here is a list of some items that use the Windows NT Registry information:

■ **The Windows NT kernel**. The kernel uses the Registry on startup to determine what device drivers to load and the order in which to load them.

■ **Device drivers**. Device drivers use the Registry to view hardware configuration settings to determine the proper way to load.

■ **The Windows NT system**. Many parts of the Windows NT system use the Registry to determine user settings and other configuration options.

■ **Application programs**. Many application programs use the Registry for various parameters, such as the location of important files that the program uses.

Items that Modify the Registry

The Windows NT Registry can be modified in a variety of ways. The list below gives some examples of items that may modify the Windows NT Registry:

Part
VI

Ch
28

- **The Windows NT Setup program**. This program creates the Windows NT system, including the default Registry information. This program can also be used to repair or update information in the Registry.

- **Other setup programs**. As programs are installed under Windows NT, their setup programs may modify the Registry to include configuration information for that program.

- **Application programs**. Application programs may modify the Registry after they have been installed to adjust user-defined settings or to change operation settings.

- **NTDETECT.COM**. When Windows NT starts, the hardware configuration is built and information is sent to the Registry. On Intel x86-based computers, this is handled by the NTDETECT.COM program. On RISC-based computers, the ARC firmware is used to build the entries into the Registry.

- **The Windows NT kernel**. The Windows NT kernel also helps to build and enter hardware data into the Registry. It will also send data about itself to the Registry.

- **Device drivers**. Device drivers send information about the system's resources that they use. Items such as hardware interrupts (IRQs), DMA channels, memory access, and so on, are examples of the type of information that is sent to the Registry. Most of this data is similar to the DEVICE= commands used in the CONFIG.SYS under MS-DOS.

- **Windows NT administrative tools**. Administrative tools, such as Control Panel, User Manager, and so on, make changes to the Windows NT Registry. In many instances, using these programs is the preferred method over manually modifying entries through the Registry Editor.

Replacing and Supplementing INI Files

The INI structure of Windows 3.1 was useful up to a point. However, it required the computer to use AUTOEXEC.BAT, CONFIG.SYS, WIN.INI, PROTOCOL.INI (with networked Windows for Workgroup systems), and SYSTEM.INI for all of its configuration. The command styles, or syntax, used in one file didn't always mean the same thing in another. Plus, Windows 3.1 also had a Registry which was used to keep track of file associations and so on. With all of these different files, which were all handled differently, the Windows NT and Windows 95 Registries were used as a way to centrally consolidate all the needed system information.

Why Keep INI Files?

If the Windows NT Registry is designed to replace the INI file entries used by Windows 3.1, why is it even necessary to keep INI files on a Windows NT system? The answer is that some Windows 16-bit programs won't work properly if they cannot find certain INI entries. If you are *absolutely sure* that you won't run any older 16-bit Windows programs that need to access the INI files, then you don't need to have the WIN.INI or SYSTEM.INI files. But, in most cases, it is probably wise to keep the files available to insure that programs work properly.

How the Registry Is Organized

The Registry uses a tree-like structure, similar to the format of files and folders used in the Windows NT Explorer (see fig. 28.1). The top most level is comprised of a structure known as *keys*. The keys are primary containers for the rest of the Registry information. The next level of the structure contains *subkeys* which are similar to subfolders under the Windows NT Explorer. In these subkeys you may find more subkeys or *values*. The values consist of an item name and value. These values are the actual configuration items used by Windows NT to configure the system.

Finally, items known as *hives* are the actual files comprising the Registry. These hives divide the Registry information and store it onto disk for use by Windows NT. The purpose for using multiple files to store Registry information is to allow different users and settings to be used on a single Windows NT machine. Figure 28.1 shows the Registry Editor. Table 28.1 describes the types of items located in the Registry.

Table 28.1 Registry Items

Item	Description
Keys	These five sections make up the core trees of the Windows NT Registry. Each handles a part of the Windows NT environment settings.
Subkeys	Subkeys are similar to Explorer's folders or DOS subdirectories. These subkeys further break up the key categories of the Registry. Subkeys can be nested inside other subkeys.
Hives	A hive is a unique type of tree structure because it has a corresponding file in the \SYSTEM32\CONFIG subdirectory of the

continues

Part

VI

Ch

28

Table 28.1 Continued	
Item	**Description**
	Windows NT directory. The combined hives essentially make up the Windows NT Registry.
Values	Values are the lowest part of the Registry structure. Values actually define the settings that Windows NT uses. Values are composed of three parts: the value name, the data type, and the value or parameter.

FIG. 28.1

This screen shot of the Registry Editor shows the tree structure used by the Windows NT Registry.

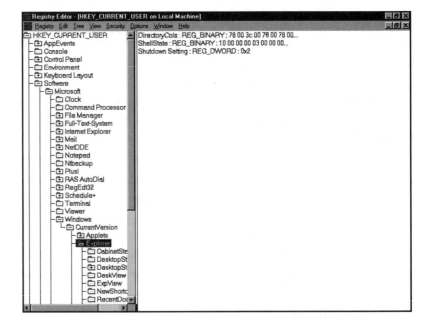

If you compare the Registry structure to the INI file structure, the INI headings, which were items contained in brackets, most closely resemble keys or subkeys. Windows 3.1 INI files did not allow for nesting of headings unlike the Registry's nesting of subkeys. The INI value strings correspond to the Registry values; however, the Registry values are not limited to strings.

Registry Keys

The Windows NT 4.0 Registry is comprised of five keys: HKEY_CLASSES_ROOT, HKEY_CURRENT_USER, HKEY_LOCAL_MACHINE, HKEY_USERS, and HKEY_CURRENT_CONFIG. The HKEY_CURRENT_CONFIG key is new to Windows NT 4.0, while the other four were also part of the Windows NT 3.5x Registry. The Registry keys break up the Registry into related sections, making it easier to locate or modify the appropriate subtrees and values.

HKEY_CLASSES_ROOT   This key contains similar data to the original Windows 3.1 Registry. It contains OLE information and file associations. This key is replicated in HKEY_LOCAL_MACHINE\SOFTWARE\Classes. Items located in this key are configured through the File, Open With command in the Windows NT Explorer. Use of the Windows NT Explorer is the preferred method for setting entries in this key.

HKEY_CURRENT_USER   This key contains configuration settings for the user that is currently logged into the computer. This key is also stored as a hive, which is stored as a file on the computer. Each user has a file which becomes this key when the user logs on to the computer. The user's file contains the first five letters of the account name and is followed by three digits. The data in this file can also be accessed from HKEY_USERS under the SID subkey of the user.

This key contains seven default subkeys: Console, Control Panel, Environment, Keyboard Layout, Printers, Program Groups, and Software. These subkeys are discussed in greater detail in the "HKEY_CURRENT_USER Subkeys" section later in this chapter.

HKEY_LOCAL_MACHINE   The information in this key stays the same no matter which user, if any, is logged on to the machine. This key contains configuration information for the Windows NT computer. It also contains both hardware and software settings and is used by device drivers and the Windows NT system to configure hardware devices. This key is used by the Windows NT boot process to determine what devices to load and how to load them.

The HKEY_LOCAL_MACHINE key has five subkeys: HARDWARE, SAM (which stands for Security Account Manager), SECURITY, SOFTWARE, and SYSTEM. These subkeys are discussed later in this chapter under the section titled, "HKEY_LOCAL_MACHINE Subkeys."

HKEY_USERS   This key contains information about the system default settings and settings for the user who is currently logged on. The settings for user currently logged on is also found in the HKEY_CURRENT_USER key. The .DEFAULT subkey contains the settings for the system default settings. The system default settings are used when the initial login dialog box is displayed. The current user information is named by the SID of the user who is currently logged on.

HKEY_CURRENT_CONFIG   This key is new to Windows NT 4.0 and Windows 95. It contains information about the current hardware and software configurations used by the Windows NT machine. Hardware information in this key is also found in HKEY_LOCAL_MACHINE\SYSTEM\CurrentControlSet.

Part

VI

Ch

28

Registry Subkeys

Registry subkeys are containers for Registry values or other subkeys. These subkeys are used to break up the Registry information further into logical groupings. There are default subkeys in each major key, and in some instances, subkeys may be added depending on the user logged in or the system configuration used.

HKEY_CURRENT_USER Subkeys The HKEY_CURRENT_USER key contains the profile information for the user who is currently logged on. This profile includes desktop settings, network connections, environment variables, and so on. This information allows multiple users to have their own personalized system setup on a single machine. This key contains information that was stored in the WIN.INI file under Windows 3.1.

This key is also mapped in the HKEY_USER key with the SID of the user. When the user logs into Windows NT, the user profile is loaded into the Registry. If the user does not have a profile, the HKEY_CURRENT_USER is built from information found in HKEY_USER\.DEFAULT.

Similar data may exist in both the HKEY_CURRENT_USER key and the HKEY_LOCAL_MACHINE key. When this occurs, data in the HKEY_CURRENT_USER key takes precedence over the information in the HKEY_LOCAL_MACHINE key. This typically occurs with environment variables or software settings. This is also very important to remember when manually editing the Registry.

The HKEY_CURRENT_USER key contains seven default subkeys: AppEvents, Console, Control Panel, Environment, Keyboard Layout, Software, and UNICODE Program Groups. Table 28.2 describes the contents of the default subkeys.

Table 28.2 HKEY_CURRENT_USER Subtrees

Subtree	Description
AppEvents	The AppEvents subkey contains information about the Windows NT events. Items such as sound associations for events and event labels used by the system are listed in this key. Changes to the event labels will be reflected in the Sounds icon in the Control Panel. The sounds associated with those events are set also in the Sounds icon in Control Panel.

Subtree	Description
Console	This subkey contains information concerning the MS-DOS prompt window or any other character-mode applications. This includes window sizes and fonts, for example. These options are usually set in the Control menu for each character-mode window. You will not see any settings for the Command Prompt unless changes have been made that are different from the default, such as changing the font settings or screen colors.
Control Panel	The Control Panel subkey contains many options that are set in the Control Panel program. This subkey also includes information located in the WIN.INI and CONTROL.INI files if the system was upgraded from Windows 3.1.
Environment	This subkey contains environment variables for a user. This includes information that was stored in the AUTOEXEC.BAT file using MS-DOS. These values are also set in the System icon in the Control Panel application.
Keyboard Layout	This subkey contains the active keyboard information for use with international settings. These options are usually set in the Control Panel under the International item.
Software	This subkey uses the same layout of HKEY_LOCAL_MACHINE\SOFTWARE, however, it contains software settings for the current user. Typically, this is application-specific information and is configured using the setup program or the program itself. This information was typically stored in the WIN.INI or a private INI file under Windows 3.1.
UNICODE Program Groups	This subkey contains information about UNICODE Program Groups. This subkey is usually empty unless Windows NT has been installed over a Windows 3.1 installation.

HKEY_LOCAL_MACHINE Subkeys   The HKEY_LOCAL_MACHINE key contains important system information about the local Windows NT machine. The information in this key is used by the Windows NT system, device drivers, and certain applications to configure the hardware and software information. This information is used regardless of

Part

VI

Ch

28

the user that is logged into the system. Even if no user is logged into the system, this key provides the information to be used by the Windows NT system.

Not all subkeys are able to be modified manually by a user. For example, the HARDWARE subtree is built when the computer successfully starts the Windows NT system. When the computer is shut down, the information is discarded. No files are kept containing the information found in the HARDWARE subtree, therefore, trying to modify the information in this subtree is not practical.

Also, the SAM and SECURITY keys cannot be modified by the user through direct editing. Much of this information is in binary format and is hard to modify manually anyway. While the information can be viewed, modification is not allowed through the Registry Editor program and is not recommended even if another program allows direct editing of these subkeys.

As mentioned previously, the information in HKEY_CURRENT_USER takes precedence over information found in HKEY_LOCAL_MACHINE if data is similar. However, some items, like device drivers, only use the HKEY_LOCAL_MACHINE key for information, so even if the data is found in HKEY_CURRENT_USER, it is not used.

The HKEY_LOCAL_MACHINE key contains five default subkeys: HARDWARE, SAM, SECURITY, SOFTWARE, and SYSTEM. Table 28.3 describes the contents of the default subkeys.

Table 28.3   HKEY_LOCAL_MACHINE Subtrees

Subtree	Description
HARDWARE	This subtree is used to handle the physical hardware of the Windows NT machine. The HARDWARE subkey is recreated each time the Windows NT system is started successfully.
SAM	The SAM (Security Account Manager) key provides security information for user and group accounts for a Windows NT machine. It also handles security information for Windows NT Server domains.
SECURITY	This key is different than the SAM key because it only contains information about the local security policy.
SOFTWARE	This subtree contains information about the software installed on the local Windows NT machine. This subkey also contains

Subtree	Description
	information that is used by certain software programs as well as miscellaneous configuration data. This subkey uses the same structure as HKEY_CURRENT_USER\SOFTWARE, but contains information that is used regardless of the current user.
SYSTEM	This subkey provides information concerning the Windows NT startup, device driver loading process, Windows NT services, and other items controlling the Windows NT system.

HKEY_LOCAL_MACHINE\HARDWARE Subtrees   Even though data in this subtree is dynamically built and user modifications aren't needed, understanding the values in this subtree helps an administrator to troubleshoot hardware problems. The HARDWARE subtree contains three default subkeys:

- **DESCRIPTION**. The DESCRIPTION subkey contains hardware descriptions and information about the hardware.

- **DEVICEMAP**. This subkey contains one or more values to specify the Registry location of the driver information.

- **RESOURCEMAP**. The RESOURCEMAP subkey maps the resources to the device drivers so that they can be used.

The DESCRIPTION subkey contains the information that is built from the computer's firmware, NTDETECT.COM, or the Windows NT Executive. How this information is collected depends on the platform that Windows NT is run on in the following manner:

- If the computer is an Intel x86-based computer the database uses the NTDETECT.COM program, run on the Windows NT startup process, to build the database.

- If the computer is a RISC-based computer, then the database uses the computer's firmware to build the database.

- If Windows NT is run on any other OEM platform, then the OEM must provide its own version of NTDETECT.COM.

N O T E   Network adapters are not found when most hardware devices are, during the hardware detection phase of Windows NT startup. Network settings are handled either through the Windows NT Setup program or by the Control Panel, Network item. ■

The DEVICEMAP subkey contains values that describe a path or port name for a specific subkey found in the HKEY_LOCAL_MACHINE\SYSTEM\ControlSet*xxx*\Services subkey. This specific subkey contains information about the device driver.

The RESOURCEMAP subkey lists the resources used by a device driver. These resources are items such as: IRQs, DMA channels, I/O ports or memory addresses, etc. Most of this information is not in text format, therefore, the Windows NT Diagnostics program is better suited to view most of these settings.

HKEY_LOCAL_MACHINE\SYSTEM Subtrees   The HKEY_LOCAL_MACHINE\SYSTEM subtree contains startup information that has to be stored rather than built during the startup process. A complete copy of this hive is saved in the SYSTEM.ALT file in case the SYSTEM subtree becomes corrupted. In the SYSTEM subtree you will find the following subkeys:

- **Clone**. This subkey is used to make a copy of the control set used when the Windows NT system successfully starts. This cloned control set is used to build the last known good control set.

- **ControlSet001, 002, 003, or 004**. These subkeys are multiple control sets which store important system information. There are usually only two control sets listed in the Registry, ControlSet001 and ControlSet002. However, up to four control sets may exist. These multiple control sets can be used if the system does not start properly. These control sets are selected by hitting the Spacebar immediately after selecting Windows NT at the boot prompt.

- **CurrentControlSet**. The CurrentControlSet is a link to the control set that was actually used to start the system. If you want to make modifications using the Registry editor, then you should modify the CurrentControlSet, not any of the other control sets.

- **Select**. This subkey is used by the Windows NT system to determine which of the multiple control sets to actually use when the system is started. The Default value determines which control set to use. This subkey also contains values for the LastKnownGood control set and the Failed control set.

- **Setup**. This subkey is used by the Windows NT Setup program. Do *not* attempt to change these entries! These entries should only be modified by the system.

To better understand the subkeys that handle the control set information, it is important to examine how the sets are used when Windows NT starts. When the system starts, the Select subkey is used to determine which control set to use. The control set that is listed in the Default subkey is normally used. If the startup is "good," usually meaning no critical or severe errors, then the clone subkey is used to construct the LastKnownGood control set value in the Select subkey. The control set that was used to start the system is then mapped to the CurrentControlSet subkey.

If the system fails or the user selects the LastKnownGood option, The LastKnownGood control set will be used instead of the Default control set. The Default control set is then mapped to the Failed value in the Select subkey. The CurrentControlSet is then mapped to the control set in the LastKnownGood entry of the Select subkey. The successful control set is still maintained as the LastKnownGood control set as well.

Registry Values

The last levels in the Registry tree structure are values. These values contain the actual configuration information. The Registry values are similar to the text values used in the Windows 3.1 INI files. However, Registry values are not limited to being text strings; they can have different data types. Values are made up of three parts: the value name, the data type, and the actual value entry.

Table 28.4 describes the different data types used by Registry values.

Table 28.4 Data Types Used by Registry Values

Item	Description
REG_BINARY	This data type stores data in raw binary format. Only one value is allowed per entry. It is displayed in hexadecimal format when using the Windows NT Registry Editor. Hardware component information is typically stored in the raw binary format. For example: RasComponents:53 65 72 76 65...
REG_DWORD	Numeric data that is 4 bytes long. Only one value is allowed per entry. Device drivers and services typically use this type of value. For example: MajorVersion:0x00000004 (4)
REG_EXPAND_SZ	This is a special type of data string (readable text) that can have variable information included using percent (%) marks. This allows for variable information, such as the location of the Windows NT system, to be specified. Only one value is allowed for each entry. For example: PathName:"%SystemRoot%\system32\rasman.exe"

Part

VI

Ch

28

continues

Table 28.4 Continued

Item	Description
REG_MULTI_SZ	Multiple string values are allowed in a single entry. This allows for many strings or lists to be used in an entry. NULL characters (spaces when using the Registry editor) separate each value entry. For example: Use:"Service yes yes"
REG_SZ	This type allows for human readable text to be used in the entry. Only one value per entry is used. This data type is the most commonly used type for most Registry settings. Values used in the older INI structure essentially used this data type. For example: Title:"Remote Access Autodial Manager"

Registry Hives and Files

Hives are files used to make up the Windows NT Registry. A hive has the original hive file which is located in the \SYSTEM32\CONFIG subdirectory of the Windows NT directory, a LOG file also located in the \SYSTEM32\CONFIG subdirectory of the Windows NT directory, and a repair file located in the \REPAIR subdirectory of the Windows NT directory. Each user on the Windows NT machine has an individual hive file that contains user information and configuration settings for that user. Table 28.5 shows the Registry Hive files and corresponding filenames.

Table 28.5 Registry Hives and Filenames

Registry Hive	Filename
HKEY_LOCAL_MACHINE\SAM	SAM & SAM.LOG
HKEY_LOCAL_MACHINE\SECURITY	SECURITY & SECURITY.LOG
HKEY_LOCAL_MACHINE\SOFTWARE	SOFTWARE & SOFTWARE.LOG
HKEY_LOCAL_MACHINE\SYSTEM	SYSTEM & SYSTEM.ALT
HKEY_CURRENT_USER	USER### & USER###.LOG or ADMIN### & ADMIN###.LOG
HKEY_USERS\.DEFAULT	DEFAULT & DEFAULT.LOG

The Registry tries to ensure the correctness of the Registry; it tries to prevent the database from being corrupted if a change is made and the system goes down unexpectedly.

If a change were to be made in one section, but a crash prevented another related section from being updated, then it is possible that the Registry would become corrupted. Windows NT prevents this from happening by ensuring that changes to the Registry either work or don't work. Even though the changes may not take effect, the Registry will not contain a mixture of old and new values. This transaction-based method of ensuring the correct Registry structure is handled by a process known as flushing.

Flushing occurs after changed Registry data either ages past a certain number of seconds or when an application explicitly instructs the Windows NT system to flush the data. Only when a flush occurs will data be written to the Registry. The flush process occurs for all hives, except the SYSTEM hive, in the following manner:

1. Before any data is written to the Registry, any changed data is written to the LOG file for the appropriate hive. This data, along with a map of where in the hive the data exists, is written to the LOG file should the computer fail during the write to the Registry.

2. After data is written to the LOG file, the LOG file is flushed. This ensures that all changed data is written to the LOG file without any failures.

3. The Registry writing process now begins. The first sector of the hive file is marked so the system knows that the writing process has started, but not been completed.

4. The changes to the appropriate data in the Registry are made.

5. After all the changes are made to the appropriate hive file, the hive file is then marked as completed.

If the system fails anytime after the hive file is marked as started and before the hive file is marked as completed, the Windows NT system will try to recover the data the next time Windows NT is started. The appropriate LOG file is used to determine what changes were made and what changes need to be completed. After a hive file is updated, the LOG file is not used until that hive's data is modified again.

Also located in the \SYSTEM32\CONFIG subdirectory of the Windows NT system directory is a file called SYSTEM.ALT. The SYSTEM.ALT file contains a copy of all the information in the SYSTEM file. After changes are written to the SYSTEM file, the same changes are then written to the SYSTEM.ALT file. This is done to ensure that there is a correct copy of the SYSTEM file should a power failure, or some other event, corrupt the SYSTEM file. The SYSTEM file is a critical file used during the startup process and this extra safeguard is used to help provide better reliability.

The SYSTEM.ALT file is similar to a LOG file, but rather than reapplying changes, the system switches from the SYSTEM file to the SYSTEM.ALT file when the Windows NT system is started. This method is used only for the SYSTEM file because some of the

Part

VI

Ch

28

startup elements in this file may prevent the Windows NT system from reaching the point where reapplying data from a LOG file normally occurs.

Exploring the Interaction Between the Registry and Windows NT

Now that we've talked about the Registry, let's take a look at an example of how the settings in the Registry interact with the Windows NT system. We'll look at the Run dialog box, found on the Start button, then Run item. The Run command keeps track of files that you've run previously and can display them in a drop-down list in the Run dialog box. The previous commands, as well as the order in which to list them, are kept in the Windows NT Registry.

To view the interaction between the Registry and Windows NT, do the following:

1. Before you start, be sure that you've run several commands using the Run dialog box. If you haven't, choose Start, Run and type **WINMSD** in the Run dialog box. Close the Windows NT Diagnostic program and open the Run dialog box again. Run another program, such as WINMINE, and close that program. The drop-down list in the Run dialog should look similar to figure 28.2.

FIG. 28.2
The Run dialog box shows items that have been previously run and are now shown in the drop-down list. This information is stored in the Windows NT Registry.

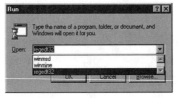

2. Start the Registry Editor program by choosing Start, then Run and typing **REGEDT32** in the Run box. This starts the Windows NT 4.0 Registry Editor.

3. The properties for the Run drop-down list are different for each user, so the information we're looking for is in the HKEY_CURRENT_USER key. Find the HKEY_CURRENT_USER key window in the Registry Editor to display the tree for that key.

4. In the HKEY_CURRENT_USER window, expand the SOFTWARE subkey. You can expand the subtree for an item by double-clicking that item.

5. In the Software subkey, find and expand the Microsoft subkey. Most of the Windows NT items that are configured for each user are located in this subkey.

6. After expanding the Microsoft subkey, find and expand the Windows subkey. Then, expand the CurrentVersion subkey.

7. The Run dialog box is part of the Windows NT Explorer desktop, so we'll find the information in the Explorer subkey. Expand the Explorer subkey.

8. The settings for the Run dialog box are located in a subkey called RunMRU. So, the entire path to view the settings of the Run dialog box is located in: HKEY_CURRENT_USER\Software\Microsoft\Windows\CurrentVersion\Explorer\ 1RunMRU. Figure 28.3 shows the Registry Editor with the tree expanded down to the RunMRU subkey and its values.

FIG. 28.3

This screen shot of the Registry Editor shows the RunMRU subkey and its values. This subkey contains the items to be displayed in the Run dialog's drop-down list, as well as the order to display them.

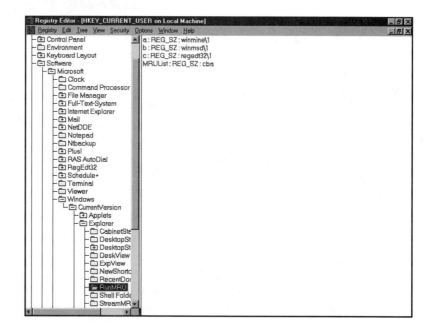

9. On the right side of the Registry editor, you should see the settings for the Run dialog box. Depending on what items were run from the dialog box, you should see a value called "a" with an entry of "winmine/1" or something similar, a value "b" with an entry of "winmsd/1" or something similar, etc. Each of these letter values represent an item to be displayed on the drop-down list in the Run dialog box.

Part

VI

Ch

28

10. Below all of the letter values, you should see a value called "MRUList." This value controls the order in which the items are to be displayed on the drop-down list. When an item is selected from the list, it moves to the top of the list. This is designed to make it easier for the user to select the last command that was run using the Run dialog box. The "MRUList" value should display something like "cba" depending on the order that the commands were run. The letters correspond to the programs to which the a, b, and c values have been assigned.

11. Close the Registry Editor. If you want, run some more programs from the Run dialog box, then view the Registry entries again to see how they have changed. For now, just view the entries; don't try to modify them. In the next chapter, titled "Backing Up and Editing the Registry," you'll see how to use the Registry Editor to modify the Registry. From there, you may want to go back into the RunMRU subkey and see if you can change the order of the items in the Run dialog drop-down list.

Many of the Explorer's settings are handled by the Registry. The Registry values change as a user does everyday tasks in Windows NT. This illustrates how important the Registry is to the operation of Windows NT.

INI Entries in the Registry

If you install Windows NT 4.0 over an existing Windows 3.1 or Windows for Workgroups 3.11 system, many of the INI file settings will be mapped to the Windows NT Registry. The Registry also contains an entry which allows you to see where in the Registry the INI settings are mapped. To view this information, view the following in the Registry:

> HKEY_LOCAL_MACHINE\SOFTWARE\Microsoft\WindowsNT\CurrentVersion\
> IniFileMapping\

N O T E If an application tries to write to one of the entries of an INI file that is listed in the IniFileMapping key by using the Windows NT Registry API, then the information is written to the Registry. If the INI section is not listed in the IniFileMapping key or if the application does not use the Windows NT Registry API, then the information is written to the INI file. ∎

Table 28.6 shows the sections of the WIN.INI file that are mapped to the Windows NT Registry.

Table 28.6 WIN.INI Sections Mapped to the Registry

Section	Registry Path
[colors]	HKEY_CURRENT_USER\Control Panel\Colors
[compatibility]	HKEY_LOCAL_MACHINE\SOFTWARE\Microsoft\Windows NT\ Current Version\Compatibilty
[desktop]	HKEY_CURRENT_USER\Control Panel\Desktop
[devices]	HKEY_LOCAL_MACHINE\SOFTWARE\Microsoft\Windows NT\ Current Version\Devices
[embedding]	HKEY_LOCAL_MACHINE\SOFTWARE\Microsoft\Windows NT\ Current Version\Embedding
[extensions]	HKEY_CURRENT_USER\SOFTWARE\Microsoft\Windows NT\ Current Version\Extensions
[fonts]	HKEY_LOCAL_MACHINE\SOFTWARE\Microsoft\Windows NT\ Current Version\Fonts
[fontSubstitutes]	HKEY_LOCAL_MACHINE\SOFTWARE\Microsoft\Windows NT\ Current Version\FontSubsititutes
[intl]	HKEY_CURRENT_USER\Control Panel\International
[mci extensions]	HKEY_LOCAL_MACHINE\SOFTWARE\Microsoft\Windows NT\ Current Version\MCI Extensions
[network]	HKEY_CURRENT_USER\Network\Persistent Connections (network printers) KEY_LOCAL_MACHINE\SYSTEM\Control\ Print
[ports]	HKEY_LOCAL_MACHINE\SOFTWARE\Microsoft\Windows NT\ Current Version\Ports
[printerPorts]	HKEY_LOCAL_MACHINE\SOFTWARE\Microsoft\Windows NT\ Current Version\Printer Ports
[sounds]	HKEY_CURRENT_USER\Control Panel\Sounds
[TrueType]	HKEY_CURRENT_USER\SOFTWARE\Microsoft\Windows NT\ Current Version\TrueType
[Windows Help]	HKEY_CURRENT_USER\SOFTWARE\Microsoft\Windows Help
[Windows]	HKEY_LOCAL_MACHINE\SOFTWARE\Microsoft\Windows NT\ Current Version\Winlogon

Table 28.7 shows the sections of the SYSTEM.INI file that are mapped to the Windows NT Registry.

Part

VI

Ch

28

Table 28.7   SYSTEM.INI Sections Mapped to the Registry

Section	Registry Path
[boot]	HKEY_LOCAL_MACHINE\SOFTWARE\Microsoft\Windows NT\ Current Version\WOW\Boot
[boot.description]	HKEY_LOCAL_MACHINE\SOFTWARE\Microsoft\Windows NT\ Current Version\WOW\Boot.description
[drivers]	Replaced by: HKEY_LOCAL_MACHINE\SOFTWARE\Microsoft\ Windows NT\Current Version\Drivers32
[keyboard]	HKEY_LOCAL_MACHINE\SOFTWARE\Microsoft\Windows NT\ Current Version\WOW\Keyboard and HKEY_CURRENT_USER\ Keyboard Layout
[mci]	HKEY_LOCAL_MACHINE\SOFTWARE\Microsoft\Windows NT\ Current Version\MCI and HKEY_LOCAL_MACHINE\ SOFTWARE\Microsoft\Windows NT\Current Version\ Drivers.desc
[mci32]	HKEY_LOCAL_MACHINE\SOFTWARE\Microsoft\Windows NT\ Current Version\MCI32 and HKEY_LOCAL_MACHINE\ SOFTWARE\Microsoft\Windows NT\ Current Version\ Drivers.desc
[NonWindows App]	HKEY_LOCAL_MACHINE\SOFTWARE\Microsoft\Windows NT\ Current Version\WOW\NonWindowsApp
[standard]	HKEY_LOCAL_MACHINE\SOFTWARE\Microsoft\Windows NT\ Current Version\WOW

Table 28.8 shows the sections of other INI files that are mapped to the Windows NT Registry.

Table 28.8   Other INI Sections Mapped to the Registry

Section	Registry Path
CONTROL.INI	
[Current]	HKEY_CURRENT_USER\Control Panel\Current
[Color Schemes]	HKEY_CURRENT_USER\Control Panel\Color Schemes
[Custom Colors]	HKEY_CURRENT_USER\Control Panel\Custom Colors
[Patterns]	HKEY_CURRENT_USER\Control Panel\Patterns
[Screen Saver]	HKEY_CURRENT_USER\Control Panel\Screen Saver
[MMCPL]	HKEY_CURRENT_USER\Control Panel\MMCPL

Section	Registry Path
[Drivers.Desc]	HKEY_CURRENT_USER\Control Panel\Drivers.Desc
[Userinstallable.drivers]	HKEY_CURRENT_USER\Control Panel\Userinstallable.drivers
PROGMAN.INI	
[groups]	HKEY_CURRENT_USER\SOFTWARE\Microsoft\Windows NT\ Current Version\Program Manager\Groups
[restrictions]	HKEY_CURRENT_USER\SOFTWARE\Microsoft\Windows NT\ Current Version\Program Manager\Restrictions
[settings]	HKEY_CURRENT_USER\SOFTWARE\Microsoft\Windows NT\ Current Version\Program Manager\Settings

Registry Size Limits

The total Registry size can be controlled to prevent it from taking up too much hard disk space. One of the disadvantages of the Windows 3.1 INI structure was that no limits were placed on the number or size of the INI files. Windows NT tries to prevent this by allowing the user to set a limit on how large the Registry can get. This total size includes all of the hive files, including hives for all users, regardless of which user is logged on.

The Registry limit is located in the following subkey KEY_LOCAL_MACHINE\SYSTEM\ CurrentControlSet\Control and the value name is RegistrySizeLimit. The value is a REG_DWORD data type and must be 4 bytes long, otherwise it will be ignored. The default RegistrySizeLimit is 8M. A RegistrySizeLimit of 8M will allow about 5,000 user hives to be created without reaching the limit. The 8M number is determined by taking 25 percent of the size of the paged pool, which is, by default, 32M. However, if the paged pool size is modified, the RegistrySizeLimit will also be affected.

Keep in mind that the RegistrySizeLimit is a maximum limit. It does *not* allocate that much space beforehand. Therefore, setting a large RegistrySizeLimit will not reduce the amount of hard disk space until it is needed. Also, a large RegistrySizeLimit can not guarantee that that much space will actually be available.

Even though the limit may be set, it is not checked until after the first successful loading of a user profile hive. This prevents the system from failing to start because the limit has been reached. Therefore, even if the limit is exceeded, the Windows NT system will be able to start successfully.

There are two ways to set the RegistrySizeLimit: either through Control Panel or through direct editing of the Registry. To change the RegistrySizeLimit through Control Panel,

Part
VI

Ch
28

open the Control Panel window and choose the System icon. In the System Properties window, choose the Performance tab. In the Performance property sheet, click the Change button in the middle right side of the sheet. The Virtual Memory window will be displayed. At the bottom of the window, a Registry Size box will be displayed with the current and maximum Registry size. To change the maximum size, enter the new size in the Maximum Registry Size (MB) box.

The RegistrySizeLimit value in the Registry is located in the following key path:

HKEY_LOCAL_MACHINE\SYSTEM\CurrentControlSet\Control

The RegistrySizeLimit can be viewed or modified from this area in the Registry. The value is a REG_DWORD value and, if it is longer than 4 bytes, it will be ignored. The preferred method to modify the Registry limit is through the System icon in Control Panel.

Using the Windows NT Diagnostics Program to View Registry Settings

Windows NT provides a Diagnostics program to view many hardware, software, and Windows NT settings. The Windows NT Diagnostics program is called WINMSD.EXE and is located in the SYSTEM32 subdirectory where Windows NT is installed. Figure 28.4 shows the Windows NT Diagnostics program.

FIG. 28.4
The Windows NT Diagnostics program (WINMSD.EXE) can be used to view certain Registry settings as well as other hardware and software configurations.

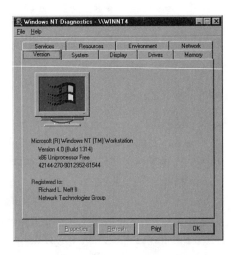

The Windows NT Diagnostic tool provides more than just Registry settings. Also, not all the Registry settings are available to be viewed under the Diagnostic program.

N O T E You can only view information with the Windows NT Diagnostic tool; you can not edit information. This helps prevent changes from being made to the Registry by accident and is a good program for other users who may not be familiar with the Registry to learn about certain Registry settings. ▪

The Windows NT Diagnostics tool contains nine tabs to select specific information about Windows NT. The following lists and describes the nine tabs/property sheets located in the Windows NT Diagnostic program:

- **Version**. Shown in figure 28.4, this property sheet displays the version number of Windows NT, the build number, and the registered user of the Windows NT software.

- **System**. The System tab displays a property sheet identifying the type of computer that is running the Windows NT system. This property sheet includes information about the BIOS and the processor.

- **Display**. This property sheet displays information about the display hardware and the device driver being used for the display. This sheet displays information about the resolution mode and colors, the video chip type and memory, and the version information about the video drivers.

- **Drives**. The Drives property sheet displays the recognized floppy disk drives, hard disk drives, and CD-ROM drives on the Windows NT computer. The drive information is grouped into a tree-like structure similar to the Registry or Explorer objects. Selecting a drive displays another window with two tabs: General and File System.

- **Memory**. This property sheet displays lots of different memory statistics and configuration information. It includes items such as handle, thread, and process totals, the amount of physical memory available, and pagefile information.

- **Services**. The Services tab displays a property sheet with a list of all the Windows NT services that are available and the status of those services. If you click on the Devices button located in the lower right corner, then the list will change to display the devices and their status. You can double-click on either a service or device item and a window will be shown displaying more detailed information about that service or device. This new window will contain two tabs: General and Dependencies.

- **Resources**. The Resource property sheet contains five buttons on the bottom: IRQ, I/O Port, DMA, Memory, and Devices. When one of the buttons is clicked, the corresponding information is displayed in the list window. This property sheet is very useful in determining what hardware options are available when installing new hardware devices.

Part

VI

Ch

28

■ **Environment**.   This property sheet allows you to display system and user environment variables for the Windows NT system. The central window displays the variable and the value assigned to it. Two buttons, System and Local User, allow you to view either system environment variables or local user environment variables.

■ **Network**.   The Network tab displays a property sheet with four buttons on the bottom: General, Transports, Settings, and Statistics. Clicking the General button displays items like the access level of the user currently logged on, the workgroup or domain that the computer is currently connected to, and network version. Selecting the Transports button displays the items like the transport address or whether the transport uses a WAN. The Settings button lists many of the variables that affect network operation. The Statistics button displays the current network statistics of the Windows NT machine.

The Windows NT Diagnostics tool is an ideal way to view many of the Windows NT configurations without viewing the Registry. Of course, the Windows NT Diagnostics tool does not display all of the values contained in the Registry. It primarily displays information found in HKEY_LOCAL_MACHINE, although other key information is displayed as well. The Windows NT Diagnostics also do not allow you to modify the information in the Registry; you can only use it to view the information.

To view an example of information stored in the Registry that is displayed using the Windows NT Diagnostic program, do the following:

1. Start both the Windows NT Diagnostics program (WINMSD.EXE) and the Registry Editor (REGEDT32.EXE) by using the Run command on the Start menu.

2. Size the windows so you can see information on both windows.

3. In the Registry Editor, select the HKEY_LOCAL_MACHINE window. Expand the SYSTEM subkey tree.

4. From the SYSTEM subkey, expand CurrentControlSet. Then, expand the Services subkey.

5. You should find a subkey called EventLog. This is information about the Event Log service of Windows NT. Highlight this subkey by clicking it with the mouse. You should now see Event Log information in the right-hand window.

6. Once you see the information in the right side of the Registry Editor, select the Windows NT Diagnostics window or double-click the entry from the taskbar.

7. To view information about Windows NT services, click the Services tab in the Windows NT Diagnostics program window. Click the Services button at the bottom of the property sheet to insure that services, not devices, are being listed.

8. In the Services list, find the EventLog item. Once you find it, either double-click the item or highlight it and click the Properties button. Another window will be displayed with a General property sheet. Be sure that the General property sheet is displayed.

9. If needed, move the two program windows so you can see the information from both programs. You should notice a Registry value in the Registry Editor called "ImagePath" which displays the path to the program, SERVICES.EXE, that handles the Event Log service.

10. You should also notice that the same path is displayed in the Pathname: item in the Diagnostics program. Other values correspond with items in the Registry program, even though the Registry program may display them differently. Browse through some of the other services in both the Registry Editor and the Windows NT Diagnostics tool to see how they correlate with each other.

11. When you are finished, close the Registry Editor and the Windows NT Diagnostics tool.

Comparing the Windows NT and Windows 95 Registries

If you've worked with Windows 95, you've probably noticed that the Windows 95 Registry is similar to, but slightly different from, the Windows NT Registry. While the knowledge of the Windows 95 Registry may help your understanding of the Windows NT Registry, there are some notable differences between the two Registries.

Windows NT versus Windows 95 Registry Files

The Windows 95 Registry consists of only two files: USER.DAT and SYSTEM.DAT. These files are located in the Windows 95 directory. The Windows NT Registry consists of many more files, depending on the number of users. These files are located in the \SYSTEM32\CONFIG directory of the Windows NT directory. The Windows NT Registry files also have corresponding LOG files.

Backup copies of the Windows 95 Registry are named USER.DA0 and SYSTEM.DA0 and are kept in the Windows 95 directory. Backup copies of the Windows NT Registry are kept in the \REPAIR subdirectory of the main Windows NT directory. The extensions on the files may vary, but usually consist of a single underscore character.

Windows NT versus Windows 95 Registry Structure

The Windows 95 Registry also differs slightly in its structure from the Windows NT Registry. The Windows 95 Registry contains the five Registry subtrees: HKEY_CLASSES_ROOT, HKEY_CURRENT_USER, HKEY_LOCAL_MACHINE, HKEY_USERS, and HKEY_CURRENT_CONFIG. The Windows 95 Registry also adds a sixth subtree called HKEY_DYN_DATA for information about devices conforming to the Plug-and-Play specification.

While both Registries contain some of the same keys, the subkeys and values may differ dramatically. Also, in order to maintain a high level of backward compatibility, the Windows 95 system may still use more information from INI files than the Windows NT system. The Registry Editor is different for the two operating systems as well.

N O T E   Windows NT 4.0 installs the Windows 95 Registry Editor (REGEDIT.EXE) if it is not installed over a Windows 3.1 installation. If it is installed over a Windows 3.1 system, it installs the Windows 3.1 Registry Editor. Surprisingly, the Windows 95 Registry Editor that is installed can modify the Windows NT 4.0 Registry. However, the REGEDT32.EXE program should be used to modify the Windows NT 4.0 Registry. ■

From Here...

The Windows NT Registry is designed to replace the older Windows 3.1 INI files structure. It provides a central database of the Windows NT configuration settings. It is composed of keys, subkeys, and values. Its values can be modified directly or through other Windows NT items, such as Control Panel.

For information on topics related to the Windows NT Registry, see the following chapters:

- Chapter 27, "Registry Overview," is a basic introduction to the Windows NT Registry.
- Chapter 29, "Backing Up and Editing the Registry," describes how to manually edit the Registry and how to back up the information in the Registry.
- Chapter 30, "Restoring and Repairing the Registry," provides information for when the worst happens. It contains information on restoring or repairing the Registry back to its correct state.
- Appendix A, "Registry Customization Tips," discusses some useful entries in the Registry that can be modified to customize the Windows NT computer.

CHAPTER 29

Backing Up and Editing the Registry

by Christa Anderson

In the previous chapter, you learned the parts of the Registry and the job of each part. Now, you're ready to tackle the job of editing it.

But first, a couple of warnings:

■ Nine times out of ten you won't need to touch the Registry. Most of the settings it contains can be changed using the Control Panel.

■ If you make a mistake editing the Registry, you can kill your NT installation and have to rein stall. Don't change anything unless you know exactly what you're changing and why you're changing it.

I know that you've probably heard these warnings before, but it seems that every time that I think that it's unnecessary to point these things out, I see another magazine article about how people are trashing their system Registries by editing them directly. (Seeing these articles usually makes me wonder if these are the same people who see "Do Not Touch" signs as a signal to handle something.) ■

When is this trip necessary?

You'll see some examples of times that you really might have to edit the Registry.

Understanding the importance of backups

Learn which properties of the Registry make it imperative that you back up before editing it.

Backing Up the Registry

See how you can save copies of the Registry before editing it.

Indirectly modifying the Registry

What actions will modify the Registry's contents?

Using the Registry Editors

Learn which of the two editors you'll use for your purposes.

When Is This Trip Necessary?

Under what kinds of situations will you potentially need to edit a system Registry? Basically, when you can't do whatever you need to do from the Control Panel. It seems that Microsoft would prefer that you never touch the Registry, so situations in which you would do so are not always heavily documented. Here are some suggestions, both from my experiences and from those of some of the members of a good Internet NT newsgroup **comp.os.ms-windows.nt.misc**. You can also find examples of situations in which you'll use the Registry Editor in TechNet articles and the Knowledge Base.

Removing Improperly Deleted Files

If you delete an executable file without using the Add/Remove Programs utility in the Control Panel, then the program will continue to appear in the list of removable programs, and you won't be able to delete it. For example, if you've installed TechNet on your system to keep up with the latest Microsoft information, you can delete it from Explorer—NT won't stop you. However, when you start up the Add/Remove Programs utility, you'll notice that TechNet is still listed as an installed program. Try to uninstall it, and you'll see an error message like the one in figure 29.1.

FIG. 29.1
Deleting an application, rather than uninstalling it, can cause problems.

To solve this problem, you have to open the Registry and find the Uninstall key. In this case, it's HKEY_LOCAL_MACHINE\Software\Microsoft\Windows\CurrentVersion\ Uninstall\TechNet0696US. However, it's simplest if you just use REGEDIT to look for occurrences of the word "Uninstall" throughout the entire Registry until you find the one that looks like what you want. Then delete the application's entry, as shown in figure 29.2.

The entry will be deleted from the Add/Remove Programs list. To complete the process, search the Registry for any other entries relating to TechNet.

Resolving Software Incompatibilities

Some software requires tweaking to run with other software. For example, the README file for the Maxtrox Millennium video driver notes that it may be necessary to set

User.SynchronizeEngine to avoid problems with communications programs. (Video settings are located in HKEY_LOCAL_MACHINE\System\CurrentControlSet\Services.) The exact setting is in the driver documentation—don't mess with this unless necessary.

FIG. 29.2
To remove an improperly deleted application from your system, you may have to edit the Registry.

Tweaking User Logon

You can use the Resource Kit to set up some custom logon options, but if you don't have it, you can accomplish the same thing by editing the Registry. For instance, if you don't want to have to log in every time you reboot NT, you can follow these steps:

N O T E If you make this change to your system, you can force a login by exiting NT and holding down the Shift key during reboot. If you've just logged off and want to log back on as a different user, hold down the Shift key after you log off. ■

1. Add a new value, AutoAdminLogon, to HKEY_LOCAL_MACHINE\Software\ Microsoft\Windows NT\Current Version\Winlogon, make its value a text string (REG_SZ), and set it equal to 1.

2. In this same key, add the value DefaultPassword, make its value a text string, and set it equal to the password of the account that you want to use.

3. Set the value of DefaultUserName (this entry should already be there) equal to the login name of the account.

Your Registry Editor should now look like the one shown in figure 29.3.

FIG. 29.3

Add entries to the WinLogon key to automate login.

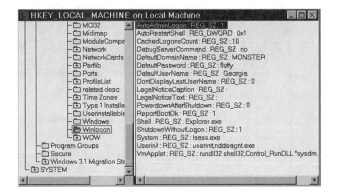

Reboot the system, and the Desktop will come up without requiring you to log in.

CAUTION

I've included this procedure because it's a neat trick and a good example of how you can customize your system, but be careful *which* account you set up with an automatic login. It's probably a bad idea to do this with an account with administrative privileges. First, you obviously don't want just anyone to be able to be an administrator, and second, this setting puts the login account's password into the Registry in human-readable form.

Disabling System Shutdown

You're able to shut down the system without logging in. This is nice for those times that you picked the wrong option in the Shut Down menu and logged off instead of shutting down. However, it's also a security breach, if you are concerned about unauthorized people being able to restart the system (perhaps with a DOS floppy). If you've gone to the trouble of disabling the Big Red Switch, then it's worth finishing the job and removing the Shutdown option from the login screen.

To do so, go to HKEY_LOCAL_MACHINE\Software\Microsoft\Windows NT\Current Version\Winlogon, and set the value of ShutdownWithoutLogon equal to 0. Log off, and when you log back on again, the Shut Down button will be grayed.

From these examples, you can see that there really *are* times when you might legitimately edit the Registry. For the rest of the chapter, we'll talk about how to do it safely.

Understanding the Importance of Backups

The Registry editors are your pathways to the workings of your system. Some of the changes that you can make here take effect immediately, other changes aren't apparent until you reboot the system. For example, try out the following exercise just to see how you can change the system configuration.

From the Start menu, choose Run, and type **REGEDT32.EXE** to start the NT system editor. (As was noted in Chapter 31, and as we'll discuss further in the course of this chapter, REGEDT32 is for viewing/editing the NT system setup; REGEDIT is for those parts of the system configuration that are for 16-bit applications.) Once you've opened the Registry Editor, you should see a screen that looks like the one shown in figure 29.4.

FIG. 29.4
Each window of the 32-bit Registry Editor displays an open subtree in a hive of the Registry.

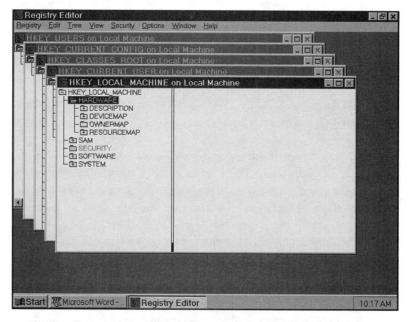

We're going to work with a relatively harmless portion of the Registry called Current User. (When you need to edit the Registry, you'll often be working in one of the hardware sections, but this gives you the idea and it's hard to do any damage here.) If it's not already in front, click the title bar of HKEY_CURRENT_USER on Local Machine, and move to the Colors key of the Control Panel key. (Open up the Colors key so that it looks like figure 29.5.)

N O T E The Registry is visually organized like the old Windows File Manager, but its parts are called values and keys rather than files and folders. ■

FIG. 29.5

The Colors key of the HKEY_CURRENT_USER subtree sets the colors used by the system display.

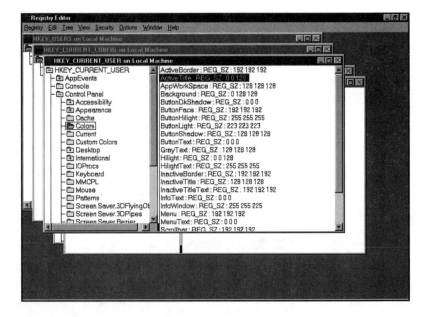

Edit the entry for Active Title. If you're using the Windows default color scheme, it should be 0 0 128—a nice medium blue.

> **N O T E** Windows colors are set by mixing values ranging from 0 to 256 of red, green, and blue (in that order). The higher the value, the higher the color intensity. If you're interested in playing around with this, it's safer to run Windows Paint, choose to edit the color palette, and then plug in various values for red, green and blue in the dialog box that appears. ■

When you double-click the entry, you'll be able to edit it in a dialog box like the one shown in figure 29.6. Change the entry to 100 0 128.

When you close the dialog box, nothing seems to have changed, but if you run REGEDIT.EXE and look at the corresponding setting there you'll notice that it's also set to 100 0 128. You won't be able to see the effects of your edit until you log off and log back on again, at which point your dialog boxes' active title bars will be an obnoxious shade of purple.

And there's the rub. Changing colors is relatively harmless, but the point is that you could make a change like that that wasn't harmless, and forget about it until the next time that you logged on. If you were lucky, you'd have just made some kind of undesirable change that you might or might not know how to restore from the Control Panel. If not, you might not be able to log back on, or boot the system at all if you'd powered it down. Before you do anything to the Registry, *back it up*.

FIG. 29.6
To edit a Registry value entry, double-click the value.

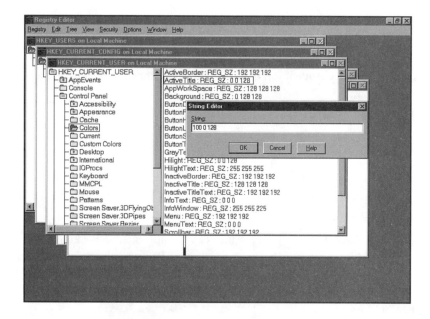

Backing Up the Registry

You can back up your system Registry in any one of several ways:

- Automatically
- Using NT Backup
- Using REGBACK.EXE from the Resource Kit
- Updating the Emergency Repair Disk (to a limited extent)

Although you can back up Registry keys with REGEDT32 and restore those saved keys, you can't back up or restore the entire thing that way because the Registry is in use when the system is running. As we'll discuss in Chapter 30, "Restoring and Repairing the Registry," you'll need to reboot the system for restorations to take effect.

Automatic Backups

Every time you successfully boot your computer, a copy is made of your system's Registry hives: Software, Default, System, Security, and Ntuser.DAT. The corresponding LOG files, which you can see in the SYSTEM32 directory with the Registry files, are not text logs of the files that you can view in Notepad, but backups. When rebooting, if you choose to activate the Last Known Good option, then you'll have the option of restoring the Registry from these backups.

The automatic backups only work from boot to boot—they don't serve the purpose that an Undo feature does in many applications. If you make a change during an NT session that you'd like to keep and then make a change that is disastrous and reboot, you'll lose the desired change if you boot with the Last Know Good configuration.

Using NT Backup

Apart from the automatic method, the easiest way to back up the Registry is to include it in your regular backups. It's a little cumbersome because you don't have the option of backing up only part of it using NT Backup, but it's a good idea anyway. Should you ever need to completely reinstall the operating system, having a backup copy of the Registry will keep you from having to reconfigure the entire system.

To back up the Registry using NT Backup, start the Backup utility, select the partition with your system files on it, and choose Backup from the menu. You'll see a dialog box like the one shown in figure 29.7.

FIG. 29.7
You can back up the entire Registry while protecting user data.

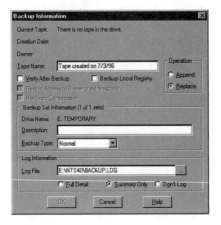

Notice that, by default, Backup Local Registry is not checked. (I'm not sure why this is the case, because I can't imagine a situation in which you wouldn't want a backup of your system in case of accidents; and you certainly don't *have* to restore it, but that's the way it's been since version 3.1.) Check it, and when you run the backup the Registry information will also be saved to tape.

N O T E   If you select a partition to back up and notice that the Back Up Local Registry option is not available, make sure that you're backing up a partition with the system files. Other partitions won't have Registry information to save. ■

Using REGBACK.EXE

You can back up the hives of the Registry with the REGBACK utility that comes with the Resource Kit. Run the program, and you can back up your Registry to a hard disk or floppy. If you don't have a tape drive, this is the best way to back up your system's configuration. Why not just use RDISK? First, those hive backups are incomplete (as is discussed later in this chapter). Second, unlike the Registry information saved with RDISK, you do not have to go through the restoration screens to restore these backups.

The syntax is pretty straightforward:

```
regback DestinationDirectory
```

where `DestinationDirectory` is the name of the directory to which you'll save the hive files. If you see an error message telling you that a file must be backed up manually, you'll need to use the alternate syntax to save it to a named file:

```
regback filename hivetype hivename
```

where `filename` is the name of the file to which you're saving it, `hivetype` is the type of hive (either machine or users—these are the only types that can you can or need to back up—and `hivename` is the name of one of the upper branches in either HKEY_LOCAL_MACHINE or HKEY_LOCAL_USER. If you're using the manual backup method because you saw an error message while doing the normal backup, `hivename` should be the name of the branch that did not back up.

Using REGEDT32 to Back Up the Registry

Alternatively, those who don't have the Resource Kit can use the Save Key option in REGEDT32's Registry menu to back up the individual keys of the non-volatile hives, as illustrated in figure 29.8. If saving to a FAT volume (a good idea, as the files will be accessible if you must boot from a DOS floppy), the file names cannot have extensions.

FIG. 29.8

Save Registry keys to a file for later restoration.

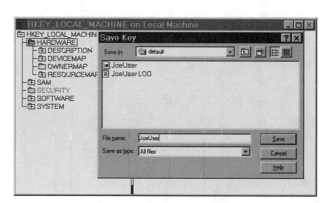

To back up the Windows NT Registry, highlight a key in a hive (you can't save an entire hive at once) and choose Save Key from the Registry menu. Save the key to a named file (it's a *very* good idea to name it according to what key it is so you can find it again). If you put it in the Repair directory of your NT installation, then that may help you remember where you put it when the time comes to restore it.

N O T E   Saving a key using the Save Subtree As option will not save a restorable version of the key; that option is for taking text "snapshots" of a Registry key. ■

After you've saved the files, you can either restore those keys to the Registry from REGEDT32 or, if you can only boot to DOS but can access the system directories (another reason to format them with FAT, rather than NTFS), you can copy the backups to the SYSTEM32 directory. We'll discuss these procedures in more detail in Chapter 30, "Restoring and Repairing the Registry."

Using REGEDIT.EXE to Back Up the Registry

By means of this simple process, you can use REGEDIT to take a "snapshot" of your Registry before doing anything drastic.

TIP   Name your backup Registry something that identifies it by date or reason, so that if you make more than one backup at different times you can tell which one you want when it comes time to restore.

To back all or part of the Registry to a file, choose Export Registry File from the Registry menu. You'll see a dialog box like the one shown in figure 29.9.

FIG. 29.9
You can choose to export either the entire Registry or one of its keys.

By default, you'll export only the currently expanded branch, but if you click the other radio button you'll export the entire thing as a file with a .reg extension.

CAUTION

Files with the .reg extension are associated with REGEDIT. If you activate one of them while in My Computer or the Explorer, you will automatically merge them with the Registry—perhaps replacing a more recent version. You will *not* be prompted as to whether this is your intention.

However, this capability is somewhat less helpful in Windows NT than it is under Windows 95 because NT does not have a real-mode version of REGEDIT that you can run from the command line if NT won't start. To prepare for serious problems, you're better off using REGEDT32's Save Key feature.

Regularly Update Your Emergency Repair Disk　When you installed NT, you had the option (which I hope you took) of creating an Emergency Repair Disk. Part of the information that that disk contains is the Registry database, so that you can restore your system to where you left it by rerunning the installation program. It's a desperate measure, but at times it's your only alternative to installation.

When repairing your system, be discriminatory about the parts of the Registry that you replace. When you update the Emergency Repair Disk, not all of the Registry files are updated: only the System and Software ones are. The account and security information are not. Therefore, if you completely restore the Registry from the Emergency Repair Disk, you'll retain the system colors and loaded drivers that you had chosen, but the account database will be returned to the two accounts that you get when you install: Administrator and Guest. When repairing, stick to replacing the parts of the Registry that are actually updated on the disk.

The Repair Disk is only as good as your last version of it. For it to be most useful, you must keep it current whenever you make changes to your system. Run RDISK regularly to update the information on your Emergency Repair Disk.

Indirectly Modifying the Registry

Just about everything you do to configure the system will change the contents of the Registry. Whether it's changing the system colors, adding a new user to the User Manager list, or changing the video driver, you'll change the contents of the hive in which that data is registered.

As discussed earlier in this chapter, it's also possible to change the contents of the Registry by activating an exported copy of it so that it merges with the rest of the file and overwrites the present contents. With this exception, however, it's difficult to indirectly make harmful changes to the Registry without meaning to.

Difficult, but not impossible—for example, it's perfectly possible to delete a user account (rather than disabling it) and then to later want to restore it, complete with its original security ID. For those times when it's easier to restore a configuration than fix it, it's a good idea to have a backup of the system Registry.

Using the Registry Editors

After you've backed up the system, the mechanics of editing the Registry are pretty simple: find the key you want, and either edit the existing value, add a new one, or (rarely) delete the existing one.

Using REGEDIT

If you've installed NT into a new directory instead of over an existing Windows 3.x installation, your copy of REGEDIT will look like the one that comes with Windows 95, as shown in figure 29.10.

FIG. 29.10
REGEDIT as it appears in a new Windows NT installation.

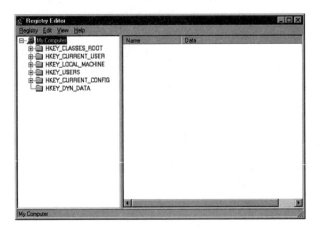

N O T E   If you installed NT into a Windows 3.x directory, running REGEDIT will display the old Windows 3.x Registry that only controls file associations and OLE. When you log on to NT, this information will be integrated into the 32-bit Registry in HKEY_LOCAL_MACHINE_SOFTWARE\ Windows 3.1 Migration Status\REG.DAT. ■

Searching the Registry   When it comes to finding keys and you're not sure where they are, REGEDIT has an advantage over REGEDT32—you can use it to search either only a part of the Registry or the entire thing at once. Choose Find from the Edit menu, and you'll see a dialog box like the one in figure 29.11.

FIGURE 29.11

From within REGEDIT, you can search the entire Registry database at once.

Sometimes, the Registry will contain more than one match. To move to the next one, just press F3. Your current location is visible on the bottom of the Registry Editor. Once you've found a match, you can either edit it there or open the appropriate hive in REGEDT32.

Using REGEDT32

The 32-bit Registry Editor has many more options than does REGEDIT. As such, it is more powerful, but it is also more dangerous. For instance, it's possible to delete entire hives of the Registry with REGEDT32, something that you can't do with REGEDIT whether you're using the Windows 3.x or Windows 95 interfaces.

 TIP If you're new to the Registry, you may want to enable an option that will prevent you from accidentally hurting anything on your first trip in. Open the Options menu and turn on Read Only mode, and you'll be able to open value editors—but the changes won't stick. Turning off Save Settings on Exit does absolutely nothing to preserve the Registry; that setting applies only to the appearance (fonts, windows sizes, and window arrangements) of the Registry Editor, not to its contents.

The Find Key Tool   The chances that you'll ever be wandering blindly through your system's Registry, looking for values to change, are pretty slim. Generally speaking, when you need to edit the Registry directly you'll know exactly which value you need to change. What you might *not* know, however, is exactly where that value is located, or you might find it too time-consuming to navigate there. Additionally, sometimes you'll need to change related values in more than one place—for example, when you're deleting the record of an application from the Registry that you deleted using the Explorer rather than the Add/Remove Programs utility.

To move quickly to a specific location in the Registry, use the Find Key tool available in the View menu. You'll see a dialog box that looks like the one in figure 29.12.

You can only use this tool to search for keys within the current hive. If the first match you encounter doesn't look like the one you want, you can press F3 to move to the next one.

FIG. 29.12
The Find Key tool in the 32-bit Registry is slightly more limited than the Find tool available in REGEDIT.

Editing Existing Registry Entries   Once you've found a value that you want to edit, the actual editing process is very simple. You can double-click it to bring up the appropriate editing dialog box for the type of value—string, multiple string, Dword (32-bit) or binary—that's required. (When you have a value selected but not open for editing, you can also choose to open one of the appropriate editing dialog boxes from the Edit menu, but this extra step isn't necessary.)

Most often, you'll be editing string values using the dialog box shown in figure 29.13.

FIG. 29.13
The easiest values to edit are string values.

When you've changed the entry, click OK and the change will be entered in the database. The change may not be visible until you log off and log back on, however.

Adding New Keys and Values   You can add new values anywhere in the Registry, and new keys anywhere except in the root of HKEY_LOCAL_MACHINE. It's not very common to need to add new keys, but fairly usual to add new values to an existing key (as in the previous example of how you can edit the Registry to automate the logon process).

The process is much the same either way. Select the existing key for which you want to create a subvalue, then choose Add Value (or Add Key) from the Edit menu. If adding a value, you'll see a dialog box that looks like the one in figure 29.14.

FIG. 29.14
To create some configurations, you'll have to add values to the Registry, not just edit existing ones.

Once you've added the value and its entry, it will appear in the right-hand pane of the Registry Editor like the other values.

Part

VI

Ch

29

Deleting a Value or Key   Generally speaking, the only values or keys that you'll need to delete are the ones that you add—for example, if you add them in the wrong place and wish to correct your mistake.

The process of doing so is quite simple: select the key or value to delete, and choose <u>D</u>e-lete from the <u>E</u>dit menu. By default, you'll see a dialog box (refer to fig. 29.17) asking you to verify that you want to make the deletion. (You can turn off this feature from the Options menu, but I'd recommend leaving it on so that it's harder to accidentally delete the wrong value or key.)

> **CAUTION**
>
> When you delete a key, you delete all of its related subkeys as well. Double-check what you're doing before deleting *anything* in the Registry—there's no Undo option to fall back on.

Editing Another System's Registry   To administer other systems' Registries from your system, you can use the <u>L</u>oad Hive command in the <u>R</u>egistry menu. Loading a hive into memory does not affect the current key; rather than replacing it in memory, it makes the loaded hive a subkey of the current one. When you load a hive, it remains part of the current Registry until you either remove it from memory with the <u>U</u>nload Hive command or reboot the system.

 TIP

Look in HKEY_LOCAL_MACHINE\SYSTEM\CurrentControlSet\Control\Hivelist to see a list of the hives available for loading.

To edit a hive from another computer, go to the root of HKEY_USERS or HKEY_LOCAL_MACHINE and choose <u>L</u>oad Hive from the <u>R</u>egistry menu. The dialog box that you see works just like any Open dialog box—you'll be able to load the hive whether it's on a network-accessible hard drive, a floppy disk, or your local hard drive. You can identify saved hives by their lack of extension: unlike Registry keys exported using REGEDIT, saved hives cannot have any extension at all if they're saved to a disk formatted using FAT.

N O T E   The <u>L</u>oad Hive command is only available when you're at the root of a subtree, with none of its keys open. ▪

After you've identified the hive to be loaded, you'll see a dialog box like the one shown in figure 29.15, in which you'll need to enter a key in which the hive will be contained.

FIG. 29.15
Choose a key name for the hive that you're loading into memory.

Choosing a file that isn't a hive (such as an exported Registry file) won't hurt anything; you'll just see an error message like the one shown in figure 29.16, and REGEDT32 will boot you back into the main screen.

FIG. 29.16
You can't damage the system by loading an invalid file into memory as a hive.

Assuming that you chose a valid hive file, however, you'll see the hive loaded into memory in the subkey name you specified, as shown in figure 29.17.

FIG. 29.17
Loaded hives appear as keys of the current subtree.

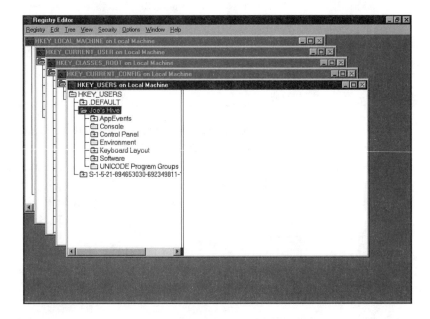

From here, you can edit the keys and values in the loaded Registry hive as described earlier in this chapter.

When finished, you'll need to save the key as a file so that it can be restored to the other computer's Registry. From the Registry menu, choose Save Key (*not* Save Subtree As, which creates a text file) and save the selected key to a filename. If you're saving the key to a FAT volume, it can't have an extension. Once you've saved the key, you can use the Restore command from the Registry menu to enter the changed data back into the other system's Registry.

Loading another system's hive into memory is good for those times when you can't access the system on the network. When you can, however, just choose to open that system's Registry. From the Registry menu, choose Select Computer, and choose an NT machine from the list. (Obviously, if a networked computer doesn't have a compatible Registry, you can't edit its configuration in REGEDT32.) You'll be able to load HKEY_USERS and HKEY_LOCAL_MACHINE into memory; you can't open the other keys in your Registry.

Reviewing Registry Snapshots   Sometimes, you don't need to change anything; you just want to see how part of the Registry looks. If that's the case, the easiest (and safest) way of getting that look is to save part of the Registry as a text file and then open it in a text editor such as Notepad. You can also use this method to save a copy of dynamic keys such as HKEY_CURRENT_CONFIG that can't be saved or loaded as hives.

To save a Registry subtree as text, activate the section to save, then choose Save Subtree As from the Registry menu. Choose a file name as you normally would (no extension is required—this file will be readable in Notepad without it), and click OK. You'll then be able to open the file in Notepad or Wordpad and use their Find utilities to search for keys and values.

From Here...

If you follow the instructions in this chapter, you should be able to edit the Registry database directly. Just remember that most of the time it's possible to do what you need to do without ever opening REGEDT32, and back up regularly, and you should be fine.

In the next chapter, we'll talk about how to recover from those times when you're *not* fine.

- For more about backups and automating them, turn to Chapter 14, "Ensuring Data Security."

- For an overview of the Registry and its structure, turn to Chapter 28, "Understanding the Registry."

- To learn how to restore the backups you've created, turn to Chapter 30, "Restoring and Repairing the Registry."

CHAPTER 30

Restoring and Repairing the Registry

by Christa Anderson

If you're reading this chapter, it's likely that you either are having a really bad day or are trying to avoid the possibility that something might go wrong in the future. In this chapter, we'll discuss how to restore the backups you created, and how NT's automatic backup feature tries to keep you out of trouble.

As always, the most important part of recovering your system's configuration information is to back it up. If you don't back it up, you can't restore it. For more information about how to back up the Registry database, turn to Chapter 29, "Backing Up and Editing the Registry." ■

Overview of common problems

Turn here to learn what kinds of problems may require you to restore or repair the Registry, and what kinds of problems a new Registry *can't* help you with.

Automatic Registry repair

Learn about NT attempts to protect your system configuration.

Restoring the Registry from a backup

Turn here to learn how you can restore your system to health.

Overview of Common Problems

Perhaps these problems aren't exactly common (for your sake, I hope not), but these are some of the most likely scenarios that might require you to restore the Registry database.

- **Deleted Accounts.** Account information is stored in the Security and Security Accounts Manager. When you restore the Registry, you restore the account information.

- **Bad Video Combinations or Drivers.** Although it's difficult to really mess up your video (with the Display settings showing you what it looks like and the video drivers insisting that you test and approve before making the change), if you really try, you can do it. If you've messed up these settings, then restoring the Registry can get your system useable again.

When Can't Backups Help?

Unfortunately, a backup of the Registry is not a universal cure-all. If any of the following occurs, then you may be faced with reinstallation.

N O T E Reinstalling the system doesn't mean that the Registry backups are useless—for example, you can use NT Backup to restore a system Registry on a new system. The point, however, is to avoid reinstallation. ▪

- **Deleted system files.** If you accidentally erase files, then you'll need to run Setup from the CD or reinstall from backups (assuming that that's still possible) or reinstall the system entirely.

- **Lost data due to a deleted partition.** If you delete a disk partition that has data on it, then the data will be lost. Although you may be able to restore the partition, the data will still be lost.

- **Dead hardware.** If you have a dead hard disk, then you'll need to reinstall the system anyway. However, you may be able to get back your Registry from backups once you've completed the installation.

In general, if the problem is dead hardware or deleted data files, then Registry backups can't help you.

Automatic Registry Repair

The most fundamental part of the Registry is the CurrentControlSet, stored in the SYSTEM hive. The information it contains describes the system enough to get it booted, including such information as the loaded device drivers, memory management, language used, system time, and so on. If you don't have any of the other Registry hives loaded, you can boot the system with this one. However, if you don't have this crucial hive, you can't boot the system to NT at all.

Because it is so important, NT makes this information as difficult as possible to lose. Every time you boot, NT backs up the SYSTEM file to SYSTEM.ALT. You cannot delete, move, or rename the SYSTEM or SYSTEM.ALT files in the SYSTEM32\CONFIG. (You *can* boot to DOS and delete them from there, but the chances of this happening accidentally are pretty limited.)

If you do manage to delete the SYSTEM file (or otherwise make it inaccessible to the system) and reboot, you'll still be able to boot because of the SYSTEM.ALT backup. If SYSTEM isn't available, SYSTEM.ALT is automatically loaded into memory, renamed to SYSTEM, and then copied as SYSTEM.ALT. This process is invisible to the user: the blue screen may be up longer, but that's the only difference.

If SYSTEM is still available, you still may not want to use it. Once you've booted the system and logged on, then the previous SYSTEM.ALT is overwritten and replaced with the data in the SYSTEM file used to get the system that far. It's possible to boot and log on even with an unusable system (for example, one with the wrong video driver installed), so if you know that you've made an error in your system setup, it is imperative that you do not log on to try to fix the problem. It's much easier to let Windows NT do the fixing for you, if it can.

In that case, you'll need to activate the Last Known Good/Hardware Configuration when that option becomes available during boot. When you press the space bar, as prompted, you'll see what purports to be a list of available configurations, but (unless you have more than one hardware profile created) is, in fact, a list of one: the last one with which you booted. Activate it, and the system will boot using the configuration information that it used the last time. Any new hardware information will be lost, but at least you'll have the system up.

TIP   You can create a vanilla hardware configuration in the Control Panel, setting it up with the System applet and defining the services and hardware recognized with the Server and Services applets. If you create an alternate hardware profile, you'll always see the Last Known Good/Hardware Configuration menu during system boot.

If neither SYSTEM nor SYSTEM.ALT are available or contain bootable information, you'll have to use the Emergency Repair disk to repair the installation. Boot the system with the setup boot disk, and then choose to repair the installation when given the choice. Insert the Repair disk when prompted, and Setup will copy the necessary files from the disk to get the system up and running.

N O T E   By default, when you repair an installation and choose to have Setup evaluate your Registry files, by default it will only overwrite the files that need repairing. You can choose to update other parts of the Registry if you like, however. ▪

Restoring the Registry from a Backup

Even though NT has its own failsafes when it comes to preserving the Registry, it's always a good idea to keep backups. First, if you keep your own backups, you're not limited to the last configuration that worked—you can save incremental versions of the Registry and then restore the one that you want. Second, the more backups you have, the more likely it is that one of them will work. If you lose the Emergency Repair Disk, then you'll need extra backup to restore your registry.

We discussed the mechanics of how you can back up your Registry in Chapter 29, "Backing Up and Editing the Registry." Armed with those backups, in this section you'll learn how to restore them.

Using NT Backup

The easiest way to restore the Registry is with NT Backup. If you've been backing up regularly and saving a copy of the Registry each time that you did so, then you'll be able to choose the date of the Registry that you want to reload.

 If you're restoring data to your system, you don't have to restore the Registry saved on the same tape. You can restore the data from one tape and the Registry from another—just indicate the files that you want to restore.

To restore the local Registry, start the Backup utility, catalog the tape, then make sure that you've checked Restore Local Registry in the Restore Information dialog box. The Registry files will be restored along with any other selected data.

Restoring Files Using REGREST

If you don't have a tape drive but do have the Resource Kit, then you can use REGBACK to back up your system Registry and REGREST to restore it. These utilities are the command-line equivalent of the Save Key and Restore Key menu options in REGEDT32. Using REGBACK is easy: put a formatted disk in the drive and type **REGBACK C:\newDirectory** (where newDirectory is the name of the location to copy to) to copy all the hive files to the disk.

After you've created the backup with REGBACK, you can restore each hive to its place in the system with REGREST. The syntax is

```
regback newDirectory saveDirectory
```

where *newDirectory* specifies the source of the backed-up hive file that will replace a hive file in the CONFIG directory, and *saveDirectory* is the name of the location to which you want to copy the old Registry files. By default, REGREST will attempt to replace all files in the CONFIG directory with a like-named file in the backup directory, and will copy all hive files to the directory that you specify. These directories must be on the same volume.

For example, regrest c:\hivefiles.bku c:\install.sav copies the files in c:\hivefiles.bku to the CONFIG directory, and then backs up the files that were in the CONFIG directory to c:\install.sav. The changes will take place when you reboot the system.

A warning appears if there are hives that must be restored manually or if there are errors. To restore a file manually (for example, if you saved it to another name using REGBACK), then the syntax is a little different. Type the following:

regrest newFilename saveFilename hivetype hivename

where *newFilename* is the name and location of the file to be copied to CONFIG and re-named, *saveFilename* is the name and destination of the file to be copied to the backup location, *hivetype* is either "users" or "machine," and hivename is one of the hives in either HKEY_LOCAL_MACHINE or HKEY_LOCAL_USERS. Once again, the changes will not take place until you reboot the system.

Restoring Files Using RDISK

If you can get to the hard disk at all, you can copy the system files from a backed up location if you previously saved them. (If you have not previously saved them, you'll restore the system files to the way they were right after installation.) Now, while your system is still up and running, try running RDISK. You'll see a dialog box that looks like the one in figure 30.1.

FIG. 30.1
Running RDISK
regularly creates
backups that can
help you restore
your system.

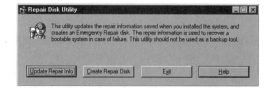

N O T E Copying all of the configuration information will take a while—be patient. ■

You can use this utility both to create or update an Emergency Repair Disk and to save the files that make up the Registry database to a backup location: the REPAIR directory.

If you look in the REPAIR directory of your Windows NT installation, you'll notice some files there that look startlingly similar to those in SYSTEM32\CONFIG. You'll see the SYSTEM, SOFTWARE, DEFAULT, SAM, SECURITY, and NTUSER files in both locations. The only difference between these two sets of hive files is the rate at which they're up- dated. Unlike the set in the CONFIG directory, which is updated every time you reboot the system (whether you've changed anything or not), the set in the REPAIR directory is only updated when you run RDISK and choose the Update Repair Info option.

This repair information can be used when you've lost the configuration information in the main directory, or if the directory is corrupted. (Recall that, because the information in the REPAIR directory is not automatically updated every time that you make a change to the system, if you really mess up the system, this set of backups is not affected.) If the system is not normally bootable, then, you've got an alternative to repairing the installa- tion with the Emergency Repair disk.

1. Boot to a DOS floppy.
2. Copy the files in the Repair directory back to SYSTEM32\CONFIG.
3. Reboot as you would normally, without the floppy.

Your system should boot with the same configuration that it had the last time you backed up the Registry files.

 TIP This is yet another reason to install NT on a FAT partition. If your REPAIR directory is on an NTFS partition, you won't be able to get to it when you boot from a DOS floppy.

Using the Emergency Repair Disk

If you haven't backed up the Registry to the Repair Directory but have kept your Emer- gency Repair Disk current, or the problem is more complicated than just corrupted

Registry files, then you can restore your configuration with the Repair Disk. This process is more complicated than just copying some files, but it can restore your system.

1. Reboot the system using the NT Workstation installation boot disk, as though you were entirely reinstalling.

2. When given the option, choose "R" to repair installation.

3. Choose which parts of the installation that you want evaluated and, if necessary, repaired. Make sure that you choose to evaluate the Registry—even if its files are gone, this option will not be checked by default.

4. When prompted, choose the files to restore from the Emergency Repair Disk. If only some of the files are corrupted or missing (for example, the SYSTEM file), then Windows NT will have that file checked already. You can choose to replace other files as well, however.

5. Insert the Emergency Repair Disk when prompted, and then reboot, when prompted.

When you reboot your system, it should be restored to the saved configuration.

Restoring Part of the Registry

Restoring the Registry is not an all-or-nothing proposition. Recall from Chapter 29 the discussion of how you can load hives from other systems into memory for editing. Well, once you've made the edits, you need some way of integrating that information with the original Registry.

Using REGEDT32   In the 32-bit Registry, that method is called the Restore option. To restore a key, select the key that you want to replace with the one saved to disk, and then choose Restore from the Registry menu. You'll see a dialog box that looks like the one shown in figure 30.2.

FIG. 30.2
You can save keys, edit them, and then restore them to the original Registry.

Choose carefully; the file that you select here will replace the currently selected key unless it's currently in use.

The Restore option may look like the Load Hive Option, but it is not. Rather than being a method of placing a key in memory for editing purposes, the Restore option replaces the currently selected key with the one that you choose. This makes it a potentially dangerous option—there are no guarantees that the saved key that you choose will fit in the Registry in the place you specify. This is one of the reasons why it's imperative to name save keys carefully, so that you know what you're restoring when you do.

Using REGEDIT   It's also possible to restore part of the Registry from REGEDIT. In the Registry menu, two options are Import Registry and Export Registry. The files that you export are text files that you can open in any text editor—even DOS's EDIT or Windows 3.x's Notepad. This is the advantage to exporting files with REGEDIT: if you want to be able to edit the Registry when away from the Windows NT machine and then integrate your changes with the original, this is how you'll have to go about it. Although Save Subtree As in REGEDT32 creates text files, there's no way to make those text files part of the Registry again.

We discussed the mechanics of exporting Registry files in Chapter 29, "Backing Up and Editing the Registry." After you have those exported files, you can import them back into the Registry, with one caveat: You can't import the System key of the Local Machine subtree, or NT will report a license violation. In fact, for those who are skimming:

N O T E   The only part of the Registry that you can't import with REGEDIT is the System key in HKEY_LOCAL_MACHINE, as it's in use by the system. ▓

The only catch is that this restriction means that you can't export the entire Registry and import it as a unit, as the SYSTEM restriction prevents you from doing so. For those used to working with Windows 95's Registry Editor, which will let you import or export anything, this can be a little frustrating, but this difference has to do with Windows NT's security architecture.

In any case, to import a previously exported registry key, choose Import from the Registry menu. You'll see a dialog box like the one shown in figure 30.3.

FIG. 30.3
Choose an exported
file to import back
into the Registry, and
it will automatically go
where it belongs.

You can only import Registry files that you exported from REGEDIT, so you need only look through the Registry files for the one you want. Choose the file, then click OK, and it will be imported back into its previous place in the Registry. You don't have to be sure that you're in the proper key—the file will automatically go where you exported it from.

When the file is fully imported, you'll see a dialog box telling you so.

From Here...

Whether it's automatic, part of your data restoration process, or done by hand, restoring the Registry is a pretty straightforward process—*if* you back it up ahead of time. Although NT will create a backup copy each time you successfully boot the machine, it's a good idea to save the Registry when doing your regular backups, or at least each time that you change the system configuration, so that you can get it back if you have to restore.

- ■ To learn more about backup and restoration services, turn to Chapter 14, "Ensuring Data Security."
- ■ For an overview of the Registry, turn to Chapter 28, "Understanding the Registry."
- ■ To learn how to back up your system Registry, turn to Chapter 29, "Backing Up and Editing the Registry."

Administering a Windows NT Workstation

Administration Overview

by Jim Boyce

Although this book focuses on Windows NT Workstation rather than Server, system and user administration still are important topics. You might need to create or manage user accounts on a workstation, share resources on the network, or control access to resources. And, administering a workstation on a peer-to-peer network includes balancing its performance as a server versus its performance as a workstation.

Fortunately, Windows NT provides a good set of administrative utilities to help you manage your workstation and its user accounts. This part of the book focuses on those tools and the concepts behind them. ∎

Managing Users

As you probably read in Chapter 16, "A Brief Primer on Networks," Windows NT uses two mechanisms to facilitate security authentication on the network: workgroups and domains. A *workgroup* is a collection of computers organized under a particular name (their workgroup name). Organizing computers into workgroups simplifies locating and accessing shared resources on the network by enabling the system manager to organize the network into logical groups of computers that share a common purpose. Rather than browsing the entire network for a shared resource, the people in the Accounting department, for example, could simply browse the Accounting workgroup. Instead of browsing through 200 computers, they need only browse through 20.

The primary disadvantage to workgroups is the fact that for a user to access a resource on a computer, he or she must have a user account on that computer. Giving access to a single user to resources on a broad range of computers therefore becomes complex. Even if your network consists of only twenty computers, you still would have to create twenty user accounts for each user if you wanted them to be able to access resources on every computer.

Domains add centralized user authentication to the workgroup model. Rather than requiring each user to have an account on a computer to access its resources, the user needs only an account on the domain's controller with membership in a group that has been granted access to the shared resource. By centralizing the user accounts, you greatly simplify system and account management. Perhaps equally important, you can administer user accounts from any node on the LAN, including through Dial-Up Networking connections. In addition, Windows NT includes a set of Windows 95-based administration tools to complement the Windows NT-based tools.

 Workgroups are most appropriate for relatively small networks in which users generally do not access one another's resources, but instead access resources from a central server. Domains are most appropriate in larger networks, networks with multiple servers, or any size network in which peer-to-peer resource access is common. The benefit of simplified administration is well worth the additional cost to install Windows NT Server on at least one computer on the LAN.

Regardless of whether you are using a workgroup or domain security model, the actual process for administering users is the same. The Windows NT User Manager enables you to create and modify accounts and impose various restrictions on accounts. With User Manager, you also can manage user profiles and set account policies. Chapter 32, "Administering Users," covers the User Manager in detail.

Managing Servers Properties

Because of its peer-to-peer networking features, it's a good bet you will want to share resources on your workstation with other users. The following sections briefly describe typical server administration tasks you'll probably perform on your workstation.

Managing the File System

Managing the file system is an important task on any computer, regardless of whether the computer is serving as a workstation or server. You need to weed out old files to keep space available for new ones, compress files to conserve available space, defragment the disk, and perform other routine maintenance. You also might need to make files and directories available to other users, which involves assigning access permissions to those resources.

Windows NT provides three primary mechanisms for administering disks—Explorer, Disk Administrator, and File Manager. Explorer incorporates most of the disk management functions, enabling you to format disks, compress files (NTFS volumes only), and run such tasks as defragmenting and checking the disk for errors. Disk Administrator adds other functions such as drive letter assignment and the ability to convert a partition from one format to another (such as FAT to NTFS). File Manager is included mainly for users of previous versions of Windows NT who are most comfortable with the File Manager interface. File Manager does not, however, support the same level of features as Explorer.

 T I P You won't find File Manager on the Start menu or desktop. Instead, choose Start, <u>R</u>un, and enter **winfile** in the <u>O</u>pen text box on the Run dialog box.

Disk administration, including coverage of Explorer and Disk Administrator, is examined in detail in Chapter 33, "Managing Server Properties."

Managing Printers

By far, one of the most common uses for peer-to-peer networking is sharing printers. Managing printers and print queues therefore becomes an important administration task for users who are sharing their printers on the LAN. Windows NT provides a unified mechanism to manage all printers—the Printers folder. Contained in the Printers folder are icons for each of the computer's installed printers and an Add Printer icon that activates a wizard to help you install a new printer.

Part VII
Ch
31

Through the Printers folder, you can add and remove printers, set printer properties, and manage printer queues. You can perform these tasks on printers connected to your computer or to remote printers for which you have the necessary management privileges. To learn more about managing printers, refer to Chapter 33, "Managing Server Properties."

▶ **See** "Managing Printers," **p. 749**

Monitoring and Controlling System Performance

In addition to managing user accounts and shared resources, you might also be concerned with optimizing your computer's performance. Another aspect of system management includes tracking and balancing the performance of various components, particularly when your computer is sharing resources. You might need to balance your computer's CPU time between functioning as a workstation for you and a server for other users.

System performance monitoring is covered in detail in Part III, "Optimizing System and Application Performance." Chapter 33 explains some of the other, less complex means at your disposal for monitoring and tuning system performance. ●

CHAPTER 32

Administering Users

by Jim Boyce

Every experienced administrator knows that managing user accounts and network access is a major facet of system administration. Because of the way Windows NT's security works, it often becomes necessary to administer user accounts on workstations as well as servers.

In this chapter, you learn about the tools that Windows NT provides to simplify user and group account management. You also learn about access permissions and how to use those permissions to securely control access to resources. ■

User accounts

A key facet of system management is understanding the role user accounts play in system security and managing those accounts.

Resource access

Rights, permissions, and group membership enable you to apply a fine degree of control over shared resources.

User profiles

User profiles enable an administrator to provide a consistent interface and work environment for users, as well as apply system-wide and network-wide restrictions.

Policies

In Windows NT 4.0, policies supersede many settings and characteristics of the user profile.

Creating and Modifying User Accounts

Unlike an environment like Windows for Workgroups and Windows 95, Windows NT requires a user to have a pre-existing user account either on the computer from which he or she is logging on, or a domain. Assume, for example, that you have created a small peer-to-peer network with Windows NT Workstation on all computers.

To log on to the computer, user A must have a user account on his local computer. To access a network resource, such as a shared folder on a remote computer, user A must have an account on that remote computer. If your network contains 20 workstations, and you want user A to be able to access shared peer resources on all computers on the network, user A must have a user account on every computer on the network. You can see that in this situation, creating user accounts will be an important, time-consuming task.

In a domain, however, a user need have only one account within the domain to access resources across the network. The primary domain controller (PDC) authenticates access requests by users for resources in the domain. Although domains greatly simplify security and user account management, you still need to create and manage accounts in the domain.

 T I P To create a domain, you must use Windows NT Server on at least one computer on the network. This server will function as the primary domain controller (PDC). Other computers on the network running Windows NT Server can function as backup domain controllers (BDC). The BDC improves overall performance by offloading some of the authentication overhead from the PDC and also provides redundancy should the PDC fail.

Therefore, a task you'll probably perform fairly often is creating and managing user accounts. Windows NT simplifies the entire process by bringing all account control under one interface: User Manager. You'll use User Manager any time you need to create a new account to enable a user to access resources on your computer, create accounts in a domain, or modify existing accounts. If a user forgets his account password, for example, you can modify his account by changing his password so he can once again access the system.

Overview of User Manager

User Manager enables you to create user accounts and groups, assign users to groups, set access permissions for groups and individual users, create trust relationships, define account policies, and perform other administrative tasks. To start User Manager, choose Start, Programs, Administrative Tools, and User Manager. Figure 32.1 shows the User Manager program window.

FIG. 32.1

User Manager enables you to create and manage user accounts and access permissions.

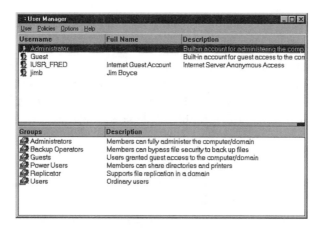

Part
VII
Ch
32

N O T E On a domain controller, User Manager for Domains performs the same function as User Manager, and is essentially identical except for the addition of a few features that enable you to select and work with domain-wide accounts.

User Manager for Domains enables you to manage user accounts on a domain controller as well as accounts on individual workstations and members servers (servers that do not function as primary or backup domain controllers). You can install User Manager for Domains on any Windows NT Workstation or Windows 95 computer, enabling you to manage user accounts on other computers besides your own. To learn how to manage accounts in this way, see the section "Administering Accounts Remotely," later in this chapter. ■

User Manager enables you to perform the following administrative functions:

- Create and modify user accounts
- Create and modify groups
- Set account policies
- Grant user rights
- Set up auditing
- Create and modify trust relationships

In order to understand how to perform these tasks with User Manager, you first need to understand the concepts of groups and individual user accounts.

Understanding Accounts and Groups

You must have a valid, pre-existing user account to log on to a computer running Windows NT. If the workstation is participating in a workgroup and not a domain, you must have an account on that workstation itself. If you are logging on from a computer in a domain, you must have an account in the domain (or in a trusted domain).

A user account not only identifies each user with a name and other optional information, but also defines how and when a user can log on, which resources he or she can access, and which level of access the user has to those resources. In effect, the user account defines all aspects of your access to the computer and network. Each user account includes a password for security.

In addition to existing as an individual account, users can belong to specific *groups*. A group is a collection of users who typically have similar job or resource access needs. For example, assume you have a folder on your computer to which you want to give every department manager access. You don't want other users in their departments to have access to the folder. So, you might create a group called DeptHeads and grant DeptHeads access to the folder. Then, each department head's user account would be added to the DeptHeads group.

From this example, you can see that groups simplify resource administration by enabling you to assign and control permissions on a broad basis. Instead of assigning permissions for a specific resource to every user, you can assign a very specific set of rights to a group, then give those rights to users simply by making them members of the group. In this way, groups provide a means of logically organizing users and access rights.

Windows NT supports two types of groups:

- **Global group.** Global groups can contain user accounts only from within the domain in which the group is created. A global group can be granted permissions in other domains through a trust relationship between the domains.

- **Local group.** A local group can contain users and global groups, which enables you to collect users from multiple domains into one group and manage them collectively. Local groups can be assigned permissions only in the domain in which the group is created.

By far the most common use for groups is simplifying the process of controlling access to shared resources. You first create a group and grant that group access to a specific resource. Then, you make a member of the group the user to whom you want to grant access to the resource. Later, if or when you need to change the level of access to the resource, such as restricting the ability to make changes, you apply the appropriate permissions to the group. Each member of the group inherits those permissions for the shared resource. This is considerably easier than changing the permissions for each individual account in the group.

Understanding Trust Relationships

In order to understand how to apply local and global groups, you need to understand what a trust relationship is and how it works. A *trust relationship* is a special logical relationship between domains. In a trust relationship, one domain trusts another domain's users. The *trusting domain* allows users who have accounts in the *trusted domain* to access resources in its domain. For example, assume that Domain A is the trusting domain, and Domain B is the trusted domain. A user from Domain B can access resources in Domain A.

A trust relationship can be unidirectional or bidirectional. Just because Domain A trusts Domain B doesn't mean that B trusts A. You must explicitly set up the trust relationship between the two domains to be bidirectional if you want it to be so. Figure 32.2 shows the relationship between multiple domains that are involved in trust relationships.

Trust relationships is a fairly complex topic that goes beyond the scope of this chapter. For a more complete description of trust relationships and how to work with them, refer to *The Windows NT 4.0 Installation and Configuration Handbook*, from Que.

FIG. 32.2
To make a trust relationship bidirectional, you must explicitly set it up as such.

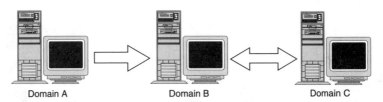

Domain A   Domain B   Domain C

Domain A trusts Domain B   Domain B trust Domain C, and Domain C trusts Domain B

Local versus Global Groups

As explained in the last section, Windows NT supports two types of groups: global and local. A global group enables you to group together accounts from one domain under one group account name. A global group can contain member accounts only from within the domain in which the group is created—it cannot contain members from other domains. After creating the group, you can grant to a global group permissions and rights in its own domain, on individual workstations or member servers, and in trusting domains.

N O T E A global group cannot contain local groups or other global groups; it can only contain user accounts. Also, you can't create global groups on a computer running Windows NT Workstation. You can create global groups only through a computer running Windows NT Server as a domain controller, or on a computer on which you've installed User Manager for Domains (creating domain accounts across the network on the domain controller). ■

A local group enables you to group together under one name accounts from one or more domains. The local group can contain individual users and global groups from outside the local domain only if those users and groups belong to a trusting domain. The primary purpose for local groups is to enable you to quickly assign permissions to resources within a domain to users and groups in the local domain and to users and groups in other domains that trust the local domain.

N O T E   A local group can't contain other local groups, but it can contain global groups.   ▪

You can think of local groups as being designed to grant access to resources in the local domain, both to users in the local domain and users in other domains. You can think of global groups as a mechanism for exporting accounts outside of the local domain. Figure 32.3 illustrates the relationship between local and global groups and users in trusted domains. Both Domain A and Domain B contain individual user accounts and global groups.

FIG. 32.3
The local group in Domain A is being used to enable users from both domains to access resources in Domain A.

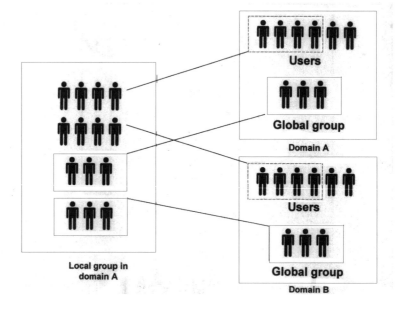

Local group in domain A

Users

Global group

Domain A

Users

Global group

Domain B

Built-In Groups

Windows NT includes a selection of built-in user accounts and groups. The Administrator account, which you create when you install Windows NT, is essentially a built-in account. You can't delete or disable the Administrator account, but you can rename it. The Guest account is another built-in account. You can't delete the Guest account, but you can rename and disable it.

The built-in groups supported by Windows NT are described in table 32.1 and listed in the following sections.

Table 32.1 Built-In Groups

Group	Type	Automatic Contents
Administrators	Local	Domain Admins
Domain Admins	Global	Administrator
Backup Operators	Local	None
Server Operators	Local	None
Account Operators	Local	None
Print Operators	Local	None
Power Users	Local	Setup user
Users	Local	Domain Users
Domain Users	Global	Administrators
Guests	Local	Domain Guests, Guest
Domain Guests	Global	Guest
Replicator	Local	None

Part
VII

Ch
32

Administrators   Members of the Administrators group enjoy almost complete access to and authority over the domain, server, or workstation containing the group. A member of the Administrator group can access any file or directory on a FAT file system, but, administrators don't have complete, automatic access to directories and files on NTFS systems. Unless the owner of a file or directory grants access, even administrators can't access the resource. An administrator can, however, take ownership of the resource to gain access to it.

▶ **See** "Understanding NTFS's Structure," **p. 248**
▶ **See** "Exploring NTFS's Advantages," **p. 258**

Domain Admins   Every domain includes a global group named Domain Admins, which is automatically added to the local Administrators group. Therefore, all members of Domain Admins are domain administrators. You can assign a user as a domain administrator in one of two ways—add the user to the Domain Admins group, or simply add the user to the local Administrators group in the domain. By adding the Domain Admins group to the Administrators group in other domains, you enable the designated users to administer multiple domains with a single account in their home domain.

Backup Operators   This local group is designed to enable users to perform backup functions. Users in the Backup Operators group can back up and restore files, log on to the system locally, and shut down the system. Backup Operators do not have the ability to change security settings or perform other administrative tasks.

▶ **See** "Optimizing and Automating Backup Services," **p. 322**

Server Operators   The Server Operators group is designed to enable its members to manage servers. Users in this group can log on to the system locally, share and unshare resources, format disks on the server, back up and restore files, and shut down servers.

Account Operators   Users in this group can create and manage user accounts in the domain. They can create and modify user accounts and groups, but can't assign user rights. Instead, they can create accounts and assign those accounts to groups that have been set up by an administrator.

Print Operators   The Print Operators group can log on to servers locally, shut down a server; and share, unshare, and manage printers.

Users   The most common group is Users. Members of this group can log on locally to a workstation, member server, or domain, but can't log on to a primary or backup domain controller.

Power Users   Power Users are like Users with some Administrative rights. Power Users can create and modify user accounts (only modifying those they create). They also can add accounts to the Users, Guests, and Power Users groups. Power Users also can share and unshare files and printers on local workstations or servers.

Domain Users   All user accounts in a domain automatically become members of the Domain Users group. The Domain Users group is part of the local Users group, which makes all of its members users of the domain.

Guests   Members of the Guests group on a domain have rights similar to Users. They can log on through a network client and access domain resources. Like Users, they cannot log on locally to a server, but instead must do so across the network.

Domain Guests   The Guest user account typically is included in the Domain Guests group, which is a member of the local Guests group. Members of the Domain Guests and Guest group enjoy guest privileges in the domain to which they are logged on. To grant guest privileges across multiple domains, include the Domain Guests group in the local Guests groups of the other domains that trust the logon domain.

Replicator The Replicator group is a special group to facilitate file and directory replication.

▶ **See** "Replicating Directories," **p. 748**

Applying Accounts and Groups The most important point for you to understand is that groups enable you to simplify administration and resource access. Instead of having to grant specific rights to each user, you simply create groups with specific rights, then assign users to those groups as needed. It's also important to understand that a user can be a member of many groups, and that one group can contain another. And, you can add specific rights to a user if that one user is the only one who needs that right—you don't have to create a group to give the user that right. You might consider doing so anyway, however, because you might have another user in the future who also needs the same right.

In the following sections, you'll learn how to use User Manager to create and manage accounts and groups.

Part VII

Ch 32

Controlling Views and Selecting Users

You can sort the view in User Manager to display names according to their account names or long names. By default, User Manager sorts by account name. To switch between these two view methods, choose View, then Sort by Full Name or Sort by Username.

When you've selected the view you prefer, you can select one or more user accounts from the list. To select an account, just click it. To select more than one account (so you can apply changes to all the selected accounts with one operation), hold down the Ctrl key and select accounts. If you want to select all accounts that belong to a specific group, choose User, Select Users. User Manager displays the Select Users dialog box (see fig. 32.4). Click the group whose member accounts you want to select, then click the Select button. Repeat the process until all of the desired accounts are selected. Then, close the dialog box to return to User Manager.

FIG. 32.4
Select all members in a group using the Select Users dialog box.

To work with the user database for a domain other than your home domain, choose User, Select Domain. From the resulting Select Domain dialog box, choose the domain you want to administer, then choose OK.

N O T E   The Select Users and Select Domain commands are available only with User Manager for Domains. User Manager, which is included with Windows NT Workstation, does not include these commands because they apply to domains rather than individual workstations. ■

Creating User Accounts

User Manager is the tool you use to create and modify user accounts. When you create an account, you specify general information such as the user's name and password, and also apply permissions and set other logon restrictions. The following sections explain the steps for creating a user account.

N O T E   The following sections explain how to create an account. To modify an account, just double-click the account in User Manager, then use the techniques and controls explained in the following sections to set account properties. ■

Specifying General Account Information   To begin creating a user account, choose User, New User to display the New User dialog box shown in figure 32.5. In the Username text box, type the name for the new account. This is the name by which the user will log on to the computer or domain.

FIG. 32.5
Start the account by specifying basic information such as user name and password.

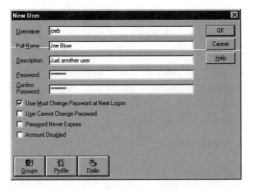

Next, type the user's full name in the Full Name text box. Type an optional description, such as the user's office location or job title, in the Description text box. Click in the Password text box and type the password you want to assign to the account, then click in the Confirm Password text box and type the password again. This is the password the user will provide with his account name when he logs on.

Four checkboxes on the New User dialog box control general account properties:

■ **User Must Change Password At Next Logon.** Mark this checkbox to force the user to change his password the next time he logs on. Windows NT will prompt the user to change the password.

■ **User Cannot Change Password.** Mark this checkbox to prevent the user from being able to change his password.

■ **Password Never Expires.** Mark this checkbox if you want the user's password to continue to be valid indefinitely. You or the user can change the password at any time.

■ **Account Disabled.** Mark this checkbox to disable the account. You might create a template account to use for creating other accounts, and disable the template account to prevent users from possibly logging on with it. Or, you might disable an account if it won't be used for a while.

T I P If a user forgets his or her password, just assign a new password to the account, then give the user the new password.

Part
VII
Ch
32

Setting Group Membership In addition to specifying general information, you need to specify to which groups a user belongs. To do so, click the Groups button to display the Group Memberships dialog box shown in figure 32.6.

FIG. 32.6
Use the Group
Memberships
dialog box to
specify group
membership for
an account.

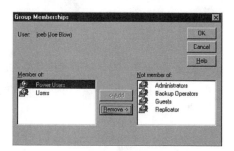

Depending on the type of environment in which you're creating the account (domain or not), User Manager will automatically add the account to the Users or Domain Users group. Other groups you can add appear in the Not Member Of list. To add other memberships, select the desired group and choose the Add button. To remove group membership for a group, select the group from the Member Of list, then choose Remove.

You can specify the group to be assigned as the primary group. The primary group association affects only users who log on using Windows NT Services for Macintosh or who run POSIX programs. To specify the primary group, select a group in the <u>M</u>ember Of list, then click the <u>S</u>et button.

N O T E Because the primary group applies only to a domain, the <u>S</u>et button appears only when running the User Manager for Domains. ▪

When you're satisfied with the group membership assignments for the account, choose OK.

Choosing a Profile The next step in creating an account is to specify a user profile, home directory, and logon script. To do so, click the <u>P</u>rofile button to display the User Environment Profile dialog box (see fig. 32.7).

N O T E Some services add to the options you can set in the User Environment Profile dialog box. This section covers the default properties. ▪

FIG. 32.7
Set a user profile,
home directory, and
logon script.

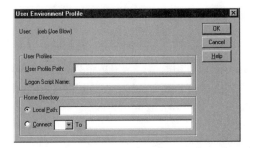

A profile is a special file Windows NT uses to store user settings such as desktop configuration, colors, sound assignments, and other user-definable properties. Each computer maintains a default user profile. If a user logs on and no profile is specified, the default profile is used. This profile then becomes the user's profile.

N O T E Profiles are covered in more depth later in the section "Managing User Profiles." ▪

 T I P To support roaming users who log on from various nodes, store the profile on a network server that will be available to the user each time he logs on. This will provide the user with the same consistent, custom interface settings each time he logs on, regardless of which computer he uses.

To specify a user profile for the account, type the path to the profile file in the User Profile Path text box. For example, you might specify **\\server\profiles\billg.usr**, which defines the path to the file in UNC format. If you're working with multiple accounts, you can use an environment variable in place of the user's name. For example, assume you're working with six different accounts, so you can't specify a single file for the profile. Instead, you'd enter something similar to **\\server\profiles\%username%.usr**. User Manager replaces the variable %username% with each user's name to create or read the appropriate profile.

In the Logon Script Name text box, enter the path to the logon script file for the account. You can specify the name of a batch (BAT) file, command (CMD) file, or executable (EXE) file. Typically, logon scripts are stored in the *systemroot*\System32\Repl\Import\ Scripts directory.

The Home Directory group on the User Environment Profile dialog box lets you specify the location of the user's home directory. This is the directory Windows NT will make active when the user logs on. In most cases, the user's home directory is the directory in which he stores his personal files.

You can specify a home directory on the user's local computer or on a server. To specify a local directory, choose the Local Path option button, then type in the associated text box the local disk and directory, such as **C:\Users\Fredf**.

N O T E If a user logs on from the same computer all the time, you should use a local home directory on the user's computer to save network traffic and server disk space. Users who roam and log on from various nodes should have a home directory on a server so their home directory "follows" them and is always available. ■

To specify a shared network directory as the user's home directory, choose the Connect option button. Then choose a drive letter from the associated drop-down list. In the To text box, type the UNC path to the shared directory, such as **\\Server\Users\Fredf**.

TIP If you're working with multiple user accounts, you can use the %username% environment variable in the home directory path. User Manager will replace the user's name with the environment variable.

Setting Logon Hours   To specify when a user can log on to the system, click the Hours button in the New User dialog box to display the Logon Hours dialog box (see fig. 32.8). You might, for example, allow logon only during the week, but not on weekends.

Part
VII

Ch
32

FIG. 32.8
You can control when
a user has access to
the system.

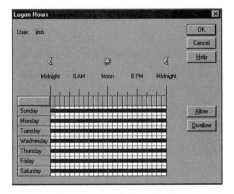

By default, the user can log on at any time. To disallow logon during a specific period,
select the period of time to disallow in the desired day(s), then choose Disallow. To disallow the same hour in every day, click the gray bar at the top of the hour column to select
the hour for the entire week. Then choose Disallow.

N O T E   Disallowing logon applies only to server logon—it does not affect the user's ability to
log on to a workstation locally. You might, for example, disallow logon to a server
during a specific period every week to run backups on the server. The ability to set logon hours is
available only through the User Manager for Domains. ■

Setting Logon Restrictions   In addition to controlling when a user can log on, you also
can specify from which computers the user can log on to a domain. This enables you to
restrict which computers a user can use to access the domain. To control logon, choose
the Logon To button on the New User dialog box to display the Logon Workstations
dialog box shown in figure 32.9.

FIG. 32.9
You can specify from
which computer(s) a
user can log on.

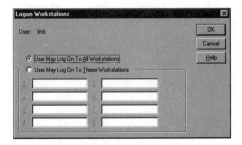

If you want to enable the user to log on to the domain from any computer, choose the User
May Log On To All Workstations option button. To restrict access to specific workstations,
choose the User May Log On To These Workstations option button. Then, enter up to
eight workstation names in the text boxes.

Setting Account Type and Expiration Most accounts in a domain are global, but you can create a local account. To specify the account type and expiration, choose the Account button on the New User dialog box to display the Account Information dialog box shown in figure 32.10.

FIG. 32.10
Specify when the account expires, and its type.

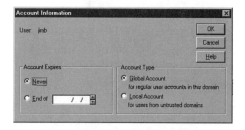

You might want to cause an account to expire for a variety of reasons. For example, the user might be a temporary employee, or need only the account during a specific project. To specify that the account should expire, choose the End of option button, then use the associated spin control to set the date on which the account will expire. The account will expire on midnight of that date. If you don't want the account to expire, choose the Never option button (the default).

You also use the Account Information dialog box to specify the type of account. Choose either the Global Account or Local Account option button, depending on your requirements. In a domain, most accounts will be global.

Part
VII

Ch
32

Creating Groups

In addition to creating and modifying user accounts with User Manager, you also can create and manage groups. After you create a group, you can add existing user accounts to that group. The following sections explain how to create local and global groups.

Creating a Local Group To create a local group, choose User, New Local Group to display the New Local Group dialog box shown in figure 32.11. In the Group Name text box, type the name you want to give the new group. You can use any combination of uppercase and lowercase letters, except for the following:

    " / \ [ ] : ; | = , + * ? < >

In the Description text box, type an optional description for the group.

Next, you can begin assigning users to the group. Or, you can leave that task for later. To put it off, just choose the OK button. To add users now, click the Add button to display the Add Users and Groups dialog box (see fig. 32.12).

FIG. 32.11
Create local groups
with the New Local
Group dialog box.

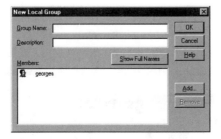

FIG. 32.12
You can add users to a
group through the Add
Users and Groups
dialog box.

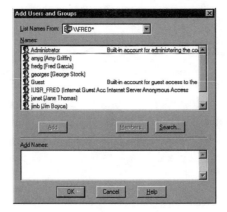

From the Names list, select all the groups and users you want to add to the new group.
Then, choose Add. If you want to view the members of one of a listed existing group,
select the group and choose the Members button. To delete a user or group from the
group, click in the Add Names text box, highlight the name(s) to be deleted, then press
Del. To search for a name or group locally or in a specific domain, choose the Search
button.

Creating a Global Group   You create a global group in much the same way you create a
local group. In User Manager, choose User, New Global Group to display the New Global
Group dialog box (see fig. 32.13). As when creating a local group, type the group name in
the Group Name box and an optional description in the Description box.

N O T E   You can create global groups only with User Manager for Domains. This ability is not
present in the User Manager utility included with Windows NT Workstation. ■

FIG. 32.13
Use the New Global
Group dialog box to
create global groups.

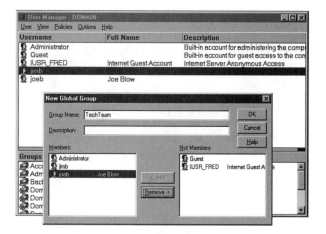

To add users to the group, select their names from the Not Members list and choose Add.
To remove users from the group, choose their names from the Members list and choose
Remove.

About Permissions

In Windows NT, *permissions* play an important role in conjunction with user and group
accounts to ensure a high level of security over resources such as folders, files, and printers. You can apply permissions in two different ways. First, each object can be associated
with its own set of permissions, often called *object permissions*, which control local access
to the resource. For example, you might set the permissions on a folder so that the Users
group has read-only access to the folder. Anyone in that group who logs on to the workstation locally will be restricted to read-only access to that folder.

In addition to local object permissions, you can apply *share permissions* to resources that
are shared on a computer. These permissions determine what level of access remote
users across the network have to the shared resource. Consider the previous example in
which we assigned read-only object permission to a folder. You can share that folder, then
assign a set of share permissions that are different from the local object permissions.
Therefore, members of the Users group (in this example) would have one set of permissions for the folder when they log on locally to the workstation and a different set of permissions when they access the resource from across the network.

Part
VII

Ch
32

There really is little difference between object permissions and share permissions except in the methods you use to assign those permissions. Therefore, both object and share permissions and how to set them are covered in detail in Chapter 33, "Managing Server Properties."

Understanding and Assigning Access Rights

A *right* grants a user (or group) the authority to perform a specific action. When a user logs on to an account to which a right has been granted, either directly or through group membership, that user can perform the task associated with the right. The following list describes the specific user rights:

- **Access this computer from network.** This right enables a user to connect to the computer from across the network.

- **Act as part of the operating system.** This right enables the user to act as a trusted part of the operating system—a right granted automatically to certain subsystems.

- **Add workstations to domain.** With this right, a user can add workstations to a domain, which enables those workstations to recognize the domain's user accounts and global groups (enabling logon from those workstations). You can set this right only when running User Manager for Domains.

- **Back up files and directories.** This right enables the user to back up files and directories on the computer, and supersedes file and directory permissions. Note that this right does not enable the user to view file or directory contents unless he has explicit permission to do so.

- **Change the system time.** With this right, the user can set the computer's system clock.

- **Create a page file.** This right allows the user to create a page file.

- **Create a token object.** With this right, the user can create security access tokens.

- **Create permanent shared objects.** This right enables the user to create permanent shared objects such as device instances.

- **Debug programs.** This right allows the user to debug programs.

- **Force shutdown from a remote system.** This right enables the user to force a system to shut down from a remote node (such as a dial-up connection).

- **Generate security audits.** This right allows the user to generate security log entries.

- **Increase quotas.** This right enables the user to increase the object quotas.

- **Increase scheduling priority.** This right enables the user to boost the scheduling priority of a process.

- **Load and unload device drivers.** This right allows the user to dynamically load and unload device drivers. When you're managing a domain, this right applies to the PDC and BDC(s). Outside of a domain, the right applies only to the computer on which the right is assigned.

- **Lock pages in memory.** With this right, the user can lock pages in memory, preventing them from being paged to disk.

- **Log on as a batch job.** This right enables the user to log on to the system as a batch queue facility.

- **Log on as a service.** This right enables the user to perform security services.

- **Log on locally.** With this right, a user can log on to the system locally. In most cases, you don't want users to have the right to log on locally to a server, PDC, or BDC for security and performance reasons.

- **Manage auditing and security log.** This right enables a user to manage auditing of files, directories, and other objects.

- **Modify firmware and environment values.** This right allows the user to modify system environment variables.

- **Profile single process.** This right enables the user to profile a process.

- **Profile system performance.** This right enables the user to profile overall system performance.

- **Receive unsolicited device input.** This right enables the user to receive unsolicited input from a terminal device.

- **Replace a process level token.** This right enables a user to modify a process' access token.

- **Restore files and directories.** With this right, a user can restore files that have previously been backed up. Note that having backup permission does not give a user restore permission, and vice versa.

- **Shut down the system.** This right enables the user to shut down the computer.

- **Take ownership of files or other objects.** With this right, a user can take ownership of files, directories, and printers. When you're managing a domain, this right applies to the PDC and BDC(s). Outside of a domain, the right applies only to the computer on which the right is assigned.

Part
VII

Ch
32

■ **Bypass traverse checking.** This right enables a user to traverse directory trees, even if he lacks the permission to traverse a directory. This right doesn't supersede ownership or permissions. If you don't have the necessary permission to see the contents of a directory, you still won't see its contents, although you can traverse the directory.

■ **Log on as a service.** This right is designed to allow processes to register with the system as a service.

N O T E   Don't confuse *rights* with *permissions*, which are different. A right applies to system-wide objects and tasks, and permissions apply to specific objects such as files and printers. Also, many of the advanced user rights listed above are applicable only within the framework of a custom application or subsystem. ■

Generally, you control user rights by placing the user in a group whose rights you've already assigned. You also can assign rights on an account-by-account basis. To assign rights, open User Manager and choose Policies, User Rights to display the User Rights Policy dialog box shown in figure 32.14.

FIG. 32.14

Assign user rights to groups with the User Rights Policy dialog box.

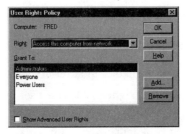

From the Right drop-down list, choose the right you want to assign. Then, if the desired group is not already listed in the Grant To list, choose the Add button to display the Add Users and Groups dialog box (see fig. 32.15).

If you want to assign only the selected right to various groups, select the groups from the Names list, then choose Add. To add the right to specific users, click the Show Users button to cause User Manager to display individual accounts as well as groups in the Names list. Choose the name(s) from the list, then choose Add. When you're satisfied with the list, choose OK to return to the User Rights Policy dialog box. Repeat the process for any other rights you want to assign.

FIG. 32.15
You can assign the selected right to any combination of users and groups.

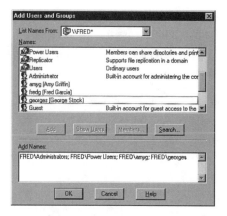

Administering Accounts Remotely

As mentioned at the beginning of this chapter, you can install User Manager for Domains on a computer running either Windows NT Workstation or Windows 95 and administer accounts in a domain across the network. The client administration tools are contained on the Windows NT Server CD in the \Clients\Srvtools folder. This folder contains other administration tools you can use remotely.

Part
VII

Ch
32

The system administration utilities included with each Windows NT 4.0 platform for administration work not only across the LAN, but also across a Dial-Up Networking connection. You therefore can manage remote domains and resources through a dial-up connection to the remote network.

The tools for managing Windows NT from a Windows NT platform include:

- **Event Viewer.** This utility enables you to monitor security, system, and application events in your system.

- **Server Manager.** This utility enables you to view the status of users connected to the server, control shared resources, start and stop services, synchronize the domain, add computers to a domain, and perform other server-related management tasks.

- **User Manager for Domains.** With User Manager you can view, create, modify user accounts and groups, create trust relationships, and set auditing options.

- **DHCP Manager.** The DHCP Manager enables you to specify TCP/IP parameters and set other options for a DHCP server.

- **Remote Access Admin.** With the Remote Access Admin utility you can start and stop RAS services on a RAS server, monitor port use, control user access, view active users, and perform other RAS administration tasks.

- **Remoteboot Manager.** This utility enables you to manage remote booting of DOS- and Windows-based PCs that boot across the network from a Windows NT server.
- **WINS Manager.** The WINS Manager enables you to perform configuration and management tasks on WINS servers.

In addition to the administration tools for the Windows NT platforms, Windows NT Server also includes Windows 95-based versions of Event Viewer, Server Manager, and User Manager. These tools enable you to manage a remote Windows NT server or workstation across the LAN or a dial-up connection from a Windows 95 workstation.

Installing the Tools

The Windows NT versions of the system administration tools are located on the Windows NT Server CD in the \Clients\Srvtools\Winnt folder. This folder contains folders for each of the supported Windows NT platforms—Alpha, Mips, Intel, and PowerPC. To install the Windows NT server tools, open the \Clients\Srvtools\Winnt folder and execute the file Setup.bat.

The Windows 95-based versions of the Windows NT system administration tools are located in the \Clients\Srvtools\Win95 folder on the Windows NT Server CD. To install the tools under Windows 95, follow these steps:

1. On the Windows 95 workstation, open the Control Panel and double-click the Add/Remove Programs icon.
2. Click the Windows Setup tab to display the Windows Setup page.
3. Click the Have Disk button.
4. Enter (or browse to) the \Clients\Srvtools\Win95 path on the Windows NT Server CD, then select the folder and choose OK, then OK again.
5. On the Have Disk dialog box, place a check beside the Windows NT Server Tools item, then choose Install.

After you have installed the administration tools, you'll find shortcuts to the tools in the Start menu. To access these shortcuts, choose Start, Programs, and Windows NT Server Tools.

Connecting Remotely

You can use the Windows NT administration tools across the LAN by simply opening the needed utility, then specifying which workstation, server, or domain you want to manage.

If you want to manage a system through a dial-up connection, however, you first must establish a connection to the remote LAN. The following sections briefly explain how to connect from Windows NT and Windows 95 computers.

Connecting from Windows NT   To connect to a remote server using Windows NT Workstation or Server, create a Dial-Up Networking connection to the server. For an explanation of Dial-Up Networking and how to create dial-up connections, refer to Chapter 20, "Using Dial-Up Networking."

Connecting from Windows 95   If you have not already done so, you need to create a Dial-Up Networking connection to the remote LAN containing the computer or domain you want to administer. To create a new connection to a RAS server on the remote LAN, follow these steps on the Windows 95 workstation:

1. If you don't have a modem installed on the Windows 95 computer, first install the modem through the Modems object in the Control Panel.

2. Open My Computer and double-click the Dial-Up Networking folder.

3. Double-click the Make New Connection icon. Windows 95 displays the Make New Connection wizard dialog box shown in figure 32.16.

FIG. 32.16

Specify a name and modem for the remote connection.

Part
VII

Ch
32

4. Type a name for the connection in the text box, then choose a modem from the Select a modem drop-down list. If you need to configure the modem, click the Configure button and use the resulting modem property sheet to configure the modem. Choose OK when you're done.

5. Click Next, then enter the area code and phone number for the remote dial-up server in the Area Code and Telephone Number boxes (see fig. 32.17). From the Country Code drop-down list, choose the country in which the server is located. Then, choose Next.

FIG. 32.17
Specify the area code and phone number for the connection.

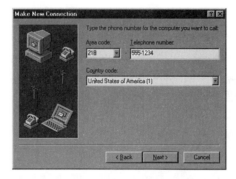

6. Click Finish to create the new connection.

7. In the Dial-Up Networking folder, right-click the connection you just created and choose Properties.

8. Click the Server Type button to display the Server Types dialog box (see fig. 32.18).

FIG. 32.18
Use the Server Types dialog box to set protocol and other connection options.

9. Select the PPP option from the Type Of Dial-Up Server drop-down list.

N O T E Although Windows NT 4.0 is not listed in the PPP option along with Windows 95, Windows NT 3.51, and Internet, Windows NT 4.0 uses the same PPP protocol for remote access as these other systems. ■

10. Verify that the Log on to network checkbox is enabled (checked).

11. In the Allowed Network Protocols group, enable the protocols you will need for the connection. If you are connecting only to administer the remote network, domain, and workstations, you need only the NetBEUI protocol. Note, however, that whatever protocol you choose for the connection must be enabled by the RAS server to which you're connecting. If the remote server is configured to support only TCP/IP for dial-in, for example, you must use TCP/IP for your connection.

TIP If you are using TCP/IP for your remote connection, you can use different settings for the remote connection that are different from your local TCP/IP settings. To specify TCP/IP settings for the connection, click the TCP/IP Settings button to display the TCP/IP Settings dialog box (see fig. 32.19). Set the desired settings, then choose OK. Note that it is generally best to let the server assign your IP addresses automatically.

FIG. 32.19
Enter TCP/IP settings for the connection in the TCP/IP Settings dialog box.

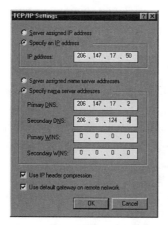

Part
VII

Ch
32

12. Choose OK, then OK again to close the property sheet for the Dial-Up Networking connection.

When you need to connect to the remote network to administer its systems, open the Dial-Up Networking folder on your Windows 95 computer and double-click the connection's icon. After the connection is established, you can start the administration tools and connect to workstations, servers, and domains on the remote LAN.

Managing User Profiles

User profiles enable a user's desktop settings and other interface and operating parameters to be retained from session to session. If a user's profile is stored on a server on the domain, the user can have the same interface and settings regardless of which computer he or she uses to log on to the domain. In addition, profiles enable you to control the types of changes a user can make to his or her working environment. The following section provides an overview of profiles.

Understanding Profiles

A *profile* is a group of settings stored in a special type of Registry file that works in conjunction with a set of folders and shortcuts to create the user's working environment.

When a user logs on, Windows NT reads the user's profile and structures the Windows NT desktop according to the settings in the profile. These settings include such things as desktop colors, sounds, and other Control Panel settings; specific accessory application settings (Notepad, WordPad, and so on); network printer connections; and other user environment settings.

The first type of profile you can assign to a user is called a *personal profile*. The personal profile can be changed by the user from one logon session to another, subject to certain restrictions in the profile itself. This type of profile enables a user to make changes to his or her profile and retain those changes for future logon sessions.

The second type of profile is called a *mandatory profile*. A mandatory profile is almost identical to a personal profile, except that changes do not carry from one session to another. A user has the ability to change certain settings even with a mandatory profile, but those changes are not stored permanently in the user's profile. The profile reverts to its original state for the next logon session.

 T I P   The only difference between a personal profile and a mandatory profile is the name of the Registry file. A personal profile has the file extension DAT, and a mandatory profile uses the file extension MAN. Profile files are explained in more detail in the next section.

If a user has no profile, Windows NT uses a *default profile* from the user's logon workstation. That profile is then saved as the user's profile for future logon sessions.

Profiles serve two primary purposes:

- Provide a unique user interface configuration for each user, and allow that configuration to move with the user from workstation to workstation.

- Enable the administrator to control the types of changes a user can make to his or her working environment.

How Profiles Are Created and Stored

Profiles consist of a Registry file named NTuser.dat, which is a cached copy of the Windows NT Registry subtree KKEY_CURRENT_USER, and a user-specific directory structure containing various shortcuts. NTuser.dat contains settings that define the computer's hardware, installed software, and environment settings. The directory structure and associated shortcuts define the user's desktop environment and application environment.

Local user profiles are stored in a folder matching the user's name within the Profiles folder. The Profiles folder typically resides under the system root, such as \WINNT\PROFILES. The profile for a user named joeb, for example, would be stored in the folder \WINNT\PROFILES\JOEB.

When a user logs on, Windows NT checks the user's account to determine whether it contains a user profile path. If the path is available and the user's profile exists on the path, Windows NT opens and uses the profile. If no profile exists on the path, or no path is specified, Windows NT creates a profile folder on the local computer for the user. Windows NT then copies the contents of the Default User profile folder to the user's profile folder. In addition, the contents of the All Users folder is used to define the user's desktop. When the user logs off, any changes he has made to his working environment are stored in his new profile folder and profile Registry file.

Specifying a Profile Path

You specify a profile path for a user with the User Manager. In User Manager, double-click the user's name whose profile path you want to set. Or, select the user's name and choose User, Properties to display the User Properties dialog box. Click the Profile button to display the User Environment Profile dialog box (see fig. 32.20). In the User Profile Path text box, type the path to the folder containing the user's profile.

FIG. 32.20
You can set a logon script and home directory in addition to a profile path in the User Environment Profile dialog box.

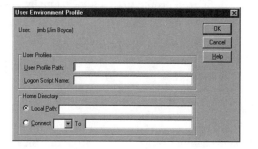

Supporting Roaming Users

A *roaming user* is one who logs on to the network from more than one computer. For consistency, these users should use the same profile regardless of the logon location, giving them a consistent desktop and user settings from one logon session to the next. To ensure that consistency, these users should use a *roaming user profile*.

The only differences between a local profile and a roaming user profile are where the profile is stored and how it is accessed. You can implement a roaming profile in one of three ways.

New Roaming Profile   In each of the three methods for creating a roaming profile, you rely on the user profile path to specify the location of the user's profile. This path must reside on a server to which the user will have access regardless of the logon location. You specify the profile path in the user's account when you create or modify the account through the User Manager as explained in the previous section.

The first method for creating a roaming user profile is to specify only the profile path in the user's account and allow the user's profile to be created automatically from the default profile the first time the user logs on to the domain. Profile changes in subsequent logon sessions will be stored to the user's profile in the specified profile path.

Preconfigured Roaming Profile   If you do not want the default profile to be used to create the user's profile, you should create a profile for the user and copy it to the user's profile path. When the user logs on, that preconfigured profile will be used. Note that you still must specify the path to the user's profile in his account. Profile changes in subsequent logon sessions will be stored to the user's profile.

> **N O T E**   You can't copy a profile using Explorer or other file management utility. Instead, you must use the System object in Control Panel to copy the profile. See the section "Copying Profiles" later in this chapter for an explanation of how to copy profiles. ■

Mandatory Roaming Profile   If you want to restrict changes to a roaming user profile, create a mandatory roaming profile. Specify the path to the user's profile directory in his account. Then, copy a preconfigured profile to that folder. Finally, rename the profile Registry file NTuser.dat to NTuser.man, turning the profile into a mandatory profile. When the user logs on, Windows NT uses the mandatory profile to create the user's work environment. Although the user can make changes to his desktop, those changes are not stored in his profile when he logs off.

Copying Profiles

You probably will want, on occasion, to copy profiles from one location to another. For example, you might need to copy a profile to a user's profile path on a network server so that profile will be applied the next time the user logs on. As mentioned previously in this chapter, you can't copy a profile simply by using Explorer or other file management utility. Instead, you must use the System object in Control Panel.

To copy a profile, open the Control Panel and double-click the System icon. Then, click the User Profiles tab to display the User Profiles page shown in figure 32.21.

From the list of stored user profiles, select the profile you want to copy. Then, choose the Copy To button to display the Copy To dialog box. In the text box on the Copy To dialog box, type the path to the folder in which you want to copy the profile, or click the Browse button to browse for the folder. Click OK when you're satisfied with the folder location.

FIG. 32.21
All profiles created on the computer appear in the User Profiles page.

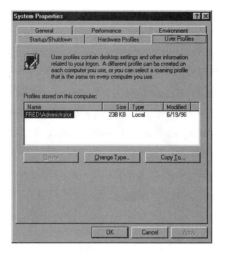

How Profiles Are Updated

Under Windows NT 3.5x, user profiles are stored as a single file with either a USR file extension (personal profile) or MAN file extension (mandatory profile). Installing Windows NT 4.0 causes 3.5x local personal profiles to be converted from a single file to a folder containing the user profile and directory structure with shortcuts. Roaming profiles are treated differently, however.

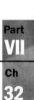

Part
VII
Ch
32

Windows NT retains the 3.5x profile in its original location and creates a new user profile that incorporates the old profile in the new Windows NT 4.0 format. This means that both profiles are available. If the user logs on from a Windows NT 3.5x workstation, the old profile is used. If he logs on from a Windows NT 4.0 workstation, the new profile is used. Only one profile at a time is updated, so changes that the user makes when logged on under the old profile are not incorporated into the new profile, and vice versa.

When Windows NT creates the 4.0 roaming profile from the 3.5x profile, the old user profile is incorporated into the NTuser.dat file. Other settings in the old profile are used to create a directory structure with the same name as the profile file, but with a PDS extension. If the user name is janet, for example, the directory structure for the 4.0 profile is created under the folder janet.pds.

Although the profile file names change, you don't have to make any changes to a user's account to specify the new profile path. During logon, Windows NT 4.0 recognizes when a 3.5x user profile is specified for an account, and automatically looks for the appropriate 4.0

profile. If the user's account specifies the path \\server\profiles\fredz.usr, Windows NT automatically looks for \\server\profiles\fredz.pds. If the user's account specifies a mandatory 3.5x profile, Windows NT performs a similar name translation to open the correct 4.0 profile.

Although Windows NT automatically looks for a new mandatory profile if a 3.5x profile is specified in the user's account, it does not automatically upgrade mandatory profiles to 4.0 format. Instead, you must manually update the profiles using the following steps:

1. Log on to a computer under the user's logon name to create a user profile with the settings you want to apply to the account.

2. Log off, then log back on as administrator.

3. Open the System object in Control Panel and click the User Profile tab to display the User Profile page.

4. Copy the user profile to the user's profile path, giving it a name that matches the 3.5x user profile name, but using the PDM file extension.

5. Open the user's new profile folder and rename the Registry file NTuser.dat to NTuser.man.

Because upgrading mandatory profiles manually can be particularly time-consuming, you should consider using system policies as an alternative to mandatory profiles. System policies are explained later in the section "Using System Policies."

 TIP   Because Windows NT 4.0 does not include the User Profile Editor included with previous versions, you might want to use system policies in place of all user profiles. The System Policy Editor included with 4.0 enables you to define the same types of settings as previously available under the User Profile Editor, along with many others.

Using System Policies

Windows NT Server 4.0 introduces a new utility called the System Policy Editor that enables you to edit the *system policy*. A system policy is a combination of user and computer settings that control a user's working environment. In effect, system policies combine a user profile with a computer profile. Just like a user profile, the user policy overwrites the settings in the current user branch in the Registry. The computer policy overwrites the settings for the current local machine branch of the Registry.

The system policy is stored in a file named NTConfig.pol, located in the Netlogon folder of the primary domain controller. When a user logs on, Windows NT checks the Netlogon folder for NTConfig.pol, and if the file exists, uses its contents to overwrite the current user and local machine portions of the user's Registry. Because it is applied to all users who log on to the domain, the system policy provides a means of ensuring a consistent and uniform policy for all users. Even so, you can customize the system policy for specific users, computers, and groups, giving the system policy considerable flexibility. Customizing the system policy is covered in detail later in this chapter in the section "Customizing the System Policy."

 TIP The Netlogon folder does not exist on the PDC by default. To apply a consistent system policy across the domain, you must first create the Netlogon folder in the root of the PDC's hard disk. Then using the System Policy Editor, you create a system policy file and store it in the Netlogon folder. You can specify a different location for a specific user's policy file, but you must do so from the user's computer. This technique, which can overcome conflicts for users who log on from multiple domains, is explained later in the section "Using Manual Update Mode."

Using the System Policy Editor

The System Policy Editor is installed automatically when you install Windows NT Server. Its executable file, poledit.exe, is located in the Windows NT root folder (such as \WINNT). To start the System Policy Editor, choose Start, Programs, Administrative Tools, and System Policy Editor. Figure 32.22 shows the System Policy Editor window.

Part
VII

Ch

32

FIG. 32.22
You create and modify the system policy with the System Policy Editor.

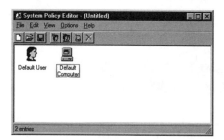

Using System Policy Editor Under Windows NT Workstation

Although the System Policy Editor isn't included with Windows NT Workstation, you can run the utility under Workstation. First, expand the files System Policy Editor files from the appropriate platform folder on the Windows NT Server CD to your computer's hard disk. For Intel platforms, for example, the folder is \I386. To expand the files, open a command prompt and use the following sample commands, specifying appropriate drive letters and paths for your system:

```
expand  d:\i386\poledit.ex_  c:\winnt\poledit.exe
expand  d:\i386\poledit.cn_  c:\winnt\help\poledit.cnt
expand  d:\i386\poledit.hl_  c:\winnt\help\poledit.hlp
```

continues

continued

Next, you need to copy the template files from a working copy of System Policy Editor on a Windows NT Server computer. The two files, common.adm and winnt.adm, are located in the \%systemroot%\inf folder on the server (such as \WINNT\INF). Copy these two files to the INF folder on your Windows NT Workstation computer. Now you're ready to run System Policy Editor on your computer.

Customizing the System Policy

The system policy can contain settings for all users (Default User), all computers (Default Computer), as well as entries for specific users, computers, and groups. When you first start the System Policy Editor, it is empty. To add the Default User and Default Computer objects to the policy, choose File, then New Policy. System Policy Editor adds icons for the Default Computer and Default User to document the area of the editor.

N O T E You don't have to add the Default Computer and Default User settings to the system policy. Instead, you can simply add custom settings for specific users, groups, and computers. The users' profiles will then be used to define their working environments, rather than the system policy. ▄

To modify user settings that apply to all users, double-click the Default User icon, or select the Default User icon and press Enter or choose Edit, Properties. System Policy Editor displays a Default User Properties page (see fig. 32.23) that you use to view and modify user settings.

FIG. 32.23

The Policies page of the Default User Properties sheet enables you to control settings that affect all users' operating environments.

To view or change a setting, expand or collapse the branches in the Policies page. Each branch contains checkboxes that control various settings. Some checkboxes work alone, and others work in conjunction with other controls, such as text boxes and sliders. When you select such a checkbox, these additional controls appear at the bottom of the property page.

The six branches on the Policies page are:

- **Control Panel.** The settings in this branch enable you to deny access to the Display icon in Control Panel and specify other settings that determine the actions, if any, the user can take to change his display.

- **Desktop.** Use this branch to specify wallpaper and color scheme settings.

- **Shell.** This branch contains numerous settings that enable you to control the user's desktop. Some of the restrictions you can apply with this branch include hiding drive icons in My Computer, hiding the Network Neighborhood, disabling the ability to shut down the computer, and hiding all objects on the desktop.

- **System.** With this branch you can prevent the user from accessing the Registry editing tools and restrict the ability to run applications to only those you specify.

- **Windows NT Shell.** This branch contains two sub-branches that enable you to specify custom desktop and application settings, such as a custom Startup folder and custom Network Neighborhood.

- **Windows NT System.** Use this branch to specify whether or not the Autoexec.bat file, if any, is parsed (executed) on the user's computer at logon.

Double-clicking the Default Computer icon displays a Policies page containing settings that control the computer's hardware (see fig. 32.24).

Part
VII

Ch
32

FIG. 32.24

The settings for Default Computer override the Registry settings in HKEY_LOCAL_MACHINE at logon.

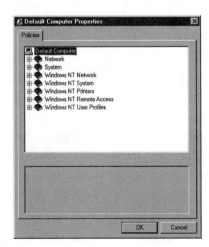

The seven branches on the computer's Policies page are:

- **Network.** Use this branch to specify whether the system policy is updated automatically from the PDC or manually from a different path. See the section "Using Manual Update Mode" later in this chapter for more information on controlling the location of the system policy for specific users.

- **System.** This branch contains two sub-branches that enable you to control SNMP settings and specify which programs, if any, run automatically at startup.

- **Windows NT Network.** With this branch you can specify whether or not Windows NT automatically creates the hidden administrative shares *<drive>*$ and Admin$ when Windows NT starts.

- **Windows NT System.** This branch lets you control logon options such as logon banner and automatic logon. The File system branch controls short file name options and whether the last access file attribute is updated. The FTP logon branch controls various FTP server settings.

- **Windows NT Printers.** Use this branch to control whether the spooler shares its printer information with other printer servers, to set print spooler priority, and to enable an audible warning for errors that occur on remote print servers.

- **Windows NT Remote Access.** With this branch you control a selection of settings that determine connection parameters for RAS.

- **Windows NT User Profiles.** This branch controls settings that determine how user profiles are read.

In general, the settings in the Default User and Default Computer Policies pages are self-explanatory. After you've specified settings as desired, you can add other computers, users, or groups. By adding specific users, groups, and computers to the system policy, you can override the Default User and Default Computer settings for specific users. This ability gives you great flexibility in customizing the system policy while still maintaining consistency where desired.

To add other users, groups, or computers, choose Edit, then Add User, Add Computer, or Add Group. System Policy Editor displays a dialog box that enables you to type the name of the entity or browse for the name. When you add an entity, an icon for it appears in the document portion of the System Policy Editor window. As with the Default User and Default Computer icons, you can double-click the icon for the entity to change its settings. The settings for a user correspond to the settings for the Default User explained previously. The settings for a computer correspond to the settings for the Default Computer explained previously. Settings for a group correspond to user settings (such as the Default User).

After you've applied settings as desired, save the system policy in an appropriate location (choose File, Save As). If you're creating a system policy to apply across a domain, create a Netlogon folder in the root of the PDC, then save the system policy as NTConfig.pol in the Netlogon folder. If you're using manual update mode (described in the next section), save the system policy in whichever folder you'll be specifying for the manual update.

Using Manual Update Mode

When a user logs on, the system policy is taken from the user's logon domain rather than the domain in which the computer resides. This can cause potential problems. Assume, for example, that user joeb has his account in Domain A. Occasionally, he logs on from Domain B, which has a trust relationship with Domain A. Even though he is logging on from Domain B, his system policy comes from Domain A.

Further, Domain B doesn't use system policies. When joeb logs on, the system policy from Domain A overwrites the computer profile settings on the local computer. Joeb then logs off and user maryg, whose account resides in Domain B, logs on. The computer profile settings are not updated; the settings from the Domain A system policy remain in effect. This could result in potential problems or inconsistent logon for maryg and other Domain B users who log on to the same computer.

To overcome this problem, you can implement system policies on all domains. When a user logs on, the system policy from his own domain overwrites the policy in place from the last user. If you don't want to use system policies on all domains, you can instead use *manual update mode* for the system policy. Using manual update mode ensures that the system policy is read from a specific server, regardless of who logs on or where their account and default system policy reside. In effect, this means you are assigning a specific system policy to the computer.

To use manual update mode, follow these steps:

1. Log on to the computer for which you want to specify manual update.
2. Open the System Policy Editor.
3. Choose File, Open Registry to open the Registry on the local computer. The icons Local Computer and Local User appear in the document area to indicate you're editing the local Registry.
4. Double-click the Local Computer icon to open its property sheet.
5. Expand the Network branch and the System policies update sub-branch to display the Remote update setting (see fig. 32.25).

Part
VII

Ch
32

FIG. 32.25

Use the scroll bar beside the settings area to view all of the settings for remote update.

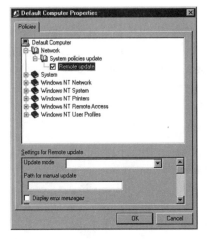

6. Enable the Remote Update check box.

7. In the settings area of the page, set the update mode to manual.

8. In the path text box, type the path where the system policy file will be stored.

9. Choose OK and close the System Policy Editor, choosing Yes to store changes to the Registry.

N O T E The settings for remote update include two checkboxes. The checkbox labeled Display Error Messages, when enabled, causes error messages to be displayed when the system policy can't be applied. The checkbox labeled Load Balancing, when enabled, allows computers running Windows 95 to read the system policy from more than one logon server, which can avoid a bottleneck on large networks in which many users access the same system policy file. ▨

Setting Account Policies

The *account policy* determines how passwords are handled for all user accounts and controls global logon parameters. You should rely on the account policy in conjunction with the system policy to provide complete control over logon behavior.

To specify account policy settings, first open User Manager and select the domain whose account policy you want to set. Then, choose Policies, Account to display the Account Policy dialog box (see fig. 32.26).

FIG. 32.26
Specify global logon
parameters with the
Account Policy dialog
box.

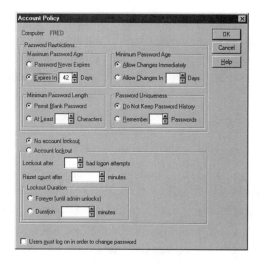

The following list summarizes the settings you can specify in the Account Policy dialog
box:

Part
VII

Ch
32

- **Domain.** This read-only entry specifies the name of the domain whose account
  policy you're modifying.

- **Maximum Password Age.** Use this group to specify when, if ever, user passwords
  expire. You can specify a value between 1 and 999 days, or choose Password Never
  Expires to allow users to keep the same password indefinitely. Use this option to
  force a user to change his or her password after the specified period of time has
  elapsed.

- **Minimum Password Age.** Use this group to specify how long a password must be
  used before the user can change it. For example, you might want to restrict a user's
  right to change his or her password in the first few weeks of employment.

- **Minimum Password Length.** Use this group to specify the minimum number of
  characters each password must be. You can specify a value from 1 to 14 characters
  as the minimum. For best security, you should not use the Permit Blank Password
  option. Specifying a larger number of characters for a password helps reduce the
  risk that an unauthorized user could guess or hack the password.

- **Password Uniqueness.** This group enables you to control whether a user can reuse an old password. If you don't care how often or soon a user can reuse a password, choose the Do Not Keep Password History option button. Otherwise, specify
  a value from 1 to 8. Preventing the user of old passwords helps increase system
  security by preventing unauthorized access through old, compromised passwords.

- **No Account Lockout.** If you choose this option, users are never locked out of the system, regardless of the number of failed login attempts they make (such as specifying an incorrect password). Although this option accommodates novice or infrequent users who tend to forget their passwords, locking users out after a specific number of failed logon attempts increases system security.

- **Account Lockout.** Use this option and group to specify how many failed logon attempts a user can make before being locked out of the system, and how soon the user can re-attempt logon.

- **Lockout Duration.** This option specifies the duration of time this user's account is locked. Choosing Forever requires the system administrator to unlock the account. Or you can specify the length of time in minutes the account will be locked.

- **Forcibly Disconnect Remote Users From Server When Logon Hours Expire.** Mark this checkbox if you want the user to be automatically logged off when the logon time defined for his account expires. (This item appears only when administering the account policy for a domain.)

- **Users Must Log On In Order To Change Password.** If you mark this checkbox, a user whose password has expired must have an administrator set a new password for his account. If this checkbox is cleared, the user can change his password without notifying the administrator.

When you're satisfied with the account policies, choose OK to close the dialog box.

From Here...

This chapter provided an overview of concepts and tools you need to administer user accounts, groups, and security options such as rights, permissions, and policies. The following chapters will help you administer other parts of the system.

- Chapter 6, "Advanced and Custom Setup Issues," explores other administration-oriented tasks that pertain to Windows NT installation.

- Chapter 33, "Managing Server Properties," explores server-related management tasks such as directory replication, file system management, and managing printers.

Managing Server Properties

by Jim Boyce

Windows NT Workstation's peer-to-peer network capability means that even though your computer's primary function is that of a workstation, it can also function as a server. Your workstation might be sharing files and folders or acting as a print server. It's therefore important for you to understand a range of server management concepts and tasks as they relate to your workstation. ∎

Share resources

Sharing resources involves not only making a resource available to other users on the network, but controlling access to it through share permissions

Protect local resources

You use object permissions to control access to local resources, and those permissions can be different from share permissions on the same object.

Replicate directories

Directory replication is an excellent mechanism for mirroring and distributing files across a LAN.

Manage printers

Windows NT enables a high degree of control over printers and the appearance and scheduling of users' print jobs.

Controlling Resource Access

As explained briefly in Chapter 32, "Administering Users," you can apply two different sets of permissions to an object. One set, called *object permissions*, applies local access to the object. The object permissions determine the level of access users and groups have to a resource when they are logged on locally to the workstation and accessing the resource locally.

The other set of permissions, called *share permissions*, apply to a resource that is shared on the network. The share permissions determine the level of access users and groups have to the share resource from across the LAN. The types of permissions you can apply for both share and object permissions are the same. Also, you apply share permissions in much the same way as object permissions, with only a slight variation in how you initiate the process. This chapter explains permissions and how to set them, both for objects and shares.

Understanding Permissions

In Windows NT, permissions determine the authority a user has to access certain types of resources such as files, directories, printers, and other objects and services. The permissions that apply to specific objects depend on the object's type. The permissions for a printer, for example, are different from the permissions for a file. In addition, file permissions vary according to the type of file system being used. You have much finer control over access on NTFS file systems than FAT file systems.

N O T E You can set object and share permissions on individual files under the NTFS file system. You can't set permissions on individual files in a FAT file system, although you can set a file's attributes. On both file systems you can set share permissions on a folder, although FAT supports only a limited set of permissions compared to the full range offered by NTFS. ■

You can apply the following permissions as object permissions and share permissions to directories on NTFS volumes:

- **No Access.** This permission prevents the user from accessing the directory in any way, even if the user belongs to a group that has been granted access to the directory.

- **List.** With this permission the user can only list the files and subdirectories in this directory and change to a subdirectory of this directory. The user can't access new files created in the directory.

- **Read.** This permission enables the user to read and execute files.

- **Add.** With this permission a user can add new files to the directory, but can't read or change existing files.

- **Add & Read.** This permission combines the Read and Add permissions.

- **Change.** With this permission a user can read and add files to a directory, and change the contents of existing files.

- **Full Control.** With this permission a user can read and change files, add new files, change permissions for the directory and its files, and take ownership of the directory and its files.

- **Special Directory Access.** This selection enables you to set a group of permissions that include Read, Write, Execute, Delete, Change Permissions, and Take Ownership.

You can assign the following permission to files on NTFS volumes:

- **No Access.** This permission prevents the user from accessing the file, even if he belongs to a group that has been granted access to the file.

- **Read.** This right enables the user to read and execute files.

- **Change.** With this right the user can read, modify, and delete the file.

- **Full Control.** This right enables the user to read, modify, delete, set permissions for, and take ownership of the file.

- **Special File Access.** This selection enables you to set a group of permissions that include Read, Write, Execute, Delete, Change Permission, and Take Ownership.

N O T E Don't confuse *rights* with *permissions*. Rights apply globally and permissions apply to specific objects. ■

Part
VII

Ch
33

On a FAT file system, you can assign the No Access, Read, Change, and Full Control share permissions to a shared folder, but you cannot apply permissions to specific files on a FAT file system. Instead, files are subject to the share permissions applied to the directory that contains them. Perhaps more important is the fact that you can't set object permissions on directories or files on a FAT file system. This essentially makes it impossible to provide any degree of local protection for FAT volumes, although you still can protect FAT volumes from unauthorized access by remote users. If a user can log onto a computer, he can gain access to any folder or file in a FAT volume on that computer.

A set of additional permissions enable to you control access to printers. These printer-related permissions are:

- **No Access.** This permission prevents any access to the printer and its queue.

- **Print.** Users with this permission can print to the printer, but can't change the queue or any other printer properties.

- **Manage Documents.** This permission enables a user to control settings for individual documents in the queue, and to pause, resume, restart, and delete documents in a queue. It does not provide print permission, which must be granted separately.

- **Full Control.** This permission gives a user complete control over a printer, including printing and managing documents. The user also can delete a printer and change its properties.

N O T E Unlike folders and files, printers receive only one set of permissions that apply both to local users and remote users. ▪

Now that you understand permissions, you're ready to begin applying them. The following section introduces sharing, which will lead you to applying share permissions.

An Overview of Sharing

One of the most common server-related tasks you'll perform on a workstation is setting up disk resources to be shared. Windows NT Workstation's peer-to-peer network capability is an important mechanism for sharing data, even on networks that contain dedicated servers running Windows NT Server or other network operating systems. For example, peer-to-peer sharing enables you to share resources among departments or workgroups on the network without imposing an additional load on the dedicated server(s). Because only a select group of users needs access to the shared resources in this example, placing the resources on a dedicated server is probably not efficient use of it.

Using peer-to-peer resource sharing brings up a few important considerations. First is security. As explained in Chapter 32, "Administering Users," a user must have an account on a workstation to access any resources the workstation is sharing. Or, if Windows NT Server is installed on the network and domains are being used, the user must have an account in the workstation's domain (or in a trusted domain). This means that if you're not using domains, a workstation sharing its resources must contain a local user account for every user on the network who needs to access those resources. Domains therefore provide a much simpler means of managing accounts and resource access.

▶ **See** "Creating and Modifying User Accounts," **p. 704**

Another important consideration for resource sharing is consistent resource availability. Once you've shared a resource on a workstation, that resource will continue to be available regardless of who is logged on to the workstation, and even when no one is logged onto the workstation. This means that you, as an administrator or primary user of the workstation, can set up a resource to be shared, and have that resource available even when you're not logged on to your workstation. Perhaps more important, you can prevent other users who do log on to the workstation from removing the resource from sharing.

To share a resource on a workstation, you must log on to the workstation as a member of the Administrators or Power Users groups. Only these two groups contain the built-in ability to share and stop sharing directories and printers. Someone who logs on to the workstation as a member of the Users group, for example, will not even see the sharing commands in Explorer or other places from which an Administrator or Power User would be able to share resources. This control over who can and can't share resources is an effective means of ensuring security (unauthorized shares can't be created) and continued resource availability (shared resources can't be removed from sharing by an unauthorized user).

The only thing that will prevent other users on the LAN from accessing a shared resource on a workstation is if someone shuts down the workstation. You can take steps to slow down users from shutting down a workstation, but can't prevent it altogether (there's nothing you can do to prevent them from punching the power button, for example).

The Disable Shut Down Command in the Shell branch of the system policy (user) removes the Shut Down command from the Start menu for any user to whom the policy is applied. Also, the option Enable Shutdown From Authentication Dialog Box in the \Windows NT System\Logon branch of the system policy (computer) removes the Shut Down command from the Logon dialog box for the selected computer, preventing the user from choosing to shut down the computer during logon.

▶ **See** "Using System Policies," **p. 732**

A better option than using the system policy to remove the shutdown command, however, is to set the user rights on each workstation to prevent users from shutting down the computer. With this method, the Shut Down command still appears in the Start menu, and the Shut Down the Computer and Restart the Computer options still appear in the Shut Down Windows dialog box. But if the user doesn't have the right to shut down the computer, Windows NT displays an error message to inform the user that he can't shut it down. The user still retains the right to log off, however.

Part

VII

Ch

33

TIP Give your users a reminder each time they log on not to shut down or turn off their computers. To do so, open the System Policy Editor and open the Default Computer object. In the \Windows NT System\Logon branch, enable the Logon Banner option. In the text box for the setting, enter a reminder such as "Don't shut down; log off instead."

Applying Share Permissions

You typically set share permissions when you share an object, and you can modify those permissions at any time. You can set permissions using more than one method, which vary according to the type of resource. You can share directories and files through Explorer or File Manager. This section focuses on Explorer to explain how to apply share permissions.

Before you can set permissions on a directory, you must share the directory. To do so, follow these steps:

1. Open Explorer (or a folder window), then locate and select the directory.

2. Right-click the directory and choose Sharing to display the Sharing property page (see fig. 33.1).

FIG. 33.1
Use the Sharing property page to share a directory.

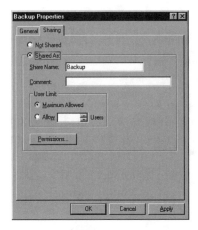

3. Choose the Shared As option button.

4. Windows NT uses the directory name as the default share name. If you want to use a different name, highlight the name in the Share Name text box and type a different name.

5. Type an optional comment for the share in the Comment text box.

6. In the User Limit group, specify the maximum number of users who can connect to the share, or choose the Maximum Allowed to allow an unlimited number of users to access the share.

7. Click the Permissions button to display the Access Through Share Permissions dialog box (see fig. 33.2).

8. To change a permission, select the group you want to change from the Name list, then select the desired permission from the Type of Access drop-down list.

FIG. 33.2
By default, Windows
NT grants full control
to everyone.

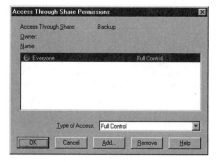

9. To add a group or user, click the <u>A</u>dd button to display the Add Users and Groups dialog box.

10. Select the users and groups you want to add, then choose <u>A</u>dd, followed by OK.

11. Repeat step 8 to change the permissions for specific groups and users, then choose OK.

N O T E To set permissions on a directory that is already shared, open Explorer and select the directory. Or, open a folder window and select the directory. Then, right-click the directory and choose S<u>h</u>aring. Click the <u>P</u>ermissions button to begin changing or adding permissions. ▨

You can set share permissions on individual files only on NTFS volumes. To set permissions on files, select the files in Explorer, then right-click a file in the selection and choose P<u>r</u>operties. Click the Security tab, then click the <u>P</u>ermissions button to display the File Permissions dialog box (see fig. 33.3). Adding and modifying group and user permissions is then similar to the process described previously for directories.

Part
VII

Ch
33

FIG. 33.3
You can set permis-
sions on individual
files on NTFS
volumes.

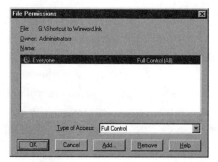

In addition to using Explorer or folder windows to share folders and files, you can use File Manager. If you've been using a previous version of Windows NT, then File Manager should be familiar to you. Although the same features are available in File Manager as in

Explorer, you might prefer to use Explorer because it brings all disks, printers, and other objects under a common interface. To run File Manager, choose Start, Run, and enter **winfile** in the Open combo box of the Run dialog box.

 One advantage File Manager has over Explorer is its support for MDI, enabling you to open multiple document windows to view different (or the same) folders within the File Manager application window. Explorer doesn't support MDI, but Explorer does enable you to expand the folder tree without actually opening a folder. This means you can open a folder and select files in the folder, then collapse/expand the tree to locate another folder. You then could drag the selected files from the opened folder to the other folder.

If you want separate windows, such as to see different views of the same folder, just open another instance of Explorer.

Managing Shared Directories with Server Manager

Although you can use Explorer to manage shared directories, you can also use Server Manager to manage them. Using Server Manager has the advantage of bringing all shared directories into a single list, making it easier for you to view all shared directories at once. In addition, Server Manager enables you to manage shared resources on other computers across the network.

Server Manager is included with Windows NT Server and installs by default when you install Server. Server Manager is not included with Windows NT Workstation. You can, however, run Server Manager under Workstation. To do so, open the \Clients\Srvtools\Winnt folder on the Windows NT Server CD, and copy the file Srvmgr.exe to your Windows NT system directory, and copy the files Srvmgr.cnt and Srvmgr.hlp to your Windows NT Help folder. Then, run Srvmgr.exe.

Replicating Directories

In a networked environment, particularly in a domain, it's often helpful to be able to duplicate a set of directories and their files to more than one computer. Logon scripts are a good example. Because backup domain controllers can authenticate user logon, you should duplicate logon scripts from the primary domain controller to the backup domain controller(s) to reduce network traffic—rather than pulling the logon scripts from the PDC, the BDCs can open them locally. Duplicating directories in this way is called *directory replication.*

You can use directory replication to replicate any type of file. For example, you might want to replicate macros, document templates, forms, or any other type of data files needed by multiple users.

A computer that copies its directories to other computers is *exporting* those directories. A computer that receives the copied files *imports* those directories. Computers running Windows NT Server can export and import directories. Computers running Windows NT Workstation, however, can only import directories. This chapter explains how to configure directory import under Windows NT Workstation. For a discussion of configuring directory export under Windows NT Server, refer to the *Windows NT Installation and Configuration Handbook*, from Que.

Importing Directories

You use the Directory Replication dialog box to establish the import of directories to a computer. The following steps explain the process:

1. Open the Control Panel and double-click the Server icon.
2. In the Server dialog box, choose the Replication button to display the Directory Replication dialog box.
3. Choose the Import Directories option button to enable directory import.
4. In the To Path text box, specify the path to the local directory in which you want the imported directories stored (by default, \Winnt\System32\Repl\Import).
5. Click the Add button under the From List to display the Select Domain dialog box.
6. Select the domain containing the computer from which you want to import, then select the computer itself.
7. Choose OK to close the Directory Replication dialog box, then choose OK to close the Properties dialog box.

Managing Printers

Setting up printers to be shared across the network is a relatively simple process under Windows NT. Some of the concepts involved in printer sharing are not self-evident, however, and understanding these topics will help you set up and manage print servers and shared printers.

Overview of Local Printing

A *print device* under Windows NT is any physical output device such as a printer or plotter. Print devices are represented in Windows NT by virtual printer objects referred to in Windows NT terminology as *printers*. Each printer is represented by a printer driver,

Part
VII

Ch
33

which is a program that converts the general graphics commands generated by Windows NT and applications into printer commands specific to each print device. A PostScript driver, for example, converts application print output to PostScript commands to drive the print device.

Printers are associated with different output locations. A printer might be associated with an LPT port, for example. Or, the printer might be associated with a file or remote print share. In effect, this means that print output can be redirected to a file or across the network to a remote printer with little or no setup by the user. Once the printer is associated with the remote device or file, Windows NT takes care or routing the data accordingly.

Because it is a multitasking, multi-user environment, Windows NT naturally supports multiple concurrent printers and print jobs. Documents that are pending printing reside in a *print queue*. The queue is controlled by a print server (such as a Windows NT Server computer or Netware server). The print server processes the documents in the queue, sending them in turn to the print device.

When you print to a local printer (one connected directly to your computer), the print job is sent from the application to the printer (print driver), which processes the document and places it in a local queue for the specified printer. Windows NT then takes care of moving the document from the queue to the print device. Through multitasking and multithreading, printing is handled in the background, enabling you to regain control of the workstation to continue working while the document(s) print. In fact, you can resume work almost immediately on a document that is printing.

Remote Printing

The Windows NT network redirector enables you to easily print to a remote shared printer as if it were a local printer. You simply create an association between the printer on your computer with the remote share. After this one-time configuration, you can print to the remote printer just by selecting the appropriate printer from your application's Print Setup dialog box. You create the association between your local printer and the remote share when you set up the printer on your workstation. Or, you can use the Ports property page for the printer to associate the printer with a remote share (see fig. 33.4).

If the remote share has already been set up on your workstation, its entry appears in the list. To connect to a newly established share or one you have never used, you can click the Add Port button, select Local Port, then specify the name for the remote share (such as \\server\sharename).

FIG. 33.4
Choose an existing
port or click the Add
Port button to connect
the printer to a new
remote printer share.

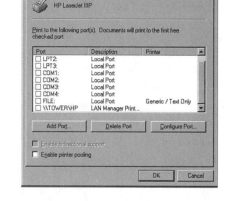

N O T E When you print to a remote printer share, you're actually printing through two different
queues. The print job goes first to the local printer's queue then Windows NT sends the
documents in the queue to the remote printer. The print job moves so quickly from the local
queue to the remote queue that if you need to modify the print job in some way (delete it, for
example), you'll have to do so in the remote print queue, rather than the local queue. ■

Windows NT greatly simplifies printer setup, particularly for the inexperienced user. Users on Windows NT or Windows 95 workstations can connect to remote printers shared by a Windows NT print server without first having the necessary printer driver installed. When the client connects to the server, your workstation automatically downloads and installs the necessary printer driver on your computer. For example, assume you need to print to a new remote printer, and have never used that type of printer before (so the printer driver isn't installed on your computer). Further, you don't have the Windows NT CD to install the needed driver. Fortunately, you don't need the CD. You simply open the Network Neighborhood, locate the shared printer, then right-drag it to your desktop. Your workstation automatically downloads the driver from the server, and you're ready to print.

N O T E The required printer driver must be installed on the remote print server for your
computer to be able to automatically download the driver. ■

When a new printer driver is installed on a Windows NT print server, Windows NT clients that connect to that shared printer automatically download the new driver. Windows 95 clients, however, do not automatically update the driver. Instead, these clients must manually update the driver. To update a driver under Windows 3.x, you must have the updated

Part
VII

Ch
33

Windows 3.x version of the driver, and install it as you would any other Windows 3.x printer driver. Under Windows 95, you can update the driver by deleting the existing printer and running the Add Printer wizard to reinstall the printer from the remote network server.

Computers running MS-DOS and Windows 3.x also can connect to and use printers on Windows NT print servers. Unlike Windows NT and Windows 95 clients, however, these clients must install the printer driver manually because automatic installation ability isn't built into the remote operating system. For the same reason, Windows NT clients that connect to print servers running other operating systems such as LAN Manager 2.x or Novell Netware must install drivers manually.

Installing a Printer

Under Windows NT, you can install a printer in three primary ways:

- **To your computer.** You can install a printer driver on your computer to service a printer connected to your computer.

- **For your computer, but connected to a remote computer.** You can install a printer driver on your computer to enable you to use a printer connected to another computer on the network.

- **To a remote computer.** You can install a printer driver to a remote computer running Windows NT Server or Workstation, setting up the driver on that computer (not on your own) to enable other users on the network to use the remote printer.

Windows NT brings all printer access and management under one object—the Printers folder. Use the Printers folder to install new printers.

Installing a Local Printer Through the Printers Folder   Installing a printer through the Printers folder is easy, thanks to a wizard that steps you through the process. Because the wizard simplifies the task, this section just provides an overview of how to start the wizard and what information you'll need to provide to set up the printer.

To start the Add Printer wizard, open My Computer and double-click the Printers folder. In addition to icons for any printers that are already set up, the Printers folder contains an Add Printer icon. Double-click the Add Printer icon to start the Add Printer wizard.

When the Add Printer wizard starts, it prompts you to specify whether you are installing a local printer or connecting to a remote print server. If the printer is connected to your computer, choose the My Computer option button and click Next. The Printer Wizard then displays a list from which you can choose the manufacturer and model of the printer you're installing. Select the appropriate printer and choose Next.

Next, Add Printer prompts you to select the port for the printer (see fig. 33.5). In addition to local LPT and COM ports, you can select the FILE: port to configure the printer to print to a file, rather than to a physical port. The printer driver will prompt for a file name each time a user prints to that printer. You'll also find port listings for previously-connected network printers, enabling you to redirect the driver to a network print server.

FIG. 33.5
Select the port for the printer.

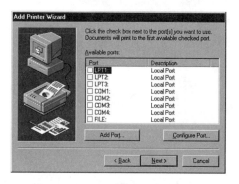

 To add another port selection, choose the Add button and follow the prompts to add the necessary port. To configure an existing port, select the port and then click the Configure Port button. You'll be presented with a dialog box to set appropriate properties for the port.

You can select more than one port for the driver. This enables you to use a single driver for multiple printers, forming a *printer pool*. The printers behave as a single logical printer, and Windows NT prints to the first available port. After you choose the port(s) for the printer, click Next.

N O T E   For specific tips on creating and using a printer pool, see the section, "Using a Printer Pool," later in this chapter. ■

The wizard then prompts you for a name for the printer. This is the name by which the printer is listed on the network and to your own local applications. You also have the option of setting the printer as your computer's default printer. Make the appropriate selections and click Next.

In the next dialog box (see fig. 33.6), you have the option of sharing the printer on the network. Choose the Shared option button to share the printer. When you choose the Shared option button, you then have the option of installing drivers for other clients such as Windows 95 or other Windows NT platforms. To ensure that the drivers are available for all users who might want to print to the printer, select all of the operating platforms present on your network. Then, click Next. The remainder of the installation process is

Part
VII

Ch
33

self-explanatory. If you selected other platforms to install, the wizard will prompt you for the location of the driver files. For Windows NT 4.0 and 3.51, you'll find the drivers on the respective Windows NT CDs. The Windows 95 drivers are located on the Windows 95 CD.

FIG. 33.6

You can copy drivers for multiple platforms when you install a printer.

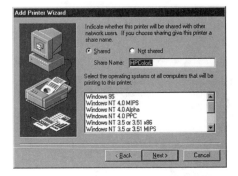

Installing a Remote Printer Through the Printers Folder

You can install a printer driver on your local computer to enable you to access a printer on a remote print server. If the remote server already contains the driver for your platform, you don't need the driver source files yourself—the Add Printer wizard will instead copy the driver files across the network from the remote print server. Otherwise, you simply supply the path to the files (either locally or through a network location).

To install a remote printer for your computer, open the Printers folder in My Computer and start the Add New Printer wizard. When the wizard prompts you in the first wizard page to choose the location of the printer, choose the Network printer server option button. After you click Next, the wizard browses the network and prompts you to select the printer you want to install (see fig. 33.7).

FIG. 33.7

Select the computer to which the printer is connected, then select the printer itself.

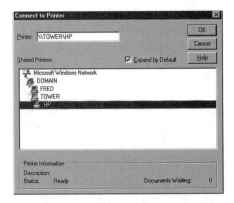

Select the network printer you want to install, then choose OK. Then click Finish in the next dialog box to complete the installation. The wizard will copy the file automatically across the network.

Installing a Printer to a Remote Server In addition to installing a local or network printer on your computer, you can install a printer to a computer across the network. This means you can install a printer driver to a server across the network, extending your ability to manage devices and resources remotely. Although the process for installing a remote printer isn't intuitive, it's extremely easy once you know how.

In essence, all you have to do is run the Add Printer Wizard on the remote computer. To do so, first log on to the local workstation as a member of a group with the necessary access rights to create printers (Administrator, Power User). Then, open the Network Neighborhood and locate and open the folder for the remote server. Or, choose Start, Run, and enter the computer's name (such as \\ *server*) in the Open text box, then choose OK. When the remote computer's folder opens, you'll see a Printers folder along with any other resources shared by the remote computer. Double-click the remote Printers folder to open it.

In the remote Printers folder, double-click the Add Printer icon. The Add Printer Wizard dialog box shown in figure 33.8 appears. The Remote Print Server option button is automatically selected with the remote server's computer name specified. Choose Next, then select the ports to be associated with the remote printer. Choose ports on the remote printer to be associated with the printer, not ports on your local computer. Continue with the wizard to set up the printer, including enabling sharing if desired, as explained in the previous sections. When the wizard is finished, you'll see an icon for the new printer in the remote Printers folder.

Part
VII

Ch
33

FIG. 33.8
Running the Add Printer Wizard on a remote computer installs a printer on that remote node.

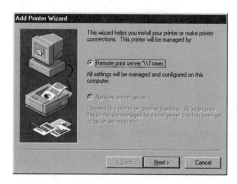

Setting Printer Properties

Whether you're working with a local or remote printer, you control its options by setting the printer's *properties*. You can access and set a printer's properties through Explorer, the Network Neighborhood, or the Printers folder. Just locate the printer in Explorer, the Network Neighborhood, or Printers folder. Right-click the printer, then choose Properties from the context menu.

Explorer, Network Neighborhood, and Printers folder offer a better method of setting printer properties because unlike Print Manager, they provide a unified interface to all of the printer's properties in a tabbed property sheet. To view a printer's property sheet, select the printer in Explorer, Network Neighborhood, or Printers folder, then right-click the printer and choose Properties.

N O T E The various printer properties are generally self-explanatory to the average system administrator. For help with a specific property, display the page containing the property control, then click the Help button. ■

Sharing a Printer

You have the option of sharing a printer when you install the printer (explained previously in the section, "Installing a Printer"). You also can share a printer at any time after it is installed. To do so, follow these steps:

1. Locate the printer in Explorer, Network Neighborhood, or the Printers folder.

2. Right-click the printer and choose Properties to display the printer's property sheet.

3. Click the Sharing tab to display the Sharing property page (see fig. 33.9).

FIG. 33.9

Use the Sharing page to share a printer.

4. Choose the Shared option button, then type in the Share Name text box the name by which you want the printer shared.

5. Click the Security tab to display the Security property page, then click the Permissions button to display the Printer Permissions dialog box (see fig. 33.10).

FIG. 33.10

Use the Printer Permissions dialog box to control which users can access the printer.

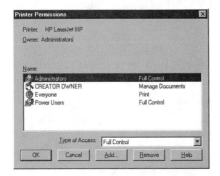

6. Add and remove groups and users as desired, then choose OK.

N O T E   See the earlier section, "Controlling Resource Access," for information on setting access permissions. ▨

7. Choose OK on the printer's property sheet to close the sheet.

Managing Print Queues

As a system administrator, you're probably familiar with managing print queues. Rather than deal with the subject in depth, this section briefly explains how to access print queues using the new Windows NT 4.0 interface.

To access a printer's queue, locate the printer in the Printers folder, Network Neighborhood, or Explorer. Select the printer and press Enter, or just double-click the printer. When you do, the printer's queue window will open (see fig. 33.11).

FIG. 33.11

Use a printer's queue window to control pending print jobs and other printer functions.

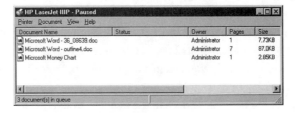

Part
VII

Ch
33

Any pending print jobs appear in the printer's queue, including an indication of the job's status. In addition to pausing and resuming specific print jobs, you also can pause and resume the printer itself, which places all pending jobs on hold.

If you have the necessary access privileges, you can set the properties of each document in the queue. Otherwise, you are restricted to setting properties only for jobs that you have created (depending on your group membership and corresponding access permissions).

To view and set a pending document's properties, double-click the document, right-click the document and choose Properties from the context menu, or select the document and choose Document, Properties. A property sheet for the document appears (see fig. 33.12), which lets you schedule the job, set its priority, set page and paper properties, and set specific printer properties for the print job.

FIG. 33.12
Use a document's property sheet to control how and when it prints.

Using a Printer Pool

As briefly explained previously in this chapter, you can use one printer driver to control multiple printers. Two or more identical printer devices associated with one printer is called a *printer pool*. For example, assume that your print server has two identical HP LaserJet 4 printers, one connected to LPT1 and the other connected to COM2 (or to another LPT port). Rather than install two separate instances of the HP LaserJet 4 printer and manage them separately, you can install one copy of the driver and tie multiple printer ports (in this case, LPT1 and COM2) to the driver. Because one printer driver controls all printer devices in the pool, all devices in the pool act as a single logical device. For example, setting printer properties affects all print devices in the pool.

The primary advantage to using a printer pool, other than simplifying configuration, is that a printer pool overcomes the potential bottleneck of a stalled printer. If one printer runs out of paper, the server simply sends the remaining pending print jobs to the next available printer in the pool. When the stalled printer comes back online, the server again begins sending documents to it. Printer pools also minimize the amount of time any one user must wait for a print job to be completed, because the next available printer is always selected for the next pending print job.

You can associate print devices across the network with a printer pool. In the previous example with the HP LaserJet 4 printers connected to one server, you might also have two other LaserJet 4 printers connected to two other computers on the network. All four of these printers can be pooled under one driver, and configuration changes will apply to all four.

 T I P Because you can associate network ports to a printer driver along with multiple local ports, the print devices in a printer pool don't have to be connected to the same physical server. If your users retrieve their own print jobs from the printer, scattering printers in a pool across the network can be very confusing to the users, because they have no way of knowing which printer will actually print their job.

If the workstations are running the Windows NT Messenger Service, the users will receive messages informing them when the print job is complete and specifying on which port the job was printed. Even so, it's a good idea to connect multiple printers in a pool to the same server, or localize the printers in one office or workplace area. Also, consider using separator pages to separate users' documents from one another.

**Part
VII**

**Ch
33**

To set up a printer pool, first install the printer driver on the computer that will act as the printer server. Then, open the Printers folder and display the property sheet for the printer. Click the Ports tab to display the Ports property page, as shown in figure 33.13.

In the Ports page, select all of the currently installed local ports to which the common printer devices are connected. To add remote printers to the pool, click the Add Port button to display the Add Port dialog box. Select Local Port from the list, then choose OK. In the Port Name dialog box, type the name for the remote printer, such as *server*\ *printshare*, then choose OK. Windows NT checks the network for the shared printer, and if it exists, add the remote share to the Ports list on the printer's Ports property page.

Next, choose Close to close the Add Port dialog box (or add other ports if desired, then choose Close). In the Ports page, enable the newly-added remote ports by enabling their check boxes. When you have selected all of the appropriate ports, choose OK. Your printer pool is now set up.

FIG. 33.13

Use the Ports page to associate multiple ports, locally and across the network, with a single printer driver.

Using Custom Separator Pages

When you configure a network printer share, consider enabling separator pages for the printer. Separator pages print at the beginning of each new document to identify the print job, its owner, and other information that helps the person managing the printer route the print job to the right person.

You can choose one of three standard separator pages by opening the printer's property sheet, then choosing the Separator Page button from the printer's General property page. Click the Browse button, then select the separator page file you want to use. Separator page files are ASCII files containing special commands that configure the printer and retrieve data during printing to incorporate that data (such as user and document name) on the separator page. The three default separator pages are described in Table 33.1.

Table 33.1 Default Separator Files

File Name	Description	Compatibility
Sysprint.sep	Prints page before each document	PostScript
Pscript.sep	Switches printer to PostScript, but doesn't print a separator page for each document	PostScript
Pcl.sep	Switches the printer to PCL and prints a separator page before each document	PCL

To create a custom separator page, copy one of the existing separator pages (whichever is appropriate to the printer in question). Edit the new file with a word processor such as WordPad. Change the commands in the file as desired. Table 33.2 lists the separator page commands.

Table 33.2   Separator Page Commands

Command	Function
\	The first line of the separator file defines the command delimiter for the file. In this example, the \ character is used as the delimiter, but you can specify a different character, if desired.
\N	Specifies the user name of the user who submitted the print job.
\I	Specifies the document number.
\D	Specifies the date the document was printed.
\T	Specifies the time the document was printed.
\L*xxx*	Prints all characters following the \L (*xxx*) until another command delimiter is encountered or until the defined separator page width (see \W*nn*) is reached.
\F*pathname*	The contents of the file *pathname* are printed, unmodified, beginning on the next line.
\H*nn*	Sends the hexidecimal code *nn* to the printer, enabling you to send printer control codes to the printer.
\W*nn*	Specifies the width in characters of the separator page. The default width is 80 characters, and the maximum width is 256 characters.
\B\S	Prints characters using single-width block characters until \U is encountered.
\E	Page eject.
n	Skip *n* number of lines. Specify a value of 0 through 9. Specifying 0 causes printing to move to the next line.
\B\M	Prints characters using double-width characters until \U is encountered.
\U	Turns off block character printing.

Part
VII

Ch
33

Setting Printer Server Properties

In addition to setting printer-specific options, you can set global print server options for each print server. To locate these print server options, open the Printers folder on the server and choose File, Server Properties to display the Print Server Properties sheet shown in figure 33.14.

FIG. 33.14

The Print Server Properties sheet controls print server settings globally for the server, rather than by specific printer.

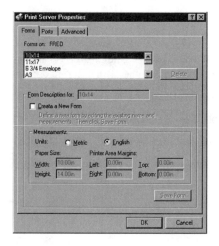

Using Forms   Windows NT uses the term *forms* to refer to page printer configurations. A form defines the page size and print area margins. Each form is identified by name and is associated by the printer administrator with a specific printer tray. Rather than choosing which tray to use, which could be difficult if the printer is located across the network or the user is unfamiliar with the printer, the user can instead choose which form to use. The print server automatically determines from which tray to pull the paper.

Windows NT includes a number of predefined forms. You can view these predefined form settings by opening the Printers folder on the print server and choosing File, Server Properties. The Forms page (refer to fig. 33.14) contains a list of the forms on the print server. As you select a form, its settings appear in the Measurements group of controls. To create a new form, enable the Create New Form check box, which enables the controls in the Measurements group. Specify the desired settings for the new form, then type a new name for the form in the Form Description text box. Then, click the Save Form button to save the form in the list.

To associate a form with a specific tray, open the printer's property sheet and click the Device Settings tab to display the Device Settings property page. Under the Form To Tray Assignment branch, click the tray in question, then select a form from the list of forms in the bottom half of the page. Repeat the process for other trays you want to assign.

When you're running a Windows application under Windows NT, you can select which form to use to print a document. You can use multiple forms within the same document. For example, when creating a letter, you might use a form named Envelope for the first page, a form named Letterhead for the second page, and a form named Letter for all other pages. How you assign forms to different parts of a document depends on the application. To choose a form at print time, open the application's Print dialog box, then click the Properties button. The available forms are listed in the Paper Size drop-down list. Select the form you want to use, then make sure the Paper Source option is set to Automatically Select Correct Tray. The print server then will determine which tray to use based on its settings.

To set the default form for a printer (to be used if no form is specified), open the printer's property sheet by right-clicking the printer in the Printers folder and choosing Properties. Click the Device Settings tab to display the Device Settings page. In the Device Settings box, select the tray for which you want to set the default form. Select the desired default form from the list of available forms at the bottom of the property page. When you've assigned the necessary form(s), choose OK to close the property sheet.

Setting Ports   The Ports page of the Print Server Properties sheet enables you to configure existing ports on the print server, as well as add and delete ports. This page is identical to the Ports page for each printer, but applies globally to the server.

Setting Advanced Properties   The Advanced property page enables you to set the location of the Windows NT spooler folder, as well as other advanced print server options. The spooler folder is the folder in which pending print jobs are spooled until sent to the print device.

The other options on the Advanced page are:

- **Log Spooler Error Events.** If enabled, this option causes spooler errors to be written to the system log.

- **Log Spooler Warning Events.** If enabled, this option causes spooler warnings to be written to the system log.

- **Log Spooler Information Events.** If enabled, this option causes spooler information events to be written to the system log.

- **Beep On Errors Of Remote Documents.** Enable this check box to have the print server beep when errors occur.

- **Notify When Remote Documents Are Printed.** Enable this check box if you want the print server to notify users when their print jobs are printed.

Part
VII

Ch
33

From Here...

This chapter examined general server-related issues that will help you configure your workstation to provide shared resources to other users. You also learned how to configure local object permissions to protect resources locally on your workstation. The following chapters and appendixes offer information on related topics:

- Chapter 6, "Advanced and Custom Setup Issues," explains how to modify Setup and use other techniques to distribute Windows NT in a multiuser environment.

- Chapter 32, "Administering Users," explores a variety of issues that relate to user and group account administration.

Appendixes

Registry Customization Tips

by Christa Anderson

Earlier in this book, we discussed some of the ways in which you can use NT 4.0's Registry Editors to safely change your system's configuration. But the Registry editors are not the only tools that exist to help you customize your system. A number of shareware and freeware utilities exist to help you either work with your Registry or use your Registry more effectively. ■

These utilities come from a variety of sources:

- Sites on the World Wide Web (either directly or via ftp links)
- Windows NT forums on the Microsoft Network
- CompuServe utilities forums

TIP If you find a site or forum that has utilities you like, be sure to return regularly and check it out. New shareware and freeware are uploaded all the time, and by the time that you read this book, more utilities will certainly be available.

In this appendix, we'll organize the utilities more or less by function, including:

- Registry editing tools
- Customization tools that use the Registry
- Registry backup tools

Registry Editing Tools

One of the things that really seems to irritate NT utility authors is that it's hard to make universal changes to the Registry. They're right, as you probably noticed when reading Chapter 29, "Backing Up and Editing the Registry." The process of finding and editing Registry keys and values is time-consuming. Therefore, it's not surprising that among the first Registry utilities I found was a search-and-replace function.

Registry Search and Replace, developed by Steven J. Hoek Software Development and now in its second incarnation, is a search-and-replace tool that works in conjunction with the Registry Editor. (If you click the Registry button that you see in figure A.1, you'll open REGEDIT, but it's not necessary to do so for the utility to work.) Using this utility, you can search for instances of a word (as data or a key) in the Registry, replace all instances with a predefined value, or replace each instance with a value that you supply at the time.

The downloadable unregistered copy of this utility is fully functional but only good for 25 uses—after that, you'll need to register it to get the full-blown version.

Another search-and-replace utility that you can use to manage your Registry files is (help-fully) called Search and Replace. This utility, shown in figure A.2, is not Registry-specific but can be used to do text searches within any text document. It's handy for those times

FIG. A.1

The Registry Search & Replace utility searches all branches of your registry for matches.

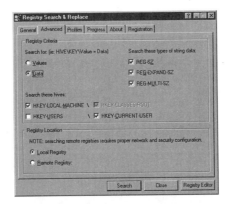

App

A

FIG. A.2

Search for text strings in exported Registry files to find the one that you want to import.

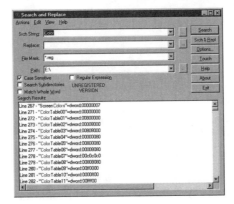

when you're sorting through exported Registry files looking for the one you want—if you know a specific line that will be in one but not in others, you can search for that line and thus identify the correct exported Registry to import.

The registered version of this utility also has a replace function that you can use to quickly make changes to your Registry or to other files.

A smaller (but free) Registry search utility is called **grep reg**, created by Opalis. This text-based utility does not include a replace function, but will return for you a complete list of all the places in which a text string occurs in the Registry. For example, I use Lotus' AmiPro for much of my in-house word processing. To see how the presence of AmiPro on my system affects the Registry, I ran a search for it. The partial output looks something like this:

```
SOFTWARE\Classes\CLSID\{0003002F-0000-0000-C000-000000000046}\ : AmiPro
➥Document
```

```
SOFTWARE\Classes\CLSID\{0003002F-0000-0000-C000-000000000046}\Ole1Class\ :
➥AmiProDocument
SOFTWARE\Classes\CLSID\{0003002F-0000-0000-C000-000000000046}\ProgID\ :
➥AmiProDocument
SOFTWARE\Classes\.sam\ : AmiProDocument
SOFTWARE\Classes\.sam\AmiProDocument\ShellNew\FileName : amipro.sam
SOFTWARE\Classes\AmiProDocument\ : AmiProDocument
SOFTWARE\Classes\AmiProDocument\protocol\StdFileEditing\server\ :
C:\AMIPRO\AMIPRO.EXE
➥SOFTWARE\Classes\AmiProDocument\shell\open\command\ : C:\AMIPRO\AMIPRO.EXE
```

Admittedly, grep reg doesn't have the functionality of the first utility, but it's a good quick and dirty way of finding out where something's mentioned in the Registry.

> **CAUTION**
>
> Be very careful when using any search-and-replace function to edit the Registry. It's easy enough to make a mistake when you're making changes by hand—imagine the havoc that you can wreak with an automated editor!

Desktop Tools That Use the Registry

As messing with the Registry is not the first purpose of many utility authors, most shareware applications are not intended specifically for editing the Registry. One, however, is Somar Software's **DumpACL**, which creates a breakdown of user security information that you can use to evaluate your system's security. Based on the results of the dump, you can change your system's security settings to close holes. Essentially, it's a tool intended to make sure that system users don't have more access to a system than is absolutely necessary, whether in terms of printer permissions, file permissions, or registry permissions. You can also customize the output. Some sample output for this product appears in figure A.3.

Once you've gotten the dump, the assumption is that you can then edit the Registry (or printer setup) to close any system holes. As you can see in the pull-down menu in figure A.3, you can use this utility to examine the security settings for a variety of your NT settings.

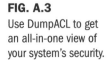

FIG. A.3
Use DumpACL to get
an all-in-one view of
your system's security.

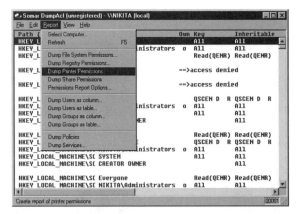

App
A

Registry Backup Tools

As we've discussed ad nauseam in the body of this book, one of the most important things that you can do with the Registry is back it up regularly. Now, although I haven't found any tools specifically intended for backing up the Registry on a regular basis, there are certainly tools that can help you automate the backup process and thus accomplish the same thing.

One of these is WinAt, a utility that comes with the NT Resource Kit but is also available for downloading from the Web. WinAt is a nice little utility that enables you to schedule any scripted command—in this case, backing up the Registry files using either NT Backup or the COPY command. The only catch with WinAt is that the scripts you give it must be non-interactive, or else the point is lost. You can see the opening screen of WinAt in figure A.4.

> **N O T E** All events in WinAt are assigned an ID number (shown in the far left column of the entry in figure A.4). When you remove an event, that ID number does not become available for future scheduled events, but this does not mean that erased events are still scheduled. ■

Another NT utility that offers a similar feature is called Remote Process and Shutdown. The remote process part of this application permits you to define a task to occur before shutting down the system—in this case, perhaps backing up the Registry to another directory. As you can see in figure A.5, you can define a complete set of listings to set up a remote process.

FIG. A.4
Use WinAt to schedule
regular backups of
your data and Registry.

FIG. A.5
Define a set of
parameters to back up
the registry before
shutting down, whether
on your own system or
a remote one.

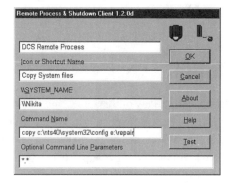

Once you've created the entry and clicked OK, this event will be added to the taskbar and a folder will be created for it.

The ability to back up a remote system's Registry is an important one due to one limitation of NT Backup: you can't use it to back up a remote system's Registry. (This is for security reasons—don't expect this to change in future releases of Windows NT.) However, if you can run a remote process on someone else's system and that system is equipped with a tape drive, you can ensure that that person's Registry gets backed up on a regular basis.

 You can't use NT Backup to back up a remote Registry, but you can use an application such as this one to run a backup or copy utility on a remote system.

Where Do I Get These Tools?

The problem with getting NT system tools isn't that they're not out there—it's just that they're in so many different places that it can get confusing trying to figure out where to go. These, however, are some of the good places to find NT utilities.

N O T E You might wonder why I haven't included any Usenet binary groups here. The simple answer is that when I've looked there, I haven't found anything. Usenet NT groups, however, can be an excellent source of troubleshooting advice. ▦

On the Web

If you search for NT utilities on the Web, you're likely to come up with dozens of hits. However, one of the best of them, the iNformaTion site at **http://rmm.com/nt**, has links to hundreds of NT (and other) utilities. It's also updated regularly, so you won't find yourself browsing through lists of utilities and finding that the most recent utilities were written in 1993.

Another good source is Digital's Free and Shareware Programs for Windows NT site at **http://www.windowsnt.digital.com**. This site holds not just utilities, but all kinds of third-party applications for NT.

ftp Sites

If you've got Web access (and, if you're running NT Workstation 4.0 and you've got a SLIP or PPP connection to the Internet, you do—the OS comes with the Internet Explorer) and are downloading files via the Web, you're probably accessing ftp sites without realizing it. In case you don't have Web access at a particular machine, however, here are some sites to check out for NT utilities:

- microsoft.com
- ftp1.rmm.com

T I P Those are two especially good ones—for others, check out Tile.net at **http://tile.net/ftp-list/viewlist.html**. It's a very good index of ftp sites, alphabetically organized by subject.

On CompuServe

Microsoft no longer maintains an official presence on CompuServe—the slack has been taken up by the Windows User Group Network (WUGNET). Two good sources for NT shareware are the Windows Shareware forum (GO WINSHARE) and the Windows Utility Vendor A forum (GO WINUTA). I find these forums to be better sources of utilities than the NT users forums, although these users forums are an excellent place to get troubleshooting advice.

On the Microsoft Network

Since Microsoft pulled out of CompuServe, the main interactive Microsoft support has been on Microsoft's network. The only catch, of course, is that MSN is (as of summer 1996) only available if you've got Windows 95. Try looking in the Microsoft forum's Utilities section.

N O T E   Windows NT version 4.0 is not expected to include MSN in the box, but the software for the online service will be available as a separate package. ■

These are some of the utilities that you can use to customize your system configuration, or to help you do so. With the large numbers of shareware authors out there, you're not limited to using only the tools that Microsoft provides for working with NT. ●

The Windows NT Advanced Technical Reference CD

by Brian Underdahl

You need good tools to fully exploit the information in the *Windows NT Workstation 4.0 Advanced Technical Reference.* The programs you'll find on the CD-ROM that accompanies this book provide many useful and powerful tools designed to help you make the most of Windows NT 4.0. The programs we've selected complement the book by enabling you to quickly make use of the tips and techniques you'll learn while reading the *Windows NT Workstation 4.0 Advanced Technical Reference.* ◼

System Requirements

You must have Windows NT 4.0, either Workstation or Server version, installed and operating on your system, as well as a CD-ROM drive to use the CD-ROM. Although many of the programs on the CD-ROM will run on Windows 95, the programs were specifically selected for their Windows NT 4.0 compatibility. You also should have at least 16M of RAM, although you'll find performance will be much better with additional memory. A Pentium processor is recommended, except for the program versions we've included specifically for the Alpha processor.

Using the Windows NT Workstation 4.0 Advanced Technical Reference CD-ROM

The *Windows NT Workstation 4.0 Advanced Technical Reference* CD-ROM has a specially designed interface that makes it easy to explore the programs on the CD-ROM and to install those programs you want to try out. With just a few clicks of your mouse, you can enjoy this easy-to-use Guide to the CD-ROM.

Having Problems Viewing the Guide to the CD-ROM?

With some display adapters it may be necessary to use small fonts rather than large fonts in order to properly view the Guide to the CD-ROM. To change to small fonts, right-click the Windows NT 4 desktop, select Properties, and use the Settings tab to adjust the settings. Select Small Fonts in the Font Size list box. You may need to test the new settings before you can apply the change.

For each program on the CD-ROM, there is an accompanying description file that tells you about the program. In most cases, after you read the description, you can choose to quickly install the program by simply clicking the install button. A few programs have special installation requirements, which are explained in the description file.

When you place the CD-ROM in your computer, the Guide to the CD-ROM program will run automatically. If the Guide to the CD-ROM does not run, it is probably because you have disabled the Autorun feature for your CD-ROM drive. In this case, simply double-click AUTORUN.EXE on the CD-ROM to run the program. You may also open the Start menu, open the Run item, and enter **d:\autorun** (where *d* is the drive letter of your CD-ROM drive).

When the Guide to the CD-ROM program starts, you will first see the dialog box shown in figure B.1. Select Continue to begin using the program.

FIG. B.1

Select Continue to begin the Guide to the CD-ROM program.

The first time you run the CD-ROM, several DLLs and OCX controls—necessary to run the Guide to the CD-ROM and to install the programs on the CD-ROM—will be copied to your computer. After these files are installed, they will remain available; when you want to use the CD-ROM in the future, they will not have to be installed again.

To view the Readme files or select programs to install, select the different items available on the Guide to the CD-ROM form. The different programs are arranged in several folders according to type, making it easy for you to find what you need. Each item listing also includes contact information for the software author, and most include additional Readme files you can view. Figure B.2 shows the Guide to the CD-ROM.

FIG. B.2

The Guide to the CD-ROM makes it easy for you to select the programs you want to install.

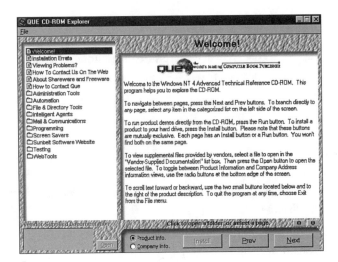

App B

Because system configurations can differ, we cannot guarantee that every program will function properly on all computers running Windows NT 4.0. We have verified the operation on a fairly typical Windows NT 4.0 installation, but as they say in the ads, "your mileage may vary." Most of the programs are 32-bit applications designed specifically to take advantage of the special features provided by Windows NT 4.0. Many of these programs also run under Windows 95.

Important Information About Shareware

Shareware distribution gives users a chance to try software before buying it. If you try a shareware program and continue using it, you are expected to pay a small fee to register your copy of the program. Individual programs differ on details. Some request registration while others require it. Some specify a maximum trial period, either a set number of days or uses. In some cases, the software will cease to function, or offer a reduced number of functions when the trial period expires. With registration, you get anything from the simple right to continue using the software to an updated program with a printed manual. The Readme files provide details on how to register and what benefits you'll receive from doing so.

Copyright laws apply to both shareware and commercial software. The software author has not given you the right to continue using their software without registration simply because they have chosen to use shareware distribution. Each of the software authors has given us permission to include their software on our CD-ROM.

Software authors use shareware distribution methods for several reasons. One of the most important is that this method enables the author to keep the cost to you as low as possible. Another is to provide you the opportunity to try out valuable software without the hassle of returning it for a refund if it isn't what you need. But this system works only if you keep up your end of the bargain. Remember, if you don't register shareware you use, there's no incentive for the software author to produce new shareware products or update versions of existing ones.

So after you've tried out the shareware on the CD-ROM, please make one of these choices: register the software you find yourself using, and uninstall any you don't find useful.

Technical Support

For problems with a particular shareware or evaluation application, please contact the software author using the information listed in the Readme file associated with the program. Note, however, that many software companies offer a higher level of support to registered users, which is yet another reason for you to register any software you intend to use.

For issues relating to the content and/or quality of the CD-ROM, contact:

App

B

Macmillan Technical Support
201 W. 103rd St.
Indianapolis, IN 46290

Voice: 317-581-3833

Internet: **support@mcp.com**

CompuServe: GO QUEBOOKS

Internet and Online Resources

by Jim Boyce

Although we've tried to include a rich selection of information for you in this book, naturally we can't cover every topic, nor can we cover a topic in minute detail. Fortunately, a wealth of technical reference information exists for Windows NT, and much of that information is available on the Internet and from other online services. This appendix lists reference sources you should find useful for installing, configuring, using, and tuning Windows NT Workstation.

The resources described in this appendix fall into four general areas:

- *Ftp sites.* You can use the ftp utility included with Windows NT or your Web browser to access a variety of ftp sites that contain support files, shareware, and other resources for Windows NT.

- *Mailing lists.* By subscribing to Internet mailing lists, you can automatically receive periodic information about Windows NT and related topics.

- *World Wide Web sites.* Everyone and his grandmother has a Web site, and you can be sure there are many Windows NT-related sites.

- *Commercial online services.* Online services such as CompuServe and America Online offer forums where you can find reference data and resource files for Windows NT, as well as communicate with other Windows NT users.

ftp Sites

The ftp (file transfer protocol) utility is included with Windows NT, and functions as a command-line program. For help using ftp, refer to Chapter 23, "Using Basic TCP/IP Services." For a detailed explanation of ftp, you can turn to the *Windows 95 Communications Handbook* (Que, 1996).

Microsoft

Ftp address: **ftp.microsoft.com**

The Microsoft ftp site provides access to a wealth of information and support files for Windows NT direct from the source—Microsoft. The Windows NT resources available from the ftp site are:

- */bussys.* This folder contains numerous subfolders with data and files for network clients, Microsoft Exchange, Internet Information Server, Windows NT, and other Windows NT-related topics.

- */developr.* This folder contains reference data and files for developers, and includes topics for C++, Visual Basic, and other development environments and tools.

- */Softlib.* This folder provides access to Microsoft's software library, which contains support files for a variety of Microsoft products, including Windows NT.

- */msdownload.* This folder contains support and beta files for a variety of Microsoft products, including Windows NT.

- */Services.* This folder contains background and reference information about many of Microsoft's support services such as Education and Certification, TechNet, and more.

WinSite

Ftp address: **ftp.winsite.com**

This ftp site, which used to be managed by the Center for Innovative Computing Applications (CICA), is now managed by a group called WinSite. You'll find a wide selection of files for not only Windows NT, but for Windows 3.x and Windows 95. The software available there runs the full gamut from games to utilities, in both shareware and freeware. This is a busy site, but has recently expanded to a new T1 line, so you should be able to access the site consistently.

Mailing Lists

By subscribing to an Internet mailing list, you can receive periodic announcements and news through your e-mail account. You might find the following Internet mailing lists of use in conjunction with Windows NT and related products.

Microsoft WinNT News

This news service is a periodic mailing by Microsoft and contains news and tips related to Windows NT. To subscribe to WinNT News, access Microsoft's WinNT News Web site at **http://www.bhs.com/microsoft.winntnews/** and fill out the form located there. Or, send an e-mail message containing the text **subscribe winntnews** as the first line of the message to **winntnews-admin@microsoft.bhs.com**. To unsubscribe to WinNT News, send a message with the text **unsubscribe winntnews** to the same address.

Microsoft DevWire

The Microsoft DevWire list is geared toward programmers and contains news, product information, seminar schedules, and other reference information. To subscribe, send an e-mail message containing the text **subscribe DevWire** to **devwire@microsoft .nwnet.com**.

Microsoft WinNews

The monthly mailing contains information about Microsoft, Microsoft products, training, press releases, and other information. To subscribe, send an e-mail message containing the text **subscribe winnews** to **enews99@microsoft.newnet.com**.

World Wide Web Sites

The Web sites related to Windows NT are too numerous to cover here. Listed below are a few sites with a good range of information and links to other Windows NT-related Web sites.

App
C

Microsoft Corporation

URL address: **www.microsoft.com**

When you reach Microsoft's home page, select the Products link, then select Windows NT Workstation (or Windows NT Server) from the products drop-down list. Then, click Go. This will take you to a page containing links to information about Windows NT and related products and services.

You'll also find a wealth of information on Microsoft's Support page. On Microsoft's home page, select Support, then select the country or U.S. region in which you're located. You'll find information about user groups, solution providers, technical support, training, and other information.

Macmillan Information SuperLibrary

URL address: **www.mcp.com/que**

This Web site provides industry news, press releases, software, and access to books and other resources about Windows NT and other computer/industry topics.

WINDOWS Magazine

URL address: **www.winmag.com**

The WINDOWS Magazine site provides news, software, demos, and other information relating to Windows NT, Windows 3.x, and Windows 95. You'll also find access to current and past issues of WINDOWS Magazine.

Commercial Online Services

You'll find useful sources of information about Windows NT—as well as support files, shareware, and freeware—on commercial online services such as CompuServe and America Online.

CompuServe

CompuServe contains a number of good forums devoted to Windows NT and related products and services. The following are a few:

- *Microsoft Connection.* Forum name: **MICROSOFT**. This forum provides access to numerous other Microsoft-related forums.

- *Windows NT Forum.* Forum name: **WINNT.** This forum, which is managed by the Windows User Group Network (WUGNET), will put you in contact with other Windows NT users and Microsoft support staff, and provide access to a large collection of Windows NT files and applications.

- *Macmillan Computer Publishing Forum.* Forum name: **MACMILLAN.** This forum, hosted by Macmillan Computer Publishing, gives you access to news, software, demos, books, and other sources of information.

America Online

America Online provides forums devoted to Windows NT and related topics. The following are a few:

- *Windows NT Resource Center.* Keyword: **WINNT.** This area provides access to message areas, Web sites, files, and other information about Windows NT and Windows 95.

- *WINDOWS Magazine.* Keyword: **WINMAG.** The WINDOWS Magazine area offers message areas, reviews, software, and access to current and past issues of WINDOWS Magazine.

App
C

Windows NT Workstation Command Reference

by Sue Plumley

This appendix contains the most common commands that you can use at the command prompt in Windows NT Workstation. In addition to commands, I've included syntax, pertinent switches, and parameters to help you use the commands. For a complete listing of commands, use NT Workstation Help.

Bold text is text you type; italic text indicates a variable. ■

Subsystem Commands

Subsystem commands are older 16-bit commands included to maintain MS-DOS compatibility. There are many subsystem commands you can use in NT; see Windows NT Help.

edit

Starts the MS-DOS Editor in which you can create and modify text files.

edit [[*drive:*] [*path*] *filename*]**/b /h /nohi**

/b

Displays MS-DOS Editor in black and white, for a monochrome monitor.

/h

Displays the maximum number of lines your monitor can display.

/nohi

Lets you use an 8-color monitor with the Editor as opposed to NT's normal 16-color use.

edlin

Starts Edlin, a line-oriented text editor that you can use to create text files.

edlin [*drive:*] [*path*]*filename* **/b**

/b

Ignores the end-of-file character.

expand

Expands compressed file(s); used to retrieve files from distribution disks.

expand [**-r**] *source* [*destination*]

-r

Renames the expanded files.

source   Specifies the files to expand; use a driver letter, colon, directory name, file name, or a combination. You can use wild cards.

destination   Specifies where the files are to be expanded.

mem

Displays a screen showing used and free memory in the MS-DOS subsystem.

mem [/program|/debug/|/classify]

/program or **/p**

Displays the memory status of programs currently loaded into memory.

/debug or **/d**

Displays the memory status of programs currently loaded and of internal drivers, plus other programming information.

/classify or **/c**

Displays the memory status of programs loaded into conventional memory and the upper memory area.

Native Commands

Native commands refer to those commands used with the 32-bit operating system, including many of the MS-DOS commands you may be familiar with.

App

D

attrib

Displays or changes a file's or directory's attributes, such as read-only, hidden, archive, and so on.

attrib [+r|-r][+a|-a][+s|-s][+h|-h] [[*drive:*][*path*]*filename*] [/s]

+r -r

+ sets the read-only file attribute, and - clears the attribute.

+a -a

+ sets the archive file attribute, and - clears it.

+s -s

+ sets the file as a system file, and - clears the system file attribute.

+h -h

+ sets the file as hidden, and - clears the attribute.

/s

Specifies to include all subdirectories in the process.

cd

Changes directory, or displays the name of the current directory.

cd [**/d**] [*drive:*] [*path*] [..]

/d

Changes the current drive and the current directory to the specified drive and path.

[..]

Changes back to the parent directory.

chkdsk

Checks a disk for errors, bad clusters, and so on, and then displays a report of the results.

chkdsk [*drive:*] [*path*]*filename*] [**/f**] [**/v**] [**/r**]

/f

Fixes errors chkdsk finds.

/v

Displays the name of every file in the directory as it checks the disk.

/r

Recovers readable information from bad sectors.

comp

Compares the contents of two files and displays a report when finished.

comp [*data1*] [*data2*] [**/d**] [**/a**] [**/l**] [**/n**=*number*] [**/c**]

data1 and *data2*

Specifies the location and the name of the first and then the second file or set of files; you can use wild cards.

/d

Displays differences in decimal format.

/a

Displays differences as characters.

/l

Displays the line number on which the difference occurs.

/n=*number*

Compares the first *number* of lines of both files.

/c

Designates the comparison is not case-sensitive.

date

Displays the date or lets you set the date.

date [*mm - dd - yy*]

mm - dd - yy

Sets the month, day, and year; separates the dates by periods, hyphens, or slash marks. The month can be a number from 1 to 12; the day can be 1 through 31; and the year can be 1980 through 2099 (80 through 99).

App
D

del

Deletes file(s).

del [*drive:*][*path*]*filename*[;...][**/p**][**/f**][**/s**][**/q**][**/a**]

/p

Asks for confirmation before deleting the file.

/f

Deletes read-only files.

/s

Includes specified files in all subdirectories of the current directory.

/q

Does not prompt for confirmation before deleting.

/a

Deletes files based on specified attributes: **r**ead-only, **h**idden, **s**ystem, or **a**rchive.

help

Displays a list of the commands and a brief description of each.

help *command*

path

Sets a search path for executable files.

path [[*drive:*]*path*[;...]] [**%path%**]

When used by itself with the command, clears all search-path settings and specifies a search in only the current directory.

%path%

Appends the current path to the new setting.

print

Prints a text file, in the background if your printer is connected to your system's serial or parallel port.

print [**/d:***device*] [*drive:*] [*path*]*filename*[...]

/d:*device*

Specifies the name of the print device, such as LPT1, LPT2, and so on. You can also specify a network printer by its sharename [*servername**print_share*]. You can use multiple files on one command line.

recover

Recovers any salvageable information from a bad disk.

recover [*drive:*] [*path*]*filename*

start

Starts a separate command prompt window.

start [*"title"*] [/**d***path*] [/**i**] [/**min**] [/**max**] [/**separate**] [/**low**] [/**normal**] [/**high**] [/**realtime**] [/**wait**] [/**b**] [*filename*] [*parameters*]

"title"

Enter a title to display in the Command Prompt's window title bar.

/**d***path*

Startup directory.

/**i**

Transfers the CMD.EXE startup environment to the new window.

/**min**

Starts the Command prompt session with the window minimized.

/**max**

Starts Command prompt session with the window maximized.

/**separate**

Starts 16-bit Windows program in a separate memory space.

/**low**

Starts the application in the idle priority class.

/**normal**

Starts the application in the normal priority class.

/**high**

Starts the application in the high priority class.

/**realtime**

Starts the application in the high priority class and runs in real time.

/**wait**

Starts the application and waits for it to terminate.

/**b**

Doesn't create a new window. Use Ctrl+break to interrupt the application, if necessary.

App
D

type

Displays the contents of a text file.

type [*drive:*][*path*]*filename* [...]

xcopy

Copies files and directory trees quickly by reading data into memory and then copying to the destination.

xcopy *source* [*destination*] [/w][/p][/c][/v][/q][/f][/l][/u][/s]

/w

Displays a message you must respond to before copying begins.

/p

Prompts for confirmation of each copied file.

/c

Ignores errors when copying.

/v

Verifies each file as it is written to the destination.

/q

Suppresses display of xcopy messages.

/f

Displays source and destination filenames while copying.

/l

Doesn't copy files but displays a list of files that would be copied.

/u

Updates only files from the source that exist on the destination.

/s

Copies directories and subdirectories, unless they're empty.

N O T E   There are many more switches for the xcopy command; see online help for more information. ■

Configuration Commands

Configuration commands enable you to configure the MS-DOS subsystem and affect only the MS-DOS subsystem. Many configuration commands are included only for compatibility and have little or no use to Windows NT Workstation because Windows NT uses its own set of commands. For that reason, no configuration commands are included here; for more information, see online Help in Windows NT.

TCP/IP Commands

Use TCP/IP commands to communicate with hosts such as UNIX. You must have the TCP/IP network protocol installed to use these utilities. Many of the switches are not shown here because of limited space. For more detailed information, see Windows Help.

finger

Displays information about a user on a specified system running the Finger service.

finger [-l] [*user*]*@computer*[...]

-l

Displays information in long list format.

user

Specifies the user you want information about.

@computer

Specifies the server on the remote system.

ftp

Transfers files to and from an ftp service node.

ftp[-v][-d][-i][-n][-g][-s:*filename*][-a][-w:*windowsize*][*computer*]

-v

Suppresses display of remote server responses.

-d

Enables debugging, displaying all ftp commands passed between the client and server.

App

D

-i

Turns off interactive prompting during multiple file transfers.

-n

Suppresses `auto0login` upon initial connection.

-g

Disables filename globbing.

-s:*filename*

Specifies a text file containing ftp commands.

-a

Uses any local interface when binding data connection.

-w:*windowsize*

Overrides the default transfer buffer size of 4096.

computer

Specifies the computer name or IP address of the remote computer to connect to.

N O T E   There are many ftp commands you can use at the Command Prompt; see NT Help for
more information. ■

hostname

Displays the current host's name.

hostname

netstat

Displays current TCP/IP connections and protocol statistics.

netstat [-a] [-e] [-n] [-s]

-a

Displays all connections and listening ports.

-e

Displays Ethernet statistics.

-n

Displays addresses and port numbers in numerical form.

-s

Displays per-protocol statistics.

ping

Verifies remote host connection.

ping [-t] [-a]

-t

Pings the specified computer until interrupted.

-a

Resolves addresses to computer names.

rcp

Copies files between computers running NT and rshd (the remote shell daemon).

rcp [-a] [-b] [-h] [[-r]*source1 source2... sourceN destination*

-a

ASCII transfer mode.

-b

Specifies binary image transfer mode.

-h

Transfers source files marked with hidden attribute on the NT computer.

-r

Recursively copies the contents of all subdirectories of the source to the destination.

source and *destination*

Must be in the form [*computer* [.*user*] [:]]*filename.*

TCP/IP Utilities

The following two utilities are used to work with an LPD server. There are more TCP/IP utilities; refer to NT Help for more information.

lpq

A diagnostic utility that displays the status of a print queue from a host running the LPD server.

lpq -**S** *server* -**P** *printer* [-**I**]

-**S** *server*

Specifies the name of the computer that has the printer attached to it.

-**P** *Printer*

Specifies the name of the printer.

-**I**

Indicates that you want a detailed status.

lpr

A utility used to print a file to the host running the LPD server.

lpr -**S** *Server* -**P** *Printer* [-**C** *Class*] [-**J** *Jobname*] [-**O** *option*] *filename*

-**S** *Server*

Specifies the name of the computer attached to the printer.

-**P** *Printer*

Specifies the name of the printer.

-**C** *Class*

Specifies the content of the banner page for the class.

-**J** *Jobname*

Specifies the name of this job.

-**O** *option*

Indicates the type of file.

filename

The name of the file to be printed.

Network Commands

Use the following network commands when your NT Workstation is attached to a network. There are many more network commands; see NT Help for more information.

net help

Lists names and descriptions of network commands.

net help [*command*]

net computer

Adds or deletes computers to the Windows NT Server domains.

net computer *computername* [**/add|del**]

net file

Displays the names of all open shared files on a server.

net file [*id*[**/close**]]

id

The identification number of the file.

/close

Closes an open file and releases locked records.

net helpmsg

Displays help about a network error message.

net helpmsg *message#*

message#

List the four-digit number of the Windows NT message you received.

net print

Displays or controls print job and printer queues.

net print [*computername*]*job*#[**/hold**|**/release**|**/delete**]

computername

The name of the computer sharing the printer queues.

job#

The ID number assigned to a print job in a printer queue.

/hold

When used with the *job*#, holds a print job waiting in the queue.

/release

Releases a held printer job in the queue.

/delete

Removes a job from a printer queue.

net start commands

A group of commands that start services or utilities, such as the Event log, Remoteboot, Schedule, Server, Spooler, and so on. Precede the name of the service with **net start**, such as **net start remoteboot** and **net start snmp**. ●

Windows NT Glossary

by Jim Boyce

abstraction   Isolating different layers of a system from one another using standards, enabling the layers to communicate, but also allowing for the layers to change internally.

access permission   A rule associated with a resource, such as a file, folder, or printer, that regulates who can use the resource and how they can use it.

access privileges   Similar to access permissions, but applied to resources by Macintosh users.

account   See user account.

account lockout   A security feature that prevents an account from being used if a set number of failed logon attempts occurs within a given time period.

account policy   Defines how passwords are created and used on a computer or domain, including password length, password life, and so on.

administrative account   A user account that includes membership in the local Administrators group on a computer or in a domain, providing administrative access to services and resources.

administrative alerts   Warning messages sent to a predefined group of users to warn of significant system events, such as security problems or hardware failures.

administrator   A member of the Administrator's group who is responsible for creating user accounts, managing the file system and security, and performing other system management tasks.

Alerter service   Works in concert with the Messenger service to generate and deliver administrative alerts.

API   Application Programming Interface; a set of predefined routines that a programmer can use to accomplish low-level tasks.

asymmetric multiprocessing   Method of multitasking in which one CPU is dedicated to running the operating system, and other CPUs run applications and perform other non-operating system functions.

attributes   Characteristics of a file that define its state, such as read-only, hidden, system, as well as creation/modification date. In the NTFS file system, any data associated with a file (file name, data, and so on) is called an attribute.

audit policy   Defines the types of security events that will be logged on a computer or domain.

auditing   Tracking and recording specific types of events, such as logons, file access, driver initialization, and so on.

authentication   Validation of a user's account information at logon.

Backup Domain Controller (BDC)   A domain controller that serves as a backup to the primary domain controller.

BDC   see *Backup Domain Controller.*

boot loader   Defines the information necessary to boot the operating system, such as the location of the operating system files.

boot partition   NTFS or FAT volume containing the operating system files required to boot the system.

browse   View resources available on the network.

browse list   A list of all servers and domains on the network that is managed by the browse master.

browse master   See *master browser.*

buffer   An area of memory set aside as a temporary storage area for data.

built-in groups   Default, predefined groups in Windows NT.

C2-level security   A standard defined by the US government for secure computing systems.

cache   An area of memory that stores recently-used data to increase access speed.

caching   The process of using a cache.

cleartext passwords   Passwords that are not encrypted.

client   A computer that uses resources shared by another computer (a *server*).

computer account   An account in the security database for a computer running Windows NT.

Computer Browser service   The Windows NT service that enables browsing of shared network resources.

computer name   The name by which a computer is known on the network.

connect   To assign a drive ID, port name, or computer name to a shared resource so it can be accessed.

connected user   A user who has connected to a shared resource.

controller   A domain controller.

DCOM   Distributed Common Object Model, formerly known as Network DDE (Dynamic Data Exchange); provides a client/server framework to enable applications to communicate and share data and objects across a network.

default gateway   The routing device on the LAN that enables local traffic to be routed to other networks on the Internet.

default profile   The profile used to define the user's work environment if no other profile is specified. See *system default profile* and *user default profile*.

device   Any component in a computer that functions as a discrete entity, such as a hard disk, display adapter, network interface card, and so on.

device driver   A program that acts as an interface between the operating system and a device.

DHCP Relay Agent   A software component that relays DHCP and BOOTP broadcast messages between a DHCP server and client across an IP router.

DHCP   See *Dynamic Host Configuration Protocol.*

dial-up networking   Software mechanism used to provide network connections through a modem or modem-eliminator such as a null-modem cable. Also referred to as Remote Access Services in Windows NT.

directory replication   The process of copying directories and their contents automatically from a replication server to one or more other computers.

Directory Replicator service   The Windows NT service that handles directory replication.

disabled user account   A user account that has been turned off and cannot be used to log on to the system.

App
E

disk configuration information   Information such as drive letter assignments, stripe sets, mirrored sets, and other disk data stored in the Registry.

disk duplexing   Using a second disk with its own controller to create a complete copy of the contents of a disk to ensure data security.

disk mirroring   Using a second disk or partition to create a complete copy of the contents of a disk or partition in order to provide fault tolerance.

disk striping   The process of writing data across multiple disks to increase disk performance.

DNS   See *Domain Name System.*

DNS name servers   A server that processes requests for resolving host names into IP addresses.

domain   A collection of computers in a Windows NT network that share a security account database.

domain controller   A server that authenticates security requests in a domain.

domain database   See *SAM.*

domain model   The manner in which a single domain is constructed or multiple domains are grouped together for centralized management.

domain name   For TCP/IP, the name by which a network is recognized on the Internet. For Windows NT domains, the name by which a domain is recognized on the LAN.

domain name space   Database structure used by DNS.

Domain Name System   A program that runs on an Internet-connected computer system (called a DNS server) and provides an automatic translation between domain names and IP addresses. The purpose of this translation process, called resolution, is to enable Internet users to continue using a familiar name even though the service's IP address may change.

dual boot   System in which the user can select between two different operating systems at system startup.

Dynamic Host Configuration Protocol (DHCP)   An optional TCP/IP service that automates the assignment of IP addresses and other IP information (such as default gateway) to a TCP/IP client.

environment variable   A string variable that stores system-wide data such as the current system path.

event   Any occurrence that requires notification of certain users or logging.

event logging   The process of recording events to a log file.

everyone   A group category that applies to all users.

export path   The path to which directories are replicated under directory replication.

export server   A server that exports directories through directory replication.

extended partition   A special disk partition in which multiple logical drives can be created.

FAT   See *file allocation table.*

fault tolerance   Providing redundancy for a file system or server to avoid lost data or services due to a disk or system failure.

file allocation table (FAT)   The data table used in the FAT file system to maintain the list of disk clusters and their allocation states.

file system   The overall structure by which files are stored.

file transfer protocol (ftp)   Program used to transfer files across a TCP/IP connection.

FQDN   See *fully qualified domain name.*

frame   A packet of data transferred between two devices.

free space   Space on a disk drive that is not yet allocated to store data.

ftp   See *file transfer protocol.*

fully qualified domain name (FQDN)   Under DNS, the name of a node defined by its domain and host name.

global group   Type of Windows NT group that can contain user accounts only from its own domain, but which can be given access in trusting domains.

group   A collection of user accounts used to apply a common set of rights and privileges to those accounts.

group account   A collection of user accounts (see *group*).

group memberships   The groups to which a user account belongs.

group name   The name of a group account.

guest account   A special account that provides logon ability to users who do not have an account on the computer or in the domain or in a trusted domain.

HAL   See *Hardware Abstraction Layer.*

Hardware Abstraction Layer (HAL)   The Windows NT operating system that serves as an interface between the executive components and the system's hardware.

Hardware Compatibility List (HCL)   The list of hardware tested and certified by Microsoft as being compatible with Windows NT.

App

E

HCL   See *Hardware Compatibility List.*

home directory   A directory defined at logon for storing a user's files and programs.

hop   A transfer between two routing devices.

host   Any device connected to a network that uses TCP/IP.

host name   The name by which a device is known on the network.

HOSTS file   A local ASCII file used to supplement domain name resolution under DNS.

HTML   See *HyperText Markup Language.*

HyperText Markup Language (HTML)   The code used to define a World Wide Web page.

IDE   Integrated Drive Electronics; refers to the fact that a disk's controller circuitry is built onto the disk, rather than a separate adapter.

IIS   Internet Information Server; a set of tools that enable a Windows NT Server computer to function as an Internet server.

import   The process of copying directories and their contents from a replication server.

import computers   Computers that import directories from a replication server.

import path   The path from which directories are replicated from a replication server.

Internet Protocol (IP)   The portion of the TCP/IP protocol that is responsible for addressing and sending IP packets across the network.

Internet router   A device that serves to route traffic between networks.

IP address   Unique address that identifies a node on a TCP/IP network.

IP router   A device that routes traffic between TCP/IP networks.

kernel   Core components of an operating system that perform low, system-level services.

KEY   A branch of the Registry that can contain other keys (subkeys) and values.

LAN   See *local area network.*

LMHOSTS file   An ASCII file used to supplement name resolution under WINS.

local area network (LAN)   A group of computers and other devices connected together to share resources.

log off   To stop using a network.

log on   To specify a user account name and password to gain access to a network.

logical drive   A unit of storage recognized by a drive letter in an extended partition.

logon hours The hours during which a user can log on to a computer or domain.

logon script A file, such as a batch file, that executes automatically when the user logs on.

mandatory user profile A user profile that cannot be changed by the user.

mapping Associating a resource name with a resource, such as associating a drive ID letter with a remote shared directory.

master browser A network name server that maintains a list of servers and domains on the network; also called a browse master.

master domain A domain trusted by all other domains in a master domain model.

maximum password age The length of time a password can be in use before the system requires the user to change the password.

member servers Computers running Windows NT Workstation or Windows NT Server that do not function as domain controllers; also called stand-alone servers.

Migration Tool for NetWare Utility included with Windows NT that simplifies migrating NetWare accounts and other information to a Windows NT server.

minimum password age The minimum amount of time a password can be in use before it can be changed by the user.

minimum password length The minimum number of characters a password must contain.

mirror set A redundant set of data, such as two synchronized hard drives that contain the same data.

multiple-boot System configuration in which the user can choose from more than one operating system at startup.

Network DDE service Windows NT service that enables DCOM (see *DCOM*).

node Any device on the network; also called a *host* under TCP/IP.

NT file system (NTFS) File system designed for and implemented in Windows NT to provide increased security and other features beyond the standard FAT file system.

NTFS See *NT file system*.

one-way trust relationship Relationship between two domains in which domain A trusts domain B for user authentication, but domain B doesn't trust domain A for user authentication.

owner Person, device, or service that determines how an object can be accessed.

partition Area of a disk that functions as a unique storage area.

pass-through authentication Process by which a computer being logged onto passes the authentication request to a domain controller for authentication.

App
E

permissions   Settings that define who can use a resource and how they can use it.

ping   TCP/IP utility used to test the connection between two hosts.

Point-to-Point Protocol (PPP)   A standard framing and authentication protocol.

Point-to-Point Tunneling Protocol (PPTP)   A protocol enabling users to access remote networks securely across the Internet.

pool, printer   A group of printers on one server that act as a single logical unit.

PPP   See *Point-to-Point Protocol.*

PPTP   See *Point-to-Point Tunneling Protocol.*

Primary Domain Controller   A computer running Windows NT Server that has primary responsibility for authenticating logon requests and maintaining the security database.

primary partition   An area of a disk recognized as a single storage area, which can be used to store an operating system.

RAID   See *Redundant Array of Inexpensive Disks.*

RAS   Remote Access Services (see *dial-up networking*).

Redundant Array of Inexpensive Disks (RAID)   An array of hard disks that serve collectively as a single, logical storage device, providing data redundancy and increased performance.

Remote Access Service (RAS)   See *dial-up networking.*

replication   The process of copying a directory and its contents to one or more other computers.

roaming user profiles   User profiles stored in a central, network-accessible location that follow the user to whichever node he uses to log on to the network.

routing   The process of transferring data packets between networks.

SAM   Security Accounts Manager; the security database that contains user and group accounts and related security data.

SCSI   See *Small Computer System Interface.*

security database   See *SAM*; also called the directory database.

server   Any computer that provides services or resources to another computer.

share name   Name by which a shared resource is known on the network.

share permissions   The access permissions applied to a shared resource.

shared directory   A local directory shared on the network.

shared network directory   A remote directory shared on the network.

shared resource   A resource such as a directory or printer that is shared on a network.

SID   Security ID; serves as a unique identifier of a device on the network for security authentication.

Small Computer System Interface (SCSI)   Defines a bus standard by which multiple devices can be connected to a computer.

spooler   Software that handles the printing of documents.

spooling   The process of sending a document to a spooler.

stand-alone servers   See *member servers*.

stripe set   Data stored across multiple partitions that are recognized as one logical drive; provides performance gain but not fault tolerance.

stripe sets with parity   A stripe set that includes parity data to provide fault tolerance.

subkey   A registry key within another key; similar to a subbranch or subdirectory.

subnet   A portion of a network with a different subnet number from the primary network.

subnet mask   An octet (32-bit value) used to distinguish the network part of an IP address from the host portion.

swap file   A file on disk used to simulate memory.

system default profile   The user profile in place when no user is logged on.

system partition   Partition that contains hardware-specific files required to load Windows NT.

system policy   Group of settings that define the computer and software environment; overrides the settings in current local machine key of the registry.

App E

TCP   See *Transmission Control Protocol*.

TCP/IP   See *Transmission Control Protocol/Internet Protocol*.

thread   A unit of execution within a process.

Transmission Control Protocol (TCP)   The portion of TCP/IP responsible for transmitting data packets.

Transmission Control Protocol/Internet Protocol (TCP/IP)   The protocol used by nodes on the Internet.

trust   A relationship between domains in which one domain allows another to authenticate security for it.

trust relationship   See *trust*.

two-way trust relationship   A trust relationship between two domains in which each trusts the other to authenticate security.

UNC name   Uniform Naming Convention name; the full name of a resource consisting of the computer name and resource name in the form *computer**resource*.

user account   A collection of group memberships, rights, privileges, and other settings that define a user's ability to log on to a computer or domain and use the computer's or domain's resources.

user account database   See *SAM*.

user default profile   The user profile that is used if no other profile has been defined or is available for the user; see also *system default profile*.

User Manager   Windows NT utility for managing user accounts, group accounts, and rights.

User Manager for Domains   Windows NT utility for managing user accounts, group accounts, and rights across a domain.

user profile   A group of settings that define a user's operating environment.

user rights   Defines the user's level of access to a computer or domain.

VDD   Virtual device driver.

VDM   Virtual DOS Machine; the operating environment of a DOS application running under Windows NT.

virtual memory   Disk space used to simulate memory.

volume   One or more partitions that have been formatted for a specific file system.

volume set   A volume comprising space in multiple partitions, possibly on different physical disks; see also *volume*.

WAN   See *wide area network*.

wide area network (WAN)   A network connecting different geographical areas.

Windows Internet Name Service (WINS)   A Windows NT-based name resolution service; see also *Domain Name System*.

Windows NT Server   Version of Windows NT providing additional features and services for connectivity and system administration.

WINS   See *Windows Internet Name Service*.

workgroup   A group of computers organized under the same logical name to simplify browsing of shared resources on those computers.

Workstation service   The Windows NT service that enables the computer to act as a client on the network.

Index

X

Z

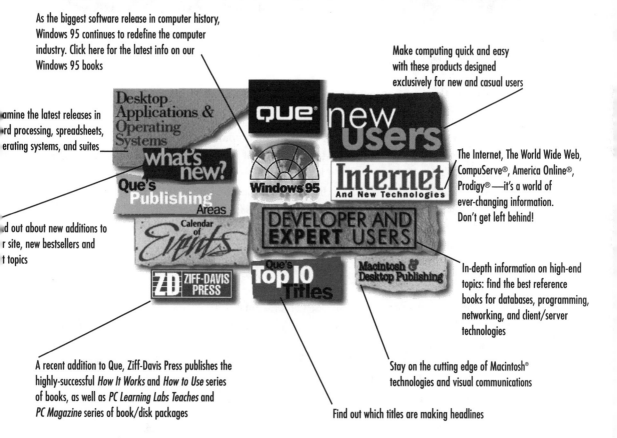

Before using this disc, please read Appendix B, "The Windows NT Advanced Technical Reference CD," for information on how to install the disc and what programs are included on the disc. If you have problems with this disc, please contact Macmillan Technical Support at (317) 581-3833. We can be reached by e-mail at **support@mcp.com** or on CompuServe at **GO QUEBOOKS**.

License Agreement

By opening this package you are agreeing to be bound by the following:

This software is copyrighted and all rights are reserved by the publisher and its licensers. You are licensed to use this software on a single computer. You may copy the software for backup or archival purposes only. Making copies of the software for any other purpose is a violation of United States copyright laws. THIS SOFTWARE IS SOLD AS IS, WITHOUT WARRANTY OF ANY KIND, EITHER EXPRESSED OR IMPLIED, INCLUDING BUT NOT LIMITED TO THE IMPLIED WARRANTIES OF MERCHANTABILITY AND FIT-NESS FOR A PARTICULAR PURPOSE. Neither the publisher nor its licensers, dealers, or distributors assumes any liability for any alleged or actual damages arising from the use of this software. (Some states do not allow exclusion of implied warranties, so the exclusion may not apply to you.)

The entire contents of the disc and the compilation of the software are copyrighted and protected by United States copyright laws. The individual programs on this disc are copyrighted by the authors or owners of each program. Each program has its own use permissions and limitations. To use each program, you must follow the individual requirements and restrictions detailed for each. Do not use a program if you do not agree to follow its licensing agreement.